MASTERING

Digital Printing

Second Edition

Harald Johnson

THOMSON

COURSE TECHNOLOGY ™

Professional ■ Trade ■ Reference

A DIVISION OF COURSE TECHNOLOGY

Mastering Digital Printing, Second Edition

CREDITS

FRONT COVER:

TOP RIGHT: *Courtesy of David Saffir*
TOP LEFT: Homestead, *courtesy of Bobbi Doyle-Maher*
BOTTOM LEFT: *Courtesy of Martin Juergens*
BOTTOM RIGHT: Sonic Color Loom,
© *1998-2004 Howard Berdach*

BACK COVER:

TOP RIGHT: *Flowers by Harald Johnson and Jasc Software*
TOP LEFT: *Courtesy of Canon USA*
BOTTOM LEFT: *Epson's R800 Stylus Photo inkjet printer courtesy of Epson America, Inc.; HP's Designjet 130 inkjet printer courtesy of Hewlett-Packard Company.*

PART OPENERS:

PART I: *Digital Printing Basics*
Courtesy of Joel Meyerowitz Photography
PART II: *The Main Event: Inkjet Printing*
Courtesy of Hewlett-Packard Company
PART III: *Beyond the Basics*
Courtesy of Mike Chaney, author of Qimage
APPENDIX:
Courtesy of Renata Spiazzi

SVP, Thomson Course Technology PTR:
Andy Shafran

Publisher:
Stacy L. Hiquet

Senior Marketing Manager:
Sarah O'Donnell

Marketing Manager:
Heather Hurley

Manager of Editorial Services:
Heather Talbot

Senior Acquisitions Editor:
Kevin Harreld

Associate Marketing Managers:
Kristin Eisenzopf and Sarah Dubois

Project Editor/Proofreader:
Marta Justak

Technical Editor:
C. David Tobie

Course Technology PTR Market Coordinator:
Elizabeth Furbish

Copy Editor:
Jenny Davidson

Interior Layout Tech:
Jill Flores

Cover Designer:
Mike Tanamachi

Indexer:
Sharon Hilgenberg

Dedication

To my wife, Lynn.

Foreword

In early 1989, I was facing two upcoming art shows—one in New York and one in Tokyo— of large format prints of my photographic images. The task was daunting: 50 images in an edition of 25, each printed 30 × 40 inches. My humble darkroom was clearly not up to such a task, not to mention the fact that the negatives for many of the key images had been forever lost during a shipment from San Francisco to Los Angeles. What to do? Whenever faced with a problem, I have only had to turn around and find that the answer was staring me right in the face. The same was true on this occasion.

With the help of my longtime friend, R. Mac Holbert, we were able to meet the challenge of finding a way to output digital images that would: (1) print in B&W as well as in color, (2) print on a wide variety of papers, (3) print at a resolution that approached that of photography, and (4) be permanent.

By using custom software programs and printing with an IRIS printer on non-traditional substrates, we finally succeeded, and the resulting shows of my images in New York, Tokyo, and Los Angeles were not only widely acclaimed, but the worlds of photography and art were introduced to a new printmaking model.

Few innovations are the result of one person's efforts. In our case, this was especially true. Without the help of John Bilotta, Charles Wehrenberg, Steve Boulter, David Coons, Jack Duganne, Al Luccesse, Mike Pelletier, Henry Wilhelm, Susan Nash, and Ruthanne Holbert, Nash Editions—which we officially opened in July 1991, as the world's first professional, digital printmaking studio—would never have become a reality.

The digital revolution rolls along. The people, the tools, and the materials continue to evolve. I applaud Harald Johnson's efforts to provide a comprehensive guidebook to digital imaging and to chronicle the past, the present, and the future of this exciting medium.

Graham Nash

Nash Editions

Acknowledgments

Don't believe it if anyone tells you that second editions of books are easier to create; they're not. And the task would have been impossible without the help of many supporting players.

First, I thank all the energetic people on the publishing side who provided their professional and enthusiastic support. The publishing team includes Andy Shafran, Kevin Harreld, Sarah O'Donnell, and the sales and marketing staff. On the production side, my kudos go to Marta Justak, Jenny Davidson, Jill Flores, and Sharon Hilgenberg who contributed to the making of this book.

Technical editor C. David Tobie again provided his insightful and knowledgeable input.

I also want to thank my expert readers who kept me from looking too foolish: Eric Everett, Ted Ginsburg, Mark Gottsegen, Dr. Mark Mizen, Mark Rogers, and Dr. Ray Work III.

Further, I called on many other experts and information sources in writing this book, and though they are too numerous to list individually, I am nonetheless grateful for their help.

More thanks go to all the product and brand managers, PR managers and outside PR reps, and owners of the companies who supplied me with information, material, and encouragement.

Finally, I want to acknowledge the many and varied online discussion lists that I follow. They have provided me with ideas, inspiration, and a connection to thousands of creative and thoughtful people around the world. And, speaking of inspiration, much appreciation goes to the many photographers, artists, and printmakers who contributed their images and their stories to this book.

About the Author

Harald Johnson has been immersed in the world of commercial and fine-art imaging and printing for more than 25 years. A former professional photographer, designer, and creative director, Johnson is an imaging consultant, the head of his own marketing communications agency, and the creator of DP&I.com (www.dpandi.com), the digital printing and imaging resource for photographers and digital/traditional artists.

Contents

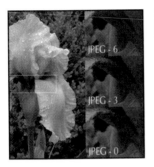

5   Determining Print Permanence   145

PART II : THE MAIN EVENT: INKJET PRINTING

6   Selecting an Inkjet Printer   181

7   Choosing Your Consumables   213

8   Making a Great Inkjet Print   249

9 **Finishing and Displaying Your Prints**   **279**

PART III : BEYOND THE BASICS

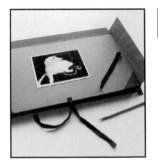

Introduction

I remember very clearly how it happened.

I had just entered the art gallery on South Dixie Highway in West Palm Beach on an extended trip to Florida. The local newspaper had promised new photographic work by artist John Paul Caponigro, son of famous landscape photographer Paul Caponigro. John Paul's digital composites of landscape elements and images of floating rocks were fascinating, but it was the style of the limited-edition prints that really caught my eye. They were rich and velvety, not like the cold and hard photographic prints I was used to. There was something special about these prints, although I couldn't put my finger on what it was.

When I found myself standing next to the artist, I asked him how he produced them, and he explained that they were digital prints or "giclées." I only followed about half of what he was saying, but the memory of those vivid and luscious prints stayed with me. Soon, I started seeing more of digital printing. I went to outdoor art festivals, and there were artists and photographers selling their digital prints. I went to galleries, and there they were again. Ads in magazines mentioned them; the art websites had them. The signs were clear enough: I had to find out more about digital printing.

In addition to photographing South Florida's beaches—one of my favorite subjects—that winter, I started my research. During a trip to the West Coast, I got in some more exploring. In Los Angeles, I visited photo galleries and saw wonderful inkjet panoramas by German filmmaker Wim Wenders and gorgeous flower blowups by Harold Feinstein. I also visited the print studio of Jack Duganne, who first used the term giclée in this context (see Chapter 1 for more details). In Seattle and Vancouver I saw even more examples. The range of subjects and artistic techniques was all over the board, but the common thread was the digital imaging and printing process. I was hooked.

Now back in Virginia, where I normally live, I got busy. I had a group of my best 35mm transparencies scanned (this was before I bought my first digital camera) and started printing my images with different printmakers around the U.S. I also bought a desktop inkjet printer and started doing my own prints.

I now regularly produce a wide range of digital prints that I've sold, exhibited, and just printed for the heck of it. In general, I've absorbed digital printing into my creative life.

Through my interest in learning about and printing my own imagery in this digital way, I discovered that I was not alone. There are literally tens of thousands of photographers, artists, and printmakers who are looking for the answers to the same questions I had. They want to know how to create and produce their images and their art by using the new digital technologies that are changing our lives. If you're one of those people, you've come to the right place!

—Harald Johnson

Whom This Book Is For

Written for photographers, digital and traditional artists, printmakers, art educators, and art marketers, *Mastering Digital Printing, Second Edition* is the first and still most complete reference to the new world of digital printing for photography and fine-art. Whether you're an amateur or serious hobbyist, an aspiring or even a veteran professional, if you're interested in spreading your creative wings and you want to learn more about this powerful art medium—this book is for you.

What You'll Find in This Second Edition

The first edition of this book introduced readers to a revolution that, although barely a dozen years old, has enabled photographers and artists the world over to create and produce their work in a way that has never been available to them before with high-quality digital printing.

What's new in the Second Edition?

- Every page of the book has been reviewed, overhauled, updated, or revised.

- References to equipment, supplies, hardware, and software have been reviewed and updated. New products have been highlighted wherever possible.

- Many of the examples, images, and artwork have been updated or replaced.

- New chapters or sections have been added or broken out. These expanded topics include: scanning; finishing, coating, and displaying prints; RIPs and special printing software; and new alternative digital output methods.

Even more than before, *Mastering Digital Printing, Second Edition*, is the definitive guide to the world of high-quality digital output.

Note: *While this book discusses techniques for and uses images created on both Macintosh and PC/Windows platforms, many of the screen-shot images were created on a Macintosh, and they may look somewhat different from what you see depending on your computer setup. You'll also notice that the book's figures and illustrations show different types of interfaces and dialog boxes, depending on the operating system and software versions used. I like variety!*

How This Book Is Organized

Mastering Digital Printing, Second Edition is divided into three parts. These parts are further subdivided into eleven chapters and the appendix as follows:

Part I: Digital Printing Basics

- Chapter 1: "Navigating the Digital Landscape"
- Chapter 2: "Understanding Digital Printing"
- Chapter 3: "Creating and Processing the Image"
- Chapter 4: "Understanding and Managing Color"
- Chapter 5: "Determining Print Permanence"

Part II: The Main Event: Inkjet Printing

- Chapter 6: "Selecting an Inkjet Printer"
- Chapter 7: "Choosing Your Consumables"
- Chapter 8: "Making a Great Inkjet Print"
- Chapter 9: "Finishing and Displaying Your Prints"

Part III: Beyond the Basics

- Chapter 10: " Using a Print Service"
- Chapter 11: "Special Printing Techniques"

Appendix

The appendix is your jumping-off point for finding more in-depth information. The Gallery Showcase, Resources, and Glossary are all introduced with links to the author's DP&I website for further exploration.

Keeping the Book's Content Current

Everyone involved with this book has worked hard to make it complete and accurate. But, as we all know, technology waits for no one, especially not for writers and book publishers! Digital printing and imaging is a moving target, and it's hard for anyone to keep up with its dizzying pace of change. This book can only be a snapshot of the techniques and technologies, products and models currently available. For updates, corrections, and other information related to the content of the book, feel free to visit the following two sites:

- www.muskalipman.com/digitalprinting
- www.dpandi.com (DP&I.com—the author's online, digital-printing and imaging resource)

And, if you have any suggestions for additions or changes to revisions of this book, contact the author at: *harald@dpandi.com.* You may not receive an instant response, but all messages are answered eventually.

C-print

inkjet

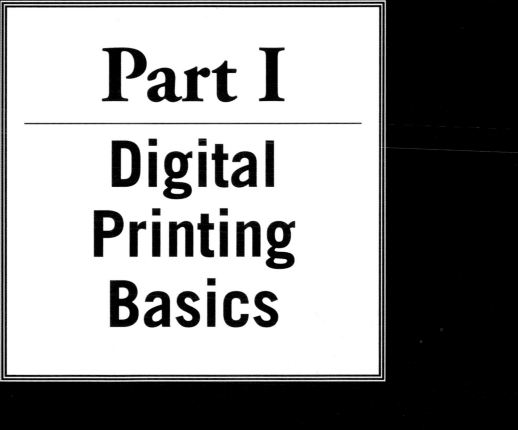

Part I

Digital Printing Basics

1

Navigating the Digital Landscape

Like the early explorers who probed the fringes of the known world with their new sextants and square-rigged ships, photographers and other artists continually experiment with and adopt new technologies, and digital printing is the latest in a long line of artistic innovations. With photographers stepping out of their toxic darkrooms and other artists embracing digital workflows, everyone wants to know more about what digital printing is—and what it isn't. This chapter puts digital printing into context and gives you a basic understanding of its role in the printmaking process.

Birth of the Digital Printing Revolution

While artists have been using computers to create and even output images for decades (see the sidebar entitled "Computers, Art, and Printmaking: A Brief History"), things didn't really take off until two groups on opposite sides of the U.S. started to put their attentions on a new way of imagemaking.

Jon Cone's Computer-Assisted Printmaking

In 1980, Jon Cone, who was educated and trained as a traditional fine-art printmaker and who owned an art gallery in New York City's SoHo district, founded an experimental and collaborative printmaking studio in the waterfront town of Port Chester, New York. There, from 1980 to 1984, printmaker Cone worked with artists in the media of silkscreen, intaglio, relief, monoprint, and photogravure.

Sensing, however, that the computer could be an advantageous tool for experimental printmaking and wanting to break away from the pack of other printmakers, many of whom were horrified by what he was doing, Cone started experimenting with scanners and learning computer programming. Combining his skills as a master printmaker and a recent computer geek (he was mesmerized by the *1984* Apple Macintosh TV commercial), he started to shift into a hybrid approach, combining traditional printmaking with a digital component to create what could be best described as computer-assisted original prints and multiples.

Left: A long collaboration—Jon Cone (at left) and artist David Humphrey working with the IRIS inkjet printer in 1996. Right: Computer-assisted printmaking and one of the early digital projects printed and published by Cone Editions Press—*Dr. Jewel*, 1986, David Humphrey, digital photogravure etching with aquatint, hard ground, relief plate, and hand stamp.

Courtesy of Cone Editions Press/www.coneeditions.com

This was nothing like the push-button inkjet printing that we know today. Cone's collaborative artists would create a digital master either with computer software, by placing objects on the scanner's glass, by painting onto separation mylars—whatever it took to create an image and turn it into a digital state. Cone would then often output the digital files to negative or positive film on a Linotronic imagesetter, and, in turn, those films would be used to burn silkscreen, photogravure, and etching plates for the final printing on a traditional etching press. An alternative technique was to use a digital Canon copier to create outputs that were used to transfer the image under pressure and with the help of acetone onto printmaking paper.

All this was very technical and time-consuming work, but the results were stunning, and Cone's innovative digital editions were shown and sold in New York until 1990 when Cone and his studio relocated to a small, rural village in Vermont to continue with his digital-printmaking experiments.

By 1992, Cone had added inkjet printing to his repertoire, but the story now backs up a little and shifts to the West Coast.

Graham Nash and Digital Fine-Art Printing

The photographic side of the equation didn't gel until the paths of six people—a rock star and his best friend, an art publicist, a sales rep, a computer wizard, and a silkscreen printer—unexpectedly intersected in early 1989 in California. Rock musician Graham Nash (of the legendary group Crosby, Stills, and Nash) had been quietly collecting photographs for years. On the road with the band, Nash and his best friend Mac Holbert, who was also CSN's tour

Crosby, Stills, and Nash in the
studio, 1977

© *1977 Joel Bernstein*

manager, would always hit the local galleries and swap meets looking for visual treasures. In the process, Nash amassed a world-class collection of vintage and contemporary photographs.

Nash also took photographs every chance he got, and it was only a matter of time before he caught the computer bug and started scanning and manipulating his images on the computer screen. Now, this was in the early days (mid '80s), when the scanning was crude and the printing was even worse.

Holbert, who had computerized the band's accounting process early on, was soon helping Nash with his digital experiments. The two could see the potential of working digitally, but a decent print of what they were viewing on the monitor had so far eluded them. No photo lab had yet figured out how to print from digital files, and the existing digital print devices just weren't up to the task of high-resolution output.

If Nash wanted to start printing and showing his digitally processed black-and-white images, he was going to have to change gears and move to a new level. He decided to invent a way to do it himself, and to do that, he needed to raise some money, and he needed some help.

Enter Charles Wehrenberg, a San Francisco art publicist and writer. Wehrenberg was a friend of Nash's and a well-known figure in New York and West Coast high-art circles. Once he understood that Nash wanted to sell his photo collection to raise the money to invest in a way to print his photo art, Wehrenberg came up with a plan. He arranged for the collection's sale through New York's venerable auction house, Sotheby's. Their PR machine would beat the drum, and Nash would handle the media like the pro he was.

However, Wehrenberg added a twist to the idea. To increase the buzz for the event and for what Nash was trying to do, Wehrenberg orchestrated a concurrent art show of Nash's own photography at the Simon Lowinsky gallery, to be held in New York the day before the Sotheby's sale.

Charles Wehrenberg (left) and Simon Lowinsky, April 1990
© 1990 Sally Larsen

The exhibition was scheduled for the following spring (1990), and Nash began pulling together 16 unique portraits taken over many years of touring with the band. But, there was a major problem. Most of the original negatives (and even the prints) had disappeared when Nash sent them to an art director, and they never returned. All he had were the contact sheet proofs to work from, and these were much too small for making the large display prints the gallery wanted—at least using normal photographic methods.

During his search for high-quality digital output, Nash had discovered Jetgraphix, a design research lab affiliated with UCLA across town from his Encino (Los Angeles) home. Run by former ad agency art director John Bilotta, the studio was a test site for Fuji's experimental, large-format inkjet printers of the same name (Jetgraphix). Nash was intrigued by the prints Bilotta could make, but the resolution was so low ("dots as big as your head") that when Nash asked if he knew of anything better, Bilotta handed him a sales brochure for something called an *IRIS printer*. (Another person who received a Bilotta brochure was a silkscreen printer named Jack Duganne; more about him shortly.)

Steve Boulter, the West Coast sales rep for Boston-based IRIS Graphics, had been showing test samples and passing out brochures for their new graphic arts, pre-press proofing machine to anyone he could. Boulter was pushing his company to get the IRIS into the hands of more photographers and artists, but the company didn't see much point to it—they were in the commercial graphics business, not the fine-art business. Boulter, however, believed in his idea and continued to make the rounds of art studios and businesses involved with art production. One of his big sales at the end of 1988 was to The Walt Disney Company in Burbank, which was using the machine to output hardcopy color prints in conjunction with their top secret, computer animation process.

Wehrenberg was already familiar with the IRIS. Artist Richard Lowenberg had shown him some early sample prints, and Wehrenberg liked what he saw. A lot. He called the IRIS company for more information, and they relayed the call to Steve Boulter who happened to be visiting San Francisco. Soon, Boulter was standing at Wehrenberg's dining room table showing off more samples. Impressed all over again, Wehrenberg picked up the phone to call Graham Nash, and he put Boulter on the line to set up a meeting.

Boulter flew to L.A. the following week (in April, 1989), and Nash was equally amazed at the quality of the IRIS prints. He instantly realized that this was the solution to his two-part problem of getting images out of his computer and also making the prints for the Lowinsky show.

However, there was a remaining glitch: how to get the images *into* the IRIS printer. The machine was meant to be hooked up only to large, proprietary, pre-press systems, not home scanners or Macintosh computers. Boulter knew just the person to solve the problem: David Coons. Coons was a color engineer for Disney, and he was helping the company make the transition from analog to digital animation. (Coons would receive an Academy Award in 1992 for co-developing Disney's ground-breaking computer animation production system.) Coons was also the one in charge of running the new IRIS 3024 printer that Boulter had sold them. Boulter introduced Coons to Nash, and soon, Coons was on the team.

David Coons and the IRIS 3024 in a well air-conditioned room at Disney, 1990.

Courtesy of David Coons
www.artscans.com

Working off-hours at Disney and using custom software programs that he wrote specifically for the project, Coons scanned and retouched Nash's proof prints, downloaded them to the IRIS, and printed the edition of images onto thick, Arches watercolor paper.

Nash ultimately met his April 24, 1990 Lowinsky exhibition deadline, and the following day's sale at Sotheby's brought in $2.17 million, a record for a private photographic collection. The world's first series of all-digitally printed, photographic fine art drew crowds and raves in New York and, as the show traveled, in Tokyo and Los Angeles. (A set of those prints later sold at auction at Christie's for $19,500.)

Self Portrait, Plaza Hotel, New York, by Graham Nash, 1971. Printed by David Coons in September, 1989, as one of the original portfolio prints shown at the Simon Lowinsky gallery in 1990.

Courtesy of Nash Editions
www.nasheditions.com

The plan had worked perfectly; digital prints were on the art map.

Even before the show, while Coons was moonlighting at Disney to output the print portfolios, Nash, Boulter, Wehrenberg, Coons, and eventually Holbert were kicking around the idea of setting up a shop to produce these new digital prints on a commercial basis. Coons was already experimenting with non-Nash images including several for artist Sally Larsen, who was Wehrenberg's wife.

Graham Nash soon bought one of the $126,000 IRIS machines and installed it in July 1990 in the small garage of an old house he owned in nearby Manhattan Beach, a suburb of Los Angeles. By August, Steve Boulter had moved into the top floor of the garage, and David Coons was making the long commute from Burbank each day with nine-track computer tapes of images that needed printing for a new edition of Nash portraits to be shown in Tokyo in November, 1990.

Remember our friend, serigrapher Jack Duganne? He soon found out about what was going on in Manhattan Beach. It wasn't far from his studio in Santa Monica, so Duganne, who could see the digital writing on the wall, started bringing digital tapes of his art clients' scanned images over for printing. By February, 1991, he was printing on the IRIS himself as a Nash Editions' employee. Duganne took to the IRIS quickly, developing new printing procedures and in the process becoming Nash's master printmaker. While there, Duganne also came up with the term *giclée,* but more about that later.

The work for outside clients continued to grow, and as Coons and Boulter began to spend less time at the Manhattan Beach studio, it became clear that someone would need to manage this new business enterprise if it were going to succeed. Coons had been running things while Nash and Holbert were on the road with CSN, but when the last tour ended in June, 1991, Holbert moved down from his home in Santa Cruz and took over the managing of the shop. On July 1, 1991, Graham Nash and Mac Holbert officially opened Nash Editions, the world's first professional, all-digital printmaking studio.

Left: Steve Boulter sits in the new, converted garage studio of Nash Editions trying to drum up business, August 1990. There was no computer hooked up to the IRIS printer then, only a nine-track tape drive (visible at left of printer). Right: Jack Duganne (front) and Mac Holbert at Nash Editions, 1993. Duganne removed the IRIS covers to make them easier to maintain.

Courtesy of Nash Editions

Mac Holbert (left) and Graham Nash in 1997 at Nash Editions.

Courtesy of Nash Editions

The Revolution Takes Off

By 1993, a mere handful of digital printmaking studios—including Nash Editions (L.A.), Harvest Productions (Anaheim, California), Cone Editions (Vermont), Adamson Editions (Washington, D.C.), Digital Pond (San Francisco), and Thunderbird Editions (Clearwater, Florida)—were busy on both U.S. coasts. All were using IRIS inkjet technology to make fine-art prints for photographers and artists. Soon, there were a dozen similar shops (many set up by Jon Cone), then many dozen, then scores. Today, there are anywhere from 2,500 to 5,000 professional or commercial printmakers making digital prints for artists the world over.

However, just as important, and the reason many of you are reading this book, is the fact that there are now many tens of thousands of individual photographers and artists, from amateurs to pros, who are able to print high-quality images in their own studios, homes, and offices. No longer constrained by the high costs of traditional printing methods, the production of "artistic" prints has been put in the hands of the greatest number of people—the artists and the imagemakers themselves.

The importance of the pioneers of this movement cannot be overstated. They not only laid the technological foundation for the entire high-quality, digital printing phenomenon, but even more importantly, they established its identity and gave it a face. These art revolutionaries provided the essential "proof of concept" that the new process needed before it could blossom and evolve. They, and those who immediately followed, deserve the credit for creating an industry. Together, they opened the door to the promise of digital printing, and the early adopting photographers and artists walked right in. And that door is swinging wider all the time.

Computers, Art, and Printmaking: A Brief History

1946

The first large-scale, general-purpose digital computer, the Eniac, is activated at the University of Pennsylvania.

1950

Mathematician Ben Laposky makes "oscillograph" images on screen of cathode-ray tube.

1959

CalComp launches first digital plotter to output computer images to print.

1965

Computer images begin to be exhibited as artworks.

1967

E.A.T. (Experiments in Art and Technology) formed to promote collaborative efforts between artists and engineers.

C.A.V.S., (Center for Advanced Visual Studies), founded by Gyorgy Kepes, opens at M.I.T.

1968

The Machine, as Seen at the End of the Mechanical Age exhibition at The Museum of Modern Art, New York.

Some More Beginnings exhibition at the Brooklyn Museum, New York.

Cybernetic Serendipity exhibition at the Institute of Contemporary Arts, London.

1971

Art and Technology exhibition at the Los Angeles County Museum of Art.

1973

First computer "painting" software created at the Xerox Palo Alto Research Center by Richard Shoup.

1976

IBM introduces the 6640, the first continuous-flow inkjet system.

1977

Applicon announces first color continuous-flow inkjet printer.

Siemens launches first piezoelectric inkjet printer.

1981

IBM introduces its first personal computer.

Canon introduces its Bubble Jet thermal print technology.

1984

Apple introduces the Macintosh line of computers.

HP releases first thermal inkjet printer (2225 ThinkJet).

Computers, Art, and Printmaking: A Brief History (continued)

1985

New York master printer Harry Bowers claims to make first digital color photo print.

Jon Cone opens Cone Editions Press for computer-assisted printmaking.

1987

The IRIS Graphics 3024 inkjet printer is launched for the pre-press proofing industry.

1989

David Coons outputs first IRIS fine-art print (of singer Joni Mitchell) for Graham Nash.

1990

Adobe Systems releases image editing software Photoshop 1.0, developed by John Knoll and Thomas Knoll.

First all-digitally printed, photographic fine-art show (Graham Nash) at the Simon Lowinsky gallery, New York.

Sally Larsen's *Tunnels Point Transformer* is the first digital fine-art print included into the permanent collection of The Metropolitan Museum of Art (New York).

1991

Nash Editions opens for business.

Jack Duganne (while at Nash Editions) first uses the term "giclée."

Maryann and John Doe start Harvest Productions.

1994

Epson introduces the Stylus Color—the first, desktop, photorealistic inkjet printer.

Durst first shows its Lambda digital laser imager, making it possible to output digital files directly to a color photographic development process.

1997

International Association of Fine Art Digital Printmakers (IAFADP) forms.

Digital Atelier: A Printmaking Studio for the 21st Century demonstration at the National Museum of American Art of the Smithsonian Institution, Washington, D.C.

1998

Jon Cone debuts DigitalPlatinum for IRIS monochromatic system.

MacDermid ColorSpan announces its Giclée PrintMakerFA, the first wide-format digital printer created specifically for fine-art market.

Roland DGA releases its Hi-Fi JET wide-format, pigmented 6-color printer.

2000

Jon Cone releases the PiezographyBW system for multi-monochromatic printing.

Epson launches the Stylus Photo 2000P, the first desktop inkjet printer to use pigmented inks.

2001

Opening of the Beecher Center at The Butler Institute of American Art (Ohio), the first art museum in the United States dedicated to digital art.

010101: Art in Technological Times exhibition at the San Francisco Museum of Modern Art.

BitStreams exhibition at the Whitney Museum of American Art, New York.

Digital: Printmaking Now exhibition at the Brooklyn Museum of Art, New York.

Giclée Printers Association (GPA) forms.

2002

Lexmark introduces first 4800-dpi desktop inkjet printer (Z65).

Epson unveils first 7-color, pigment-ink desktop inkjet printer (Stylus Photo 2100/2200).

Cone Editions introduces ConeTech PiezoTone quad black inkjet inks.

Epson unveils first 2-picoliter ink droplet (Stylus Photo 960).

HP introduces first switchable 4- to 6-ink desktop inkjet printer (Deskjet 5550).

2003

HP introduces first 8-color desktop inkjet printer with 3 blacks (Photosmart 7960).

Cone Editions launches PiezographyBW ICC system for monochromatic inkjet printing.

Digital Printmakers Guild forms.

Professional Digital Imaging Association (DPIA) forms.

2004

Epson releases first 1.5-picoliter ink droplets and first desktop inkjet printer with Red and Blue plus Hi-Gloss inks and Gloss Optimizer (Stylus Photo R800).

Canon launches first desktop inkjet printer with 8 ink tanks including Red and Green (i9900 Photo Printer).

(Sources: John Bilotta, Steve Boulter; Canon USA, Jon Cone; David Coons; Andrew Darlow; Digital Atelier; Jack Duganne; Durst U.S., Epson America, David Hamre; Mac Holbert, Hewlett-Packard Company, Martin Juergens, Preservation of Ink Jet Hardcopies, 1999; Marilyn Kushner, Digital: Printmaking Now, Brooklyn Museum of Art, 2001; Graham Nash; The New York Times; Mike Pelletier; Roland DGA, John Shaw/DPIA, Barbara Vogt Stability Issues and Test Methods for Ink Jet Materials, 2001; Charles Wehrenberg; Henry Wilhelm)

Defining Digital Printing

Just what is digital printing anyway? The way I like to describe it is by being more specific and using the words "high-quality digital printing." This phrase defines the boundaries of a complex topic and helps us focus on the subject of this book. So, let's break down *high-quality digital printing* into its components. This may seem like an elementary exercise, but it's important to understand the territory we're about to enter.

High Quality

High quality means better than normal or above average. This is not ordinary printing but something at a higher level. Something more akin to art. ("Photo quality" is another term often used for this in relation to inkjet printing.)

Of course, talking about art gets tricky. People have been debating its definition for thousands of years, and it certainly won't end here. However, I equate "high quality" with "art," so for our purposes, art (and I use the term *very* broadly) is created by individual photographers and/or artists—they can be the same or not, and I'll sometimes call the combination "photographer-artists"—even if it's only as a hobby or sideline. Whether it's destined for the walls of the Louvre or the walls of a living room or corporate boardroom, art is meant to be displayed, to be admired—and yes, even bought and sold, and to provide inspiration and an emotional connection with the artist or the viewer's own thoughts and feelings.

The world of commercial art, which includes the fields of graphic design, advertising, and marketing communications—commercial imagemaking—are on the edges of this universe, and I'll cover them in a limited way. But, we won't spend much time with the digital printing technologies that produce signs and banners, brochures, billboards, event graphics, building wraps, and vehicle signage. While photographers and artists can—and frequently do—use commercial technologies to create their high-quality work, that world is not the primary focus of this book.

Digital

Here's the basic concept: Digital means using numbers to represent something, and that's exactly what a computer does. A normal image is converted into numerical data (a long string of ones and zeros) that describe or quantify each sample point or "pixel" (short for *pic*ture

One of two large murals (and five other pieces) that were commissioned by the Boston Federal Reserve Bank from digital artist Dorothy Simpson Krause in 2000 (and completed in the fall of 2003). Krause used historical documents and photographs from the bank's archives to create the 60 x 151-inch mural, which is composed of five panels printed on a Mutoh Falcon II inkjet printer.

Courtesy of Dorothy Simpson Krause
www.dotkrause.com

*el*ement, the basic unit of image information) in terms of certain attributes such as color and intensity. This data can be stored, manipulated, and ultimately transformed with digital printing technologies back into a normally viewed image (see Chapter 2 for an in-depth look at this).

Printing

Traditional (analog) printing is a mechanical process that uses a physical master or "matrix" for making repeatable prints. Commercial and even traditional fine-art printing presses use pressure or impact to transfer the image from a carrier, plate, or blanket—the matrix—to the receiving paper. Similarly, with old-style photography, the negative or a transparency is the matrix through which light travels to expose the print.

Digital printing is different, however. There is no pressure or impact, and there is no *physical* matrix. The matrix now sits in the computer in the form of digital data that can be converted repeatedly, with or without any variation, into a print by any photographer-artist who either does his own printing ("self-printing") or who uses an outside printing service. (I'm intentionally avoiding all the permutations and variations of computer-to-plate and other forms of commercial digital printing, although there's no reason they can't be used.)

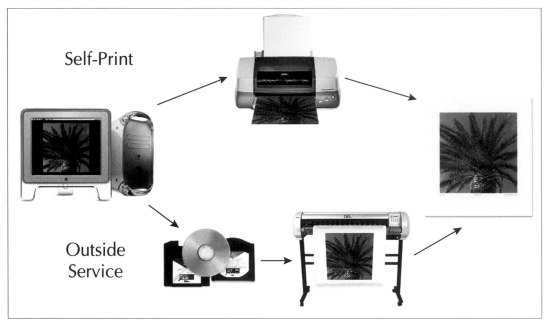

Digital printing workflow: from digital matrix to hardcopy print.

Putting Prints in Their Places

The worlds of photography and traditional fine-art printmaking have been historically separated by a kind of psychological barrier. Art exhibitions of fine-art prints don't usually include photographs. Photo exhibits don't also have etchings, for example. And as far as the practitioners themselves go, traditional artists such as painters or printmakers have not commonly also been photographers, and the reverse has also been true. The techniques and the language of each field have been different—until now.

Computer technology in general, and digital printing in particular, is the big gorilla straddling the fence and spilling over onto the once-separate arenas of photography and fine-art printmaking. The whole field of image and art production is rapidly changing, and if you plan to be an active player in this new world, you have to know something about the old one. It's time for a quick review to give you some perspective.

What's a Print?

Unlike paintings or drawings, most prints exist in repeatable, multiple examples. Images are not created directly on paper but with another medium or on another surface (a master or matrix), which then transfers (or in the case of digital, "outputs") the image to paper. More than one impression or example can be made by printing the same image on a new piece of paper. The total number of impressions or prints an artist or photographer makes of one image is frequently called an *edition*. Following are the three major types of prints that apply to the making of art. (Traditional fine-art printmakers maintain that only they make what can be truly called "prints," but I take a wider view.)

Photographic Prints

Photographers have been making prints of their images ever since the pioneering days of the medium in the 19th century. While Louis Daguerre (1839) and before him Nicéphore Niépce (1829) were able to produce the first, fixed photographs, it was William Henry Fox Talbot's 1840 invention of the Calotype process that allowed photographers to make an unlimited number of positive paper prints from the same negative.

I roughly categorize traditional photographic prints into three technology groups: black-and-white, color, and alternative process.

Jackson Lake by William Henry Jackson, albumen print, c. 1892.

Library of Congress, Prints and Photographs Division, Detroit Publishing Company Collection

Black-and-White Prints

Normal black-and-white photography is metallic-silver based. The chemical processing of a silver-halide emulsion that has been exposed to light via an enlarger creates a lasting image made up of tiny bits of silver that absorb, rather than reflect, light. Correctly processed black-and-white prints on fiber-based paper are essentially permanent; they will last for hundreds of years without image deterioration. "Silver-gelatin print" is the art-world description for a normal black-and-white print.

Traditional black-and-white developing in a chemical darkroom.

Courtesy of Seth Rossman www.msrphoto.com

Color Prints

Although the early photographers had hoped to produce color images from day one—and they partially succeeded but with awkward and time-consuming processes like Autochrome, dye-transfer, and tricolor carbro prints—real color photography didn't actually begin until 1935 when Kodak launched its famous Kodachrome transparency film. Then in 1939, Agfa introduced the first paper for printing from color negatives using the "chromagenic development" (color coupler) method. The basic process is this: The chemical development of a certain type of silver-halide emulsion creates products that react or "couple" with special compounds to form color dyes and a resulting color image. Unlike the metallic-silver prints of black and white, color prints are composed of dye emulsion layers that are sensitive to different light spectra and that create images when developed, primarily in RA-4 or EP-2 processing. The three emulsion layers are: red-sensitive producing cyan dyes, green-sensitive producing magenta dyes, and blue-sensitive producing yellow dyes.

Alternative Process

Fitting somewhere between (or outside, depending on your point of view) black and white and color are the alternative or non-traditional photo print processes. They're "alternative" primarily because they tend to be handmade or use custom techniques that are, in many cases, resurrections—or continuations—of antique methods for printing photographs. Examples include: cyanotypes, kallitypes, gum bichromates, platinum and palladium prints, salted paper and albumen prints, van dykes, bromoils, and sepia (or other) chemically toned prints. Many of these are made by contact-printing large negatives and most are monochromatic (cyanotypes are blue, which is why they're also called "blueprints;" more recent diazotype process blueprints are positive instead of negative, earning them the nickname "bluelines").

Jill Skupin Burkholder is a practitioner of one of the oldest and most painterly of the traditional photographic processes: bromoil, which begins with a bleached silver print and ends with a pictorial version of the image that has been artistically interpreted using a brush and lithography ink. Left: *Trees and Stream* (2001).

Courtesy of Jill Skupin Burkholder
www.jillskupinburkholder.com

Liquid emulsions, image transfers, and emulsion lifts are alternative printing processes for color photographs.

Traditional Fine-Art Prints

Fine-art printmaking has a glorious history that extends back to the time of the 16th century and Albrecht Dürer. Here is a brief rundown of the major types of traditional fine-art prints (also called "fine prints" or "works on paper").

Relief Prints

The artist sketches an image on a wood block or other surface and then cuts away pieces from the surface, leaving only the raised image. Ink is then applied to the surface with a roller and transferred onto paper with a press or by hand-burnishing or rubbing. The recessed, cutaway areas do not receive ink and appear white on the printed image. Relief prints are characterized by bold dark-light contrasts. The primary relief techniques are *woodcut* (the earliest and most enduring print technique), *wood engraving* (made from the end-grain surface of blocks and offering more precision and detail), and *linocut* (printed from linoleum; well-suited for large areas of contrasting colors).

Intaglio Prints

Intaglio (pronounced "in-tal-yo") comes from the Italian word *intagliare*, meaning "to incise." An image is incised with a pointed tool or "bitten" with acid into a metal plate, usually copper or zinc. The plate is covered with ink and then cleaned so that only the incised grooves hold the ink. The plate and dampened paper are then run through a press to create the print. The intaglio family of printmaking techniques includes: *engraving* (an engraved line has a sharp and clean appearance), *drypoint* (results in heavier, softer-looking lines than those in an engraving), *mezzotint* (yields soft tonalities ranging from gray to black), *etching* (results in a characteristically raised surface), and *aquatint* (an etching process yielding a textured and toned image).

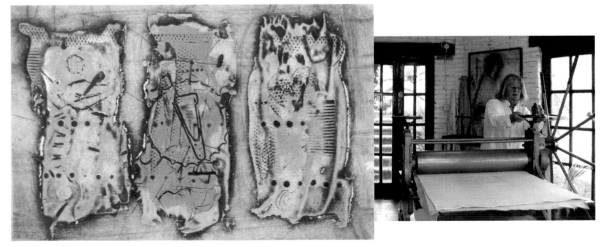

Right: Spanish painter/printmaker Maureen Lucía Booth works with her etching press in her studio in the Sierra Nevada foothills near Granada. Left: *The Three Graces*, drypoint, additive (etching), by Maureen Booth (2002).
Courtesy of Mike Booth/WorldPrintmakers.com

Lithography

Invented in 1798, lithography is a "planographic" process that was championed by artists such as Henri de Toulouse-Lautrec, Goya, Picasso, Degas, Braque, and Miro. To make a lithograph, the artist uses a greasy medium such as crayon or tusche to create an image on a stone or metal plate. The surface is then dampened with water, which is repelled by the greasy areas, sticking only to the sections of the plate that have not been marked by the artist. Printer's ink is then applied to the plate with a roller. This, in turn, sticks only to the greasy sections, as the water protects the rest of the plate. The stone or plate is then covered with paper and run through a printing press to create the print.

Screenprints (Serigraphy)

This technique was popularized by artists like Andy Warhol who exploited its bold, commercial look. To make a screenprint, an image that has been cut out of a material (paper, fabric, or film) is attached to a piece of tautly stretched mesh. Paint is then forced through the mesh—the "screen"—onto the sheet of paper below by means of a squeegee. The uncovered areas of the screen allow the paint to pass through, while the areas covered by the image shapes do not. For works with more than one color, a separate screen is required for each color. Screenprints, silkscreen, and serigraphy are different words for the same process.

Monotypes/Monoprints

As their names imply, *monotypes* or *monoprints* (the words are often confused and sometimes used interchangeably) are prints that have an edition of a single impression. The artist creates an image on a smooth, flat surface, which is then covered with dampened paper and run through a printing press or rubbed with the back of a spoon or with another tool, or even the artist's hand. Only one unique print results.

Digital Prints

Announcing a new, major, high-quality printing category—digital prints! Claiming that this is an official classification in a rapidly evolving field is a risky, even foolish, endeavor, but you have to start somewhere, and this is a place to draw a line in the sand. At the very least, we can consider digital printing to be a new tool for photographers and artists who want to expand their artistic options.

While there is no end to the inventiveness of rival terminology—"giclées," "IRIS prints," "inkjets," "virtual paintings," "digigraphs," "limited editions on canvas," "digital pigment prints," "pigmented inks on archival paper," (do I need to go on?), let's keep it to one overall term for the moment—*digital prints*, which I define as prints resulting from a digital master or matrix. Whether they are "originals" or "reproductions" is another issue, which I discuss below.

Of course, artists being artists, all these nice and neat categories are frequently violated. For example, wedding and portrait photographers are famous for coating and embellishing their prints. Kolibri Art Studio, a leading serigraph atelier in Torrance, California, offers both serigraphic and digital printing to artists who will sometimes start with a digital reproduction and add serigraphic embossing, texturizing, or gold-leafing on top. New York City's Pamplemousse Press creates digital editions that combine IRIS printing with

Printing Cousins: Offset and Digital Offset

Offset Lithography: While technically not a fine-art printing process, offset lithography is frequently used in printing art reproductions, usually only in large editions where economy of scale brings the unit cost down. This is how everyday art posters (as well as brochures, magazines, and newspapers) are printed. The "offset" part of the name comes from the principle of transferring the image from the revolving plate to a rubber blanket before final transfer to the paper (see Figure 1.1). Because of the similarity of terms, and because they both fall under the "planographic" category, fine-art lithographs are sometimes called "original lithographs" to distinguish them from commercial offset prints.

Digital Offset/Indigo: Here's a new printing technology that's mainly commercial but with an artistic edge: digital offset color. Indigo, originally an Israeli/Dutch company but now a division of HP, is an example (see Figure 1.2).

Indigo uses a laser imager, special liquid ink (ElectroInk), and a thermal offset system to print the image. It's fully digital from creation to printing, which means that there is no film, no imagesetters, no plates, no photo-chemicals, and no press make-ready.

You're mostly likely to find an HP Indigo Press at a normal print shop, but the output is anything but normal! It produces offset litho-like quality but in short-run jobs (100–500 is a good average range) and in full color. And, because it's all-digital, each piece can be unique. What that means is that you could customize a print run so that names, languages, or even images could change *per print*. This is a great new way to print art exhibition catalogs, calendars, and invitations.

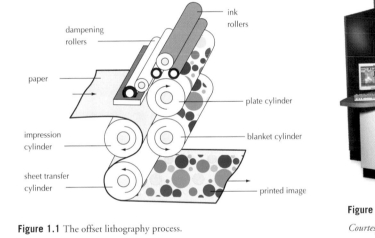

Figure 1.1 The offset lithography process.

Figure 1.2 The HP Indigo Press 3050.
Courtesy of Hewlett-Packard Company

construction and relief techniques. Members of the Digital Atelier printmaking studio love to use digital prints as the base or ground and then add painting, collage, encaustic, and emulsion transfer techniques. (See Chapter 11 for more on this.)

Why Go Digital?

Digital imaging and printing have changed the rules of visual communication. Making original prints or reproductions (see next page), especially at a large size and in color, used to be costly, cumbersome, or difficult for the individual photographer or artist. No longer. The advantages of digital printing are clear:

Cost

Once the initial setup and proofing stage is complete, digital prints can be made on an as-needed basis. This is true print-on-demand. You want one print to test a market or an image? No problem. You want 100? Also no problem. By contrast, conventional non-photographic,

The author's digital print, *Pelican Jetty.*
© 2001-2004 Harald Johnson

print production methods require the entire print run to be produced all at once. The result is a pile of inventory that probably took a pile of cash to make (also known as the "Now What Do I Do with that Stack of Prints in My Garage?" syndrome).

Consistency

Because digital source files are stored on computer hard disks or on other digital storage media, they can be reused over time to produce identical results, assuming the media, inks, and hardware/software have not changed. In theory, the first and last prints in an edition of 100 produced over a ten-year period should look identical.

Storage

Related to the above, digital art takes little physical room when stored on disk. Digital files can be long-lasting *if* the digital data remains intact and there is a way to read it. Another benefit is for artists working with traditional media who can have their completed originals scanned and stored for future use in print editions. Not only does this safeguard the image, but it allows artists to sell their originals without having to worry about reclaiming them later for reproductions.

Larger Sizes

Size is not much of an issue with digital, especially with wide-format inkjet printers, which come in four-, five-, and even six-feet-wide models; and that's not even considering the "grand-format" printers, more often used for commercial work. Printing on roll paper, the length of an inkjet image is only limited by the printer's software. For even larger prints, images can be "tiled" and assembled in pieces. And, of course, the same digital source file can be cropped, blown up or shrunk, and printed in many sizes.

Artistic Control

If you print your own images, you have complete control of the process. You decide on the best machine to use, you select the best paper-and-ink combination, you decide if you want to run the colors a little heavier on the next print. You have no one else to blame or to praise. You also get the immediate feedback of seeing what's working in print and what's not.

Photographer John Livzey has the flexibility to print what he wants when he wants in his own home studio.
Courtesy of John Livzey Photography/www.livzey.com

Freedom & Flexibility

Before the digital printing revolution, average photographers could not make their own color prints without a large investment in equipment and the space to house it. Or, they had to go to a photolab, where their printing choices were limited. Now, with desktop printing equipment, almost anyone has the freedom to print what they want, when they want. Using the same image file, a photographer-artist can experiment with different sizes, croppings, or unconventional media. New images, variations, or new editions can be sampled and tested at minimal cost and with little risk, one at a time.

Who's Doin' Digital?

The digital revolution (including the Internet) has created opportunities for photographers, artists, and imagemakers to create and distribute their work in ways that were not even dreamed of ten or even five years ago. While many like to sidestep categories, it's still useful to attempt some kind of lumping together, if only to allow more understanding of the widespread reach of digital imaging and printing.

Also, art buyers and marketers tend to think in terms of classifications: pop art, Old Masters, that sort of thing. The same with juried art shows and contests, which by necessity need to categorize entries and awards to keep the whole system of judging art somewhat manageable. So here goes my attempt at classifying the *creators* of high-quality digital prints (see Gallery Showcase for some good examples from each group). Printmakers, as a group, get their own special chapter (10).

Photographers/Imagemakers

The digital wave has definitely broken over the photographic/imagemaking field, and most photographers are riding it (they'll drown if they don't). It's only logical considering that photography was born out of the technological innovations of Niépce, Talbot, Bayard, and Daguerre in the 19th century. Some say that the digital revolution is as important as the invention of color photography, even photography itself. Of course, there will always be the few purists and hold-outs who thumb their noses at technological advances, but if you are reading this book, you are probably not one of them.

Left: Photographer Gary Goldberg creates images in a wide range of sub-specialties including fashion and beauty.
Right: Goldberg checks a print in his Florida studio.
Courtesy of Gary Goldberg Photography/www.garygoldbergphoto.com

Some of the photographers who are emerging from their smelly darkrooms and into the digital light are merely using digital printing to output their existing work with little intervention. Others are playing a more active digital role, either shooting with a digital camera or scanning in their film-based images before beginning the work of color correcting, retouching, and in general, improving what they have. Many are taking full advantage of what digital imaging and especially printing can offer them.

A good example is Gary Goldberg, a new Toronto resident (from Florida) who covers a lot of bases in the digital game. He's a commercial photographer now shooting all-digitally and working with ad agencies, record companies, and other types of businesses to create his portrait, fashion, and advertising images. However, he also photographs weddings, does digital restorations of damaged photographs, and markets his own fine-art prints at art shows and through online services. And it's those last two job categories, in addition to printing his portfolios, that put his several inkjet printers to most use.

Goldberg is also not hesitant in using the online display and marketing services of Shutterfly.com and Pictage.com, both of whom utilize the digital printing technologies covered in this book for their products (read more about this in Chapter 10).

Traditional Artists

The painters, watercolorists, and sketch and pastel artists who have taken up digital printing techniques to publish and reproduce their work are currently producing a large number of commercially sold, digital prints. Artists can either have a transparency made of their original work, take it to a digital printmaker for direct digital scanning, or digitize it themselves with their own digital camera or scanner (if the original is small enough). The digital file is then typically printed on either paper (watercolors, drawings, or pastels) or canvas (oils or acrylics) to produce an edition.

Left: *Blue Bird*, available as a fresco and also as a limited edition giclée and hand-embellished print. Right: Traditional artist Steve Bogdanoff works on one of his unique frescoes in his New Orleans studio.
Courtesy of Bogdanoff Gallery/www.bogdanoff.com

American artist Steve Bogdanoff is known for his interpretive *fresco secco* paintings. (*Fresco secco,* where the artist applies paint to dried plaster, is one of the two classic fresco techniques. *Buon fresco,* which is the art of painting on freshly spread, moist lime plaster with pigments suspended in a water vehicle, is the other.) Influenced by ancient Greek art among others, Bogdanoff replicates in his own version of the fresco from scenes depicted in myriad wall murals, friezes, reliefs, and statues starting with the Greek Bronze Age through the end of the Renaissance.

Bogdanoff has his frescoes photographed, drum-scanned, and put on a CD. He then does all the image editing on his computer in preparation for his own digital prints on paper via inkjet printing in his New Orleans studio (on an Epson Stylus Pro 4000). In this storefront gallery, he displays not only his fresco originals but also his limited-edition prints, some of which are hand-embellished with acrylic washes. The prints have definitely become a hit, and Bogdanoff admits that a substantial part of his revenue comes from them.

Digital Artists

A blurry, hard-to-define kind of group, this is the forward edge of digital art. It includes artists who draw or paint on the computer, who heavily manipulate and alter their photo-based art, who create "machine art" with mathematical formulas or fractals, or who combine traditional and digital techniques to produce new forms of hybrid, mixed-media art. Since their originals exist only in the computer, digital printing is the primary method used to output their work.

Left: *Reflections,* available as a made-to-order print, either signed and dated or in limited edition.
Right: Digital artist Ursula Freer at work in her New Mexico studio.
Courtesy of Ursula Freer/www.ursulafreer.com

These are the artists who are truly partners with the computer, using it as a tool no differently than Monet used a brush. This is what used to be called "computer art," but that term is much too old-fashioned and imprecise now to cover the amazing range of today's digital artists.

New Mexico artist Ursula Freer has a traditional art background, but seven years ago she went all-digital. "It has totally changed my way of creating art," she says. "The medium is quite amazing; there seems to be no end to the possibilities for creative expression and great freedom for communicating ideas."

In her studio, Freer works with digital photos taken with her digital camera, software and filters, and also what she calls "screen painting" by using a digital graphics tablet. She produces her own inkjet prints on fine-art paper, and she markets them through galleries and her website. In addition, Freer has started to do digital art photography and printing for other artists in her local area.

Gaining Ground: A Question of Acceptance

Artists have been criticized for adopting new technologies since they first rubbed colored dirt on the walls of the caves at Lascaux, France. Oil-on-canvas was considered heresy by the tempera-on-wood-panel crowd in the mid-1400s. Photography was blasted as a perversion in the early 19th century. The same with lithography. And it is no different with digital technology, which many photographer-artists—the true opportunists that they are—have readily adopted.

While the digital printing boom includes everyone from aging Baby Boomers who are creating family photo prints in their home offices to professional artists selling fine-art prints through galleries, it is the latter group who are pushing the edges of print quality, durability, and acceptability. However, it has not been an easy road to gain the public's and the art community's acceptance. First attempts at digital printing were crude and focused on the technology itself. But art typically expands to absorb new technologies, and after the initial, giddy, "look what I can do" phase, photographers and artists have evolved to the point of focusing on a true artistic goal: moving us with their images.

A seminal event on the path to digital acceptance was the printmaking artist-in-residency, *Digital Atelier: A Printmaking Studio for the 21st Century*, at the National Museum of American Art of the Smithsonian Institution (now the Smithsonian American Art Museum) in Washington, D.C., which ran for three weeks in 1997 (see Figure 1.3). All five founding members of Unique Editions (Dorothy Simpson Krause, Karin Schminke, Bonny Lhotka, Helen Golden, and the late Judith Moncrieff) were present, and this was probably the first time the public got to interact with computers in a workshop setting at a major museum (this event is now part of the permanent collection of the Smithsonian). Krause, Schminke, and Lhotka would go on to be Digital Atelier, the well-known printmaking collective (see more about them in Chapter 11).

Another watershed event marking the art world's acceptance of digital art was when the Brooklyn Museum of Art staged its *Digital: Printmaking Now* exhibition that ran from June through August, 2001. The second largest art museum in the U.S. put a huge stamp of approval on digitally created art.

Digital prints (primarily inkjets) are now part of the permanent collections of New York's Metropolitan Museum of Art, the Museum of Modern Art, the Whitney Museum of American Art, the Corcoran Gallery in Washington, D.C., and the Art Institute of Chicago. Even the Louvre, The Musee D'Orsay, the Hermitage, both National Galleries

Figure 1.3 Unique Editions, aka Digital Atelier, in the learning center at the groundbreaking event *Digital Atelier: A Printmaking Studio for the 21st Century* at the National Museum of American Art of the Smithsonian Institution in Washington, D.C., in 1997. From left: Dorothy Simpson Krause, Karin Schminke, Bonny Lhotka, Helen Golden, and the late Judith Moncrieff (in back).

Courtesy of Digital Atelier/www.digitalatelier.com

(U.S. and UK), and the Library of Congress are now reproducing some of their most important holdings by way of digital printing.

However, digital printing is not just for museums. Most professional photographers are now creating their portfolios from digital prints, and the National Geographic headquarters in Washington, D.C., uses both a Durst Lambda and a Fuji Frontier to do 90 percent of its for-the-public and internal photographic printing.

The proof is in the acceptance of digital printing technologies by large and small art galleries, mini and custom photo labs, online photo services, and by e-commerce businesses that are providing art buyers with high-quality prints that fit somewhere between inexpensive posters and unobtainable originals. Then, there are the hotels, shops, corporations, and other businesses that have gotten into the digital act, commissioning, purchasing, and displaying both original and reproduction digital prints for customers and clients to enjoy (see Figure 1.4).

Figure 1.4 This exhibition of photographer Andrew Darlow's limited-edition inkjet prints on watercolor paper took place at Renny & Reed, world-renowned florist and event design firm on Park Avenue in New York City in 2004.

Courtesy of Andrew Darlow/www.andrewdarlow.com

Schools are also promoting digital printing. Andrew Behla, an educator and color management consultant, offers a 10-week course ("Mastering Fine Art Digital Printing") in the spring and fall quarters at UCLA Extension in Los Angeles. This course is attended by artists, photographers, and printmakers.

And more local and regional art festivals, shows, and contests are adding "digital " categories to their official entry rules, although their definitions and requirements are sometimes confusing to artists.

To be sure, there were questions and problems with digital printing early on. The first IRIS inks were notorious for their ability to fade right off the paper. But subsequent improvements in ink formulations and in ink/paper matching have ended most of those arguments. Probably the remaining obstacle to the full acceptance of digital print methods today is the faulty perception that this type of art is "mechanical" and, therefore, inferior in some way. Nothing could be further from the truth.

Let's face it, people who are used to slower, more traditional practices sometimes have a hard time adjusting to newer, automated ways of doing things. "The harder it is to make, the better it is" seems to be a commonly held belief among the public and even some artists when discussing art. But technical methods including automation do not necessarily diminish the value of the creative works aided by them. Besides the obvious examples of lithography and photography, look further back in art history. Michelangelo used teams of assistants as did Leonardo DaVinci. Artist David Hockney claims that painters such as Caravaggio, Ingres, Velasquez, and Vermeer all used either a *camera obscura* or a *camera lucida* lens system to speed up and improve the initial drafting step in their paintings. In his 2001 book, *Secret Knowledge: Rediscovering the Lost Techniques of the Old Masters*, Hockney, who himself is one of the world's best-known living artists, makes the argument that artists were enthusiastically using lenses and mirrors (the highest of high-tech at the time) in creating their art 400–500 years ago. It's a small step from optics to computers and digital workflows, and Hockney's book has helped open people's eyes to the fact that technology has always been an important part of art creation.

The computer and other digital tools are just that—tools. Used in the hands of a perceptive, talented artist or photographer, a computer is not subordinate to brushes, palette knives, or enlargers. The fact is, the artist's own hand lies heavy on most of the steps in the making of digital art. Using cameras, scanners, digital tablets, and a whole host of image-editing software, photographers and artists have a personal and intense relationship with their images as they guide them through the various stages of creation, manipulation, and finally, printing. The aesthetic decisions are always the artist's. In most cases, this is not mechanical art; this is imagery that emanates directly from the mind and the soul of the artist.

Digital Decisions

Photographers and artists tend to fall into a couple of large groups when it comes to digital printing. Knowing what these are up front and matching your interests to them can help you better navigate through the digital landscape.

Doing It Yourself vs. Sending It Out

If you want to get involved with digital printing, you must soon make an important decision: do the printing yourself or send it out to a printmaking studio or print-service provider, atelier, or even an online printing service. There are advantages, disadvantages, and consequences to each route.

Doing Your Own Printing

Some artists love the thought of working with their own printing equipment. Photographers especially, with their tradition of working in a darkroom full of enlargers, timers, and other technical equipment, are a driving force in the growth of "self-printing." (Note: The following applies more to "serious" artists, but anyone at any level can learn from this discussion.)

Advantages of Photographer-Artists Printing Their Own Work

- **Personal involvement, flexibility, and full control of the entire process.** It's your printer, your paper, your inks, your everything. You can test, and re-test, and test again. You can change settings, paper, anything you want, when you want. You are in control. Doing it yourself, once you've figured out the system, gets you on the road to making prints very quickly. You can also fine-tune and output your prints on your schedule, one at a time, or in small quantities.

Photographer Steven Katzman in full control in his digital darkroom. Photography by A.F. Uccello.

Courtesy of Steven Katzman
www.stevenkatzmanphotography.com

- **Once a breakeven point on your initial capital investment is reached,** *print costs can be less.* After you've locked down your workflow settings and procedures, the extra cost of making additional prints is marginal—only the cost of paper, ink, and overhead.

A DO-IT-YOURSELF WARNING! What tends to happen with a lot of self-printing artists is that they start off printing for themselves, then doing a favor for an artist friend, then buying some more equipment, then taking in a couple more print clients to pay for the equipment, and before you know it, they are in the printmaking business, not the art-making business. That is exactly how many of today's printmakers started.

Disadvantages of Self-Printing

■ **Potentially steep learning curve and time commitment to acquire the printmaking craft.** Digital printing is both an art and a craft, and just having the equipment does not guarantee you will know what to do with it. Learning how to work with a new technology takes time, and lots of it. This is time that could be spent doing other things or creating more art. Do you also do your own auto body work or your own roof repairs?

■ **Sometimes significant upfront investment in hardware, software, and consumables (especially for the larger formats).** Add to that the perpetual, ongoing costs of self-printing that include: overhead (rent, utilities), your time or labor (your time is worth something, isn't it?), consumables (paper, inks), maintenance, software/hardware upgrades, and continuing education and training. If you're in the business of art, an accountant would call all of this your "cost of goods sold."

Of course, if you are doing this as a hobby or in your off-time, then these obstacles are less of a consideration.

Using an Outside Printmaker or Printing Service

An old saying in the art world goes, "The artist is the eye, the printmaker is the hand." Because printing techniques can be complicated, and considering the traditionally collaborative nature of fine-art printmaking, many photographers and artists use a "print-for-pay" service to create their final work.

Advantages of Using a Print-Service Provider

■ **You work with seasoned printing professionals and take advantage of top-of-the-line technology that is more quickly updated.** An experienced printmaker brings to the table a vast knowledge of materials and artistic approaches that have been tried and tested many times before you walk in the door. Besides helping to guarantee a higher-quality result, a printmaker can act as an aesthetic guide and be a valuable art advisor.

Mark Staples (right) of Staples Fine Art in Richmond, Virginia, confers with artist Durwood Dommisse about the digital prints Staples is producing from Dommisse's landscape oil paintings.

Courtesy of Mark Staples
www.staplesart.com

- **Up-front investment to test the market or your expectations is low.** Depending on the size and the process, an investment of anywhere from $50 to $500 is all that's needed to produce a trial print (unframed). This is a good way for an "emerging artist" to see if their work is going to sell. Or for a photographer to try out a new or exotic printing process. A corollary to this is that since your investment is low, you are free to drop a printmaker or service at any point and move on. You haven't lost much.

- If you're a professional artist, prints may be more acceptable to galleries or art buyers if produced by a well-known printmaker. The best printing studios apply a "chop" to every print going out the door. Typically an embossed logo in the print's lower left or right corner, this is a seal of approval indicating that the work has met the printmaker's quality standards. A well-respected printmaker's chop is a marketing tool for the artist; knowledgeable art marketers and buyers will recognize it instantly. The downside is that some—not all—of the more famous printmakers charge accordingly.

Disadvantages of Using an Outside Printing Service

- **Loss of some control and flexibility.** The print is in the printmaker's hands, not yours. The final result will depend, in part, on their skill level and your ability to communicate what you want to their craftspeople. If they think it's good enough, but you don't, you have a problem.

- **Time delays going back and forth.** No matter how good or how fast an outside printmaker is, there is still a lot of back-and-forth downtime between artist and printer. Getting to the final approved proof and to that first finished print sometimes can take weeks.

- **Ongoing, per-print costs are higher.** Using a printing service may not be worth it economically if you are creating large prints for sale and your prints sell for much less than $500. Run the numbers and see how much profit is left over after the costs for initial setup, prints, coating, "curating," shipping, and framing have been added up. Of course, if your prints are selling for four-figure amounts, this is not a problem!

It is also possible to take *both* paths down the print road. Some artists and photographers using print-for-pay services will make internal proofs on their own equipment to fine-tune their work in progress. This also comes in handy since most printmakers prefer to have a hard-copy proof (sometimes called a "match" or "guide" print) to look at and work from. On the flip side, some self-printers do the majority of the work themselves, but save the largest or most complicated pieces for a professional printmaker.

(For more on working with outside printmakers, see Chapter 10.)

Reproductions or Original Prints?

While there continues to be debate about this, many art professionals in the art community have come to the following definition: A *digital reproduction* is a multiple print or exact copy of an original work of art that was created by conventional means (painting, drawing, etc.) and then reproduced by using any of the digital print technologies described in this book. A giclée print (see "What's In a Name" below) of an original oil painting, for example, is a digital reproduction. (Note that not everyone agrees with this definition. Even some of the artists in this book use the term "giclée" for their original work.)

An *original digital print* uses the same output methods, except the original does not exist outside of or apart from the computer. There is still an original, but it's *in* the computer. Or as some would have it: the "printing matrix" exists only as a digital file. (This is similar to the

Print Council of America's definition of traditional printmaking methods where "the impression or print is made directly from the original material by the artist or pursuant to his or her directions; the image does not exist unless it is printed.") Therefore, a print made from a digitally captured, scanned, or manipulated photo is an original digital print. (Even traditional photographs have always been considered "multiple" original prints.) So is a print made from what a digital artist creates with a digital graphics tablet or related software.

Printmaker Lester Wilson of Greencastle Photo Service, Greencastle, Indiana, checks a digital reproduction from his ColorSpan Giclée PrintMaker FA inkjet printer (in background).

Courtesy of Seth Rossman

These two main divisions represent two different ways of looking at the digital printing process. (Of course, there are other ways, too.) Why is all this nitpicking important? Because in the world of art, the idea of "originality" is carefully considered by many galleries, art festivals, and art buyers. Just as the label "photograph" can affect a work's desirability, acceptance, and price, so too do the labels "reproduction" or "original print."

An original print of JD Jarvis' *The Unwoven Tale* was featured in a group exhibit at the Cork Gallery at Lincoln Center, New York City in 2004. The artist explains: "The piece is an example of the amalgamation or synthesis of natural media digital painting techniques and tools, and algorithmic or machine-art imagery created inside a filtering software."

Courtesy of JD Jarvis/
www.dunkingbirdproductions.com

What's in a Name: The Story of Giclée

One thing that became quickly apparent to the early digital pioneers was the lack of a proper name to describe the prints they were making. By the close of the 1980s, IRIS printers were installed all over the world and spinning off full-color proofs in commercial printing plants and pre-press shops. These prints were used to check color and get client approvals before starting the main print run. They definitely were *not* meant to last or to be displayed on anyone's walls. Most people called them "IRIS prints," or "IRIS proofs," or, more simply, "IRISes."

However, this wasn't good enough for the new digital printmakers like Maryann Doe of Harvest Productions and Jack Duganne, who was the first printmaker (after David Coons) at Nash Editions. They wanted to draw a distinction between the beautiful prints they were laboring over and the quickie proofs the commercial print-ers were cranking out. Just like artist Robert Rauschenberg did when he came up with the term "combines" for his new assemblage art, they needed a new label, or, in marketing terms, a "brand identity." The makers of digital art needed a word of their own.

And, in 1991, they got it. Duganne had to come up with a print-medium description for a mailer announcing California artist Diane Bartz' upcoming show (see Figure 1.5). He wanted to stay away from words like "computer" or "digital" because of the negative connotations the art world attached to the new medium. Taking a cue from the French word for inkjet (*jet d'encre*), Duganne opened his pocket Larousse and searched for a word that was generic enough to cover most inkjet tech-nologies at the time and hopefully into the future. He focused on the nozzle, which most printers used. In French, that was *le gicleur*. What inkjet nozzles do is spray ink, so looking up French verbs for "to spray," he found *gicler*, which literally means "to squirt, spurt, or spray." The feminine noun version of the verb is *(la) giclée*, (pro-nounced "zhee-clay") or "that which is sprayed or squirted." An industry moniker was born.

However, the controversy started immediately. Graham Nash and Mac Holbert had come up with *digigraph*, which was close to "serigraph" and "photograph." The pho-tographers liked that. But, the artists and printmakers doing reproductions had adopted *giclée*, and the term soon became a synonym for "an art print made on an IRIS inkjet printer."

Today, giclée has become established with traditional media artists and some photog-raphers. But, many photographers and other digital artists have not accepted it, using, instead, labels such as "inkjet print," "pigment print," or "(substitute the name of your print process) print."

For many artists, the debate over giclée continues. Some object to its suggestive, French slang meaning ("spurt"). Others believe it is still too closely linked to the IRIS printer or to the reproduction market. And some feel that it is just too pretentious. But, for many, the term giclée has become part of the printmaking landscape, a generic word, like Kleenex, that has evolved into a broader term that describes any high-qual-ity, digitally produced, fine-art print.

Bartz Studios is pleased to announce a new and exciting process by which the work of Diane Bartz will be reproduced in a strictly limited edition of less than 50 pieces. Some of our special paintings will be re-created in this new medium through a totally revolution-ary digital process called Gicleé by Nash Editions. Gicleé is a French term de-scribing the spraying of ink onto paper. Nash Editions uses the finest archival qual...

Figure 1.5 From the Bartz Studio newsletter for ArtExpo California, fall 1991. This is the first known use of the word *giclée* in print.

Courtesy of Diane Clapp Bartz/http://bartz.com/studio

One problem, of course, is that when a term becomes too broad, it loses its ability to describe a specific thing. At that point, it stops being a good marketing label—and make no mistake about it, giclée is a marketing term. When everything is a giclée, people become confused, and the process starts all over again with new labels.

This is exactly what happened when a new group formed in 2001—the Giclée Printers Association (GPA)—and came up with its own standards and trademarked term: *Tru Giclée*. The GPA is concerned with reproduction printing only, and its printmaker members must meet nine standards or principles in order for them (and their customers) to display the Tru Giclée logo.

In 2003, recognizing that only a small number of printmakers could meet the requirements of Tru Giclée, the GPA instituted a lower-threshold standard, *Tru Décor,* which applies to the much larger decor-art market.

Others have also jumped on the giclée bandwagon with such variations as *Platinum* Giclée (Jonathan Penney's term for his black-and-white printmaking process), *Canvas Photo* Giclée (a California photo printmaking shop), and Heritage Giclée (Staples Fine Art's trademarked term for their brand of giclée printmaking).

Giclée logos from (left) the Giclée Printers Association and (right) Staples Fine Art.
Courtesy of Giclée Printers Association (www.gpa.bz) and Staples Fine Art

giclée (zhee-clay) *n.* 1. A type of digital fine-art print. 2. Most often associated with reproductions; a giclée is a multiple print or exact copy of an original work of art that was created by conventional means (painting, drawing, and so on) and then reproduced digitally, typically via inkjet printing. First use in this context by Jack Duganne in 1991, Los Angeles, California

State of the Art: The Digital Revolution

It's been estimated by research company IDC that more than 15 *billion* digital images will be printed in the U.S. by 2005 and according to research firm I.T. Strategies, that the digital fine-art print market is growing at an astonishing rate of 27 percent annually, faster than the art market as a whole. Digital printing, although only a dozen or so years old, is enabling artists and photographers around the world to create and produce their work in ways never thought possible before: on-demand, inexpensively, and with superb and consistent quality.

The industry and the technology are still embryonic; there is a lot of change and evolution yet to come. We're still only in the early stages of this amazing story. And glimpses of what is on the horizon show a future that is truly astounding. "Smart inks," wireless printing, Organic Light-Emitting Diode (OLED) technology, three-dimensional imaging, more colors, better software, more artist control—we all have a lot to look forward to. Or, as digital artist Bonny Lhotka puts it, "I believe this is the most exciting time to be an artist."

Now that we've discovered and taken in a bird's-eye view of the digital landscape, it's time to explore the essential, start-up information you'll need before you start printing.

2

Understanding Digital Printing

At its core, digital printing is simple. A binary data stream drives a print engine to render a digital image on an output device. End of story? Not quite. Like any production process, digital printing requires the right tools and the right information to make the right choices. Let's begin at the beginning.

A Digital Primer

Photographers and artists are all, basically, image makers, so let's start by looking inside a digital image.

Anatomy of a Digital Image

First things first. Ninety-five percent of all the images that photographers and artists end up printing digitally are binary images, also called *raster images*, also called *pixel-based images*, also called *bitmaps*. Confused yet? The term bitmap itself sends some people running for shelter. One reason is because Adobe Photoshop, considered the top image-editing software program, has a mode option called "bitmap" that converts an image into the crudest (1-bit per pixel) form. That's unfortunate because there's a lot more to bitmaps than that. In fact, bitmaps are the key to the Chamber of Secrets of digital printing.

To put it simply, a bitmapped image is a collection of pixels (**pic**ture **el**ements) arranged on a rectangular grid (it's a *map* of a bunch of *bits*); see Figure 2.1. Each pixel can be described or "quantized" in terms of its color and its intensity or value. The more pixels there are and/or the more the depth of information per pixel, the more binary digits (the little ones and zeros that the computer understands) there are, and the more detailed the image (see "Pixels and Bit Depth" for more about this).

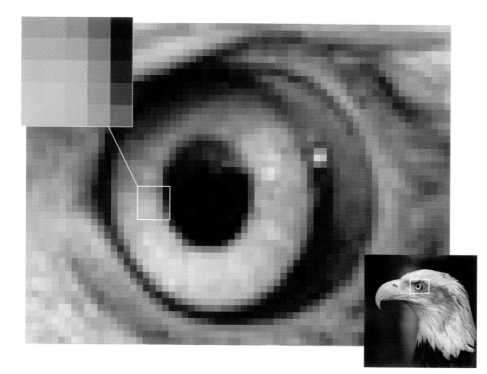

Figure 2.1 Pixels—the building blocks of all bitmapped images.

© 2001 Gregory Georges

That other five percent of digitally printed images are called *vector-based* or *object-oriented*. Instead of a bunch of pixels arranged on a grid, vector graphics are made up of mathematical formulas that describe each object in an image in terms of its outline shape, line weight, fill, and exactly where it is on the page. Logos, type, and any hard-edged, flat-colored art are perfect for the vector format (see Figure 2.2). And that's why vector art often comes from drawing programs like Adobe Illustrator, Macromedia Freehand, or CorelDRAW. To further complicate matters, a bitmap image can be placed within a vector file, and inversely, some bitmap files contain certain vector information.

The problem with vector art is that since it doesn't actually exist except as a formula, there needs to be a way to interpret it and bring it down to earth and onto the printed page. And the primary way to do that is through the computer language of Adobe PostScript, which complicates the digital printing process (see more about PostScript in Chapter 11). Alternatively, you can convert the vector graphic into a bitmap through the process of "rasterizing," and you're back in bitmap business. (A "raster" is a grid-like organization of image elements.)

Figure 2.2 Logos are typical vector graphics.

There are three things you need to know about bitmaps to fully understand the nuances of printing digital images: *pixels and bit depth*, *resolution*, and *halftoning and dithering*. (Color is another issue, but because it's such a huge subject, it gets its own chapter— Chapter 4.) Let's take them one at a time.

Pixels and Bit Depth

Pixels are the basic elements that make up a bitmap image. Pixels actually have no shape or form until they are viewed, printed, or otherwise "rendered." Instead, they are little points that contain information in the form of binary digits or "bits" (ones and zeros—a "0" represents something, a "1" represents nothing or empty space). Bits are the smallest unit of digital information.

A 1-bit image is the lowliest of all bitmaps. There are only two digits to work with—a 1 and a 0, which means that each picture element is either on or off, black or white (I'm keeping this to a simple one-color example to start with). But a 2-bit image is much more detailed. Now you have four possibilities or values for each pixel: 00, 01, 10, 11 (black, white, and two shades of gray). Keep going, and you see that three bits yields eight values, four bits 16, eight bits 256, and so on (see Figure 2.3). In mathematical terms, this is called the power of two: 2^2 equals four choices (2×2), 2^8 is 256 choices ($2 \times 2 \times 2 \times 2 \times 2 \times 2 \times 2 \times 2$). Generally speaking, a one-color digital image needs to be at least 8-bit (256 tones) to be "photorealistic" or "continuous-tone" in appearance. Study the eye image variations in Figure 2.3, and you'll see what I mean.

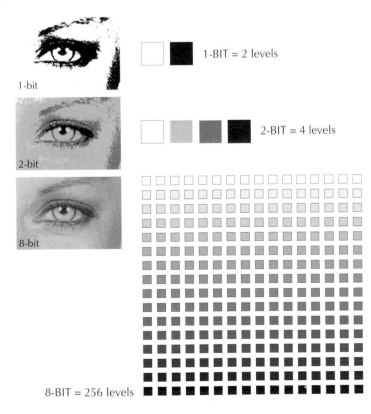

Figure 2.3 The more bits, the more realistic the image.

1-bit

2-bit

8-bit

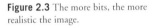

1-BIT = 2 levels

2-BIT = 4 levels

8-BIT = 256 levels

Digital Equivalents

8 bits=1 byte

1024* bytes=1 kilobyte (KB)

1024 kilobytes=1 megabyte (MB)

1024 megabytes=1 gigabyte (GB)

1024 gigabytes=1 terabyte (TB)

it's 1024 and not 1000 because of the way the binary system works with its powers of two—in this case, 2^{10}.

So far, we've only talked about bits in terms of black, white, or gray. Since most people work in color, you now have to apply the same thinking *to each color component of the image.* So, in a 24-bit (8 bits per color) RGB image, there are 256 possible values of Red, 256 of Green, and 256 of Blue, for a grand total of—are you ready?—16,777,216 possible values, tones, or colors for *each pixel* (see Figure 2.4). A CMYK color image is described as 32-bit, or one 8-bit channel for each of the four printing colors: cyan, magenta, yellow, and black or "K." There is no more color information with CMYK; it's just allocated differently than RGB. (For more about color and color models, see Chapter 4.)

Figure 2.4 Color bit depth.

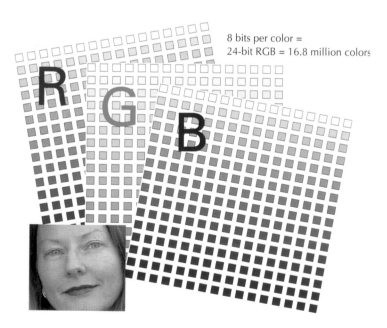

8 bits per color =
24-bit RGB = 16.8 million colors

Whether an image has one, two, four, eight, or even more bits of information per pixel per color determines its *bit depth.* The higher the bit depth, the more detailed and realistic the image. (You don't have to stop at 8 bits. Current input technology allows for up to 16 bits of information per channel—see Chapter 3 for the pluses and minuses of going "high-bit".)

Resolution

This seems to be the single most confusing word in all of the digital imaging world. And it doesn't help that there are different terms and definitions for camera resolution, scanner resolution, monitor resolution, file resolution, and printer resolution. Since this is a book about printing, let's concentrate on the last two: *file* and *printer resolution*.

File or Image Resolution

In basic terms, the resolution of a digital, bitmapped image is determined by how many pixels there are. This is called *spatial resolution*. If you have a scanned image and can count 100 pixels across (or down) one inch of the image (remember, bitmapped images actually have no physical size until they are rendered into a tangible form; at that point, you can measure them), then the resolution is 100 pixels per inch or 100 ppi. Technically, it's pixels per inch (*ppi*) when you're talking about image files, monitors, and cameras. But it's dots per inch (*dpi*) when it comes out of a printer because, if it's an inkjet, the printer's software translates the pixels into tiny little marks or dots on the paper (see "Dots, Drops & Spots" box).

An image's resolution will, in part, determine its quality or the degree of detail and definition. The more pixels you have in a certain amount of space, the smaller the pixels, and the higher the quality of the image. The same image with a resolution of 300 ppi looks much different—and better—than one of 50 ppi at the same relative output size (see Figure 2.5).

Figure 2.5 Image resolution affects detail and definition. Left: 50 ppi, Right: 300 ppi.

However, there's a downside to more pixels. The higher the ppi and/or the greater the bit depth, the more space the files take up, the slower they are to edit and work with, and the harder they are to print since extra pixels are simply discarded by the printer or can cause it to choke, stall, or even crash. The goal is to have a file that's just big enough for the job, but not so big that it causes extra headaches.

So what is the best file or image resolution for digital printing? There is no standard rule-of-thumb for all digital devices as there is with commercial offset lithography. There, it's well accepted that the ppi-to-lpi ratio (lpi is the "screen frequency"), which is also called the "halftone factor," should be somewhere between 1.5 and 2.0. In other words, if you have an image that will be printed as a poster by a commercial print shop, the normal screen frequency would be 150 lpi. Multiply that by 1.5, and you get 225 ppi. Substitute 2.0, and you get 300 ppi. So your best image resolution in this example of commercial offset printing is usually between 225–300 ppi at final print size.

However, with most high-quality digital processes, there is no "lpi" in the same sense as with offset. In the early days of inkjets, some people used the $1/3$ Rule: Take the highest resolution of the printer and divide by 3. For example, an older Epson inkjet printer with a 720 maximum resolution would require a 240 ppi file for optimal results (the "Magic Resolution Number"). But then Epson printhead-based printers started coming out with 1440, then 2880, and now 5760 resolutions. One-third of 5760 is 1920 ppi, an absurdly high and unnecessary image resolution. Some photographers and artists still swear by the 240-ppi formula for even the latest models of desktop printers, claiming, correctly, that, for *desktop* Epsons, the "native driver resolution" is still 720, so the $1/3$ Rule remains in effect. (According to Epson data, the "input resolution"—the resolution that data is rasterized at—is 720 "dpi" for desktops and 360 "dpi" for wide formats.) However, Epson now recommends 300–360 ppi *at the size you intend to print* as their current Magic Number; if you get below 240 you may start to see a difference in image quality, and conversely, you won't see any improvement with bitmapped images by going over 360 ppi. (Note: unlike bitmaps, vector art is "resolution-independent," which means that you can blow it up or down without any loss of definition or clarity.)

Hewlett-Packard (HP) has an "internal render resolution" of either 600 dpi or 1200 dpi, depending on the quality setting, and they recommend 150–200 ppi (or even up to 300 ppi) *at final size* for their inkjet printers. (HP likes to call it "pixels per printed inch" or PPPI.) They claim that scientists doing satellite photo reproduction for the government on their printers typically find that 125 ppi is adequate. In my own experience, 200 ppi is a good image resolution target for most HP inkjet printers.

Canon, also with a native printhead resolution of 600 dpi on many of its inkjets, says that an image must be greater than 180 ppi "to avoid pixelation that shows as staggering in contrast points." They go on to recommend 200 ppi (see Table 2.1) as the target with 300 ppi as the maximum needed for their inkjets. (To see what printheads look like, go to the "Inkjet" section near the end of this chapter.)

For continuous-tone printers that don't use halftoning or dithering (explained below), try to have your image resolution match the printer resolution. Most dye sublimation printers are around 300 dpi, so make your final image also 300 ppi. Same for LightJets and

Table 2.1 The Magic Numbers of Inkjet File Resolution

Brand	Manufacturer's PPI Recommendation *at Final Size*
Canon	200–300 ppi
Epson	300–360 ppi
HP	150–200–300 ppi

Lambdas, which are, respectively, 300 dpi and 400 dpi at their maximum settings; an image resolution of 300 ppi should work well for them, too.

Chances are that if you are anywhere between 240 to 360 ppi in terms of image resolution at final print size, you're going to be fine with most digital print devices, although the best answer is to either test several resolutions with the intended output device and evaluate the resulting prints, or ask a printmaker for recommendations if you're using an outside printing service.

Measuring Image Resolution

Here are the most common measurement methods:

- **By pixel array or dimension:** Some people just say, "Here's a 1600×1200 image" (pixels is understood). Once you're familiar with certain files sizes, you'll automatically know what a 1600 × 1200-pixel image (or any other size) will do.

- **By total number of pixels:** Multiply the number of horizontal pixels by the vertical ones, and you've got the total number of pixels or the pixel dimensions. A 1600×1200 image totals out at 1,920,000 pixels or about 2 megapixels.

- **By pixels per inch and image size:** As long as you know both the intended output size and the ppi, you're set. For example, an uncompressed, 24-bit, RGB, color 300-ppi image set to an output size of 4 × 5 inches is just over a 5-megabyte (MB) file.

Pixel dimensions are one method of measuring image resolution. (See more about sizing and scaling images in Chapter 3.)

- **By file size:** Take the total number of pixels (pixel dimensions), multiply that by 3 (total RGB color bit depth—24 divided by 8), and you've got the file size in *bytes* (one byte is eight bits). Divide that by one million, and you have the *approximate* final file size in megabytes. Example: 1600×1200 pixels = 1,920,000 pixels. 1,920,000×3 = 5,760,000 bytes or 5.76 MB. Pretty close.

- **By single-side measure:** Film-recorder users typically refer to the width of the image in pixels. A standard "4K file" is one that measures 4,096 pixels horizontally (as already stated, the reason it's not 4,000 pixels is because of the way the binary system works). Because most film-recorder output ends up as standard 35mm transparency film, the other dimension (2,730 pixels) is understood to be in the correct proportion to the first and isn't mentioned.

(For a much more complete look at determining the size, scale, and resolution of your digital files—including the use of odd/even or integer resolution numbers, see Chapter 3.)

Printer Resolution

Pull on your tall boots because we're now going to be wading in deep!

How capable is the printing device of reproducing the information in an image? You may have the highest-resolution image imaginable, but if the printer isn't able to output all the fine details you've worked so hard on, you've wasted your time. There are two main types of printer resolutions to be concerned about: *addressable* and *apparent*.

Addressable Resolution

Digital printers have to translate all those nebulous image pixels we learned about into real dots of ink or spots of dyes. The number of different positions on the paper where the printer is able to place the little dots per unit area is its addressable resolution. Think of it

---

Commercial LPI vs. DPI

Spatial resolution is a measure of how finely the image information is grouped to be reproduced or rendered by the output device. With the digital imagesetters used in commercial printing, this is where the line screen (or screen frequency) comes into play.

Using the typical 150 lines per inch (lpi) as the assumption, the printing dots are arranged in rows that are placed 1/150" apart. The spatial resolution is then 150 lpi. Now output the same image at 85 lpi, and you've lowered the spatial resolution (and reduced the detail of the image). See Figure 2.6 for an exaggerated example.

How does lines-per-inch (lpi) relate to dots-per-inch (dpi)? A 150 lines-per-inch image will probably be output on a commercial imagesetter at 2,400 dots per inch. The addressable resolution of this device is, then, 2400 dpi; the spatial resolution is 150 lpi. The 2400 dots are used to print the 150 lines.

Clear as mud, right?

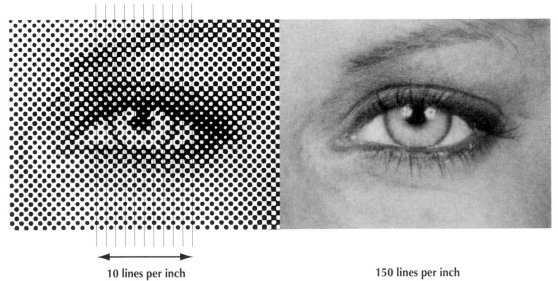

10 lines per inch   150 lines per inch

Figure 2.6 Two spatial resolutions for the same image for offset printing.

as each dot or spot having its own address on the paper, and all this is measured in dots per inch (dpi). (Imaging scientists actually have other ways of talking about resolution, too, but I'll leave the arcane terms and definitions to them.)

Do you know the story of the blind men and the elephant? Six blind men encountered an elephant for the first time. Each touched a separate part of the beast and was then asked to describe the whole animal. They did so but in very different ways. The elephant was either like a snake, a wall, a spear, a fan, a tree, or a rope depending on which blind man spoke.

And so it is with "addressability" and dots per inch. Those numbers you see listed on every print device's spec sheet and in every advertisement only give you part of the picture. And each print-device manufacturer talks about it differently.

Take inkjet printers. The Epson Stylus Pro 4000 printer's maximum resolution is listed as 2880 × 1440 dpi (Note: virtually all digital-printing devices have multiple modes that allow for more than one resolution setting; naturally, only the maximum is advertised. The smaller the resolution numbers, the faster the printing, but the lower the image quality). The maximum resolution on the HP Designjet 130 is 2400 × 1200 dpi. For the Canon i9900, it's 4800 × 2400 dpi.

So what do these numbers mean? The 2880 (or 2400 or 4800) refers to the horizontal axis and is the maximum number of dots the printer can cram into one inch *across* the paper, or in the direction of the printhead's travel (see Figure 2.7). The other number (720, 1200, or 1440) is the maximum number of dots the printer can place in one inch *down* the paper (in the direction of the paper feed).Keep in mind that these are not separate little dots standing all alone; they are frequently overlapping or overprinting on top of each other.

Figure 2.7 Inkjet printers have the higher-resolution numbers in the horizontal or printhead-travel direction.

Printer image courtesy of Hewlett-Packard Company

Why are the horizontal numbers usually higher? Because it's a lot easier to position the printhead precisely than it is to position the paper precisely. As software developer Robert Krawitz explains it, "The printhead typically doesn't actually lay down a dot every

1/2880th of an inch in one horizontal pass. What happens is that different nozzles on the printhead pass over the same line or row to fill it in. It might require up to eight passes to print all of the intermediate dot positions and complete the row. This interleaving of dots is sometimes referred to [in the case of Epson] as 'weaving.'" (See Figure 2.8.)

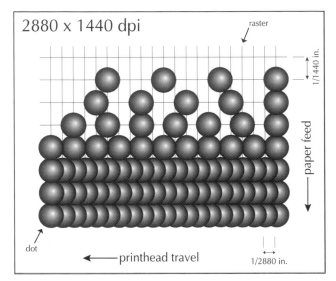

Figure 2.8 Multi-pass droplet offsetting or "weaving" is one factor affecting an inkjet printer's addressable resolution. (Note: the dot sizes and positions are representative only; actual printing dots are more variable.)

The idea is the same for the other inkjet brands, although each has its own way to arrive at the maximum resolution numbers. HPs do things like "color layering" to change both horizontal and vertical resolutions. Canons combine "dot layering" with other factors including small ink droplets, small nozzle structure, and a small nozzle pitch (the distance between nozzles on the printhead) to reach high dpi numbers.

What does all this mean? Honestly, not that much. Is 2880 × 1400 really 36 percent higher—if you simply multiply the two numbers together—than 2400 × 1200 dpi resolution? I've seen outputs from many printers with these stated maximum resolutions, and I would be hard-pressed to say one is that much better than the other.

The theory is that higher printer resolutions produce finer details and smoother tonal gradations. This is true up to a point, but you eventually reach a position of diminishing returns. The negatives of high dpi—slower printing speeds and increased ink usage—eventually outweigh the positives, especially if you can't really see the differences. (For more about this, see "Viewing Distance & Visual Acuity" below.)

When it comes right down to it, the dpi resolution numbers on a spec sheet are irrelevant. They only tell a very small part of the story, just like the blind men's elephant. There are many factors that go into what really counts—the *image quality* a particular printing device is capable of producing. Factors like printer resolution, the number of ink colors, the size of the ink droplets, the precise positioning of the dots, how the inkjet nozzles are arranged and fire, the order of the colors, the direction of printing, and the screening or dithering pattern of the image pixels—they all come into play. My advice: Don't put too much stock in the dpi numbers alone, and don't use them to compare printers of different types or brands. Instead, use dots-per-inch resolution only to weigh different models of the same brand. Then, at least you're talking the same language.

Dots, Drops, & Spots

If all this talk of dots, drops, and spots is making your head hurt, it's time to sort all this out. I asked inkjet expert Dr. Ray Work, an internationally recognized authority on the subject, to help me clarify the differences from an inkjet printing point of view.

Dots: A dot is the mark on the paper or other inkjet receptive material resulting from the printing of one or more drops of ink. It is the smallest component of an inkjet-printed image.

Drops: A drop (or droplet) is that small amount of ink that's ejected from the orifice in the inkjet printhead that lands on the paper and forms a mark or dot.

Spots: With printing, a spot is the same as a dot.

When inkjet printers translate pixels into printed dots, it's not a 1:1 conversion. Each pixel typically requires lots of dots depending on its color and value.

In addition, inkjet printers can place multiple drops per dot. Some HP printers can generate up to 32 ink drops for every dot yielding over 1.2 million colors per dot.

And there's more. Inkjet printers can eject drops from their printheads one at a time and place them at different positions on the paper or on the same position. They can eject one or more drops on the same position to form one dot. They can eject drops of different sizes, which results in different size dots. They can eject bursts of drops that combine in flight prior to landing on the paper to form a single dot.

All of these amazing options are in play with the inkjet printers on the market today. (Learn more about inkjet printers in the "Comparing Digital Printing Technologies" section.)

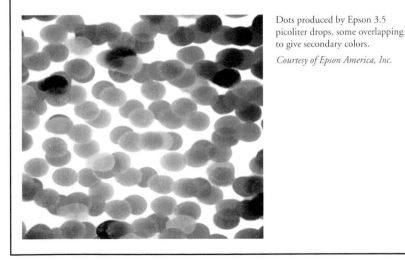

Dots produced by Epson 3.5 picoliter drops, some overlapping to give secondary colors.

Courtesy of Epson America, Inc.

Apparent Resolution

Continuous-tone printers such as digital photo printers and dye sublimation devices (explained in the "Comparing Digital Printing Technologies" section) are unique in that their spatial and addressable resolutions are the same. That is, each image pixel ends up being a "device pixel" at the printer end. There is no halftoning, dithering, or screening involved; the full pixel information in terms of color and tone/value is output directly to paper. Contone printers are playing a different game on the digital ball field.

Since these types of printers can only list relatively lowly 200 ppi, 300 ppi, or at the most, 400 ppi as their addressable resolutions, the manufacturers have come up with a marketing term—"apparent resolution"—to put them on equal footing with all the inkjets that are claiming much higher numbers.

Using the Océ LightJet 430 photo laser printer as an example, here's how it works. The LightJet accepts 24-bit, RGB color data. We know that each color is 8-bit, which represents 256 possible values per pixel. The equivalent commercial halftone printing device would need a 16 × 16 cell to equal that same 256 levels (16 × 16=256). (If you don't know what a halftone cell is, don't worry; you'll learn about it soon. Just stick with me for now.) So if you take 300 ppi (one of the LightJet's two resolution settings) and multiply that by 16 (16 cell units per pixel), you get 4,800. That's 4,800 "dots per inch of apparent resolution." They're not really dots in the same way that inkjets have dots, but that's what the makers of these devices have come up with as a way to do battle with the army of inkjet printers covering the land. Unfortunately these "virtual dots" are of no use in forming sharp-edged vector elements, so dye subs and photo printers are at a disadvantage in printing fine text.

Some inkjets themselves have used "apparent resolution" to compete in the marketplace. The now-discontinued-but-still-in-use, drum-based, wide-format inkjet printers IRIS and ColorSpan's Giclée PrintMakerFA have addressable resolutions of 300 dpi (the IRIS was replaced by the IXIA, which is still being sold). However, they both claim 1800–2000 dpi "apparent resolution," based on either variable-drop technology, the ability to layer color dots, or additional ink colors, or all three.

Variable-sized and overlapping dots are clearly visible on an IRIS print on Photo Glossy paper (40x blowup).

Courtesy of Martin Juergens

What About Type?

Any type or text that's part of a bitmapped image is no different than the rest of that image, and it will print with the same resolution of the image file. (Note: while Photoshop versions 6 and later support clean, vector type, you can't print it that way without first going through a PostScript printer or interpreter, or a file conversion to PDF format and printing from Adobe Acrobat (see more about PostScript and PDFs in Chapter 11). Although other factors such as paper surface quality and the kind of printing technology used can definitely have an impact, it's the printer's resolution—addressable, not apparent—that mainly determines the quality of the printed, *bitmapped* type. A high dpi (dots per inch) will generally yield higher-quality type with smoother edges while a low dpi produces type with ragged edges (see Figure 2.9).

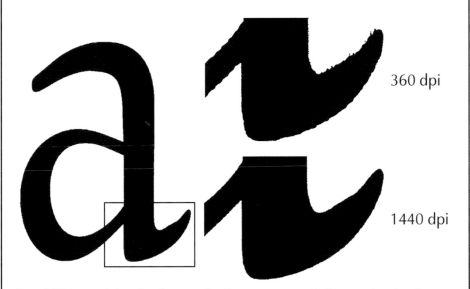

360 dpi

1440 dpi

Figure 2.9 Printer resolution affects the type quality. Here, type was scanned in Bitmap mode to show the differences.

If you're printing from a drawing or page-layout program, the rules change somewhat. Adobe Illustrator and InDesign (version 1.5 and later) don't require a freestanding PostScript interpreter for good-looking type. Other programs like Quark XPress need PostScript font support from a utility program like Adobe Type Manager (ATM) if your operating system doesn't already have PostScript font support built in. In any of these cases, if you're printing through an inkjet's native printer driver, the type quality will still vary with the resolution of the printer. However, as soon as you bring in a PostScript interpreter, things improve significantly.

Viewing Distance & Visual Acuity

Another aspect of printer resolution commonly overlooked is the relationship between *viewing distance* and *visual acuity.*

Viewing Distance: It matters how close you or your viewers are to your prints. Consider the ubiquitous billboard that *could* be printed at a high resolution but never is. If you've ever seen a billboard up close, you know that the dots are huge. Yet, billboards are perfectly readable at the distance from which they are meant to be viewed—across the street or driving down the road.

The key point here is that you don't need more printer resolution than you need. Normal people will stand back to view a large image, and they will get up close to a small one. This means that larger or fewer dots are more acceptable on big prints destined to be viewed from further back.

Viewing distance can have an impact on the choice of printer resolution.

Courtesy of Joe Nalven
www.digitalartist1.com

If you're wondering how to estimate standard viewing distances, photographer Joe Butts gives this formula: 1.5 × the diagonal dimension of the art piece. To calculate the diagonal, it's $a^2 + b^2 = c^2$. For example, to figure the viewing distance for an 8 × 10 print: 8 squared plus 10 squared is 64 plus 100 equals 164 inches. The square root of 164 is 12.806 or rounding it off, 12.8 inches. Multiplying by 1.5, the viewing distance would be 19.2 inches (see Table 2.2). Similarly, the normal viewing distance for a large 40 × 60-inch print is about 9 feet. You won't see many dots from there!

Viewing distance, however, is only one-half the story.

Visual Acuity & Maximum Resolving Power: The ability of the human eye to distinguish fine detail is called *visual acuity*, and it is directly related to distance. As you move farther away from the visual source, you reach a point where you no longer see the detail, and everything merges together. This can be determined scientifically by using alternating black-and-white lines of a specified width and then measuring the angle made from the eye to these lines at the maximum resolvable distance. It has been shown that the visual acuity of a normal eye with 20/20 vision is somewhere between 30 seconds of arc (when lighting is "ideal") and one minute of arc (when the lighting is "ordinary"). This is the maximum visual resolution possible for most humans.

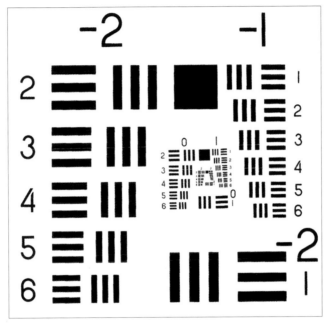

A standard USAF 1951 resolution target for measuring visual acuity.

Courtesy of Edmund Industrial Optics

From this information, all kinds of interesting formulas [c = 2 × d × tan(RADIAN ANGLE SYMBOL ÷ 2)] and conclusions can be drawn (see Table 2.2). One is that at any given viewing distance, you gain nothing by having higher resolution than the maximum resolving power of the eye because no finer details can be perceived. This is the upper limit, so there's no point going beyond that.

However, things are not so simple. These resolving power charts are based on high-contrasting, black-and-white lines or letters (see illustration above and think of the chart at your eye doctor's office). The images that most of us print are anything but that. We have complex patterns of dots or device pixels, overlapping dots, and all the rest. So how does Table 2.2's "details per inch" relate to the dots per inch of inkjet printing? It is generally believed that printer resolution (dpi) must exceed maximum visual resolution ("depi") by a significant amount, on the order of double, triple, or more.

Plus, as digital imaging writer and publisher Wayne Cosshall explains it, there are other issues like presentation. If you print on fine art or textured paper, you could get away with a lower resolution because the paper's texture will create its own detail and somewhat fool the eye. Also, if you frame a print behind glass that lowers the contrast of the print a little, so again, you can get away with less print resolution.

Table 2.2 Viewing Distance & Visual Acuity

Print Dimensions (inches)	Standard Viewing Distance[1] (inches)	Maximum Visual Resolution (Ordinary)[2] (details per inch)	Maximum Visual Resolution (Ideal)[3] (details per inch)
4×6	10.8	318	637
8×10	19.2	179	358
13×19	34.5	100	199
30×40	75.0	46	92

[1] *Formula: 1.5× diagonal of art.*

[2] *"Ordinary" means reduced illumination on the target and its surroundings.*

[3] *"Ideal" means bright illumination on the target and its surroundings.*

The formula numbers give you a place to start, but your own experience and your own style of printing and displaying will determine which printer resolutions will work best for you.

This entire concept of viewing distance and the eye's maximum resolving power was brought home to me in dramatic fashion when I visited well-known documentary and fine-art photographer Joel Meyerowitz at his studio in New York City. Meyerowitz had just started experimenting with in-house inkjet printing, and he wanted to see how it compared to traditional C-prints, which he was used to getting from the top photo labs in New York.

He and I both analyzed two 11 × 14-inch prints made of the same image he had photographed in Tuscany (see Figure 2.10). Using a loupe (magnifier), I could see the difference between

Figure 2.10   Left: *White Road* by Joel Meyerowitz (2003). Details at right show comparison of C-print and HP Designjet 130 inkjet print at high magnification. The inkjet colors are truer to the original, and when viewed at a normal viewing distance, the inkjet dot structure disappears.

Courtesy of Joel Meyerowitz Photography/www.joelmeyerowitz.com

the cloudy smoothness of the C-print and the discrete dots of the HP Designjet 130 print. At first I was discouraged, but then Meyerowitz had me put the loupe away and view both prints from a normal viewing distance. *Voilá!* The inkjet print was beautiful and actually superior. The colors were better differentiated and richer, and there was an overall sharpness that surpassed the traditional lab print. "The inkjet print is more alive," Meyerowitz enthused. "It's just plain better, and I've been looking at color prints for more than 30 years."

The theory worked: When viewed at a normal distance, the inkjet dots had merged into one continuous-tone image.

Halftones, Contones, and Dithers

There are three common ways to produce continuous-tone images such as photographs with any printing method, whether analog or digital: with *halftone screening, contone imaging*, or *alternative screening (dithering)*. All three have roles in the digital printing process, and each printer manufacturer uses its own method and guards it closely. This is the real Secret Sauce of digital printing.

Halftone Screening

Since the late-19th century, continuous-tone (or "contone") images have been rendered by the process of "halftoning." Since smooth transitions of grays or colors are impossible to print with analog or even digital devices (remember, all computers and digital printers use binary information that is either on or off, one or zero), images that use halftoning have to be broken down into tiny little dots or spots (I use the two words interchangeably). The darker portions of the image have larger spots with less space between them; the lighter areas have smaller spots with more space to reveal the paper underneath (see Figure 2.11).

Figure 2.11 Halftones are optical illusions tricking us into thinking we're seeing continuous tones.

At the right viewing distance, our brains then merge all the spots together to give us the impression that what we're seeing is one smooth image. (Hold the page with the apple farther and farther away from you to see.) It's just a trick—an optical illusion.

By knowing all this you can affect the coarseness or smoothness of printed images in a number of ways. With digital printing, depending on the capabilities of the device and the software used to drive it, you can vary the number of spots, the size of the spot, the closeness of the spots to each other, and the arrangement of the individual color spots that make up the final image.

While old-school halftoning utilized the process of photographing images through glass or film screens (hence the terming "screening"), most of the halftones these days are made digitally. These *amplitude-modulated (AM) screening* halftones are created on digital devices that place dots that are either round, elliptical, or rectangular on a grid-like cell made up of little squares. Each halftone dot is actually made up of clusters of printer dots. The more printer dots in a cell, the bigger the halftone dot, and the darker that cell appears. Also, the more cell squares (the bigger the grid), the more shades of gray or color available.

For example, a two-by-two cell can yield five possible tones (the paper is one) as follows (see Figure 2.12):

1. no dots, all you see is the paper

2. one dot, 25% tone

3. two dots, 50% tone

4. three dots, 75% tone

5. four dots, 100% tone (solid, no paper showing)

This is a simple example. Expand the cell to be, say, 16 squares across, and you now have a lot of possible tones that can be printed (see Figure 2.13).

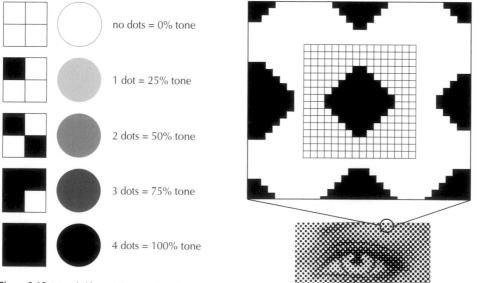

Figure 2.12 A 2×2 halftone cell can produce five tones.

Figure 2.13 A 16×16 halftone cell (center with gridlines) with the halftone dot growing from the center out.

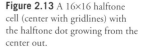

Commercial digital printing systems, imagesetters, and some binary, digital desktop printers such as color and B&W lasers use digital halftoning as part or all of their image-rendering methods.

Contone Imaging

Digital continuous-tone or contone imaging, most clearly seen in digital photoprinting and dye sublimation devices, works differently. Image pixels are still involved, but instead of using halftoning as a middleman to break the various tones in an image apart, contone devices translate the pixel information directly through the printer to the paper. As the image is being rendered, the printer is, in essence, asking each image pixel, "which color and how much of it?" Therefore, the more pixels or the higher the bit depth, the better the image. Because the printed image is made up of overlapping dyes of each primary color with no spaces between them, the color transitions are very smooth and the resulting images are very photorealistic (see Figure 2.14).

Figure 2.14 Contone imaging, in this case with a Durst Lambda digital laser imager, produces photorealistic images with overlapping dye colors.

Alternative Screening (Dithering)

Certain branches of digital printing, specifically inkjet and electrophotography, now use a relatively new screening type: *frequency modulated (FM) screening* or *stochastic screening* to produce near- or at-continuous-tone images where the dots are smaller and more irregular than halftone dots. Perfectly shaped, regularly spaced halftone dots are replaced with more randomly shaped, irregularly placed ones. If you know what a commercial mezzotint screen looks like, you're not too far off (see Figure 2.15).

This is where *dithering* comes in. In the dictionary, dithering means "nervously excited or confused." Dithering is simply an alternative to halftoning and is the process of breaking down a continuous-tone image into a bunch of tiny, confused, excited little spots in a "stochastic" or random arrangement. Dithering, sometimes in combination with halftoning, has been successfully implemented by inkjet and color laser printers to output a full range of tones and image detail.

HP, for example, combines halftoning with what it calls PhotoREt Color Layering Technology on many of its desktop inkjets. PhotoREt layers the color dots

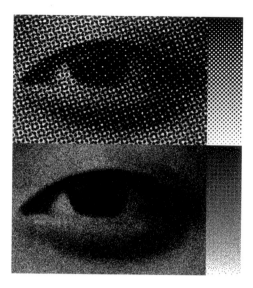

Figure 2.15 A simulation comparing halftone screening (top) with frequency modulated screening (bottom), 30x magnification.

Eyes courtesy of Martin Juergens; panels courtesy of Wasatch Computer Technology

on top of each other and dithers them with *error diffusion*, which is a common dithering method (others include ordered-matrix dithering and threshold dithering). Error diffusion means that the error in creating a specific color—say green, which has to be made up of the only colors the printer has available, primarily for green: yellow and cyan—is spread to the adjacent dots. If one is too green, the next one over is made to be less green. And so on. If you stand back and look at the print, it all balances out, and what you see is "green." (Note that there is no green ink in 99.9 percent of all inkjet printers; Canon's i9900 is the lone desktop exception at the time of this writing. All the green—or any of the other colors of the rainbow—must come from a visual blending of primary colors that the printers *do* have.)

Epson employs its own proprietary algorithms (an algorithm is the mathematical set of instructions the printer software uses to control and precisely place the ink droplets) for what it calls AcuPhoto Halftoning, actually a type of error-diffusion-type dithering.

Canon uses what it calls Precision Color Distribution Technology for its dot layering technique to ensure uniform color.

Moving away from inkjets, the Xerox Phaser 7750 color laser printer uses a combination of digital halftoning and a special dithering pattern to render the image (see Figure 2.16).

Why is all this talk about dithers and halftones important? Because the type of screen rendering will partially determine the "look" of an image when printed using that particular screening or halftoning technology. This is a big part of what makes up a print's "digital signature." When you get experienced enough, you will be able to spot the differences between the specific types of digital output. And you can make your purchase or service choices accordingly.

The bottom line is that when you're at the upper end of digital printing quality, including inkjet, you've pretty much entered the world of continuous-tone imaging. The dots touch with no space between them, and the four or six (or more) colors are layered next to or on top of each other to blend together and form a smooth image. The dividing line between continuous-tone and screened images, at least with high-quality, 8-bit digital printing, is disappearing.

Figure 2.16 The Xerox Phaser 7750 color laser printer uses both halftoning and dithering. *Fantasy Island* artwork by Ciro Marchetti.

Courtesy of Xerox Corporation and Ciro Marchetti/www.ciromarchetti.com

Printer Drivers and Printing Software

Printing software allows you to access and interface with your printer. Before you can print from a drawing, painting, image-editing, or page-layout program, the printer software program must be correctly installed onto the computer, usually from the CD that comes with your printer. (Photo-direct printers that take media cards don't require computers, and the printer software can be accessed directly from the printer itself).

Every print device requires a particular "printer driver" for the specific operating system of the computer. (Note that it's your computer's operating system that you match to the printer, not the software application.) You must have the right driver for your printer in order to support all the printer's features (paper selection, quality level, and so on) and to tell the print engine how to correctly render the image's digital data. If you change your operating system, you may need to install an updated printer driver, which you can normally download from the printer-manufacturer's website.

When you select "print" from your application's File menu, what you get is a series of menu screens and dialog boxes for that particular printer driver (see Figure 2.17). If you have a PostScript printing device, you need to use a PostScript driver and select it.

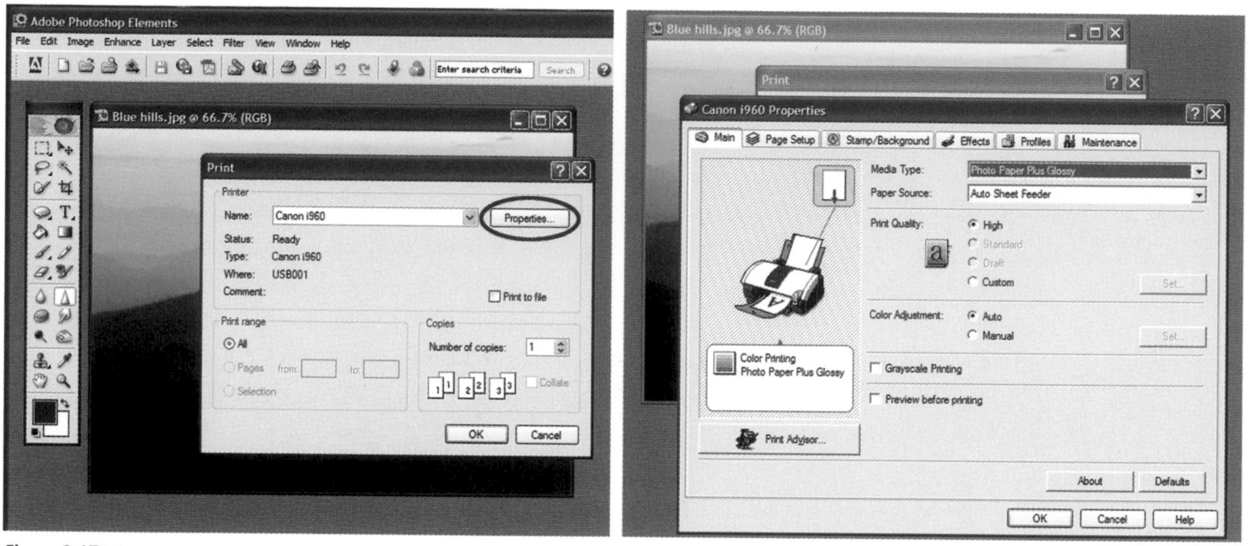

Figure 2.17 The printer driver at work. Left: The basic print dialogue box from Windows XP Home when accessed via Adobe Photoshop Element's "Print" command. Make sure the proper printer is selected (Canon i960 inkjet printer); then click Properties (red oval). Right: The Properties screen lets you specify that printer's important options and settings, or it will open further screens as needed.

Table 2.3 Digital Printing Technologies for High-Quality Output

type	examples	max. output size	inks/dyes	media
Digital Photo Print				
Wide-Format	Durst Lambda	50"×164'	photo dyes	photo paper
	Océ LightJet	76"×120"	photo dyes	photo paper
Digital Minilabs	Fuji Frontier	12×18"	photo dyes	photo paper
	Noritsu QSS	12×18"	photo dyes	photo paper
Dye Sublimation				
	Olympus P-440	8×10"	ribbon: dyes	special paper
	Kodak Pro 8500	8×10"	ribbon: dyes	special paper
Electrophotography				
	Xerox Phaser 7750	12×47"	dry toner	normal paper
Inkjet				
Continuous-Flow	IXIA (formerly IRIS)	35×47"	dye inks only	anything flexible
Drop-on-Demand:				
Thermal	HPs, Canons, Lexmarks	all sizes	dye or pigment	large range
Piezo	Epsons, Rolands, Mimakis, Mutohs	all sizes	dye or pigment	large range
Solid Ink	Xerox Phaser 8400	letter/legal	solid resin ink	many options

After you've made your selections and hit the final "OK" or "Print" button, the printing software converts the digital file's data into a form that the printhead(s) can use to form the image on the paper. (We'll get into more step-by-step printmaking details in Chapter 8.)

Although all inkjet printers come with their own printer driver software, there are times when you may want to bypass the supplied driver and use a specialized one. Many of these come in the form of third-party RIPs ("raster image processors") that can offer functions that the default printer drivers can't. For much more about RIPs and other specialized printing software, see Chapters 6 and 11.

Comparing Digital Printing Technologies

Artists have always experimented with new printmaking materials and techniques, and a list of them would be a long one. But the process of creating high-quality digital prints has, for the majority of photographers and artists working today, coalesced around four major output methods or technologies: *digital photo print, dye sublimation, electrophotography*, and *inkjet*. To be sure, there are plenty of other digital processes that a photographer-artist can use (solvent- and UV-curable-based inkjet printing, electrostatic or "e-stat" from reprographic shops, thermal wax/resin transfer, and blueprint reprographics, to name

for self-printing? (cost)	image quality	comments
no	excellent	A standard for high-quality digital output for many
no	excellent	photographers. Limited media choices. Print costs are high.
no	excellent	Found in photolabs and discount chains; perfect for
no	excellent	inexpensive, high-quality photo prints.
yes	very good	Used by pro and advanced-amateur photographers for low-
yes	very good	volume, high-quality images and proofs. Fast.
maybe	up to very good	Great for comps, proofs, and general design work.
no	can be excellent	The original IRIS technology but updated. Some fine-art printmakers still swear by its quality.
yes	up to excellent	The most common type of inkjet printer; found everywhere.
yes	up to excellent	The other common type of inkjet printer, including all Epsons.
yes	up to very good	A popular option for designers and illustrators; produces very saturated colors; fast.

just a few), but these are either more obscure, more expensive, or too low on the quality scale, so we won't be covering them here in any detail.

Naturally, there are different ways to categorize all these technologies. One is by format size: *narrow* (or desktop) format is anything under 24 inches in width; *wide* (or large) format is everything 24 inches wide or more (this is media size, not the size of the printer). Another way is by drum versus "plotter" configuration (based on the original CAD plotters used to produce computer-generated charts and graphics). What I've chosen to do, instead, is to group them by their logical (in my opinion) imaging characteristics. (Note: products, brands, and models current at the time of this writing.)

Digital Photo Print

Until recently, and apart from the IRIS printing process, photographers who wanted actual photographic output (reflective or backlit display) produced from their digital files had to make an intermediate negative or transparency with a film recorder and then use a conventional enlarger to make the final print. But in 1994, a new type of printer was developed that could print directly from a digital file without the need for the intermediate transparency step. The photo processing industry has never looked back.

I break this category down into two groups: *wide-format digital photo print* and *digital photo process.*

Wide-Format Digital Photo Print

This is top-of-the-line, continuous-tone photo output, and you'll only find the pricey devices for doing this in photo labs, repro shops, service bureaus, and "imaging centers." (See Chapter 10 for more about how to work with outside print providers.) I like the term "digital photo print;" others use words like "digital C-print" or "laser photo printing," although not all devices use lasers.

How Does It Work?

Either using three-color lasers (red, green, blue) or light-emitting diodes (LEDs), these wide-format printers produce extremely high-resolution prints on conventional, light-sensitive, color photo paper that's processed in the normal wet-chemistry photographic manner (although other processing "back ends" can be used). There is no screening, halftoning, or dithering of the image.

Italy-based Durst popularized this category of digital printers, and it now has several models of the Lambda digital laser imager plus other variations including the Theta and the Zeta printers, each with its own market niche. Using continuous roll feeding, the smallest (Lambda 76) can print a single image up to 31 inches by 164 feet, and the largest (Lambda 130/131, used at National Geographic Magazine's headquarters) prints up to 50 inches by 164 feet in one shot. Even larger sizes can be printed in sections or tiles. Two resolution options (200 or 400 dpi) yield an apparent resolution of 4000 dpi. (see the "Apparent Resolution" explanation earlier in this chapter.) For color depth, the input is at 24-bit, output is interpolated to 36-bit using RGB lasers to expose the photographic paper. There are approximately 800 Lambdas installed around the world.

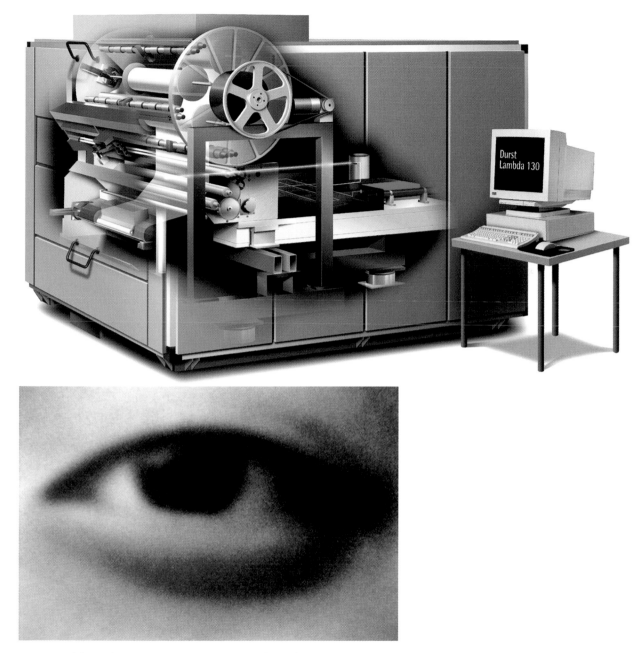

Top: Durst Lambda 130 digital laser imager. Bottom: 30× magnification from a Durst Lambda 76 print. This use of the human eye, which includes a full range of tones from highlights to shadows, as a visual reference for making image-quality comparisons comes from photography conservator Martin C. Juergens.

Courtesy of Durst U.S. (top) and Martin Juergens (bottom)

The Océ LightJet 430 has a maximum output size of 50 × 120 inches, and the newer 500XL model can go up to 76 inches wide (the older 5000 model prints to a maximum of 49 × 97 inches). The spatial/addressable resolution is either 200 dpi or 300 dpi with an apparent resolution of 4000 dpi. As with the Lambda, the input is 24-bit, interpolated to 36-bit output color space (12-bit per RGB color). The LightJet uses three RGB lasers for exposure, and a unique 270-degree internal drum platen for media handling (the media is held stationary within the drum while a spinning mirror directs laser light to the photographic material).

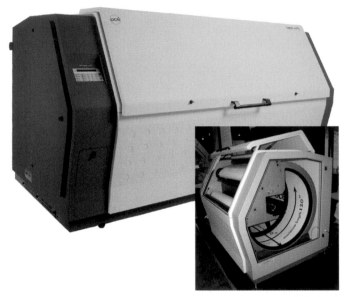

The Océ LightJet 500XL (top) and 430 photo laser printers.

Courtesy of Océ Display Graphics Systems

Another high-end, large-format printer is the ZBE Chromira, which uses LED lights instead of lasers. The print is processed in normal RA-4 chemistry through a separate processor. There are two models and two sizes, 30 or 50 inches wide, with no limit on length. Yielding 300 ppi resolution (425 ppi "visual resolution" with ZBE's proprietary Resolution Enhancement Technology), this is another expensive piece of hardware (but less costly than a LightJet or Lambda), so you'll find one only at a photo lab or service bureau.

Digital Photo Process (Digital Minilab)

Digital photo printing isn't limited to high-end, large-format devices. In fact, you may not realize it, but most photo labs and photo minilabs today use the same technology to print everything from Grandma's snapshots to professional prints. These are the ubiquitous "digital minilabs" found at many photo retailers, drugstores, and big-box merchandisers like Wal-Mart and Costco.

How Does It Work?

Digital minilabs made by Agfa, Noritsu, and Fuji are the standard at many photofinishing labs and the new online processors described in Chapter 10. The Fuji Frontier (see Figure 2.18) was the first digital minilab used for the mass retail market. It's a complete system that takes input from conventional film, digital camera, digital media, or prints (with onboard flatbed scanner) and outputs to digital media or prints via wet-chemistry processing. There are several different models of the Fuji Frontier, and the largest output is 10 × 15-inch prints.

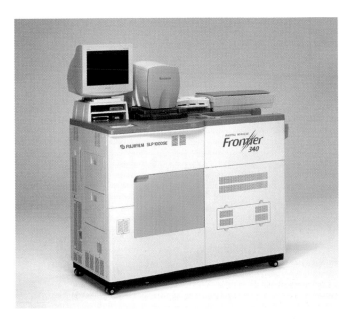

Figure 2.18 Fuji Frontier 340 digital lab system.

Courtesy of Fuji Photo Film USA, Inc.

Digital Photo Print: For What and for Whom?

Photographers like the output from digital photo print/photo process because it looks like a real photograph. In fact, it *is* a real photograph! Larry Berman, a photographer who is a regular on the art show circuit, has most of his prints done on a Noritsu digital printer at his local Costco. Berman pays only $2.99 for a 12 × 18 print that can also yield two 8 × 10s. The costs for the wide-format variety (Lambda, LightJet, Chromira) are comparable to wet-darkroom prints from a custom lab, but the digital versions will soon be replacing the traditional ones as their materials become extinct.

The primary drawbacks with digital photo print are that paper choices are limited, and you can't do this yourself because the devices are much too expensive for self-printers to own.

Dye Sublimation

Dye sublimation (also known as "dye diffusion thermal transfer" and typically called "dye sub") is for high-quality photo and digital snapshot printing (and pre-press proofing). Dye-sub printing has a loyal following among some photographers who prefer it to inkjet printing.

How Does It Work?

With dye sub a single-color ribbon containing dye is heated by a special heating head that runs the width of the paper. This head has thousands of tiny elements that, when they heat up, vaporize ("sublimate") the dye at that location. The gaseous dye spot is then absorbed into the surface of the paper. Since the paper receives separate cyan, magenta, yellow, and sometimes black passes of the dye ribbons to make up the final image, the resulting layering of color provides a smooth, seamless image. Photo dye-sub printers only have 300 or so dpi resolution, but they can deliver continuous tone images because of this layering and the way the dyes diffuse or "cloud" into the paper. Some dye subs add a protective layer (a clear UV laminate) as a fourth and final step after the single-color passes.

Examples of dye-sub printers include: Olympus P-440, and P-10; Kodak Pro 8500 and Photo Printer 6800; and Sony DPP-EX50.

The Olympus P-440 Photo Printer is a dye-sub printer that produces realistic, continuous-tone images

Courtesy of Olympus America, Inc.

Dye Sub: For What and for Whom?

Dye sub is popular with pro and advanced-amateur photographers who want continuous-tone, photographic image quality. Prints speeds can be very fast: 20 seconds per 5x7 on the Kodak 6800, or 75 seconds for letter-size on the Olympus P-440. Also, certain types of dye-sub prints are more scratch-resistant than with inkjet.

While dye sub yields photographic quality to the naked eye, disadvantages are the high cost of the larger format or specialized printers—Kodak's 6800 is targeted to event photographers and studios, and it's priced at $3,000, the high cost of the consumable supplies, and the limited choice of special papers and ribbons (glossy and matte only).

Fuji Pictrography

Many top photo labs and retouch studios, especially those involved with the fashion and beauty industries, use the Fuji Pictrography printer (models 3500 and 4500) for high-quality prints and proofs, also known as *Fujix prints*. Pictrography uses a unique, single-pass, four-step process (see Figure 2.19). A sheet of photosensitive "donor" paper is exposed to laser diodes (LD). A small amount of water is applied to create the dye image on the donor paper with heat. The dye image is then transferred to the "receiving" paper with a combination of heat and pressure. Finally, the receiving paper, with its transferred dyes, is peeled off and separated from the used donor paper. This is not photographic paper, although Fuji claims the equivalent image permanence. Only special Fuji paper can be used. Two resolutions (267 dpi and 400 dpi) are available with a maximum paper size of 12×18 inches (4500 model only).

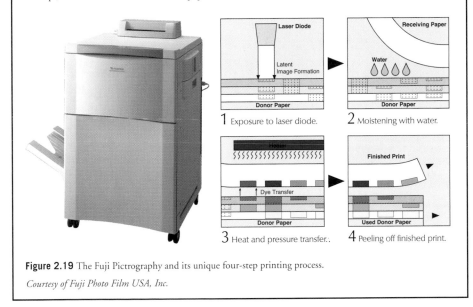

Figure 2.19 The Fuji Pictrography and its unique four-step printing process.

Courtesy of Fuji Photo Film USA, Inc.

Electrophotography (Color Copy/Color Laser)

Also called "xerography" ("xeros" for dry, "graphos" for picture), electrophotography involves the use of dry toners and laser printers or printer/copiers. (The liquid-toner version or "digital offset" was described in the last chapter.)

How Does It Work?

Many color lasers use hair-thin lasers to etch a latent image onto four rotating drums, one each for the four printing colors (see Figure 2.20). The drums attract electrically charged, dry, plastic-based pigment toner and then transfer the image to an intermediate transfer belt and then to the paper where it is fused. Other laser printers transfer the toner directly to the paper without the intermediate step.

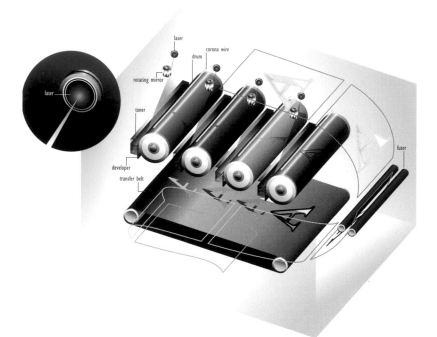

Figure 2.20 Single-pass, color laser print technology by Xerox.

Courtesy of Xerox Corporation

Older technology devices image one layer/color at a time; the trend now is to "single pass" printing, which speeds up the process considerably. Maximum output size is typically 12 × 18 inches, although the Xerox Phaser 7750 can handle 4x6-inch postcards up to 12x47-inch banners. And in some printers, laser imaging is replaced with light-emitting diodes (LEDs).

Most color lasers these days offer up to 1200 × 1200 dpi resolution and use their own combinations of stochastic and halftone screening for color rendering. (See earlier discussion about stochastic and halftone screens.)

Examples of electrophotographic printers include color lasers from the Xerox Phaser, Canon CLC, and Konica Minolta Magicolor lines.

Xerox Phaser 7750 color printer.
Courtesy of Xerox Corporation

Electrophotography: For What and for Whom?

Traditionally used as proof printers by pre-press departments and production printing operations, color laser printers are becoming more short-run printing presses in quick-print shops as well as businesses. They are also used as primary color output devices in graphic arts departments and design studios, and now, by artists—especially photographers. Indiana photographer Seth Rossman likes this type of output. "For photographers, it's an almost perfect medium. I use it in continuous-tone mode, which gives it more of a dithered effect, so no dots."

Electrophotographic printing is fast and reasonable, with 8x10 prints under $1.00 at many retailers, and images can be printed on a small range of substrates including matte paper and commercial printing stocks. "If you want top-quality photo prints from a color laser printer," says photographer Phillip Buzard, "the paper must be very smooth and very white."

The main disadvantages of electrophotography are the limited maximum output size (usually 12x18 inches) and the high initial cost of the machines if you're self-printing. The image has a slightly raised surface when viewed at an angle, especially on glossy or cast-coated stock, but the colors can be very bright and saturated. Depending on the type of screening and resolution used, prints sometimes have a lined or halftone-dot look (see Figure 2.17 earlier in this chapter).

Inkjet

For the most flexibility in terms of choices of printer brands and types, inks, papers, sizes, and third-party hardware and software support, you can't go wrong with inkjet. There are photo printers, proof and comp printers, you name it. As far as quality goes, I've seen high-resolution desktop, thermal and piezo inkjet prints on glossy and semi-gloss paper that rival—even surpass—any traditional photographic print. In addition, certain inkjet print combinations exceed all other standard, color-photo print processes in terms of projected print longevity or permanence.

Simply described, inkjets use nozzles to spray millions of tiny droplets of ink onto a surface, typically paper. While earlier devices had an obvious digital signature, the newer printers are so much further along that many inkjet prints can now be considered continuous tone for all practical purposes.

There are two main types of inkjet technologies: *continuous flow* and *drop-on-demand*, which is further subdivided into thermal, piezoelectric, and solid ink (see Table 2.3). (We'll go into more detail about inkjet printing in Part II.)

Continuous Flow

Although this is the original technology that started the high-quality, digital-printing boom, continuous flow has become much less popular over the years. The most famous example is the IRIS printer, which is no longer manufactured although there are many of these printers still in use. The IRIS has been replaced with the ITNH company's IXIA, pronounced "zia."

How Does It Work?

A single printhead moves along a rod above the paper that is wrapped around a rotating drum. The printhead encloses four glass nozzles (one for each of the printing colors: cyan, magenta, yellow, and black) that are each connected to a bottle of translucent dye ink. In each head is a tiny vibrating piezoelectric crystal that pushes out a million ink droplets per second. As the ionized ink droplets exit the nozzle, some receive an electrostatic charge; some don't. The charged ink droplets are deflected away from the drum and recycled. But the uncharged ones—our heroes—pass through the deflector and end up hitting the paper to form the image. Although the IRIS/IXIA has a maximum resolution of only 300 dpi, its apparent resolution is more like 1800–2000 dpi due to its variable dot size and overlapping dot densities.

The drum-based, IXIA inkjet printer—successor to the IRIS.

Courtesy of ITNH, Inc.

Continuous Flow: For What and for Whom?

The main advantage the IRIS/IXIA is the wide range of media accepted plus the high image quality and the ability to produce deep, rich blacks. When printed on textured fine-art paper, these prints have a beautiful velvety look, but the slow print speed (30–60 minutes per print) plus the time-consuming maintenance and manual paper mounting have reduced demand for these expensive ($45,000) drum machines.

Drop-on-Demand

This is where most of the inkjet action is. The reason it's called drop-on-demand is because only the ink droplets that are needed to form the image are produced, one at a time, in contrast to continuous-flow where most of the ink that's sprayed is *not* used. The three main categories of drop-on-demand, inkjet printing are: *thermal, piezo,* and *solid ink.*

Thermal

How Does It Work? This process, which was invented in 1981 by Canon ("Bubble Jet Printer"), is based on the heating of a resister inside the printhead chamber (see Figure 2.21). As the resister heats up, a vapor bubble surrounded by ink is formed, and the increase in pressure pushes an ink droplet out of the nozzle in a printhead. After the bubble collapses, more ink is drawn in from the ink reservoir, and the cycle repeats.

Wide-format, thermal inkjet printers used to come in either drum or plotter formats, but the MacDermid ColorSpan Giclée PrintMakerFA, the only drum-based, thermal inkjet printer specifically designed for fine-art applications, was discontinued in 2003 (although ColorSpan makes several other more commercial plotter inkjets that are also used for fine-art output).

Both narrow-format (desktop) and wide-format thermal plotter printers (also called "bar printers") have printheads that move back and forth on a rail or bar over the paper, which is

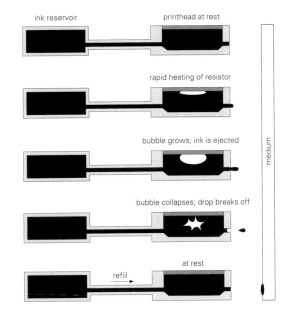

Figure 2.21 The thermal inkjet process.

Courtesy of Martin Juergens

pushed incrementally by a stepper motor after each head pass. Some printheads with their nozzles are integrated into the ink cartridges and are replaced with each ink change. Others are separate from the inks but still need replacing. Still others come in the form of a monolithic printhead assembly that holds the ink cartridges. See Figure 2.22 for several types.

Figure 2.22 Three types of thermal printheads and ink carts: (left) HP integrated print cartridge with ink tank and printhead, (center) HP separate printhead and ink cartridge, and (right) Canon ink tanks and one-piece printhead and holder (inset).

Examples of thermal inkjet printers include—*Wide-format:* HP Designjet 130 and 5500, Canon image PROGRAF W6200 and W8200, ColorSpan DisplayMaker X-12, and ENCAD NovaJet 1000i. *Desktop:* Canon i9900, HP PhotoSmart 7960 and Designjet 30, and Lexmark P707.

The HP Designjet 130 six-color printer (with optional stand) can print on media 24 inches wide.

Courtesy of Hewlett-Packard Company

Thermal Inkjet: For What and for Whom? The largest number of inkjet printers sold in the world today fall into this category. They're affordable and widely available with up to excellent image quality that rivals photographic prints.

Piezoelectric

How Does It Work? When certain kinds of crystals are subjected to an electric field, they undergo mechanical stress, i.e., they expand or contract. This is called the "piezoelectric effect," and it's the key to this popular brand of digital printing, called "piezo" for short (and not to be confused with "piezography," which is described in Chapter 11). When the crystalline material deflects inside the confined chamber of the printhead, the pressure increases, and a tiny ink droplet shoots out toward the paper (see Figure 2.23). The returning deflection refills the chamber with more ink.

Both the wide-format and desktop models of piezo printers come only in plotter versions with the printhead assembly going back and forth over the paper to create the image. Piezo printheads are typically single units with all colors included; they are a permanent part of the machine and usually need no replacing.

Examples of piezoelectric inkjet printers include—*Wide-format*: Epson Stylus Pro 4000, 7600 and 9600; Roland Hi-Fi JET Pro-II, Mimaki JV4, and Mutoh Falcon II. *Desktop*: Epson Stylus C84, Stylus Photo R800 and 2200.

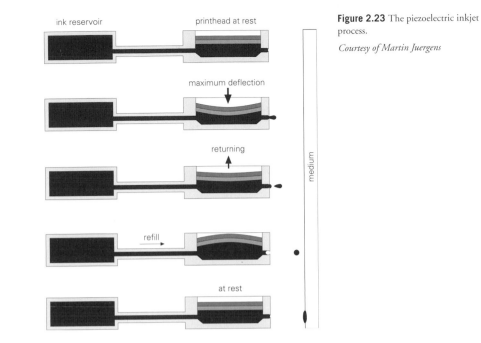

Figure 2.23 The piezoelectric inkjet process.

Courtesy of Martin Juergens

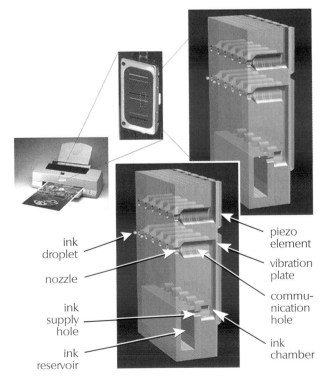

Epson's Micro Piezo printhead.

Courtesy of Epson America, Inc.

Epson's Stylus Pro 4000 features ink droplet sizes down to 3.5 picoliters and 17-inch wide printing.

Courtesy of Epson America, Inc.

Piezo Inkjet: For What and for Whom? In the desktop category, there's only one piezo player, and that's Epson. With six- to seven-color inks in dye and pigment versions, these are the printers that have historically owned a significant share of the photographer-artist, self-printing inkjet market. Other manufacturers join Epson in the wide-format category. As with thermal, piezo inkjet printers are widely available and produce up to excellent image quality.

Solid Ink

How Does It Work? Formerly called "phase change," solid ink technology is the inkjet oddball. The Xerox Phaser 8400 (Xerox is the only real player in this category) is a true piezoelectric inkjet, but there are several surprises. First, the pigmented colors come in the form of solid blocks of resin-based inks, although the ink still ends up as a liquid after heating (hence the term "phase change"). These printers also have the affectionate nickname "crayon printers," from the resemblance of the ink sticks to children's crayons.

And instead of a smaller, reciprocating printhead assembly, there is a single printhead that extends nearly the width of the paper with 88 nozzles in each of four rows. The same piezo substance we've already learned about shoots the ink droplets out as before, but in another twist, the ink doesn't go onto the paper; instead, the ink goes onto a turning offset drum that is kept warm so the ink doesn't solidify. The drum then transfers (in a single pass) the still-molten ink to the paper under pressure to form the image.

The inner workings of the Xerox
Phaser 8400 solid-ink color printer.

Courtesy of Xerox Corporation

Solid Ink: For What and for Whom? With ink that sits on top of the paper creating a definite relief effect, the colors are brilliant and sharp since the ink drops don't spread or bleed. However, even at 2400 dpi, "near-photographic" might better describe the image quality. Solid ink inkjet is fast, it prints on a variety of media, and it yields highly saturated images that some photographers, designers, and illustrators love. Disadvantages include limited output size (letter/legal) and relatively poor image permanence (Xerox claims only "a year or more" with office lighting, "over several years" with dark storage).

With all this new, accumulated information about pixels, hardware, and printing technology under our belts, let's move our attention to what it takes to create and process a digital image.

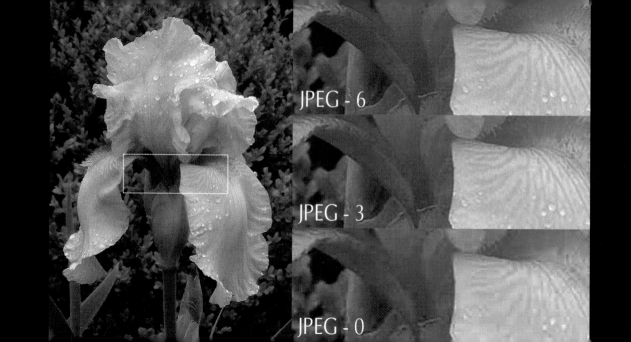

JPEG - 6

JPEG - 3

JPEG - 0

3

Creating and Processing the Image

Art and technology have never been more intertwined than they are now. Digital technology may be the tool, but the act of creation springs from the mind—and heart—of the artist. Let's look at how digital images are created and processed.

Image Input

If printing is close to the last step in the making of digital art, then one of the first steps is inputting or acquiring the image or the image elements. Most photographers and artists work with source material. Photographs, sketches, scans—these are the raw materials that, when combined with a creative vision, end up as an image worth printing.

It's like making a fire. Before the flames can blaze, you've got to go out and gather the wood. And if you've spent much time camping, you know that the drier and higher-quality the wood, the bigger and better the fire.

As with many things digital, the boundary lines between categories are not hard and fast. For example, digital cameras do the same basic thing that scanners do. But because the digital world has decided that a camera is one thing, and a scanner is another, I'll break image input down similarly.

Note: For a description of the equipment you'll need for setting up your own print studio, see Chapter 8.

Scanning

Scanning means sampling a reflective or transparent object (usually flat) point by point and turning that information into a usable digital file that can be processed in the computer and, for our purposes, ultimately printed.

Scanning is done by scanners, and here's how they work. Light generated in the scanner itself is either reflected off or transmitted through a piece of art or film via a mirror-and-lens system (see Figure 3.1) and onto a grouping of light sensors, which are actually tiny CCDs (charge-coupled devices) or in some cases CMOSs (complementary metal oxide semi-conductors) or CISs (contact image sensors). The thousands of individual sensor elements, one per image pixel, are either arranged in single or triple rows, called, respectively, *linear* or *tri-linear arrays*.

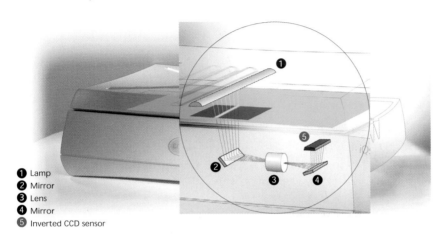

1 Lamp
2 Mirror
3 Lens
4 Mirror
5 Inverted CCD sensor

Figure 3.1 Flatbed scanners use lamps, mirrors, lenses, and sensor arrays to produce digital files. The Creo iQsmart has a unique inverted CCD sensor that minimizes dust accumulation on the CCD surface.

Courtesy of Creo

The scanner's image is then formed (in the case of CCDs) like this: As the scan progresses line by line down the original object, the light that is reflected or transmitted strikes each sensor, which transfers that information in the form of increasing voltage to something called an A/D (short for analog/digital) converter. The A/D converter then transforms the voltage into the binary values (our favorite ones and zeroes) that are sent to the computer. Once inside the computer, the scan is now a digital file that can be viewed, manipulated, and printed.

In the context of digital printing, the type and quality of a scan can be critical to the final printed output. Therefore, let's start off with an overview of some important things to know about the scanning process. The types of scanners and what they do follows.

What You Need to Know about Scanning

There are some key issues about scanners and printers that need to be understood by anyone hoping to become proficient with high-quality digital imaging and printing. These issues or factors are: *color depth, dynamic range*, and *resolution*.

Color Depth

Remember our friend "Bit Depth" from the last chapter? Color depth is just another way to say bit depth for scanners, and the same principles apply. A normal color original (print or film) will require a minimum 24-bit scan (8 bits of information per RGB channel; all scanners scan in RGB) to reproduce with adequate fidelity. This is the old "millions" scanner setting (actually, it's 16.8 million as we learned in Chapter 2). However, since some of the scanned bits are invariably corrupted or lost to electronic noise, using a scanner with a higher color depth like 36-bit is preferred. A 36-bit or "high-bit" scanner records 12 bits per color channel, which translates into 68.7 *billion* possible values or colors per pixel.

(Most modern scanners are 12-bit scanners. Even some that say they're 16-bit are really only using 12 bits of data carried in a 16-bit format that is more efficient for computers.)

Aren't these millions and billions of colors simply overkill? Maybe, if you consider that until recently with the introduction of Adobe Photoshop CS, almost no one could edit or work with these high-bit files, and consequently, they were always down-sampled or converted by the scanner into 24-bit images. However, the advantages of adding more information up-front (more raw material or "headroom" to work with) in the scanning stage has become more obvious to people, especially those working with film versus those scanning prints where the density range is much lower (see below for more about that).

Keep in mind that many high-bit scanners still output the files in 24-bit (some do true 48-bit output). Why only 24-bit output? Because humans can't really see 48 bits, and also because computer monitors operate in 24-bit mode (although most digital printers *can* accept 48-bit data, which is usually converted on the fly to 24-bit).

However, you still want to be scanning in high-bit mode because a 36-bit scanner has more steps in the range of densities between deep shadows and light highlights than does a 24-bit scanner. (Truthfully, there are no more 24-bit scanners; they're either 36-, 42-, or 48-bit.) A 24-bit scan means 8 bits per RGB channel, which equates to 256 possible brightness levels per channel (0–255, where 0 is pure black and 255 is pure white). A 36-bit color scan means 12 bits per channel or 4,096 possible values. That's a lot more tonal possibilities. And this is especially important in the dark shadows of positive or reversal film (which with negatives turn into highlights) where you want as many steps to differentiate unique detail as possible. Shadow detail is frequently what makes or breaks an image.

The downside—and there's always a downside—to scanning and then editing high-bit image files is that increasing the bit depth increases the file size arithmetically. However, as scanning expert David Coons says, "Double the file size is a small price to pay for the 256-times increase in luminance accuracy you achieve by moving to 16-bits per channel."

Dynamic Range

Many people get the terms color or bit depth and dynamic range confused. Both are important and related, but they are different. Think of a stairway: the number of steps is a function of the bit depth (8-bit equals 256 steps), and the height of the entire stairway is the dynamic or density range from Dmin to Dmax (see Figure 3.2).

Scanning book author Wayne Fulton (see more about him later) has an even better analogy when he says, "More bits are needed simply to store data with high dynamic range, but the bits do not create dynamic range,

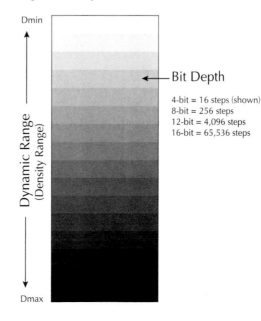

Figure 3.2 The digital stairway. The number of steps is a function of Bit Depth; the height of the stairway is the Dynamic/Density Range.

Bit Depth
4-bit = 16 steps (shown)
8-bit = 256 steps
12-bit = 4,096 steps
16-bit = 65,536 steps

they only allow it to be stored. Just like a large wallet is needed to hold a great sum of money, but having a large wallet does not necessarily mean the wallet is full of money."

There are actually two different, but related, types of *dynamic range*. There's *scene dynamic range*, which is how much tonal information an input process or medium can capture. It usually applies to camera systems, and it's expressed in terms of photographic *exposure value* or *f-stops*. Color reversal film, for example, has a scene dynamic range of 7 f-stops.

Then there's *density range*, which is the difference in density between the lightest and darkest areas of an image. It's the numerical range from the minimum density (Dmin) to the maximum density (Dmax). If the Dmin is 0.3 and the Dmax (also called *optical density*) is 3.9, then the density range is 3.6 D.

Density range applies to digital input devices like scanners, but it can also describe imaging material, such as printing paper or photographic film. Reversal film (transparencies), for example, has a wide density range (3.3–3.6 D) but a narrow dynamic range (7 f-stops). Anyone who works with slides quickly realizes that, while the blacks are black and the whites are bright, the shadows and highlights are very compressed. Slides are great for viewing or projecting (what they were invented for), but for capturing all the subtle tones in a scene, negative film, with its wider dynamic range but lower density range (2.4 D–3.0 D), is much better. Other types of art materials also have their own inherent density ranges. Photographic prints have an average range of around 2.0 D; watercolors, even less.

How does all this affect scanning? Several ways. First, you need to make sure you consider what type of art you will be scanning before deciding on a scanner to purchase or a service to use. And for that, density range and D values are important factors. When dealing with transparencies with very dense blacks, you'll want the widest density range and the highest Dmax you can get so you can pull out the details from those dense areas. But with certain kinds of reflective art, it's not as critical because the prints themselves have a low density range, and many low- to mid-priced scanners will do the job. (Unfortunately, because of a lack of standards, advertised density ranges and Dmax specs, as with "resolution" on inkjet printers, serve mostly marketing purposes. Use them to compare scanner models by the same manufacturer, but be leery of any cross-brand comparisons. In fact, comparative price at a given time is usually the best indicator of scanner performance.)

Scanner Resolution

I've saved the best for last. Or I should say, the most complicated. Some of this necessarily overlaps what was discussed in the last chapter about image and printer resolution, but I'm adding another piece of the resolution puzzle.

Most of the sales information for scanners highlights the dots-per-inch (dpi) resolution. Technically, there are no dots in scanning, just samples. It should really be "samples per inch" (spi) or pixels per inch (ppi), but that battle of terminology has been lost to the scanner industry. Whenever you hear anyone mention dpi in the context of scanning (as I tend to do), understand that they are also saying ppi. It's still about pixels.

The more sensor elements per unit area, the higher the *optical resolution* of the scanner, and, in general, the more information and detail the scanner is capable of capturing. Flatbed scanners use the same naming system as inkjet printers to trumpet their resolutions: 2400×4800 dpi, for example. In this case, 2400 means the number of CCD elements across

A scanner with a wide density range will help pull details out of the top of this banyan tree in South Florida.

the bed of the scanner. They don't really cover the full width of the scanner but only a portion of it because they receive the image focused by a lens. The 4800 refers to the other dimension and is achieved, as with inkjets, by motor stepping (this is sometimes called "hardware resolution"). It's the lower number—the optical resolution—that counts. Film and drum scanners also use dpi, but they usually only list one number such as 4000 dpi.

Many scanners also list an *interpolated resolution*, which is invariably a larger number. Here, sophisticated software is used to add extra pixels where there were none before. However, this is fudging the pixel data, and it should not be a consideration when weighing scanning or scanner choices.

A certain amount of knowledge of how scanning resolution affects printing is necessary, so to get to the heart of the matter, I've gone to the source: Wayne Fulton. Fulton is the author of what I believe is the most understandable and helpful book on the entire subject: *A Few Scanning Tips*, www.scantips.com. What follows in an interview format are some of the most common scanning resolution questions and Fulton's answers.

■ How do I choose a scanning resolution? You scan for the capability of your output device, which means that you choose a scan resolution based strictly on the needs of the monitor or printer that will display that image. For images viewed on computer (video) screens, scan resolution merely determines image size. Since ppi and dpi both mean pixels per inch, then if you scan a print of 6 inches at 100 dpi, you will create 600 pixels, which will display on the screen as 600 pixels in size. If you scan a 1 inch print at 600 dpi, you still have 600 pixels. And those 600 pixels will still fill 600 pixels on any screen (although the width of those pixels will depend on the type of screen).

- *But I'm scanning for printing. What about printers?* Printers are very different from monitors or computer screens. Scan resolution does NOT determine image size on the printer as it does with monitors. The size of the original scan area in combination with Scaling (see below) determines printed image size. Lower resolutions may look fuzzy, and higher resolutions may look better, but the printed size on paper will be the same at any scan resolution. The size is changed by the Scale or Magnification setting of the scanner.

- *What is Scaling? What is Resampling? What's the difference?* Scaling is a word that means stretching or compressing the image pixels to fit a specified area of paper, and it is very different from changing the size by resampling. Scaling is accomplished by simply changing the value of the number used as resolution when the printer calculates the spacing of the pixels on the paper (ppi, pixels per inch). Scaling only changes the future pixel spacing on paper so the image prints at a different size. Scaling is a simple operation, but the concept is a little abstract.

There are two ways to scale an image: (1) after the scan and (2) during the scan. Scaling after the scan is discussed in "Sizing with Image Editing" later in this chapter, so we'll concentrate on scanner scaling here.

The scanner's scaling control is simply a calculator to help with the arithmetic. The settings for a sample 4x4-inch reflective color print scanning at 300 dpi are shown in Figure 3.3. If the scaling factor is 100%, then the scanning resolution (or Source or Input) is 100% of the printing resolution (or Target or Output). The 100% means that the image is scaled to print at the same original size at the specified printing resolution. (If you switch to scan 35mm film at 4000 dpi at 100%, and you print it just like that, it will indeed print at original film size at 4000 ppi or at the same small size of a 35mm film frame: .94 × 1.42 inches.)

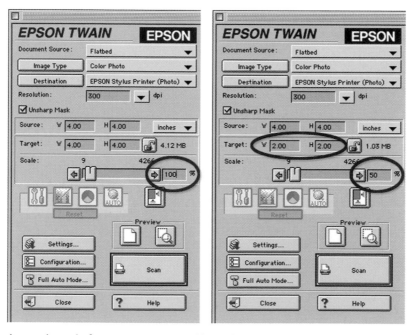

Figure 3.3 Left: Sample scan showing a scaling factor of 100%. Note how Source and Target dimensions are equal. Right: When the scaling factor is changed to 50%, the target print size is cut in half.

If you change the scale factor to say 50% and keep the same 300 dpi, then the scanner will scan at 50% of the 300 dpi value, or at 150 dpi scanning resolution, to create the right number of pixels to print half size—or 2x2 inches—at 300 ppi (see Figure 3.3 again). The image will be scaled to print at the specified 300 ppi that you asked for. So, if you want to scale the image's printed size during the scan, do NOT change the scanning resolution setting like you would to change the size on the computer monitor; you'll always get the same printed size at 100%. Instead, leave the scanner's resolution setting at 200 or 300 dpi (for prints), or whatever is appropriate for your printer, and instead use the Output or Target field to modify the output size, which in turn modifies the scaling.

Keep in mind that the output resolution number is just a note or comment that is carried along with the image. This is the scaled resolution, or the printing resolution, and it is just a number, a numerical value, nothing more. It only matters to the printing software, to tell it how to size the scanned image pixels on that output device later. Scaling is intended for printing.

(Caution! You may not be aware of the actual scanning resolution when scaling. The real calculated scanning resolution is not shown [on most scanners], and there is a risk that if you don't pay attention, you might exceed the scanner's optical rating without realizing it. You can happily set the resolution to 300 dpi and the scaling to 300% to get a larger image size. The scanner scans at 900 ppi in that case, but you might have a 600-dpi scanner, which must interpolate to do what you've asked. No hand comes out to slap you, but you've just exceeded the optical capability of the scanner. A few scanners may refuse, or may show red numbers then, but most are silent. You typically don't have any warning of this, you just have to be careful and realize how it works. Interpolated results won't be as sharp as you expect.)

Resampling is very different from scaling. Scaling does not affect any pixel, but resampling changes *all* pixels, and the total number of pixels in the data become different. Resampling is a drastic procedure that actually recalculates all of the image's pixel color data values to produce a different size of image. Most people know that image-editing programs like Photoshop are usually used for resampling, but scanners can resample, too. Look at a 1200-dpi flatbed scanner. This scanner has 1200 CCD cells spaced 1/1200 inch apart. A 1200-dpi scanner can therefore only scan samples at 1200 dpi horizontally. When you scan at, say, 520 dpi, the scanner must resample the 1200-dpi scan line to 520 dpi. Some scanners use the Bilinear resampling method (creates the new pixel to be the color interpolated from linearly weighting the value and distance of the old pixel on either side of the new pixel on the same row) and some use Nearest Neighbor (creates the new pixel simply to be the same color of the one closest to the adjacent old pixel) to resample the scan line horizontally. Some users claim it is better to always scan at full optical resolution and then resample back to the desired dpi in an external program. Their point is that programs like Photoshop have all of the rows and columns available for Bicubic resampling (creates the new pixels from the color of two pixels in either direction), and your computer has much more memory and processor power than the scanner.

Resampling is just *interpolation*, either *downsampling* (reducing image size by discarding data and detail, replacing many pixels with a few) or *upsampling* (increasing size to a larger image by fabricating additional data, replacing a few pixels with many). It is always better to resample to reduce the image size, rather than to resample to increase the image size.

(For more about scaling and resampling when image editing, see "Sizing with Image Editing" and also Chapter 11.)

■ *What's the deal about scanning with integer numbers?* Some claim that you can scan at less than full optical resolution, but you should scan only at values of full optical resolution divided by integers (1, 2, 3, 4, 5, etc.). So, for a 600-dpi scanner, the idea is that you should scan only at 300 or 150 or 100 or 75 dpi. Some scanners provide *only* these integer divisor choices as presets, and others provide them mixed in with other options (see Figure 3.4). The idea is that an integer divisor makes resampling easier, with better results, because the new and the old pixel grids are always aligned. Scan at the next higher integer resolution, and then downsample (resample) slightly to the desired size (externally). For example, scan at 600 dpi and resample to 520 dpi size later. Even divisors of 2, 4, 8 are likely better than odd divisors like 3 or 5, but any integer divisor is probably better than other values, like 333 dpi.

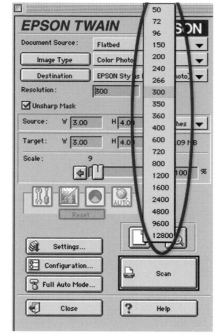

Figure 3.4 This Epson Perfection 2400 Photo scanner provides various resolution presets including several integer divisors (1200, 800, 600, 400, 300, 240, 200, 150, 96, 50). Custom resolutions can also be used.

- *How much resolution do I need when scanning prints?* Scanning *color* prints can rarely yield more detail when scanned at more than 300 dpi. Enlarging photo prints suffers quality losses, at least if enlarged to much degree. A 2x enlargement may be acceptable, but 3x starts being poor. Enlarging film is the much-preferred procedure.

- *How much resolution when scanning film?* When you realize that the primary purpose of modern photo film is to be enlarged (perhaps with a few exceptions such as X-rays), you can see that scanning film at 3000 dpi or more is to good effect. When you need large images to print big at high-scaled resolution, that resolution creates the pixels that effectively give the magnification necessary to print the enlarged print. Film scanners give you those large images while retaining very good image quality.

As to how far to go with film scanning resolution, there is no one answer for this; there are several choices and varying opinions. The best single answer is that the scanned image size should be appropriate for the intended purpose. There is no question that it must be big enough to do the job, but a huge image greatly larger than the requirements can be a rather fanciful indulgence. Except that when enlarging film, there can be subtle yet real reasons for scanning at the film scanner's optical maximum resolution. Or, when maximum resolution is too ridiculously huge, an intermediate step for a smaller goal is to scan at the next larger integer divisor of maximum. The scanner simply functions a little better at maximum or at an integer divisor of maximum. The smaller, desired final image size then can be resampled in a photo editor, followed by modest sharpening. Integer-divisor scanning is a small factor, but the increased quality can often be detected. A good way to bet is that the photo editor will do the resampling better than the scanner.

- *Are there any downsides to scanning film at highest resolution?* Yes, there is a memory cost to high-resolution scans. While image quality is usually the most important consideration with scanning, also realize that large images consume large memory and make computers struggle. The memory cost for an image increases with the square of the resolution. When you multiply the scan resolution by 2, the memory cost goes up by 4 times. As memory goes up, file size goes up, too. A 35mm negative scanned at 2700 dpi in 16-bit mode is 55.5 MB in size. A 5400-dpi scan of the same negative at the same scaling is 222.2 MB.

- *Which is better: scanning prints or film?* Scanning film is better than scanning prints. Film has more detail and contrast available; prints don't. Film is meant to be enlarged; prints are already enlarged. When scanning for enlargement, scan from the film if possible.

Testing Scanner Resolutions for Print Quality

Reading words and theories about scanning resolution guidelines are one thing, but seeing and evaluating printed test results in terms of detail rendering and overall image quality are even more valuable. I asked advanced-amateur photographer Mark Segal in Toronto to test two different scenarios with a film scanner: (A) starting at optical maximum resolution, at what point does the resulting printed image start to deteriorate? and (B) can you really see differences between odd and even integer divisor resolutions on prints?

To do the tests, Segal took a 35mm color negative he shot of the Cairo Tower (Egypt) a few years ago and scanned it on his Konica Minolta DiMAGE Scan Elite 5400 film scanner scaled to print 6.7 by 10 inches on his EPSON Stylus Pro 4000 desktop inkjet printer. This is one of his normal workflows. This image (see Figure 3.5) was selected because its details, diagonals, highlights, and shadows lend themselves well to observing the consequences of different resolution settings.

Figure 3.5 The test image of Cairo Tower in the center of Cairo.

Courtesy of Mark Segal

The scanned images were produced as "scanner raw" files with no sharpening or repairs and no color correction, and they were output in 8-bit mode and printed at 1440 dpi. What you see shown are scans of the actual prints made on the Epson 4000.

(Note: Konica Minolta has a slightly different way of talking about scan resolution terminology and of setting up their scanner software. There are separate Input and Output resolution list boxes (see Figure 3.6). The Input resolution shows how many pixels per inch are scanned. The Output resolution shows what the resolution of the printed image *would be* for the print size and magnification factor indicated. What ultimately matters with resolution is this Output resolution or how many pixels there are spread across how many inches.)

In Test A, Segal scanned his negative at several Input resolutions starting at the maximum (5400 dpi) and decreasing them with each scan, maintaining his desired output sizing (6.7 × 10 inches). As you can see in the cropped and enlarged portions of the resulting prints, the images only start to degrade at his 1704/240 dpi test with the biggest deterioration at 860/120 (Figure 3.7).

For Test B, Segal tested an EVEN integer divisor of 5400 dpi (2700/383 dpi), an ODD integer divisor (1800/255 dpi), and a non-integer resolution of 2800/395, again with all scaled to print at the same desired output size (see Figure 3.8). Studied at a normal viewing distance, the ODD 1800/255 is slightly inferior to the other two, although it's unclear if that's a function of its odd-integerness or of its lower resolution. The other two look identical. However, looking through a 6x magnifier, there is an almost imperceptible improvement with the 2700/383 over the 2800/395, which indicates that there actually is a difference when scanning with integer divisors, although the practical benefit is debatable.

So what's the conclusion of these tests? Says Segal in his analysis, "If you don't look at prints with a powerful magnifier, there is a wide latitude of scanner settings to produce similar quality results."

I agree. While there may be slight advantages to scanning at higher resolutions (including optical maximum resolution), the proof of quality is in the printed output, and I encourage all photographer-artists to do these kinds of tests themselves to determine the best scanning resolutions for *their* workflows. You may conclude, as Mark Segal has, that you don't need as much resolution as you once thought.

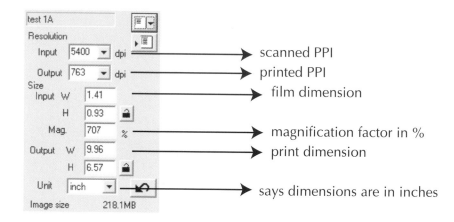

Figure 3.6 The DiMAGE Scan Elite 5400 interface.

Courtesy of Mark Segal

Types of Scanners

There are four basic types of scanners or scanning systems to consider for high-quality printing purposes. *drum, film, flatbed,* and *specialty.*

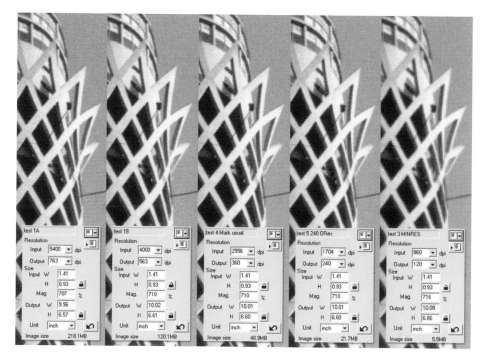

Figure 3.7 Test A with Input/Output resolutions (from left): 5400/763, 4000/563, 2556/360, 1704/240, and 860/120. Scanned directly from the Epson 4000 test prints.

Courtesy of Mark Segal

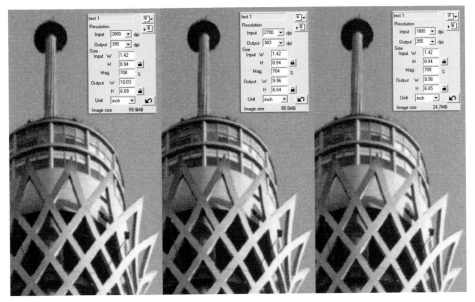

Figure 3.8 Test B: testing ODD and EVEN integer divisors. From left: 2800/395, 2700/383, and 1800/255 dpi.

Courtesy of Mark Segal

Sending Out for Scans

Not everyone has his own scanner, and even if you do, there will be times when you'll want to send out your images to a scanning service for "digitizing." Some of the reasons include: you have large-sized artwork and don't want to be bothered scanning it in sections, you don't want to spend the big bucks for a good camera-scan-back system, or you want a pro to do your scanning and match your colors with minimal proofing.

David Coons, who, with his company ArtScans Studio, is considered by some to be the top fine-art scanning service provider in the world, says, "Anybody just getting started with high-quality digital printing should send out some initial scanning and printing just to get their feet wet, and also to get a sense for what good quality looks like.

"When deciding which scanning service to use, make sure the shop is experienced at the kind of work you need. Talk with other artists who are happy with the services they use."

Left: ArtScans' David Coons and Caroline Dockrell; right: John Silva and Stephen Canthal prepare to scan a painting. The scanner, affectionately dubbed "Audrey 1," moves over the artwork on a track.

Courtesy of David Coons/ArtScans Studio, Inc.

Drum Scanners

It used to be that using a drum scanner was the only way to have a high-resolution scan made, and many photographers-artists still purchase drum scans from scanning-service providers. Using photomultiplier tubes (PMTs) instead of CCD chips, old-style drum scanners are big, finicky machines that can take up half a room, although newer, desktop models are now available. The artwork—typically a transparency or a small print—must be flexible, and it is wrapped around a clear cylinder or drum that spins while a focused light source on a track shines through or on it and onto the image sensors. Drum scanners can produce wonderfully large, high-quality images with great dynamic range and resolutions that can approach 12000 dpi. These outsourced scans aren't cheap, though. Figure paying $50–$100+ per drum scan depending on the file size.

California fine-art photographer Anil Rao has his 6×7-cm medium format transparencies drum scanned at Calypso Imaging of Santa Clara for two main reasons: (1) very high-

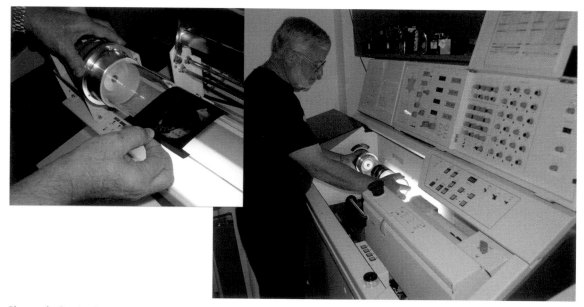

Photoworks Creative Group imaging center in Charlottesville, Virginia, uses a drum scanner for certain scans requiring large blow-ups (they also have a Nikon Coolscan 8000ED). Left: Ron Hurst mounts a 4x5 transparency on the plexiglass drum at a separate mounting station; right: he inserts the drum into the scanner.

Courtesy of Photoworks Creative Group

resolution scans so he can make large prints without sacrificing sharpness and density, and (2) high maximum density (Dmax) that he feels cannot be matched by other types of scanners.

"Print quality is very important to me in my photography," says Rao. "Therefore, I want to start out with the best possible scan. The drum scans from Calypso are 'raw' scans and just record what is there on the film. They are not adjusted for color, contrast, or sharpness. As a result, the scans initially seem flat and dull (they almost never match the original tranny); however, they are full of information. I often find more detail and colors in the scan than I did when viewing the film on the light box. I like working with this wide palette to realize my vision in the final print."

While there are still plenty of drum scanners around in specialty imaging centers, pre-press shops, and service bureaus, there are now more scanning alternatives for photographer-artists.

Film Scanners

These specialized desktop scanners have become very popular with photographers who want to do their own scanning of negatives or transparencies. Film scanners have taken over the position of drum scanners for many wanting high-quality scans. Instead of the light moving past the original on a spinning drum, here the film moves ever-so-slightly past the light source, which with many brands is a cold-cathode, mercury fluorescent lamp, or, in other cases, an array of LEDs. Depending on the price, film scanners can handle 35mm up to 4 × 5-inch sizes.

Because film has to be enlarged more than prints, and also because film has a wider density range and more contrast, most film scanners have correspondingly higher optical resolutions. A maximum resolution of 4000 dpi is standard for many desktop film scanners with others going even higher.

Two of Konica Minolta's 35mm film scanners: left: DiMAGE Scan Elite 5400 with an impressive 5400-dpi optical resolution and built-in Kodak DIGITAL ICE image correction; right: DiMAGE Scan Dual IV with 3200-dpi resolution and Digital Grain Dissolver.

Courtesy of Konica Minolta Photo Imaging USA

A different type of film scanner is made by Denmark's Imacon, and their Flextight models have a unique way to handle the artwork (several models also scan reflective prints). The film is bent in a drum-like shape except there is no drum! There's only air between the sensor and the film, which is held in place by its edges. They call it a "virtual drum," and there's no need for the mounting liquids, gels, or tape that drum scanners require. The resolution is high (up to 8000 dpi, non-interpolated) and with a price tag to match.

Other desktop *film*-scanner makers include: Nikon, Canon, Microtek, and Polaroid.

Upgrading Your Scanner Software: The software provided with the scanner you purchase usually does a fine job. However, some have found that separate third-party software does even better. The two most popular scanner software applications are VueScan and SilverFast.

VueScan: VueScan is an advanced scanning program that works with most flatbed and film scanners (it's updated continuously) to produce scans that have excellent color fidelity and color balance. Developer Ed Hamrick says that VueScan is the world's most popular scanner software, used by over 50,000 people world-wide, and I don't doubt it. It's reasonably priced ($60 or $80), works with Mac, Windows, and Linux, and it only takes a few minutes to download and install (www.hamrick.com).

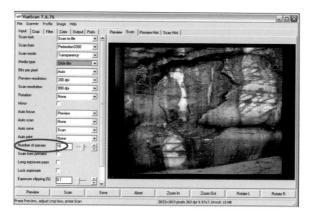

The VueScan interface from photographer Tom O Scott showing one of the features he likes best—the ability to go up to 12 passes on a scan. He finds this crucial for eliminating dust and noise.

Courtesy of Tom O Scott
www.tomoscott.com

I've tried it myself, and it's very intuitive. Photographer Tom O Scott also uses it. "I love the incredible amount of control you have over the scan in VueScan," he says. "There are dozens of options you can configure for every type of film. One feature I like is the ability to set a different resolution for preview scans versus final scans. Also, I really like to "serialize" the output files. A '+' at the end of the file name increments each scan by one so you don't overwrite your files."

SilverFast: LaserSoft's Silver-Fast Ai scanning software, which works as either a stand-alone or Photoshop plug-in, is even more powerful than VueScan, but it also costs more (the price varies by scanner model). This is a very professional scanning application that's more like a suite of features or modules. Version 6 includes: Smart Removal of Defects (SRD), Selective Color Correction (SCC), Selective Color to Gray (SC2G), Grain and Noise Elimination (GANE), remove multiple color casts (MidPip4), adjust and process any negative for optimum results (NegaFix), and generate ICC color profiles (IT8 Target Calibration).

"I've been using SilverFast Ai for more than four years," says publisher and professional landscape photographer Jerry D. Greer. "With the additional IT8 calibration, custom IT8 targets, SilverFast guide book, and a little time to master the program, a photographer can transform a mediocre scanner into a professional imaging tool."

For Mac or PC. www.lasersoft.com

Flatbed Scanners

Like photocopiers, flatbed scanners are basically boxes with a flat glass plate that you put the artwork on (face down). This can be photo or artwork prints, books, even 3D found objects like seashells (see "Scanograms" box). A moving CCD array travels the length of the bed scanning as it goes. Earlier flatbeds could only scan reflective art, but the newer generation can now do a decent job with transparencies and film negatives as well; these are sometimes called "dual-media" scanners. These either use an adapter or special lid construction that allows light to shine from above onto the CCD sensors, or they have special drawers with film holders built into the base of the scanner (see Figure 3.9).

Several manufacturers such as Microtek, Canon, HP, Agfa, Umax, and Epson make a wide range of flatbed models with resolutions from 600 × 1200 dpi to 4800 × 9600 dpi. Photographer Tom O Scott uses the transparency adapter on his Epson Perfection 3200 Photo to process photos from his Mamiya 7ii medium-format film camera. "My scans with the 3200 are fantastic," he

Figure 3.9 The Microtek ArtixScan 1800f flatbed features a "dual-platen" design to accommodate a variety of reflective, positive, and negative film originals—from 35mm up to 8×10 inches.

Courtesy of Microtek Lab, Inc.

says. "I got some cans of compressed air to keep the glass clean, and the results are far better than the photo lab was giving me for their usual 'production scan.' It takes a while when you scan at high resolution, but if it's a good photo, the wait is worth it."

Automatic Dust-Busting with Digital ICE

If you've ever spent hours retouching or cloning out dust, scratches, and other imperfections from scanned images, you know what a tedious chore that can be. And this is where options like SilverFast and Kodak's (formerly Applied Science Fiction's) Digital ICE can be tremendous time-savers.

Digital ICE ("ICE" informally stands for Image Correction and Enhancement) is a combination of hardware and software, and a film-scanner manufacturer must implement it at the time of manufacture. It's a special technology that uses infrared to locate flaws on color films (it doesn't work on silver-halide black-and-white films, and Kodachrome is problematic due to its unique dye structure), isolate them on a fourth "defect" or "D" channel, and then automatically delete them, leaving the image clean. Another way of doing this—besides manual "dust busting" or cloning—has been by slightly softening or blurring the image, which isn't always the best way to deal with this problem, as you can imagine. Instead, Digital ICE works from within the scanner during the scanning process.

"It's astonishing what ICE can do," says Mark Segal, who provides an example in the nearby pair of images. "Scanning time is slower, but the before-and-after difference is night and day."

Other related image-enhancement and correction tools from Kodak such as DIGITAL GEM and DIGITAL ROC are also integrated into some film scanners as the DIGITAL ICE[3] Suite, but GEM and ROC along with DIGITAL SHO are also available as Photoshop plug-ins and are covered in "Plug-ins and Filters."

Digital ICE at work: (left) a 1958 slide taken by Mark Segal in Zermatt, Switzerland, shows its age. Right: the same slide rescanned on the Konica Minolta DiMAGE Scan Elite 5400 but this time with ICE turned on.

Courtesy of Mark Segal

"Scanograms"

"Photograms" have been around since the invention of photography, but it seems as though they're being resurrected through digital imaging and printing. I call them "scanograms." Just lay any not-too-thick object on a flatbed scanner and have at it. Of course, scans made this way can also be incorporated into any subsequent artwork as backgrounds or whatever is desired. Let your imagination run wild!

Scanning book author Wayne Fulton made this scan from small seashells that he placed—very carefully to keep from scratching the glass—on his flatbed scanner's glass bed.

Courtesy of Wayne Fulton
www.scantips.com

There is another type of flatbed scanner that does a superb job of scanning, and those are the higher-end, professional flatbeds (aka "super flatbeds") that offer resolutions that match drum scanners (more than 5000 dpi). The best of these give photographers, photo labs, and wide-format digital printmakers exceptional quality scans in a smaller footprint.

For example, the Creo iQsmart[3] (see Figure 3.10) features 5500 × 10000 dpi optical resolution, a productivity of 85 scans per hour, optional oil mounting station for better quality on cracked or scratched films, and "XY Stitch" technology, which is where the scan head moves on both X and Y axis for more consistent imaging across the entire scanning area and maximum resolution, regardless of original size.

Figure 3.10 Sister of the famous EverSmart Supreme scanner, the Creo iQsmart[3] produces scans from many sizes of originals, reflective or film.

Courtesy of Creo

"The Creo EverSmart scanner has become the cornerstone of our scanning services," says Bill Smith, owner of Boston Photo Imaging, a professional photo lab specializing in archiving, collections, and reproductions. "Our largest order to date was 350,000 scans from one customer, and the Creo's combination of high capture quality, flexibility to accept diverse originals, and speed to handle the large volume made it possible."

With price tags in the low- to mid-five figures, Creo scanners are for serious digital imagers. However, high-end scanners of this type also double as film scanners, so they can be worth the investment depending on the need. Other super-flatbed makers include Fujifilm and Microtek.

Specialty Scanners

There are other scanning systems—including such names as BetterLight, Jumboscan, and Cruse—that don't fit neatly into the categories above. These are very high-end reproduction scanners used primarily by museums, universities, and research institutions. (For more about digital back uses including BetterLight, see the "Photography" section next.)

The Jumboscan by Lumiere Technology in Paris uses a unique up-to-360-Megapixel 12000×30000 pixel RGB or "6 band/13 band multispectral" camera with the largest CCD sensor array in the world: 78×195mm in size! The camera and JumboLux elliptical light projectors that sweep across the subject in synchronization with the CCD array can be aimed to scan objects on walls, floors, easels, and copytables. Currently being used by research (Rochester Institute of Technology), education, and government institutions (U.S. Library of Congress) as well as museums (the Louvre in Paris and the National Gallery of London), the JumboScan is the world's only scanner that captures images with up to 6 or 13 filters instead of the normal 3 (RGB) at very high definition for highly color-accurate fine-art reproduction.

Figure 3.11 The Cruse Synchron Table scanner. This is the latest evolution of the Cruse reproduction scanners where the bed moves under the stationary light and image sensor.

Courtesy of Cruse Digital Equipment

The other Rolls Royce of scanners is the Cruse Synchron. Invented by Hermann Cruse and manufactured in Germany, this behemoth comes in a couple of styles and several models (see Figure 3.11), and it is a sight to see. Weighing in at 1,940 lbs. and priced around $110K, the Synchron CS 285 ST-FA has a maximum resolution of 14000 × 26000 dpi, generates 1.1 GB files, and it can accept originals up to 59 × 88 inches (that's more than seven feet across!). This model scanner has a fixed light source and scan head with the artwork on a vacuum table moving underneath. Many Cruse scanners also have a "variable texture" feature that allows you to vary the lighting to emphasize the raised texture patterns on the original art.

Photography

Since photography in general and digital photography in particular are subjects that fill many worthy books, we'll only hit the highlights as they relate to digital printing.

Photographers have the most experience in this area since capturing images is already their primary activity, either with analog or digital cameras. Traditional artists, on the other hand, are mainly concerned about digitizing finished artwork, and they tend to rely on outside professionals such as printmakers or photographers. And finally, many digital artists use cameras (and scanners) for inputting image elements that are later manipulated on the computer.

There are two main ways to capture images with photography: with traditional *film photography* and *direct digital capture.*

Film Photography

Many photographers still prefer to work with film and then scan it in the ways that we've already covered. For traditional artists reproducing existing artwork with film, the art is photographed with a camera that typically produces a medium- to large-format transparency (color negatives are harder to deal with in scanning), which is then scanned on a high-end scanner. The skill of the photographer in dealing with image squareness, lighting, exposure time, focus, film choice, and more is paramount. Photographing art is an art in itself, and it takes a lot of experience and training to do it right.

Although film is losing ground steadily in the face of the digital onslaught, many have not abandoned it yet. "As I write this," says John Castronovo, owner of Tech Photo & Imaging in Fairfield, New Jersey, "the best film capture is still superior to digital. However, I'm afraid that the knowledge of how to use film is dying as fast as the technology itself. There are serious reasons why one might want to shoot and scan film, and in our lab, we find that we still need to do both, depending on the requirements of the job.

"One of the nicest things about large format film is that it captures more data than we will probably ever need in the reproduction process. An 8×10 transparency can yield well over a gigabyte of usable data, and most importantly, all that information recorded in the transparency is automatically there for the taking at any time in the future. Few people would ever scan artwork at such resolutions expecting that someone *might* have a need for it sometime down the road. Moreover, a transparency is its own proof. Unlike digital, it needs no translation to manifest itself in our analog world.

"You have to admit that the quality of large format film plus a drum scan has never been in question," Castronovo continues. "However, digital is more convenient for most

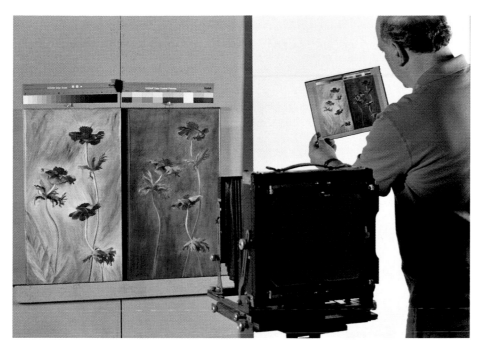

Photo lab owner John Castronovo holds an 8×10 transparency after photographing the traditional art of Liron Sissman. "You can't beat a large-format transparency as its own proof," says Castronovo, who shoots either film or digital depending on the requirements of the job.

Courtesy of John Castronovo, Tech Photo & Imaging

people, and now that we're at the point where 'more than acceptable results' are possible to obtain using digital capture, and given that most people are driven to expediency, direct digital scanning is quickly replacing film for art reproduction."

Advantages of Film Photography

- Traditional, universal workflow with reliable results.
- Medium- and large-format film advocates claim film still has the quality edge over digital.
- Film is its own proof; nothing else is required to view it.
- Film is the safe and permanent standard.

Since the ultimate goal of a film-photography-based workflow is to end up with a digital file, the obvious question is: Why not just start off with digital to begin with?

Digital Capture

Digital cameras and digital camera backs are all the rage (41 million were sold in 2003 worldwide) and are gradually replacing their analog ancestors (film cameras). Here are some reasons why:

Advantages of Digital Capture

- There's no lag time from exposure to the final image. You see it, you got it.
- Lack of film grain means digital captures are very smooth and clean.
- Since there's no film, you don't have to buy it, store it, or process it. Or worry about it being X-rayed at airports!
- Digital proponents say camera-back captures are sharper, clearer, and show more detail than film.

While the debate continues over whether film or digital is better for the highest-quality imaging and printing (many feel that digital equals or exceeds 35mm quality but film still wins in larger formats), capturing images with either a digital-capable camera or a digital camera back continues as a growing trend.

What You Need to Know about Digital Cameras

Using lenses to focus light and create an image in the same way film cameras do, digital cameras or "digicams" are basically little scanners, and all the things we've learned about pixels, file sizes, and resolution apply here equally as well (i.e., more is better). The main difference is that the cameras in this category are primarily "area array" devices. A single, light-sensitive sensor (CCD or CMOS), which is made up of tiny elements in a checkerboard or mosaic pattern that are individually coated to be sensitive to red, green, or blue light, is exposed through a lens to the light reflecting off the subject. The camera converts the analog signal into binary information, and bingo, you have a digital file.

Everyone thought that the revolutionary Foveon X3 image sensor (introduced in 2002) would change the digital camera industry forever, but with only Sigma and more recently Polaroid offering Foveon sensors in their cameras, it just hasn't happened (yet). Instead of sensing elements that capture only one color at a time, each Foveon chip has three photo detector layers to capture a different color—one each for red, green, and blue (see Figure 3.12). As a light ray sinks into the sensor, first blue, then green, then red is absorbed. So, what's the big deal? The resulting image can be sharper and with higher resolution.

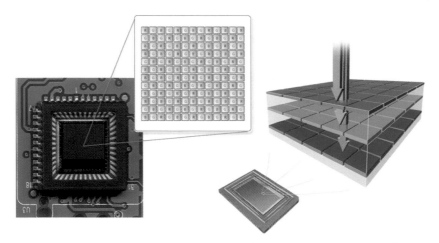

Figure 3.12 Two digital camera sensor technologies—left: a small 2 Megapixel CCD sensor and a simulated area array pattern of the individual elements; right: the newer Foveon X3 layered chip.

right: © 1998-2002 Foveon, Inc.

Digicams come in myriad styles and types. Pick up a photography magazine or walk into any camera store, and you'll see that there are point-and-shoots, "prosumer," professional, and studio cameras for every possible use and occasion. They are usually categorized and marketed by their maximum number of recorded pixels, e.g., 2048 × 1536 (that's horizontal by vertical). This is the advertised CCD resolution, which is arrived at by simply multiplying the two numbers together and rounding off to the closest million-pixel decimal. For example, 2560 × 1920 pixels equals 4.9 or just 5 Megapixels (abbreviated as 5 MP).

A 5-MP camera is considered to be the minimum for capturing images that can yield decent quality at moderate print dimensions. Consider a 5.1-Megapixel camera like the Nikon Coolpix 5700 that has a maximum resolution of 2592 × 1944 pixels. An opened and decompressed file at 300 ppi would yield a very good 6.4 × 8.5-inch print but not much more unless you reduce the ppi (cut the ppi to 150 and the print size doubles).

If you move up to something like Canon's PowerShot Pro1 (see Figure 3.13), you're dealing with 8 MP and a maximum resolution of 3264 × 2448 pixels resulting in an 8 × 11-inch print (or more if you reduce the ppi).

The next step up with digital cameras is to the top-of-the-line digital SLRs. This is the rarefied world where the flagship cameras of the major brands live: Olympus' E-1 (5 MP), Nikon's D100 (6.1 MP), Canon's EOS 1Ds (11.1 MP), Fuji FinePix S3 Pro (12 MP), and the Kodak DCS Pro SLR/n (13.5 MP). One main advantage of these dSLR cameras (besides the higher pixel count) is the ability to interchange lenses, just like traditional SLR cameras.

Figure 3.13 Canon's 8-MP PowerShot Pro1 digital camera.

Courtesy of Canon USA

With a few exceptions such as the use of a camera-RAW file format, a file from a digital camera is treated exactly the same as a file from a scanner. And it isn't only the pixel count that matters (although that's an important part of the equation—see Table 3.1 for a summary of print sizes in relation to pixel dimensions). Other factors that affect image and ultimately print quality include: the quality of the lenses, the size and type of the image sensors (most sensors are still smaller than a 35mm film frame), the type and size of individual sensor elements (Fuji offers two sensitivities in its Super CCD SR sensors), and the camera software that processes the images.

Table 3.1 Pixels & Print Sizes[1]

Image Resolution	Megapixels	Printed @ 200ppi	Printed @ 300 ppi
640 × 480 pixels	.3 MP	3.2 × 2.4 in.	2.1 × 1.6 in.
1024 × 768	.8	5.1 × 3.8	3.4 × 2.6
1280 × 960	1.2	6.4 × 4.8	4.3 × 3.2
1600 × 1200	1.9	8.0 × 6.0	5.3 × 4.0
2048 × 1536	3.2	10.2 × 7.7	6.8 × 5.1
2592 × 1944	5.0	13.0 × 9.7	8.6 × 6.5
3264 × 2448	8.0	16.3 × 12.2	10.9 × 8.2
4256 × 2848	12.1	21.3 × 14.2	14.2 × 9.5

[1]*Does not include any special scaling programs, use of RIPs, etc.*

You basically get what you pay for, which means that as you spend more, your ability to print larger, higher-quality images increases.

Digital Camera Backs

While purists argue that digicams still can't equal the quality of a well-exposed, processed, and scanned medium- or large-format piece of film, the ground shifts when you start talking about *digital camera backs* (also called digital scan backs). With these devices that typically attach to large- and medium-format cameras such as Hasselblad and Mamiya, you're on a different level of quality that either approaches or exceeds large film formats, depending on who is talking.

These digital backs are used mostly by professional commercial and advertising photographers in a high-production environment. Exposures are instantaneous, so all light sources including flash can be used, and some models give the photographer the option of working untethered from the computer to capture hundreds of high-resolution images. For example, Imacon's Ixpress digital backs have a companion Ixpress Image Bank device with a storage capacity of more than 850 132-MB images and power for up to eight hours of constant shooting.

Imacon's Ixpress 528C (22 Megapixel) digital back attached to a studio camera.

Courtesy of Imacon USA

Some of the most popular digital backs include (with their maximum pixel dimensions): Leaf Valeo 22 (22 MP), Imacon Ixpress 528C (22 MP), Phase One P25 (22 MP), Sinar Bron 54M (22 MP), Kodak DCS Pro Back Plus (16 MP), and Fuji Luma II (11 MP).

Digital Drawing/Painting

Not really a way to acquire or capture an image, digital drawing or painting involves artists creatively inputting their ideas directly into the computer. It can be done with drawing or painting software applications, image-editing programs, or the many niche programs, plug-ins, and filters that are available to artists working digitally.

Let me admit right up front that there is a lot of overlap between this category and the next one, image editing. The dividing line where image creation becomes image processing is very fuzzy. Much art is made with a feedback loop of trying something, going back and fixing it, then trying again. And that's one of the main advantages of working digitally. Experiments and variations with a computer can be done quickly, and if done right, they're reversible.

BetterLight Scan Backs

BetterLight scan backs provide large, high-resolution files with extraordinary detail and sharp focus, wide dynamic range (BetterLight claims 11+ f-stops), great control of color and tones, and adjustment of density (exposure) in less than $^1/_{10}$th f-stop steps.

The technology that BetterLight uses is completely different than the other single-shot backs with area-array sensors. Working like a flatbed scanner turned up on its side, the BetterLight gathers the information for the image in one continuous scan as the light is collected by three, individually filtered rows of pixels (tri-linear scanning array or CCD).

Because the CCD sensor slowly moves across the image plane, scans can take minutes. This results in two limiting issues: (1) the subject cannot move, and (2) continuous lights rather than electronic flash must be used.

However, if you're willing to live with those two conditions, then you will be amazed at the quality of the resulting captures. For example, the top-end model of BetterLight at this writing was the expected Super 10K-2, which features a native maximum resolution of 10200×13800×3 pixels (422 MP)! (BetterLight gets to multiply the pixel dimensions by 3 since they have "real" pixels for each of the three colors throughout the image.) If I were to plug those numbers into Table 3.1, the resulting print sizes would be 51×69 inches (@200ppi) and 34×46 inches (@300ppi)!

The primary users of BetterLights are professional photographers involved with advertising, catalog, commercial/industrial, art reproduction, and museum/archiving applications. One is Benjamin Blackwell who creates digital archives of artwork for the UC Berkeley (California) Art Museum, as well as other museums and clients. Figure 3.14 shows his setup using a BetterLight scanning back on a 4×5 camera. He uses 4200°K HID (ceramic metal halide High Intensity Discharge) lights, which produce much less heat and more light per watt than tungsten.

Blackwell's image files for museums, artists, and printers can range from 300—549 MB in size!

Figure 3.14 A BetterLight scanning-back system is used by photographer Ben Blackwell to digitally capture artwork at the UC Berkeley Art Museum. Inset shows two of the BetterLight inserts with a CCD sensor that moves across image plane.

© Ben Blackwell
www.benblackwell.com;

inset: Courtesy of BetterLight, Inc.

One way to get a handle on digital drawing and painting work is to look at the software used to create it. I'll give a short summary of some of the major program players to give you a feel for them. And again, keep in mind that my category dividing lines are not impermeable. Many programs can both help create and edit images, and many artists own several types of software and use them all, even in a single image. (See Table 3.2 for an overview of the major image-editing software applications, including drawing/painting programs.)

Painter

Corel Painter is a digital painting program that simulates traditional media. With 30 mediums and more than 400 new brushes in Painter 8, this is the premier "natural-media," digital painting and sketching tool. It's a complex program that is a little daunting for some, but the results are pretty amazing if you hang in there long enough to explore it.

You can create images from scratch, or you can enhance what you already have, and Painter is completely compatible with Photoshop so you can exchange layers between the two. Digital artist Bobbi Doyle-Maher, for example, moves between Painter and Photoshop as she develops her photo-based and layered images (see Figure 3.15). "One of the big advantages of working digitally is the ability to accomplish layering with great speed. I compare digital layering with the glazing that the Old Masters did with paint. To gain the luminous look and depth of many of the paintings we admire today, the artist started with a tonal underpainting, followed by glazes of color, then waited for the glazes to dry before they could proceed. A similar process can be done with a computer, and the results are exciting indeed!"

Figure 3.15 Below: Bobbi Doyle-Maher used Painter's Mixer palette to paint highlights on the backs of the cows. Above: The final digitally painted and layered *Homestead* image.

Courtesy of Bobbi Doyle-Maher/ www.rabbittwilight.com

Other Paint Programs

There are many other digital drawing and painting programs that artists use. A few of the most popular:

Studio Artist: Synthetik Software's Studio Artist isn't as well know as Painter, but those who use it love it. Based on the idea of a music synthesizer, it's a "graphic synthesizer" with an unusual interface, and one of its great strengths is in letting you take an existing source image and going wild with it. The number of editable controls is astounding, which makes it an experimenter's dream. There are also plenty of brushes and textures for straight digital painting, plus added functions for video processing, morphing, warp animation, and even "intelligent-assisted (auto) painting." One common complaint about images processed in Photoshop is that the various "Photoshop effects" from common filters and plug-ins become obvious and hackneyed. Studio Artist's approach helps to avoid this problem.

As with other painting programs, Studio Artist is a good companion to Photoshop. Hawaii artist Diana Jeon likes to start an image in Photoshop, bring it into Studio Artist to add different painted or sketched effects, and then wrap it all up back in Photoshop for final printing.

CorelDRAW/PhotoPaint: Primarily used as an illustration/page-layout program, CorelDRAW is now packaged with Corel PhotoPaint (for image editing and painting) and R.A.V.E. (for creating animations and vector effects for the Web) into the CorelDRAW Graphics Suite. While originally a dual-platform application, Version 12 of the Graphics Suite is for Windows only.

Digital artist Carol Pentleton, who also runs the online gallery The Digital Artist, uses CorelDRAW exclusively in the creation of her images. She loves the flexibility, the transparency of use, and the quality of the tools, and her favorite feature is the infinite mutability of fills she can get with the program. Pentleton outputs her images to both IRIS and a proprietary digital-oil-on-canvas printing process. "I love the color saturation and the smoothness of the transitions of the prints," she says.

Illustrator and Freehand: I put Adobe Illustrator and Macromedia Freehand in the same grouping because they often trade places on most artists' lists for best vector-based, drawing or illustration program (CorelDRAW is the other contender). Digital artists have found good uses for vector-based drawing programs, using them in combination with other software. New York artist Howard Berdach works this way by starting off his images as shapes in Freehand. Brought into Photoshop, the elements are colorized, layered, and then layered some more (see Figure 3.16). "When my images are 'done,' they're often just starting points to the next version," he says. Printed output is to Epson, Roland, and IRIS wide-format inkjet printers.

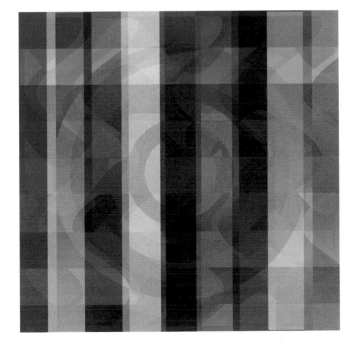

Figure 3.16 Howard Berdach's *Sonic Color Loom,* created in Freehand and Photoshop.

© 1998-2004 Howard Berdach
www.howardberdach.com

NaturePainter: The new Windows-only NaturePainter Digitas Canvas (NaturePainter.net) is a moderately priced, entry- to mid-level painting program. It's designed to be more for learning how to paint, and you can paint in any style with tools like brushes, palette knife, and the ability to mix paint to experiment with color. "NaturePainter is a brilliant, user-friendly program," says UK amateur artist Malcolm Randall. "It has a very short learning curve, but it can suit the most seasoned digital artist, as well as the beginner. The end result can look just like an oil painting."

Machine Art

I learned the term "machine art" from digital printmaker and New Mexico-based artist JD Jarvis, although let's be clear that the machine doesn't make the art. As Jarvis explains, "machine art is the imagery of the computer's soul. What is truly 'digital art' is the work that begins in the mind of the artist with the notion of synthesis. Using all the software tools and all the traditional processes together to make something that we have not yet seen—this is the power and the challenge of working digitally to make Art."

Machine art includes three-dimensional modeling where 3D artists who use programs such as Maya (Alias), Bryce (Corel/DAZ), Poser (Curious Labs), and LightWave 3D (NewTek) to create entire universes that only exist at the interface of the computer software and their imaginations. And, this is also the world of fractal mathematics and algorithmic art. Using filters, texture and pattern generators, commercial or free software, custom computer coding, scripts, or pure mathematical equations, digital artists spend hours, days, and weeks with precise calculations that are performed by the computer and ultimately rendered into print or other 2D or 3D forms.

Digital artist Renata Spiazzi has been using the computer to create art since 1991. Trained in traditional techniques, Spiazzi didn't want to imitate other media but wanted to see what the computer could really do (Figure 3.17). When she discovered the original Kai's Power Tools (KPT) filters, she was hooked. "I'm frequently asked 'which 3D program are you using?' The illusion of 3D is very powerful and very expressive in the results I get from KPT (she uses all the versions including the older ones). However, even though I keep thinking that I should learn a 3D program, I still use Photoshop and filters, and occasionally Painter and a few other 2D programs. I also experiment with fractals, which are fascinating, but most of the time a fractal gives an object but not a complete image. In order to make a painting of it, I feel I have to transfer it to Photoshop and work on it to have what I call 'a symphony.'"

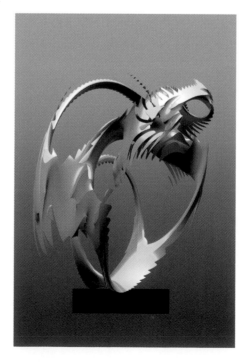

Figure 3.17 Renata Spiazzi's *My Golden Eagle*, from her series *Impossible: Works I Wish I Could Sculpt*, which was created mainly with KPT5 Frax 4D.

Courtesy of Renata Spiazzi www.spiazzi.com

Image Editing

Once you have the raw materials of an image in your digital workspace, you're ready for image processing or editing. Image editing can be as simple as taking a single image and making sure it looks the way you want it to look, that it's the right size, and that it has the correct file format. But for many, that's just the beginning. This is where many photographer-artists spend most of their time in creating their complex imagery. Compositing, layering, montage/collage—this is where it all happens. This is the stage on which much digital art is played out.

Image editing is a full-length subject on its own, so I'll only concentrate on three aspects of it: *software, plug-ins,* and *filters,* and that part of the image-editing workflow dealing with *sizing and scaling.*

Image-Editing Software

Most photographers and artists use some form of image-editing software. This is not an absolute requirement—you could print an image from a word-processing program if you wanted, but to get the most out of your images and your printing, you'll want to have and use an image editor.

Which is the best image editor? There is no easy answer to that question. Besides the obvious requirement that you be able to drive a printer from the software—or be able to place the image into another type of program (page-layout, for example) to drive a printer, the other requirements of an image-editing program depend on what you want to do to process or improve your images. Minimum features to look for: layer editing, support for

Table 3.2 Image-Editing & Painting Software

Program	Maker	Platform	Used for
CorelDRAW/PhotoPaint	Corel	PC + Mac	DRAW: page layout, illustration Suite12 : PC only PhotoPaint: image editing, painting
Freehand	Macromedia	PC + Mac	vector illustrations, print and web design
GIMP	(open source)	PC + Mac	photo retouching, image composition, image authoring
Illustrator	Adobe Systems	PC + Mac	vector illustrations, print and web design
NaturePainter Digital Canvas	Urban Pursuit	PC only	painting
Photoshop	Adobe Systems	PC + Mac	image editing, painting, web graphics
Photoshop Elements	Adobe Systems	PC + Mac	image editing, photo retouching, web graphics
Painter	Corel	PC + Mac	painting, photo and image editing
Paint Shop Pro	Jasc Software	PC only	painting, photo and image editing, web graphics
Qimage	Digital Domain	PC only	image-viewing/printing software
Studio Artist	Synthetik Software	Mac only	painting, photo and image editing

various file and input/output formats, masking, cloning, painting and retouching, Photoshop plug-in compatibility, and color management support.

Here is a summary of the most popular, image-editing software used to help photographer-artists process and prepare their images for printing. (If you're using a paint program, many image-editing functions are available within that program, although you will still want to consider having a separate image editor, too.)

Photoshop

Adobe's Photoshop is the gold standard of image-editing software for most serious digital photographer-artists. It's the most expensive, the most complex, and for many, the most intimidating piece of software they will ever own.

I was intimidated at first, too. I had Photoshop 2.1 sitting in a corner unused for a couple of years; I was scared to death of it. Then I upgraded to version 5.5 and decided it was time to learn it. Many, many hours later, the veil finally lifted. Now, with the later versions, including version 8 ("CS"), I don't know how I existed without Photoshop. I use it constantly for image editing, and because of that, it's as familiar as an old sweater. Not that I know everything there is to know about it. I don't. I consider Photoshop a lifetime learning experience.

What's so great about Photoshop?

- With CS, broad support for the first time of both 16-bit and camera RAW images. This is high-level, high-powered stuff for serious digital imagers and printers.

- Full CMYK color support including custom CMYK separations, which are essential for commercial printing or pre-press work. In addition, support for important L*a*b* color.

- Comprehensive color management options that are hard to match elsewhere. This is an important aspect of high-quality digital printing. A key part of this is the ability to "soft proof" or show you what an RGB image will look like printed to an inkjet or other digital device (starting with Version 6). See the next chapter for more about this.

- All kinds of sophisticated image-editing tools including, with CS: Shadow/Highlight adjustment, Match Color for making colors in separate images consistent, Color Replacement for changing color while retaining texture, an enhanced File Browser for viewing and opening image thumbnails, and Photomerge for panorama stitching (which was only available in Photoshop Elements until Photoshop CS).

- A final advantage is Photoshop's redundancy. There are many ways to do the same thing, which can be a big plus in terms of flexibility and tailoring the program to your needs.

In basic terms, if you're in the *business* of digital imaging and printing, you'll want Photoshop. If not, you may not need all the horsepower that Photoshop offers. Depending on your goals, one of the following software programs may be all you require.

Photoshop Elements

Adobe's Photoshop Elements is a trimmed down Photoshop targeted to those doing digital photography. If that's all you're doing, then Elements may be all you really need. It combines image editing, photo retouching, and web-graphics creation, and it has most of the core functions of Photoshop like Levels, Color Balance, and other features that are in some cases only available through the use of outside work-arounds.

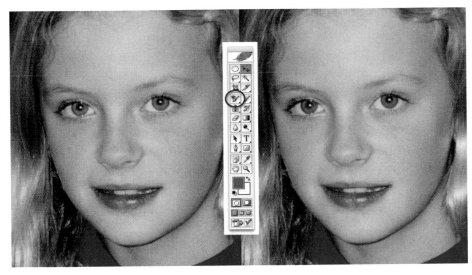

Photoshop CS's Color Replacement tool lets you change color while retaining the original texture and shading.

From a high-quality, digital printing point of view, the main drawbacks to Elements are: (1) its rudimentary color management function where Photoshop is much more advanced, (2) no 16-bit or camera RAW image support where there is in Photoshop, and (3) only elementary CMYK color support, which is where Photoshop really shines.

However, it is possible to get very satisfactory results from Elements without the tremendous learning curve and sticker shock associated with the full-blown Photoshop that, honestly, is just too much for many to handle. Elements sometimes comes bundled with other hardware or software, and one secret that many don't know about is that it also supports some full-version Photoshop plug-ins that work on RGB images.

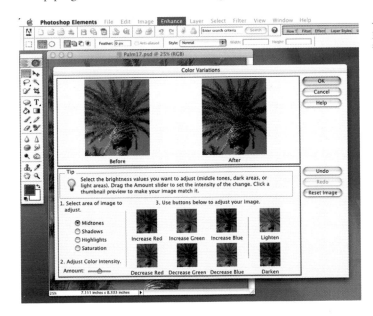

Adobe Photoshop Elements is a powerful yet easy-to-use image-editing software package.

Paint Shop Pro

Paint Shop Pro ("PSP") by Jasc Software is a great program for the average user, especially for the price, which is about a sixth of Photoshop's. You can both create and edit images with it. There are text and drawing tools, photo and perspective correction and enhancement tools, a fast background eraser, web design tools, and a powerful full-blown scripting engine that allows users to record, play, and edit any series of repetitive or creative tasks within the program (similar to Actions in Photoshop). And as with Photoshop, there are layers, adjustment layers, and layer blending modes. It's very Wacom-compatible, and it even has Levels and Curves adjustments. On the drawback side, Paint Shop Pro lacks the 16-bit support, CMYK, LAB, and other advanced modes of Photoshop, and it offers only the simplest of color management, but compared to Photoshop, PSP is very easy to use. My main complaint is that it's only for the PC; there is no Mac version.

Jasc Software's Paint Shop Pro is a lower-priced, image-editing alternative to Photoshop.

Courtesy of Jasc Software

The GIMP

GIMP is an acronym for GNU Image Manipulation Program. It's a freely distributed ("open source") program, which means that unlike commercial software, The GIMP is under continual development by a group of volunteers and enthusiasts around the world. The GIMP is meant for doing things like photo retouching, digital painting, and image composition and editing. "I've found everything I was looking for in The Gimp," says artist Pat Thompson. "I'm astounded by all the color-manipulation tools and options. It has layers, color management including Lab color, an optional animation module, and several tool options I'd never heard of before."

The GIMP is expandable and designed to be augmented with plug-ins and extensions. It's written and developed on the UNIX platform, although it also runs on Windows and Mac (OSX only). To use The GIMP, you'll need only enough computer expertise to download it and follow simple directions. For printing, Windows users activate the normal printer drivers, and Mac users can print through the related but independent Gimp-Print printing package.

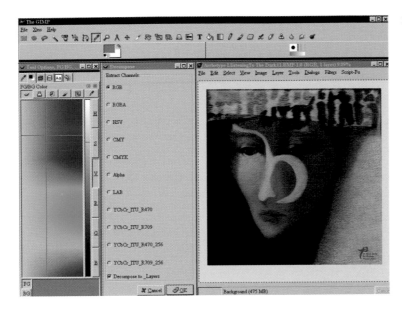

Pat Thompson's *Archetype Listening to the Dark* being edited with The GIMP.

Courtesy of Pat Thompson

Qimage

Qimage fills it own unique category. It's a powerful image-viewing and printing software package (PC only) that optimizes print quality, especially from low-resolution images. As such, I will discuss it in more depth in Chapter 11.

Professional Online Image Editing

Don't want to do your own image adjustments? Plenty of online photo sites now offer simple editing including corrections such as red-eye removal, but one online service provides professional-level image-editing. Image-Edit & Art by DigitalCustom (www.image-edit.com) can handle serious projects remotely, including: face and skin repairs, motion effects, color changes, photo restoration, and digital hand coloring. The company stresses that the work is artist-executed, not automated, and performed by skilled digital artists.

Plug-ins and Filters

There are dozens and dozens of plug-ins and filters that add to and extend the range of other software. Most are algorithm-based and made for changing, tweaking, and wholesale modifying of images. I can't mention them all, but here are some popular ones that I or friends and colleagues of mine have used to work with Photoshop and most other image editors.

■ *DIGITAL ROC, SHO,* and *GEM (Kodak):* Photoshop plug-ins that automatically correct, restore, and balance the color and contrast/brightness of digital images (ROC); reveal the detail in the shadows and automatically optimize contrast and exposure (SHO); and reduce digital image noise and grain (GEM). Photographer Elliott Landy gets full use out of these plug-ins, especially ROC, for his vintage rock-and-roll images that stretch back to the '60s (see Figure 3.18). "We use Digital ROC to restore the colors of the original," says Landy, who outputs exhibition prints to an HP Designjet 30/130 printer. "Although similar results might be obtainable by using Photoshop's tools, we've tried and it's real hard to come close to what this plug-in does in a moment."

Figure 3.18 Elliott Landy's famous *Nashville Skyline* album cover photo of Bob Dylan (1968). Before Digital ROC corrections (left) and after (right).

©Elliott Landy
Landyvision.com

- *PhotoKit (Pixel Genius):* A photographer's plug-in toolkit comprising 141 effects that offer accurate digital replications of analog photographic effects. PC or Mac.

- *buZZ (Fo2PiX):* Image-editor plug-ins for adding painterly filter effects to images. Can be stacked to combine effects. PC or Mac. "It's seldom that I fall so totally in love with a plug-in filter as I have with buZZ filters," says digital artist SkyDancer (www.sky-dancers.com), who is also an independent buZZ dealer. "The ability to remove unwanted and distracting detail from an image without distortion, loss of focus, color, or edges is wondrous in itself. To be able to then save all of my individual settings and filter stacks as a recallable parameter file is frosting on the cake. This filter can turn even a so-so photograph into a work of art."

- *Photo/Graphic Edges (Auto FX Software):* Version 6.0 includes a suite of 14 artistic effects for photographs, including the flagship "10,000 edges" (that's right; 10,000!). Plug-in for Photoshop, Photoshop Elements, Paint Shop Pro, and CorelDRAW, or stand-alone application. PC or Mac.

- *Filters Unlimited (I.C.NET):* 350 filter effects combined into one single Photoshop-compatible plug-in. Combines with Photoshop Actions to create almost unlimited effects. Says photographer Keith Krebs (www.p-o-v-image.com), "Filters Unlimited is 'raw cocoa' for the hearts of filter-addict 'chocoholics.' Not only does it allow me to organize and archive all the FilterFactory based filters that would otherwise make for an unwieldy menu in Photoshop or Paint Shop Pro, but it comes with a bunch of truly useful filters of its own. And Filters Unlimited provides an interface that allows you to interactively edit pre-existing plug-ins and create new ones, seeing the results of edits in the live preview window."

Sizing with Image-Editing

So what do you do with all that great image-editing software? With digital technology, images can be tweaked and improved to an infinite degree. Almost anything you can imagine, you can do with digital image editing. This is not a guide to image-editing (there are plenty of good ones available), and I will illustrate the key steps in creating, processing, and printing an image in Chapter 8. However, this is a good point to review one part of the image-editing workflow that always confuses people and that I introduced in the scanning section earlier. I'm talking about scaling or resampling to change a print's size.

As we learned earlier, *scaling* means stretching or compressing an image's pixels to fit a certain size on the paper. This is also called *resizing. Resampling,* on the other hand, accomplishes the same thing but in a different way.

Let's see how this works with a hypothetical, bitmapped photo image. (Although I'm using Photoshop CS here, you should be able to take similar actions with other image editors with only slight modifications).

In Photoshop's Image Size dialogue box (Image > Image Size), you are confronted with an array of settings and options (see Figure 3.19).

The top portion is titled *Pixel Dimensions,* and it merely measures the number of pixels across (Width) and the number down (Height). The number of pixels determines the amount of information or detail contained in the image; more is better.

Figure 3.19 Photoshop's important Image Size screen.

The next section down is titled *Document Size,* and this is where the critical decisions about image size and resolution are made. The key to how this section works is the little check box at the bottom called *Resample Image.* By either checking or unchecking that box, you are committing yourself to either *scaling* (*resizing*) or *resampling,* and as we already know, they are very different things. Let me explain the impact of this important choice.

With the Resample box *unchecked,* there is now a direct correlation among height, width, and resolution. If you change one, the others change, too. But, in this case—and this is the important point—*you are not changing any pixel data!* You can prove this to yourself by changing the Resolution number while keeping an eye on the Pixel Dimensions; they won't budge (see Figure 3.20). In essence, what you are doing is taking the same number of pixels and spreading them over a larger or smaller amount of space. You are only *scaling or resizing* the image, and since you're not actually printing pixels but dots, the printer driver's (or RIP's) dithering or screening method will try to cover up the differences, usually successfully.

Following this latter method with my hypothetical image, if I have Resample Image unchecked and change the Resolution from 300 ppi to, say, 200 ppi, the Document Size has now magically changed from 8×5.4 inches to 12×8.1 inches. In other words, the image is now larger in size because I lowered the image's

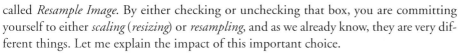

Figure 3.20 With Resample Image unchecked, decreasing the resolution from 300 ppi to 200 ppi increases the print size without affecting the pixel information.

file resolution. Conversely, I could shrink the image by increasing the resolution. But, again, this only works with the Resample Image box *unchecked.*

If you *check* the Resample box, you are *resampling* or *interpolating* the pixel information in the image to reach a desired height and width while at the same time maintaining a fixed resolution (see Figure 3.21). You are adding or deleting pixels depending on whether you are going up in size (*upsampling*) or down (*downsampling*). Either way, realize that you are changing *all* the pixel information and, therefore, the image itself. (The Interpolation Method—Bicubic, Bilinear, or Nearest Neighbor—determines *how* the new pixels are created.) This action degrades the image to some degree, usually resulting in a loss of sharpness. I try to avoid this

whenever I can, but it's not always possible and a judicious amount of re-sharpening is then employed.

An alternative to image-editor sizing (reducing or enlarging) is to have the printer driver or RIP, if one is used, do it. Results can vary so it's best to test this method for yourself.

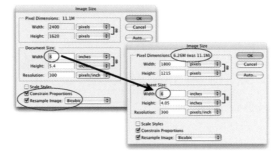

Figure 3.21 With Resample Image checked, you can change the print size while keeping the same image resolution, but at a cost.

File Formats, Image Compression, and More...

Image processing also requires an understanding of file formats and image compression before a final image can be printed, transported, or stored.

File Formats

Image files are stored, shipped, saved, and opened in specific formats. Depending on which platform you're on (PC or Mac) and which version of Photoshop or other major image-editing programs you have, there might be up to two dozen file formats to choose from. But for most photographers and artists working with digital printing, there are only a few real choices.

Camera RAW

More and more digital cameras give you the option of capturing the image in the camera's RAW format, sometimes called by other names like *NEF* by Nikon. Why RAW? Instead of the normal procedure where the image's information is processed and adjusted behind the scenes by the camera's software, with RAW you get everything the image sensor captured. RAW has it all, and usually with more bit depth (12 bits per channel).

You won't be printing from it, but image editors like Photoshop CS will open a RAW file with its Camera Raw import plug-in, which allows a lot of control over the image's pre-processing before it's converted to one of the normal editing formats that follow.

Native Format

If you do a lot of work in Photoshop, the native format (PSD) is the one to use for preliminary work (CDR is CorelDRAW's native format; RIFF is Painter's). It saves all layers, channels, paths, etc. in the most flexible way. However, native files can get very unwieldy with all the layers and adjustments, and while you can usually print from PSD, final work destined for output is usually saved in a format like TIFF.

TIFF

Tagged Image File Format (TIFF) is the standard image file format accepted by virtually all painting, image-editing, and page-layout programs. And starting with Photoshop 6.0, TIFFs have most of the same layers, vector shapes, paths, and channels that exist in the native PSD format. What most people do is store the master, layered PSD file and make a flattened TIFF copy for sending to the printer (yours or anyone else's) or for importing into a page-layout program. TIFFs also compress very nicely (see below) and support color management profiles. Macs and PCs each deal with TIFFs differently; if you're sending your file out for printing, make sure you find out which version they want (see Figure 3.22).

Figure 3.22 Photoshop CS offers plenty of options for saving in TIFF format, although not all are compatible with other or older applications.

EPS

EPS stands for *Encapsulated PostScript*, and while on the surface it may seem even better than TIFF because it supports both bitmapped and vector-based art, it's not the best choice for most photographer-artists. As you'll learn in Chapter 11, EPS requires a PostScript workflow, either in the form of a PostScript-enabled printer, RIP, or through a PDF workaround. Graphic designers use EPS files all the time, but usually for importing vector art into page-layout programs that will ultimately be sent to a PostScript imagesetter. If you're placing bitmapped image files into QuarkXPress or InDesign, you're better off using TIFFs, which also process faster than EPS files.

PDF

PDF (Portable Document Format) is gradually becoming the standard transport format for complex graphics including text and images. With a PDF (which is in reality a PostScript file that has already been pre-interpreted by a RIP), all the fonts and images have been converted to objects that can be seen by anyone with Acrobat Reader, which is freely available. PDF file sizes can be tiny, depending on the image type, and this file format will continue to play a large role in all types of digital printing.

To make a PDF, you'll need to use Adobe Acrobat or some form of PDFWriter, if your software program includes it; some applications (such as Photoshop and InDesign) also create PDFs directly. If you're using Acrobat, its Distiller function acts like a PostScript RIP, converting an intermediate PostScript file into a PDF. This is one way to get around having to have a RIP or a PostScript printer if you're printing EPS elements to an inkjet printer from a page-layout program.

There are also plenty of other file formats out there, but they're used mostly for specific purposes that usually have little applicability to the digital printing of high-quality bitmapped images. Examples: DCS, a version of EPS; PICT (Mac)/BMP (PC), mainly for internal Mac or PC use; GIF and PNG, primarily for web compression; and PCX, for limited Windows use.

(For information about color models such as RGB and CMYK, see the next chapter.)

Image Compression

Compression is used primarily to shrink a file's size for transport or storage. With digital art files reaching into the hundreds of megabytes, this is sometimes a necessity, at least for transport. There is normally no reason to compress a file while you're working on it, but if you have to compress, it's critical to understand the difference between the two categories: *lossless* and *lossy*.

The lossless variety compresses without removing any color or pixel data from the file. Lossy removes data. (Obviously, lossless is the way to go whenever possible.) The most common file-format compression techniques are the following.

Name That File

File extensions are those three- or four-digit characters after the dot on file names. The problem is: Macs don't need them (and until OS X didn't use them at all), and PCs require them. This isn't an issue if you are staying in your own closed-loop world: your computer, your printer. But as soon as you have to send a file to someone else—a professional printmaker or service bureau, for example, you have to make sure everyone is speaking the same language.

PC users won't be able to recognize a file without the correct file extension. And Macophiles can have the same problem with PC files, depending on its type and name. So the safest thing to do is consistently name your files correctly right off the bat: all lowercase, no weird characters, no spaces, and with the correct file extension.

LZW

LZW (stands for *Lemple-Zif-Welch*, in case you're wondering) is a lossless compression process. It's part of the TIFF format (GIF, too) and can be used whenever you're saving a file (it's one of the few TIFF options available prior to Photoshop 6, 7, and CS). It doesn't compress as much as JPEG and is not supported by all output devices or outside service bureaus. Use it sparingly or not at all. While a LZW-compressed TIFF file will take up only about half as much room on your hard drive, keep in mind that it will take longer to save and open the file when using this option.

ZIP

ZIP is another lossless TIFF compression option in later versions of Photoshop. It works best with images containing large areas of single color.

JPEG

JPEG is the standard *lossy* format for bitmapped images. You can easily adjust the amount of compression and, with it, the quality of the image. The more you compress, the worse the image gets, eventually showing visible artifacts and breaking up into small image blocks. Amazingly, and as my test in Figure 3.23 shows, even JPEGs set to "Low" can produce usable results, while the "0" (lowest) setting can reduce a file's size more than 94 percent (although you would rarely use this setting because of the poor quality). Keep in mind that JPEG compression (or any compression option except LZW) of TIFF files will make them unopenable to many programs, including older versions of Photoshop. In addition, all layers are lost with JPEGs.

Figure 3.23 A low-resolution digicam image as an uncompressed TIFF (left), with, from top, medium to low JPEG compressions. The "0" (lowest) quality shows obvious compression blocks.

JPEG2000 supposedly has the highest image quality per compression ratio, but it's been in the works since 1998, and as of this writing, has barely made its presence known (as an optional plug-in in Photoshop CS). Other specialty compression options include wavelet compression (LuraWave, Wavelet Image) and fractal compression (MrSID), both of which offer high compression along with high image quality.

CAUTION! While it's fine to print from JPEG, avoid opening a JPEG file and resaving it in the JPEG format. Depending on the quality setting, you will loose data each time, and if you keep doing it, you could end up with a bowl of digital mush. The best thing to do is open a JPEG and immediately Save As to a TIFF or a native image-editing format.

File Transport, Storage, and Archives

The image files that photographers and artists create tend to be large. No, huge is a better word. I can still remember working with files in the late '80s that were in the five or ten megabyte range. Those were big files then. Now, I regularly work with files that exceed 200+ MB! Like dust balls, image files constantly accumulate, and when they're also large, they can become a problem when you have to take or send them somewhere, or when you want to store and archive them for the future.

Transporting

If you need to get an image file to someone, you have three basic choices: send it electronically (e-mail, FTP), drop it in the mail or call FedEx, or get in the car and take it yourself. If you're sending it electronically, you could use one of the lossless archiving utilities such as StuffIt (Mac) or Zip (PC); just make sure that the person on the other end has the same program, or they may not be able to open it (self-extracting archives are another answer for those who don't have the program). JPEGs are also a possibility if made with high compression settings.

If you're physically sending or taking your files, CD-Rs (700 MB), CD-RWs (650 MB), and DVDs (4.7 to 9.4 GB) are commonly used to move files around. However, if you're sending your files out to a print service provider, make sure you talk to them first about acceptable file and transport formats (as well as resolution, color management profiles, etc.)

Storing

All the above methods will also work for storing your in-progress as well as finished image files. You can either save files onto transportable media and store them somewhere safe (in a separate location, if you're a stickler for security), or you can buy auxiliary hard drives and/or tape backup systems to do the same thing. Many digital imagemakers do both: using external hard drives with capacties of up to 1 terabyte for primary storage and removable disks like CDs or DVDs as extra backups. With data storage space becoming less costly all the time, many power users are now even moving to multiple hard drives in a RAID (Redundant Array of Inexpensive Disks) configuration to store their huge files.

Archiving: Managing Your Images

Sometimes, the biggest problem with archiving is not the storage space, but knowing where everything is. This is called "digital asset management" or "image management," and there are lots of software products available to help you keep things straight.

A couple of built-in image managers include Photoshop CS's enhanced File Browser and Apple's iPhoto for Macintosh (only). Photoshop's File Browser may not be as powerful as a third-party asset-management software, but it's sometimes easier to work with files directly in the program where you're likely to be using them. File Browser lets you view, sort, and process image files, and you can use it to rename, move, and rotate images. It uses flags, key words, and editable metadata to quickly organize and locate "image assets."

iPhoto is part of the Max OS X operating system, and it's a combination image-importer, browser, and organizer that, besides letting you retouch and crop images, helps you collect and store them into albums.

And speaking of albums, Adobe Photoshop Album is a separate (and inexpensive) software package that's designed to integrate with Photoshop Elements. It organizes and finds images by date or keyword tags, and it also does basic image editing like cropping, adjusting brightness, and removing red eye. PC only.

Other lower-priced options for image management are these "picture viewers" or image browsers: ACDSee (ACD Systems), ThumbsPlus (Cerious Software), and IrfanView (shareware). All these are also PC-only.

Serious digital asset managers also use more sophisticated third-party programs like Extensis Portfolio, Canto Cumulus, and iView MediaPro. For example, Portfolio creates a database of assets on your hard drive and helps you catalog and retrieve digital files including images, clip art, movies, audio, and more. You can create previews, digital watermarking, and customizable thumbnails and slide shows. Portfolio can track any image coming into the computer via several types of searching, and you can also access an image catalog from any application with only one keystroke. Portfolio's latest versions include NetPublish, an add-on module that automates the process of dynamically distributing Portfolio catalog contents through the Internet. Full-featured websites can be created in seconds. PC and Mac.

Canto Cumulus differs from Extensis Portfolio in that it catalogs assets (images) where they're *from*, not where they reside on the hard drive. This allows you to keep track of images on outside CDs and other removable media. However, Cumulus does not dynamically update the locations of files when they're changed or moved. It also includes powerful search capabilities and multiple-size thumbnail previews. PC and Mac.

iView MediaPro (see Figure 3.24) also has search tools and allows a variety of thumbnail sizes (up to 640x640pixels) including smaller ones to speed the search process. There are a host of powerful editing and organization tools, including "folder watching" and the ability to track assets dynamically, shown with a question mark when the asset is not present and a square with a blue arrow when the cataloged assets are on the local computer, or on a connected hard drive or removable drive. Folder paths also can be reset after burning to disk or backing up to other media.

Each catalog can contain over 100,000 media files, including most image, sound, and video formats (JPEG, TIFF, MP3, .mov) plus many Raw digital camera files. "iView MediaPro is indispensable as a digital camera file editing tool," says Andrew Darlow, professional photographer and digital imaging consultant. "With very fast Raw file previews (processor dependant) at highly magnified levels, it can create HTML galleries and contact sheets, batch resize and rename files, make slide shows, and do many other important tasks in a very efficient manner." PC and Mac.

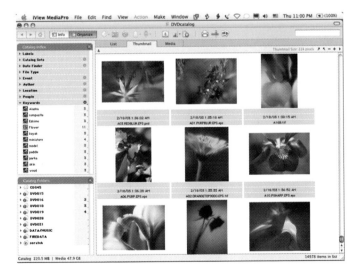

Figure 3.24 This screen shot from the Mac OS X version of iView MediaPro illustrates the thumbnail view with medium-sized thumbnails(256 x 256 pixels). Under each thumbnail are lines with customizable fields, (in this case showing the file name and modification date). To the left, in the Organize Panel, is file information including an automatic sorting function based on embedded file information. Keywords can also be easily created with drag -and-drop simplicity.

Courtesy of Andrew Darlow
www.andrewdarlow.com

To fully understand the digital printing process, you have to become an intimate friend of color. It's now time to tackle one of the most important and complex digital subjects of all.

4

Understanding and Managing Color

Color—and how it affects your printing—is one of those mysterious subject pits. Many people have a hard time wrapping their minds around digital color, so as I've done before, I'll break it down into bite-size pieces.

Color Basics

To understand color, we need a quick course in color theory.

What Is Color?

Color is what happens when our eyes perceive different wavelengths of light, which is that part of the electromagnetic spectrum that occurs roughly between 380 and 760 nanometers. A namometer ("nm" or one billionth of a meter) measures the distance between the crests of a light wavelength. Wavelengths shorter than 380 nm are outside our ability to see them, and they're called *ultraviolet* or *UV*. Wavelengths just over 760 nm are likewise invisible and are called *infrared* or *IR*.

There are lots of other types of electromagnetic radiation like X-rays, microwaves, radar, and radio, and those are also invisible because our eyes and the rest of our vision apparatus are sensitive only to a tiny slice of the energy pie (380–760 nm). This is called the *visible spectrum*, or more commonly, just *light* (see Figure 4.1).

The basis of color is *trichromacy*, which refers to the three color channels or receptors of the human retina. What this means is that with only three primary colors in either the subtractive or additive color systems, all—or most—of the other colors can be created.

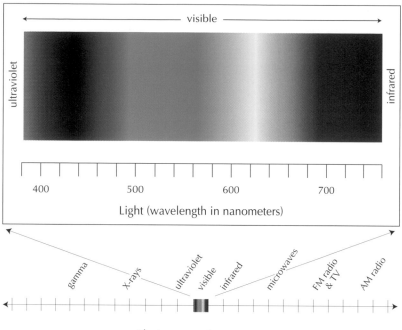

When you add this to the idea of "visual blending" covered in Chapter 2, you begin to understand how we are able to print and view color images.

With *subtractive color*, light is reflected off objects that absorb some of its wavelengths and let others continue on. Our eyes interpret those remaining wavelengths as color. In other words, the color of an image on a piece of paper is what's left over *after* the ink and the paper have absorbed or subtracted certain wavelengths (see Figure 4.2). If green and red are absorbed, what we end up seeing is called blue, which is in the 400–500 nm range. If cyan and magenta are absorbed, we see yellow. If we keep subtracting wavelengths by piling on more dyes or pigments, we end up with black. (See Chapter 7 for a more in-depth look at printing inks and color.)

Figure 4.2 When full-spectrum white light that contains all wavelengths (left) strikes the sky portion of the print, the red wavelengths are absorbed (subtracted), and the green and blue ones are reflected back to produce the cyan color we call "sky blue." All the wavelengths are reflected back from the white clouds since there are no dyes or pigments there.

The subtractive primary colors are Cyan, Magenta, and Yellow. The secondaries are Red, Green, and Blue (see Figure 4.3).

The *additive color* system, which applies to light coming from a computer monitor or stage lighting, is different in that if you add colors, you ultimately end up with white, not black. The additive primaries are Red, Green, and Blue. The secondaries are Cyan, Magenta, and Yellow.

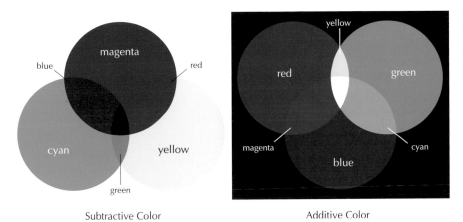

Subtractive Color   Additive Color

Figure 4.3 The subtractive primaries (left) and the additive primaries (right). Notice how the overlaps (secondary colors) become the primary colors of the other system (and at the same time the complement of the remaining primary).

Here's how color is created on computer monitors. Traditional cathode-ray-tube (CRT) monitors have "guns" that shoot electron beams toward the inside of the screen where they strike a phosphor coating. When a beam hits a red phosphor, it gets excited and emits light—light of a wavelength perceived as red. The same thing happens with the green and blue phosphors. As the voltage of a gun changes, so does the intensity of the light. (Flat-panel, LCD monitors work differently by using filters to either block the light or allow it to pass. There are no electron guns; instead, tiny transistor switches—one each for red, green, and blue—sit in front of each screen spot and control the light through polarization.)

Corresponding to the binary data in the digital file, each pixel on a monitor screen is made up of combinations of red, green, and blue in varying intensities (256 levels in 8-bit mode). All the other secondary colors come from differing combinations and values of the three primary colors. As the intensities (brightness) of the individual colored pixels increase, they get lighter.

Light Sources and Color

Light sources also have their own "colors" associated with them. That is, you can draw a *spectral curve* of the light source with each wavelength charted (see Figure 4.4).

The type of light source will affect anything displayed under it, and this is where the dreaded word *metamerism* comes into play.

Metamerism (pronounced *me-TAM-er-ism*) is greatly misunderstood as only being a "problem" with certain types of inks, when in fact, it is a normal phenomenon relating to how we see color. I'll discuss the ink-problem aspect of it in Chapter 7, but for now I define

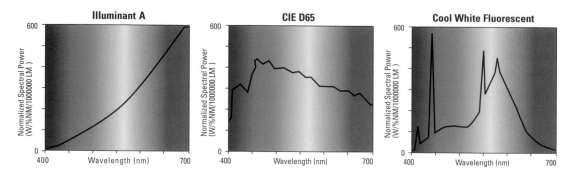

Figure 4.4 The spectral curves of two standard CIE Illuminants (A is for tungsten or incandescent, D or more specifically D65 is a standard daylight source) and a popular fluorescent or F source.

Courtesy of GretagMacbeth

metamerism as: When two different color objects have the same color appearance to a normal human viewer under one light source (*metameric match*) but look different under another light source (*metameric mismatch*).

Since the light source has a major impact on how the colors are perceived, the light along with the object and the human observer form the triumvirate of what we know as color. See more about light sources and viewing in the "Room with a View" box.

Measuring Color

With standard light sources and a model of human vision, we can measure and quantify the light spectra that form colors in our minds by using one of these three measuring devices:

Densitometers compute density by directing light onto a surface and measuring the amount of light returned through filters. They don't read color directly but can calculate relative densities of color patches. Not commonly used by photographers-artists except in certain situations.

Colorimeters measure light through filters like densitometers, but the filters and the internal circuitry match human vision much more closely. "Colorimetry" standardizes two of the three color variables (light source and observer) and then works with the third (object). Colorimeters are frequently used for monitor profiling (see below).

Spectrophotometers, also called "spectros," measure the full light spectrum in even more detail than colorimeters. Either handheld or adaptable to mounting tables or with suction cups, spectrophotometers can measure reflective prints, and in some cases, monitor displays and transmissive film. Spectros (including the related spectrocolorimeters) are often used in higher-end profile-generating packages.

GretagMacbeth's Eye-One Pro spectrophotometer being used for printer profile building.

Courtesy of GretagMacbeth

Color Attributes

One way of defining color is by the three attributes of *hue, saturation*, and *brightness*. Each plays an important role and shows up over and over again in the imagemaking process.

- *Hue* is a primary descriptor of a color. Red is a hue. Yellow is a hue. A hue is the name from that region of the spectrum where most of a color's wavelengths dominate. A spectral curve diagram showing reflected Red would show wavelengths peaking around the 700nm range.

- *Saturation* (also called "chroma" by traditional artists) describes how pure or vivid the color is. Since most real-world colors combine more than one wavelength, the fewer the extraneous colors, the more saturated the color.

- *Brightness*, a primary function of vision, means how light or dark a color is.

These three attributes are visually represented by color spaces, which are next.

Color Spaces

One of the problems with color is that it's so subjective. In order for people all over the world to talk about color in the same way, what's needed is a common language to quantify and discuss it. In 1931, an international group called the Commission Internationale de L'Eclairage (CIE) met in England and developed a method to describe color for the "standard observer." This effort resulted in the very powerful tool called *color spaces*.

Color spaces (sometimes called *color models*, although they are technically different things) are crucial to working with and communicating about digital color. They exist to quantify it; to take it out of the subjective and instead to give it names and numbers.

A color space is an abstract, three-dimensional range of colors. Photographer Joseph Holmes describes it as something like a football standing on its end with white at the top and black at the bottom. A line drawn top to bottom through the center includes all the grays. The various hues of the visible spectrum wrap around the ball as the colors go from gray on the inside to their most colorful (saturated) on the outside.

Color consultant C. David Tobie uses the analogy of a tent. The three corners of the tent are attached to the ground with three tent pegs: Red, Green, and Blue. How far you move the pegs out determines the size of the tent or color space. The tent is held up in the center by a pole, which is its gray axis. Raising or lowering the tent on the pole changes the gray balance and the *white point*, which is where the pole supports the top of the tent. Colors further away from the pole are more saturated, those closer, less.

You'll notice that the two color space descriptions just given closely match the three color attributes of hue, saturation, and brightness.

Here are the three most important color spaces for photographer-artists:

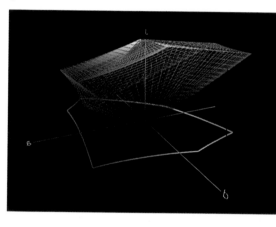

Somewhere between a football and a tent, this wire-frame representation of the sRGB color space shows LAB coordinates and L-dimension toning. To get the full effect, ColorThink (www.chromix.com) allows you to spin the graph to see the 3D volume in motion.

Graphing by CHROMiX ColorThink

LAB

The original CIE color space (XYZ) was adopted in 1931, and it identifies color coordinates in a three-dimensional curved space. It was adapted to become the familiar shark-fin-shaped CIE xyY Chromaticity Diagram (see Figure 4.5) for easier displaying in 2D space. (*Chromaticity* refers to the color properties of hue and saturation only.)

Between them, "x" and "y" define any color's *hue* and fullness of color or *saturation*. The "Y" is a little hard to grasp since it runs perpendicular to the plane of view, and it indicates the *lightness* or luminance of the color. In this sense, the xy diagram is the color tent viewed from above.

Because of difficulties with non-uniform color spacing in the XYZ model, improvements were made, and in 1976, the CIE added the LUV and then the now-famous CIE LAB (or just "LAB," also written "Lab") color space. The type of LAB used in color conversions is ICC LAB, which defines three variables in three-dimensional space: L* (pronounced "L-star"), a*, and b* (see Figure 4.6). L* refers to lightness, ranging from 0 (dark) to 100 (light). a* refers to the "magenta/cyan" axis ranging from -128 to 127; positive numbers are "magenta-ish," and negative ones are "cyan-ish." b* refers to the "yellow/blue" axis also ranging from -128 to 127; positive numbers are "yellow-ish," negative ones are "blue-ish." (The reason the color words are in quotes is because the terms are loose. One person's blue may be another's cyan. It's the numbers, not the words, that count.) Any particular color that you can see can be pinpointed by its three LAB coordinates. For example, a spot of blue sky could be identified as L* = 64, a* = -15, b* = -42. (If you want to get even more color geeky, you'll want to explore the concept of ΔE, spoken as *Delta-E*, where each ΔE unit represents the *just-noticeable difference* between any two LAB colors.)

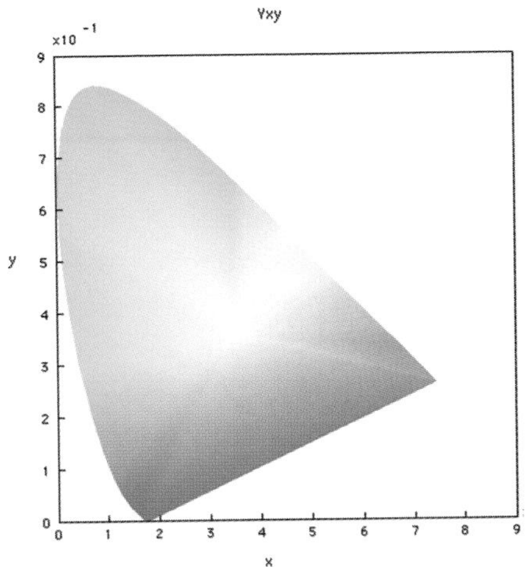

The LAB color space most closely represents how humans see. It's the one that Photoshop uses for its mode changes. It's the one that color management systems (see below) generally use as a *reference space* to relate their input and output behaviors. It's the largest of all the common color spaces, and it includes most of the colors in the RGB and CMYK gamuts. Best of all, LAB is not dependent on any particular device, ink, or process. It just is, offering universal color definitions.

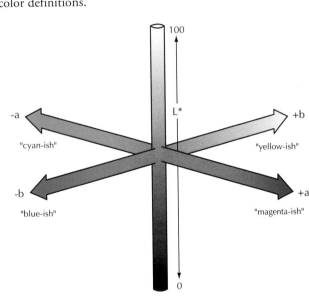

Figure 4.5 The CIE xyY Chromaticity Diagram, which represents (in two dimensions) the color range of human vision.

Graphing by CHROMiX ColorThink

Admittedly, it's a little hard to understand LAB, which is why you may not be spending much time there except for some specialized purposes.

RGB

RGB is the dominant color space for digital artists. It's based not only on the viewable colors on a television screen or computer monitor, but also on the fact that red, green, and blue form the basis of the *tristimulas*

Figure 4.6 The three-dimensional ICC LAB color space.

model of color perception, which scientists have now discovered corresponds to how our nervous systems perceive color.

RGB is the default space for most digital cameras and scanners (*all* scanners scan in RGB; if you're getting CMYK scans, the scanner operator or the software is converting the data), and it's the preferred space for film recorders, digital photo print, and most desktop inkjets. That last one may surprise you, but even though inkjets must print real inks on real paper in CMYK fashion, they prefer RGB files, and some people actually call them "RGB devices." I wouldn't go that far, but it is true that Epson printers, for example, are RGB-based, and if you send CMYK information to an Epson through its normal printer driver, it will first convert the data to RGB and then back again to CMYK for printing! (The use of a CMYK RIP will bypass this workflow.)

RGB is *device-dependent*, which means that the color you end up with depends on the device you send it to or the RGB space you define it in. This is what I call "The Circuit City Phenomenon." Go into any appliance store like Sears or Circuit City, and pay a visit to the television department. Stand there in front of the wall of TVs for a moment, and you will instantly understand the problems of working with color. Even though every TV may be set to the same channel, all the screens look different! The same with digital devices. Some have large color gamuts, some don't. Some clip colors, some don't. Fortunately, advanced image-editors like Photoshop help you control some of these uncertainties.

Color Space Gamuts

One of the important, distinguishing characteristics of each color space is its *color gamut*, which defines the entire range of possible colors in that system (it can also apply to material and devices like monitors and printers). The larger or "wider" the gamut, the more colors available. Although most people believe that the gamut of RGB is larger than that of CMYK, color expert Steve Upton of CHROMiX explains that that's a myth. "I usually describe them as different and use 'a circle drawn over a triangle so they both have portions outside the other' as a description." Figure 4.7 shows how some CMYK colors fall outside the RGB gamut, making them unviewable or *clipped*. This is also called being *out-of-gamut*, or in color tent terms, outside the tent.

Also realize that these 2D diagram plots don't tell the whole story since they represent only one view of a 3D color space.

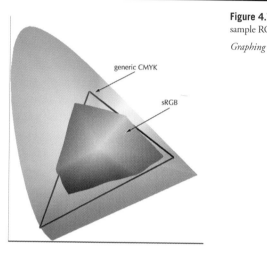

Figure 4.7 The different gamuts of two sample RGB and CMYK color spaces.

Graphing by CHROMiX ColorThink

generic CMYK

sRGB

RGB comes in several sub-varieties called RGB *working spaces* in Photoshop, which currently only recommends four of them (see Figure 4.8). While all RGB files are generically called "RGB," when you're actually working on images in Photoshop, you have the option of picking different working spaces for them (starting with Photoshop 6, you no longer have to choose only one). Leaving out the more obscure, from largest gamut to smallest, the default *RGB* working spaces in Photoshop are: *Adobe RGB (1998), ColorMatch RGB, AppleRGB,* and *sRGB.*

Adobe RGB (1998)

The is the largest of the default RGB color working spaces and a good choice for digital artists. It pretty much covers the gamut range of the common CMYK devices including inkjets plus digital photo printers. You'll rarely be out of gamut with Adobe RGB, yet it's not as unwieldy as the larger LAB space.

ColorMatch RGB

Originally designed for Radius PressView monitors, this is another good working space for the photographer-artist. The color gamut is smaller than for Adobe RGB but larger than the other working spaces on this list. ColorMatch RGB is well-accepted by the color industry, so most people know how to handle it. It has been considered the best choice if you plan to do a lot of CMYK commercial printing, although Adobe RGB is gaining ground for this usage.

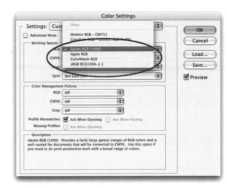

Figure 4.8 The four currently recommended RGB working spaces in Photoshop (version 7 and 8 or CS).

AppleRGB

This is a holdover from the old Apple 13" Trinitron monitor days. It's gamut is only slightly larger than sRGB. Not recommended for print.

sRGB

Even though this is the default working-space setting for Photoshop and other hardware and software manufacturers, including those making digital cameras, this is probably not the best choice for a color working space. It's mainly for people working with web images, and it should be avoided by those hoping to output their files to the broadest range of print devices. The color gamut is small, and many deep, saturated colors, especially greens, blues, and some yellows, may be clipped or discarded, depending on the output device. As print provider John Castronovo puts it, "Always working in sRGB can be like having training wheels on a bike—safe but limiting."

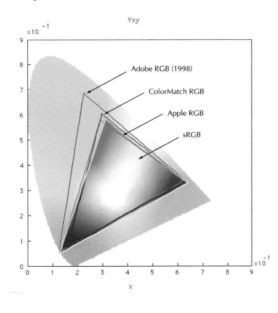

The relative gamuts of the four major RGB working spaces. Keep in mind that these only represent one view of the 3D color spaces.

Graphing by CHROMiX ColorThink

CMYK

CMYK is another device-dependent color space (actually a series of device-dependent color spaces with infinite possible variations). CMYK is short for Cyan, Magenta, Yellow, and Black ("K" for Key), which are the four subtractive process-printing colors. Why four instead of three? In theory, (and taking another peek at Figure 4.3), CMY should be enough to make all the colors, but real-world inks aren't pure, and the extra black component is needed to add the snap or depth to the printed image and to solve other print-specific problems.

Many photographer-artists don't pay enough attention to CMYK, but it's important, especially when you realize that much of the world's printing is ultimately CMYK-based. In fact, *all* inkjet printers print in CMYK (or CcMmYK, or CMYKRB, or whatever variant), even if they are expecting RGB input. An RGB-to-CMYK conversion is being done somewhere along the line (unless you're using a CMYK RIP where you control the conversion), so it helps to know something about CMYK.

CMYK is the de facto standard of the commercial printing industry so you will undoubtedly run into CMYK for that reason, too. Anytime you want to create an advertisement, a brochure, or any project that will end up being printed on an offset lithography press, you (or someone else) will need to convert your images to CMYK. By using Photoshop's CMYK preview functions in combination with ICC profiles (see below) set up for the type of printing anticipated, you can get a fairly good monitor representation of how things will look in a particular CMYK, without permanently committing yourself to that printing space. This keeps you from being surprised at the final printing step, and it lets you make appropriate image adjustments in advance.

Which Color Space Is Best?

There are many theories (even some fights) about this. Keeping in mind that you'll need to come up with your own answers depending on your needs and goals, here are some recommendations:

1. In general, work and save your master files in one of the larger RGB spaces. You can always *repurpose* a file to a different color space like CMYK as needed.

2. For a specific, all-purpose working space, choose either Adobe RGB or ColorMatch RGB. Experiment with other boutique working spaces if you want, but if you're unsure, stick with the major ones.

3. If you have very specific needs that only involve one type of CMYK printing, and you want tight control of your printing colors, it might be advantageous to work in CMYK. But if you have *any* inkling of reaching out to other service providers or of other uses for your images, work in the larger RGB spaces. (If you come from an offset printing background as I did, you might feel more comfortable working with CMYK numbers, but my advice is to transition to RGB as quickly as possible.)

4. The same advice goes for sRGB. If you're working for web output or sending camera files around, then sRGB might make the best sense. However, if you're going to print, or if you're not sure which type of printing you'll be doing, pick one of the larger RGB working spaces.

Tape the following Color Cheat Sheet to your monitor until you have it memorized:

Converting from One Space to Another

Chances are, you will have to convert from one color space into another at some point. There are several things to keep in mind:

1. Convert as few times as possible. Converting color spaces permanently alters a file's color information. Only do it if and when you have to. When you convert from RGB to CMYK, for example, *you've forever lost* the richer information of RGB. And you can't get it back!

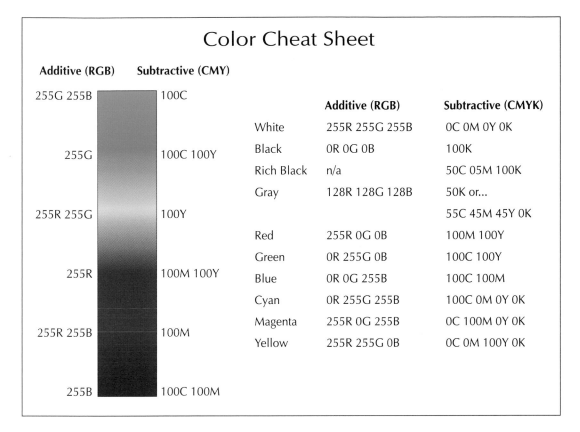

Color Cheat Sheet

Additive (RGB)	Subtractive (CMY)
255G 255B	100C
255G	100C 100Y
255R 255G	100Y
255R	100M 100Y
255R 255B	100M
255B	100C 100M

	Additive (RGB)	Subtractive (CMYK)
White	255R 255G 255B	0C 0M 0Y 0K
Black	0R 0G 0B	100K
Rich Black	n/a	50C 05M 100K
Gray	128R 128G 128B	50K or...
		55C 45M 45Y 0K
Red	255R 0G 0B	100M 100Y
Green	0R 255G 0B	100C 100Y
Blue	0R 0G 255B	100C 100M
Cyan	0R 255G 255B	100C 0M 0Y 0K
Magenta	255R 0G 255B	0C 100M 0Y 0K
Yellow	255R 255G 0B	0C 0M 100Y 0K

2. If you're using a print-service provider that needs to end up with CMYK, have *them* make the RGB-to-CMYK conversion; they'll have more control over the process. Do all your image-editing in RGB but use their provided ICC profile to preview on your monitor how it's going to look in CMYK.

3. On the other hand, if you're using page-layout programs to create ads, brochures, etc., for commercial offset printing, you could do the RGB-to-CMYK conversion yourself (most commercial printers hate receiving RGB files), *as long as you've received conversion specifications from the printer.* When in doubt, and if a commercial printer can't or won't give you an ICC profile (and many won't), you could use Photoshop's built-in CMYK preset profiles as a last resort, especially the SWOP-standard ones, to get you in the ballpark.

4. A more recent, more flexible page layout workflow involves placing your RGB images directly into the layout software (InDesign is a must for this!) and then converting that layout for different uses later, often by saving out device-specific PDF files.

What Is Color Management?

Color management is one of those terms like health maintenance. Everyone has a vague idea of what it is, and most admit it's important, but few actually understand it.

The crux of the problem is this:

1. Human eyes can see more colors than can be reproduced by digital devices—scanners, cameras, monitors, or printers.

2. The color gamuts of *all* scanners, cameras, monitors, and printers are *different*. The color you see depends on the device that's producing it. Monitors can display more colors than can be printed; some printing colors cannot be seen on a monitor.

3. Color reproduction is like a funnel. As you move down the art production line from input to onscreen display to final print, the color gamut, in general, shrinks (you lose colors).

4. Monitors and printers see color in completely different ways. Monitors use the additive color system; printers use the subtractive. Colors printed on paper look dull and dreary compared to their brighter and more energetic monitor counterparts.

The result of this quadruple threat is that images don't always end up the way you imagine them in your mind or how you see them on the monitor.

The goal, then, behind managing your color is simple enough: WYSIWYP. What You See Is What You Print. Color management in its most generic and simplistic form merely means rendering color across different devices—digicams, scanners, monitors, print devices—in a predictable, repeatable way.

Sometimes you're lucky. You buy a new inkjet printer, you hook it up, and your prints come out looking gorgeous right off, and they continue to do so forever. Yeah, right. The reality is this: an image can pass through many hands and be affected by many variables on its way to final output—digital cameras, scanners, computer hardware and operating system, image-editing software, the viewing environment, monitors, and printer software. At any one of those checkpoints, an image can be compromised. Even at the last step of printing, you could be dealing with different inks, paper, and even different printing technologies. A lot can go wrong on an image's path to glory, and, unfortunately, it usually does.

Enter *color management systems* (CMS). A CMS is a software solution to the problems facing all digital imagers. It's a way to smooth out the differences among devices and processes to ensure consistent color all along the art production chain.

Some claim that there's a lot of fuss about nothing here. All you have to do, they say, is use your experience with image file information plus monitor and printer settings, and simply get familiar with how color "A" on the monitor relates to color "A" on the printed piece. If it's different, you either fiddle with your monitor settings or tweak the image file itself until you get a good monitor-to-print match (this is called "reverse proofing").

There are several problems with this approach. First, it requires a closed-loop system: the same person, the same monitor, the same print device, the same inks, the same paper, the same everything. As soon as you involve other people or other systems (such as with an outside print provider) that aren't *identical* to yours (and they won't be), your control and predictability is out the window. Second, it takes a lot of time and experience to work "by the numbers" to match digital files to prints. And finally, you can't "soft proof" (accurately preview on the screen) an RGB image without correct calibration and characterization profiles (this has only become possible starting with Photoshop 6.0).

Welcome to ICC Color Management

In 1993, the International Color Consortium (ICC) was formed by eight industry vendors including Adobe Systems, Eastman Kodak, Apple Computer, and Microsoft. Their goal was to create and encourage the use of an open, cross-platform color-management system to make consistent color reproduction a reality. The ICC Color Management System comprises three components:

1. A device-independent color space, also known as the *Reference Color Space*. CIE's XYZ and LAB are the two related color spaces chosen by the ICC; XYZ for monitors, LAB for print devices. To get consistent color across different devices, a *transform* (a fancy word for a mathematical process) is needed to convert the colors from one device to the other. It's all about *from* and *to*. Source and destination. Monitor to printer, for example. But what actually happens is that the transformation takes place through an intermediary color space or PCS (Profile Connection Space).

2. *Device profiles* that characterize each device. An ICC device profile—note that the Mac world calls them *ICC* profiles, and the PC world, *ICM*, but they're really the same thing—is a digital data file that describes a device's capabilities and limitations. It's like an equivalence dictionary, and it works like this: If you characterize (or profile) any input, display, or output device by relating its specific color space values to a known reference space, then any image file moving from one profiled device to another can be rendered so that the image looks the same (has the same values). This can apply to scanners scanning images, monitors displaying images, and printers printing images, and there are ICC profiles for each situation. The profile is actually a fingerprint of the device or process, and it helps each new device in the chain understand what that image is supposed to look like—objectively.

3. A *Color Management Module* (*CMM*) that interprets the device profiles and maps one color gamut to another. CMMs are also called *color engines*, and they use device profiles and *rendering intents* (see "What Is Your Intent?") to "map" any out-of-gamut colors into a reproducible range of colors by the next device. (As you move down the production line from capture to display to print, the color gamut gets smaller and smaller. Think of the funnel.)

Apple uses ColorSync as its color architecture, while Microsoft uses the comparable Image Color Matching (ICM 2). Both ColorSync and ICM 2 rely on CMMs and ICC-standard device profiles (with .icc file extensions) that contain information about how to convert colors from one color space and color gamut into another. Photoshop can use ColorSync or ICM 2 on each platform but by default uses the built-in Adobe ACE color engine for its CMM. This makes highly consistent cross-platform color possible in Adobe applications.

The bottom line on CMS is this: instead of using eyes and a brain, which are easily fooled, a color management system utilizes cold, hard, unbiased numbers. Easiest thing to do is just delete this part. It's already explained above in text and with ILL0405.A CMS helps you calibrate, characterize, and finally print your images accurately and predictably. It's more than WYSIWYP, it's WYSIWYPET—What You See Is What You Print, Every Time. At least, that's the theory.

A quick note: To utilize a CMS, you also need to have an ICC-savvy image-creation or image-editing software program. There are actually three possible places to do color management: (1) at the printer driver level, (2) at the application level, and (3) at the operating system level. The application level is best.

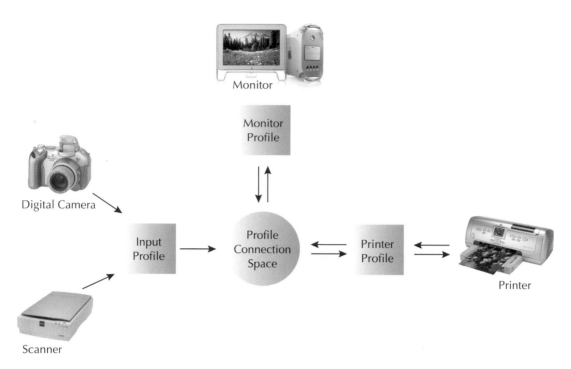

The ICC CMS workflow. The input side (left) is only one-way because color isn't viewed or output on cameras or scanners.

Photoshop is the ultimate ICC-aware software since Adobe, its maker, is a founding member of the ICC. (Adobe Photoshop LE is not ICC-aware, but Photoshop Elements is in a limited way.) Painter, CorelDRAW, PhotoImpact, and Paint Shop Pro are also ICC-aware to varying degrees. You also need an ICC-friendly operating system, but with the exception of WindowsNT, virtually all currently used ones are.

Assuming that you now believe in color management, let's see how it actually works with our two main areas of device concern—monitors and printers.

Monitor Calibration and Profiling

Good monitor-to-print coordination starts with the monitor in a two-step process: *calibration* then *profiling*. The point of monitor calibration is to bring the screen back to a group of standard settings for *white point* (the color of white), *white luminance* (the brightness of white), *gamma* (a simple curve to relate to the eye's non-linear response to light), *black point* (the darkest black the monitor can display), *gray balance* (neutrality of grays), and *tonal response* (how evenly a gray ramp runs from black to white). When you calibrate a monitor (more accurately a "display" that includes the monitor and video card and driver), you actually change its settings and its behavior, and those new settings are in effect every time you start up the computer. And that, in turn, affects how you view and correct your images. If, for example, your monitor is set too bright, then your prints may end up too dark because you erroneously tried to darken them onscreen to look better. That's why monitor calibration is so important for a correctly color-managed digital workflow.

What Is Your Intent?

Rendering intents are the guidelines or the rules that color engines follow to handle their color gamut transformations or "mapping." Here are the official ICC definitions with my comments following:

- *Perceptual.* The full gamut of the image is compressed. Gray balance is preserved but *colorimetric* (measured color) accuracy is not. This preserves the visual relationship of all the colors as a single unit. Everything stays relatively the same (including in-gamut colors), but not absolutely the same, so it's a good choice if you've got a lot of out-of-gamut colors.

- *Relative Colorimetric.* The *white point* (the lightest area) of the actual medium is mapped to the white point of the reference medium. The colors map accordingly. This one changes only the colors that are out-of-gamut, which will, by necessity, be compressed. Useful when proofing a commercial printing press on an inkjet printer. Often preferable for general printing, as long as out-of-gamut colors, if any, have been dealt with in advance.

- *Absolute Colorimetric.* The white point of the source profile maps to the white point of the reference illuminant. The colors map accordingly. This allows a proof of dull gray newsprint to be made on bright white proofing stock, with the newsprint gray emulated by ink. Otherwise, AbCol is just the same as RelCol.

- *Saturation.* The saturation of the pixels in the image is preserved, perhaps at the expense of accuracy in hue and lightness. This is typically used for business-type graphics where vividness is the most important thing; color accuracy takes a back seat. It's not normally recommended, although after Steve Upton suggested giving it a try when I wasn't happy with a profile's saturation, I did and found that certain images gained more punch this way. Color expert C. David Tobie offers that a well-designed Saturation intent may suit general photographic needs, and is especially useful for flowers, red sports cars, and other brilliant content.

Any of the four ICC rendering intents can be selected in Photoshop.

Monitor profiling is step two, and it measures and describes the personality of *that* particular monitor. Profiling doesn't actually change anything, it just keeps track of how the monitor is set up. You calibrate *before* you profile, although in many instances, calibration and profiling occur in a continuous process, especially if you're using third-party software packages.

Monitors should be calibrated and profiled regularly; weekly is a good target. As Pennsylvania digital printmaker Jim Davis recommends, "first thing Monday morning, calibrate your monitor. It takes 10 minutes, and then you are set for the week."

There are two basic ways to calibrate and profile a monitor: eyeballing it visually using software alone, or using a measuring tool on either a non-calibrator ("dumb") or calibrator ("smart") monitor.

A "smart monitor includes its own measuring device (colorimeter) that's attached to the screen and wired back into the computer's processor. The instant feedback from the colorimeter allows the system to adjust each individual RGB gun as part of the calibration process. The advantage of this system is that color management is automatic; the RGB guns are adjusted for you. One disadvantage to such a system is the higher cost. Others include: specificity (calibration system works only with that monitor), uniqueness (calibration process for other monitors can't use the same software and targets), update dependency (new OS versions may not be compatible), and complexity (conflicts may occur with the special cabling and connections). Examples of smart monitors include the Sony Artisan Color Reference System and the LaCie Electronblue with BlueEye Vision calibration.

Dumb (non-calibrator) monitors are calibrated through the computer's video board or card and the front panel controls. The card's lookup table (LUT) is altered, which changes the monitor settings. Non-calibrator monitors, which are what most people use, are perfectly capable (especially with third-party help) of being calibrated. The only downside is that because some data has been clipped by the video card, you may see fewer available color values, depending on how far you stray from the monitor's native settings. Some software/hardware packages can compensate for this loss by allowing the user to adjust the color guns through the front panel controls, offering the same level of control as "smart" monitors at a lower cost.

So What's the Standard?

If monitors should be regularly calibrated to a known standard, the next question is: to what standard? Although the prepress/graphic design portion of the color-viewing industry is based around a white point of D50 (5000K), many digital workers have shifted their monitors to D65, a much cooler, brighter color. Although a lot of this is personal preference and also dependent on the monitor and room brightness levels, D50 is too dim and yellow to my eye, and D65 seems to match a nearby D50 viewing light more closely, even if that sounds illogical. I also choose a gamma setting of 2.2, which seems better-suited to most computer systems.

Eyeballing It

Adobe Gamma (a Photoshop accessory for Mac and Windows) or Monitor Calibrator (an Apple OS utility) is a straightforward, wizard-like, visual calibration process (other image-editing applications have their own versions of this), so I'm not going to walk you through it. After a series of steps that include adjusting the monitor for white point, contrast and brightness, and phosphor RGB output levels, you end up with a monitor profile that Photoshop and other ICC-savvy applications must have to display colors correctly on screen.

The main reason I'm giving Adobe Gamma (or similar visual procedures) scant mention is because I don't think it's the best way of calibrating a monitor. It's very dependent on the viewing environment, plus many people have a hard time evaluating and comparing colors, and that's partly what these built-in software calibrators rely on.

To be sure, eyeballing it is better than no calibration at all, but if you have the option, go with a third-party, instrument-based calibration/profiling system.

Using a Measuring Device

This is a better way to do monitor calibration and profiling because it's based on objective measurements, not just your visual opinion about how good your monitor's display looks.

Hardware-based profile-generating programs do two things for monitor color: (1) calibrate your monitor by automatically measuring test patches and adjusting a combination of the RGB guns and the video board, and (2) create a monitor ICC/ICM profile that your editing software refers to when displaying images. An ICC *display profile* contains a small group of numerical values in table form for the monitor's brightness, contrast, RGB gain, and backlight, depending on what exists on a given device, as well as a copy of the video card corrections (see Figure 4.9). When a display or monitor profile is correctly stored on your system, any ICC-aware application can use the profile to tweak the onscreen display and make it more objectively accurate. If you also have a printer profile (see below), that profile can be added to the mix to adjust the display.

Where is this profile stored? It varies. For OS X Macs, it's in any of several Libraries (System is discouraged, Root Library is recommended for universal use, User Library is for personal use) in the Profiles folder within the ColorSync folder, in each case. For Windows, it's in the Color Directory, but that location varies with the version of the OS.

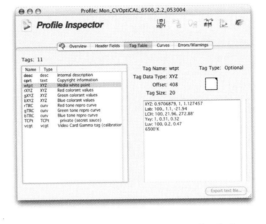

Figure 4.9 An inside peek at a monitor profile's tags as viewed in the CHROMiX Profile Inspector.

ColorThink courtesy of CHROMiX

Because profiling is such a hot topic, there are lots of companies competing for your color management dollars. At this writing, the main higher-level, device-and-software choices for monitor calibration and profiling are: ColorVision Spyder with OptiCAL, Monaco OptixXR, and GretagMacbeth Eye-One Display or Eye-One Photo with Match 2 software. The instruments used by ColorVision, Monaco, and GretagMacbeth (EyeOne Display) are colorimeters, while the EyeOne Photo device is a spectrophotometer.

CAUTION! Make sure you only use a measuring device made for the type of monitor you have. Some suction cups can cause problems when used on LCD displays.

X-Rite's MonacoOPTIXXR colorimeter for calibrating and profiling CRT and flat panel displays.

Courtesy of X-Rite, Inc.

What About Input Profiles?

Input profiles for digital cameras and scanners are part of the ICC color management scheme, and the process involves scanning a pre-measured target and then constructing a profile based on the RGB value differences. In reality, though, many people don't profile their inputs. Why not? The primary reason is that device characterization requires that all variables remain constant. With digital cameras, for example, that means the light cannot change. Clearly, this will never happen except in a controlled, studio environment. With scanners, it means that the settings must always be the same, but many prefer to fiddle with the software to get the best scan they can. Also, color-negative scanning is extremely difficult to profile.

However, with that said, more and more scanners are supporting proper profiling, and this can save you a lot of time in profile tweaking. So, if you have a very controlled, consistent workflow with either a scanner, digital camera, or a scanning back, then, yes, you can definitely benefit from an input profile that is passed along with the image. Photographer-artists, however, who don't fall into this category are probably better off learning how to capture a full range of values with neutral graytones and then bringing that image file into a color-managed system from that point on.

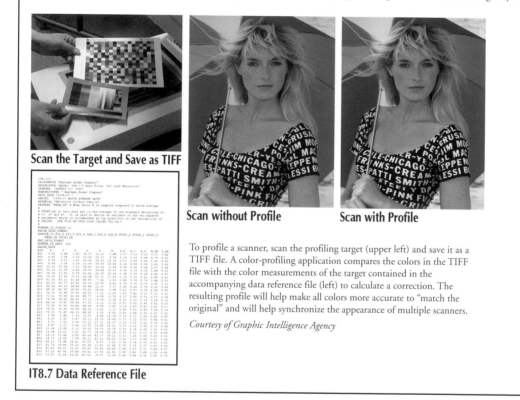

Scan the Target and Save as TIFF

Scan without Profile

Scan with Profile

IT8.7 Data Reference File

To profile a scanner, scan the profiling target (upper left) and save it as a TIFF file. A color-profiling application compares the colors in the TIFF file with the color measurements of the target contained in the accompanying data reference file (left) to calculate a correction. The resulting profile will help make all colors more accurate to "match the original" and will help synchronize the appearance of multiple scanners.

Courtesy of Graphic Intelligence Agency

Printer Calibration and Profiling

As with monitors, getting printers to output what you want consistently is, at its best, a two-part process: *calibration* and *characterization* (or *profiling*).

Printer Calibration

The reason I qualified the sentence above with "at its best" is because while printer calibration is always desirable, it is not always possible, nor common. Also, there is some confusion about the definition of the term "calibration" when talking about printers. It sometimes refers, with inkjets, to procedures for aligning printheads and for cleaning ink nozzles, and others think it is the same thing as printer characterization or profiling, but it is not. In the context of color management, calibration means changing the printer's behavior to bring it into a predictable state where ink densities and tonal values are known and stable. In order to get accurate color and to take advantage of color management (and to make the profiles I'll be describing next), a printer has to be consistent in its output, and calibration forces it to be that.

While many high-end digital printers (usually working in conjunction with equally high-end RIPs) offer printer calibration with the use of on-board densitometers or spectropho-tometers, many inkjets do not have a built-in form of calibration. Notable exceptions are the more commercial, large-format printers from ColorSpan, Encad, and HP.

One of the few desktop inkjets to offer this function is the HP Designjet 30/130 inkjet printer, which has its own automatic, closed-loop color calibration procedure. What hap-pens first is that a test pattern is output by the printer. After allowing the ink to dry for a short time, the printed page is fed back into the printer and analyzed automatically by a built-in optical sensor. The sensor measures the different color patches, and correction curves are created that will then alter the output of the printer and bring it back to its pre-determined base point.

Another way to calibrate a printer is by using a RIP that provides this calibration function in conjunction with a meas-uring device. Two popu-lar such RIPs geared to photographer-artists are StudioPrint (by ErgoSoft, PC only) and ImagePrint (by ColorByte), and both have calibration features (see "Linearization" box). (For more about RIPs, see Chapter 11.)

The HP Designjet 30/130 is one of the only desktop inkjets with built-in color calibration. Note how the process calibrates for a specific paper type and print quality.

A final thing to do with any printer that cannot be calibrated is simply to re-profile it if colors start to drift or look wrong. This is what Epson suggests for its desktops, even for the higher-end Stylus Pro 4000 (the larger-format 7600, 9600, and 10600 use optional RIPs that can be calibrated or the Epson Color Calibrator).

Is not being able to calibrate a printer a major issue? It depends on your tolerance for vari-ability. It's more important for printers that are used for proofing and press emulation where there's no room for color error. For normal bitmap-image printing with inkjets, it may not be as vital, but it's still desirable.

Linearization

Linearization (sometimes called *optimization*) is related to and is a type of printer calibration.

A theoretically perfect printer should be able to take any input value—say 50% black—and print it out with that exact same density on the paper. Unfortunately, due to something called *dot gain*, and also because printers aren't always perfect, or they may have been perfect at one point but have now drifted off course, that 50% black may be printing at the equivalent of 54% black. Multiply this by every percentage and every color combination, and you can see where having this kind of "nonlinear" response undermines the whole concept of accurate color printing.

One solution is to *linearize* the printer periodically so that a 50% value will end up 50% on the paper. Many RIPs support linearization (see image).

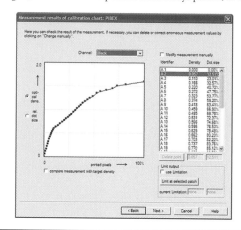

ErgoSoft's StudioPrint 10 RIP performs a linearization step in its "calibration" process when it has you print out a Density Target and instrument measure it. Shown is the Target Measurement Window with a graphic representation of the printer's density curve from which a final calibration or "density adjustment" is made by the RIP to adjust input-to-output values.

Courtesy of Amadou Diallo
www.diallophotography.com

Printer Profiling

Once a printer is calibrated (or you've decided it's stable and printing consistently enough), you can characterize or profile it. In a color-managed workflow, this is where *output device or printer profiles* come into play. Compared to monitor profiling, you're dealing with an even wider range of variables with printers. Fortunately, all these variables are taken into account by printing and then measuring targets with an instrument and creating ICC profiles from those measurements (see Figure 4.10).

Figure 4.10 *To profile a color printer, first print the color management target, then measure the target using a device connected to the color profiling package to create an ICC profile. Popular instruments for profiling include the ColorVision SpectroPRO spectrocolorimeter (left) and the X-Rite DTP41 spectrophotometer.*
Courtesy of ColorVision, Inc. and X-Rite, Inc.

Here's what happens behind the scene: LAB values are created when the printed profiling target is measured, and these LAB values are compared to reference values already known for that target. Two-way lookup tables (LUT) are then calculated in both the RGB or CMYK>LAB and LAB>RGB or CMYK directions, and you end up with a profile that characterizes *that* printer on *that* day with its combination of settings, inks, and paper. Finally, when you're ready to print using *those exact same settings*, inks, and paper, you select that ICC profile in your image-editing software, and out comes a much-improved print!

One thing to emphasize about printer profiling is that it's not the printer that's profiled! Instead, it's the combination of printer resolution and driver settings, ink, and paper. Change one variable, and you need a new profile. That's why it's common for photographer-artists to have many different printer profiles, one for each printer/ink/paper combination.

Where do printer profiles live in the computer? The locations vary depending on platform and OS version. They are basically the same as with the monitor profiles.

A printer profile's lookup table data as seen through the CHROMiX ColorThink Color List.

ColorThink courtesy of CHROMiX

A World of Profiles

Where do printer profiles come from? There are three main sources: generic or canned, custom-made remote, and do-it-yourself with profile-building software (see Table 4.1). (For information about acquiring and using printer profiles with outside service providers such as photo labs with Fuji Frontiers or printmakers, see Chapter 10.)

Table 4.1 Printer Profiles

| | Generic | Custom | DIY | |
			scanner-based	spectro-based
user level	beginner and up	serious amateur and up	amateur/serious amateur	professional
convenience level	very easy	easy	moderately difficult	difficult
supported printers	OEM only	all	all	all
type of profile	RGB	RGB/CMYK	RGB/CMYK	RGB/CMYK + specialty
cost	free	$100 average per profile	$79 to $329 per package	$1,000 to $10,000 per package

A Room with a View?

Color is subjective to start with, and if you're going to be viewing it and making decisions about its rightness or wrongness, you need to reduce the variables in your viewing environment. Here are some tips:

- Use (or create) a neutral gray for your monitor's desktop color. Extraneous colors will alter your perception of the colors of the image you're working on.

- Pay attention to everything in your field of view that could affect your color judgement. Ceilings, walls, and floors should be neutral gray, if at all possible. You can buy flat, neutral gray paint (Standard Gray Neutral 8) or mix it yourself.

- By the same token, don't let anything behind you contaminate the image onscreen. Wear neutral-colored clothes when correcting critical images onscreen. This is not as silly as it sounds. Hard-core digitalists have been known to only wear black turtlenecks and remove all jewelry to make sure the monitor is not reflecting back unwanted colors. No bright lights, no colorful posters from Hawaii.

- If you just can't control the light in a room, at least make a hood for the monitor to shield it from distracting light. Black Foam Core material available at any art supply store works great.

- Make the overall ambient light in the room dim and low. Adjust shades or blinds over windows, and if you use rheostats on light fixtures, realize that they affect the light's color temperature (incandescents get redder as you turn them down). If you can't darken your room, consider using an LCD monitor, as they offer a brighter display, and can be used effectively with higher levels of ambient lighting.

- If possible, use a graphics-standard viewing booth and/or lightbox for viewing and evaluating prints. These devices illuminate at an industry standard 5000° Kelvin (also called D5000 or just D50) and have dimmers so you can match the brightness of the monitor to the prints when soft proofing. Excellent viewing booths are made by GTI and Just Normlicht to provide both transparency viewing (*luminance*) and reflection-copy viewing (*illuminance*) in the same unit.

- If a viewing booth is out of the question for evaluating prints, at least try to think about and carefully select the artificial lights for the print-viewing area. Incandescent tungsten light (regular light bulbs) is the worst choice; it's too heavy on the red end of the color spectrum. Regular fluorescent tubes ("cool whites") have their own quirks, like having spectral spikes in the green and blue ranges and changing color as they warm up and as they age. Quartz or tungsten halogen lamps are whiter and preferred by some, but specialized professional lamps from Ott-Lite and Solux are even better for bringing you closer to industry standards. (See more about displaying prints in Chapter 9.)

Generic Profiles

Canned or generic profiles come in two basic varieties: (1) preloaded in the printer-driver software by the manufacturer for use with its recommended inks and media, and (2) available from third-party providers of inks and media for use with their products. Keep in mind that these profiles are made for *all* printers of the type you have. They don't take into account any individual characteristics of *your* printer or anything that's specific to your workflow. They're made for the average printer, and for that reason, they may or may not be adequate for your needs. Consider them as starting points to get you in the ballpark of good printing.

Generic profiles are often free, especially if the supplier is trying to sell you something else. However, you can also buy them from several sources for under $50 each. The emphasis is on the word *each*. If, for example, you needed a profile for an Epson 2200 running original Epson inks on Arches Infinity Smooth paper, that's one profile (see Figure 4.11). If you wanted to switch to Arches Infinity Textured paper, that requires another profile. Hahnemuhle Photo Rag? Yet another, and from a different vendor. You can see why people collect *lots* of profiles.

■ Instead of (or in addition to) the standard light of a viewing booth, some prefer to aim for the specific light of the final display environment. Creating prints for gallery display? Consider having a "gallery wall" lit with quartz halogen. Know your prints are heading for an office environment? Set up a fluorescent area for print evaluation.

■ As a last resort for print viewing, find a room with a window (keeping in mind that a north daylight contains more blue) and use indirect, midday daylight (no direct sun!).

Left: Joel Meyerowitz has a viewing area in his New York City studio outfitted with various lights and lamps including natural window light. Here, he analyzes HP inkjet prints of his famous 9/11 images. Right: GTI's Soft-View combination transparency/print viewer at work (on left). Both sets of lights can be independently dimmed to match monitor luminance.

(right) Courtesy of GTI Graphic Technology, Inc.

Figure 4.11 *Most third-party paper suppliers like Arches provide free downloadable ICC profiles for many popular inkjet printers.*

Courtesy of Arches North America

HOME	COMING SOON	PRODUCT INFO	ICC PROFILES	GALLERY FEATURE	SPECIAL OFFER	CONTACT US	WHERE TO BUY

Arches Infinity ICC Profiles | Each download includes installation instructions, use in Photoshop, output print settings, and the printer specific profile.

Printer	Driver/RIP	Ink Set	WT g/m²	Paper	ICC Profile		Size
Epson 2200	Epson	Epson UltraChrome	230/355	Smooth	AISM _EPS2200Ultra.zip		231k
			230/355	Textured	AITX _EPS2200Ultra.zip		232k
Epson 7600	Epson	Epson UltraChrome	230/355	Smooth	AISM_EPS7600Ultra.zip		231k
			230/355	Textured	AITX_EPS7600Ultra.zip		231k
Epson 9600	Epson	Epson UltraChrome	230/355	Smooth	AISM_EPS9600Ultra.zip	NEW!	1.17mb
			230/355	Textured	AITX_EPS9600Ultra.zip	Nash Editions Profiles	1.17mb
Epson 10000	Epson	Epson Archival	230/355	Smooth	AISM_EPS10000Arc.zip		221k
			230/355	Textured	AITX_EPS10000Arc.zip		221k
HP5000	HP5000PS	HP UV	230/355	Smooth	AISM_HP5000UV.zip		235k
			230/355	Textured	AITX_HP5000UV.zip		234k
Roland Hi-Fi Jet	Onyx	Roland Pigment	230/355	Smooth	AISM_RolHIFIPig.zip		416k

Also realize that profiles require that you use specific printer settings. You cannot change these settings without invalidating the profile. (You can also adjust or modify profiles.)

As an aside, you may not realize that the built-in Media Type or paper settings on inkjet printers actually invoke the canned profiles provided by the manufacturer. If you have an ICC-aware image-editing or profile-managing program, or if you just look in the computer's system folder that houses them, you can see all the same profiles as those showing in the printer settings dialog box.

Custom-Made Remote Profiles

The next step up in printer profile quality is to have someone with professional-grade equipment (spectrophotometer- or spectrocolorimeter-based) make custom profiles for you. These will be more accurate because they're specifically created for your unique set of variables including inks, paper, environment, driver settings, etc. It typically works like this: you download a single-page target with numerous color patches that have known values (see Figure 4.12) and print it out to exact instructions that include printing with uncorrected settings—you want to capture the good *and* the bad about your printer. You send that printed page to the profile maker who then scans it, builds a profile, and either e-mails or ships it back to you on a CD (or allows you to download it from the Web). You need to carefully record all the printer settings when you make the test print and then use those same settings for all your printing with that profile (which can also be edited or tweaked if needed). Costs average around $100 or less. Again, that's for *each* separate ink/paper/printer combination.

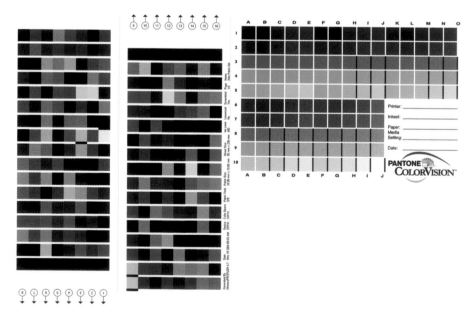

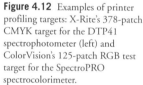

Figure 4.12 Examples of printer profiling targets: X-Rite's 378-patch CMYK target for the DTP41 spectrophotometer (left) and ColorVision's 125-patch RGB test target for the SpectroPRO spectrocolorimeter.

Courtesy of X-Rite, Inc. and ColorVision, Inc.

If you don't want to invest the time or money into a profile-making system of your own, and you don't anticipate many printer/ink/paper changes, this can be a good solution. Many claim that custom profiles yield the best results of all the profile options.

Custom, remote profiles can be purchased from providers such as CHROMiX/ColorValet, InkjetMall.com, digitalartsupplies.com, and from independent color consultants.

DIY Profiling

As with monitor profiling, you can purchase a profile-making package and create your own printer profiles. Profile-making systems either bundle the printer-profile function with monitor calibration or sell it separately. Doing it yourself has the highest start-up cost (several hundred to several thousand dollars), but if you anticipate needing a lot of profiles, and aren't fazed by the learning and experimenting curve, this may be your best choice.

The workflow is the same as with custom profiles: a reference target is output to your print device using identical print settings, ink, and paper as the final prints made with the resulting profile. Those same patches are then measured with either a regular flatbed scanner or patch reader (low cost, less accurate options) or a spectrophotometer or spectrocolorimeter (more expensive but more accurate). The variances are recorded by the software in the form of an ICC printer profile for *that* particular combination of variables.

Printer profiles can also be edited or fine-tuned by most profile-building and profile-managing software programs.

Caution: Please keep in mind that profiling software contains licensing restrictions; just because you bought the software does not mean you are free to distribute profiles built with it!

Some of the most popular profile-making packages include (at the time of this writing):

Scanner- or Patch-Reader-Based: ColorVision ProfilerPLUS, ColorVision PrintFIX (see Figure 4.13), Digital Domain Profile Prism, and MonacoEZcolor.

Figure 4.13 Designed for amateurs to prosumers, ColorVision's PrintFIX is the first affordable, integrated hardware/software product for printer profiling. As a plug-in for Adobe Photoshop or Photoshop Elements, PrintFIX prints a target that's read back into the computer with a USB patch reader. The software quickly creates an RGB ICC profile for supported inkjet printers.

Courtesy of ColorVision, Inc.

Spectro-Based: ColorVision ProfilerPRO, ColorVision SpectroPRO, GretagMacbeth Eye-One Photo, GretagMacbeth ProfileMaker, MonacoPROOF, and MonacoPROFILER.

These choices include everything from inexpensive scanner-based packages to multi-thousand-dollar packages with everything you would ever need to create and edit profiles. However, you may not need everything. For example, if you're only interested in printing RGB files on a desktop inkjet printer, some of the more sophisticated options would be wasted on you, and your money wasted on them.

Profiling Multi-Channel Printers

Multi-channel printers are those that have more than the basic four CMYK inks (if inkjet). For inkjets, six colors (including light cyan and light magenta) are very common, but there are also printers with up to 12 colors!

Some people question whether current profiling packages, few of which support multi-channel profiling, can produce adequate profiles for these printers.

The consensus so far is yes, they can. This makes sense when you realize that you still end up with an RGB or CMYK file, the data from which is then split up into each individual ink channel by either the printer driver or the RIP, if one is used.

A Color-Managed Workflow

Let's get this out of the way first: The easiest way to obtain *adequate* print quality is to use the original equipment manufacturer's (OEM) papers, inks, and printer settings. They've already been optimized to work together, and all you have to do is follow the instructions.

But, because most photographers, imagemakers, and artists hope to squeeze the last drops of quality, longevity, and uniqueness out of their images, they're willing to go a little further to get the color they want.

Since space doesn't allow me to explore all the choices and complexities of various color-managed workflow options, I will pick and explain one common digital workflow: Photoshop soft-proofing with profiles for inkjet printing.

Using Profiles and Soft-Proofing with Photoshop

We finally now have a set of color standards (ICC) and understandable, affordable tools to implement them. A color-managed workflow with a calibrated monitor and the use of either generic, custom, or do-it-yourself printer profiles can give you accurate, consistent color. It does work if you spend the time to understand and work with profile-generating and profile-savvy software. Using printer profiles should be seriously considered if:

1. You're using non-OEM-recommended, third-party ink or media (paper).
2. You're using OEM inks and media but want to compensate for their variations over time.
3. You're discovering that your printer is inconsistent and you want to characterize its current behavior.

I will now walk you through a few steps of a color-managed workflow. This will be an abbreviated tour focusing primarily on the color-management aspects; I go into a more complete printing workflow in Chapter 8. I'll be using Photoshop CS on a Mac with OS X 10.3.4, a calibrated monitor, and an older Epson Stylus Photo 1280 workhorse printer.

In terms of media, I've accumulated lots of different paper samples (haven't we all!), and I wanted to see how a 35mm color negative scan sent to me would print on something different: Hawk Mountain Papers' 100-percent cotton Merlin Photo. A perfect assignment for a custom profile made with GretagMacbeth's Eye-One Photo profiling system.

1. Open and Convert

A color-managed application like Photoshop must first know what to do with tagged or untagged documents. "Tagging" means associating a required Source profile to the file. In this case, there was no source profile since I received the scan from someone who doesn't know about such things (not an uncommon situation). Also, profiling a color negative scan is very problematic, and it's often better to simply capture a good, full-range scan, and take it from there.

I open the scan of my two nieces Kira and Katie in Photoshop and immediately *assign* my typical working space: Adobe RGB (1998)—see Figure 4.14. This gives me a "bigger tent" to work in. I can change the profile later.

The scan needs some work, and I do some basic image editing with Levels and Curves to darken it, remove the overall green tinge, and more (not shown). This is now my new master file.

Figure 4.14 Raw scan and assigning the Adobe RGB (1998) working space.

Photo courtesy of Karen Inga Morgan

2. Soft-Proof

One of the best ways to implement profile-based color management is with the use of Photoshop's RGB soft-proofing function. Soft-proofing RGB files (you could always soft-proof CMYK) is a great advancement to digital image-editing from Photoshop (beginning with version 6).

Soft-proofing means proofing an image onscreen with the use of one or more ICC profiles so you can get an idea of how the image is going to print. The image is viewed through the visual filter of both a printer profile *and* a monitor profile. Photoshop will change the way the image looks based on these output (and input if you have one) profiles.

Soft-proofing works like this in my current situation:

1. I duplicate the new master image (Image > Duplicate) for use as a visual reference. This is a temporary image that stays untouched.

2. On the working image, I use the Proof Setup dialog box (View > Proof Setup > Custom) to create the proofing space I want (see Figure 4.15). Under Profile, I choose the custom output (printer) profile I had made earlier with the Eye-One Photo package. The Intent tab let me pick a rendering intent for converting from document space to proofing space. The Simulate and Use Black Point Compensation checkboxes offer options that give different renderings of the image. I don't worry if the soft-proofed image (still on my screen) looks less than perfect; I'm getting a preview of how it will print if I didn't do anything to fix it.

3. Now it's time to make any final edits based on the previewed image. The best way is with adjustment layers, viewing both the reference and new image side by side (see Figure 4.16). In this case, I only need to flatten out the contrast in their faces a little with an RGB curve.

4. As a last step, I view the final image full-screen (use the "F" key), check for any out-of-gamut colors (View > Gamut Warning), and, if needed, make any last-minute tweaks. I can see that the bright red top is out of gamut,

Figure 4.15 Setting up Photoshop's RGB soft-proofing function with the custom DIY profile made for this combination of printing variables.

but I don't worry about it because I can preview the effect with View > Proof Colors. Both Gamut Warning and Proof Colors are working from the base of the Profile I've selected.

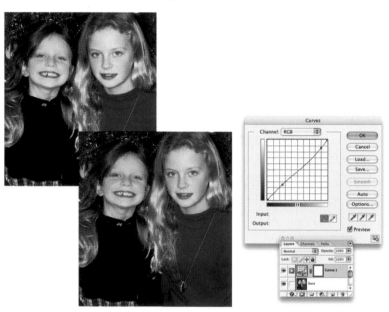

Figure 4.16 Soft-proofing at work: the master, reference RGB image (top left) and the new, soft-proofed preview image after a curve is pulled to flatten the contrast on the faces.

If I'm sending this file to someone else for output, I would save it as a flattened TIFF, which automatically embeds the assigned Adobe RGB (1998) profile to it. That way, anyone opening the file would know how I wanted it to look. However, since I'm printing it myself, I don't have to take this step but can print directly from the layered PSD file.

A few final notes about soft-proofing in Photoshop:

■ This applies to any profile-managed desktop printing: *Don't double dip your color management!* By that, I mean don't use an ICC profile *and* have the printer driver do its own color adjusting. While various Epson, Canon, and HP models have differing configurations, the key is to turn off color adjustment, whether that occurs within the ColorSync/ICM section, or outside it. Failing to do this can lead to unpredictable and usually disastrous results.

- The validity and quality of this soft-proof process is directly related to how well you've calibrated your monitor. Don't skip—or skimp on—that step.

- It's important to realize that as great a tool as digital soft-proofing is, you will never match an onscreen preview to a final print *exactly*. It just isn't going to happen. You can get close—much closer now than ever before—but you still need to understand the limits of your hardware and digital workflow and make allowances for them in your own way.

3. Print

Because I had already created a custom ICC printer profile for this printing combination, I select it in the Print with Preview window and print. (For both Mac and Windows, it's Print with Preview > Show More Options > Color Management > Print Space > Profile > your custom profile. See Figure 4.17.)

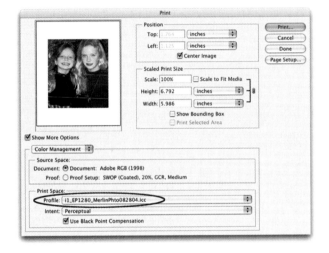

Figure 4.17 Choosing the custom printer profile in the Print with Preview dialog box.

The print on HawkMountain Merlin Photo is great; much better than a control print made without any color management

Color management works!

———

With a better understanding of color under our belts, it's now time to take a look at one of the most controversial and often-debated topics in the digital printing universe: print permanence.

Som.
24 hrs.

Bock.
24 hrs.

EAM

Som.

Bock.

5

Determining Print Permanence

Although substantial improvements in ink and paper manufacturing plus the knowledge gained from controlled testing have brought us to a point where some digital prints can now potentially outlast their traditional counterparts, the issue of image stability and print life remains a contentious one.

Anyone who's concerned about print permanence must grapple with two simple questions:

1. How long is long enough?
2. How do I know if a print will actually last that long?

How Long Is Long Enough?

Several years ago, I innocently asked a well-known watercolorist exhibiting at an art festival why she only had photographic reproduction prints on display next to her originals and not inkjets. She almost tore my head off, fuming that she had lost a good customer when the prints she had sold him had faded in about a year. For her, that clearly wasn't long enough.

Who Cares?

First, some people don't believe there is a problem. They argue either that they can always reprint the image if it fades or that longevity and permanence are properly the work of conservators, not artists, and that *all* images fade and deteriorate over time. (Van Gogh's painting *Irises*, which today hangs in New York's Metropolitan Museum of Art, is badly faded. The original "pink background" that Van Gogh wrote his brother Theo about is now almost snow white.)

Digital artist and printmaker JD Jarvis feels that digital work is held up to more rigorous demands than any other artwork. A gallery owner once was worried that his digital prints weren't waterproof. "As if watercolors, photos, and lithos are?" he asked. "I'm making art, not foul-weather gear."

Notwithstanding the above arguments and anecdotes, most photographer-artists working digitally are rightly concerned about print permanence.

Image-stability researcher Henry Wilhelm (see more about him below) brings the point home with a dramatic example. "The entire era of picture taking from 1942 to 1953 when people were using box cameras and Kodak's new Kodacolor print process is lost forever," he once explained to me. "*There is not one single known print* that survives today in reasonable condition; they are *all* severely stained and faded." Pictures and prints are important to people. Maybe not all of them, but that doesn't mean that *none* of them are! And in the digital age, this becomes even more important because, chances are, the digital files will not survive, but the prints will. "It's always been about the print," says Wilhelm, "and we can actually produce right now, at very low cost, extremely stable photographs and prints in color. Do we want to? Ask anybody, "Which would you rather have: a longer-lasting print or a shorter-lasting one?" What do you think the answer will be?"

Family photos have value, but most color prints from the '40s, '50s, and even '60s are now faded or stained. Compare my family's Kodalux print on the left from 1968 with the Kodak black-and-white print on the right from 1953, which, apart from a slight yellowing on the edges, is otherwise in perfect condition. Both were stored in the same shoe box.

I believe most photographer-artists sensibly want to be confident that the prints they are making—for themselves or for sale or gift to others—will last for a reasonable amount of time under normal conditions. (What "reasonable amount of time" and "normal conditions" actually mean is, of course, up for grabs.) As digital printing researcher Dr. David

Matz says, "Everything will change with time and will change faster under less-friendly conditions. But doesn't it make sense to start with the most stable materials that will change the slowest?"

The Meaning of Permanence

If we're going to talk about print permanence, then we should at least agree on what that means. Unfortunately, that's no easy task. Here are some different ways to define it.

Image Stability: The dictionary meaning of image stability is "resistance to chemical decomposition," but for the purpose of printing an image, we're talking about what photo conservator Martin Juergens calls "the stability of image-forming substances." These include the inks or dyes (together termed *colorants*) and the paper and coating materials (the *media*) used to produce the print. It's the inherent stability of not only the colorants and the media separately, but the ink/media *combination* that is vitally important.

Archival: Although ink and paper manufacturers love to throw around the term "archival," there is no uniformly accepted definition of what is archival and what is not. In fact, the word just means that something is in an archive, being stored, but not necessarily monitored or preserved. "Archival" has become a marketing term, and it's been appropriated by just about anyone with something to sell in the printing business. They would have you believe that archival—and hence, their product—means "long-lasting," when in fact it may not mean that at all.

Lightfast: Lightfast means resistant to fading. But for how long? The permanence, or fading characteristics, of many pigments used in traditional art materials are well-established. Colors rated by ASTM International as "Lightfast I" should last as long as pigments known to have retained their color more than 100 years. (See more about the ASTM's tests below.) However, as permanence researcher Joy Turner Luke explains, ASTM members stress that it's never possible to predict how many years a particular color will last since future display and storage conditions are unknown.

Other testing organizations (primarily WIR and RIT/IPI—see later) attach usable-life predictions to lightfastness. In essence, they're saying: "Based on certain display or storage assumptions, a print similar to the one tested should last for X years without noticeable fading or should only change this much in terms of its colors or densities." As we will shortly see, there are dangers with this approach.

Permanence: Permanence refers to resistance to *any* physical change, whether it be from light, heat, acids, etc. As an example, an ink can be lightfast but impermanent because it is prone to fast fading when exposed to atmospheric contaminants. How long is permanent? The U.S. Library of Congress, which is responsible for the care of 125 million cultural artifacts, uses "as long as possible" as its goal for preserving and making available to the public its vast collections.

Because no one really knows what permanent or "archival" is, they are relative terms that anyone can claim. In the end, you—the photographer-artist—must decide how long is long enough.

The Granny Standard

Since there is no accepted time-length standard for image permanence, I decided to invent one. Consider this a benchmark or reference for determining what is "long enough." Here's what I propose:

The Granny, Three-Generation Permanence Standard

The standard answers the following question based on this assumption: A pregnant 30-year-old digital artist and fine-art photographer makes a color print of her favorite image and frames and displays it proudly in her living room. On her son's 30th birthday, the artist gives him the framed print as a present just after his baby daughter is born. The son hangs the print in his living room and then gives it to his daughter on *her* 30th birthday. It's now been 60 years. **Question:** Has the print lost any of its image quality or experienced any noticeable fading or other deterioration? (It turns out that Granny was pretty smart and kept a duplicate copy in an acid-free envelope stored in a dark, dry dresser drawer all these years. When her granddaughter asked the question, she was able to pull that print out and compare it to the family heirloom version.)

The Granny Standard is 60 years of time, which I believe is long enough to be concerned about a color print's permanence. (Note: Determining the measuring criteria and the acceptable limits of fading/color shifting is, of course, another issue and covered later in this chapter.)

What Affects Permanence?

In addition to the inherent instability of colorants and media—everything disintegrates eventually—there are a whole host of enemies willing and able to do damage to your beautiful prints. No matter which type of digital print technology is used, certain *influencing factors* (environmental conditions) can and will affect print permanence. Here are the main culprits to worry about.

Light & UV Radiation

Light negatively affects prints through a complicated combination of processes including photo-oxidation, photo-reduction, photocatalysis, and other photochemical reactions that are not completely understood. But, we're all familiar with one of the results of light striking a print's image: fading. Any one who has seen a faded or discolored poster in a store window knows what this means.

Most fading occurs at the higher-energy end of the light spectrum, especially near the border where visible light becomes invisible UV radiation (in the 380–400 nm range). UV rays—natural light plus fluorescent and some halogen lamps emit significant amounts of UV radiation—can be very damaging to printed images. Regular window glass (or Plexiglas) can do a lot to filter the shorter UV wavelengths (see Figure 5.1), but beyond that simple procedure, every material—including inks, dyes, and papers—has its own spectral sensitivity and will be affected by light in a different way. In general, the higher the intensity and/or the longer the exposure, the worse the damage from light.

What Can Happen?
- Image fading
- Color balance changes
- Yellow stain formation

Figure 5.1 The print on the left was displayed on a wall for nine months with a standard glass covering in a frame. The one on the right is exactly the same except it was framed without glass. The increased fading is probably due to UV exposure and/or atmospheric contamination. Scientists at the U.S. National Bureau of Standards (NBS) found that UV wavelengths were about three times more damaging than the visible spectrum. The graph at bottom shows the NBS relationship between the wavelength of the radiation and the resulting relative damage. This helps explain why even standard window glass (with a UV cutoff at around 330 nm) is effective in slowing down fading, at least to some extent.

Courtesy of inkjetART.com

Relative Damage of Solar Wavelengths

Temperature

Any student of chemistry knows that as the temperature goes up, chemical reactions speed up as well. So it stands to reason that a photochemical reaction such as light fading will be accelerated by higher temperatures. Studies have found this to be true in general. High humidity also frequently aggravates the situation. Extremely low temperatures, on the other hand, can also be a problem when some materials will become brittle or even crack.

What Can Happen?

- Color fading

- Increased yellowing, especially in light or paper-white areas

- Dye migration causing uneven densities and color hue shifts

Water & Humidity

Water in its liquid form or as moisture in the air can have a big—negative—impact on prints, primarily those made with dye-based inks and/or on non-porous surfaces. Water dripping, spills, water leaks, flood damage—these are just some of the most obvious potential problems. The original, uncoated IRIS prints were so sensitive to moisture that unknowledgeable framers ruined prints with only their own saliva while talking near them! High humidity can also cause problems and is often linked with higher temperatures to make things even worse.

What Can Happen?

- Ink migration, smearing, loss of sharpness, bleeding, and spreading (see Figure 5.2)

- Changes in density (increase!) and hue shifts with higher humidity

- Dark storage print life that decreases with higher humidity

- Stains, mold, and fungal growth with high humidity

Paper Comparison (8 Weeks at 73°F)

20 % RH   50 % RH   80 % RH

Glossy Photo Paper (Microporous)

Glossy Photo RC Paper (Microporous)

Figure 5.2 This group of images shows the effect of high humidity on image sharpness. Note how the enlarged 0.4-mm black line bleeds into the adjacent background area on certain resin-coated (RC) papers as the humidity increases. From a study by Creative Memories; printed with dye-based inks on an Epson Stylus Photo 890 printer.

Courtesy of Dr. Mark Mizen/Creative Memories

Atmospheric Contaminants

Not only are air pollutants such as cigarette smoke, cooking fumes, nitrous oxide, and sulfur dioxide dangerous for most prints, but ozone levels in possible combination with UV radiation may also cause severe problems (see "The Dreaded Orange Shift"). And all of that is exacerbated by open air flow across the face of a print, which is one reason why you want to frame all prints under glass or acrylic (Plexiglas) or store them in an album or in sleeves. The resulting problem is also known as "gas fading."

What Can Happen?

- Density loss, especially with inkjet dyes vs. pigments

- In some cases, severe color balance change

The Dreaded Orange Shift

The problem of atmospheric contamination was rudely brought to everyone's attention in 2000 by the Orange Shift fiasco. What happened was that some people's inkjet prints made on Epson's Premium Glossy Photo Paper (PGPP) inexplicably experienced severe color shifting, turning bright orange, sometimes within 24 hours of being printed! But, this didn't happen to everyone; it was completely dependent on where you lived, what your local environment was like, and whether your prints were covered or not. It turned out that PGPP was Epson's first paper to use a "microporous" coating to improve image quality. Unfortunately, this coating acted like a sponge, soaking up any ozone or other atmospheric contaminants and speeding up the exchange of gases to the cyan dye in the inks. The cyan rapidly faded, and that left only the yellow and magenta, which combined to produce orange ("differential fading"). (For those who didn't have the problem, the prints were—and continue to be—fine.)

Epson, along with everyone else (photographer Bob Meyer points out that this was not just an Epson problem), was caught off-guard, and they ultimately released new types of paper coatings to help put the problem behind them.

This situation pointed out the importance of air flow over the surface of the print. It is now universally recommended that prints destined for long-term display should be framed under glass or plastic or otherwise protected from atmospheric contaminants.

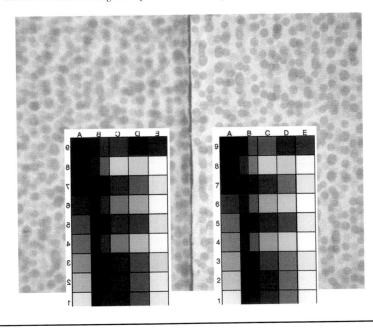

Photographer Bob Meyer's Bair Test Chart images at bottom show an Epson Premium Glossy Photo Paper print before (left) and after exposure to his "ozone chamber," which involves placing the print at the bottom of an electronic air filter, a known ozone source. The larger images were taken of a neutral gray patch on a similarly orange-shifted print (plus a control) with a microscope (150x magnification) by Roger Smith at the University of New Brunswick, Canada. Before is on the left; after is on the right.

Courtesy of Roger Smith (top) and Bob Meyer (bottom); Bair Test Chart: www.inkjetart.com/custom/index.html

Acidity

As I discuss more in Chapter 7, acidic components in either a print or the accompanying support, backing board, or mat can be destructive eventually. Many inkjet papers on the market are, in fact, produced with an acidic paper base. These papers may have good light stability but will typically have worse dark stability.

What Can Happen?
■ Paper yellowing over time
■ Slow destruction of print materials

Catalytic Fading

There are even more obscure ways for prints to fail. One is called "catalytic fading," where two or more inkjet inks in combination may fade quickly, even if the individual ink components wouldn't on their own.

Poor Handling

And finally, folding, creasing, smudging, scraping, fingerprinting plus poor display and storage procedures—all are possible, and all can reduce the permanence of prints (especially with inkjet prints that do not generally have a protective coating).

Determining Permanence: Standards and Tests

With some notable exceptions—when British painter J.M.W. Turner was accused by paint manufacturer William Winsor for using fugitive pigments, he allegedly responded, "It's your business to make paints; it's my business to use them"—artists, collectors, and curators have been concerned about image permanence for many, many years. According to artist and educator Bruce MacEvoy, English chemist Walter Russell and amateur painter Capt. William de W. Abney published a report in 1888 (*Report on the Action of Light on Watercolors*) that put to rest the debate about whether watercolors faded under certain kinds of light. They did.

Why Test?

As with many areas of human endeavor, knowledge about print permanence can be gained from scientific testing. Just like dropping feathers and apples from tall buildings to investigate the effects of gravity, tests can help explain real-world phenomena if they're carefully constructed and performed under accepted standards. Once you have an idea of what can cause the deterioration of a print (the "hypothesis"), you can test for it.

Image-quality researcher Mark McCormick-Goodhart believes a well-designed test: (1) provides insight into what we can expect to happen over time, (2) helps to delineate how products compare and what products are best-suited to a particular application, and (3) helps end-users create appropriate storage and display conditions.

Types of Tests

Print permanence tests fall under several broad categories:

Accelerated vs. Real-Time Testing

Accelerated testing exposes a printed sample or specimen to much higher levels of light or whatever is being tested than would occur under normal conditions. This simulates in a short amount of time any deleterious effects, if any, that a print might experience.

Real-time testing, on the other hand, just lets the test run over the course of weeks, months, or even years under normal display or storage conditions. (There is a variation of this: real-world testing under extreme conditions; see the next "Indoor vs. Outdoor Testing" section.)

Problems with Reciprocity

Accelerated tests are based on the *reciprocity* law, which says that, using light-fading as the example, the total amount of fading is equal to the total amount of energy exposure (time × intensity). Doubling the time but halving the intensity would yield the same effect (e.g., 10 klux of exposure for 1 year should equal 1 klux for 10 years). That's the theory. However, one of the major problems with accelerated testing is the concept of *reciprocity failure*, which means that the predicted results of high-intensity, short-time exposure do *not* equal the actual results of low-intensity, long-term exposure as they should. Or, the law doesn't always work.

For example, Henry Wilhelm has reported that accelerated tests of color photographic prints usually produce *less* overall fading and *less* yellow stain accumulation than the equivalent light exposure taken over the months or years of normal display. In other words, accelerated tests can *underestimate*, by a factor of 2–4, the amount of print deterioration that will occur during actual, real-world display conditions. (One of the reasons for this is if the test fails to properly account for all factors that affect image stability; factors that may only reveal themselves after a long period of time.)

Indoor vs. Outdoor Testing

Once the accelerated vs. real-time decision is made, the next sticking point is whether indoor or outdoor tests are better for determining the longevity of prints. By "indoor," I mean that the test conditions mimic the environments in which most fine-art prints will find themselves: living rooms, offices, gallery walls, museum spaces, etc. This is where most of the manufacturer-contracted testing by inkjet and film companies using fluorescent or xenon arc exposures would fit.

"Outdoor" tests are typically done either outdoors or with outdoor, real-world conditions prevailing. An example is what Q-Panel Weathering Research Service does (Q-Panel also performs accelerated laboratory tests, and it makes and markets testing equipment). In its Florida and Arizona facilities, Q-Panel conducts fade-resistance testing with real-world sunlight on outside exposure racks, either glass-covered or not (see Figure 5.3). This is considered a "worst-case" scenario where high sunlight and UV levels combine with high temperatures and high relative humidities to provide an extreme environment. "If your product can survive in Florida and Arizona," explains Q-Panel's Eric Everett, "it can probably survive anywhere in the world, from the hot and humid climate of New Orleans to the arid, high-UV conditions of Saudi Arabia."

The theory is that sunlight is full-spectrum and contains all the components of light plus UV and infrared radiation (heat) that can fade a print. The high dosage of these sunlight test exposures also can speed up the testing procedure so that results can be obtained in weeks instead of the years that normal real-world tests would take. This is exactly how many industries—automotive paint, for example—test and improve their products.

Others groups, including individual photographer-artists, do their own versions of sunlight or "window tests" (see "Do Your Own Permanence Testing" later). There were even

What Are Normal Display Conditions, and How Are They Measured?

What's normal? It depends on where you are and whom you ask. According to independent researcher Barbara Vogt, the average amount of light an image is exposed to in U.S. homes is about 215 lux (lux is an illumination measurement) with the temperature and humidity at an average of 21° C and 50% RH (relative humidity). The Eastman Kodak Company says that 120 lux (with 23° C and 50% RH) is a good, overall estimate for "typical home display." Henry Wilhelm has adopted 450 lux for 12 hours per day (24° C and 60% RH) to simulate "standard," indoor display conditions. Photographer Stephen Livick along with fade researcher Bill Waterson have settled on 275 lux as "average home daylight lux display level." The Montreal Museum of Fine Arts uses 75 lux and 100 lux illumination levels for its exhibits, which it rotates between display and dark storage. David Matz has measured the light levels in his house. One wall (with art) in his living room gets three hours of sunlight each day at an intensity of 50,000 lux; when the sunlight leaves, the room lighting drops to under 2,000 lux.

Conclusion? There are no normal display conditions! In fact, there isn't even agreement that lux should be the measurement used. While the photographic world promotes lux since it's based on the human eye's response to light, prints are also affected to a significant degree by the shorter wavelengths (320–400 nm) that typically go undetected when using lux as the metric.

Are there other options? ASTM International and researchers like Q-Panel's Eric Everett recommend watts per square meter (W/m2) for the irradiance level and joules per square meter (J/m2) for the total radiant exposure. And how are these measurements taken? Unfortunately, only with expensive radiometers or testing devices equipped for it.

The foyer in this house is lit by a combination of diffused, indirect window light and overhead incandescent spotlights. The midday illumination level at the sailboat painting is around 200 lux.

Figure 5.3 Q-Lab Weathering Research Service Test Facilities in Florida and Arizona perform fade-resistance testing of ink and media samples on outdoor racks, both glass-covered (right) and not.

Courtesy of Q-Panel Lab Products

some infamous tests done with inkjet prints taped to the top of a car traveling around Southern California for months at a time. Now that was an extreme test!

Detractors of these outdoor tests point out that they don't accurately represent the real-world conditions of indoor prints, and that they may introduce unknown and known factors such as the heat generated by the sun that could skew the results.

Comparative vs. Predictive Testing

This is a key testing issue. Is the goal of the test to give results so that different print products can be compared, or is it to give an effective lifespan prediction for any one print? Big difference.

A *comparative test* uses a consistent test method and compares how different choices for colorants or media, for example, perform under that test. How long did it take Sample A to lose X percent of its density? Sample B? Sample C? A rank ordering of the results can then be compared. Assuming identical test conditions, you're testing for the *relative* changes among the samples.

A *predictive test*, on the other hand, uses a consistent test method under a specific set of conditions and then projects those results out to a predicted lifetime before a predetermined amount of deterioration would occur. It's a calculated guess of a print's "useful" or "service life."

Predictive tests are problematic. Because of reciprocity failure and the very likely chance that the test conditions *will never* be matched exactly, predicted life-years should be viewed skeptically. Compounding the problem is the fact that (1) manufacturers often do not clearly disclose the conditions of predictive tests, and (2) people often don't read the fine print and pay close attention to the conditions on which the tests are predicted.

Visual vs. Measurement Testing

The simplest way to test print deterioration is to run different samples under one test and then look at the samples and visually compare them with a control set that wasn't exposed to the test conditions. For a lightfastness test, the controls are either covered up next to the test samples, or they're stored in the dark nearby. Visual tests are usually run by individual artists because they're relatively easy to do. Just line up the samples and visually decide which you like best, or in the case of a lightfastness test, which appear to have faded the least.

Most testing labs and serious testers, however, run instrument-measured tests (using either a spectrophotometer, colorimeter, or densitometer). Printed color samples are measured before, during, and after the test is complete. The test ends either when a stated period of time has elapsed, a certain amount of irradiance (exposure) has accumulated, or a specified densitometric *endpoint value* is reached (see "What Are Endpoints"). The measurement values are then computed or graphed for analysis (see Figure 5.4).

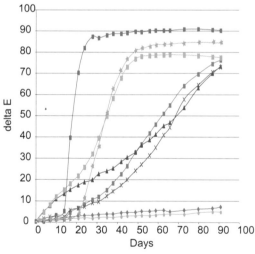

Fade Resistance Range For 8 Colors

Figure 5.4 A graph of fade resistance for eight lithographic inks using total color change expressed in ΔE (Delta-E) units.

Courtesy of Q-Panel Lab Products

Dark Fading Tests

The fading of prints occurs under two main types of unrelated conditions: dark storage and light display. *Dark fading* (also called "thermal image degradationÆ or "dark aging") is usually the result of the *inherent instability* of the colorants and the media, or because of the effect of other influences such as heat, humidity, and environmental contaminants. Dark fading can be exacerbated by high temperatures and/or humidity, and this type of test is frequently conducted in high-temperature ovens or "accelerated aging chambers" using the Arrhenius test method.

What Are Endpoints, and Why Are They Important?

Many instrument-measured tests currently use densitometric endpoints—the point at which a test sample fails and the test ends. Initial starting densities are recorded on different neutral gray, pure color, and minimum density ("paper-white") patches. When repeated measurements of the patches show that one has reached its allowed percentage of density change, that patch has reached its endpoint.

Wilhelm Imaging Research uses a unique, endpoint criteria set that is visually weighted. Instead of uniform percentages across the board, WIR has employed focus groups and other psychometric factors to determine what changes are more acceptable than others. For example, most people will tolerate a Caucasian flesh tone going more red or pink but not more green. Also, WIR's blue density change for paper-white has a higher limit that allows the paper to go yellower before failing. Wilhelm colleague Mark McCormick-Goodhart believes that's because the human eye is adapted to campfire light, and we tend to accept some visual yellowing.

The selection of the endpoints is very important in densitometric-based testing. If you want a sample to appear to be more long-lasting, all you have to do is increase the endpoint percentage so that it takes longer to reach it. That's why some don't agree with the industry standard 30-percent or more density loss. "Our opinion is that the 30–35-percent fade rate is too generous," says InkjetMall's Jon Cone. "While it makes for impressive ratings, it does not meet users' expectations, especially when you realize that the threshold in humans for detecting fade is 5 percent."

ADDENDUM: Wilhelm and McCormick-Goodhart are now working on a new test method that is based not on densitometric endpoint criteria, but rather on CIELAB colorimetry. This is partly due to all the complexity in digital printing including multiple ink colors, unique black generation, etc. It is not known when this new test method will be accepted, although ASTM methods and other testers are already using variations of spectrophotometric measurements and Delta-E comparisons.

A typical result of dark fading is the formation of yellow stain on color photographic or inkjet prints. Dark fading is not limited to dark storage, but since it is primarily due to the instability of the materials, it starts the moment the print is made and takes place independently and at the same time as any light-caused fading if the print is displayed.

Different types of colorants or media will have different dark-fading rates, and the only way to know for sure is to wait for it to happen or to test it. Wilhelm Imaging Research now includes "dark storage stability—including paper yellowing" as an official category in its Display Permanence Ratings (DPR). In fact, Wilhelm now states that they won't provide a DPR of greater than 100 years for any print material unless Arrhenius-accelerated dark storage stability test data indicates that the print can indeed last longer than those 100 years without noticeable deterioration.

Lightfastness Tests

All prints will *photodegrade* in the presence of light. That means that they undergo a photochemical reaction when exposed to lightwave photons, and they start to deteriorate. The changes can be in the form of fading, darkening, or changing hue (color). The more resistant a print is to this inexorable process, the more lightfast it is.

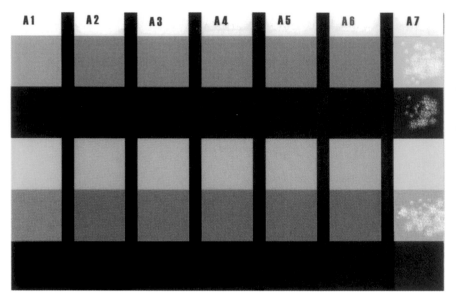

Photographer Stephen Livick and colleague Bill Waterson collaborate on sunlight fade tests. This image shows the results of 700 hours of full sun exposure (approximating 70 years on a 275-lux, daylight-illuminated interior wall) on inkjet prints with five different protective coatings. The original, uncoated strip is at far right (A7). According to Livick, the white spots are from the pigment or manufacturer's white base simply flaking off.

Courtesy of Stephen Livick
www.livick.com
and Bill Waterson
waterson@ainet.com

The light doesn't have to be a high-noon bombardment of Florida sunshine either. Although direct and indirect sunlight or unfiltered fluorescent light tends to accelerate fading more than incandescent light, the weak light from a 75-watt bulb hanging near a print can be enough to fade it as well. It all depends on the *duration* and the *intensity* of the light exposure. High intensity for a short time has the same effect—*in theory*—as low intensity for a long time. (See reciprocity failure above.)

One problem with lightfast testing is that it may or may not take into account all the other factors that cause prints to fail. Is it really just the light that makes a print fade? Or is it also the humidity, the temperature, and the air quality? As you might expect, it's usually all those things and possibly even others that have yet to be discovered.

Another problem with lightfast tests is that the methods and test protocols vary from tester to tester. From endpoints to reference display conditions and light-source choices, there is no uniformly accepted way to conduct a lightfastness test (also see more about this in "Your Mileage May Vary"). Creative Memories' Dr. Mark Mizen has a good analogy to fit this state of affairs: "It's as if Ford decided to measure gas mileage only going downhill while Chrysler chose a level road. Both methods would give a gas mileage, yet the numbers would be very different and would not allow a fair comparison."

You can see why this testing business is so tricky.

Other Tests

Other important tests that are currently being carried out or being developed by standards groups include:

- Gas Fading (for air pollutants, air flow, and ozone)

- Waterfastness (for waterfastness and outdoor durability: the drip test, the pour test, the standing water evaporation test, the standing water plus gentle wipe test, and the water smear test) (See Figure 5.5.)

- Humidity-fastness

- Fingerprint Test (for handling damage)

- Chemical and Biological Stability (to test resistance to attack by chemicals and biological agents)

Choosing the Light

One big debate around lightfastness testing is this: What type of light source should be used in the testing? Here's a quick rundown of the three main choices.

Fluorescent has been the favorite of the major testing organizations and manufacturers for years, but it has obvious flaws, including not accurately simulating most indoor lighting conditions due to its unusual spectral power distribution (see accompanying illustration). Fluorescent is useful for prints destined for display exclusively in stores or offices, but many doubt its appropriateness otherwise.

Natural sunlight is the original light source, and because it covers the spectral range with ultraviolet, visible, and infrared radiation, many use it for testing. Some, however, question its validity since added variables (like heat) are introduced. Also, natural sunlight may vary from season to season.

Xenon arc lamp testing is done with a special device (see illustration on page 161 and Figure 5.9 in this chapter) that provides the best available approximation of full-spectrum sunlight. Using filters to simulate either sunlight through a window or direct outdoor exposure to sunlight, the other advantages of xenon arc testing are that the variables can be controlled, and the results are fast. The main disadvantage is the cost of the expensive machines.

What's the answer? ASTM's approach is to specify in their D4303 standard that at least two of four different light-source conditions be tested and then compared: filtered xenon to simulate daylight, outdoor sunlight in Arizona, outdoor sunlight in Florida, and special fluorescent lamps (these may be removed in the next version of the standard). (See more about ASTM's testing standards next).

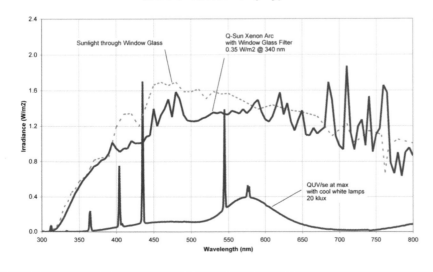

SPD's of Various Lamp Types

The spectral power distributions (SPDs) of three common light sources: sunlight through glass (gray), xenon arc (red), and cool white fluorescent (blue). Note how closely the sunlight and xenon match yet how different the fluorescent is.

Courtesy of Q-Panel Lab Products

Figure 5.5 Part of a waterfastness test from the author's testing of several inkjet papers. Top: portions of the print tests were cut out and immersed into separate containers of water. Bottom: After only 24 hours of water immersion, the differences were striking among three different ink/paper combinations.

Accelerated Testing Standards

Since real-time observation of print deterioration is, for the most part, impractical—the products used to make the print would be off the market by the time the test ended—accelerated tests have been developed to help us out.

The basic idea is simple: By using high-intensity light and/or any of the other influencing factors, the tester can speed up what would normally happen to a print over the course of many years.

While there is currently no single, universally accepted testing standard that applies to print permanence, there is a long history of testing methodology that guides today's testers, and several organizations have developed scientific procedures and standards for different kinds of permanence tests. Unfortunately, they're all different! The two most important types are the *ISO/ANSI* and *ASTM* standards.

ISO/ANSI

The International Organization for Standardization (ISO)—and formerly the USA-member-body organization American National Standards Institute (ANSI)—have been developing or promoting standards for the testing of everything from toothpaste to photographic film for decades. The older standards ISO 10977 (1993) and ANSI IT9-9 (1996) deal with photographic color image stability, and they regulate such things as the preparation of test samples, how the tests are to be carried out, how the temperature and humidity are to be controlled, and how the results are to be evaluated. An updated standard that deals specifically with photographic images is currently being prepared by ISO committee WG-5/TG-3 (ISO 18909). With Steve Puglia of the U.S. National Archives as its chairperson and Henry Wilhelm as its secretary, the group is working on a new set of standards (tentatively titled "Methods for Measuring the Stability of Color Pictorial Images") that will finally cover digital prints.

The new standards, which supposedly will still focus on print-life predictions, will be released in stages over the next several years. This ISO group represents most of the heavy-hitters in the digital printing field (Kodak, Epson, HP, Canon, Ilford, Agfa, DuPont, Fuji, et al.), so they move very slowly and very carefully with so much marketing power at stake.

ASTM

ASTM International (formerly the American Society for Testing and Materials) has been in the testing business since the late 1800s, but their work in developing standards for testing art materials is the most relevant here. Their subcommittee D01.57 on Artists' Paints and Related Materials developed the D4303 standard that describes the basic method to test the lightfastness (only) of artists' paints including oil, acrylic, alkyd, watercolor, and gouache. (They have also created standards for colored pencils and soon, pastels.) The D4303 standard requires that colors be subjected to a specific amount of irradiation (measured in watts per square meter and megajoules per square meter, not lux) in several tests using different light sources including xenon arc and outdoor sunlight in Florida and Arizona. Each paint or pigment can then be assigned a lightfastness category based on the Delta-E difference between samples before and after exposure. Walk into any art supply store, pick up a tube of paint, and you will see written "Lightfastness I" or similar. That is the result of ASTM testing.

Even more interesting to us is the fact that this same group is now developing a draft of a standard specification for printed color digital imagery (primarily inkjets) that will include some form of the ASTM D4303 standard. Under the guidance of the subcommittee's chair, Mark Gottsegen, ASTM is getting the ball rolling with a demonstration ("ruggedness") round-robin cycle of tests on a small selection of inkjet samples (see Figure 5.6).

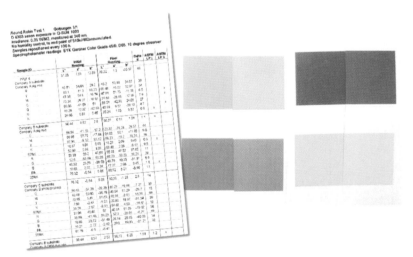

Figure 5.6 Preliminary portion of a table-top xenon arc test (with before and after color patches at right) of a few digital and photographic ink/media combinations. This is just the first of 27 total round-robin test results that would ultimately be averaged and published as a demonstration of what ASTM's testing standards can provide to the digital imaging community

Courtesy of Mark Gottsegen

Since D4303 is a complex standard that requires instrument measurements, the ASTM has also developed two simpler ones. Standard D5383 describes a method for exposing color samples indoors to sunlight coming through a closed window. Three to five outside observers then rate each sample by comparing it to a Blue Wool Reference (see next section) that shows the same amount of color change. Standard D5398 is similar and even simpler since it doesn't require outside observers, and it can be used by any artist to evaluate the lightfastness of his or her own materials.

How will these new ASTM standards affect the world of digital printing? Because they are an all-volunteer organization and not really in the business of testing themselves, ASTM is hoping that the major manufacturers start doing their own tests based on the ASTM standards, which, importantly, make no predictions of print-service life.

Blue Wool Lightfastness Standard References

The Blue Wool Lightfastness References were, and still are, aimed at those who work in the textile industry. The European version is part of the ISO standards, and it gets its name from the dyed blue wool fabric bands or swatches that are used to visually compare fading rates. Much like a litmus test, Blue Wools act as a visual reference or "dosimeter" for users like museums to determine when too much light has fallen on an artwork so it can be removed from display. Blue Wools also are used as a timing device for knowing when to end a lightfastness test (although they have become less important or needed with the introduction of accurate testing instruments that can control exposure times and intensity). There are eight levels or references, with #8 being essentially permanent and #1 being fugitive (each is roughly twice as light-resistant as the one before) (see Figure 5.7).

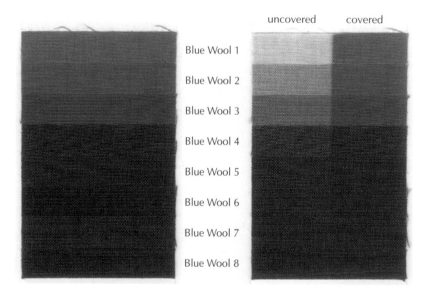

uncovered   covered

Blue Wool 1

Blue Wool 2

Blue Wool 3

Blue Wool 4

Blue Wool 5

Blue Wool 6

Blue Wool 7

Blue Wool 8

Figure 5.7 ISO Blue Wool references after an actual 10-week south-window test. Left is before the test; right is after. Test sample is half-covered to keep those references from being exposed to light.

Blue Wool References courtesy of TalasOnline.com, which calls them "Blue Scales"

In the U.S., the Blue Wool References are manufactured differently, but because they are more difficult to use, many U.S. printmakers use the European ISO ones.

The Blue Wool References are not just for sheep shearers and textile dyers. As a simple, comparative reference, digital printmakers, especially European ones, are now also using Blue Wools to indicate in general terms how permanent a print is or could be. For example, British artist and giclée printmaker Colin Ruffell refers to his large-format prints achieving "a Blue Wool 6 rating, which is the minimum lightfastness requirement to meet the British and international standards set by The Fine Art Trade Guild in the UK for limited edition prints."

Who's Doing the Testing?

There are three kinds of groups doing print permanence testing and making permanence claims: *independent testing organizations* and *researchers*, *manufacturers* and *marketers*, and *individual photographer-artists*.

Testing Organizations and Independent Researchers

These are the scientists, the university-based, non-profit research laboratories, and the independent labs that do the most well-publicized testing of print permanence.

Wilhelm Imaging Research (WIR)

Henry Wilhelm (see Figure 5.8) is the dominant figure in both photographic and now digital print permanence testing. He wrote the ground-breaking book *The Permanence and Care of Color Photographs* (1993), he is on the key industry standards committees (ISO) and panels, and he is a consultant on image permanence to such prestigious institutions as the Museum of Modern Art in New York.

Figure 5.8 Image-stability researcher Henry Wilhelm at the Maine Art Gallery in Kennebunk.

© 2000 Mark H. McCormick-Goodhart

Wilhelm Imaging Research (WIR) is based in the college town of Grinnell, Iowa, and does both independent contract testing on prototype materials for companies as well as generic testing for public consumption. When you see permanence claims made by ink vendors or inkjet printer makers, there's a good chance that WIR did the tests from which the results were drawn.

For the lightfastness portion of its well-known Display Permanence Ratings (see Table 5.1), WIR runs accelerated, measured, predictive testing based on continuous, high-intensity light exposure (35 klux with glass-filtered cool white fluorescent illumination) conducted at 24° C and 60% RH. Using Wilhelm's visually-weighted criteria set, the results are then extrapolated to a reference display condition of 450 lux for 12 hours per day and represent "the years of display for easily noticeable fading, changes in color balance, and/or staining to occur." (WIR also conducts separate tests of other environmental conditions.)

While there may be debate about the applicability of WIR's predictive ratings, I believe they can be valuable when used for relative comparisons. For example, if WIR rates ink/paper combination "A" at 73 years and ink/paper combination "B" at 25 years, then if I'm interested in a print's permanence, I will choose ink/paper combination "A" for my production, all other things being equal. In other words, don't use the WIR years for actual service-life predictions; use them as a basis for comparison and choice of materials. Also, look for significant differences in ratings. If one material is rated at 70 years and another at 75 years, both may, in fact, perform similarly.

IPI/RIT

The Image Permanence Institute (IPI) at the Rochester Institute of Technology (RIT) is a university-based, nonprofit research laboratory in Rochester, New York, that's devoted to scientific research in the preservation of visual and other forms of recorded information. Under the direction of James Reilly, IPI is the world's largest independent lab with this specific scope, and they have sponsors who include the likes of Eastman Kodak Company, 3M Company, Fuji Photo Film Company, and Polaroid Corporation.

The IPI tests for lightfastness (using high-intensity xenon arc and fluorescent) and the effects of pollutants and heat and humidity on photos, inkjet prints, and other imaging media. Normal test conditions used for high-intensity fluorescent tests include exposing color samples for 10 or 14 weeks to 50 klux light with normal airflow. IPI is one of the few facilities in the world equipped to test materials for gas pollutants at different concentrations, temperatures, and humidities. They can study the effects of sulfur dioxide, nitrogen dioxide, hydrogen sulfide, and ozone.

Instead of publicizing any test results as WIR sometimes does, IPI only provides them to the companies that contract for the tests. Those companies then—not IPI—are free to draw their own conclusions and use them in their marketing claims. For example, Red River Paper and inkjet ink supplier MIS both promote the longevity of their respective products as tested by IPI/RIT, and they show the results of those tests on their websites.

Q-Lab Weathering Research Service

The testing service of this Ohio-based company is an accredited independent lab and run as a separate division of Q-Panel Lab Products, which makes testing products such as xenon arc chambers. Q-Lab Weathering Research Service performs accelerated laboratory light-stability and

Q-Panel's Eric Everett and a Q-Sun table-top xenon arc test chamber.

Courtesy of Q-Panel Lab Products

weathering tests as well as natural, environmental exposure tests using its Florida and Arizona locations. (Atlas Laboratory Weathering Testing provides similar services.)

Independent Researchers

Independent researchers like the aforementioned Barbara Vogt and Joy Turner Luke also conduct scientific testing. Traditional artist, art educator, and color expert Luke has been doing volunteer, prototype testing for the ASTM since the 1970s. In her northern Virginia studio, she conducts daylight tests controlled by ISO Blue Wool References. She follows the ASTM standard D5383 to the letter (she helped write it) and has been doing inkjet lightfastness testing on her own for more than seven years. She recently added xenon arc testing to her repertoire (see Figure 5.9) and also "Do Your Own Permanence Testing" later in this chapter for more about Luke).

Figure 5.9 Permanence researcher Joy Turner Luke in her studio working with an Atlas SUNTEST XLS+ xenon testing instrument (furnished by Atlas Material Testing Technology for her ongoing research).

Manufacturers, Vendors, and Distributors

Some manufacturers (Kodak, for example) do their own tests and use the results in promoting their products. Others, like Epson, HP, and Canon (who also do some internal testing as well), contract with independent testers, like WIR or IPI/RIT, to perform their tests and then use the results in their marketing.

Epson, which was bruised by the infamous Orange Shift problem, is now very careful about its permanence claims. For example, here's the small print it typically uses with its inkjet printers: "Lightfastness rating based on accelerated testing of prints on specialty media, displayed indoors, under glass. Actual print stability will vary according to media, printed image, display conditions, light intensity, humidity, and atmospheric conditions. Epson does not guarantee longevity of prints."

Table 5.1 Epson Stylus Pro 4000 – Print Permanence Ratings

Epson Stylus Pro 4000 – Print Permanence Ratings

Display Permanence Ratings and Dark Storage Ratings (Years Before Noticeable Fading and/or Changes in Color Balance Occur)[1]								
Paper, Canvas, or Film Media Printed with UltraChrome Pigmented Inks	Displayed Prints Framed Under Glass[2]	Displayed Prints Framed with UV Filter[3]	Displayed Prints Not Framed (Bare-Bulb)[4]	Dark Storage Stability Rating at 73°F & 50% RH (incl. Paper Yellowing)[5]	Resistance to Ozone[6]	Resistance to High Humidity[7]	Resistance to Water[8]	Are UV Brighteners Present?[9]
Epson Premium Glossy Photo Paper (250)	85 years	98 years	60 years	>200 years	now in test	very high	high	no
Epson Premium Semigloss Photo Paper (250)	77 years	>150 years	55 years	>200 years	now in test	very high	high	no
Epson Premium Luster Photo Paper (250) [roll]	71 years	165 years	48 years	>200 years	now in test	very high	high	yes
Epson Premium Luster Photo Paper (250) [sheet]	71 years	165 years	48 years	>200 years	now in test	very high	high	yes
Epson Premium Semimatte Photo Paper (250)	67 years	133 years	47 years	>200 years	now in test	very high	high	yes
Epson UltraSmooth Fine Art Paper	108 years	175 years	57 years	>200 years	now in test	very high	high	no
Somerset Velvet for Epson (255 and 505 gsm)	62 years	124 years	37 years	>200 years	now in test	very high	high	some
Somerset Velvet for Epson w/PremierArt™ Spray[10]	166 years	>200 years	75 years	>200 years	now in test	very high	high	some
Epson Velvet Fine Art Paper (sheet)	61 years	125 years	34 years	>200 years	now in test	very high	high	some
Epson Velvet Fine Art Paper w/PremierArt™ Spray[10]	82 years	>150 years	55 years	>200 years	now in test	very high	high	some
Epson Textured Fine Art Paper	82 years	160 years	68 years	>200 years	now in test	very high	high	no
Epson Watercolor Paper Radiant White (sheet)	92 years	>200 years	68 years	>200 years	now in test	very high	high	yes
Epson Enhanced Matte Paper[11]	76 years	155 years	45 years[10] 110 years	>200 years	now in test	very high	high	yes
PremierArt™ Water Resistant Canvas for Epson	now in test	now in test	now in test	now in test	now in test	very high	high	no
PremierArt™ Water Resistant Canvas for Epson	now in test	now in test	now in test	now in test	now in test	very high	high	no

(Black-and-white prints made with the full-color Epson UltraChrome inkset)

Epson Premium Glossy Photo Paper (250)	135 years	130 years	76 years	>200 years	now in test	very high	high	no
Epson Premium Semigloss Photo Paper (250)	118 years	>150 years	74 years	>200 years	now in test	very high	high	no
Epson Premium Luster Photo Paper (250) [roll]	95 years	>200 years	58 years	>200 years	now in test	very high	high	yes
Epson Premium Luster Photo Paper (250) [sheet]	95 years	>200 years	58 years	>200 years	now in test	very high	high	yes
Epson Premium Semimatte Photo Paper (250)	76 years	170 years	57 years	>200 years	now in test	very high	high	yes
Epson UltraSmooth Fine Art Paper	>140 years	>175 years	>130 years	>200 years	now in test	very high	high	no
Somerset Velvet for Epson (255 and 505 gsm)	90 years	>160 years	60 years	>200 years	now in test	very high	high	some
Somerset Velvet for Epson w/PremierArt™ Spray[10]	>250 years	>150 years	135 years	>200 years	now in test	very high	high	some
Epson Velvet Fine Art Paper (sheet)	115 years	125 years	112 years	>200 years	now in test	very high	high	some
Epson Velvet Fine Art Paper w/PremierArt™ Spray[10]	178 years	>145 years	118 years	>200 years	now in test	very high	high	some
Epson Textured Fine Art Paper	140 years	>165 years	120 years	>200 years	now in test	very high	high	no
Epson Watercolor Paper Radiant White (sheet)	>150 years	>200 years	130 years	>200 years	now in test	very high	high	yes
Epson Enhanced Matte Paper[11]	>180 years	>200 years	>150 years (8)	110 years	now in test	very high	high	yes
PremierArt™ Water Resistant Canvas for Epson	now in test	now in test	now in test	now in test	now in test	very high	high	no

Notes on These Tests:

[1]Display Permanence Ratings (DPR) are based on accelerated light stability tests conducted at 35 klux with glass-filtered cool white fluorescent illumination with the sample plane air temperature maintained at 24°C and 60% relative humidity. Data were extrapolated to a display condition of 450 lux for 12 hours per day using the Wilhelm Imaging Research, Inc. "Visually-Weighted Endpoint Criteria Set v3.0." and represent the years of display for easily noticeable fading, changes in color balance, and/or staining to occur. (See: Henry Wilhelm, "How Long Will They Last? An Overview of the Light-Fading Stability of Inkjet Prints and Traditional Color Photographs," *IS&T's 12th International Symposium on Photofinishing Technologies*, sponsored by the Society for Imaging Science and Technology, Orlando, Florida, February 2002: *<http://www.wilhelm-research.com/articles_ist_02_2002.html>*. See also: Henry Wilhelm, "How Long Will They Last? – Part II An Overview of the Permanence of Digitally-Printed Photographs and Applicable Print Permanence Test Methods," *IS&T's 13th International Symposium on Photofinishing Technology*, sponsored by the Society for Imaging Science and Technology, Las Vegas, Nevada, February 2004: *<WIR_ISTpaper_2004_02_HW.pdf>*.) High-intensity light fading

continued

Table 5.1 continued

reciprocity failures in these tests are assumed to be zero. Illumination conditions in homes, offices, and galleries do vary, however, and color images will last longer when displayed under lower light levels; likewise, the life of prints will be shortened when displayed under illumination that is more intense than 450 lux. Ink and paper combinations that have not reached a fading or color balance failure point after the equivalent of 100 years of display are given a rating of "more than 100 years" until such time as meaningful dark stability data are available (see discussion in No. 5 below). The image permanence data listed here were obtained from tests with prototype SP4000 printers, as well as with SP7600 and SP9600 printers (all three printers use identical 110 ml and 220 ml Epson UltraChrome ink cartridges). These data may change somewhat as tests are completed with production SP4000 printers and samples of current media. From time to time this document will be updated with new test results.

[2]In typical indoor situations, the "Displayed Prints Framed Under Glass" test condition is considered the single most important of the three display conditions listed. All prints intended for long-term display should be framed under glass or plastic to protect them from staining, image discoloration, and other deterioration caused by prolonged exposure to cigarette smoke, cooking fumes, insect residues, and other airborne contaminants; this precaution applies to traditional black-and-white and color photographs as well as inkjet and other types of digital prints.

[3]Displayed prints framed with ultraviolet filtering glass or ultraviolet filtering plastic sheet generally last longer than those framed under ordinary glass. How much longer depends upon the specific print material and the spectral composition of the illuminate, with some ink/paper combinations benefitting a great deal more than others. Some products may even show reduced life when framed under a UV filter because one of the image dyes or pigments is disproportionately protected from fading caused by UV radiation and this can result in more rapid changes in color balance than occur with the glass-filtered and/or the bare-bulb illumination conditions. For example, if a UV filter protects the cyan and magenta inks much more than it protects the yellow ink in a particular ink/media combination, the color balance of the image may shift toward blue more rapidly than it does when a glass filter is used (in which case the fading rates of the cyan, magenta, and yellow dyes or pigments are more balanced in the neutral scale). Keep in mind, however, that the major cause of fading with most digital and traditional color prints in indoor display conditions is visible light and although a UV filter may slow fading, it will not stop it. For the display permanence data reported here, Acrylite OP-3 acrylic sheet, a "museum quality" UV filter supplied by Cyro Industries, was used.

[4]Illumination from bare-bulb fluorescent lamps (with no glass or plastic sheet between the lamps and prints) contains significant UV emissions at 313nm and 365nm which, with most print materials, increases the rate of fading compared with fluorescent illumination filtered by ordinary glass (which absorbs UV radiation with wavelengths below about 330nm). Some print materials are affected greatly by UV radiation in the 313–365nm region, and others very little. "Gas fading" is another potential problem when prints are displayed unframed, such as when they are attached to kitchen refrigerator doors with magnets, pinned to office walls, or displayed inside of fluorescent illuminated glass display cases in schools, stores, and offices. Field experience has shown that, as a class of media, microporous "instant dry" papers used with dye-based inkjet inks can be very vulnerable to gas fading when displayed unframed and/or stored exposed to the open atmosphere where even very low levels of ozone and certain other air pollutants are present. In some locations, displayed unframed prints made with microporous papers and dye-based inks have suffered from extremely rapid image deterioration. This type of premature ink fading is not caused by exposure to light. Polluted outdoor air is the source of most ozone found indoors in homes, offices, and public buildings. Ozone can also be generated indoors by electrical equipment such as electrostatic air filters ("electronic dust precipitators") that may be part of heating and air conditioning systems in homes, office buildings, restaurants, and other public buildings to remove dust, tobacco smoke, etc. Electrostatic air filtration units are also supplied as small "tabletop" devices. Potentially harmful pollutants may be found in combustion products from gas stoves; in addition, microscopic droplets of cooking oil and grease in cooking fumes can damage unframed prints. Because of the wide range of environmental conditions in which prints may be displayed or stored, Display Permanence Ratings for the bare-bulb illumination condition will not be listed for paper/ink combinations of known susceptibility to gas fading. For all of the reasons cited above, prints made with microporous papers and dye-based inks should always be displayed framed under glass or plastic.

[5]Prints stored in the dark may suffer slow deterioration that is manifested in yellowing of the print paper, image fading, changes in color balance, and physical embrittlement, cracking, and/or delamination of the image layer. These types of deterioration may affect the paper support, the image layer, or both. Each type of print material (ink/paper combination) has its own intrinsic dark storage stability characteristics; some are far more stable than others. Rates of deterioration are influenced by temperature and relative humidity; high temperatures and/or high relative humidity exacerbate the problems. Long-term dark storage stability is determined using Arrhenius accelerated dark storage stability tests that employ a series of elevated temperatures (e.g., 57°C, 64°C, 71°C, 78°C, and 85°C) at a constant relative humidity of 50% RH to permit extrapolation to ambient room temperatures (or other conditions such as those found in sub-zero, humidity-controlled cold storage preservation facilities). Because many types of inkjet inks, especially those employing pigments instead of dyes, are exceedingly stable when stored in the dark, the eventual life of prints made with these inks may be limited by the instability of the paper support, and not by the inks themselves. Due to this concern, as a matter of policy, Wilhelm Imaging Research does not provide a Display Permanence Rating of greater than 100 years for any inkjet or other photographic print material unless it has also been evaluated with Arrhenius dark storage tests and the data indicate that the print can indeed last longer than 100 years without noticeable deterioration when stored at 73°F (23°C) and 50% RH. Arrhenius dark storage data are also necessary to assess the physical and image stability of a print material when it is stored in an album, portfolio box, or other dark place. The Arrhenius data given here are only applicable when prints are protected from the open atmosphere; that is, they are stored in closed boxes, placed in albums within protective plastic sleeves, or framed under glass or high-quality acrylic sheet. If prints are stored, displayed without glass or plastic, or otherwise exposed to the open atmosphere, low-level air pollutants may cause significant paper yellowing within a relatively short period of time. Note that these Arrhenius dark storage data are for storage at 50%

RH; depending on the specific type of paper and ink, storage at higher relative humidities (e.g., 70% RH) could produce significantly higher rates of paper yellowing and/or other types of physical deterioration.

[6]Tests for resistance to ozone are conducted using an accelerated ozone exposure test (conducted at 23°C and 60% RH) and the reporting method outlined in: Kazuhiko Kitamura, Yasuhiro Oki, Hidemasa Kanada, and Hiroko Hayashi, "A Study of Fading Property Indoors Without Glass Frame from an Ozone Accelerated Test," *Final Program and Proceedings – IS&T's NIP19: International Conference on Digital Printing Technologies*, sponsored by the Society for Imaging Science and Technology, New Orleans, Louisiana, September 28 – October 3, 2003, pp. 415–419.

[7]Changes in image color and density, and/or image diffusion ("image bleeding"), that may take place over time when prints are stored and/or displayed in conditions of high relative humidity are evaluated using a humidity-fastness test maintained at 80°F (27°C) and 80% RH. Depending on the particular ink/media combination, slow humidity-induced changes may occur at much lower humidities – even at 50–60% RH. Test methods for resistance to high humidity and related test methods for evaluating "short-term color drift" in inkjet prints have been developed over the past six years by Mark McCormick-Goodhart and Henry Wilhelm at Wilhelm Imaging Research, Inc. See, for example, Mark McCormick-Goodhart and Henry Wilhelm, "An Overview of the Permanence of Inkjet Prints Compared with Traditional Color Prints," *Final Program and Proceedings – IS&T's Eleventh International Symposium on Photofinishing Technologies*, sponsored by the Society for Imaging Science and Technology, Las Vegas, Nevada, January 30 – February 1, 2000, pp. 34–39. See also: Mark McCormick-Goodhart and Henry Wilhelm, "Humidity-Induced Color Changes and Ink Migration Effects in Inkjet Photographs in Real-World Environmental Conditions," *Final Program and Proceedings – IS&T's NIP16: International Conference on Digital Printing Technologies, sponsored by the Society for Imaging Science and Technologies*, Vancouver, B.C., Canada, October 15–20, 2000, pp. 74–77. See also: Mark McCormick-Goodhart and Henry Wilhelm, "The Influence of Relative Humidity on Short-Term Color Drift in Inkjet Prints," *Final Program and Proceedings – IS&T's NIP17: International Conference on Digital Printing Technologies*, sponsored by the Society for Imaging Science and Technology, Ft. Lauderdale, Florida, September 30 – October 5, 2001, pp. 179–185. See also: Mark McCormick-Goodhart and Henry Wilhelm, "The Correlation of Line Quality Degradation With Color Changes in Inkjet Prints Exposed to High Relative Humidity," *Final Program and Proceedings – IS&T's NIP19: International Conference on Digital Printing Technologies*, sponsored by the Society for Imaging Science and Technology, New Orleans, Louisiana, September 28 – October 3, 2003, pp. 420–425.

[8]Data from waterfastness tests are reported in terms of three subjective classes: "high," "moderate," and "poor." Both "water drip" tests and "standing water droplets/gentle wipe" tests are employed.

[9]Fluorescent brighteners (also called "UV brighteners," "optical brighteners," or "optical brightening agents" [OBA's]) are white or colorless compounds added to most inkjet and other papers in order to make them appear whiter and "brighter" than they really are. Fluorescent brighteners absorb ultraviolet (UV) radiation, causing the brighteners to fluoresce (emit light) in the visible region, especially in the blue and green portions of the spectrum. Fluorescent brighteners can lose activity – partially or completely – as a result of exposure to light. Brighteners may also lose activity when subjected to high temperatures in accelerated thermal aging tests and, it may be assumed, in long-term storage in albums or other dark places under normal room temperature conditions. With loss of brightener activity, papers will appear to have yellowed and to be "less bright" and "less white." In recent years, traditional chromogenic ("silver-halide") color photographic papers have been made with UV-absorbing interlayers and overcoats and this prevents brighteners that might be present in the base paper from being activated by UV radiation. It is the relative UV component in the viewing illumination that determines the perceived "brightening effect" produced by fluorescent brighteners. If the illumination contains no UV radiation (for example, if a UV filter is used in framing a print), fluorescent brighteners are not activated and, comparatively speaking, the paper appears to be somewhat yellowed – and not as "white." This spectral dependency of fluorescent brighteners makes papers containing such brighteners look different depending on the illumination conditions. For example, prints displayed near windows are illuminated with direct or indirect daylight, which contains a relatively high UV component, and if an inkjet paper contains brighteners, this causes the brighteners to strongly fluoresce. When the same print is displayed under incandescent tungsten illumination, which has a low UV component, the brighteners have little effect. Another potential drawback of brighteners is that brightener degradation products may themselves be a source of yellowish stain. These problems can be avoided by not adding fluorescent brighteners to inkjet photographic papers during manufacture. When long-term image permanence is an important consideration – or may eventually become an important consideration – papers with fluorescent brighteners should be avoided.

[10]PremierArt™Print Shield, an easy-to-apply spray for protecting inkjet prints (supplied in aerosol spray cans) is available from Premier Imaging Products, Inc. <www.Premierimagingproducts.com>, 121 Lombard Street, Oxnard, California 93030; tel: 805-983-1472; fax: 805-988-0213. Epson UltraSmooth Fine Art Paper is supplied by Epson and its authorized dealers in the U.S., Canada, and LatinAmerica.

[11]When exposed to low-level air pollutants that may be present in ambient indoor air, Epson Enhanced Matte Paper is highly susceptible to yellowing over time. Therefore, it is not recommended that prints made with the paper be displayed without framing under glass or a UV-filter.

Extracted portion of Wilhelm Imaging Research's May 1, 2004 document.

Kodak, on the other hand, has taken a slightly different marketing tack by claiming for its Ultima Picture Paper that "other inkjet testing methods that only evaluate light fade, for example, don't present an accurate view of real-world picture display conditions." Their tests also include heat, high humidity, and air quality (ozone). Wilhelm is now doing some of this too, but the manufacturers may or may not choose to report all the data.

Some vendors and distributors also do their own testing. InkjetART.com does both internal and contract fade testing on some of the papers and inks that it sells, and Jon Cone's InkjetMall.com does 1,000-hour xenon-based fade tests with its in-house ink brand compared to others. "Our testing is brutal when we look at how one ink/paper does against another," Cone says. Digital printing supplies distributor LexJet Direct contracts with WIR to test its products.

The problem with vendor-sponsored tests and claims, besides an obvious bias, is that they tend to generalize and simplify what is a very complex interaction of separate elements that can contribute to significantly different results depending on the display or storage conditions. There just is no standardized "miles-per-gallon" way to describe print permanence. At least not yet.

Your Mileage May Vary

Permanence claims and estimates will vary depending on the specific display or storage conditions any print experiences. Using WIR's lightfastness tests as the model, it's easy to see why this is. The point of print failure (David Matz calls it "the death point") is reached based on the total, cumulative light exposure. The way that's figured is by multiplying the lux level by the time of exposure, which yields the total, cumulative amount of light in *lux-hours*.

Let's say WIR has determined that the death point of a particular ink/paper combination is reached at 100 million lux-hours (that's the equivalent of 30,000 lux over 3,333 hours or 139 24-hour days). Extrapolating the results to WIR's "standard" indoor conditions of 450 lux for 12-hour days, you would end up with a usable print life of 50 years. But if the intended conditions are more like a museum where 100 lux might be used, then all of a sudden that same ink/paper combination now becomes a 228-year rating. Or, if the print is going in your south-facing living room where 5,000 lux will hit it each day, the print's lifetime has just shrunk to 4.6 years. Big difference.

Kodak raised some eyebrows in early 2004 when they announced their Ultima Picture Paper that "delivers inkjet prints that last more than 100 years." Sounds good until you read the small print and discover that Kodak's reference display environment is 120 lux for 12-hour days, which they support with "typical home" studies. Simply replacing 120 lux with WIR's 450 lux would instantly drop that 100-year longevity prediction to 26.7 years! This is why reading the fine print on these tests is so important.

Individual Artist Testing

There are many photographer-artists who, in an attempt to compare products and get accurate information about *their specific* materials and methods, do their own permanence tests. For example, working photographic artist Steven Livick (in collaboration with Bill Waterson) combines lux-hour-measured, outdoor-sunlight testing with the use of inkjet coatings to help him determine the longevity of his large-scale murals.

Others who do their own testing include photographer and monochromatic inkjet expert Paul Roark and also photo artist Barry Stein, who constructed a fluorescent fade tester for under $50 that allows him to test with and without a glass filter and to adjust the light level from 20 to 60 klux (see Figure 5.10).

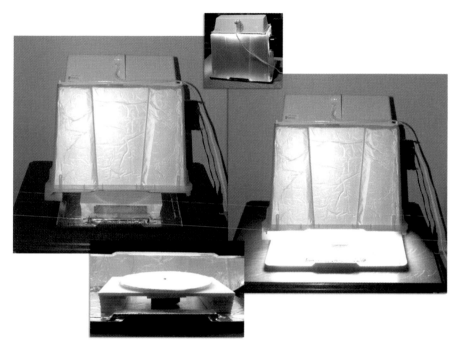

Figure 5.10 Barry Stein made this fluorescent light-testing device from inexpensive parts including a foil-lined trash can, light fixture, and fan. Bottom inset shows the turntable for rotating samples made from pieces of Foamcore and a small motor. All this for under $50.

Courtesy of Barry Stein
www.BSteinArt.com.

For more ideas about individual-artist testing, see "Do Your Own Permanence Testing" below.

So How Long Will It Last?

I started off this chapter asking two simple questions: How long is long enough? and How long will it last? That second one is the hardest to answer. Because there is no *one* answer; because it all depends. Even the best outside permanence tests and manufacturers' claims will only give you a generalized guesstimate of what's going to happen to *your* prints. There are just too many variables. What is the atmospheric pollution level where the print will be displayed or stored? What is the UV component of the light coming in from the windows? What's the temperature? What's the humidity? These are just some of the influencing factors that will significantly affect the permanence of *that* print.

What Can You Do?

To get closer to knowing about the longevity of your prints—besides waiting around a few decades as they age, you have three basic options: (1) carefully study the existing test data, (2) contract out your permanence testing, or (3) do your own testing. In any case, you should also learn how to maximize print permanence.

Study the Test Data

If you're relying on outside permanence test results, make sure you understand what the test conditions and standards were and adjust your expectations accordingly. Make yourself a checklist: Accelerated or real-time? Indoor or outdoor? Comparative or predictive? Visual or measured? If measured, what device was used? What were the endpoints? If results were extrapolated, what were the reference display conditions?

By looking deeply, you can start to really understand the meaning of any test result and see if it matches your needs.

Contract Out Your Permanence Testing

The middle ground between studying and using the test data from others and doing the testing yourself (next section) is having someone else do the testing for you.

If you had the money to spend you could actually contract the IPI/RIT or WIR organizations, but we're talking thousands of dollars per test, so that's not very likely. The next step would be to go to the "artificial weathering" companies like Q-Panel Weathering Research Service or Atlas Laboratory Weathering Testing. They normally do industrial testing in the fields of textiles, plastics, paints and coatings, etc., but they could also do testing for you. For example, Q-Panel's laboratory xenon lightfastness fade tests start in the mid- to high-hundred dollar range, but the outdoor tests described earlier can cost as little as $2.40 per specimen per year (Florida and Arizona outdoor exposures under glass).

Finally, you can contract with an individual who has experience and a well-established method of doing this kind of testing. As we've already learned, there are many ways to test permanence, so the first obvious hurdle is that you have to agree with the methodology of the tester.

While this is not exactly the same as contract testing, Joy Turner Luke has an open offer to be part of her ongoing lightfastness research studies. If you have combinations of inks and paper that meet the needs of Luke's testing, she will run both natural daylight and xenon arc tests on your materials for a nominal charge of fifty cents per sample to cover handling. If you are accepted into her program, she will furnish complete instructions on sample preparation and will send test results upon completion. Contact her at: joy.luke@verizon.net.

Do Your Own Permanence Testing

Can you do your own permanence testing? Absolutely. There are as many ways to conduct a print permanence test as there are ways to make a print. However, it can be done, and I highly recommend it.

Here are the basic steps of an actual lightfastness test I conducted:

1. **Decide on what you want to test for.** I decided to test the fading of four different inkjet papers using the same desktop printer and inks.

2. **Select test type, conditions, and testing procedure or standard.** This is actually the most important step, and many people rush through it without much thought. In my case, I did an accelerated, comparative (relative), visual, lightfastness test.

3. **Set up test conditions and apparatus.** I built a crude light-testing apparatus with full-spectrum fluorescent tubes and standard window glass over the target samples (see Figure 5.11).

Figure 5.11 The author's fluorescent light-fading test unit. Fluorescents should only be used if the intended display environment relies on this type of lighting.

4. **Prepare and print the targets.** I created my own test target in Adobe Photoshop combining personal and stock images and "color ramps" (pure color patches of varying densities).

5. **Run Test.** With the targets in place, I turned on the lights and didn't turn them off, checking in each day and rotating the targets under the lights each week to make sure they all received the same average exposure.

6. **Terminate test and make evaluations.** On the 100th day (the equivalent of 6.7 "Wilhelm Years" at my light intensity), I turned off the lights and compared the test specimens along with the dark-stored references in my viewing booth and decided which ones looked best (see Figure 5.12). Those that matched their controls the closest had faded the least.

Figure 5.12 Visually comparing the targets after the lightfastness test is over.

Remember that this was just one way to do a test. I could have, instead, used a different light source, run the test longer, tested different inks on the same paper, instrument-measured the samples before and after, or changed any of the other factors. I wanted some quick, basic information to make an informed decision about what material combinations would best meet my needs for a specific display condition.

Others do it differently. Mark Gottsegen suggests a quick-and-dirty test: "Make a sample and expose half to daylight (sunlight preferred) in a south-facing window while keeping the other half in the dark. Compare after a month or two. This, of course, is very subjective and not very scientific. Using one of the ASTM standards Blue Wool Test Methods such as D5398 or D5383 is much better, and not that expensive nor hard to do."

Joy Turner Luke is one who follows the ASTM D5383 guidelines. In a recent test, she took inkjet-printed test specimens and exposed them to natural daylight (including direct sunlight) on racks suspended one foot below skylights facing upward and to the south in a heated and air-conditioned room. A card containing the eight ISO Blue Wool References was placed on each test board. The test was complete when Blue Wool 3 faded to match a Munsell 5 PB 6/4 color chip and Blue Wool 6 also showed a color change. In this case, it took 139 days. (At the same time and as part of the same test, another set of identical specimens were hung on an interior wall out of direct light in the same building for five years.)

The skylight specimens were taken down and rated visually by three human observers. Figure 5.13 reproduces the appearance of both sets of exposed specimens.

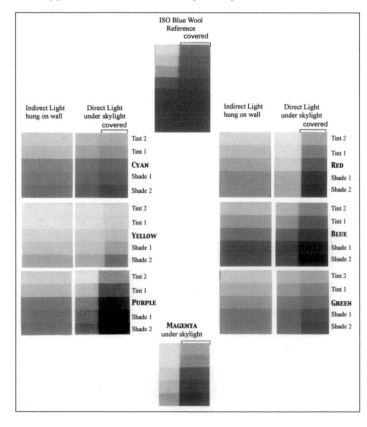

Figure 5.13 Joy Turner Luke's exposed inkjet test panels and, at top, the ISO Blue Wool Reference card. The three panels on the left of each set were hung on an interior wall in indirect light for five years. The three panels on the right of each set were exposed to daylight coming through skylights. The far right-hand section of each skylight panel was covered with a lined metal bar to protect the colors from light. At bottom is the Magenta that bleached under the skylight.

Courtesy of Joy Turner Luke

Maximize Print Permanence

Depending on whether you self-print or have someone make prints for you, there are things you can do to maximize print permanence: (see also Chapter 7 and Chapter 9 for more about inks, paper, coatings, framing, and display)

- Always select/specify long-lasting colorant and media *combinations*. The key is in matching your colorants to your media. Realize that permanence is specific to a particular type of ink or dye on a particular type of medium (paper). Don't mix them up and expect the same results.

- Study paper and coating specs. Swellable polymer coatings on inkjet papers protect against light and ozone but are more sensitive to humidity. Microporous coatings are less sensitive to humidity but more sensitive to light and ozone.

- Keep prints on display away from strong light, especially daylight, and very especially sunlight. (Your goal should be to *never* let one ray of sun strike a display print.)

- To protect against gas-air fading, display your prints behind glass or acrylic (or store them in an album or in sleeves) whenever possible. This reduces airflow and some UV exposure problems. If using fluorescent lights, filter them with glass or plastic covers to cut down on the UV emissions.

- If you can't or don't want to display prints—on canvas, for example—behind glass, consider using a coating, lamination, or spray. Keep in mind that post-print coatings sometimes add a new element to the chemical interaction of ink and media; under certain circumstances they could even reduce print life.

- Store your prints in a dark, dry, and cool place; light and moisture are real print killers. Try to minimize temperature and humidity changes; keep them as constant as possible. High temperature and humidity levels can speed up print deterioration, and very low humidity or fluctuating humidity can cause prints to crack or peel. Model conditions are 68° F (20° C) to 77°F (25° C) with 30 to 50% relative humidity. (See more print storage recommendations in Chapter 9.)

- Communicate to and impress upon anyone receiving your prints all the points above. You'll save yourself and them a lot of disappointment.

The Artist's Responsibility

Prints begin deteriorating the moment they're made. Some faster, some slower. Whether because of light, temperature, or other factors, your prints are going to degrade. Your goal should be to use your knowledge about materials and processes to make the wisest choices that will improve the permanence of your work. This applies to inkjets, digital photo prints, color lasers, everything.

Realize that there are three main factors that affect print permanence: colorants (inks, toners, etc.), media (paper, film, etc.), and display/storage conditions. (Most people erroneously think that the printing device is the main factor, but it's only important in that it can limit the others.) To optimize permanence, you need to carefully control all three factors. If you make prints to sell or give away, you've just lost one leg of the stool since you can't control the conditions where the prints will end up. But, you can do your best with the other two.

Coatings and Permanence

More and more photographer-artists are coating or laminating prints to increase permanence (see more about inkjet print coatings in Chapter 7). Stephen Livick even goes so far as to say, "Our testing shows that all digital print media must be coated for any decent longevity."

Wilhelm Imaging Research now has separate Display Permanence Ratings for some ink/paper combinations that are sprayed with PremierArt Print Shield, a lacquer-based spray designed specifically for inkjet prints. A quick review of WIR's ratings show significant longevity increases when the spray is used.

Inkjet expert Dr. Ray Work is another believer in coatings. "Coating or, better yet, laminating with a pressure sensitive lamination film will give increased protection from moisture, which can interact with other variables and accelerate image degradation," he says. "Coating or laminating is also important for microporous, fast-drying papers that can soak up air pollution and cause rapid fading."

A further twist on this subject is the new inkjet "infusion" formulation that's added as part of the papermaking process. According to its inventor John Edmunds, "This is the only type of built-in inkjet coating that actually increases the longevity of the paper and the inks that are applied to it."

A. 3 drops* of water for 45 seconds, then wiped away with a sponge.
B. Moist sponge with 3 passes.
C. 3 drops* of water for 4 minutes, then blotted with a paper towel.

A water-resistance test showing the protection of Print Shield spray coating.

Courtesy of Premier Imaging Products, Inc.

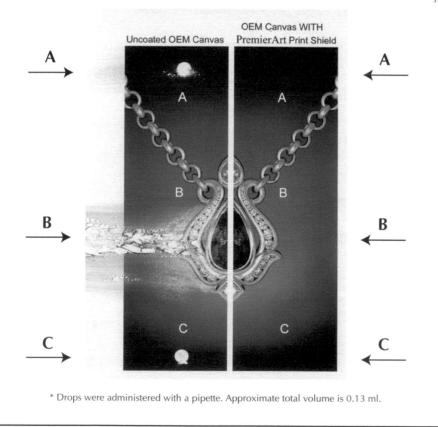

* Drops were administered with a pipette. Approximate total volume is 0.13 ml.

Knowing what we now know about the ability of printed images to fade, deteriorate, degrade, and literally become shadows of their original selves, artists cannot simply shrug off this issue of permanence, or call it "artistic freedom." The legal term *implied warranty of merchantability* (a warranty that the property is fit for the ordinary purposes for which it is used) applies to artists and photographers just like it applies to makers of other products.

The answer is simple enough: anyone selling or distributing artistic print work should determine and then include a full disclosure as to the methods and materials used, including paper and inks. In 14 U.S. states, print disclosure is not optional but is set down as law. For example, California's Civil Code (sections 1742–1744.9) requires a "certificate of authenticity" (C of A) that includes "a description of the medium or process, and where pertinent to photographic processes, the material used in producing the multiple."

In my opinion, it is the responsibility of every printmaking photographer-artist to learn about and communicate the particulars of his or her print methods and how they affect a particular print's longevity. To do otherwise is unwise at minimum, and, if prints are being sold, an actual fraud on the buying public and the entire community of other artists.

Study the technical data that's available, do your own tests if you have to, and use the best materials to make the best art you can.

———————

We've now covered what I consider to be the basics of digital printing. Let's now move to Part II and the subject that everyone is talking about: inkjet.

Part II

The Main Event: Inkjet Printing

6

Selecting an
Inkjet Printer

Inkjet printers are the output devices of choice for many photographers and traditional and digital artists. In Chapter 2, I gave a big-picture overview of the main digital printing technologies. Now, it's time to dive a little deeper and explore the world of inkjets. Whether it's a desktop or a wide-format; if you're looking for your first printer or ready to trade up; no matter if you're planning to self-print or use an outside print service—the more information you have about inkjet printers, the smarter your decision-making will be.

When you go to the grocery store, you take a list. It's the same when shopping for an inkjet printer or an inkjet printmaker. Instead of a list of items, you need to know which questions to ask. So, rather than giving you a rundown of all the printers with a detailed inventory of features and specifications (with new printers constantly coming onto the market, no book can hope to be up-to-date), I'm going to present you with nine important questions and ways to think about answering them. Add or subtract questions to suit your situation, then finalize your own list and start shopping! (The printer brands and models I mention are current as of this writing. For the latest information about inkjet printers, visit my website DP&I.com (www.dpandi.com).

(See Table 6.1 for a sample inkjet printer comparison using the following nine questions.)

1. Can I Use It to Print...?

The foundation question is: What do you want to do with the printer? It's best if you have an understanding of the type of printing you'll be doing in order to pick the best printer for the job.

You may even decide that inkjet is not the best solution for you. Looking for "good enough" quality at a lower cost per print? Consider color laser, especially for multiple copies.

Table 6.1 A Sample Inkjet Printer Comparison

Considerations[1]	Canon imageproGRAF W6200 (thermal technology)	Epson Stylus Pro 4000 (piezo technology)	HP Designjet 130 (thermal technology)
Use?			
max. output size	24 in. × 59 ft.	17 in. × up to 100 ft.	24 in. × 50 ft.
roll feed included?	yes	yes	optional (+$295); included in NR model
Age?			
announced	February 2004	November 2003	May 2004
Print Quality?			
max. resolution	1200 × 1200 dpi	2880 × 1440 dpi	2400 × 1200 dpi
max. # colors	6 (CMYKcm)	7 (CMKYcmk)	6 (CMYKcm)
smallest ink drop size	8 picoliter	3.5 picoliter	4 picoliter
Inks/Media?			
max. paper thickness	19.6 mil (.5 mm)	1.5 mm	.4 mm
dye or pigment?	pigment	pigment	"durable dye"
individual ink tanks	yes	yes	yes
tanks max. capacity	130 ml	110 or 220 ml	28 ml and 69 ml
Permanence?			
WIR rated?	n/a	up to 85 years under glass[2]	82 years under glass[3]
other rated?	approx. 75 years [4]	n/a	n/a
Speed?			
rated print speed	1.5 PPM, glossy, letter, stndrd.	4 min 3 sec./13x19"	4 min./pg., normal, glossy
# nozzles	7,680 (1,280 × 6)	1,440 (180 × 8)	1,824 (304 × 6)
Set Up?			
printer size	47" W × 22.4" D × 19.1" H	33.4" W × 30" D × 14" H	41.3" W × 16.3" D × 8.7" H
printer weight	85 lb.	83.7 lb.	48.5 lb.
connectivity (stndrd)	USB 2.0, 10/100Base-TX	USB 1.1/2.0, IEEE-1394 FW, EIO slot	USB 1.1/2.0, IEEE-1284, EIO slot
Software?			
built-in color calibration?	none	none	yes (standard)
built-in RIP?	yes (PostScript)	optional (PostScript)	optional (PostScript)
standard warranty	1 year	1 year	1 year
Cost?			
estimated U.S. price	$3,495	$1,795	$1,295 ($1,895 NR model)
cost per...	$.019/sq.ft.[5]	unknown	unknown

[1] *North American model numbers; models in other world markets may vary. Information as of September 2004.*

[2] *WIR Display Permanence Ratings on various media as of July 2004.*

[3] *WIR Display Permanence Ratings on various media as of July 2004.*

[4] *Based on Canon Inc. studies conducted using heavy coated paper, under glass, utilizing industry standard conditions and controlled temperature and humidity in an indoor environment. Results may vary based on individual environmental factors.*

[5] *On all popular Canon media.*

SOURCE: Manufacturers or their data sheets

Want top-end photographic output with the look, feel, and smell of a wet-chemistry C-print? Think about using a service with a digital photo printer (see Chapter 2 for more about these). However, there are plenty of advantages to inkjet, and it's a safe bet that an inkjet printer will meet most, if not all, of your requirements for high-quality digital output.

Even within the inkjet category, there are many choices depending on the type of printing desired. Do you want to print on CDs or DVDs? Epson makes several inkjet printers that do this. Want to combine printing with additional functions like scanning, copying, and faxing? Consider the popular "all-in-one" category with multi-function devices from Canon, Epson, HP, Lexmark, and Dell. Dying to make black-and-white or quadtone prints? Then consider either one of the newer HPs or Epsons with multiple black inks or using an inkjet that can be retrofitted to use specialized black-and-white inks and drivers (see Chapter 11). Oversized fine-art prints for gallery display? Consider wide-format printer brands such as ColorSpan, Roland, Epson, HP, Mimaki, or ENCAD.

The Epson Stylus Photo R800 desktop inkjet printer (and also the R200 and R300) lets you print directly onto inkjet-printable CDs/DVDs.

Courtesy of Epson America, Inc.

Sometimes, a printer designed for one purpose is used for another. Take the Epson Stylus C84/C86. It's really an office printer, but digital photographer-artists instantly saw its advantages—high quality, low price, waterproof, pigmented inks—and claimed it for themselves. Similarly, HP's Photosmart 7960 is a consumer printer that's great for black and white, so pro photographers immediately "stole it" for themselves.

What Size Output?

A subset of the "Can I Use It to Print…" question is: What Sizes Can I Print? This is usually a top-level question since you must, at a minimum, have a printer that can handle the largest size you intend to output. In addition, this is where the decision between desktop and wide-format printing is often made.

Desktop

As I've already defined it, desktop (sometimes called "narrow format") means anything less than 24 inches wide. This refers to the media (paper) size and not the physical dimensions of the printer. Practically speaking, the largest common paper size for desktops has been 13 × 19 inches, also called *Super B*, *Super A3*, or *A3+*. Some people, especially in the UK, like to call the A3+ format "wide-carriage" or, confusingly, "wide-format," but I'll stick with the U.S. industry standard definition. The Epson Stylus Pro 4000 prints on paper up to 17 inches wide, but I (and Epson) sometimes put this printer in the "wide-format" category, although it could, technically, fit onto a desktop—only a big one!

Left: *Bird Woman* (2004) by Ileana. Right: The artist checks digital print proofs up to 13×19 inches on her Epson Stylus Photo 2200 in her home studio. For final prints, Ileana works with an outside print-service provider to make larger prints.

Courtesy of Ileana Frómeta Grillo
www.ileanaspage.com

Desktops can squeeze more size out of their limited dimensions by turning the image sideways and printing on roll or cut-from-roll stock. Not all desktops can do this, but if you have long panoramics, roll-feeding desktops can be lifesavers. Desktops like the Epson Stylus Photo R800, 1280, and 2200 are good examples of printers that can provide this function. Keep in mind that the image length on a roll is not unlimited. For instance, on the Epson Stylus Photo 2200, the maximum printable area is either 13 × 44 inches or 13 × 129 inches, depending on your computer's operating system and the application software. (See more about printing big in Chapter 11.)

Another issue that may be important to you is the ability to make "borderless" prints. Epson introduced this capability (also called "borderfree" or "edge-to-edge printing") with its newer Stylus Photo printers, and Canon soon followed suit. Canons make borderless prints by slightly enlarging the image and overspraying beyond the edges of the paper.

Wide-Format

Any printer that can accept media 24 inches or wider is called "wide-format" (or sometimes "large-format"), with the Epson 4000 (and the classic Epson 3000) exception already noted. Another distinguishing characteristic of wide-formats is that they can generally take both roll and sheet media. Granted, some desktops can also do this (mostly Epsons), but virtually *all* wide-formats can. The reason is simple: Wide-format printers are designed for high-production environments. Service bureaus, high-volume outputers, professional printmakers—these are the typical users of wide-formats with a practical paper width of 24–60 inches or even more. If you only want to print 4 × 6-inch snapshots, you could use a wide-format, but unless you wanted thousands of them, it would be overkill—and expensive!

The Roland Hi-Fi JET Pro II can print any image size from 8-5/16" to 53-9/16" wide (210–1361 mm).

Courtesy of Roland DGA Corporation

When North Carolina painter Craig Forrest was looking to step up from a 13 × 19-inch printer to something larger, he chose a refurbished (and still on warranty) Epson Stylus Pro 7600 (24 inches wide) and skipped the Epson 4000 (17 inches wide), even though it was newer and speedier. "My local gallery had several customers who wanted larger-size reproduction prints of my paintings," explains Forrest. "These customers were looking specifically for sizes that when matted and framed would be large enough to work well over a couch or in a similar situation. The 4000 prints were just not large enough."

Any outside printmaker you use will undoubtedly have wide-format print devices. Remember, wide-formats can always print a smaller image, but a desktop can't print a larger one (with the exception of panoramics).

2. How Old Is It?

Pay attention to the age of the printers you're considering. By this, I don't mean when a particular unit was manufactured, but rather, when that particular printer model was introduced. For example, when the Epson Stylus Photo 2200 was announced in April 2002, it effectively wiped out the demand for the 2000P, which was released in May 2000 (the 2200 was also positioned as a step-up printer for those with 1280s). The same can be said for Canon's i9900, which improved on the i9100 that was announced only the year before, and the HP Designjet 5000/5500 series, which replaced the older HP2000/3000CP and 2500/3500CP series. Each of the newer products introduced innovative technology that everyone immediately wanted to have.

The HP Designjet 5000 series (5500 shown in both 42" and 60" sizes) replaced the HP2000/3000CP and 2500/3500CP series.

Courtesy of Hewlett-Packard Company

I'm not saying that older printers can't do a good job for you; they obviously can. For certain specialty uses, some older printers are highly desirable, even to the point of being sought out and stockpiled when they go out of production. The Epson Stylus Color 3000 had been around for seven years, and it was still available from Epson at the time of this writing! However, you may not want to be on the trailing edge of a technology just as a new type of printer is introduced.

How do you know when a printer is being replaced? You don't. However, by using some of the clues I've already given, you can bet that any printer that's more than 12–18 months old will soon be on the chopping block (wide-format "professional" models typically have longer life expectancies than do desktop models). Also be aware of any large price reductions in a printer model; these tend to be used to clear existing stock before a replacement model is announced.

3. What's the Print Quality?

In a nutshell, any of the newer "photo" inkjet printers can produce stunning prints. Inkjet output is now as good as—and in some respects, better than—traditional ways of printing images. High-quality, continuous-tone digital printing has finally become a reality. Here are three quality features to consider when looking at printers (keeping in mind what I said in Chapter 2 about image or print quality resulting in the combination of many factors, not just these three).

Printer Resolution: Each printer manufacturer highlights different features to help tell its marketing story, so don't worry too much about the "Battle of the Resolution" claims. The difference between 1440 dpi, 2880 dpi, 4800 dpi, and 5760 dpi is hardly discernable to the naked eye, and most newer printers are more than adequate in terms of printer resolution. Maximum dpi resolution, however, can be used to compare different models of the same brand.

Number of Colors: When possible, go for at least six colors for desktop inkjet printing (some black-and-white printmakers feel that four is all you need for multi-tone black-and-white printing). The extra two colors (usually a light cyan and a light magenta for CMYKcm) will smooth out subtle gradations, color blends, and skin tones. Four-color-only printers with lower resolutions tend to show grain in highlight areas. Epson, HP, Canon, and Lexmark all have six-color desktop printers. The seven-color Epsons 2200, 4000, 7600, and 9600 (CMYKcmk) have an extra low-density black to reduce graininess and improve the neutrality of grays. Epson's R800 has eight "channels" but only six colors: CMYK with a selectable Matte Black plus extra Red and Blue inks (see Figure 6.1). This printer doesn't need the lighter colors for smoothness since its dots are so small; it takes advantage of using other colors to increase its color range. The Canon i9900 has eight true colors: CMYKck plus an additional Red and Green. The HP 7960 also has eight colors with three blacks for excellent grayscale (black-and-white) printing.

Figure 6.1 The Epson Stylus Photo R800 with six different colors in eight channels. This was Epson's first printer with Red and Blue inks and a separate "gloss optimizer."

Six, seven, or eight colors is currently as far as desktop inkjets go, but wide-formats go even further. The ColorSpan DisplayMaker X-12 comes with 12 separate printheads, which allows you to choose different print modes and inksets. Want to print difficult colors and make spot-color matches? You could configure the X-12 to be CCcMMmYK+Orange, Green, Red, and Blue. Or, you could have both dye-based and pigment inks loaded at the same time (CMYKcm×2) and switch between them as the work requires. (The Mimaki JV4 Series printers offer a similar feature.) Of course, none of this is push-button. Highly specialized printing software is required to deal with this type of color flexibility.

Ink Droplet Sizes: The smaller the drop or dot sizes, the finer the detail and the smoother the color variations. The smallest drop size currently available (at this writing) in the U.S. is 1.5 picoliters (a picoliter is a liquid measurement unit) from the Epson Stylus Photo R800 desktop. One thing to keep in mind about dot sizes: Uncoated papers are much more forgiving of large dots, which tend to spread or bleed together and create a softer look. That's one reason some of the older printers, such as the Epson 3000 with its gargantuan 11 picoliter drop size, can still produce acceptable prints, especially when used on uncoated art and watercolor papers.

Variable droplet sizes are a further advancement for increasing fine highlight detail and for optimizing photographic quality. The Epson 3000 was the first desktop printer to incorporate variable droplet technology, but it used only one dot size per print. Following Epson models began offering differing dot sizes within an image. Now, several brands offer different drop sizes per line including IRIS/IXIA, Epson, Lexmark, Roland, and Mimaki.

Notwithstanding what I've said in this quality section, the numbers alone do not tell the whole story. More important is what your eyes tell you when looking at a print. That's why it's important to request sample prints (see the "Sample Before You Buy" note below), figure out a way to see others' prints (this is one benefit of joining a "Print Exchange"), or have prints from your files made for you on any potential printer.

Sample Before You Buy

As part of your research into printers, try to gather actual printed samples for review. For desktops, office super stores will frequently have sample prints available next to the printer on display. Online retailer inkjetART.com offers custom sample prints from several of the inkjets it sells for evaluation/comparison. (InkjetART.com also has some excellent output comparisons and recommendations on their website.)

In addition, most manufacturers will send you sample prints from their various printer models. Narrow your list down to the top few and call their 800 numbers for samples and product brochures. For desktop samples in the U.S., call these OEM pre-sales numbers:

Dell: (800) 624-9896   Epson: (800) 463-7766   HP: (800) 888-0262   Lexmark: (888) LEXMARK

The next step up is to have sample comparison prints made from your own test files. This is usually only done by vendors of the more expensive wide-formats. When printmaker Larry Thomas of Gleedsville Editions in Leesburg, Virginia, was trying to decide on which wide-format printer to buy, he sent the same test image to several different vendors who made prints for him. He then presented the prints to a panel of friends and associates for blind testing and asked them to pick the best one. He went with the printer (a Roland) that produced the winning sample.

4. What Different Inks and Media Can I Use?

Some photographer-artists consider printing merely the final step in a long digital work-flow. They're mainly concerned with accurately reproducing on paper what they've worked hard on and now see in front of them on their computer monitors. Others are true print-makers and view the selection of ink and media as an integral part of the creative process. How you locate yourself on this continuum will help determine how important inks and papers are to your decision-making process.

Inks

We'll go into much more detail about inks in the next chapter, but here are a few issues that might affect your printer-picking process.

Dye or Pigment?

Most inkjet printers come from the factory pre-configured to run either dye-based or pig-ment inks. Desktops come one way or the other, while some wide-formats let you switch between the two systems or even run them simultaneously. With Epson Stylus Pros— 7600, 9600, and 10600, you have to choose between the Photo Dye or the Archival/UltraChrome pigment version when you set up the machine. The same choice of either dye or pigment exists for the HP Designjet 5500 (there is an optional "ink changeover kit" so you can switch), and some HP Designjets run pigment-based black inks in combination with dye-based colors. With the Epson 4000, you can switch back and forth between two different ink modes: Photographic (CMYKcmkMK) and Dual CMYK (CMYMK + CMYMK)—the "MK" means Matte Black; you can switch between Photo Black and Matte Black inks to tailor the black to your specific media.

If you're concerned about OEM print permanence (also see "How Permanent Are the Prints?"), your choices are either one of the pigment-based printers (or one that can be adapted for third-party pigment inks) or a dye-based printer that can offer long-lasting prints on specific swellable-coated media. For dedicated pigment printers for the desktop, your choices are simple and all Epson. For wide-format, the field opens up considerably with Roland, ENCAD, Mimaki, Mutoh, MacDermid ColorSpan, HP, and Epson all offer-ing several models from which to choose. For long-lasting OEM dye-based prints, HP leads the pack at this writing.

Cartridges and Capacities

Out-of-the-box inkjet printers use ink cartridges or tanks to feed the printer, and in gen-eral, desktops have small cartridges, while the wide-formats have larger ink tanks, which makes them run longer before ink changing and also helps economize ink costs. At one end of the spectrum, a single desktop ink cartridge might hold as little as 17 milliliters of ink (approximately one-half fluid ounce), while the tanks on the ColorSpan DisplayMaker X-12 have a whopping 960 ml (almost a liter or 28 fluid ounces) capacity. The wide-format ENCAD 1000i has a unique intermediate ink reservoir system that maintains a constant ink supply to the printheads, and that allows you to change 700-ml ink bottles on the fly.

For desktops, Canon pioneered individual ink cartridges (one cartridge or "tank" per color), but Epson and then HP quickly responded with the same idea for several of their newer printers. Whether having separate tanks will actually save you any money (one main benefit cited) is open to debate, although separate tanks do have the benefit of reducing wasted ink from discarded multi-color carts with only one color exhausted..

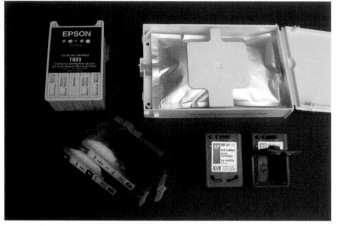

Desktop inkjets use multicolor cartridges (top left and bottom right; note the foam inserts) or separate color carts (bottom left). Most wide-formats use larger, single-color "bag-in-a-box" carts (110 ml shown).

The way around the high-price and inconvenience of tiny ink cartridges is to use a bulk ink system. These are also called continuous-flow (CFS) or continuous-inking systems (CIS), and they pump bulk ink from large containers to the printer, bypassing those puny cartridges entirely (see the next chapter for more about these). The rub is that the bulk systems can be finicky, and they only work with certain printers. (Primarily desktops utilize bulk-ink systems; wide-formats normally don't need them because of their larger capacity ink tanks.)

Metamerism

If you're concerned about metamerism (introduced in Chapter 4 and explained even more in the next chapter), you should realize that, in general, dye-based inks will exhibit less of it. It's more the pigmented inks that give many photographer-artists fits. Even though manufacturers like Epson and HP have worked hard to reduce its effects in their newer printers (Epson's adding a light black and reformulating its inks helped; so did their changing the color mixing or black-generation formulas in the printer drivers), metamerism is still a fact of digital-printing life and still a factor worth investigating in printer searches.

Third-Party Inks

The ability to use third-party inks can be an important consideration, and Epson is the clear favorite in being supported by third-party ink makers. You'll have a harder time finding these inks for HPs, Lexmarks, or Canons. Some of the older Epson models don't use the smart-chipped ink cartridges (see Figure 6.2), which make them easily convertible to third-party ink solutions. (Many of the newer "intelligent," microchipped printers can also accept aftermarket inks and bulk-ink systems, but it usually takes third-party marketers at least six months to a year to come up with workarounds for the printers after they hit the market.) Another important thing to keep in mind is that the OEMs don't like it when you replace their brand of inks (and media) with an outside source. That's understandable if you consider that they've gone to a lot of trouble to develop the right printer driver settings to match their inks and media for the best results. (And the fact that they stand to lose lots of money if you switch to Brand XYZ!) One way to help insure that you use their consumable supplies—inks, primarily—is to state that you will void the printer's warranty if you stray from the OEM flock, although this is a shaky legal position.

Figure 6.2 Two Epson smart-chipped ink cartridges. Note the green circuit boards.

Media

Most major desktop OEMs recommend their own specific papers to use with each printer model. The reasons are two-fold: (1) the engineers can optimize the print quality for a specific selection of paper and coatings, and (2) they'd like to sell you more of their own paper. So, if you like the paper selection (and prices), you're in good shape; if you don't, well, luckily, many outside companies are now offering high-quality third-party papers that work well with most inkjet printers. (See the next chapter for more about printing papers.)

Paper Options

For desktops, the widest range of OEM desktop paper choices belongs to Epson, followed by HP. While both companies offer basic choices in "photo papers" in gloss, matte, or satin/luster finishes, Epson also has "fine art" papers as a stock item for some of its desktop printers. HP does too, but only for wide-format. Canon offers only basic "photo papers."

Wide-format printers have more media options including specialty papers like artist canvas, watercolor, and translucent films (see Figure 6.3). Epson has several 100-percent cotton, acid-free, fine-art papers, while HP has a Photo Rag and Watercolor paper both made by German papermaker Hahnemuhle. Some wide-format paper is not available for desktop printers. For example, Epson's UltraSmooth Fine Art Paper comes only in rolls and in sheets starting with 13 × 19 inches, while HP's Photo Rag by Hahnemuhle comes only in 36-inch rolls.

Figure 6.3 Artist and fine-art printmaker Jan Steinman uses translucent film to produce his signature Translesce prints.

Courtesy of Jan Steinman www.Bytesmiths.com

The other way to go is to use non-recommended, third-party papers. ILFORD, Hahnemuhle, Arches, Crane, Somerset, Legion, Hawk Mountain, Red River, and Moab are only some of the paper makers or distributors offering top-notch third-party papers for inkjet printers. Larger online retailers like MediaStreet.com ("Generations," "Royal," "Renaissance") and inkjetART.com ("Micro Ceramic") also sell high-quality media under their own brand names. (InkjetGoodies.com sells its related division Moab paper line in addition to other brands.)

Paper Handling

Another important printer-deciding factor is paper handling. The drum-based inkjets (IRIS/IXIA and the discontinued ColorSpan Giclée PrintMakerFA) are famous for being able to handle very thick media (although their maximum dimensions are limited, and the manual loading and unloading is a major headache—the main reason the Giclée PrintMakerFA is no longer made). I know of an English printmaker who uses an old IRIS to print on Arches 640 gsm artist paper (the same paper used for painting).

Maximum paper thickness is an important consideration for many. Epsons shine in this category with most newer wide-format models (including the 4000) able to print on premounted papers and boards up to 1.5 mm thick. The Mutoh Falcon II can also print up to 1.5 mm, and the Mimaki JV4 Series printers can handle thicknesses up to an amazing 7 mm.

Most regular users, however, don't need to print on paper that thick. In fact, according to inkjet supplies reseller Royce Bair of inkjetART.com, most desktop users of photo/fine art inkjet papers tend to prefer thicknesses below 13 mil, typically 10-12 mil. (A mil is a measurement of thickness, 1/1,000 inch.) That same 1.5mm would equate to 59 mil, and there is no popular, unmounted paper currently that thick. In fact, the thickest inkjet papers now available are some of Epson's that are 425 and 500 gsm (30-36 mils/.76-.9 mm).

For wide-format, most people prefer 15 mil to 24 mil (17 mil average or .43mm) for fine-art sheet and roll paper; the HP Designjet 30/130 can handle up to .4 mm. Bair explains, "Beyond 25 mil, it's hard to make and use a fine-art roll paper that will de-curl or flatten out after printing."

To go along with thick-paper handling, look for a straight paper path that allows thick papers to be fed from the back of the printer (see Figure 6.4). Not all printers have this capability, so investigate it thoroughly if this is important to you. In addition, many HPs have paper paths with a 180-degree turn; this can be a real disadvantage with thicker media.

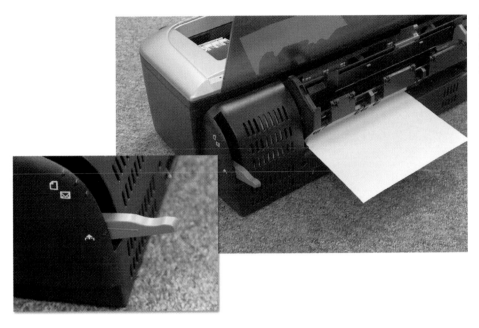

Figure 6.4 Epson's Stylus Photo 2200 has a rear-feeding option for thicker papers. The inset shows the printer's thickness lever in the correct position for inserting a sheet from the rear.

Courtesy of www.inkjetART.com

Some printers also require single-sheet feeding of certain papers (Bair advises that anything thicker than 11 mil will require hand-feeding on most desktops), while others let you stack up several (thin) sheets. Others have optional or built-in roll-feed attachments that let you print from long rolls. Your production needs will determine how important this is to you.

Another niche consideration is whether the printer has the ability to *duplex* (automatically print on both sides of the paper). HP has the largest number of desktop models that can do this.

5. How Permanent Are the Prints?

If you've been paying attention so far, you know that this is a trick question. Inkjet print permanence is a function of the ink/media combination and the storage or display conditions. The printer itself is only a factor in that it limits your choices of inks and paper.

Based on who's doing the testing and which paper is used, pigmented inks currently offer the most permanent prints available by inkjet printing (more than 100 years predicted by Wilhelm Imaging Research for several ink/paper combinations, based on WIR's test conditions). This exceeds the predicted lifespan of traditional photo prints on Fuji Crystal Archive, the longest-lasting wet-chemistry color photo paper, again according to WIR.

Inkjet printers running pigment inks (either OEM or third-party) still have the upper hand in terms of lightfastness before noticeable fading occurs, although some dye-ink/paper combinations are closing the gap. For example, WIR rates Epson's UltraChrome inks on Epson Premium Glossy Photo Paper, Epson Premium Semigloss Photo Paper, and Epson Premium Luster Photo Paper indoors under glass at 85, 77, and 71 years, respectively (again, based on WIR display conditions). At the same time, HP's #57 and #58 (Deskjet 5550) and #85 (Designjet 30/130) dye inks on HP Premium Plus Photo Paper and HP Premium Plus Photo Satin papers are rated indoors under glass by WIR at 73 and 82 years, respectively. As you can see, those longevity ratings are very close! (Don't forget that it's the specific combination of inks and paper that counts with permanence ratings. Henry Wilhelm points out that that same 73-year rating with HP inks on HP paper drops to only two years when an office supply store paper is substituted!)

HP's "durable-dye" based Designjet 130 (shown) and 30 printers are the first inkjet printers to offer predicted WIR permanence ratings (on matched HP media) in the same range as many pigment choices.

Courtesy of Hewlett-Packard Company

The conclusion on permanence? Pick your printers—along with their built-in or third-party ink and paper options—carefully if you're interested in print longevity.

6. Speed: How Long Does It Take to Print?

Newcomers to inkjet printing are, at first, enamored by the high-quality prints they can produce. Speed is usually not a primary concern. However, after a few days of watching that printhead going back and forth as the paper slowly emerges at what seems like the rate of a glacial ice flow, speed starts to become more important. And, it's especially crucial if you're hoping to achieve any sort of production output or run a business by outputting prints for others. The phrase "time is money" is nowhere more appropriate than here. That's why plotter-type, wide-format inkjets usually advertise their speeds in square-feet-per-hour (sfph) or square-meter-per-hour (smph).

One of the selling points for the Epson Stylus Pro 4000 is that it's almost twice as fast as its older cousins (7600 and 9600) in the Epson Stylus Pro model line, and the 4000's Dual CMYK ink mode is 98-percent faster than the same printer's Photographic ink mode. The ENCAD 1000i prints at 220 sfph in High Speed mode down to 30 sfph in Ultrafine mode, and it has a special heated nose and ambient airflow drying system. The ColorSpan DisplayMaker X-12 is so fast (up to 400 square feet per hour) that it has a heated-forced-air dryer to dry the ink. The HP Designjet 5500 even beats that with a top production-mode speed of 569 square feet per hour and its own integrated heater.

Desktop inkjets, on the other hand, typically advertise their pages-per-minute (ppm) rate or how many minutes it takes to print an 8 × 10-inch photo (or 4 × 6). In general, the higher the quality of inkjet output, the slower the print speed. You can check this yourself by simply changing the "quality" (or similar) mode setting on any inkjet printer and timing the same test prints. These different quality modes become especially important for the wide-formats, which often have to provide higher-speed, lower-quality production output. The Roland Hi-Fi JET Pro II, for example, has 10 different speed/quality variations for its six printheads (see Table 6.2).

Table 6.2 Print Modes, Resolution Settings, and Production Capacity for Roland Hi-Fi JET Pro II

Resolution	Direction	Passes	Sq.Ft. per Hr.
450 × 360 dpi	bi	2	300
450 × 360 dpi	uni	2	159
360 × 720 dpi	bi	4	150
360 × 720 dpi	uni	4	75
720 × 720 dpi	bi	8	75
720 × 720 dpi	uni	8	37
720 × 1440 dpi	bi	16	38
720 × 1440 dpi	uni	16	19
1440 × 1440 dpi	bi	32	18
1440 × 1440 dpi	uni	32	9

SOURCE: Roland DGA Corporation

Most inkjets have a high-speed option that changes the printer from unidirectional printing to bi-directional; the head or heads now print in both directions. (Unidirectional printing with Epsons is always from the parked-head position out toward the center of the printer.) This effectively doubles the print speed, but at a slight loss in quality, although careful use of the head alignment utility can minimize this quality drop.

For the photo-desktop category, the speed champ is clearly Canon. The i9900 Photo Printer has a rated 8 × 10 speed of approximately 50 seconds, with a 4 × 6 borderless print at 38 seconds. By comparison, the same-size 13 × 19 printer from Epson (2200) lists an 8 × 10 at either 2 minutes 6 seconds or 3 minutes 51 seconds, depending on the paper type and other variables.

What's the primary factor in determining print speed? Simple: the number of inkjet nozzles available. The more nozzles available shooting out ink over a wider printhead area, the faster the printing speed. You can easily see why the desktop Canons are so speedy: the i9900 has a total of 6,144 nozzles (768 × 8 colors), while its sister imagePROGRAF W2200 printer has even more (7,680 nozzles at 1,280 nozzles per color). To accommodate all these nozzles, the printheads are giant (over 1 inch wide). By comparison, the much-larger Epson 4000 printer has only 1,440 total nozzles and the even-larger Epson 7600 has only 672 total nozzles.

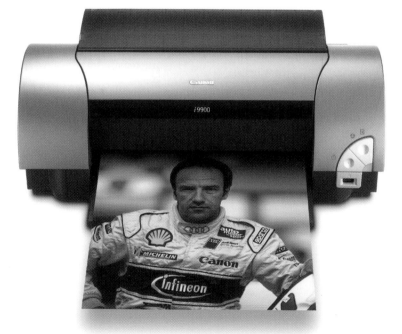

Canon's i9900 Photo Printer is the desktop inkjet speed champ.

Courtesy of Canon USA, Inc.

There are workarounds to deal with slow printing speed (beside buying a faster printer). I've gotten into the habit of having several in-progress projects ready that I can immediately move to while waiting for a slow print. Organizing my office studio, emptying the trash, that sort of thing (it also gets me out of my computer chair). If your printer allows it, you can also take advantage of unattended printing. You load several pieces of paper, hit the print button, and move onto other tasks. Finally, you can always print at a lower quality mode setting. Many photographer-artists report little or no visible difference in quality when using the next-lower setting.

7. How Easy to Set Up and Connect? How Big? How Noisy?

The first lesson that all serious digital printmakers learn is that, regardless of the marketing hype, digital printing is not a push-button operation. Don't expect magic right out of the box. To be sure, you will get something with your first print, and there will be some—perhaps many—who will be perfectly thrilled and satisfied with no need to explore further. But many others—undoubtedly you, if you've read this far—will need to learn and advance their knowledge to get the kind of superb prints that are achievable with inkjet.

Desktop

Printer Size: The size of the printer may be a minor issue for some, but if you're living in a one-room apartment and sleeping on a Murphy bed, you probably pay close attention to such things. While their shapes may vary, letter-size printers all take up about the same amount of desk space. They're approximately 16–17 inches wide, and the particular configuration of paper support and output tray extensions will determine how much desk depth you need. However, you should count on one entire section of desk devoted to an inkjet printer. Move up to a 13 × 19-inch, and you've increased your width to approximately 24 inches with only slightly more depth required. Only a few desktop printers don't fit this mold—the HP Designjet 30 is larger in comparison, and the Epson Stylus Pro 4000, which straddles the desktop/wide-format categories, is gigantic, measuring 33 inches wide and weighing a back-breaking 84 pounds.

Keep in mind that the same printer is sometimes available in two different sizes; only the media handling capacity is different. For instance, the HP Designjet 130 is the larger version of the Designjet 30. The same can be said for several Epsons; the wide-formats even use the same drivers and connection modes as their desktop siblings. The resulting short learning curve in moving from desktop to wide-format has been one key to the popularity of Epson's wide-format printers.

Setup: We've reached the point in desktop inkjet evolution where equipment setup is plug-and-play. Buy any desktop inkjet on the market, and you should be up and running in less than one-half hour. Unpack the box, hook up the printer to your computer, insert the ink cartridges, load the paper, install the printer software (from CD), maybe run a head-alignment check, and you're done. This doesn't mean that printing, itself, is plug-and-play—just the setup.

Compatibility: The first question is: "Are there drivers for my OS?" You must have printer drivers (or a RIP) that supports your computer's current operating system. This can be an important issue depending on where you are on the early-adoption-of-technology scale.

For example, after Mac OS X came out, there was only limited driver support at first by Epson for it. You either had to backtrack to an earlier OS or keep checking Epson's website to see if the OS X driver for your printer was available for downloading.

In general, most newer desktops come ready to play with all the usual OSs, both Windows and Mac; only Dell is Windows only. Again, you can usually download the most recent drivers from the printer manufacturer's website.

Want to skip the computer altogether and go direct-to-print from digital camera memory cards? Canon, Epson, HP, and Lexmark all allow this kind of direct-to-print capability. But, realize that most serious photographer-artists are doing significant image-editing with Photoshop or other software. They would rarely print raw captures right off a memory card. However, while most of these printers are aimed primarily at hobbyists, they are perfectly capable of acting like normal printers, too. Just check the specs first.

Photo-direct printers such as this HP Photosmart can read—and print from—digital camera memory cards. They can also print from a computer.

Connectivity (or Interface): This means how you physically connect the printer to your computer. Since the printer OEMs want to connect as many printers to as many computers as possible, they all offer the basic options: IEEE 1284 parallel (Windows) and USB (Windows and Mac). The newest printers also support FireWire ports. If you have an older printer like an Epson 3000, which only has parallel and Mac serial interfaces, you'll need to add an adapter card, cable, or box to get it to connect to the latest computers (plus up-to-date printer drivers).

Noise: All desktops make those characteristic back-and-forth, mechanical sounds when they print (see Table 6.3). It's a sound you get used to, and for some, it becomes the background noise of their lives!

Table 6.3 Noise Levels of Selected Printers (in printing mode)

Printer/Source	Max. Decibel Level (dB)[1]
Canon i9900	37 dB(A) 2 (in quiet mode)
HP Photosmart 7960	37-43 dB (depends on quality mode)
Lexmark P707	40 dB(A)
Epson 2100/2200	42 dB(A)
Canon W6200	55 dB
Epson 4000	50 dB(A)
Epson 7600/9600/10000	50 dB(A)
Roland Hi-Fi JET Pro II	65 dB
Common Noise Levels	
Quiet Whisper	15-20 dB
Airport terminal	55-65 dB
Subway	90 dB
Chickens inside a building	105 dB
Loud Rock Music	115 dB

[1] *A decibel (dB) is the unit used to measure the intensity of sound. Each increase of 6 decibels doubles the noise level. Twenty decibels is not twice as loud as 10 dB, but three times as loud. Sound above 130 decibels causes pain. 2 Because the human ear doesn't respond equally to all frequencies, sound meters use filters to approximate how the ear hears sound. The A weighting filter (dBA) is widely used.*

Wide-Format

Printer Size & Setup: As can be expected, wide-format inkjets are bigger and typically more complicated to set up and use (count on at least a half-day for setup). A drum-based printer like the IXIA is basically a big box about the size of a very large copying machine—four feet wide and three feet deep. Most plotter-type printers sit on their own stands, and their widths vary depending on the maximum print area. The Epson 7600 is 43 inches wide, and the 9600 is 64 inches. The Roland HiFiJET Pro II is 106 inches wide, the widest Mutoh Falcon II is 143 inches, and the largest HPs run anywhere from 78 to 96 inches wide. All are about four feet high including the stand, and they weigh in at anywhere from 200 to 550 pounds!

Add up the printer and stand, plus the space needed for paper loading and output, and any extras like a separate server or RIP station, and you'll probably end up devoting at least a portion of a room to a wide-format printer. However, some wide-format owners, like digital artist and educator Teri Brudnak, are able to maximize space by having their printers on rollers and moving them around as needed (see Figure 6.5).

Figure 6.5 Artist Teri Brudnak and her Roland Hi-Fi JET in her home studio.

Courtesy of Teri Brudnak

Connectivity/Compatibility: Most wide-formats have cross-platform OS support (Mac and Windows), although a few do not. There are more connectivity options with wide-formats. Besides standard printer drivers for direct printing, most wide-formats will give you built-in access or expansion slots for parallel, USB, FireWire, and even serial connections, plus internal or external connections (10/100base-T interfaces) for print servers, networks, and RIP drivers.

Even with the added complexities, once you nail down your workflow, wide-format operation is fairly smooth. In terms of noise, wide-format inkjets are only slightly louder than their desktop cousins. But you still have to learn to live with that bzzzz, bzzzz, bzzzz sound!

8. What About Printer Software, Drivers, and RIPs?

In addition to the required printer drivers, inkjet printers now include various software tools to make your printing more efficient (many will also come with bundled third-party software trials and demos).

Printer Management Software

Today's inkjet printers have very sophisticated software to help with various printing tasks. Take, for example, the *ink status monitor*. Lexmark's Ink Levels Indicator counts the number of dots you place and uses that to calculate the remaining ink. HPs use a smart chip on the ink cartridge to monitor how much ink has been used and how much is left. Additionally, smart chips in the HP printheads monitor the amount of ink that flows through the heads plus the status of the printhead's health. The Canon i9900 has a unique optical, low-ink sensor that pops a warning on the screen when an ink tank is getting low.

Wide-format printers offer even more-sophisticated usability features to make your print-making more efficient. For example, the HP Designjet 5500 not only checks the printhead to make sure that all nozzles are firing, but it will also try to recover as many nozzles as it can by priming and cleaning them while printing. It also has a "fault-tolerant" print mode that makes unattended printing a less-risky gamble. You go away for lunch, and the printer will not allow more than one bad print to come out. HP also offers a print-accounting function through a unique web-access interface. It not only tells you what the status of all your ink supplies is, but it can track how much ink you're using on any job, and how much paper you've used. It will even calculate exactly how much media is left on a roll whenever you change rolls, allowing you to swap media as often as you like without having to worry if you're going to run out of paper mid-print.

Joel Meyerowitz (left) and his archive manager John Saponara confer while printing with the HP Designjet 130, which includes an automatic, closed-loop, color calibration process.

Courtesy of Joel Meyerowitz Photography
www.joelmeyerowitz.com

Similarly, wide-format Epson Stylus Pros (including the 4000) have proprietary auto head alignment and nozzle-check technology. A built-in light-beam sensor precisely aligns and checks all color channels automatically, and it also reads the nozzle-check pattern and automatically cleans the printhead if any problems are found—even partially clogged nozzles.

The ColorSpan X-12 also has an image sensor that supports automatic features like analyzing and aligning the 12 printheads, eliminating banding by mapping out the sub-par nozzles, and providing color density data to external RIPs for linearization. Another separate sensor helps read color patches and ties into a color management system for color profiling.

And finally, as I already mentioned in Chapter 4, a few wide-formats, including the HP Designjet 5500 and 30/130, include an automatic closed-loop, built-in sensor color calibration process.

RIPs

As I explain elsewhere, you may not need a raster image processor (RIP). RIPs can cost as much or more than the printer itself, so weigh this carefully. In general, if you're primarily printing single, RGB bitmapped images without PostScript elements, and you're planning to use a desktop inkjet, an optional RIP is not a requirement. If, however, you want to wring the last 10 percent out of the image, a good RIP can help. For example, most RIPs can control very precisely how and where the inks are laid down. Of course, the built-in printer drivers do this, too, but it becomes more important if you use third-party inks and/or non-recommended papers that the printer wasn't designed for. Setting precise ink limits, defining at what points the light magenta and light cyans come into the image, mixing differing amounts of black with the other colors for dense shadows or "rich blacks"—these are the kinds of things RIPs can sometimes do better than the installed printer driver.

The Canon imagePROGRAF W6200 comes with a built-in Canon Graphic (PostScript) RIP.

Courtesy of Canon USA, Inc.

Only a few desktop inkjets come with optional software RIPs from the manufacturer (mainly HP and Epson), but many of the most popular printers (primarily Epson) are supported by the major third-party RIP makers.

Many wide-formats come with their own RIPs, or you can purchase a RIP separately. The Epson Stylus Pro wide-formats are sold without RIPs, but you can buy optional EFI software RIPs from Epson, or there are more than 50 third-party RIPs available for printing everything from fine art to signage. The HP Designjet 5500 comes in four different models (and in two different sizes of each) with the "ps" versions providing built-in Adobe PostScript 3 RIPs, and the non-ps versions ready to use an array of third-party RIPs. The Canon imagePROGRAF W6200 comes with its own Canon Graphic RIP.

What About Service, Repairs, and Warranties?

Just like with cars, you will want to take maintenance and service into account when picking a printer, especially a wide-format. In general, the more money you spend on the printer, the more important this becomes. One of the reasons that many printmakers abandoned IRIS printers was the cost and complexity of maintaining the already expensive machines. Printmaker Jan Steinman researched IRIS printers but ultimately bought a 50-inch Roland when he discovered that an IRIS service contract would run him $1,200 per month. (Lynn Lown, another professional printmaker, points out that the cost of a maintenance contract is a good indicator of how much maintenance an average machine will require.)

Being able to do simple parts replacements is an area where thermal inkjets have a slight advantage. When an Epson printhead goes bad, you have two options (after the warranty period): (1) spend the money to have it serviced or replaced at a service center or by an on-call technician, or (2) throw the printer away and buy another. Clearly, if you're paying $99 for a printer, you wouldn't spend double that for a new printhead, nor, conversely, would you trash a $5,000 printer because of a bad printhead. On thermal printers where the head is part of the ink cartridge, that becomes a non-issue; change cartridges and you've changed the printheads! With individual-color printheads, it's easy and relatively inexpensive to replace them.

Tech support is one reason to go with an all-OEM solution, and *not* to mix different printers, inks, and papers. The manufacturer will help you solve problems when you're using their products. As soon as you don't, fingers start pointing in other directions, and the tech support people are less willing—or able—to help.

All the major desktop printer-makers (Epson, HP, Canon, Lexmark, and Dell) offer one-year limited warranties. What this means is that you can exchange a bad printer for a new one if there are any manufacturer's defects, subject, of course, to certain conditions and restrictions. Sending back a printer due to ink clogging if you've used third-party inks won't work; that's one of the conditions. Wide-formats go even further in offering next-business-day exchange or on-site service under the standard one-year warranty, plus the ability to buy extended warranties and service contracts after that.

9. What Does It Cost?

You might think that this would be the first question, but I like to bury it at the bottom of the list. If all the questions above bring you to a choice between two printers, then make your decision on price. But never make a decision about buying or using an inkjet printer solely on cost. You may be getting a good deal, but if the printer doesn't solve your problems, what good is it?

"What Does It Cost?" is also a complex question. There's much more involved than just the cost of the printer.

Desktop

Virtually all desktop inkjet printers cost less than $1,000, most are under $500, and some are even under $50! In terms of a low printer-only cost, you really can't go wrong with the lower-end Canons, Epsons, HPs, Lexmarks, or Dells, which are made by Lexmark. They're practically giving these printers away. But remember, through a marketing strategy called *cost-shifting*, these printer manufacturers make their profit on the consumable supplies: the inks and the media. *That's* where your money will go, so make sure you figure in those costs, too.

Ink: Once you realize that ink is the most expensive part of desktop inkjet printing, you'll undoubtedly be looking very carefully at this element. Much has been said about the cost benefits of having a printer that uses individual ink cartridges or tanks. The argument goes: If you print images with a lot of blues, you will obviously run out of cyan ink before one of the other colors. And, if you have a printer that uses a combination-color cartridge (plus a separate black one), then you're basically throwing away all the unused ink when the printer indicates it's time to change ink cartridges. It's all or nothing with these combo-color cartridges. The solution is to have individual ink carts that can be changed separately as needed, and even though the savings are not always quite what people imagine, there are several desktop manufacturers (Canon, Epson, HP) who have picked up on the idea and now offer individual cartridges for some of their models.

Manufacturers have attacked this problem in a couple other ways, as well. The Epson 4000 (if you consider it a desktop printer) has not only very large ink cartridges (110 ml or 220 ml), but you can use either size at the same time. The list price of light magenta ink in a 220-ml cart (from Epson at the time of this writing) was $0.51 per milliliter; in a 110-ml cartridge, it was $0.64. In a 17-ml cart that goes into the Epson 2200, it was $0.67 per milliliter.

In the HP Designjet 30 printer, not only do the inks come in individual cartridges, but the colors typically used most often, such as light magenta and light cyan, are in larger (69-ml) carts, while others (cyan and magenta) come in smaller (28-ml) carts (see Figure 6.6).

However, the real savings with desktop inks is by getting rid of the expensive cartridges altogether. There are now several bulk-ink-delivery systems that allow you to buy and use large, more-economical ink bottles to provide bulk ink to the printer. Unfortunately, not all printers will accept this type of system, which I discuss in more detail in the following chapter.

Figure 6.6 Newer HP Designjet printers come with different-sized ink carts based on expected normal usage.

Media: The second important element in figuring ongoing inkjet costs is paper or media. Inkjet paper in cut sheets can run anywhere from $.50 to $5.00 or more *per sheet*, depending on the size and brand. Zeroing in on the U.S. standard letter size (8.5 × 11 inches), you should be able to find high-quality paper under $1.00 per sheet with quantity purchases.

One way to save money on paper is to buy it in long rolls. However, the selection for desktops is limited, and it's only practical if you have a roll adapter for your printer (unless you cut your own sheets from the roll and hand-feed them). Wide-formats, on the other hand, are set up for roll media, and that's one way they can economize paper costs. Owners of both types of printers have been known to use the wide-format's roll cutter to produce cut sheets as needed for their desktop printers.

Cost Per Print: Adding these two cost components (ink and media) together brings you to the important "Cost Per Print" (or cost per page). For one example, Epson America has provided a cost-per-print analysis for the Stylus Photo 2200 printer. In their analysis, an 8 × 10 glossy print runs $1.25 in consumable costs based on certain papers used. That is, if you make a print on the recommended paper with ink coverage that matches their assumed average image, then the total cost of the inks and the media used to produce the print should be $1.25.

So how does that $1.25 compare to other digital or traditional print costs? My local pro photo lab charges $5.50 for a single, Fuji Frontier 8 × 10 digital print from a digital file, $14.25 for a LightJet print of the same size, and $20 for a traditional enlarger print, although they are now phasing those out. Factor in the cost of the printer, software, training, and your time, and you can see where inkjet printing starts to pay for itself.

Other analyses by different media, ink, or print-device suppliers, of course, will vary, but you can use this kind of information to compare different printer/consumable options.

Wide-Format

Wide-format inkjet printers are *much* more expensive than desktops, running anywhere from $1,500 to $30,000. However, again, the purchase price is only part of the equation. Because wide-formats are widely used by commercial print-service providers who need to keep an eye on the bottom line, a Running Cost Analysis is a standard factor in selecting a wide-format. Similar to print speeds, ink and media costs are usually figured on a cost-per-square-foot basis. Since the calculations can get complex in determining ink and paper costs per unit area, Royce Bair at InkjetArt has come up with a handy Excel spreadsheet for doing it for the Epson Stylus Pro 7600 and 9600 models (only). You can find his "Cost Per Square Foot Calculator" at: www.inkjetart.com/pro/7600_9600/Pro_print_cost.xls.

Printmaker Jan Steinman has estimated that ink and media cost him about $2-$3 per square foot for the premium-quality media and pigment inks he runs through his Roland Hi-Fi JET. He knows he can reduce his costs to under $1 per square foot by using dye-based inks and cheaper media, but he recognizes that that would be unacceptable for his high-end market.

Cost Per Print can also be used for wide format. As an example, customers of ILFORD's Studio system (see "Printing Packages" for a description) are provided a cost-per-print analysis (see a partial example in Table 6.4). Only to be used as a guideline, these print costs are estimates (at the time of this writing) based on purchasing the ink and media directly from ILFORD. As you can see, an 8 × 10 RC paper print runs $0.91–$1.10 in

Table 6.4 Cost Per Print Using ILFORD Studio (media: RC paper - Roll)

Print Size (inches)	Studio 24 (Epson 7600)	Studio 44 (Epson 9600)
8 × 10	$1.10	$0.91
8.5 × 11	1.29	1.06
11 × 14	2.12	1.75
16 × 20	4.40	3.64
20 × 30	8.25	6.82
24 × 36	11.88	9.83
30 × 40	n/a	13.65
8 × 10 on 11 × 14	$1.38	1.19
11 × 14 on 16 × 20	2.74	2.37
16 × 20 on 20 × 24	5.00	4.24

[1] *Cost includes RC paper (100' roll) AND ink at standard price in U.S. dollars.*
[2] *Sizes assume full bleed unless otherwise specified.*
[3] *Ink usage is calculated at 2.6 ml/ft2 TOTAL for all 7 colors.*
[4] *Ink costs assume 110 ml cartridge for Studio 24 and 220 ml cartridge for Studio 44.*

SOURCE: ILFORD Imaging

consumable costs, depending on which printer and size of ink cartridge is used. ILFORD provides these cost estimates for different media types and for many more sizes than the ones I show.

Like high-ticket office equipment, wide-format printers can also be leased. For a few hundred dollars a month, you can have the latest in technology, and then trade up when you need to. (Of course, if you're interested in the total cost of providing a printmaking service to others, you must also add in basic business expenses like rent, waste, and overhead, but that's the subject of a different book.)

An Inkjet Summary

The days of wondering if inkjet would ever be good enough for high-quality digital output are definitely behind us. Inkjets are helping artists and photographers around the world produce work inexpensively, on-demand, and with great quality. The future for inkjet printers is only going to get rosier—more colors, better and longer-lasting inks, and more media choices. The best is yet to come.

How important is all this talk about inkjet printing equipment? It needs to be kept in perspective. As Santa Fe, New Mexico-based, fine-art digital printmaker Lynn Lown explains, "The printer is like a camera or a musical instrument; the operator is the key. A good printer or artist can make interesting pictures with simple tools. They have the hardware under control and can concentrate on ideas, images, and vision. Of course, that's easy to say."

Printing Packages

An inkjet printing option that's aimed primarily at professional photographers or photo studios is the turnkey printer package. Here are two systems that combine existing hardware and software into integrated solutions:

Epson Gemini: Marketed as an alternative to sending out to traditional photo labs, the Gemini system was in the middle of a complete update at the time of this writing. The original system included two Epson Stylus Pro 5500 inkjet printers, a PC server, proprietary software, an uninterrupted power supply, and a touch screen control for the server. An internal modem dialed up Epson and ordered its own supplies. You couldn't buy it; you leased it with a monthly charge depending on the amount of supplies used.

The rumor was that the new and improved system would be based on the Epson 4000 printer and that you could actually buy it in addition to leasing.

ILFORD Studio: ILFORD's version of this concept is its Studio Professional Digital Output system, which, at this time, is comprised of (1) *either* an Epson Stylus Pro 7600 or 9600 printer, (2) ILFORD RIPSTAR Studio RIP (non-PostScript, RGB and CMYK) with built-in profiles for (3) ILFORD media, which must be purchased separately, and (4) a complete installation and support package.

The system costs $5,399 (with Epson 7600) or $7,199 (with Epson 9600), and those prices include installation, software, hardware maintenance training, and one year of unlimited technical support. ILFORD also has leasing programs available. There is no fancy box or container as with the Epson Gemini system; these are all separate items.

OEM Wrapup

At the risk of oversimplifying what is a very complex and ever-evolving subject, let me offer a few words about the major inkjet brands (in alphabetical order) and their roles in the world of high-quality inkjet printing.

Canon: Canon introduced the world to its BubbleJet thermal technology way back in 1981. It took a while for Canon to build up its momentum in the high-quality digital printing area, but it has done so with a splash, introducing a string of innovative and high-quality printers. While Canon doesn't have quite the market penetration that Epson or HP has, their emergence onto the digital-print playing field can only be good for all of us. Desktop and wide-format.

ColorSpan: MacDermid ColorSpan's Giclée PrintMakerFA was the first wide-format digital printer created specifically for the fine-art market (in 1998), and there are still lots of happy users spinning its high-quality drum. However, that printer is no longer being manufactured, and, like the IRIS/IXIA, represents a printing style (drum-based) that has become a deadend over time. However, ColorSpan continues to move forward with several very capable plotter-type inkjet printers in its DisplayMaker line. Wide-format only.

Dell: Dell is the newcomer to this list, having only entered the printer market with a few desktops (all made by Lexmark) in March 2004. They finally released a "photo" all-in-one printer mid-2004, and it will be interesting to see how their model (of selling direct) works out in the long run. Consumer desktops; Windows only.

ENCAD: ENCAD, which is now a wholly owned subsidiary of Kodak, has a long history of making wide-format inkjet printers, mostly for the commercial and outdoor signage markets. However, its NovaJet 1000i, the first printer developed in collaboration with Kodak, offers alternatives to photographer-artists and print-service providers looking for speedy production machines. Wide-format only.

The ENCAD 1000i is the first printer developed in collaboration with Kodak, which owns ENCAD.

Courtesy of ENCAD, Inc.

Epson: Epson is a dominant force in the high-quality inkjet printing world. They are the ones who basically invented photorealistic inkjet printing. Always an innovative leader, Epson makes great printers, and you can make great prints using them. Epson is constantly upping the ante with its new models, and with the introduction of its reasonably priced Stylus Pro 7600 and 9600 models, as well as the newer 4000, Epson is helping to bridge the gap between wide-format and desktop printers. One of Epson's main challenges is juggling the diverse needs of both consumer and professional customers, and keeping them all happy. Desktop and wide-format.

Epson's Stylus Pro 7600 (right) and 9600 were the first low-cost wide-format printers.

Courtesy of Epson America, Inc.

HP: HP, which is larger than any other company on this list, is the world leader in many market segments of the digital imaging and printing field, and it has a large base of satisfied users for its various products, which are well-known for being reliable and reasonably priced. HP has now finally focused its considerable engineering and marketing muscle onto the photo/fine-art arena, and its recent product introductions, both at the prosumer and professional level (including the popular Designjet 30/130), have been well-received. The sleeping giant has awakened! Desktop and wide-format.

IRIS/IXIA: The IRIS is the printer that started this whole inkjet phenomenon, and it has been reincarnated as the IXIA from Improved Technologies, which is selling the expensive devices to fine-art photographers, artists, and printmakers. There are still many IRIS printers in use out there, but as they wear out, printmakers are either trading them in for the newer IXIA or shifting to other styles and brands of inkjet printers. Drum-based only.

Lexmark: Lexmark is well-known for its no-nonsense, inexpensive, desktop inkjet printers. However, it has been an innovator all along (first 1200-dpi printer, first sub $100 inkjet printer, first photo-direct printer), and they're slowly attempting to win over photographer-artists. With features like 4800-dpi resolution, variable ink droplets, and six colors (finally), Lexmark offers a low-initial-cost solution. Consumer desktops only.

HP's Photosmart 7960 printer is just one of many examples of the company's focus on photo market.

Courtesy of Hewlett-Packard Company

Mimaki: Another relatively unknown commodity for most photographer-artists, Mimaki makes excellent wide-formats, particularly their JV4 line with its three models: JV4-130 (54 inches wide), JV4-160 (64 inches), and JV4-180 (75 inches). Used mostly for commercial signage applications, they are perfectly capable of producing fine-art prints (1440 × 1440 max resolution). Interestingly, Harvest Productions has started making fine-art prints with the JV3 solvent-based inkjet printer. Mimakis include some innovative features like being able to combine two separate inksets of three different types into 10 printing variations. Wide-format only.

Mutoh: Like Mimaki, Mutoh is primarily known for its wide-format printers used in the point-of-purchase and poster industry. However, they're now also targeting the photo/fine-art market with their Falcon II piezo printer (see Dot Krause's use of this printer for her mural project elsewhere in the book). Featuring 8-color (CMYKLcLmOG), variable-dot printing, the Falcon II comes in 50-, 64-, and 87-inch widths with 2880 × 1440 dpi maximum resolution, the same printheads that are in the Epson 10000, and the ability to run both dye and pigment inks. Wide-format only.

Roland: Roland has staked out a strong position in the high-quality, wide-format inkjet category. As a favorite brand with many serious photographer-artists, Roland has no current plans to enter the desktop market, but intends, instead, to keep improving their wide-format pigment-based printers, solvent printers, and related products. Wide-format only.

We've been talking a lot about inks and media for inkjet printing. Let's now get more details on choosing your consumables.

7

Choosing Your Consumables

Anyone who does a lot of inkjet printing discovers very quickly that the consumable supplies (ink and media) are important keys to the whole process. Not only are they typically the most expensive aspect of digital printing in the long run, but the ink and paper will also make or break the quality of your final output.

Inks

Stating the obvious, it's important to remember that all inkjet printers use ink to form the image—not electrostatically charged toners, not RGB laser lights, not photosensitive silver halide, but liquid inks. (Solid ink printers use resin-based inks that turn into liquid after heating, but I won't be covering them here. See Chapter 2.) Which ink is the question, and there are plenty of choices. (Note: As with printers, this chapter is a snapshot of what's available at the time of this writing. Check with suppliers for their latest products or with the DP&I.com website (www.dpandi.com).

Inkjet ink formulation is a complex, scientific undertaking, with modern day alchemists spending their days paying microscopic attention to chemical and physical ink properties such as dispersants, solvents, pH buffers, solubilizing agents, viscosity modifiers, antioxidants, biocides, and more. While making informed choices about which inks to use doesn't require a Ph.D. in chemistry, a certain amount of knowledge is necessary.

Ink Components, Dyes vs. Pigments

Inks are made up of two main components: a *colorant* and a *vehicle* or *carrier*. The vehicle is the transport medium that holds or contains the colorant, and it's either solvent- or water-based, with water (*aqueous*) being the dominant type for the kind of printing that's the subject of this book, whether dye- or pigment-based—*all* Epson inks are aqueous. (Solvent-based printers are preferred for various types of commercial and sign making applications and are sometimes used for fine art.)

Added to the water base are other ingredients or additives such as *humectants, surfactants,* and *penetrants* that help the inks perform better in an inkjet-printing environment.

The colorant (technically called *dyestuffs*) gives the ink its color. Based on what we've already learned, the colorant of an ink absorbs certain wavelengths of visible light and reflects others that are then perceived by our eyes as color. Colorants come in two basic types for inkjet printing: *dyes* and *pigments,* and each has its strengths and weaknesses. See Figure 7.1 for a visual comparison of the two types.

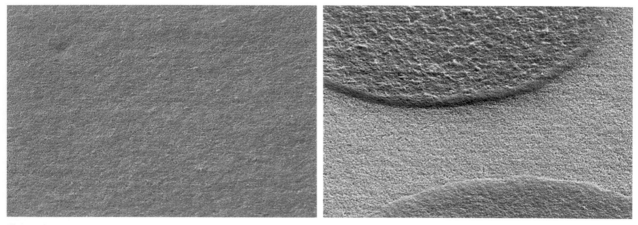

Figure 7.1   These two microscopic views show the difference between dye-based and pigment inks. Left: Dyes interact with the paper to form a uniform surface. Right: Pigment particles form a thick film on the surface of the paper.

Courtesy of Hewlett-Packard Company

Dye-Based Inks

The first inkjet inks used for photography and fine art were water-soluble dyes. In fact, some early artists even experimented with running food coloring through their IRIS printers! Dye-based inks are still a large part of inkjet printing. All thermal desktops (Canon, HP, Lexark) come ready to print with dye-based inks. Epson desktops come either in dye or pigment types.

Dyes are made up of extremely small, individual colorant molecules, and because they penetrate below the surface of the paper coating, dye-based inks provide excellent image quality with rich color depth and a gloss that's usually more uniform than with pigments. Dyes also work very well on uncoated fine-art papers that absorb the ink; the ink droplets bleed a little and tend to cover up certain printer-based problems like low dpi resolution.

The main disadvantages of using dyes for printing are higher susceptibility to light fading (in most cases), higher susceptibility to humidity influences(in most cases), higher susceptibility to environmental gases, like ozone (in most cases), and greater variability of longevity with differing media

The reason I say "in most cases" is that, in terms of longevity, certain dye-based inks and media combinations are definitely getting better. As already explained in the last chapter, HP has carefully matched its newest "durable dye" inks with specific HP media and swellable coatings in order to come up with combinations that rival the permanence predictions of popular pigment-ink solutions. The way this works is that the dyes interact with ingredients in the coated paper to gain the permanence. Print those same dyes on a different paper, and the projected permanence is significantly reduced.

Third-party ink suppliers have also gotten on board by producing improved dye-based color inksets. Futures Wales, Ltd., for example, released Futures Ink Wide Gamut dye-based inkset in mid-2004 claiming that it provided a wider color gamut than other dye inks, and that it was as durable as the leading pigments.

Pigment Inks

Unlike dyes, a pigment is a solid material comprised of many colorant molecules tightly bound together and "stacked up" in a particular order into a single particle. These "super-molecules" (actually crystalline solids) are more complex and are much larger than their dye counterparts. While a dye molecule might be 1.5 to 4 nanometers in size (a nanometer is 1/1,000th of a micrometer or a micron, which is 1/1,000th of a millimeter), pigment particles are typically in the .05–.2 micron range or 50–200 nanometers. Even though this might seem large in relation to dye molecules, these pigment particles, which have been carefully ground down to microfine sizes, are easily small enough to flow through the smallest 10-micron inkjet nozzle orifice that is 50–100 times as large (see Figure 7.2).

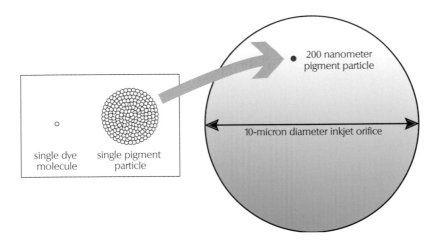

Figure 7.2 A relatively large pigment particle (left) is still very small compared to an inkjet nozzle orifice. As ink researcher David Matz likes to explain it: Think of a golf ball falling into a six-foot-diameter cup.

Recreated from diagrams of Dr. Ray Work (left) and Dr. David Matz

200 nanometer
pigment particle

10-micron diameter inkjet orifice

single dye
molecule

single pigment
particle

Because pigment particles are insoluble in water, pigments remain in a solid state dispersed throughout the liquid vehicle that will deliver them to the paper. One goal of a good pigment ink is to keep the particles suspended for a long period of time. Epson uses microencapsulation with pigment particles encased in a polymer resin medium to help with this. (Not all of Epson's pigment inks are *microencapsulated*. The Matte Black in the UltraChrome inkset, for example, is not, which makes it problematic for use on glossy or semiglossy papers where there can be "rub off" of the ink without a top coating of some kind.)

The main advantage of pigment inks is that, in general, they are more stable than dyes, being more lightfast and less sensitive to environmental gases. Why? Due to the relationship between surface area and volume, the smaller the particle size, the greater the relative surface area, and the more likely that a photo-fading agent like light or a chemical attack agent like ozone can reach it. Since pigments are more complex with many more molecular components, gases will only reach a small percentage of the colorant molecules while leaving the others untouched. In addition, the electronic structure of pigments is less vulnerable to light. The result is that, in general, pigments fade more slowly than dyes.

When it comes to humidity sensitivity, again pigments are usually better. With dyes, the printed colorant can begin to "redissolve" in high humidity and become "mobile," the last thing you want on a print. Pigments don't dissolve in aqueous vehicles, so they can't do this when exposed to high humidity.

But there are downsides to pigments: The larger particles of pigmented inks cause more light scattering at the surface, which reduces color range or *color gamut* and makes some colors look weaker or duller (see Figure 7.3). Rich reds are particularly hard to print with some pigments.

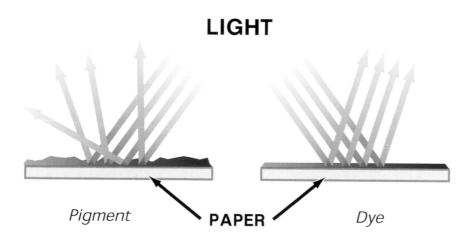

LIGHT

Pigment   **PAPER**   *Dye*

Figure 7.3 Although the paper surface itself also plays a very important role, the larger particles of pigmented inks (left) typically create irregular surfaces and more light scattering, causing colors to look duller. A print with dye inks (right) has a smoother surface that reflects the light back uniformly with more strength and saturation.

Courtesy of Lyson, Inc.

Other pigment problems include:

- A greater tendency toward *metamerism* (shifting colors under different types of lights— see other references in this book). This is a common complaint of the earlier Epson pigmented printers (such as 2000P) with neutral tones (also skintones) that turned green under natural daylight. The more recent Epson printers (2200, 4000, 7600, 9600) with their newer UltraChrome inks, are designed to help reduce this problem.

- Pigments tend to sit on top of the paper forming irregularities on the surface. In fact, some—not all—pigments are not recommended for glossy papers since they either do not dry completely, do not adhere well, or they exhibit what's called *gloss differential* or *bronzing*, where one part of the image will have a sheen or look duller and obviously different than another. (One solution to this problem from Epson is found on the R800 printer that includes not only special High-Gloss pigment inks but also a separate Gloss Optimizer layer that coats the surface.) The flip side of this problem is that pigments are also not recommended for use on uncoated, fine-art papers like Somerset Velvet or Arches Cold Press;

the inks tend to get lost in the paper's fibers and look muddy. Most pigment inks are designed to go on coated papers (Epson Durabrite pigments are an exception; they're designed for uncoated papers.).

■ A related issue with some pigments used on glossy or luster-type papers is smudging or "rub-off" where the ink can smear, especially in darker or black areas. Newer pigment ink formulations such as Epson's microencapsulated inks that "stick" better to the paper have attempted to fix this problem.

■ Pigment ink particles can separate or "settle out" over time, especially if the printer is not used on a regular basis, and this can cause inconsistent printing including weak colors. Tony Martin, President of ink supplier Lyson USA, has a couple of good analogies to illustrate this: While dye inks are like Kool-Aid or apple juice that, once stirred, never separates again, pigment inks are more like the sandy water in a river or at the beach. If you look closely, you can see the particles of sand dispersed in the water. One easy solution to the settling problem is to occasionally shake pigment ink carts or tanks, although Martin advises that it is difficult to sufficiently re-disperse the pigments with this method so that the ink returns completely to its original color intensity.

In theory, the basic trade-off between dyes and pigments has traditionally been: Dye-based inks are more "colorful" on a wide range of media but also prone to being less stable or permanent, while pigment-based inks may offer less color gamut, but they are more light-fast, humidity fast, and gas fast (see Figure 7.4). In reality, the gap is closing, and ink manufacturers are continually trying to come up with compromise solutions between color gamut and permanence.

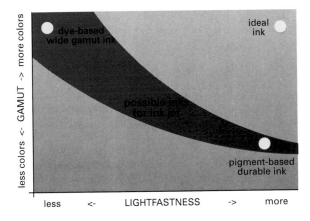

Figure 7.4 Photoconservator Martin Juergens' view of the basic trade-offs between inkjet dyes and pigments.

Courtesy of Martin Juergens

Dyes and pigments can also be mixed together for a specific result. For example, third-party ink supplier MediaStreet.com has formulated its popular Generations brand (G4, G5, G6 or G-Chrome) pigmented inks to include black-ink options that are 75-percent pigment and 25-percent dye in order to boost density and visual richness. (The other blacks and colors are all 100-percent pigment, and other Generations inksets still include the 100-percent pigment black.) The only downside to such mixtures is that there can be uneven results when one ink component changes or fades before another. MediaStreet, however, claims that their hybrid blacks still exceed the same 100 years of display life (tested by Wilhelm Imaging Research) as the other colors do, and they still offer all-pigment blacks, too. (Note that multi-monochromatic inksets are handled in a slightly different way: Pigmented black ink is mixed with a clear base stock to create the different gray shades or densities.)

Although several wide-format printers use pigmented OEM ink, the only desktop OEM option for using pigment particles as colorants is with Epson. Epson claims that all three versions or generations of its pigmented inks (Archival, DuraBrite, and UltraChrome) are 100-percent pigment-based, although many wonder about this based on the fading behaviors of some of the colors, specifically the UltraChrome yellow. For third-party pigment ink suppliers, see the next section, "OEM or Third-Party Inks."

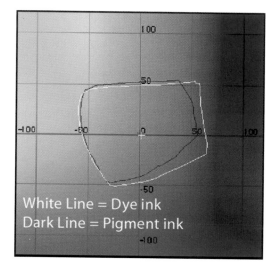

Lyson's Tony Martin points out a failing of simple 2D color gamut diagrams comparing, in this case, one OEM pigment ink to a third-party dye-based one. Although the gamuts apparently look similar, Martin explains that an actual print made with the dye inks was much more intense and brilliant. His conclusion? 2D gamut charts without the third brightness dimension do not tell the whole story between dye- and pigment-based inks. 3D charts would be more accurate.

Courtesy of Lyson, Inc.

OEM or Third-Party Inks?

The major inkjet printer manufacturers (OEMs) have inks they want you to use with their printers, and many desktops come with a starter set of cartridges ("carts") ready for installing and printing. For many people, this is all they want to know about inks, and they are content to use these standard recommended inks that can usually do a perfectly good job of making prints. After all, the OEMs have carefully researched and developed ink formulations to best match their equipment and their recommended media. For example, thermal inkjets involve the quick heating and cooling of the printhead elements to create the ink droplets. Consequently, thermal inks have to be carefully formulated with this in mind. Epson's piezo ink technology, on the other hand, is pressure-based, which has its own requirements. This is one reason why you can't simply switch inks between inkjet technologies.

While OEMs don't like it when you bypass their ink supplies (and threaten to penalize you for doing so by voiding the printer's warranty), there are some legitimate reasons to consider using third-party inks: *reduced cost, increased color gamut* and *permanence*, and *special uses*.

Warning: Putting third-party inks in your inkjet printer is not without risk. Besides potentially ruining the printer, you may be in violation of the printer's warranty, although the OEMs have little legal foundation for this. Check the compatibility specs of any third-party inks before using them.

Cost: One reason OEMs push their inks is because they make a lot of money on them. Walk into any office super store and take a good look at the inkjet supplies rack (see Figure 7.5). It will quickly become obvious that all those $35 ink-cartridge packages (plus the paper) are what provide the profits for much of the inkjet printing business. It's the old Gillette business model at work: Sell cheap razors but expensive blades.

Figure 7.5   Cartridge inks are a major profit center for the inkjet industry.

If you feel like you're feeding your printers liquid gold, consider using third-party inks that can reduce your ink bill by as much as 50–75 percent or more. A flourishing mini-industry has developed that provides compatible, non-OEM inks in various ways to consumers who want to save a significant amount of money. For example, ink supplier MediaStreet.com likes to point out that while a $100 bottle of champagne equates to $3.94 per ounce, a typical OEM desktop ink cartridge is about $24.00 per ounce. Using one of their bulk-ink systems (see below) can save you up to 90 percent in ink costs compared to single-use OEM cartridges, MediaStreet claims.

Increased Color Gamut and Permanence: Certain third-party, dye-based inks are designed to exceed OEM ink permanence. Suppliers such as Futures, Lyson, Luminos, MediaStreet, Pantone, and MIS offer extended-life dye alternatives to OEM inks (see Table 7.1). Third-party pigment inks that either match or exceed OEM color gamuts and/or longevity predictions are also available from several companies (see Table 7.2 later in this chapter).

Specialty Uses: There are some applications where the OEM inks just can't do the job as well as third-party inks. Multi-monochromatic black-and-white printing is a good example. With the exception of certain printers like HP's 3-black-ink Photosmart 7960, it's difficult to get the highest-quality black-and-white prints out of inkjet printers using stock

Table 7.1 Sample Third-Party, DYE-BASED Color Ink Brands

Ink Supplier	Brand	Acceptable Printers	Works Well with These Papers	Profiles Provided?	Comes In
Futures/EIC	Futures Ink Wide Gamut	all Piezo	various	yes	carts & bulk bottles & complete bulk system
www.futuresinkjettechnology.com					
Luminos	Preservation Series	select Epsons	Preservation media	yes, for Preservation media	carts
www.lumijet.com					
Lyson	Fotonic Photo	select Epsons	Lysonic media	yes, for Lyson media	carts & bulk bottles
www.lyson.com	Lysonic Archival	select Epsons	Lysonic media	yes, for Lyson media	carts & bulk bottles
MediaStreet *www.mediastreet.com*	Plug-N-Play (OEM-compatible inks)	various	various	no	carts & bulk bottles
MIS	factory originals	various	various	no	carts
www.inksupply.com	aftermarket	various	various	yes	carts
	OEM-compatible	various	various	yes	bulk bottles

color inks (some RIPs can help). However, there are numerous third-party solutions that expand the possibilities significantly. For examples and more about multi-monochromatic specialty printing, see Chapter 11.

The three main ways of using third-party inks are with *replacement cartridges, refill kits,* and *bulk-ink systems.*

Replacement Cartridges

Non-OEM replacement cartridges come in rebranded, OEM-compatible cartridges from ink dealers and makers (including MediaStreet, inkjetART.com, Inkjet Goodies, InkjetMall, Luminos, MIS, Pantone, and Lyson) for most of the popular inkjet printers in use today. The cartridges are either new or recycled, filled with non-OEM inks, and usually less expensive than the real deal. (You can also buy factory-original OEM cartridges from several of these and other suppliers.)

The key issues to consider are: match (How close are they in terms of quality to the OEM inks they're replacing? Are they made to OEM specifications?), *compatibility* (Are they 100-percent compatible with your inkjet printer, and is there a guarantee backing this up?), and *age* (How old is the ink?).

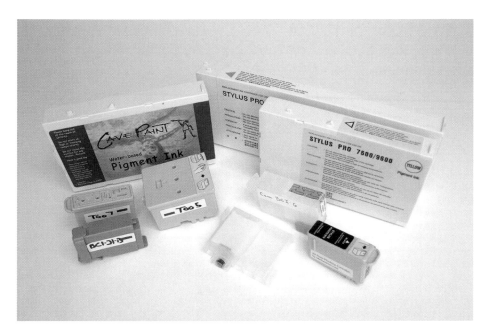

Non-OEM replacement carts come in different shapes and sizes. Shown are ink carts from Lyson, Media Street, and MIS Associates.

You can also buy virgin, empty cartridges for do-it-yourself filling with the inks of your choice from some ink suppliers like MediaStreet, Inkjet Goodies, and MIS.

Refills

If you don't mind the sometimes messy and exacting work of refilling cartridges by hand, you might consider one of the refill kits that are produced by companies like MediaStreet, WeInk.com, and MIS. These kits (see Figure 7.7) typically include syringes and blunt needles, empty cartridges, and replacement inks for select Epson and Canon printers.

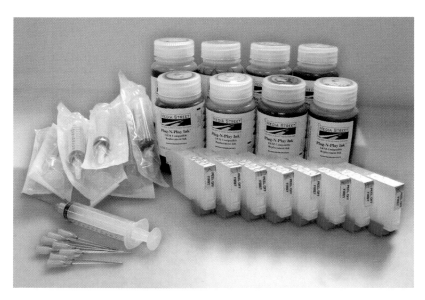

Figure 7.7 A MediaStreet Plug-n-Play refill kit from Inkjet Goodies for filling your own ink cartridges.

Courtesy of inkjetgoodies.com

Fooling the Printer

Many of the newer inkjet printers have smart-chipped cartridges with built-in microchips (Epson's are called *Intellidge chips*). Although they are advertised to help keep track of ink usage, one maybe-not-so-unintended result has been to thwart the use of cartridge refills and third-party inks. But, as soon as each generation of chips appears, entrepreneurs get busy and come up with ways to defeat and fool them.

Two inventions are auto-reset chips and chip reprogrammers or resetters that: (1) allow cartridges to be refilled, (2) make it possible to use certain bulk-ink systems and non-OEM replacement cartridges, or (3) let you get the last few prints out of a cartridge that would normally be thrown away with some ink remaining (as they are designed to be).

For example, MIS Associates sells three chip-resetting products for Epson-only inkjet printers:

Auto Reset Chips: Auto reset chips reset the ink level to full when the printer power is turned on or when a cleaning cycle is completed. They are now used in the MIS Continuous Flow Systems as well as bulk systems by other suppliers. Not recommended for refilling.

F-16 Chip Resetter: This is a hardware device that connects to the printer (Epson only) and works on Macs and PCs. It will reset the printer even if the Red "out of ink" light is on. Meant for use with MIS Continuous Flow Systems only, not for refilling.

SK168 Universal Chip Resetter: The SK168 is a self-contained unit with an internal battery and seven small pins that contact the cartridge chip (see Figure 7.6). When held against the chip for 6 seconds, it puts the chip back to its electronic FULL setting. Requires that cartridges be removed from the printer; not ideal for use with Continuous Flow Systems; great for use with refilling.

Figure 7.6 The MIS SK168 Universal Chip Resetter.

Courtesy of MIS Associates, Inc.

Bulk-Ink Systems

Bulk-ink delivery systems—variously called by their popular acronyms *CIS*, *CFS*, or *CRS*—are a definite trend among high-volume printmakers and are popular for two reasons: cost and convenience. The cost savings are obvious. Because you buy the ink in bulk, it's cheaper (the systems themselves can cost up to $350 for desktop printers, more for wide-format). And because you only need to hook up the system once and then replenish or top off the bottled ink as needed, it's much more convenient than continually having to buy, change, or refill cartridges. Another advantage is that long, unmanaged print runs can occur; you can't print all night with tiny carts, especially individual ones, but you can with a CIS.

There are several manufacturers of these bulk-ink systems, and you will also find them sold under different rebranded names. They all work the same basic way: External reservoir bottles supply ink to the printer via tubing that then connects to special cartridges that replace the printer's original ones. Here are three of the key bulk-ink players:

MediaStreet Niagara II and III Continuous Ink Flow System: The Niagara system replaces single-use inkjet cartridges with a specially modified OEM-compatible cartridge that is connected to individual reservoir bottles of ink (4-, 8-, and 16-oz.). Once installed, maintaining the ink level is as simple as visually checking each bottle.

The Niagara II is custom-built and pre-assembled for a specific Epson or Canon inkjet printer. The system comes with a choice of Generations G-Chrome, Enhanced Generations, Generations ProPhoto, Generations Elite, or Plug-N-Play inks.

The Niagara III only differs from the Niagara II in that it does not include the pre-filled carts.

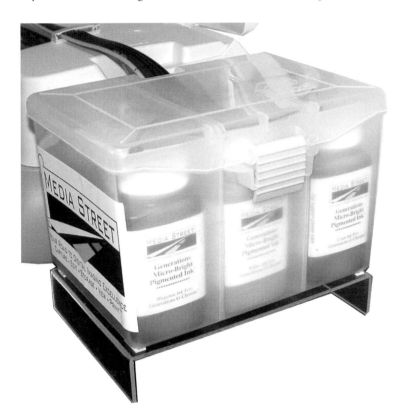

MediaStreet's Niagara II Continuous Flow Ink System that replaces standard Epson or Canon ink carts.

Courtesy of MediaStreet.com

MIS Continuous Flow Systems: Ink supplier MIS Associates was the first to create a commercial bulk-ink system, and they sell their own brand of continuous flow systems (CFS) for select Epson (only) printers, both desktop and wide-format (32 different models as of this writing). MIS Continuous Flow Systems come either prefilled with one of three types of ink (dye-based, archival color, or black-and-white) or empty with the tubes attached and with auto reset chips. Complete systems have everything you need with inks included. Estimated installation time is 30 minutes. Cartridges draw ink from a set of 4-oz. bottles kept next to the printer.

MIS will even sell you the parts to make your own CFS system. If you want to make a CFS for a printer that they do not support, this is one way to do it.

NoMoreCarts CIS: Continuous Inking Systems of North Carolina started marketing their continuous inking system (CIS) for selected Epson inkjet printers soon after MIS launched theirs. The NoMoreCarts CIS can be purchased through dealers who offer it either under that name or as a rebranded item such as InkjetArtery from inkjetART.com or LumiFlo Fluidic Ink Delivery System from Luminos. With these CIS systems, the cartridge chips for the newer printers always read full, they require no separate chip resetters, and they can run with any type of computer-printer connection regardless of the platform (Mac or PC) or OS. CIS systems from dealers usually come complete with a set of introductory inks.

Other popular bulk-ink systems include: Camel Ink Systems CRS (by WeInk), JetBlaster, and a bulk-ink system by American Imaging (see Figure 7.8).

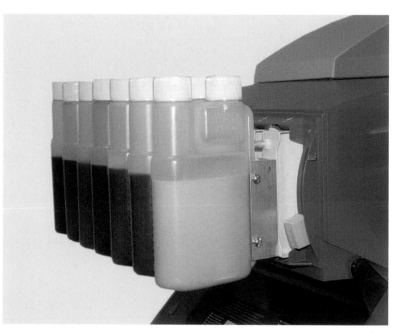

Figure 7.8 American Imaging's bulk-ink system for Epson 7600/9600 has an ingenious design with no tubes and no worries about correct ink reservoir height, which can sometimes cause problems.

Courtesy of American Imaging Corp.

Keep in mind that only specific printer models (mostly Epsons and some Canons for desktop) are adaptable for bulk-ink delivery use, depending on the physical design of the printer housing and, more importantly, the method of bypassing the printer's designated ink cartridges. Check with each manufacturer or dealer to make sure your intended printer is on the list.

Bulk Ink for Wide-Format

While bulk-ink systems have gained popular fame with users of desktop inkjet printers looking to circumvent expensive, single-use cartridges, these systems are now also available from the major suppliers for wide-format printers as well. For example, MediaStreet, MIS, WeInk, M&M Studios, and American Imaging (Symphonic Inks) offer systems for the Epson 7600/9600 and other models. Bulldog Products sells its Easy Fill Pro system for both aqueous and solvent-based printers including—besides Epson—Roland, Mutoh, and Mimaki.

Pennsylvania printmaker Diana York of Hawk Mountain Editions and Hawk Mountain Art Papers runs Generations 4 inks in both an Epson 9600 with an MIS CFS and an Epson 9500 with a JetBlaster system (see Figure 7.9).

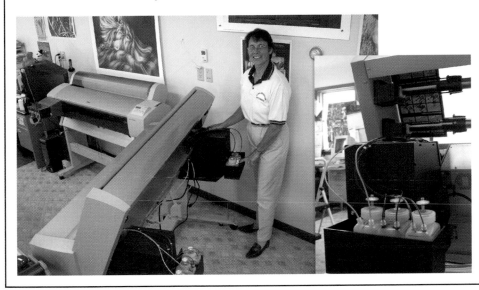

Figure 7.9 Diana York in her printmaking studio standing behind an Epson 9500 outfitted with a JetBlaster bulk-ink system. Detail at right.

Courtesy of Diana York
www.hawkmtnartpapers.com

Third-Party Overview

The use of third-party inks is increasing on some fronts, especially as photographer-artists become more sophisticated and more familiar with digital printing processes. However, you must weigh the disadvantages as well as the advantages. A few observations:

■ *Source:* Who makes which brand of ink is a closely guarded secret. There are only a handful of primary ink manufacturers, and they provide the finished inks or the raw ingredients to the well-known OEMs and third-party marketers alike. Suppliers and percentages of business held by each are constantly changing, so it's fruitless to try to pin down the ink sourcing with any accuracy.

■ *Quality:* With third-party inks, you may or may not get the same quality as you would using the OEM-recommended inks that are made for the printer. OEMs maintain that they are selling printer-ink-media systems, and that you forfeit consistent results and quality if you break that chain. That's why the best third-party inks try to exactly match the OEM's specifications for physical properties (density, viscosity, drying time, surface tension, and so on). The only way to know is to try them and find out for yourself.

Conversely, this is also one advantage of a bulk-ink system. It's well-reported that there are sometimes differences in color and quality from one OEM ink cartridge to another. Whether it's due to changing ink suppliers or other obscure reasons, the fact is that two

Table 7.2 Sample Third-Party PIGMENT Color Ink Brands

Ink Supplier	Brand	Acceptable Printers	Works Well with These Papers	Profiles Provided?	Comes In
American Imaging Corp.	Symphonic Me2	Epson 2200, 7600, 9600	various	no	bulk bottles
www.inkjetcolorsystems.com	Symphonic: Me2 Ultra	Epson 7600, 9600	various	no	bulk bottles
	Symphonic Ultra IV	various Epson	various	no, requires RIP	bulk bottles
Lyson *www.lyson.com*	Cave Paint/ PhotoChrome	Epson UltraChrome	various	yes	carts & bulk bottles
M & M Studios *www.indelibleinks.com*	Indelible Fine Art Inks	select Epsons	fine art, canvas only	no	carts & bulk bottles
www.chameleoninkjetinks.com	Chameleon	select Epsons	various	no	carts & bulk bottles
MediaStreet	Generations G-Chrome G6	various Epson	(RC) photo paper	no	carts & bulk bottles
www.inksupply.com	Generations ProPhoto G5	various	(RC) photo paper	no	carts & bulk bottles
	Generations Enhanced G4	various	various	no	carts & bulk bottles
	Generations Standard G3	various	various	no	carts & bulk bottles
	Generations Elite (Outdoor)	various	various	no	carts & bulk bottles
MIS	Glossy Pigments (GP)	select desktop Epsons	matte or glossy	yes	carts & bulk bottles
www.inksupply.com	7600 Archival Epsons	UltraChrome	matte or glossy	yes	carts & bulk bottles
	Perpetual Archival	all Epsons	various, not glossy	yes	bulk bottles
	Original Archival	all Epsons	various, not glossy	yes	bulk bottles
Pantone *www.pantone.com*	ColorVantage	select Epsons	various	yes	carts

seemingly identical ink cartridges bought from the same lot at the same time from the same source can—and do—sometimes vary. A bulk-ink system can mitigate this problem because you buy ink in larger quantities to spread over more prints before a change is needed.

There are other ways around the quality concern. Some people set up bulk-ink systems on their desktop printers and fill the bottles with cheaper-per-unit ink removed from the larger cartridges used on other printer models of the same type. This can only be done with same-generation inks—Epson UltraChrome, for example. A variation on this theme for wide-formats is simply to use larger-capacity cartridges in smaller machines. Epson 9600 220-ml. carts will work on an Epson 7600, even though the cartridges will stick out and look funny, and Epson doesn't recommend it.

- *Printer Settings and Profiles:* Realize that when you use third-party inks, the normal printer settings may no longer work since you've changed the inks for which the manufacturer designed the printer. The same goes for any printer profiles that you've made or bought. Change the ink; change the profiles.

- *Availability:* Don't forget that you'll have a harder time finding third-party inks for non-Epson printers or for the latest ones with smart-chipped ink cartridges. It usually takes third-party ink distributors 12 months or longer to come up with ways to get around the intelligent OEM ink cartridges. Of course, by this time, your one-year warranty will have expired, and you won't be so worried about voiding it.

- *Back-and-Forth:* Some third-party inks require that you flush or purge the existing OEM inks from the printhead. This is usually done with cleaning cartridges. This is especially important with third-party inks that are chemically incompatible with the original OEM inks and can damage the printer. Third-party ink makers sell purging or cleaning kits where needed. (Some printmakers make their own home-brewed concoctions.) This obviously causes some ink wastage and limits how many times you'll want to go back and forth between OEM and third-party inks. With desktops, and even more so with wide-format printers where a large amount of ink must be purged from the lines and reservoirs, the best advice is to plan on dedicating the printer to only one type of ink and leaving it that way.

Media

If inks are the left hand, then media are the right to inkjet printing. You can't have one without the other. And, even more so than with inks, the variety available is tremendous. There are coated and uncoated papers, watercolor papers, high-gloss and backlit films, canvas, satins, fabrics, vinyls, plastics, polyesters, you name it. If it can hold ink and be run through an inkjet printer, it's a media candidate for somebody.

But before you get too excited, let's back up and try to understand how media are made and how they work.

Paper

Media is what you put through a printer. It's what you print on. Because paper is the most common type of media used in inkjet printing, let's study it in more detail. (Non-paper media are described in the "Alternative Media" section.)

Types of Paper

Paper for inkjet printing falls into two main camps: uncoated and coated.

Uncoated Paper

Uncoated paper is the paper that we all know. This is the plain "bond" paper used in laser printers and copiers in every office around the world. On the opposite end of the quality scale, uncoated paper also includes those beautiful, mouldmade (made on a cylinder mould machine) fine-art papers that have been lovingly used for centuries for watercolors, drawing, and traditional printmaking (see Figure 7.10).

Figure 7.10 Arches uncoated watercolor papers in different weights and finishes can be printed on with inkjet.

There are two main components of uncoated paper: (1) the base or *substrate*, and (2) any *sizing*. The substrate forms the structure of the paper and determines its thickness, weight, and strength. Sizing can be added either internally to the substrate or to its surface to seal or bind the fibers and to provide resistance to the absorption of moisture.

Uncoated paper substrates such as newsprint are produced with an acidic process and made up of wood pulp, which contains *cellulose* fibers and *lignin*, a natural glue that holds the fibers together. The main problem with lignin is that it builds up over time and ultimately destroys the paper along with any image printed on it (lignin is what causes newspapers to yellow).

The majority of bond paper is produced via an alkaline process with AKD or ASA sizing, and it does not contain lignin. Bond paper is also *calendared* (sometimes spelled *calendered*) or smoothed between two metal rollers. However, bond paper is still not a good choice for inkjet printing except for solid-ink printers and for some inkjets like Epson's C84 and C86, which are designed to handle this bottom-of-the-barrel paper medium. Bond papers do not have an inkjet receptive coating, which leads to poorer image quality due to ink wicking or bleeding (see Figure 7.11).

Figure 7.11 Ink on uncoated bond paper, 40x magnification, showing wicking and print density loss due to ink penetration, which leads to a decrease in image quality.

Courtesy of Martin Juergens

What sets uncoated fine-art papers apart from their lowly office paper cousins are the ingredients, the most important of which is cellulose fiber. Cellulose can come from a variety of plant sources including wood (the most common) and cotton. The highest-quality art papers are made from 100-percent cotton content, usually rag trimmings (that's where the term "cotton rag" comes from). Cotton fiber contains mostly *alpha cellulose*, the purest form of cellulose, and it's this cotton content that yields highly stable fine-art paper that is more resistant to deterioration than wood-based paper. There is also no rosin sizing nor lignin (and hence no acid-forming compounds), but, instead, alkaline buffering agents like calcium carbonate are frequently used to raise the paper's pH. The surface of uncoated fine-art paper is sometimes sized with starches or gelatins.

Uncoated art papers can be used with inkjets, but normally only with dye-based inks. Arches, Rives BFK, and Somerset are three well-known brands, and they typically come in rough, cold-pressed (smoother), and hot-pressed (smoothest) finishes.

Printing on fine-art papers can be a challenge for a couple of reasons. First, the printer must be able to accept the thick paper. Next, these special papers can be full of loose fibers and dust that can clog the feeding mechanism and the delicate inkjet printheads. (Some printmakers actually sweep, vacuum, or roll with a tacky roller each sheet before printing.) If a paper is especially non-uniform or wavy, it can cause "head strikes" (the printhead strikes the paper surface), which could seriously damage the printer. Also, many art papers have deckle (rough or torn) edges that can be damaged or cause damage. Digital artist Karin Schminke, a member of the Digital Atelier printmaking group, covers deckle edges with removable tape or tapes a strip of acetate to the back of the paper to hold the edges flat.

Printing on Arches Uncoated

Since Arches Watercolor paper is probably the most well-known fine-art paper in the world, I thought I would try printing on it, especially since the history of digital fine-art printmaking started on Arches uncoated (David Coons printed the first images for Graham Nash on it in Los Angeles back in 1989), and many artists still use it for inkjet printing.

True to what I had always heard, my Epson 1280 inkjet prints on Arches Watercolor (Cold Press, 300gsm) started off dark and a bit muddy. This is due to an uncoated surface that, although sized with gelatin, still allows for a lot of ink bleeding or "dot gain" (wicking of the ink through the fibers). Using a couple of techniques provided by Royce Bair on the inkjetart.com/watercolor_printing.html website, mainly the Epson driver's Color Controls and Photoshop's Transfer function, I was able to get a reasonable print.

However, when I printed an image that was better-suited for a muted presentation (see Figure 7.12), it looked even better, especially when using a DIY printer profile I had made for this purpose.

Figure 7.12 A soft, muted image can work well on an uncoated paper. Left: *Shopping* I as printed on Arches Watercolor Cold Press 300gsm using a combination of +15 Saturation in Epson's Color Controls plus a Photoshop Transfer curve. Right: The same image but printed through a scanner-based DIY printer profile made with ColorVision ProfilerPLUS. Notice how the shadows open up in the hair, pants, and background.

© 2001-2004 Harald Johnson

Coated Inkjet Paper

This is where most of the action is for inkjet printing. Coated papers, which can include versions of the fine-art papers mentioned above, have a *receptor coating* added to the paper's surface to better receive the inks and render the image (see Figure 7.13). This coating can contain a whole host of substances such as alumina, silica, clay, titanium dioxide, calcium carbonates, and various polymers. Coatings are specifically designed to enhance a desired effect like better image quality, better binding with the ink, higher-color gamut, less ink bleeding into the substrate, greater brightness, and so on. The coating can also change the surface finish of the paper to be more glossy, matte, or anything in between.

Sulphite paper (also called "alpha cellulose" paper) is widely used and an alternative to 100-percent cotton paper. Instead of using cotton fibers, sulphite papers use pulp made from wood chips that are cooked in calcium bisulphate or sodium sulphite. After bleaching and buffering agents are added, you end up with a 100-percent alpha cellulose paper that is pH neutral. See Table 7.3 later in this chapter for examples.

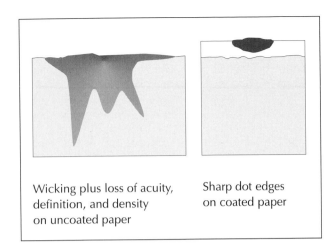

Figure 7.13 Coatings affect how the ink interacts with the paper.

Courtesy of Martin Juergens

Wicking plus loss of acuity, definition, and density on uncoated paper

Sharp dot edges on coated paper

There are so many coated inkjet papers available now, it's even hard to keep track of the categories for organizing them. But, that won't keep me from trying.

One way that suppliers like to classify coated papers is with the terms "photo paper" and "fine-art paper" (see Table 7.3). Photo papers tend to have a resin-coated (RC) component structure (see below) and a glossy or semi-glossy finish just as their traditional counterparts have. Fine-art papers frequently resemble watercolor paper. However, there is really little reason to limit your thinking to only these two categories. There are plenty of crossover choices that don't fit neatly into either camp.

Another way to classify paper is by finish or surface texture type: glossy, matte, satin, and so on. This, however, tells you very little about the type of paper and its appropriateness for use with different inks or printers.

A final way to categorize papers is by the coating technology: *microporous* or *swellable*, plus the misnamed *resin coated*. These help tell you what you can and cannot do with a particular paper.

■ **Microporous:** A relatively new solution to the problem of inkjets printing faster than the ink can dry, microporous coatings (sometimes called "particulate" or "micro-ceramic" coatings) contain very small, inorganic particles of either alumina or silica to create voids or cavities in the coating. The ink is absorbed into these cavities by capillary action, and the particles prevent the ink from spreading. The good news is that this results in very fast-drying prints that can be handled immediately and that have a high resistance to moisture and humidity. The bad news is that the open areas of the coating allow the ink to come into contact with air and all the atmospheric contaminants it contains.

This may have contributed to the Orange Shift problem described earlier, which is why all microporous prints made with dye–based inks should be displayed or stored covered or framed behind glass or Plexiglas. Microporous papers produce excellent image quality, and they can have a glossy, luster, or matte finish. These papers can work with either dye-based inks or pigment inks depending on the particular brand. (See Table 7.3 for some third-party examples.)

■ **Swellable:** Water-receptive polymer coatings for printing papers have been around since the early 1990s, but their use was limited. All that changed when people needed to find a way to reduce the fading caused by ozone and other atmospheric contaminants. Swellable coatings are made with organic polymers (gelatin is one) that swell up to surround the ink after it hits the paper. Only a very thin layer of ink is then open to direct air exposure; the rest is protected. The finishes of these papers tend to be either glossy or satiny (luster), and the image quality is excellent. Another positive is that because the swelling tends to isolate the ink drops, print permanence is increased. Negatives include being more sensitive to contact with water or high humidity and also requiring longer drying times before the print feels dry. Swellable-coated papers are for dye-based inks only. OEM swellable examples include: Epson ColorLife Photo Paper, HP Premium Plus Photo Paper, Kodak Ultima Picture Paper High Gloss, and ILFORD Galerie Classic Gloss and Classic Pearl.

The Future with Futures Coatings?

All the inkjet coatings mentioned in this chapter are added on top of the substrate after the paper is made. However, chemist and inventor John Edmunds from Futures Wales Ltd. (in Wales) has a different way of coating, although "coating" may be the wrong word to use. With his system, the coating is impregnated into the paper itself. "It's a patented infusion formulation that's added as part of the paper-making process," he explains.

Bockingford Inkjet, produced in the same St. Cuthberts paper mill in Somerset, England, as Somerset and distributed in the U.S. by Legion Paper, was the first inkjet paper to use this formulation, and Edmunds promises many more that will feature the unique coating process.

■ **Resin Coated (RC):** This is *not* a coating but a different way that papers are constructed. RC papers have been around for a long time; they are well-known in the photographic world and have now migrated to inkjets as well. Typically, a standard substrate is sandwiched between two layers of polyethylene, and one of the receptor coatings described above is then applied on top (see Figure 7.14). It's the inkjet receptive layer that determines the printing performance of the paper. The in-between polyethylene layer acts as a barrier and helps reduce wrinkling that could result from heavy ink coverage. Many microporous- and swellable-coated inkjet papers aimed at photographers are, in fact, RCs (see Table 7.3 for examples). The goal of many of these papers is to look and feel the same as a traditional photo print. Not always appropriate for pigment inks, some RCs are specially designed to accept them. Check for compatibility.

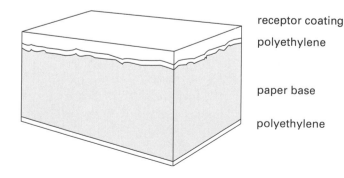

receptor coating

polyethylene

paper base

polyethylene

Figure 7.14 The layered structure of RC paper for inkjet printing.

Courtesy of Martin Juergens

Deciding on Paper

Choosing among all the different types of papers for inkjet printing can be either an exhilarating or exhausting experience. The assortment available has become bewildering. Where do you start? With the recommended printer papers.

OEM Printer Paper

Just like with inks, desktop inkjet printer manufacturers market their own lines of papers, and this is how I define "OEM" papers or media, even though some paper suppliers take issue with this since they consider themselves to be the true OEM suppliers.

In terms of choice, this is where Epson takes the lead with photographer-artists interested in high-quality inkjet media. At this writing, Epson listed seven different 100-percent cotton "fine-art" papers on its product list. This is in addition to all the other types.

HP comes in second with two different fine-art papers (by Hahnemuhle) and several photographic papers.

So, again, as with inks, the question is: Do you stick with the recommended media of the printer maker, or do you experiment with the smorgasbord of third-party choices that awaits you? And again, the answer is: It all depends. If you're happy with the recommended papers, you can be confident that they will be optimally designed for the printer's inks and printing technology. The permanence of those combinations will have been researched and well-advertised. In most cases, you know what you're getting.

But what if you want to spread your wings a little? To see what's on the other side of the door?

It's time to open that door.

Third-Party Paper

The first thing to acknowledge is that printer OEMs discourage you from using non-recommended papers. The rationale is the same as it is with inks: (1) they lose money if you buy your paper elsewhere, and (2) they lose control of the performance of their product since you are now introducing an unknown element to it. OEM-branded papers are designed to work in conjunction with OEM printers, drivers, and inks in a coordinated system.

However, because there are no smart chips embedded in papers (yet), you are free to use and print on whatever you can find, within reason. Of course, some papers will work better than others depending on your needs. See Table 7.3 for only a partial list of third-party media choices.

Key Paper Characteristics

What follows next are the key factors and characteristics you should be aware of (and questions to ask) when going paper hunting, whether for OEM or third-party brands.

Table 7.3 Sample Third-Party Media (a partial list only)

Family	Name	Substrate Type	Coating Type	Weight (gsm)	Acceptable Inks
Fine Art					
Arches *www.archesinfinity.com*	Infinity	100% cotton	microporous	230/355	dyes or pigs
Breathing Color *www.breathingcolor.com*	Elegance	100% cotton	swellable	310	dyes or pigs
Crane *www.crane.com*	Museo	100% cotton	microporous	250/365	dyes or pigs
Hahnemuhle *www.hahnemuhle.com*	Photo Rag	100% cotton	microporous	188/308/460	dyes or pigs
Hawk Mountain *www.hawkmtnartpapers.com*	Osprey	100% cotton	microporous	250	dyes or pigs
ILFORD *www.ilford.com*	Smooth Fine Art	100% cotton	microporous	190	dyes or pigs
Innova *www.innovaart.com*	Soft-Textured Art	alpha cellulose	swellable	315	dyes or pigs
Legion *www.legionpaper.com*	Somerset Photo Enhanced	100% cotton	microporous	225	dyes or pigs
Moab *www.moabpaper.com*	Entrada Bright White	100% cotton	microporous	190/300	dyes or pigs
PremierArt *www.premierimagingproducts.com*	Hot Press Fine Art	100% cotton	microporous	325	dyes or pigs
Photo Glossy					
Brilliant *www.calumetphoto.com*	Supreme Glossy	RC	n/a	270	dyes or pigs
ILFORD	Smooth High Gloss	RC	microporous	235	dyes or pigs

(continued)

Family	Name	Substrate Type	Coating Type	Weight (gsm)	Acceptable Inks
InkjetART *www.inkjetart.com*	Micro Ceramic Gloss	RC	microporous	250	dyes or pigs
Lexjet *www.lexjet.com*	Photo Gloss	RC	microporous	10 mil	dyes or pigs
Lumijet *www.lumijet.com*	Ultra Gloss	RC	microporous	260	dyes or pigs
Lyson *www.lyson.com*	Darkroom Range Gloss	alpha cellulose	swellable	320	dyes
MediaStreet *www.mediastreet.com*	Generations Gloss G-Chrome	RC	microporous	10+ mil	pigs
Pictorico *www.pictorico.com*	Photo Gallery Glossy	RC	microporous	260	dyes or pigs

Photo Matte

Family	Name	Substrate Type	Coating Type	Weight (gsm)	Acceptable Inks
Breathing Color	Sterling	100% cotton	swellable	210	dyes or pigs
InkjetART	Prem. Duo Brite Matte	alpha cellulose	microporous	225	dyes or pigs
Innova	Photo FibaPrint	alpha cellulose	swellable	280	dyes or pigs
Legion	Photo Matte	alpha cellulose	n/a	230	dyes or pigs
Lexjet	Professional Semi-Matte	RC	microporous	10 mil	dyes or pigs
MediaStreet	Generations Photo Matte	alpha cellulose	microporous	230	dyes or pigs
Moab	Kayenta Photo Matte	alpha cellulose	microporous	205	dyes or pigs

Size: As I mentioned in the last chapter, size is one of the primary factors in deciding among inkjet printers. Most inkjet papers come in normal, commercial print sizes: 8.5 × 11, 11 × 17, 13 × 19, and so on. These sizes are based on those used in the U.S. for standard office paper products (see Table 7.4). Paper marketed in Europe or other parts of the world comes in different sizes and matches the paper sizes of that area. Some paper suppliers will also list standard photographic paper sizes (4 × 6, 8 × 10, 11 × 14, and so on).

Table 7.4 Standard Paper Sizes

U.S. Name	U.S. Size	Metric Equivalent
A (letter)	8.5 × 11 inches	216 × 279 mm
Legal	8.5 × 14 inches	216 × 356 mm
B (ledger)	11 × 17 inches	279 × 432 mm
Super B/Super A3	13 × 19 inches	330 × 483 mm
C	17 × 22 inches	432 × 559 mm
D	22 × 34 inches	559 × 864 mm
E	34 × 44 inches	864 × 1118 mm

Metric Name	Metric Size	U.S. Equivalent
A5	148 × 210 mm	5.8 × 8.3 inches
A4	210 × 297 mm	8.3 × 11.7 inches
A3	297 × 420 mm	11.7 × 16.5 inches
A3+	329 × 483 mm	13 × 19 inches
A2	420 × 594 mm	16.5 × 23.4 inches
A1	594 × 841 mm	23.4 × 33.1 inches
A0	841 × 1189 mm	33.1 × 46.8 inches

Don't forget that many papers, especially high-end ones, come in sheets *and* rolls. Rolls are not just for wide-format printers, but also for desktops. For example, Digital Art Supplies carries short-width rolls of certain high-quality papers. Digital artist Bonny Lhotka takes her wide rolls to a plastic supply company where they have the right saws for cutting the rolls down to size. Rolls work well for people who not only need to print with roll-fed media but also for those who want the flexibility to cut their own sheet sizes or to roll-print quantities of images without supervision.

Substrate: How is the paper made? What is the substrate material? Wood pulp? Cotton rag content? Plastic or other synthetics? RC? This is the starting point for knowing about a type of paper.

Color: The whiter the substrate, the better the reflector under the colors, and the higher the color gamut. However, there's white, and then there's white. Some whites seem too cold. Too creamy, and it will look dreary as you lose color gamut. Again, it's a matter of personal preference. Papers have their characteristic colors, and people gravitate to them accordingly.

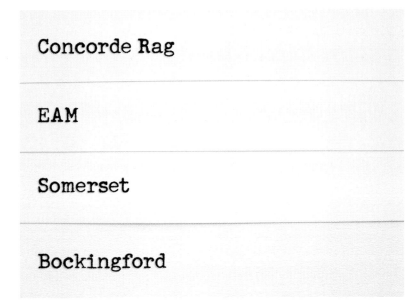

Inkjet printing papers are not just white!

Weight: The standard measurement of paper weight for inkjet papers is grams per square meter (gsm). This is more accurate than the Imperial system that measures paper by its "basis weight," or the weight in pounds of 500 sheets of standard size, usually 17×22 inches. Knowing a paper's weight is only partially useful information. A much more important thing to know is a paper's thickness, which is not necessarily related to its weight. Within one brand of paper, heavier weights may be thicker, but Brand X of one weight may be thicker than Brand Y with the same weight.

Caliper (thickness): Caliper or thickness is a more useful paper measurement since each printer model prints best with papers of a certain thickness range (and have a maximum thickness they will print). A paper's caliper is measured in *mils*, also called "points" in the commercial printing industry. One mil is 1/1,000th of an inch, and it is determined by the combination of substrate, additives, and coating. Some papers have different calipers for sheets and rolls. Legion Concorde Rag, for example, is 11 mil for sheets and 17.5 mil for rolls.

Coating: Although this was covered earlier, it bears repeating. (Note: Coating in this context refers to the pre-coating on the paper when you buy it. If you're considering any post-printing coatings or sprays, see Chapter 9.) It's very important to match the paper coating to your inks and printer type. Quality, handling issues, ink puddling, smearing, scuffing, flaking, wicking, and excessive dot gain (ink spreading) are all affected by the type—or lack—of the appropriate paper coating.

How to Identify the Coating

How do you know if you're dealing with a microporous or a swellable coating if the box or package doesn't say? I use Henry Wilhelm's "squeak test." Rub your fingers across the paper. If it grabs your fingers or sort of squeaks (most noticeable on glossy papers), you've got a microporous paper. Another easy clue is if it's designated "instant dry" or something similar, it's probably microporous.

Determining the correct printing side of a coated paper is also sometimes a problem with inkjet papers (even if the box clearly says "image side up"). Here's a trick to help you figure it out: Wet two fingers and lightly grip a corner of the paper; the side that sticks to your finger has the printable coating. With experience, you'll be able to tell the coated side just by feel.

Finish: This is the surface texture. The range is high gloss to very rough with all kinds of pearls, satins, lusters (equivalent to the photographic "E" surface), mattes, and more in between. People tend to have strong feelings about their paper finishes. Color consultant C. David Tobie says it well when he states: "Paper is like religion or politics; you will have little success preaching matte to the glossy crowd, or vice versa. Celebrate diversity."

The two finishes of Arches Infinity (Textured and Smooth) compared to Crane Museo.

pH: You want papers that are pH-neutral (pH 7) or a little alkaline because our polluted environment will add acidity over time. Acidic paper is a ticking time bomb; it will self-destruct sooner or later. Look for papers that say "acid-free" and hope they mean it. Acid-free means either that no acids were added to the paper (as with 100% cotton) or that any acids used in a wood-pulp-based paper have been removed or neutralized with an alkaline buffering agent such as calcium carbonate or magnesium carbonate, which is added to the pulp. Keep in mind that buffering may lose its effect over time. It's best if you can find out the actual pH level, which is what Crane provides in its paper specs: 7.9-8.5.

Brightness: Brightness is usually given, if at all, in terms of a rating scale of 1–100, with 100 being the brightest. Keep in mind that some papers achieve a higher brightness by adding optical brighteners.

Optical Brighteners: Optical brightening agents (OBAs) are commonly used in the paper, textile, and detergent industries. As the name implies, they're also added to inkjet printing papers and coatings to make them whiter and brighter. The way OBAs work is by absorbing UV radiation and fluorescing (re-emitting as visible light). A common OBA is titanium dioxide, which is added to the paper's outer receptor coating. You can tell if a paper has OBAs added by turning on a portable "black light" in a dark room and running it over the paper. If OBAs are present, the paper will appear to glow while a non-optical-brightened paper will appear dark or "optically dead" because no light is reflected. (This gets more complicated with a 100%-cotton paper that has no OBAs added to its coating but may have OBAs in the substrate if the original cotton trimmings contained optical brighteners.)

It's unclear what long-term effects OBAs have on print permanence. Some believe that they can possibly contribute to print deterioration, but others disagree, saying first that not all OBAs are the same, and then that the worst that can happen is a bright white paper ending up being less white (yellower) as the brightener loses its ability to fluoresce over time. According to Epson, all its standard papers have optical brighteners to improve whiteness and to inhibit the yellowing of the paper. Some paper suppliers will offer a brightened paper and a "natural" unbrightened one as an alternative. Moab's Entrada is an example.

Opacity: This becomes an issue with thinner papers, and you see this measurement on many from Epson plus a few third-party suppliers. Opacity means how opaque the paper is, or how much "show-through" (how much you can see the image underneath when stacked) there is. It's measured with a simple meter; the higher the opacity figure up to 100, the more opaque the paper. The most common application where opacity is important is in the making of specialty books and albums.

Dmax: Dmax, the maximum density reading possible at the highest black ink levels, depends on the type of inks used so this parameter may not be readily available. However, online discussion lists and other sources sometimes compare the Dmax of different papers with different inks, so if you can find the numbers (the higher the better), pay attention, especially if you like deep, rich blacks and shadows. In general, the smoother the finish, the higher the Dmax reading, all others being equal. Glossy papers typically have higher Dmax numbers than watercolor papers; dye inks higher than pigments. Many sophisticated printmakers use devices such as densitometers and spectrophotometers to calculate their own Dmax measurements with various inksets. See Table 7.5 for one example.

Table 7.5	Sample Dmax Readings[1]	
Paper	Harald's Dye-Based	Andrew's UltraChrome
A.I. 230 Smooth	1.68	1.52
A.I. 230 Textured	1.66	1.51
A.I. 355 Smooth	1.69	1.53
A.I. 355 Textured	1.71	1.48

[1]*Adapted from an actual review of Arches Infinity paper by Harald Johnson and Andrew Darlow, July, 2003. Harald's samples were printed on an Epson Stylus Photo 1280 with the OEM Photo Dye color inks. Andrew's samples were printed on an Epson Stylus Pro 7600 with UltraChrome inks. Black patch readings (using all colors) were made by Andrew using a GretagMacbeth Eye-One Pro Spectrophotometer. See the full review at: www.dpandi.com/newsreviews/reviews/ai/index.html.*

Permanence/Lightfastness: As we already know, print permanence is the result of the interaction of inks, paper, and display or storage conditions. You cannot pick only a paper and have any idea as to its permanence. You need to know at least one other part of the equation. Most paper suppliers include permanence ratings based on certain assumptions in their paper specs or marketing material. Make sure you read the fine print carefully to see how those projections are determined. (See Chapter 5 for more about print permanence.)

Free Profiles Provided: In addition to what ink suppliers provide, some paper vendors or manufacturers also furnish generic or canned printer profiles for their papers. ILFORD lists recommended printer settings for its media on its website for Epson, HP, Canon, and Lexmark inkjets.

Two-Sided: Most people print on just one side of the paper, but there are times when printing on both sides (also called "duplexing") is a real bonus. Portfolios, brochures, greeting cards, postcards, and digital books—these are all good uses for two-sided printing (see Figure 7.15). However, in such cases, you need a dual-sided, dual-coated paper on which to print. (Be careful if you think you can just print on a single-sided paper and not worry about the back. Some papers from Epson, Kodak, HP, and others have advertising or logos printed on the back side.) Also, most inkjet receptive coatings are fragile and easily scuffable. When using a dual-sided paper, you must take extra care in handling the sheets.

Examples of "duo" papers include: Bockingford Inkjet, Dotworks FS2, Epson Double-Sided Matte, Hahnemuhle Photo Rag Duo, InkjetART Duo Brite Matte, Lumijet Matte Double Sided, Moab Entrada, Pictorico Premium DualSide Photo, PremierArt Hot Press, and Red River Denali Matte Two. (See Chapter 11 for more about printing books, cards, and portfolios.)

There are very few inkjets that can automatically duplex print. One is the Xerox Phaser 8400 solid ink printer where the paper is fed back through the machine on a different paper path. Several HP Deskjets can also do it with special two-sided printing modules that hold and then automatically pull the paper back to print the reverse side.

Figure 7.15 A portfolio book created by Andrew Darlow with Lineco's PopArt post-bound digital album. Andrew printed directly onto the double-sided Lineco Digital Archival Matte paper, which has a post-binding strip with holes ready to fit into the album covers.

Album and photographs © Andrew Darlow/www.andrewdarlow.com

Cost: I've already described ink and media costs in the previous chapter, but I'll mention a cost-saver here. One trick that experienced printmakers have learned is to do the testing, color balancing, and other preliminary work on similar, but cheaper, paper. Then, when they're ready, they pull out the good stuff. This used to be hit or miss, hoping that the proofing paper would use the same settings or profiles as the expensive paper, but now, paper suppliers are starting to offer this combination with uniform coatings. For example, Hahnemuhle introduced their Art Proof paper in early 2004 specifically for "lowering the expense of non-income-earning test prints." It's 110 gsm, and they claim it saves 35–50 percent on the regular Hahnemuhle stocks. Similarly, Moab now offers Kayenta Photo Matte as a lower-cost "everyday" paper (Sulphite) plus as a proofing paper for Moab's Entrada line (100-percent cotton). Finally, Legion Digital Rag is the proofing suggestion for Somerset Velvet.

Paper Name Equivalents

Trying to sift through all the various types and names of printing papers can be a challenging task. It's made even harder when you realize that the same paper can have different, rebranded marketing names depending on who is selling it. For example, consider the following:

Hahnemuhle German Etching = Lumijet Classic Velour = Lyson Standard Fine Art = MediaStreet Royal Plush = the former ConeTech Orwell.

Sometimes, it's common knowledge when it's the same paper, but many times, as with the examples above, its not. You just have to know.

Alternative Media

I've concentrated on normal paper because it's the most common type of media. However, there are many alternatives to paper for inkjet printing. Wood veneer? Sandpaper? Aluminum foil? Open your mind to the possibilities—but at the same time, be forewarned about the possible fatal dangers to your printer whenever you put non-recommended media through it. (See more about special printing techniques in Chapter 11.)

Canvas: One of the primary media choices for both portrait photographers and artists working with canvas originals and printing giclée reproductions is canvas. Canvas, of course, has been around for hundreds of years as an artist medium, but now, specially treated canvas is also available for inkjet printing. Different canvases have different coatings, different weaves or textures, and they come either on rolls for wide-format printers or in cut sheets for desktops. For example, Fredrix, the oldest (since 1868) and largest maker of artist canvas in the U.S., also has a line of Print Canvas products. These are 100% cotton or Polyflax/cotton blends, and they come in either cut sheets or bulk rolls. Other inkjet canvas suppliers (of their own or rebranded canvas) include: Breathing Color, Bulldog Products, Hahnemuhle, Hawk Mountain, HP, Legion Paper, LexJet Direct, Luminos, MediaStreet, PremierArt, and Moab. Epson also carries a 100-percent cotton canvas, but it only comes in 24-, 36-, and 44-inch rolls.

Photographer and print-service provider David Saffir frequently uses canvas for printing client portraits. Using LexJet's Instant Dry Satin Canvas printed with UltraChromes and an Epson 9600, he either stretches the prints or mounts to board. In the example shown, his clients chose a traditional frame for the 20 × 24-inch print.

Courtesy of David Saffir
www.davidsaffir.com

Exotic Papers: There are lots of specialty papers available for inkjet printing. Paper vendor Digital Art Supplies carries an entire stock of handmade Japanese papers and even has a sampler pack devoted to them. With names like Harukaze, Kinwashi, and Yanagi, you are actually printing on mixtures of hemp, kozo, bamboo, or straw. Different from the Japanese papers found at art supply stores, these are specially treated for inkjet printing.

Red River Paper carries Silver and Gold Metallic papers that yield an unusual effect when printed with dye-based (only) inks.

Specialty Films and Plastics: While they are normal materials for sign and display print shops, backlit films, vinyls, polycarbonates, and decal media are coming under the scrutiny of photographer-artists who want to print on something different. Clear or translucent films, for example, can be used to make digital negatives, positive films for screen printing, and the kind of window art we saw in the last chapter.

■ At this writing, John Edmunds' Futures (Wales) Ltd. was announcing its own brand of durable, high-resolution, inkjet-printable film with the ability to accept up to 6000-dpi printing.

■ Pictorico's Photo Gallery Hi-Gloss White Film, used for photo reproduction, is made entirely with DuPont Melinex polyester film as the substrate (it's also coated with ceramic particles).

■ Consultant Dr. Ray Work has come up with a Cibachrome-like solution for digital photographic output. It's an all-synthetic sandwich comprised of a base of 8-mil DuPont Melinex polyester film with a microporous inkjet coating, pigment colorants that form the image, and a laminated Teflon topcoat. There is no paper. There's also nothing to degrade, and, since there's no contact with the air, there are no gas fading problems.

■ DuPont Tyvek is a spun-bonded polyolefin (a hydrocarbon polymer like polyethylene). Known mostly as a sign maker's medium, a wrap in home construction, and for FedEx and other shipping packaging, Tyvek is gaining popularity with adventurous digital printmakers willing to search it out. Artist JD Jarvis has been inkjet printing on it for years. Jarvis admits that it's been a struggle to convince collectors and gallery staff to accept it, but he has had large pieces printed on Tyvek hung vertically in galleries by hooks and bungy cords. "Tyvek has a PR problem," he says. "It's used a lot in the signage industry, but my feeling is that new tools beget new materials, and maybe even new ways to display art. Art in general is about innovation, and I maintain that digital artists, at this point, should be the most willing to innovate with any and all new materials, images, and display modes." Tyvek is available from Océ, HP, and digital supplier Azon.

Textiles and Fabrics: Inkjet printing on textiles and fabrics has come a long way, and very quickly. In addition to the well-established use of digital printing on banners and flags in commercial settings, there is an accelerating trend for printing directly onto fabrics for more utilitarian uses like home decor textiles and clothing.

The original use of this textile printing technology was (and still is) to produce commercial samples and "strike-offs" quickly and cheaply without having to go through the traditionally complicated and expensive process of cutting screens, etc. This can be very important when you realize that 95-percent of fabric designs never make it into production. However, individuals are now using their own inkjet printers to print on fabric for personal use. (A variation of inkjet printing on fabrics is the use of dye-sublimation transfers.)

JD and Myriam Jarvis hold up their Tyvek print of Le-Com-Bo, which has been shown in exhibitions hung with bungee cords attached to the grommets (inset).

Courtesy of JD Jarvis
www.dunkingbirdproductions.com

Futures Wales Ltd. has a new line of fabrics that include the same patented infusion for-mulation for inkjet printing as used with paper. These Futures Fabrics can be printed with ordinary aqueous inkjet inks, both dyes and pigments. When printed with pigment inks such as Epson UltraChromes, they can be hand-washed with little or no bleeding. They can also be ironed, stretched, twisted, pulled, and wrinkled, and they are claimed to be very durable, even when printed with dye inks. There are currently (at this writing) three Futures Fabrics available in rolls of various sizes: Gainsborough (100-percent cotton, 320 gsm), Hogarth (100-percent cotton, 230 gsm), and Landseer (polycotton, 100 gsm). Uses for the fabrics include custom wall coverings, window treatments, floor tiles, and banners. Compatible inkjet printers include HPs, Epsons, Mimakis, Encads, Lexmarks, Canons, and ColorSpans.

See more examples of printing on fabric in Chapter 11.

Finding Media

Where do you find all these wonderful printing papers and other media? With the crazy quilt of paper mills, converters, manufacturers, importers, coaters, suppliers, distributors, repackagers, dealers, and so on, it would be impossible to come up with a comprehensive list of all the media and their sources. However, there are two good ways to track down the media of your dreams: start at the top and at the bottom. By the top, I mean go to the major manufacturer/distributor websites (see some in Table 7.3) and research the features and specs of an entire product line. You can also go to the bottom of the food chain—retailers and dealers—and see what they have to offer and for how much.

Because media are so personal, it's always best to sample them yourself before deciding on a larger order. One of the best ways to try out different media is to order sample packs; most major brands offer them. If, however, the goal is to evaluate different brand samples, then go to the dealers that carry more than one brand. For example, Digital Art Supplies has "A Bit of (Almost) Everything Multipack" with paper samples from various brands and mills all in one box. They also have themed multipacks like "Dual-Sided Multipack" and "Photographer's Multipack." It's a great way to touch, feel, and try out different inkjet papers.

Matching Ink to Media

If there is one lesson to take away from this chapter, it's this: You must carefully match your inks and media to get the best and the most permanent inkjet output. Think of it as a system; everything has to work together. Some points to remember:

- If you want to print on *uncoated* fine-art paper, use dye-based inks; pigments will look muddier (Epson DuraBrites an exception). But, be aware that the dye inks may fade more quickly.

- Use pigment inks on coated papers; use dyes on both coated and uncoated papers. Check the paper specifications carefully for compatibility.

- In general, use pigment inks if you require maximum print permanence, or use a dye-ink/media combination that specifically offers greater permanence.

- If you want to use pigment inks on glossy or semi-glossy papers, carefully check for ink/paper compatibility. You may need a protective coating or spray.

- Although dye inks can usually produce brighter colors, pigments on carefully matched media can come very close to dyes in terms of color gamut.

- Pigments, in general, tend to exhibit more metamerism, although newer pigment inks have reduced the problem. Other strategies, like using certain RIPs, can also minimize metamerism.

- Try to use matching ink/media systems when possible. These can come from OEMs or from third-party suppliers.

As soon as the ink hits the paper, a chain of events takes place, and you want to understand and control the resulting physical and chemical interactions as much as possible.

You *may* have a better chance of achieving this goal with the consumables recommended by the printer manufacturer. As I've already said, companies like Canon, Epson, and HP have spent a great deal of time and money to come up with a complete system of inks, media, and printers that optimize print quality.

Carefully matching inks to media takes effort, but the results are worth it.

You can, of course, stray from the herd if you choose (taking into account certain restrictions like smart-chipped ink cartridges). Third-party providers of inks and media have also done their homework, and they offer many compatible products that compare favorably with—and are sometimes better than—the OEMs'. But, you will have to spend your own time and money to do the research needed to prove this to yourself (one of the reasons you're probably reading this book!).

The bottom line for consumables is this: Inkjet printing has finally evolved to the stage where photographer-artists can now choose a specific printer, inkset, and medium to produce the kind of output or look they have in their mind's eye. You just have to make the right choices to make the perfect match.

Enough background information; let's make a print!

8

Making a Great Inkjet Print

I can't give you instant, hard-earned experience in the digital trenches, but I can illuminate the key steps—and pitfalls—of the digital printing process. However, before you can start printing, you need the right front-end system. If you're hoping to set up a printmaking studio—on whatever scale—read on.

System Setups

The tools of a digital artist—besides curiosity, thought, feeling, and imagination—include the hardware and software that make it possible to create, process, and, ultimately, output digital prints. In addition to providing a few words about each major equipment category, I will also show you the actual setups of two artists: photographer Larry Berman's PC Digital Darkroom and digital artist Ileana's Mac Digital Studio.

Healthy Hardware: Basic Equipment Setups

Just like socialites in Palm Beach who can never be too rich or too thin, digital artists can never have too much digital horsepower or too much disk space. It's not the printers themselves (if outputting to a desktop printer) that require it; even the newest inkjet printers need only a basic setup. But when it comes to the large image files that photographers and artists process and inevitably end up with, more is definitely better.

① Left Monitor: Sony 21" 1620HT

Right Monitor: Gateway 21"

Radeon 9600 128 MB DDR ATI dual monitor card

Monaco Optix for calibrating dual monitors

② Olympus P-440 Photo Printer (dye sublimation)

③ Wacom ArtZII 6x8" serial port graphics tablet

④ APC Back-UPS Pro 1000 uninterrupted power supply

⑤ Windows XP Pro P4 2.8 GHz, 1 GB RAM dual 200 GB 7200 RPM hard drives DVD burner

⑥ Nikon Coolscan 5000ED 35mm film scanner

⑦ Epson Perfection 1640SU flatbed scanner

⑧ dual backup 160 GB USB2 external hard drives

⑨ Lexar Firewire card reader for digital camera files

Not shown:
Linksys wireless G broadband router Internet connection sharing to Win XP Pro Pro laptop

Photographer System Setup: Larry Berman's PC Digital Darkroom

Pennsylvania photographer Larry Berman, seen here working on one of his new color X-ray digital photographs, has been selling his photography at juried art shows throughout the U.S. for over 25 years. He considered this a "power user" setup when he purchased it last year. It's a 2.8 GHz P4 system with a Gig of RAM. He's also added a Nikon Coolscan 5000ED, which he uses to scan client's slides for the new art show digital jury system.

Courtesy of Larry Berman/www.LarryBerman.com, www.ColorXrays.com

Platforms, Operating Systems, and CPUs

Like fanatical sports team fans, photographers and artists are usually die-hard defenders of either the PC/Windows or Macintosh platform. The fact is, it doesn't make much difference which you go with. Most image-editing programs (but not all) and virtually all high-quality desktop printers run just as well with both. PCs tend to be cheaper and easier to find, and Macs are still preferred in an almost cult-like way by certain groups such as high-end photographers. (I also find it interesting that art galleries invariably use Macs as their office computers; must be something about the cool design!)

Each operating system's (OS) software also has its band of adherents. Microsoft Windows reigns supreme on the PC with its many incarnations, and although XP is the latest as of this writing, I know artists who still happily use Windows 95, 98, and 2000 (Windows 2000 is legendary for being rock-solid stable). On the Mac side, most Macophiles are shifting to OS X, although some are still holding on to OS 9.x for as long as they can. Once the image-editing or printer software you're running can no longer work with your old OS, it's time to upgrade it. At that point, many Windows users just opt for a whole new computer, with the latest OS built in.

CPUs and Processing Speed

The central processing unit (CPU) is the heart of your computer. Intel Pentium (3 or 4) and AMD Athlon are two obvious choices for the PC. PowerPC processors (currently G4s and G5s) on the Mac are the only realistic options.

CPUs come in different "clock speeds," which have a big impact on how fast your work gets done as the computer processes all those binary numbers. Get the fastest CPU you can afford unless you like staring at the monitor watching little hourglasses or spinning clocks while your files are processed. Note that megahertz or gigahertz ratings should only be used for comparing CPUs in the same family; it doesn't work to compare Pentium speeds with PowerPCs.

The best performance will come from using dual processors, and both PCs and Macs support that option. The only problem is that not all software will run on multiprocessors, and conflicts with critical software or drivers can more than offset the speed advantages of a dual processor system. Macs have the advantage here since OS X offers better system-level usage of dual processors than previous systems and shows far fewer compatibility issues.

RAM

The other big key to processing large image files is Random Access Memory (RAM). These days, RAM is cheap so buy all you can. Photoshop, especially, is a RAM hog, so load up on it. If you can get and utilize more than 1GB (1,000MB) of RAM, get it. You'll be smiling when your work flies off the screen.

An interesting point that digital artist Ileana makes about RAM and her art: Every time she increases the RAM in her computer, she immediately begins to compose larger pieces to take advantage of the improvement. So her work actually changes *because* of the equipment.

Connections

One of the real limitations with older computers is the printer interface or connection. Most contemporary desktop printers, whether inkjet, dye sub, or laser, require a USB or parallel (IEEE-1284) connection. Even better, upgading to a system offering USB2 or FireWire can be important for downloading large numbers of digital photos, or gaining high-speed access to scanners, drives, and printers. Older computers don't have these options, although special cards can be installed for this purpose. When nothing can connect to your computer anymore, that's usually the time to buy a new one.

Hard Drives and Other Storage and Transport

As with RAM and processing speed, large art files require a lot of storage space. It's hard to imagine that I used to work with a 10MB hard disk, but I did. Now, single file sizes in the 200–500MB range are not unusual. Since you have to store all those gigantic files somewhere, you should get the largest hard-disk storage capacity you can, 120, 250, even 500 *gigabytes*. And you might think about getting multiple hard drives configured in a RAID ("Redundant Array of Inexpensive Disks") array for spreading the data across multiple disks. Again, as with RAM, per megabyte storage costs have dropped significantly, so be generous to yourself.

For small-scale or temporary storage (or for file transport), you'll definitely want some kind of removable media system. Most file transport these days is done either with microstorage drives or on CDs (650MB) and DVDs (4–9GB). You'll either need a built-in CD/DVD writer/reader on the computer or use an external, stand-alone unit.

Displays

Again, bigger is definitely better when it comes to monitors. With the menus and palettes multiplying on the latest image-editing software, screen real estate has become a priceless commodity. Most photographer-artists work on 19"–21" or even larger screens, and some use dual monitors, one for the main image, the other for all the tools. Mitsubishi, NEC, LaCie, Apple, and Sony make models popular with photographer-artists.

Another trend is to flat-screen, liquid crystal displays (LCDs) and away from the traditional cathode ray tube (CRT) monitors, although some users still maintain that CRTs are better. (Apple has abandoned CRTs almost entirely with its current product line of displays.) Prior concerns about poor color fidelity on LCDs are fading as the quality improves and as more color profiling devices come online to deal with the new flat-screen monitors.

Video Display Cards

Powerful graphics cards are frequently needed to avoid the speed bottlenecks that intense image-processing can cause. They are also needed to run sophisticated dual-monitor setups. Matrox, NVIDIA, and AGP make good ones.

Input Devices

Most photographer-artists work with source material in one form or another that needs to end up in the computer. We've already covered digital cameras and scanners in Chapter 3; however, one tool that needs more description is the digital graphics tablet, which combines a pen or stylus and an electronic tablet that records the pen's position and action.

① Epson Stylus Photo 2200 inkjet printer

② Apple G5 2.0GHz Dual Processor
3.5 GB RAM
160GB hard drive
Mac OS X 10.3 Panther
Pioneer DVR-106 DVD-RW
ATI Radeon 9600
Pro AGP 64MB

③ Canon LiDE 30 Scanner 48-bit /1200x2400 dpi

④ 17-inch Apple Studio Display

⑤ 15-inch Apple Studio Display (Apple DVI to ADC Adapter)

⑥ Dazzle Digital Media Reader

⑦ WACOM Intuos II 6x8" USB graphics tablet

⑧ Kensington ExpertMouse Trackball

⑨ APC Back-UPS 400 Uninterruptible Power Supply

⑩ LTS Daylight Glow portable lamp

LinkSys Wireless-B Broadband Router

Not shown:
Pantone ColorVision SpyderPRO

Nikon D70 6.0 MP digital SLR camera

Digital Artist System Setup: Ileana's Mac Digital Studio

Digital artist Ileana considers her setup above average for someone expecting to make a living doing fine-art on a computer. Her dream setup when the budget and sales allow? Add a 30" Apple Cinema HD, Apple PowerBook laptop so she can work remotely, and a state-of-the-art wide-format inkjet printer.

Courtesy of Ileana Frómeta Grillo/www.ileanaspage.com

Besides the obvious help with digital painting or drawing, tablets also allow for easier retouching and other kinds of image handwork. In fact, there are many photographers, artists, and designers who have replaced the mouse on their desk with a tablet for every-day use. "I've had one for years," says Huntsville, Alabama, designer Brien O'Brien of OBGraphiX. "I use it for *everything*. My mouse is in a drawer somewhere, I think. I haven't seen it in ages."

Tablets come in all sizes, shapes, and types, and Wacom (see Figure 8.1) is the dominant player with its popular models: Graphire (basic), Intuous2 (professional), and Cintiq (work directly on the screen).

What are the most important things to look for in choosing a graphics tablet? Size (very personal), resolution (more is better), and pressure (more is still better).

A ScanDisk USB Flash drive. It's easy to carry one of these in your pocket and then just plug it into any computer's USB slot

Internet Connection

This is not really equipment-related, but it's becoming more and more necessary for pho-tographers and artists to have a high-speed connection to the Internet. Here are some com-mon uses for the Internet among imagemakers: downloading software and software updates; downloading users' guides and being connected to serialize or register some prod-ucts; researching art information; browsing and maintaining art-related websites; down-loading images from stock agencies; sending image files to galleries, colleagues, or outside printmakers; and quickly perusing and contributing to online forums and discussion lists.

The more time you spend online, the more frustrating the old 56K-dial-up connection becomes. Cable modems, DSL, and dedicated high-speed lines are the way of the mod-ern, online world.

Digital Graphics Tablets

Once artists were able to set aside that cute but clunky mouse and replace it with a stylus that allowed the hand and eye to move more naturally in creating lines and shapes, digital drawing and painting took a huge leap forward.

It's such a natural idea: a pressure-sensitive pen or stylus moves over an electronic tablet that records the pen's position and action. Just like writing with a pen on a piece of paper, only the pen never runs out of ink, and the paper never moves. And though the stylus is like a mouse in sampling relative motion (pick it up and position it somewhere else, and the on-screen cursor never moves), it can also record absolute motion (move it to another spot on the tablet, and the cursor moves, too), and it can do things that a simple mouse never dreamed of. Like being pressure-sensitive. Wacom's Intuous (see Figure 8.1) includes a batteryless, cordless pen with 1,024 levels of pressure-sensitivity. Push a little harder and the brush size or the transparency of the stroke changes.

The key features to weigh and consider when shopping for a graphics tablet are:

1. *Size:* This is a personal preference. For many, a 4 × 5 or 6 × 8 tablet is all they need. Others feel cramped with anything smaller than 9 × 12 inches. Larger tablets take up more desk real estate but allow more 1:1 scaling between the monitor and the tablet.

2. *Resolution:* The more the better because resolution affects the control of the cursor on the monitor. The working range is 1000–2540 dpi, sometimes stated as "lpi" or "lpmm" (lines per millimeter).

3. *Pressure:* The more pressure-sensitivity levels, the more natural and responsive the tablet will feel. A tablet with 512 levels will do the job, but one with 1,024 levels is even better. "Pressure-sensitivity is important," explains artist Martha Bradford, "because I try to make many of my brushstrokes gestural, meaning that starting thin and light, getting thicker and darker, and then finishing thin and light is the effect I'm after, and that comes from pressure-sensitivity."

4. *Pen Tilt:* Pen tilt is a feature that lets the stylus angle change relative to the tablet. Tilt allows for a more flexible and natural drawing style.

5. *Compatibility:* Almost all high-quality, image creating or editing software is pressure-sensitive-compatible, but check just in case. You may not be able to use a pressure-sensitive tool with a word-processor, for example.

6. If your hand-eye coordination isn't great, consider one of the newer LCD tablets like Wacom's Cintiq interactive models. Instead of drawing on a tablet and watching the monitor, you draw instead right on the monitor/tablet, which is a handy, albeit pricey option.

7. Keep in mind that graphics tablets are not just for painting or drawing. Some artists use them for everything; the only mice they deal with are the ones in the attic.

Color Management

Most photographer-artists are incorporating some type of color management into their workflows. Color management can take many forms: from simple—and free—onboard monitor calibration, to stock or custom profiles, to specialized hardware and software packages costing $5,000 and up. (For an in-depth overview of this important topic, see Chapter 4.)

Figure 8.1   Wacom's Intuos3 (6 × 8) graphics tablet with tools.

Courtesy of Wacom Technology

RIPs

A Raster Image Processor (RIP) can give you a significant amount of control over certain aspects of your output. It translates a file's data (bitmap images, vector graphics, fonts) into a single rasterized (bitmapped) file for printing at the print device's specific resolution. For more about RIPs, see Chapter 11.

Printers

See the in-depth discussion about printer choices in Chapter 6.

Quick-Start Printing Guide

In the following main section, I will go into some depth about the different printing steps, but here I want to get you printing in the shortest time possible. Consider this an overview or a skeleton approach. (Note: these are the basic steps for self-printing on a desktop inkjet printer; if you plan to use an outside printmaker or a printing service, see Chapter 10.)

Before we begin, I will make certain assumptions, namely:

1. That you have or have access to a computer system and an inkjet printer and know the basics of how both work. For this Quick-Start section, I will be using a PC laptop running Windows XP Home to print from the Adobe Photoshop Elements (2.0) program to a Canon i960 Photo Printer (see Figure 8.2).

2.   That you have scanned in, captured, or otherwise created a digital image file (see Chapter 3);

3.   That you have a reasonably calibrated monitor (see Chapter 4).

You don't absolutely *have* to have all these, but it will make what follows a little more understandable if you do.

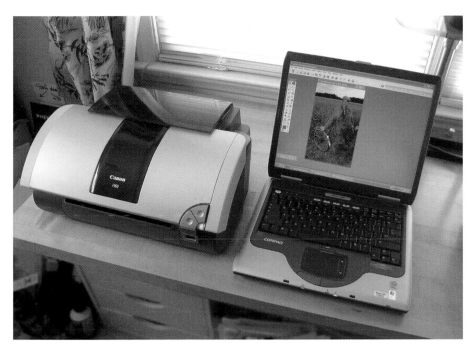

Figure 8.2 For this workflow, I'm using a laptop computer running Windows XP Home to print from Adobe Photoshop Elements 2.0 to a Canon i960 Photo Printer.

Step 1: Open and Convert the File

I had taken this photo of a farmer in Sweden some years ago, and I had it scanned at a service bureau with a Nikon Coolscan 8000ED 4000-dpi scanner. I open the raw scan in Elements and immediately Save As to the PSD format of Elements to create my working file. I start thinking about what editing needs to be done.

This is the full-frame scan of my original 35mm slide of the Swedish farmer.

Step 2: Edit and Prep the Image

Figure 8.3 The cropped, edited, and sharpened image file.

Because I decide to crop in tight on this image, and because I know that cropping permanently alters the file, I do another Save As to create a new file with the word "crop" in the title. This way, I can always go back to the earlier version and start over, if I want. I check for *squareness* and then *crop* the image to be much tighter at the top and bottom.

To continue the editing, I only do a minimal "move" by adjusting the Levels. I finish by going over the entire image removing dust spots and repairing defects wherever I see them.

Normally, I would save a print-specific version of the file at this point and then sharpen it as needed based on the type of output I'm doing. However, because I'm only doing a basic workflow, I simply duplicate the base layer and rename it "sharpen" before doing a minor amount of sharpening *to this layer*. (By doing this, I can always remove the sharpen layer to get back to where I was.) Figure 8.3 shows the resulting image and its Layers palette.

Step 3: Choose and Load the Paper

Figure 8.4 The printer is ready with the paper loaded.

I'm using Canon's Matte Photo Paper, which is a recommended paper for the Canon. After I turn on the printer, I load the paper (letter size) so that it's leaning against the back paper support with the printing side in the correct orientation (see Figure 8.4). Because this paper is thin enough, I load a few sheets.

Step 4: Select Image Settings

I first confirm that I have the right scaling and print resolution in Elements under Image > Resize > Image Size. I adjust the Printer Resolution to size the image for my paper. I now go to File > Page Setup to confirm that the paper size and orientation is correct. It is. Then I go to File > Print Preview to access more settings (I could have

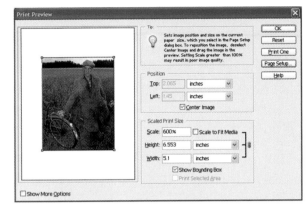

Figure 8.5 Elements' Print Preview screen.

accessed Page Setup from here, too) and to see a preview of how the image is positioned on the page (see Figure 8.5). All looks good, so I now hit the Print button.

Step 5: Select Printer Driver Settings

The Print menu confirms that I have the correct printer selected (I can change printers at this point). Now I click on the Properties button to access the printer driver settings. This is where all the goody options are for this printer (see Figure 8.6). I check the basics at the top and pick my paper under Media Type. Because I want to see first if I'm even close with this print, I start off with

Figure 8.6 The Properties button opens the various printer driver options.

the simplest Standard and Auto settings. This will hand over everything to the printer driver, and I'll know soon enough if this is the right decision or not. The last thing I do in this box is confirm that the Source Space is Document, and that the Print Space is Profile: Same as Source. I'm ready to make my first print.

Step 6: Make the Print

Before I forget everything, I write down all my settings and decisions I've made up to this point. This will be an essential record if I want to make alterations later.

Finally ready, I click the OK button, and the printer comes to life. Soon, I have my first print, and I evaluate it under the diffused window daylight of my studio space. It looks great!

Making a Print Step-by-Step

Now, let's go into more depth. In this section, I'm going to elaborate on the previous steps, add some more, and also give more options for some. I'll change printers (to HP Designjet 130), printer type (consumer desktop to professional wide-format), and media type (swellable-coated satin from microporous matte).

The image this time is a vintage shot I took in a Paris cheese shop. There is a fascination for food and beverage fine-art imagery (especially wine), so this seems like an appropriate image to print. I call what I will end up with an *original print*; if you're more interested in making reproduction prints, the same basic workflow would apply (see "A Giclée Workflow" in Chapter 10).

La Fromagerie.
© 1970-2004 Harald Johnson

The printer used in this section is the newer HP Designjet 130nr. The 130 was introduced in May 2004, and it is a 6-color (CMYKcm), thermal, wide-format inkjet printer. The "durable-dye" inks and the HP Premium Plus Photo Satin paper are OEM from HP.

For this print, I'll be working on a Mac (G4) in OS X 10.3 with Photoshop CS, but the same basic principles and procedures apply to Windows workers with only a few minor changes, which I'll note below.

As I walk you through my printing procedure, keep in mind that this is only one way of doing it. Use this workflow as a base or a point of reference; don't hesitate to change it to suit your own way of working. These steps are not carved in stone, even for me. I will sometimes change their order just for fun, or to see if there are any creative possibilities to discover.

The 11 steps in my inkjet printmaking workflow are:

1. Plan the Print.

2. Prep the File.

3. Edit the Image.

4. Save a Print-Specific Version.

5. Scale, Res, and Sharpen.

6. Select and Load Paper.

7. Select Image Settings.

8. Select Printer Driver Settings, Profile or RIP.

9. Make a Test Print (or two or three…).

10. Make Adjustments and More Test Prints.

11. Make the Final Print(s).

Step 1: Plan the Print

Just like tailors who measure twice and cut once, I spend a lot of time planning out my prints in advance. This may be less fun than jumping in and starting to image-edit, but believe me, you will save yourself a lot of headaches if you take your time with this step.

Once I've decided on my image and the rough print size, I make a full-size mockup. This is the best way to see if what you're planning is really going to work or not. The old-fashioned way is simply to cut down or tape together pieces of white poster board to equal the exact finished size of the print. (If you have an extra piece of the actual paper you'll be using, that's even better.) Then, cut out various-sized blocks of a colored paper to match the image size. I like to try out different sizes, taping them to the white backing piece. This is a very easy and good way to get a sense of a print's borders and proportions.

Full-sized mockups, done with either blocks of color or low-res versions of the actual image, are good ways to evaluate the size and proportions of a print.

A more sophisticated variation for making a mock-up is to output your actual image in a low-resolution format. For larger sizes, you may need to *tile* the image. You can do that with most page-layout and drawing programs or even in Photoshop if you add reference grid lines. I sometimes make a tiled, black-and-white mock-up with my office laser printer. The image can then be taped together and attached to the print backing sheet to evaluate the overall effect.

Again, the purpose of this important step is to have a 100-percent-size mock-up of your intended print that you live with for a while. I like to hang or tack them up in different locations around my house over the course of several days. Whenever I walk by, I stop and make a mental note. Once I'm satisfied with the image and print size, I'm ready for Step 2.

Step 2: Prep the File

Working in Photoshop CS, I verify my Color Settings RGB Working Space as Adobe RGB (1998), my favorite. I also check my monitor calibration settings or calibrate the monitor with one of the measured-calibration systems described in Chapter 4 again.

I organize my computer desktop with the appropriate folders and prepare to work on the file. This particular image was in 35mm slide format, and I had it scanned on a film scanner at my local photo lab at 4000 dpi. The 2592 × 1712-pixel file (I had pre-cropped a smaller portion to use for this) is an 8-bit RGB TIFF, and the first thing I do after opening it in Photoshop CS is Save As to the native PSD format. This now is my working file (see Figure 8.7).

Figure 8.7 The original scan is saved to a new file with a new name.

Step 3: Edit the Image

The first thing I usually do in Photoshop is check the *squareness* and the *cropping* of the image. In this case, there's nothing to square it against, so I won't worry about that. However, I do see a little too much emptiness on the right side, so I'll want to do some cropping. Because I know that I can't go back once I've cropped, I play it safe and create another Save As, this time adding the word "crop" to the title.

The image's Histogram looks pretty good; nice and full, so I don't really need to do any Levels or Curves adjustments. However, I'm noticing an overall red cast that's clearly visible in both the sidewalk outside the window and in the highlight top of the metal cheese cutter. This was obviously caused by the incandescent lights in the shop in combination with the daylight slide film. I confirm this by running the cursor over those areas and watching the Info palette numbers. Sure enough—too red.

One solution is to open an adjustment layer with Levels, and using the gray eyedropper, click on the metal cutter to make it and the rest of the image more neutral. However, I can't find a good spot where the image doesn't go too green and blue, so I try a different approach. I create a Curves adjustment layer, and in the Red channel, I pull down the end point until the red goes away. By doing it this way, the Red goes down, but the Green and Blue stay where they are. Figure 8.8 shows the final edited image along with the Curves menu. Sometimes, an image like this with different light sources (shop lighting, daylight) requires selection masks to correct such lighting issues.

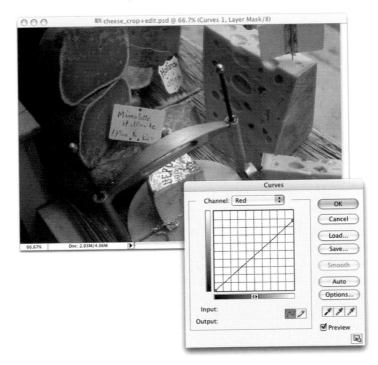

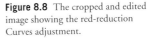

Figure 8.8 The cropped and edited image showing the red-reduction Curves adjustment.

I finish the editing by going over the entire image at 200% view, removing dust spots and repairing holes and defects.

Step 4: Save a Print-Specific Version

Once I have a finished, edited master and its companion files tucked safely away on my hard disk and on a backup CD stored in my wife's safety deposit box at the bank (you think I'm kidding?), I now make a

Figure 8.9 Work folder with the original files and the new print-specific file.

print-specific version to my edited (layered) file to continue my work. Again using the Save As command, I create a new file, adding to its name the destination printer—_HP130—or a project name or whatever makes the most sense. See Figure 8.9 to see how my project folder now looks.

Step 5: Scale, Res, and Sharpen

Because I'll be printing directly out of Photoshop, I could choose to flatten all the layers into one (Layer > Flatten Image), or I could Save As to TIFF format, which offers a flattening option. This removes the Layer palette clutter and also reduces the file size. However, because the file is relatively small, I decide to keep the file in its layered form. That way, I can easily go back and make minor adjustments to the existing layers if the printing is a little off. Note that if you're sending a file to someone else for printing, they will want a flattened TIFF *without* all the layers.

Size/Scale and Resolution: I covered the idea of sizing with image editing in Chapter 3, where I explained that *scaling* means stretching or compressing an image's pixels to fit a certain size on the paper. This is also called *resizing*. With *resampling*, on the other hand, all the pixel information and, therefore, the image itself is changed. With my cheeses, I use the scaling method to reach my desired print size.

Sharpen: There are people who say that sharpening should be done both early and again late in the workflow, but I prefer to do all the sharpening as a close-to-last last stage when I know what kind of printing I'll be doing.

There are many ways to sharpen an image—and I have yet to meet an image that didn't need it—including using Photoshop's standard unsharp masking filter (Filter > Sharpen > Unsharp Mask), using what's called the High Pass/Hard Light method, sharpening the L (Lightness) channel in Lab Color mode (keeping in mind that there is some degree of quality loss every time a file is moved into or out of Lab), or using special software, plug-ins, or procedures (such as only sharpening in 10-percent increments). For this image, I decide to use standard RGB sharpening but with a variation of the Fade Unsharp Mask effect.

I first make a duplicate image layer and start experimenting with the Unsharp Mask filter. Because this image does not have large flat areas, such as sky, I leave the Threshold setting at a lowly 1. I end up with sharpness settings of 99/.7/1.

Then I do a trick. The classic Fade Unsharp Mask (Edit > Fade Unsharp Mask) procedure involves setting the Fade mode to Luminosity and adjusting the opacity on the duplicate image layer. With this variation, I simply make a duplicate image layer, change the duplicate's blending mode to Luminosity, sharpen it, and adjust that layer's opacity; in this case to 85 percent (see Figure 8.10).

After sharpening, it's always a good idea to go over and check the image again carefully, usually at 100–200% view or more. Sharpening tends to add artifacts and to exaggerate any repair work.

Figure 8.10 Final sharpening with the Luminosity Blend Mode method. Left: the Unsharp Mask filter; right: the new sharpening layer.

Step 6: Select and Load Paper

I can't tell you how many times I've tried to print a file only to realize that I forgot to load the paper first. That's why I'm highlighting this step here.

I'll be using HP Premium Plus Photo Satin in 13 × 19-inch sheets. It's designed for use with the Designjet 130 (and 30), and I like its luster/satin surface as well as the 11.5-mil thickness (286 gsm).

After I turn on the printer (another essential step!), I load the paper in the front tray so that the printing surface is facing down (see Figure 8.11). This is different from the way many other inkjets (including most Epsons) handle paper, and it takes a little getting used to. The printer pulls the paper from the top. (Note that this printer also comes with roll feeder depending on the model, but I'm not using it here.)

With this paper there is no chance of mistaking the printing for the non-printing side as is sometimes the case with others. That's because the paper has an unusual "grainy" surface on the backside that helps stacked prints from offsetting or marring the image by providing a minuscule layer of air between the prints. Plus, there are all these HP logos printed on the back!

Certain papers can only be loaded one sheet at a time, but this is not one of them, so I load several sheets.

Proofing Paper: If I anticipate a lot of trouble, or if I'm using a very expensive paper stock, I might run my first tests on proofing paper, which only means that it costs less. Since the HP Premium Plus Photo Satin is a moderately priced paper (about $2.40 a sheet in the 13 × 19 size when you buy a box of 25), I choose to skip the special proofing paper and print right on the real stuff, primarily because I know that this printer/paper combination

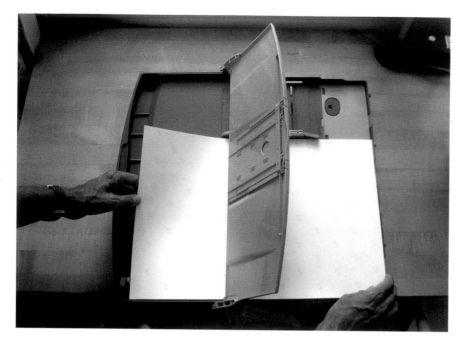

Figure 8.11 Most front-loading printers, including many HPs, require that you load the paper in trays with the printing side down.

gives predictably good results. Another solution would be to cut the paper in half so I can get two test prints out of each sheet. Since my final image is only about 9 × 6 inches, it would fit nicely on a half-sheet of 13 × 19 paper. All I would have to do is set up a new 13 × 9.5-inch size in Page Setup > Settings > Customize Paper Size (see Figure 8.12). (In Windows, it's Page Setup > Properties > Paper > Custom.) The new size now appears on the Paper Size list. If the image were larger, I could scale it down to fit just for this testing stage. Alternatively, I could pick a paper with similar characteristics in 8.5 × 11-inch format and use that. The whole point is to use less-expensive paper to proof and to see if you're even in the ballpark with the image.

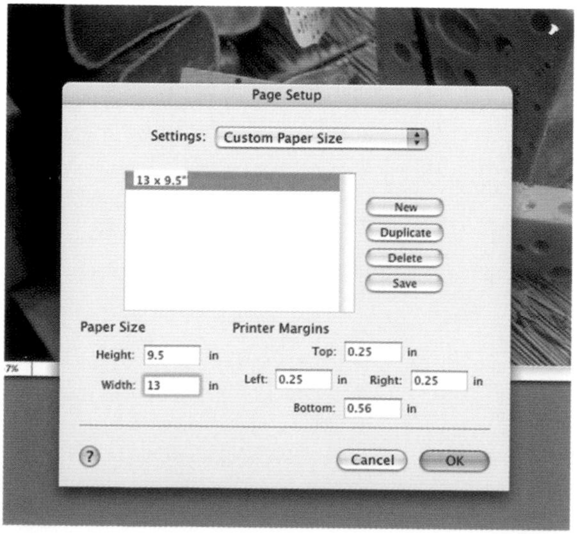

Figure 8.12 The Custom Paper Size function in Photoshop lets you create unique paper sizes for different purposes.

Step 7: Select Image Settings

In Photoshop, I confirm that I have the right sizing and print resolution settings under Image > Image Size (see Figure 8.13). I adjust the Printer Resolution to size the image for my paper. (You might want to review the section on resizing and resampling in Chapter 3 if you're still confused about this.) I use the resizing/scaling (not resampling) solution to end up with a print size of 8.6 × 5.7 inches at 300 ppi. (If you see variations in these figures in the screen shots in this chapter, it is because I'm continually experimenting with subtle size changes to see how the image and borders look.)

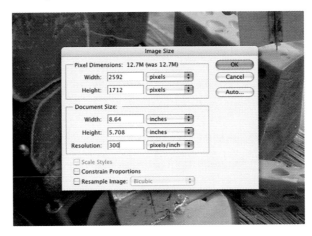

Figure 8.13 The Photoshop CS Image Size screen.

Step 8: Select Printer Driver Settings, Profile, or RIP

To access the printer driver settings for this printer, I choose Page Setup from the File menu and select the basic page options I want (see Figure 8.14). (In Windows 2000 and XP, it's Start > Settings > Printers.) These are just the rudimentary choices such as the printer I'm using, the paper size (if I were printing on a roll, I'd pick it here), the orientation (portrait or landscape), and the scale percentage.

For more, I now choose Print with Preview from the File menu and select the appropriate print options (I could have accessed Page Setup from here, too—see Figure 8.14).

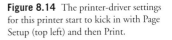

Figure 8.14 The printer-driver settings for this printer start to kick in with Page Setup (top left) and then Print.

The top portion of the Print menu is easy to understand, but the bottom (Show More Options checked), includes many options. I'll explain four of them.

Option A: Using the Printer's Basic Settings

Back in the Print menu (Figure 8.14), I confirm the scaling and sizing of the print and see a preview of how the image is positioned on the page. In the important Color Management section at bottom, I select Source Space > Document > Document: Adobe RGB (1998). This was the working space to which I had converted the image file as it is my preferred working space. If there were no working space associated with this file, it would read instead Document: untagged RGB.

For Print Space I select Profile > Same As Source because I want to start with the basic options at first. Same as Source means that there is no color conversion from working space to printer space going on (other than at the operating system level); the file is sent directly to the printer driver. This can yield very different results depending on the platform and driver color tools being used. For example, HP's color utility ColorSmart III assumes everything is sRGB, which in my case it isn't. Windows assumes the same thing, but ColorSync on the Mac is much smarter, assuming I know what I'm doing and recognizing whatever working space I have. You'll see the result in a later section.

All looks good, so I now select the Print button on this screen (top right). When that happens, I am presented with another small screen that allows me to quickly confirm settings I've already made, but more importantly, the third drop-down menu is my entrance into the key printer options, with the most important under the Paper tab being the Paper Type, Quality, and Color (see Figure 8.15). Here is where I make important choices, selecting my paper (Photo Satin), Quality (Best), and Color (ColorSmart III, HP's primary color utility). Note that Epson and Canon have similar screens that look slightly different. There's also a cool Summary option that let's me save and see what all my settings are and even fax them to someone else.

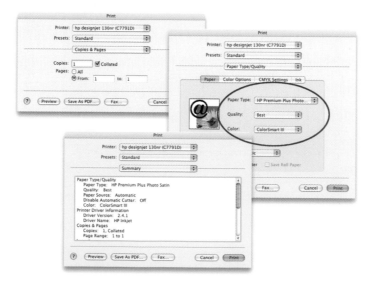

Figure 8.15 Deeper levels of printer settings for this printer include a few basics (top left), the all-important Paper Type, Quality, and Color settings (middle), and a summary of the settings chosen (bottom).

Option B: Using a Built-In ICC Profile

Next, I make a slightly different version by accessing the correct HP-supplied ICC printer profile (installed with the printer software) in the Print Space section of the main printer driver screen (see Figure 8.19). To make this work best, I want Photoshop to make the color conversion, which means I have to turn off all color management at the printer driver level. With this HP, that is accomplished by selecting Application Managed Color in the Color options tab (see Figure 8.19). This is similar to Epson's No Color Adjustment setting, and it avoids the "double dipping" problem I referred to in Chapter 4.

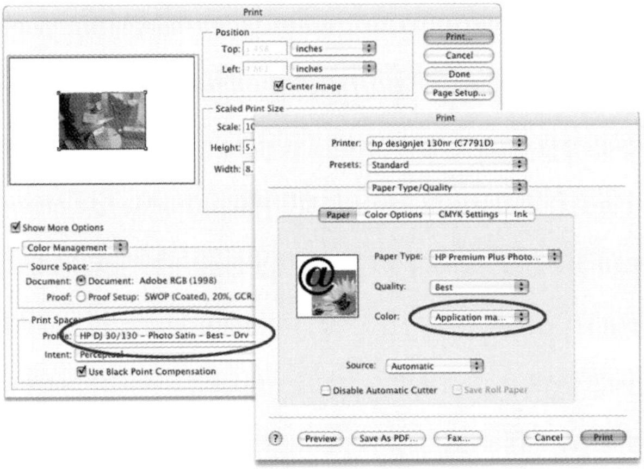

By using an ICC printer profile, this also opens up the options for Intent (I use Perceptual) and Black Point Compensation (I check it).

Figure 8.19 Selecting the supplied media profile (left oval) requires turning off color management at the driver level (right oval).

Option C: Using an Outside Printer Profile

An alternative to using the onboard printer settings and profiles is to use an outside printer profile, either one you create yourself with a profile software package as described in Chapter 4, or with a purchased custom profile. For this option, I choose the DIY Profile route.

I had already made a printer profile for this combination of inks and paper with GretagMacbeth's spectrophotometer-based Eye-One Publish (a higher version of Eye-One Photo) software, and I am ready to give it a try. I select the profile in the Print Space section and prepare to make a test print (see Figure 8.20). Obviously, if you plan to use a printer profile but haven't made one, now is the time.

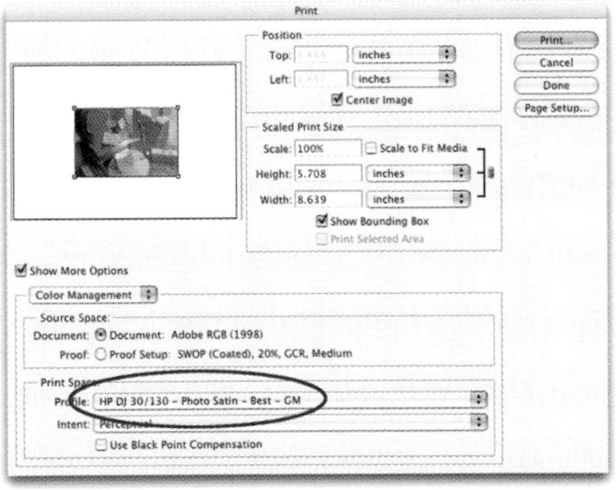

Figure 8.20 Selecting my own do-it-yourself printer profile (left oval), identified with a "GM."

Media Type Settings, Ink Output, and Dot Gain

The Media Type setting on an inkjet printer (it's called *Paper Type* or other names on different printers) determines, among other things, the amount of ink coverage or "ink laydown." This crosses over into the arcane world of *dot gain*, which is the tendency of ink dots to grow in size as they interact with different types of paper. Fibrous papers or more porous coatings set the stage for higher dot gain as the ink spreads, wicks, or bleeds into the paper. The opposite occurs on harder-coated or glossy paper surfaces where the ink tends to sit on top without much bleeding, spreading, or dot gain. The end result is that if the ink laydown or dot gain is not matched to the paper, prints can end up looking dark and muddy, or conversely, light and wimpy.

There are many sophisticated ways to control dot gain, including Photoshop's Dot Gain setting and Dot Gain Curves, but one of the easiest adjustments to make on a print that is coming out too light or too dark is simply to change the Media Type setting, which acts as a kind of dot-gain controller. (An alternative with some inkjets is to use the Color Density or Ink Density sliders (see Figure 8.16).

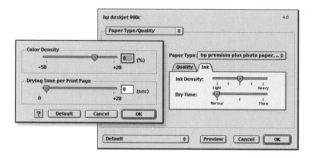

Figure 8.16 Ink density sliders are a welcome adjustment on certain inkjet printers. Epson and HP shown.

The Print Quality—or resolution—setting will also affect the amount of ink laydown. In general, the higher the resolution, the more ink will be used, although it's not true that doubling the dpi will double the amount of ink coverage. I've done tests, and the increase in total ink density from 360 to 720 to 1440 dpi is marginal, unless printing with no color adjustment, as is done for profiling targets.)

Figure 8.17 shows what the same test-strip image looks like printed on the same paper with only the Media Type settings changed. One caveat here is that, because Media Type settings include a whole package of image-quality features, changing these settings can affect other things—like color rendition—in addition to ink coverage.

While you can't always predict the results of changing Media Types without testing them yourself, a rule of thumb that usually holds true is that a setting for porous paper will yield *lighter* ink coverage on a glossy stock, and a glossy setting will do the reverse and yield *darker* ink output on a porous paper.

The bottom line to all this Media Type fiddling is that sometimes the wrong settings can produce the right results! See Figure 8.18.

Option D: Using the RIP

The HP Designjet 130 (and 30) comes with an optional HP software RIP (see Figure 8.21). The workflow is different than the previous ones because the PostScript driver supplied with the RIP must first convert the image data into PostScript page description language. Then the RIP itself takes over and converts the PostScript into a special printer language (PCL3GUI) that is sent to the printer to make the print. During all this, the appropriate printer profile is accessed, the screening pattern is applied, and the color management is done, either at the RIP or Photoshop level. (Read more about RIPs in Chapter 11.)

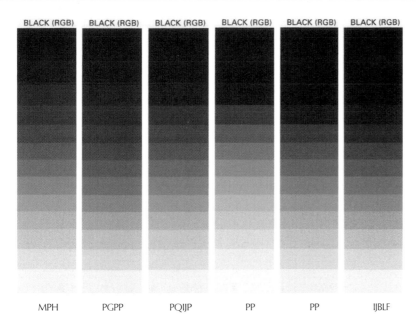

BLACK (RGB)   BLACK (RGB)   BLACK (RGB)   BLACK (RGB)   BLACK (RGB)   BLACK (RGB)

MPH   PGPP   PQIJP   PP   PP   IJBLF

Figure 8.17 The same test strip of RGB black (0R, 0G, 0B) in equal gradient steps printed with an Epson 1280 on the same paper (Epson Premium Glossy Photo Paper) at 1440 dpi with exactly the same settings, except that the Media Type was changed for each. From left Matte Paper Heavyweight, Premium Glossy Photo Paper, Photo Quality Ink Jet Paper, Plain Paper, Photo Paper, and Ink Jet Back Light Film. The Matte Paper Heavyweight setting applied the least amount of ink, and the Photo Paper or Ink Jet Back Light Film settings applied the most. Although color shifts were theoretically controlled by using a consistent No Color Adjustment setting, you can see how each setting changed the colors.

Figure 8.18 Sometimes it's right to pick the wrong setting! Here, the same image was printed with an Epson 1280 on the same paper (Epson Photo Quality Glossy Film) at 1440 dpi with only the Media Type settings changed. From left, the settings are: Photo Quality Glossy Film, Photo Quality Ink Jet Paper, and Ink Jet Back Light Film. The far-left image has the correct setting for the paper used, but I personally prefer the far-right "wrong" setting. Although it's grainier, the colors are punchier and more pleasing to my eye. It's reversed, but that's easily fixed with the "Flip Horizontal" check box that becomes active when you select this setting.

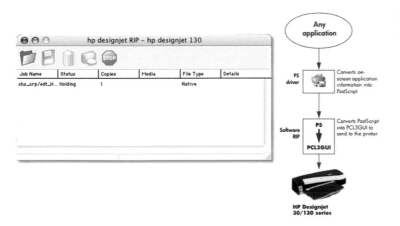

Figure 8.21 The HP RIP screen (left) with my file ready to print. Right is the basic workflow of this RIP.

Step 9: Make a Test Print (or Two or Three...)

Whichever workflow I'm following, when I'm satisfied that all the settings are correct, I am ready to send the file to the printer. (I may want to precede this step with a new Color Calibration to make sure the printer is in an optimum state. This Designjet 130 printer is one of the few that offers this option.)

The moment of truth—and an exciting one it is—comes with that first print out of the printer. This is almost never the final print, but it serves as the reference benchmark for all subsequent adjustments.

I make one test print with each of the four workflow versions already outlined. Here are my subjective comments about each:

A. Using the Printer's Basic Settings: To ease my way into this, I used Same As Source and the HP ColorSmart III utility. The print is so-so, with the colors weak overall. I quickly make another one but this time first converting my file to sRGB (remember that ColorSmart assumes all files are sRGB). That print is better with richer colors, but I know I can do much better.

B. Using a Built-In ICC Profile: For this print, I used the built-in ICC profile for the paper/resolution (Best) combination, and it's excellent. More saturated and with more contrast.

C. Using an Outside Printer Profile: Using the Eye-One-generated profile is better yet. Smooth and rich colors.

D. Using the RIP: This also results in an excellent print, but I'm actually leaning more to a couple of the others.

Left is the first print (Option A) with very basic settings; right is Option B, using the built-in ICC printer profile.

Keeping Track of Tests

A big part of printing is keeping track of what you've done so you can use your experience to improve the next prints down the line. That's why I always take the time to pull out a blank legal pad and jot down all the specifications, settings, and decisions made during each step of the workflow (see Figure 8.22).

Figure 8.22 It's a good idea to keep records of test-printing settings. These were from an earlier test printing.

Step 10: Make Adjustments and More Test Prints

You'll notice that I didn't say in this heading "Make Adjustments and *One More Print.*" I usually go through at least a few rounds of adjusting, printing, re-adjusting, re-printing, and so on. That's why it's important to take notes and to consistently number the prints as soon as they come out of the printer.

I saw some good potential in the Option B workflow (using a built-in ICC printer profile), so let's take that one a little further to get an even-better print.

Tweaks for Using a Built-In ICC Profile

This was the workflow based on the built-in HP ICC profile for the specific paper and resolution combination I'm using: HP Photo Satin paper and Best resolution. Let's try adjusting three parameters.

Print Resolution: A brief digression to explain HP's print resolutions—Normal, Best, and Max DPI—is in order. Normal on this printer means 600 × 600 dpi with eight passes of the printhead. This is the faster print mode, but the worst in terms of quality. I never use it. Best is 600 × 1200 dpi with 12 passes. Max DPI is 2400 × 1200 dpi with 12 passes. My original test print was done in Best mode, so the obvious next test is with Max DPI. The main difference between the resulting Max print and the Best one is the time it took to print it. Best took a total of 3:53 from the moment I clicked on the Print button to when the paper shot out of the printer. (Shot is the correct word since with this printer the paper flies out at the end like a missile!) Max DPI, on the other hand, took a whopping 10:16 for the same print. If the difference in quality were obvious, I might be open to taking the time to print in Max mode. However, after looking at the two prints, there is no visual difference between them, so I think I'll stick with Best.

Rendering Intent: The next thing to try is to change the Rendering Intent and Black Point Compensation (BPC). I try a print with BPC turned off and see virtually no difference (this is frequently the case). Then I try one print with each of the different intents (go back to Chapter 4 to revisit this). Saturation and Relative Colorimetric are all very close to my original Perceptual print with this image, but Absolute Colorimetric is clearly different (too blue).

Different rendering intents were tested; only one was clearly different.

Adjustment Layer: Because I'm noticing a slight darkness or dinginess in the lighter areas of the print, especially in the cheese cutter's top and bottom, I think I'll try adding an adjustment layer to make a subtle move. Opening a Curves layer in Photoshop, I click on the RGB highlight anchor point (top right) and, using my keyboard's arrow key, move it to the left one number at a time until I reach the lightness that looks right. I find a good point at 245 and stop (see Figure 8.23).

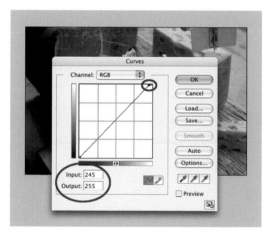

Figure 8.23 Lightening the composite RGB curve by moving the highlight end to the left helps to brighten the print.

Sure enough, the print with this adjustment, while very subtle, feels brighter and better overall.

I like it.

I have now made several test prints using four different workflows. Evaluating all my prints near a large window with diffused daylight coming in, I pick a good test print (the one I've been working on) as the final proof, and I check my notes for which settings were used to make it. As a safety measure, I transfer all the setting information to the border of the test print itself.

I have one more thing to do before making the final prints. Using the same settings as my approved test, I go back to the file, reload a sheet of 13 × 19-inch paper, and I make another print. I use the traditional printmaking term—*bon à tirer*, which means "good to print" in French—and write it on the final proof as a reminder. (If you use an outside printmaker, they will undoubtedly ask you to similarly sign off on the approved test print so they can use it as a guide against which all the final prints must conform.)

I'm ready to go.

Step 11: Make the Final Print(s)

Final prints require more planning. Test prints are disposable (or make great gift cards), but depending on how many of the real thing you'll now be printing at once, you need to think through this last step *before* you start:

- How long do the prints need to dry before they can be stacked or stored? (I'll let them air dry for several hours; glossy paper can take up to 24 hours or more. The HP paper with the grainy back takes less.)

- How many are you doing and how will you store them? Do you have an envelope or box that's big enough? (The original box the paper came is the perfect storage container.)

- How will you keep the prints from being damaged or soiled while handling? Do you have a clean worktable? Do you have cotton photo-darkroom gloves to wear? Do you have a good way—compressed air, for example—to clean off surface dust or dirt?

- Do you need to do any coating, spraying, or other type of finishing of the prints? How, when, and where will that be done?

- Are you signing and numbering the prints? When? How?

These are just some of the obvious questions that need answers; you will undoubtedly have more. In my case, since I'm only making one print for framing (and one extra as a backup), I have my drying table, acid-free glassine cover sheets (available at any art supply store), empty paper storage box, and gloves ready.

With everything in place, I re-open my final digital file, inspect and load the paper, do a quick check of the HP ink status icons on the front panel (see Figure 8.24) to make sure I have enough ink remaining for the job, verify all my settings, and hit the Print button.

As soon as the print comes out of the printer, I pick it up at the edges and carefully inspect it. It's perfect, and it goes to the drying area to lay flat while I return to the computer and print a backup copy.

A few hours later, I blow off any accumulated dust, and separate the two prints with slip sheets of glassine. To protect the edges as well as the prints in general,

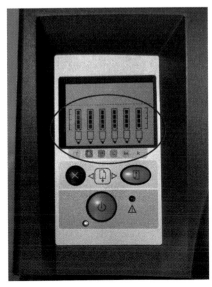

Figure 8.24 The six icons on the 130's front panel refer to the amount of ink in each of the ink cartridges. If any are flashing, they need to be replaced.

A Web Workflow

Because so many digital images end up on the Internet, here is a short workflow for preparing images for the Web. (My thanks to digital photographer and artist web-designer Larry Berman at www.LarryBerman.com for these 10 basic Photoshop steps.)

1. Convert to an uncompressed format, preferably PSD.

2. Crop and do your image adjustments. Curves, levels, cloning out dust, and so on. (Larry works at 100%.)

3. Resize to 72 ppi at whatever your long-pixel dimension is going to be. Be consistent. If you are preparing a series of images for a website, make them all the same long-pixel dimensions.

4. Add a single pixel stroke (Edit > Stroke in Photoshop). If the page is going to be black, make the stroke white; if the page is white, make the stroke black. That will let the dark areas stand out from a black page or the light areas stand out from a white page. Choose "inside" for the placement of the stroke, or it won't show.

5. Add a drop shadow if desired. This only works on a white or light-colored background, and the shadow should be right and bottom.

6. Add your copyright as a text layer. If you have a website, use that URL as the copyright so you can be found later.

7. Select the background layer and add unsharp masking.

8. Save and use the long-pixel dimensions as part of the file name to differentiate it from the full-size image in step one.

9. Image > Mode > Convert to Profile > sRGB

10. File > Save For Web. (Larry uses a setting of 40 for a progressive JPEG.)

For each image, you now have a full-sized uncompressed file, a resized version with active layers uncompressed, and the JPEG for the Web.

This is a good web workflow, and the only added suggestions I have are: (1) I also add the compression setting to the file name, for example, nordstrom_300x_50q.jpg, and (2) instead of always using a consistent JPEG setting, and depending on the situation, I sometimes try to hit a certain file size range. I adjust the setting accordingly until I have it. With experience, I can do it in one or two tries.

An example of a Larry Berman web image complete with a white stroke and a URL copyright.

Courtesy of Larry Berman
www.LaryBerman.com

I put them in the empty paper box they came in. This will keep them away from air circulation and light, and in general, keep them safe and sound until I'm ready to move to the final step: finishing, framing, and displaying—explained in more detail in the next chapter.

After the final prints are safely stored away, I congratulate myself for making a great inkjet print. You should do the same.

The workflow steps made above are meant to apply to anyone making his own inkjet prints. What's the next step after printing? Finishing and displaying. To find out about this post-printing step, turn the page.

9

Finishing and Displaying Your Prints

You've output one or more great digital prints. Now what? It's time to finish them in a way that protects and preserves them, and to show them off for the world to see.

Print Aesthetics

Because digital printing is a new art process, many wonder if the age-old rules of traditional printmaking apply to it. Canadian photographer Alan Scharf introduced me to the question of how to handle *print aesthetics*, and it's a good one. Should a digitally printed photograph look different from one printed in a darkroom? Is glossy paper or fine-art paper more appropriate? Should prints have square-cut edges or deckled ones? Plain borders, printed borders, or no borders? Equal borders all around or the traditional larger bottom border? Over-matted or float-mounted when framed or no frame at all?

One advantage of the digital printing revolution is that there are now many different looks available—everything from muted prints that evoke watercolors to glossy photographic prints and beyond. Artist and printmaker JD Jarvis believes that digital printing cries out for new approaches. "When it comes to printing or displaying digital art, think in non-traditional terms. Explore new materials and ways of displaying the work. In the long run, we stand to gain more credibility with the fine arts world by thinking outside the box it has created."

Finishing Prints

Finishing means anything after the print pops out of the printer, including drying, trimming, signing, embellishing, and more.

Drying

It's essential that your digital prints be completely dry before moving them to the next step, whether that be mounting, framing, storing, or shipping. Certain inkjet ink solvents, such as glycol, need extra time to dry, and this can take anywhere from 24 hours to several days depending on the inks and media used plus environmental factors such as temperature and humidity. Some imagemakers even let their prints dry for weeks! Fogging, misting, and clouding inside a glass-covered frame or a clear storage bag can be the result of not following this advice (see "Gas Ghosting").

High-volume printmakers solve the obvious space problems associated with drying by using commercial print-drying racks, sometimes in combination with forced-air heating systems (see Figure 9.1). These can be expensive new, but they can sometimes be picked up used from screenprinters.

Individual imagemakers have come up with their own creative approaches to print drying. For smaller prints, some, like John Nollendorfs, use hand hair dryers. "I have a hair dryer that I use to dry my test patches for profiling," he says, "and whenever I need a print to give a client quickly." However, he also recommends that people "put their prints in a drymount press for 30 seconds to one minute to minimize the gas ghosting problem (see "Gas Ghosting") prior to framing. "I think this makes more sense than letting prints sit around for a week under unknown humidity conditions hoping that this takes care of the ghosting problem."

Figure 9.1 Robert Kildoo at the drying rack at Thunderbird Editions in Clearwater, Florida. Prints are loaded from the bottom up; each rack is spring-loaded. This is a standard drying rack found in most printmaking studios.

Courtesy of Steve Carlisle Thunderbird Editions

Photographer Ken Smith lets his Epson UltraChrome (Premium Luster) prints sit for a good hour after printing. He then covers them with plain bond paper to soak up excess ink residue for a minimum of 48 hours. Then he hangs up the prints for another 48 hours (see Figure 9.2). Finally, he top-coats them with Lyson Print Guard spray. "This method is fine if I am not busy, but workspace comes at a premium, and there's only so much room to hang up prints. The place starts to look like a meat locker at times!"

Gas Ghosting

In 2003, photographers first reported on e-mail discussion lists about a specific problem called "gas ghosting" or out-gassing/fogging. Imagemakers were finding "fogging" on the inside of glass-framed prints when certain combinations of paper and inks were used for their digital printing. The initial discussion focused on Epson UltraChrome inks.

Epson took the unusual action of responding publicly, claiming that the fogging was caused by ink solvents that hadn't completely cured, and that the phenomenon primarily affected "barrier" papers (RC, as an example), and that it could occur with *any* manufacturers' inks, not only Epson inks.

The problem apparently does not occur with fine-art, matte-coated, watercolor, or cotton-rag-type papers, and the best solution seems to be with accelerated drying or curing procedures. Epson recommends interleaving stacked prints with plain paper to absorb the gasses and ink residues. If the fogging is already in evidence on the frame or bag, simply remove it with glass cleaner.

(*Epson's explanation of this phenomenon can be downloaded from www.dpandi.com/digitalnews/fogging.pdf.*)

Figure 9.2 Ken Smith likes to hang up his Epson UltraChrome (Premium Luster) prints for 48 hours as part of his drying process. "The problem is," he says, "I have only so much room to do this."

Courtesy of Ken Smith
www.klsimages.com

Deckling Your Edges

While some artists like Karin Schminke print directly onto fine-art paper with deckled edges (she has a special technique using removable tape plus strips of acetate taped to the back of the print), most prefer to tear the edges to give a deckled effect *after* printing. This takes some practice, but it's a skill that can be picked up very quickly.

Here's printmaker Jack Duganne's explanation for tearing the edges of a print: "Punch the front of the paper (where you want the tear to be) with a pin so that you can see the holes through the back of the paper. Turn the paper over and, lining up the holes made on the other side, tear against a straight edge, keeping the pressure against it and pulling the paper that you want to remove. After the tears are made, just smooth the torn paper with a rounded device like a spoon or piece of rubbing bone, and—Voilá!—a perfect deckled edge!"

For a deckled edge, gently tear the paper using the straight edge as both a guide and a cutting edge. You will notice that the paper will tear at different consistencies based on speed and pressure.

Deckling Tips

- With some paper stocks, it works well to use short tears (rather than one long one), even ripping toward the straight edge at varying angles to get a different look. All-cotton papers tear best.

- Different straight edge thicknesses will also create different tears.

- Special "deckling bars" or edges are available but not really necessary.

- Some like to wet the paper with a dampened sponge, brush, or Q-Tip, but others find this an unneeded extra step.

- It's best to practice on scraps of paper first. Then, when you're ready, move to the real print, take a deep breath, and start tearing.

Adding a Chop

What's a "chop"? It's a mark, usually embossed, on a print to identify the printmaker or the printmaking studio that produced the print. Sort of an identifying sign or house logo. Chops can add authenticity or a little flair to prints.

Chops are usually made with hand seals, which can be ordered at any good stationery or office supply store.

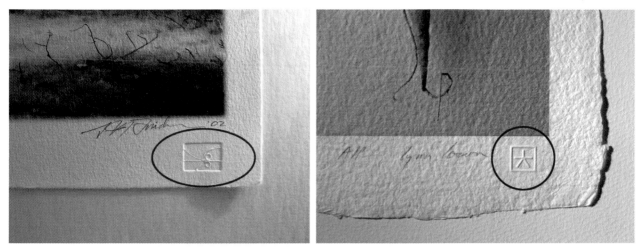

Left: Chop by New York's Marty Friedman, who for many years was a traditional fine-art printmaker with his own atelier where he did printing for such artists as LeRoy Neiman and Salvador Dali. Always a photographer, Friedman is now starting to use the chop on his digital prints, one of which is shown. Right: New Mexico digital fine-art printmaker Lynn Lown uses this chop on the work he produces at his studio. Lown trained as a traditional printmaker in intaglio, lithography, and photography, and in 1996 he opened New Media Arts, Santa Fe's first archival fine-art digital print shop.

Courtesy of (left) Marty Friedman/www.smfgallery.com and (right) Lynn Lown/www.nmarts.com.

Signing and Numbering

If you're producing an edition, you'll probably want to sign and number your prints. There are no hard-and-fast rules, although it's traditional for the signature and date to go on the right under the image, and for the edition number (if any) to go on the left. The title can go in the center. This only works if there's an empty border to sign on. If not, and the print is matted, some sign the back (lightly), and some even sign the mat, although that's not recommended since the mat and the print may eventually part company. Don't use adhesive labels on the back if you're concerned about print permanence.

Note that there's an entire movement of photographer-artists who are opposed to the principle of artificial limited editions when applied to digital prints that, in theory, can be produced endlessly without any image loss. These artists produce *open editions* and sign and number sequentially only. It's a personal choice.

If it's a limited edition, you'll write the number as a fraction: the first number (the numerator) is the number of the print; the second number (the denominator) is the full number of the edition. Like this: 15/50 or 1/250.

As for the mechanics of signing, it's conventional to sign art prints in pencil, although that won't work with glossy and other non-porous media. In that case, paint markers, gold or silver pens, or other permanent marking pens are used (Sharpie brand permanent markers have been known to fade rapidly). Some hardcore digitalists who are concerned with "differential permanence" have been known to use pens filled with the actual black ink from their printing inksets.

35/400

Embellishing Prints

Embellishing means taking a digital print and adding hand brush strokes, glitter, textures, or other artistic flourishes and enhancements to give the print a more custom look. This is also a form of "digital mixed media," and it's very popular among certain artists printing giclée reproductions since selling prices can be much higher than with non-embellished prints.

One important question about embellishing is: do you need to seal the print, and what sort of embellishing media can you use? Some experimentation may be required. For example, Toronto printmaker John Toles at Dragonfly Imaging & Printing works with artists who embellish their PremierArt WR Glossy Canvas prints (Epson UltraChrome inks) by (1) allowing the prints to dry at least 24 hours, (2) using two light coats of Print Shield protective spray coating to seal the prints, and finally (3) applying acrylic paints (not oils) by hand with a brush. In fact, some artists, like Dorene Macaulay, do much more! (See next image.)

Artist Karin Schminke advises that the type of medium and coating will determine how and if sealing is required and which materials work best. "If you are using a gelatin-based, pre-coated paper or canvas (often gloss or semigloss surfaces), they will dissolve when moistened and therefore need to be sealed before adding other media." (For more about using custom pre-coats and even more about digital mixed media printmaking, see Chapter 11.)

Other artists report success after spraying paper prints with an acrylic sealer like Krylon brand clear spray and then painting over that with acrylic medium.

Talk about embellishing! Canadian artist Dorene Macaulay embellishes her canvas prints by painting on colored, melted wax, using a blow torch, and finally gouging the surface.

Courtesy of Maureen Toles/www.dragonflyprinting.com

Coating Prints

The decision of whether or not to coat a digital print is dependent on how the print is made and what problems need solving. Some newer printers, such as Epson's R800, are starting to incorporate a form of gloss coating as a print device option, but the applications (so far) are limited, and many imagemakers are experimenting with coating their prints.

Why Coat?

The main benefit of post-coating digital prints is protection—protection against moisture, UV light damage, atmospheric contaminants, biochemical activity (molds), plus the abrasion, scuffing, and fingerprinting that always seem to occur with normal print handling.

Coatings can also be used to even out gloss differential and to punch-up or add depth to the color intensity of inkjet inks, especially pigmented ones that sometimes have a reduced color gamut. This is a well-known technique to increasing the Dmax of an inkjet print's dark shadows.

Digital artist Dot Krause used Clearstar's ClearShield Type C semigloss liquid laminate for her Boston Federal Reserve mural project (see Chapter 1). Explains Krause, "The ClearShield enriched the color while providing protection from UV light, airborne particles, moisture, and abrasion. It also made the surface of my pigment inkjet prints more flexible, enabling the canvas to be wrapped around the edges of the custom-made stretchers."

Do the coatings actually help with print permanence? This is a hotly debated issue, where some believe coatings can do more harm than good. "Many of these coatings," says artist and artists' materials researcher Mark Gottsegen, "may eventually cross-link, which makes them harder to remove should that become necessary; some may yellow or crack."

Chris Polson, whose company Twin Brooks also stretched the canvases, brushes ClearShield Type C semi-gloss liquid laminate onto Dot Krause's inkjet-printed panels for the Boston Federal Reserve Bank murals.

Courtesy of Chris Polson
www.midcoast.com/~twnbrook

While this has been a relatively unresearched area in the past with all sorts of wild claims, coating products do seem to be improving with the permanence spotlight now shining on this area of digital printing. However, reasonable caution and adequate research into claims and testing methods are in order for any imagemaker intending to use print coatings.

One popular product is PremierArt's Print Shield spray. This is a low-odor, lacquer-based, aerosol-can spray designed specifically for inkjet prints. Print Shield has even been allocated a special category in Henry Wilhelm's Display Permanence Ratings, and the results, according to Wilhelm, are very encouraging. For example, in the May 1, 2004 testing results for the Epson 4000 printer, the predicted life for Somerset Velvet for Epson and UltraChrome inks is 62 years for prints displayed under glass. The very next line on the chart shows the same paper/ink combination and again under glass, but this time a sprayed coating of Print Shield bumps the predicted lifespan up to 166 years! (Note that this is with the spray coating and glass framing, which apparently provides the almost-triple protection. The same chart shows the identical combination with only the Print Shield at 75 years.)

Do you really need to coat prints that will ultimately end up framed under glass or in an album of some type? As inkjet expert Dr. Ray Work says, "Glass is good, but coating and glass is better." Others, however, believe that if you're using long-lasting inks that are well-matched to the medium or paper, coating your (paper) prints is very optional. Canvas prints are more likely *not* to go under glass, so in that case, coating makes much more sense.

PremierArt Print Shield is a lacquer-based spray designed specifically for inkjet prints.

Courtesy of Premier Imaging Products

Other reasons to coat prints include: (1) isolating certain pigment inks that tend to smear or smudge on glossy media, (2) providing a base on which to add painted-on embellishments, and (3) giving your prints even more protection for some situations like outdoor exposure.

Types of Coatings

Coatings (also called *overcoats* or *topcoats*) come in different forms including film laminates, liquid laminates (clearcoats, acrylic varnishes, photo lacquers), and sprays. These can be further broken down into finish types from high gloss to satin or matte. Ideally, you want an inert, odorless, colorless, non-yellowing, anti-fungal coating that's easy to apply. You also want to avoid a coating that draws coating or buffering agents out of the medium, an early problem often reported that caused the coated prints to turn milky or dusty. And, you want to know that the coating is not going to shorten the life of the print.

Let's look more closely at two popular coating categories for digital prints.

Liquid Laminates

Liquid laminates are of many types—acrylics, solvent-based, water-based, and UV-curable, and they can form a protective shield on your prints. However, these post-print coatings must be carefully matched to the type of inks and especially the media pre-coatings used so that the image is not destroyed when one attacks the other. Most liquid laminate suppliers will give guidelines for this kind of materials matching.

Brushing and rolling are two popular ways to put a liquid coating onto a print. (Screening and using a "Mayer" or metering bar are two more, but they are beyond what most self-printers want to tackle.)

Brush: Liquid coatings can be brushed on with relative ease, although it takes patience and practice in order to get a thin, uniform coat. Brush choice plus correct thinning technique are essential.

Roll: Rolling on a liquid coating can be a good option for fine-art paper and canvas prints, although it can be tricky and sometimes messy. Printmakers report mixed results with roll-ons. Ken Smith uses a 4-inch super-smooth foam roller to apply Liquitex Matte Varnish (for matte finishes) and Liquitex Gloss Medium and Varnish (for gloss finishes) to his canvas prints (see Figure 9.3). "In 99 percent of the cases," Smith says, "this method works well. That other 1 percent, however, causes problems when mysterious intruders such as specs of dust are introduced to ruin the coating."

And while Australian printmaker Len Phillips also has had good luck with a fine-nap paint roller, others have switched to professional spraying systems.

Figure 9.3 Photographer Ken Smith rolls on Liquitex Gloss Medium and Varnish to coat his canvas prints.

Courtesy of Ken Smith
www.klsimages.com

Liquid Coating Tips

- Clean everything before coating: wiping down the print, vacuuming the work area and work clothes.

- For some, better protection occurs after first spraying print with an artist's fixative before liquid coating.

- To keep bubbles from forming with brush-on, try diluting with the recommended thinner and always stir—never shake—the container.

- Make sure the ink on any print is completely dry before any coating is attempted.

- Make sure any coatings are completely dry before framing or storing.

- Always test any coating method on scrap prints.

Sprays

Spraying prints is popular, but it can be dangerous to your health without the proper precautions, including a good mask and *very good* ventilation.

With spray coatings, you need to become experienced enough so that you can't see the spray marks on the paper or canvas. Several light coats are usually recommended over one thick coating. InkjetART's Royce Bair has good recommendations for spraying with Print Shield: "…produces almost invisible changes to matte or textured fine-art prints when coated with at least three light coatings that do not completely wet the print, allowing one to two minutes of drying time between each coating. The direction of the spray should be

Table 9.1 Sample Liquid/Spray Coatings for Digital Prints

Supplier	Brand Name	Type	Use On (media)	Use With (inks)	Comes In
Breathing Color www.breathingcolor.com	Giclée Varnish	water-based	fine-art paper, canvas	any pigment inkjet	750ml tin (container)
Clearstar Coatings	ClearShield Type C	water-based	waterproof canvas	non-water-sensitive pigment	quart, 1-gallon, 5-gal., 55-gal.
www.clearstarcorp.com	ClearJet	solvent-based	canvas, various	dyes or pigment inkjet	aerosol can, quart, gallon
Golden www.goldenpaints.com	MSA Varnish Archival Varnish	solvent-based solvent-based	various various, inkjet prints	various various	12-fl. oz. can aerosol can
Liquitex	Matte Permanent Varnish	acrylic polymer and paper	various canvas	experiment!	multiple-sized jars
www.liquitex.com	Gloss Medium & Varnish	acrylic polymer	various canvas and paper	experiment!	multiple-sized jars
Lumina Coatings	Giclée Jetcoat	solvent-based	fine-art paper	dyes or pigment inkjet	1-gal, 5-gal, 55-gal
www.luminacoatings.ca	AQUA Jetcoat II	water-based	canvas, various papers	pigment	1-gal, 5-gal, 55-gal
Lyson www.lyson.com	Print Guard	resin	gloss, semi-gloss, fine-art	dyes or pigment inkjet	aerosol can, pint
PremierArt www.premierimagingproducts.com	Print Shield	solvent (lacquer)	canvas, fine-art paper	dyes or pigment inkjet	aerosol can, 5-ltr.bulk
Triangle Coatings www.bulldogproducts.com	Bulldog Ultra	solvent-based	canvas is best	dyes or pigment inkjet	aerosol can, quart, gallon, 5-gal.

alternated between applications (move left to right, then up and down, then diagonally across the print). Glossy, semigloss, luster, or canvas prints should be coated once with enough spray to thoroughly wet the print's surface (the print should lay in a horizontal position so as to not cause the wet spray to run)."

Some printmakers report that aerosol spray cans sometimes deliver unpredictable results with occasional spurts and blobs landing on prints. A professional spray unit is preferred. A high-quality HVLP (high volume, low pressure) spray gun will provide a good finish with very little over-spray and less product waste than with high-pressure sprayers. High-pressure, automotive-type sprayers or high-end airless sprayers can also work, although these types of sprayers are made to spray paint and do not atomize all liquid laminates properly.

Spraying Safety

The biggest concern with spray coatings are the health and environmental hazards involved.

What can you do to be safer? Follow these safety tips:

- Because spraying produces airborne contaminants, get a good face mask like the ones professional autobody painters use.

- Wear your face mask whenever spraying, mixing, or handling coating or painting materials.

- Always wear safety approved goggles or glasses when spraying. Try to cover your hands and other areas of exposed skin.

- Never spray near open flames or pilot lights in stoves or heaters.

- Ventilation requirements (indoors): (1) only work in a well-ventilated area, (2) run ventilation continuously, and (3) continue ventilation for at least *one hour* after spraying is completed. The best sort of ventilation is a hood type with direct exhaust (through a filter) to the outside.

Two spraying operations: (left) photographer, professor, and author Stan Shire sprays with an HVLP sprayer in his basement shop next to an open sliding door, which pulls most of the material out. "In the winter, I wear a sweater," he says. His mask is a standard 3M organic vapor respirator. At right is printmaker Steve Carlisle using the same type of HVLP sprayer that's used for painting cars. That's a silkscreen sink with built-in ventilation from behind. He also has code-approved top ventilation, and he keeps a door open. His full-face mask is also from 3M.

Courtesy of Stan Shire/Community College of Philadelphia (left); Steve Carlisle/Thunderbird Editions

Two other options for those who don't want to mess around with proper ventilation and/or face masks are "spray-for-pay" and using a liquid coating machine. Spray-for-pay means finding someone else to do it for you. It may be hard to locate an individual or a shop who will take in your prints for coating without having done the printing, but it may be worth the effort to find them.

Liquid coating machines for photographer-artists are relatively new on the scene, and permanence researcher Bill Waterson has developed a working prototype that was undergoing field testing at the time of this writing (see Figure 9.4). You pour the coating solution into the tray and then pass your print manually under the roller and pull it out the other side. Cost is about $40 in materials, and of course the labor is your own. It can be constructed up to any size; the one shown is intended for 24-inch wide prints coming from an Epson 7600 printer. All materials are easily available at most hardware suppliers.

Figure 9.4 Bill Waterson's prototype of a liquid coating machine. The print is drawn under a roller and over a squeegee, which is really just an ordinary door sweep from the hardware store cut to size and then bolted in place using wing nuts for easy removal. Total cost of materials: about $40, or $65 with a stainless steel roller (shown).

Courtesy of Bill Waterson
waterson@ainet.com

Film Laminates

Film lamination is growing in popularity with photographers and artists who are producing digital output. As a frequent gallery goer and an observer of the scene, I have noticed more and more high-end galleries showing laminated photo exhibits. Joel Meyerowitz exhibits and sells laminated inkjet prints mounted on Sintra material or Plexiglas. Judith Turner, a New York architectural photographer, had an exhibition of her Times Square prints that were mounted on aluminum with no framing and no glass, just laminated with a luster finish.

Dr. Ray Work is a strong advocate for film lamination of inkjet prints. "Lamination provides extraordinary advantages," he explains. "In addition to protection from humidity and pollution, it eliminates the differential gloss frequently experienced with pigmented inks, allows different choices in surface finish, increases the color density, and improves the distinctness of the image. Lamination also improves the lightfastness and provides both physical surface durability and waterfastness. All in all, it's a good idea."

Lamination Equipment and Materials: Depending on whether you are considering hot (with heat) or cold (with adhesives) lamination, you need to pay attention to the composition of the laminate material itself. According to Dr. Work, some films are made of PVC (polyvinyl chloride). PVC yellows and cracks with age, plus PVCs contain materials that can migrate into the ink layer and chemically bleach the image, resulting in fading. The adhesives can also degrade inkjet images. "Polyester is a far better choice for a laminating film," says Dr. Work. "It is much more stable to light and ages very well, plus it contains no materials that migrate into the ink layer." To drive the point home, Dr. Work points out that the virtually indestructible, modern, plastic beverage bottle is made of polyester.

Laminating requires a laminator, and they come in all sizes and shapes from various suppliers including ProSeal, Coda, LEDCO, and LexJet. The LexJet 2700C (see Figure 9.5), engineered by a company owned by photographer Cris Daniels, is interesting because it may be the first cold-pressure laminating and mounting system designed and created for photographers and fine-art studios. It's a solid-looking machine made with 6061 anodized aluminum, stainless steel, and silicone ground-rubber rollers.

Figure 9.5 LexJet's 2700C cold-pressure laminating and mounting machine (developed by Cris Daniels, inset) may be the first laminator specially made for photographers, fine-art printmakers, and others doing high-quality digital imaging and printing.

Courtesy of LexJet.com and danielsimaging.com

The Look of Lamination: Film laminates, while being very protective, have traditionally been disparaged by photographer-artists because the resulting work has looked stiff and "plasticy." After all, this is how restaurant menus at Denny's are coated! Many have not liked the look of lamination on fine-art papers where the texture or feel of the paper is part of the overall package. However, recent film-lamination advances have resulted in very thin, very flexible overlaminate films that are only 0.5-mil thick. Once applied correctly, they basically disappear. Photographer Phillip Buzard has had canvas inkjet prints top-coated with a Drytac laminate that was so thin that "I couldn't tell it was there. The canvas texture was still apparent. There was no stiffness, and if I had wanted, I could have rolled them up."

Photographer Stephen Livick adds, "If you use a laminator, then mat and frame your prints, people will not be able to tell if the work is laminated or not, and you will add years to the life of your prints."

Mounting and Framing Prints

Mounting and framing go together, and they are a good way to protect and display your prints.

Mounting

While many photographers are successful with dry (hot) or cold-adhesive mounting of their prints to backing boards, others follow traditional printmaking methods where prints are adhered at the top only, letting the sides and bottom hang free and exposed. The idea is to have the least amount of bonding with the print so that it is free to expand and contract with environmental changes. This is called "float-mounting," and it creates its own shadow-box effect as the light falling on the print plays over the loose edges (see Figure 9.6).

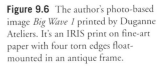

Figure 9.6 The author's photo-based image *Big Wave 1* printed by Duganne Ateliers. It's an IRIS print on fine-art paper with four torn edges float-mounted in an antique frame.

In terms of mounting materials and techniques, acid-free corners or archival linen hinges are often used. A so-called "T-hinge" requires that the print be overlaid with a mat to hide it. A variation of the T-hinge is the V-hinge, which folds up under the print, making it perfect for float mounting. Also, Japanese paper and a water-soluble adhesive such as wheat starch are popular with museums; they adhere to a basic conservation requirement that the mounting can be completely undone with no damage to the print.

The key point is to avoid non-archival material such as rubber cement or masking tape. Use only acid-free mounting, matting, backing, and framing materials. If dry mounting inkjet prints, make sure to use low heat and always test first; some inks are affected by heat more than others. You can also dry mount canvas prints, but again, test first.

Buffering or Not?

Many people are confused about whether buffered (calcium carbonate or similar substances are added to raise the pH level) or non-buffered mounting and matting material should be used with digital prints. Here are some tips:

- For certain types of prints, you do *not* want buffered papers to come in contact with the prints. For animal-based materials (leather, silk, wool) and for traditional photographic C prints (chromagenic), Cibachromes (Ilfochromes), dye-transfer prints, albumens, and cyanotypes, use pH-neutral but *non-buffered* materials.

- For traditional silver gelatin photo prints and for color inkjet prints, it's okay to use buffered papers.

- Frame Destination's Mark Rogers points out that most paper mats, while technically "acid-free," are actually just pumped full of calcium carbonate to temporarily reduce the acid content. "Just like with people who take TUMS for acid indigestion," he says, "the buffering will last many years, but eventually the mat will become acidic and need replacing. How long is debatable. For true conservation, it is preferable to start with 100-percent cotton rag mats, which are naturally acid free."

Figure 9.7 Jonathan Talbot presents his mixed-media work, many of which contain computer-generated elements, by floating the paper (with the edges showing) inside 8-ply, all-rag mats and then framing them under glass in simple, white-washed maple frames. Shown at left is *Pi Patrin*, a 3-inch-square image on 7 × 7-inch paper in a 12 × 12-inch frame. Strategic grouping on a gallery wall adds rhythm to what might otherwise be a repetitious display.

Courtesy of Jonathan Talbot
www.talbot1.com

Mats: If loose or hanging edges are not your style, then adding an over-mat (or just "mat") is probably right for you. Most mats slightly overlap the edges of the print, holding them down and also providing an uncluttered border between the image and the edge of any framing. A variation is to have the mat stop short of the edges of the print, so that the edges are exposed (see Figure 9.7). Mats come in various colors and thicknesses with 4-ply and 8-ply (thicker) as the standards.

Equality for Borders?

The traditional way to mat an image is to have equal borders on the top, left, and right, but to have the bottom border be slightly larger, usually by a factor of 1.5. (Mark Rogers says some believe that the wider bottom helps provide a base for the artwork to "sit down into.") There are various theories of why this should be, but the fact is that the trend now seems to be shifting to having equal borders on all sides. Why?

Former frame shop owner Laurie Draper explains that "the shift to cutting equal borders was due largely to the mat cutters commonly used in frame shops having three cutting stops that had to be adjusted for each changing border width. This made it time-consuming to adjust them repeatedly to cut one mat. Some frame shops adopted a new norm of cutting equal borders all around, making it faster and therefore more cost-effective for them.

However, with the growing use of computerized mat-cutters, all one needs to do now is enter the border widths and the computer determines the cut, so cutting weighted (unequal) mats is no longer more effort. Conversely, the growing use of precut mats makes equal borders a necessity so that the buyer can use the ready-made mat in either a vertical or horizontal position."

NOTE: A nifty Mat Size Calculator that was created by Ken Schuster for determining equal and unequal border sizes can be downloaded from the DP&I.com website at: www.dpandi.com.

Mats can be made with a mat cutter or bought pre-made in quantity. Many established photographer-artists buy pre-cut mats from such suppliers as pictureframes.com, unit-edmfrs.com, and framingsupplies.com.

A digital alternative to real mats is a "faux mat" created in an image-editing or drawing program and printed on the print itself. See Figure 9.8 for an example. Faux mats can be combined with real ones to produce a double-mat effect.

Framing

There are two reasons to frame a print: (1) to help protect it, and (2) to present the image or print in a professional and appealing way that separates it from everything around it while at the same time not distracting attention from the image itself. This is not an easy task with so many options for moldings, mats, and special treatments like French matting, fillets, and finished corners. Framing is a true craft and should not be undertaken casually. You either pay a professional framer, or you buy the equipment and take the time to learn how to do it yourself.

The normal process involves attaching the (paper) print to a backing board (see Mounting above), then attaching the mat (if one is used) over the print and the board with conservation/archival-quality framing tape. The whole sandwich is then ready for the frame with either a glass or acrylic front. Canvas prints can also be framed once they are either mounted on board or on artist stretcher bars.

Purchased frames are either custom-made to your specifications, or they come in pre-made standard sizes or by-the-inch kits that you assemble yourself. A sampling of frame suppliers includes: Graphik Dimensions, Frame Fit, and Frame Destination, Inc.

Frame Sizes: Standard-sized mats and frames are the way to go for keeping costs down. Print buyers are also more likely to buy art that is either matted or framed in standard sizes. The problem is photo industry frame sizes (8 × 10, 11 × 14, 16 × 20, etc.) do not match printing industry paper sizes (8.5 × 11, 11 × 17, 13 × 19, 17 × 22, etc.).

One of the author's do-it-yourself framing projects with a float-mounted inkjet print.

Another problem for photographers is that the aspect ratio of common film sizes (35mm and 4 × 5) does not match up to the proportions of all standard frames. The photographer is then faced with a choice: either crop the image (unacceptable by many photographers), or have unequal borders that maintain the integrity of the full-frame image. Most opt to live with unequal borders (or they make custom frames to fit).

This standard wood frame (Profile 952, .75-inch wide, 1.25-inch deep) from Frame Destination has exterior dimensions of 20 × 26 inches with equal 3.5-inch 8-ply mat borders added to a 13 × 19-inch inkjet print (the actual window opening is 12.75 × 18.75 inches). The frame is faced with UV-filtering acrylic (Cyro OP3).

Courtesy of Mark Rogers
www.framedestination.com

These—and other—problems caused amateur photographer Mark Rogers to start his own framing business (www.framedestination.com). "I was really frustrated with the lack of frame sizes for 13 × 19 and other print sizes from the usual suppliers," Rogers explains. "I also found it hard to find standard-size frames that would help reduce fading and not cause yellowing. So I decided to offer these products for fine-art photography." Rogers currently markets acid-free, conservation-quality frames in wood or metal, complete with CYRO acrylic glazing and Artcare-treated Bainbridge mat/mount components.

Glazing: Glazing means glass or acrylic (Plexiglas is one example) when you're talking about framing. Both types come in plain UV-filtering, anti-reflective or non-glare, and abrasion-resistant versions. With glass, the UV-filtering type is preferred except it's much more expensive than regular glass. As we've learned, even plain clear glass will block much of the UV radiation hitting a print.

Glass and acrylic each have their followings. Acrylic is lighter, more expensive, scratches easily, and is a magnet for dust and lint, but it's the best choice if you're shipping prints or if used in high-traffic or dangerous areas like a child's room. Also, some museums prefer acrylic since it's safer for priceless artwork; it will not shatter and cut the art when dropped.

Framing Tips

- Never let a print touch the glass in a frame. Why? Some inks and emulsions can react with the glass and get permanently stuck to it. Also, if condensation ever forms on the inside of the glass, the water could damage the print. Either use a mat or frame spacers to create a gap between the glazing and the art.

- Always use acid-free (and lignin-free) materials in all phases of the framing process. That goes for mats, backing boards, and the hinging or adhesive material. Much of the commercial framing done before 1980 used poor-quality materials; replace all such frames and materials.

- Isolate any questionable material from important prints with sheets of glassine or wax paper. A very common questionable material is any wood frame, since it would naturally contain acidic pulp products.

- Don't use acidic brown barrier (Kraft) paper on the back of a frame to seal against air and dust. Use instead conservation/archival-quality paper, or in a pinch, white butcher paper.

- Make sure your prints are completely dry before framing. This can be anywhere from 24 hours to several days depending on the inks and media used.

- Periodically open up your framed prints (five years is a good target) and clean them thoroughly. Replace any problem components.

Framing Alternatives

There are now many alternatives to the traditional picture frame approach to digital print display. Here are just a few:

Unusual Frames: Feeling like breaking away from the standard frame shop selection? Photographer-artist Konrad Poth makes his own frames from recycled wood from old barns and fences. Globe-trotting photographer S.R. Aull spends a year photographing a specific place (Paris, Hong Kong, Manhattan), and then he frames his traditional Ilfochrome color prints in antique wood windows and doors from each respective culture. He explains that "Each window or door represents a tangible portal combined with an image transporting the viewer to that culture and period in time."

Board-Mounted Prints: Mounting prints (using either cold or hot mounting techniques) to thick composite boards with no borders and no framing is very popular. Board materials include Foamcore, MDF, Sintra, Dibond, and Gatorfoam. These can be purchased from art supply vendors, and they come in various thicknesses and even colors. Black Gaterfoam in 3/4" is a common choice. (Gaterfoam has a polystyrene core and a wood-fiber laminate surface that resists denting. It's very rigid and smooth, and it can be used for dry or pressure-sensitive mounting.) The hanging is a bit tricky, but one solution is to glue on blocks of wood with framing wire attached. The blocks offset the print from the wall, creating a nice drop-shadow effect.

Landscape photographer Russ Davis has devised a practical and inexpensive alternative to normal framing for his Epson 7600 inkjet prints (see Figure 9.10). Using MDF board (Medium Density Fiberboard) as his backing, he covers the print/backing sandwich with a matte-finish laminate (hot press). "The laminate is non-reflecting so you see the photograph without glare," Davis says. "The edge is finished with a beveled black border, and the board-mounted prints are very durable with a surface that can be cleaned with window cleaner and a soft cloth." The MDF is not acid-free, but Davis inserts an acid-barrier (mounting tissue) between the print and the MDF.

Figure 9.10 Russ Davis uses MDF board and a matte laminate for displaying his prints.

Courtesy of Russ Davis Photography
www.russdavisphoto.com

Plexiglas, Aluminum, and More: Many modern materials are available for alternative framing. Duggal Visual Solutions is one of the largest photo and imaging labs in the world, at least by the number and type of services offered. Located right in the heart of the Photo District in New York City, Duggal is a leader in modern framing techniques and specializes in custom work for museums, galleries, photographers, and fine artists. They offer state-of-the-art framing solutions, including face-mounting images to Plexiglas, "Sandwich Plexiglas" (image sandwiched between two pieces of Plexi), anodized aluminum, and custom metal and wood bracing.

New York City's Duggal specializes in unusual mounting and framing techniques. Shown (from left): Digital photo print on floating gallery Plexi with standoffs, digital Duratrans in custom light box, and digital photo print with museum box mount.

Courtesy of Duggal Visual Solutions

Canvas: If you're printing on canvas, you can stretch the print onto the standard artist stretcher bars that painters use, complete with folded corners. Canvas prints can be mounted to board or stretched and then either wall-hung as is or placed in a frame. Following are some canvas-stretching tips from artist and printmaker Lance Amici at Torlan Studios in San Antonio, Texas.

Canvas Stretching Tips
- Leave plenty of margin on all sides for wrapping around the wood.
- Slightly sand or round off the corners of the stretcher bars before stretching to minimize tearing or hairline cracks.
- Do not stretch or roll canvas prints in temperatures below 70° F.
- If a coating seems brittle, use a hair dryer to warm up the canvas edges before stretching them.
- Do not stretch canvas prints as tightly as you would an original.

John Toles of Dragonfly Imaging and Printing in Toronto, Canada, stretches a canvas print.

Courtesy of John Toles
www.dragonflyprinting.com

Storing and Shipping Prints

After prints are finished, you have to store and sometimes ship them.

Storing Prints

If you're not selling, giving away, or displaying your prints, then you'll be storing them. Storage enclosures can take several forms, but they have the same goal: to provide your prints protection from light, dust, and physical abuse, plus to reduce the effects of high humidity and atmospheric contaminants. Here are some options and things to keep in mind:

Protective Sleeves: Clear sleeves or bags are great for storing just about any type of digital print, whether used for presentation, general protection, or final delivery. Bags are available in all sizes from such companies as inkjetART.com, digitalartsupplies.com, Lineco, and clearbags.com (Impact Images).

One of the most popular types has a fold-over flap with a resticking, self-adhesive strip (ask for the strip on the bag, not the flap—see Figure 9.11). Don't use regular envelopes or sleeves that contain acid or polyvinyl chloride (PVC) for this purpose, and never use rubber bands, paper clips, or pressure-sensitive tapes.

Archive Boxes: Archive or museum storage boxes are great for storing lots of prints, and they can also double as inexpensive portfolio boxes. Make sure they are constructed with acid-free and buffered materials, and interleave your prints with glassine or other acid-free tissue or sheeting. Metal corners add strength for stacking. Companies like Lineco, EternaStor, and Light Impressions carry these products.

Albums: While early photographic albums were made with materials that were actually harmful to prints, many contemporary albums follow ISO standards for permanence. Album pages are generally safe if they are acid-free, buffered, and lignin-free. If there are plastic sleeves or protectors, these should be made of either polyester, polypropylene, polyethylene, or polystyrene. Polyvinyl plastics or cellophane should be avoided because they are brittle and unstable.

Lineco (PopArt) carries a whole line of professional, do-it-yourself albums for digital prints. Ztra and Creative Memories are other well-known album providers.

General Print Storage Tips

- Handle prints as little as possible, but when you do, do it with great care as you would any original artwork. Wash your hands and wear white cotton gloves whenever possible.

- As with framing, make sure prints are completely dry before storing.

- Because heat and humidity significantly shorten print lifespans, store your prints in a dark, dry, and cool place. Shoot for a goal temperature of 68º F (20º C) to 77º F (25º C) with 30 to 50% relative humidity.

- Store prints flat, but not in the open. Use dust-free cabinets, acid-free boxes, archival sleeves, or albums. It's okay to stack prints but separate them with sheets of acid-free glassine or tissue.

- Don't store prints in areas with chemicals, such as in a photographic darkroom.

- Don't let prints come into contact with any objects that produce oxidizing agents, solvents, monomers, acids, or other volatile materials. An incident in 2001 illustrates this danger. Photographer Butch Hulett inadvertently put a newly made inkjet print on coated paper on top of an ordinary pillow. He forgot about it, but the next day he noticed that the print had turned a bright yellow. It was guessed that either the high acid content of the pillow's materials or chemical outgassing of formaldehyde interacted with the paper's coating to cause the problem.

Shipping Prints

What's the safest way to ship prints? In tubes or flat? Royce Bair of BairArtEditions.com uses Yazoo mailing tubes (yazoomills.com), which he believes are the strongest mailing tubes in the world. Here's how he does it: "You want tubes that are large in diameter (5–12 inches) so that your prints arrive with less curl memory, especially if you are using thicker fine-art papers in the 250-gsm or higher weights. Yazoo's 6-inch-diameter tubes will handle super-thick 425-gsm Epson Smooth Fine Art quite nicely.

"For creaseless rolling," Bair continues, "we recommend you roll the print in tissue or Pellon (a semi-transparent, acid-free material used in the sewing industry), image side in, and then loosely around a 4- or 5-inch tube, wrap a strip of junk paper around the print, secure the strip with adhesive tape (to prevent the print from unrolling; you don't want a print that's snug against the inside tube wall), slide the tube out, and then insert the rolled print into the 6-inch tube. Add tissue or padding on both ends to fill any extra space so the print doesn't move back and forth inside the tube. Use the snap-on end caps and tape them securely before shipping."

You can also ship prints flat, but it's riskier in terms of potential damage. If the prints are already matted and/or framed, they will have to ship flat. Artist Jean Anne Allen uses a two-piece (inner and outer) mirror-picture carton from a moving-supply company with the artwork inside protected with bubble wrap. "My advice," business manager Michael Allen says, "is to wrap both directions with bubble wrap and use a two-part mirror box that is the largest practical size so that it fully inserts into itself giving double-walled protection."

If possible, avoid shipping a print framed with glass; use Plexiglas instead. Some art shows and contests will refuse artwork shipped with glass. The potential for damage and injury is too high.

Displaying Prints

Print display choices range from the simple (push-pinning a print to your office wall) to the complex (museum display conditions). In fact, even in lofty museums, I've seen unframed digital prints that were attached to the walls with building nails. When it comes to displaying prints, there are few rules, and even those are frequently broken. Let's break this topic down into two components: *display aesthetics* and *display permanence*.

Display Aesthetics

Continuing the "Print Aesthetics" section that started off this chapter, there are varied theories about the best way to display prints. The purpose of the display is, of course, paramount. Are you trying to maximize print sales in a gallery setting or just mounting a pleasant arrangement that goes well with the room decor?

Artistic Intent: Sometimes, the type of print or the artistic intent determines the display method. For example, UK photographer/artist Henry Reichhold makes "walkway art," which involves covering bridges with inkjet prints attached end-to-end (see Figure 9.12). He's actually thinking beyond just bridges to other forms of walks, streets, roads, etc. that could be covered with his unique "walkable art."

Figure 9.12 Fine-art photographer Henry Reichhold stands next to one example of his "walkway art." In this case, the single piece of multiple inkjet prints spans the top walkway of London's Tower Bridge. The Canon large-format inkjet prints are glued end-to-end and over-laminated for hard use with the public walking on them, which he encourages.

Print Arrangement: Which is better? Fewer, larger pieces separated by vast wall space or many pieces clustered together in tight groupings? Entire workshops are given to artists and gallery directors so they can fine-tune their displays for maximum benefit.

Hanging Style: I have seen everything imaginable from traditional framing to prints pinned to the wall with arrows shot from bows. Use your creativity!

Famed photographer Elliott Erwitt stands with his pinned-to-the-wall HP inkjet prints of photos taken at Truman Capote's 1966 Black & White Ball. This "Color Work" show was part of a month-long series of "Magnum in May" exhibitions in New York City in 2004.

Display Permanence

We covered print permanence in general in Chapter 5, but here is more as it relates specifically to print displays. Whenever prints are on view, they are usually the most vulnerable to the factors that can decrease their longevity. Here are some basic display tips for prints:

Permanence and Print Display Tips

- Avoid displaying or storing prints outdoors.

- The lower the display light levels, the better. Lux levels of 100–200 lux is usually more than enough. Spotlights are a good choice, but turn them off when prints are not being actively viewed.

- Never expose prints to even one ray of direct sunlight.

- Display paper prints behind glass or Plexiglas. Use a protective coating on canvas prints.

- Protect against extreme temperature fluctuations with central or room air conditioners and/or heating systems. However, don't display prints near radiators, heaters, or the ducts themselves.

- Avoid high-humidity exposure by using dehumidifiers. Do not hang prints in bathrooms or kitchens unless they are sealed appropriately. To help moderate humidity fluctuations, use vapor barriers or frame desiccants like silica gel in the print frames.

- If prints are unprotected, keep them away from sources of ozone, such as air cleaners, copying machines, or other generators of high-voltage electricity.

- Follow the example of museums and limit the total amount of exposure to light any single piece of artwork receives. One way to do this is by artwork rotation, periodically moving pieces from the wall to storage.

The Print Alternative?

There has been talk of digital displays replacing real paper prints for years (just like the predictions of the paperless office!). Two contemporary examples come from Epson and MediaStreet.

Epson entered the home entertainment arena in 2004 with its LivingStation (see Figure 9.13), which comprises a flat-screen HDTV LCD projection television plus an on-board dye-sub digital printer, a CD burner, computer hookups, and digicam media card slots. The goal is to allow imagemakers the ability to move from the office to the living room to do all their work, from computer to photo viewing and printing. $3,000+

Figure 9.13 Epson's LivingStation for viewing, printing, and storing digital images.

The latest in a long line of "digi-frames" is MediaStreet's eMotion Multimedia Digital Picture Frame. This is not as high-ticket as the Epson system, but the price for the small 7-inch diagonal screen is also more comfortable: $620. It's a combination photo-art-music-movie player, and it accepts all the usual memory cards and CDs/DVDs.

There's no doubt that, eventually, every office and home will have the equivalent of a LivingStation or Multimedia Digital Frame sitting in a corner or hanging on a wall. However, that day, I predict, is many years away. People still love their prints.

MediaStreet's eMotion Multimedia Digital Picture Frame.

The print finishing points made above and the workflow steps in the prior chapter are meant to apply to anyone making his own digital prints. But what if you want to have your printing done by an outside print provider or service? To find out about this other side to digital printing, turn the page.

Part III

Beyond the Basics

10

Using a Print Service

There are advantages and disadvantages to doing your own printing. Sometimes, it makes sense to farm out some or all of the process. Let's take a closer look at the role of professional printmakers and printing services.

Note: This chapter is written mostly from the point of view of the buyer of printing services—photographer, artist, imagemaker. Printmakers should also be able to pick up some pointers, or at least understand better what is in the mind of the print buyer.

Why Use a Print Service?

Many in the digital printing industry call the category of outside print-service providers "print-for-pay," which is just a shorthand way to say: "You print this, and I'll pay you for it." This is a larger group than you might think, and it covers fine-art printmakers, service bureaus, imaging centers, photo labs with digital equipment, online vendors, forward-thinking repro and color houses, some sign and banner shops, and even instant-print chains that are expanding their services to include art reproductions. It also includes those photographer-artists who, for whatever reason, take on outside work from others to supplement their own self-printing (a common occurrence).

Who uses printmakers? Traditional artists wanting inkjet reproductions (giclées) form a large group of buyers of digital printing services. Most have no other way to reproduce their work, especially if they're producing large prints.

Photographers are another group, and one reason is that many are used to doing their own lab work, and so, do their own digital printing. "Photographers tend to want complete control over their work, but traditional artists just want to paint," is how Pennsylvania printmaker Jim Davis of The Visual Artist explains it.

And finally, there are the digital artists, many of whom (not all) frequently work at a small scale and like the immediate results of seeing their own prints coming out of their own printers.

Regardless of which category you might fit into, anyone who's involved with digital imaging or printing should at least consider using an outside printmaker. If you're on the fence about this, following are some additional reasons for using a print service. (I'll concentrate on fine-art printing, primarily inkjet, in the first section of this chapter and then look at photographic and other commercial providers at the end.)

Digital printmaker Lynn Lown (left) of New Media Arts works with Santa Fe artist and photographer Barbara Bowles.

Courtesy of New Media Arts
www.nmarts.com

Printmaking Advantages

There are many advantages and benefits to using a printmaker or outside printing service.

Knowledge, Experience, and Craft

Printmaking is a craft that takes years, even a lifetime, to perfect. Experienced printmakers are experts at what they do, and they usually have the best, most expensive equipment. Therefore, by using an outside print provider, you shift the burden of learning the craft and of keeping up with all the latest print technology to the printmaker, which frees you to concentrate on image-making.

A seasoned printing professional has seen it all and has an in-depth knowledge of materials and artistic approaches that have been tried and tested, and, accordingly, can act as your aesthetic guide and advisor. New Mexico printmaker Lynn Lown of New Media Arts notes that he has artists consistently tell him that he has helped them to take their work to the next level. "I do that by listening to them and by showing them the possible ways to go with their work," he explains.

Geoffrey Kilmer, president of Photoworks Creative Group in Charlottesville, Virginia, which offers both wide-format inkjet and photographic LightJet printing, says that "When you have a group of people working in digital output on a daily basis, it only makes sense that they have the potential to hold a much greater reservoir of knowledge in this area. And, an artist can learn some very valuable lessons in the process of working with such a professional provider."

I've used several inkjet printmakers in all corners of the U.S., and, without exception, they have all taught me something about digital printing I hadn't known before. Each outside printing project was an eye-opening experience that improved my own imagemaking process. For this reason alone, I recommend working with a professional printmaker, at least once or on an occasional basis.

Bair Art Editions in Salt Lake City, Utah, is affiliated with InkJetArt.com and is an all-Epson wide-format shop specializing in fine art print reproduction. Shown are Ted Van Horn (left) and Stephen Bair.
Courtesy of Bair Art Editions/www.bairarteditions.com

Quality

Unless you are an experienced, long-time self-printer, an outside printmaker will usually be able to give you higher-quality prints than you can do on your own. The fact is, first attempts at digital printing are typically not perfect. It takes a lot of trial and error as well as gallons of ink and boxes of paper before the printing process is humming along producing top-quality output.

This is why I often recommend that newcomers to digital printing start off by jobbing out their first few projects to an outside printmaker. This sets a benchmark of what is good and what can be achieved. Some imagemakers end up being so happy using a particular printmaker that they continue to work this way, even going so far as to fly in from other locations for the printing sessions.

Legendary rock artist Stanley Mouse (www.mousestudios.com) does his own printing and uses outside printmakers to produce his higher-quality reproduction prints. He's shown holding The Jester from the cover of the Grateful Dead songbook.

Time and Focus

Many photographers and artists believe that their time is best spent creating their art; labs and print shops are best left to others. Printmaker Lynn Lown says, "As a commercial photographer for years, it was common wisdom that you should stay out of the darkroom. You can make much more money as a shooter if you are good at that. If you are good at the lab, you should stop shooting and open one. A pro needs a lab so he or she can spend more time shooting."

Other types of image-makers may feel they are in the same boat. Digital artist Ileana explains that using a printmaker "allows me to focus on the creative aspects of making the picture. It would have taken me a lot of time and many trials to produce a piece that I would consider satisfying. Until I gain enough knowledge about printmaking, I can have my work printed quickly and easily."

For some, then, it comes down to a simple question: Do you want to spend the time yourself to learn about the printmaking process, or do you want to pay someone who's already been there and back many times?

Size and Practicality

If you need large prints, and you can't afford a wide-format printer or the space to house one, then your only alternative is to use a service provider with wide-format printers. "The one big factor that brings most of my print clients to the door is size," explains digital artist and printmaker JD Jarvis. Most of the artists I deal with have excellent printers that may print up to 17 × 22 inches, but for larger prints, they come to me. Basically, you would go to an outside printmaker when they offer services you cannot match with your own equipment, or when the cost of providing those services for a limited project outweighs the return."

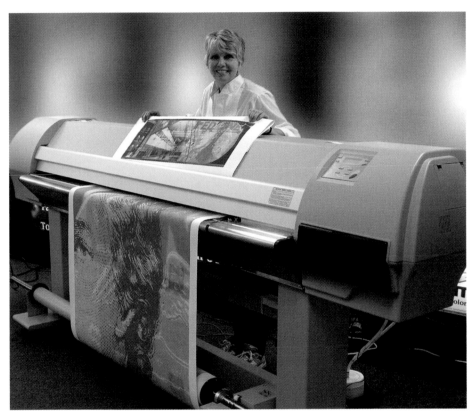

Artist Dot Krause stands behind the 64-inch wide Mutoh Falcon II High Productivity inkjet printer that produced the panels for her Boston Federal Reserve Bank mural project (see Chapter 1).

Courtesy of Mutoh America
www.mutoh.com

Similarly, there is no practical way to use certain digital technologies *without* using an outside service. Fuji Frontiers, Océ LightJets, Durst Lambdas, etc. start at $120,000 and go up, so the chances of having one of your own in the back bedroom are slim indeed. Photo labs, service bureaus, print shops, and the like are your only hope for making these kinds of prints. (See "Working with Non-Inkjet Providers".)

Cost Effectiveness

Depending on your situation, printmakers can save you money. You can have a small print made from a digital file by an outside print provider for $100 or less. This is a good way to test an image or a potential market. If the test fails, you haven't lost much. And if that particular printmaker doesn't suit you, you can simply move on to someone else.

"I don't have to keep up with products, materials, and inks, or make that significant investment," says artist Ileana. "Since I currently don't sell prints in bulk, it would take me a long time before I would see any return on my initial investment if I did it all myself."

Some of the *disadvantages* of using an outside printmaker include the following:

- Loss of some control and flexibility.
- Reduced experimentation and spontaneity that goes with doing your own printing trials.
- Time delays going back and forth.
- Ongoing, per-print costs are usually higher.

Note that some imagemakers take both approaches, doing some self-printing and farming other work out. I, myself, fall into this group.

How To Pick an Inkjet Printmaker

To select an outside print service provider, you have to do your homework and then ask the right questions. To narrow the choices of potential inkjet printmakers, interview (by phone, mail, or in person) all the candidates with the same set of questions. If you can, visit the print studios or businesses in person to get a feel for them. How they answer your questions is just as important as what they say. You are about to enter into a close, possibly long-term relationship. You want to give it the best chance of succeeding up-front.

Following are several main points you should have on your questions list before you start your investigating. (Use this list as a guide; add your own questions as needed.)

Printmaker Jim Davis places artwork on the copy board in order to capture the image on 8 × 10 film and then drum scan it. "This file will range from 800 MB to 1.2 GB in size," explains Davis. "All the color balancing is done at the time of the scan so there is no additional tweaking needed in Photoshop, only some minimal cleanup. To get away with this, I run a clean shop and make sure everything from copy board to lighting is properly balanced and aligned."

Courtesy of Jim Davis
www.visual-artists.com

Experience?

How long have they been in the business of making digital prints? Do they understand color management and take a hands-on approach to getting the best color from each file? Are they familiar with the kind of art output you're looking for, or are they a sign shop that figures digital printing is digital printing? "Find out if they have worked with other artists and whether or not they found that experience rewarding," advises printmaker JD Jarvis. "If the printer does not realize that creating work for 'fine-art' requires special attention, or if they offer that attention grudgingly, look for someone else."

Referrals?

As with any service, get referrals. How many clients or customers similar to you do they have? Can they give you any customer references? If so, absolutely follow up and contact them asking for their comments.

Also, talk to other imagemakers whose output you like, and who are happy with the printing services they use. Then contact those providers.

Samples?

At a minimum, you should evaluate several samples of a printmaker's work. Most professional printmakers are glad to send out a sample packet with a price sheet and sometimes paper swatches.

An even better idea is a test print. "The best interview," explains New Media Art's Lynn Lown, "is to have them make you a small print." You'll have to pay for it, but one-quarter-size prints can be made at very reasonable prices.

A custom test file the author had printed by Thunderbird Editions in Clearwater, Florida.

Olé No Moiré image (lower right) courtesy of Adobe Systems, Inc.

Lown also advises that those searching for a printmaker "look for someone who does other work that resembles your own. This guarantees that the printmaker is aware of your sensibility. In dealing with images, most people think about 'technology' when, really, it's about 'culture.'"

Physical Space/Location?

Where are they located? Is it local, or does it require mail, courier shipments, or online interaction to reach them (see more about online services below)? Is there a professional viewing booth? Do they encourage artists to come in and view their work in progress and interact with the staff? French printmaker Franck Bordas of Atelier Bordas explains that "We work in a large studio in the center of Paris. Many of the artists come here in person to finish and prepare their files. For this purpose, we have set up three Macintosh workstations (G4/G5) with large screens."

If possible, take a tour and look at the printmaker's operation. Does it look like a real business, or is it just a hobby in the garage?

You could never confuse Harvest Productions in Anaheim Hills, California, with a garage operation (although that's exactly how they started off). Harvest is currently the largest giclée printing company in the world. Shown are some of the 12 Roland Hi-Fi JETs they use (that's in addition to the 13 IRIS printers plus others).

Courtesy of Harvest Productions Ltd.
www.harvestpro.com

How Long Will It Take?

What is the turnaround time from file to final print? Whatever you're told, add 50 percent to come up with a more realistic schedule. And make sure you factor in shipping time, holidays, etc.

Keep in mind that print-service providers are running commercial businesses. Time is money to them, and they will want to move your project through their production flow as efficiently as possible. But the digital print process takes time, and there's no point in short-circuiting it.

Printer Profiles Provided?

One purpose of a printer-provided profile is so the imagemaker can soft-proof the image on their own computer screen to get an idea of how it will look when printed. This reduces the likelihood of a poor print, and it becomes even more important if the photographer-artist is providing a digital file. If it's a painting or other preexisting artwork that the printmaker will scan or photograph, then a profile may not be necessary; the entire workflow is in the printmaker's hands.

Fine-art photographer Paul Eric Johnson believes that "profiles are at the heart of the matter for me. Of the several companies in the San Francisco Bay area who offer LightJet printing, Calypso Imaging (see more about them below) is one of the only ones that makes their profiles readily available." (See Figure 10.1.)

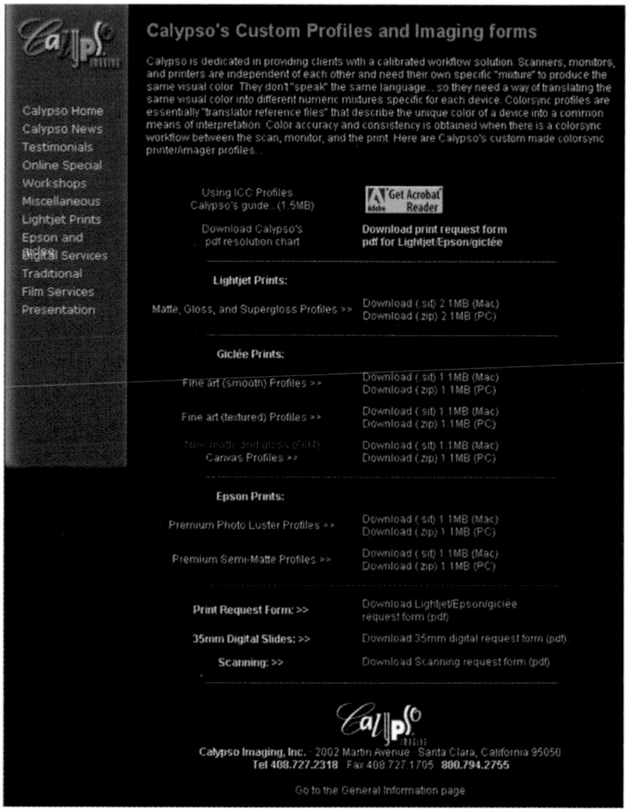

Figure 10.1 Calypso Imaging makes it easy to download their printer profiles.

Courtesy of Calypso Imaging, Inc.
www.calypsoinc.com

If printer profiles are important to the way you work, you need to ask about them. (See also "Profiles for Digital Photo Print".)

Other Services?

Printmakers do more than just print. Some offer a complete range of artist support services including finishing, canvas stretching, and shipping. Lynn Lown offers bookbinding for custom family albums and individual artist's books, while the giant New York City photo lab Duggal provides a full range of pre- and post-printing services.

Some print providers do printing for art publishers or are art publishers themselves, and they may be able to help you market your work. Len Phillips and Mark Lutz of The Art House in Brisbane, Australia, run seminars for artists to help them make the most of the giclée experience. "The success of The Art House is based on helping the artists sell their work for a reasonable return," says Phillips. "Our basic business is production, but with decades of sales experience in the wedding/portrait photography market under our belts, we have adapted these methods to the promotion and marketing of giclées. We hold seminars to introduce artists to the giclée printmaking process, sales seminars to show artists how they can make more money with reproductions, and hands-on seminars on how to enhance their reproductions with post-printing artwork to add value."

At a minimum, because they deal with so many artists, printmakers can be good sounding boards for sales and marketing ideas.

Obviously, these related services are chargeable and on top of the basic printing costs.

A staff artist embellishes a giclée print as an extra service at Harvest Productions.

Courtesy of Harvest Productions Ltd.
www.harvestpro.com

How Much?

Price is important, but even more important is how a printmaker charges. Per page? Per linear foot? Per square foot? What is included and what is not? Here are the main issues:

Creative or Pre-Printing Prep: Scans, digital retouching, extraordinary color adjustments, etc. will all incur extra charges above the printing price. There is sometimes a catch-all "image file preparation" or "set-up" fee that includes basic image-editing and file storage. Otherwise, image-editing may be called something like "system" or "computer time" and is typically billed by the hour (figure on an average of $100 or so per hour depending on your regional location).

Basic Print Cost: Digital printmakers usually charge by the output size or by the square unit measure. They take their material costs for ink, media, coatings, etc. and tack on enough to cover overhead and hopefully a profit.

For inkjet, per sheet costs (a full sheet is approximately 35 × 45 inches) can range from $200 to $400 with discounts for additional sheets printed at the same time. Keep in mind that a full sheet can be divided up into multiple, smaller images to reduce the unit cost per image. Also, certain factors like the choice of paper will affect the costs. For example, canvas usually costs more.

Per-square-foot inkjet costs can range from $15 to $35 per square foot with a minimum charge, and some, like Nash Editions, Duganne Ateliers, Jim Davis' The Visual Artist even charge by the square inch. Nash charges $0.25–0.27 per square inch on basic paper, Duganne and Davis both charge $0.10 per square inch for the first print on paper (see Figure 10.2), and Davis charges $0.16 for canvas.

Figure 10.2 Online price list for digital printmaking studio Duganne Ateliers in Santa Monica, California.

Courtesy of Jack Duganne
www.duganne.com

JD Jarvis charges by the linear inch, "Since it matches the way frame shops have structured their services." For him, all other "value added" services are separate charges.

Reorders: This is one of the benefits of digital printing. Because the printmaker will store your final digital file, you can call and reorder the same print as many times as you want for as long you want. In theory, each print will be exactly the same as the first. Because all the preliminary work has already been done, reorders cost much less than the first print.

This archiving of files and reordering sometimes comes with a cost. One systemized approach to this is from Chris Wade at Pixel Place in Hamilton, Ontario, Canada. "We tell artists that although we archive every job," he explains, "we only promise to make reprints without additional charges if they reorder within 90 days or unless they have purchased our

'Documentation Package.'" This CD package includes: (1) a copy of everything someone would need to have prints made without additional charges, except for Certificates of Authenticity, which cost $1 each; (2) a guarantee that the prints will match the first print order; (3) the freedom so that if for some reason Pixel Place went out of business, the artist would have everything they need to have prints done elsewhere.

Proofs: Proofs, usually reduced or at one-quarter-size, can make or break a printing project in terms of costs. Jack Duganne (Duganne Ateliers) charges a flat $85 per proofing session, although what constitutes a proofing session is open to interpretation. Jim Davis charges artists "$150, which includes the transparency, drum scan and a set of proofs. With my closed-loop system, I can hit my color match targets 98 percent of the time. Very seldom do I have to make a second proof. If I do, it is included in the $150 price." Chris Wade (Pixel Place) charges for proofs individually, anywhere from $16 to $48 (Canadian dollars).

Make sure you understand what's included in a proof, and how many you'll be getting.

Package Prices: Some inkjet printmakers, usually only those dealing with traditional art reproductions, will offer package prices that include an image scan, basic image cleanup and color correction, up to three reduced-size proofs, archiving, and one or more final prints. For example, Staples Fine Art in Richmond, Virginia, has four packages ranging from $165 to $450 depending on the size of the print (see Figure 10.3).

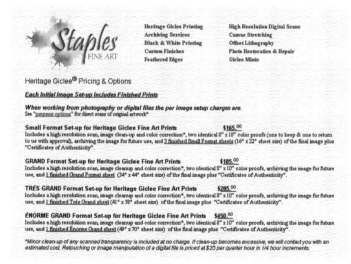

Figure 10.3 Digital print shop Staples Fine Art offers four price packages based on size.

Courtesy of Mark Staples
www.staplesart.com

Package pricing may be a good idea, or it may make more sense to price out your work *à la carte* (per item).

Warranty or Guarantee?

Does the printmaker offer a warranty or a guarantee of some kind, and do you understand what it does and does not cover?

As you can imagine, this is a very tricky area, and as proof, there are only a few major fine-art digital printmakers who offer a written warranty or guarantee (a warranty is legally different from a guarantee). Why? The main issue is print permanence, and as we learned in the earlier chapter on that subject, the printmaker has no control over how the print will be handled or displayed once it leaves the shop. There are so many environmental factors that can affect a print that the conditions for the warranty or guarantee must be specifically spelled out.

Hunter Editions in Kennebunk, Maine, is one provider who does exactly this. They offer a 30-year "Fade Free" Limited Guarantee, which basically states that its prints will be free from defects in material, workmanship, and "significant visible fading for a period of 30 years," or they will replace or refund the monies actually paid (their choice). The catch is the long list of conditions that must be met including specific display or storage specifications.

Another approach some printmakers can take is not to worry about all the details and conditions. Len Phillips of Australia's The Art House offers a "warranty," which says, in part: "All Art House giclée reproductions come with a lifetime warranty if anything should happen to the reproduction done by the Art House, and it applies regardless of the owner of the giclée reproduction. Provided we have the file to match the print being returned (with authenticity certificate where the print is from a limited edition), we will print a replacement for 50 percent of the current price. Due to copyright laws, we will require the artist to first approve the replacement and be available to re-sign the new reproduction."

While this may not technically be a warranty in the U.S. (warranties require free replacement), it works for Phillips.

Extras: File conversions, CDs or other archival media, shipping tubes, hand deckling, and other extra services like special protective coatings are all charged in addition to the above costs. Make sure you clearly understand these charges. Also, make sure it's clear who owns the final digital files—you or them?

Studio Rental: If you're really feeling ambitious, some printmakers (inkjet, primarily) will even turn over and devote their entire studios to your project. Figure on about $1,500 per day for this exclusive attention.

What To Look Out For

Not only are you looking for reasons to select an inkjet printmaker, you're also looking for any red flags for not choosing one. Here are a few things to watch out for:

Not Being Responsive

"One sure negative sign," explains artist Ileana, "would be a printmaker's lack of responsiveness and a rigid or negative reaction to my suggestions, especially if I'm dissatisfied with a print that shows defects. My printmaker must be receptive to my needs and want to work with me in accomplishing my vision (colors, inks, size, etc.). Not having this goes against the interdependent relationship that I think is needed."

I Have a Printer, Therefore I Am a Printmaker

There are printmakers, and there are printmakers. Having the equipment doesn't make you a printmaker, just like having a camera doesn't necessarily make you a photographer. There is no push-button solution to high-quality digital output; it takes time and experience.

Los Angeles fine-art printing consultant, printmaker, and UCLA digital printmaking instructor Andrew Behla (see Figure 10.4) explains it like this: "An eye for color, a knowledge of color theory, and an understanding of the digital imaging process are the foundation blocks for making successful prints. In addition, utilizing color management and developing Photoshop wizardry are two other important resources needed in the printmaker's toolbox. So, what is the most useful tool to have? Ultimately, it is your eye. Developing your own visual sensibility and effectively using your printmaking tools to facilitate the process are crucial. A music producer once summed it up for me like this: 'It's not the gear, it's the ear.' The art of digital printmaking is found in the eyes of the printmaker."

Figure 10.4 Andrew Behla reviews client prints from his Epson 7600.

Courtesy of Andrew Behla
www.behladesign.com

Ask questions and investigate everything to satisfy yourself that a printmaker does, in fact, have the eyes and the experience.

The Artist as Printmaker

Many artists take in work to print for others. One reason they do this is to help pay for the expensive printmaking equipment. One problem with artist-printmakers is that they sometimes don't have the well-rounded experience of doing work for many different people. Many will have printed only their own work, which may or may not be anything like yours. As I've said before, printing is a craft, and what you ideally want is an experienced craftsperson, not necessarily an artist, as your printmaker.

Disagreeing with me on this is digital artist Ileana. "Printmakers have to match the artist's vision," she says, "and that takes a lot of communication and know-how. To me, it is also important that they be digital artists themselves. This may not have anything to do with their actual printing expertise, but I think that they will be much more sensitive and understand the highs and lows of working with this medium."

Artist/printmaker JD Jarvis outputs a large-format edition on an HP 2500CP inkjet printer in his home studio in Las Cruces, New Mexico.

Courtesy of JD Jarvis
dunkingbirdproductions.com

So, again, it's important to carefully determine the printmaker's background.

The Artist/Printmaker Relationship

The ideal imagemaker/printmaker relationship is a true collaboration. The photographer-artist provides the image, and the printmaker provides years of experience in helping the artist best realize his or her vision. To repeat the apt phrase mentioned earlier: "The artist is the eye, the printmaker is the hand."

Photographer Paul Eric Johnson sums up this idea well. "I'm all in favor of the digital revolution, but I only want to know as much technically as is necessary to produce my desired results. After several years of working with print providers, I wouldn't even think of doing this without my trusted artistic partners." (See more about Johnson's relationship with Calypso Imaging in "Digital Photo Print.")

Even if you're only sending off digital files to a remote commercial business, two-way communication is vital. Are you able to explain what you want, and, conversely, are they understanding you? Print provider Geoff Kilmer adds, "The artist should realize there are limitations to what can be done and should respect the fact that the printmaker is also trying to make a living in the process of rendering the service. Generally, the same ethics that make up any mutually beneficial business relationship apply to an artist and a printmaker."

"The printmaker/artist relationship is the most important factor of the whole process," adds JD Jarvis. "More important than the model type of printer being used, more important than the substrate chosen to print on. And, don't be impressed by the cost, size, or publicity surrounding any one make or model of inkjet print device. Look to the output of an individual printmaker. The human factor—how skilled and how willing the printmaker is to work with you—is more important than any technical factors beyond the obvious ones you need to meet in any particular project."

And that's good advice.

David Adamson (left) and world-famous artist Chuck Close review inkjet proofs in Close's studio. Says Adamson, "The prints we make are the result of a dialogue between our knowledge of the digital process and the artist's vision and ideas. I speak the same language as the artists, and they relate to this. They trust my eye and my ideas."

Courtesy of David Adamson
www.adamsoneditions.com

A Giclée Workflow

As I mentioned in Chapter 1, *giclée* is the term used to describe a digital, inkjet, reproduction print made from a work created in another medium. Prints made from paintings, watercolors, drawings, etc. are all giclées, and the process has its own workflow. While some of the steps are similar to the ones I outlined in Chapter 8 for self-printing, the main difference is that most of the activity is the responsibility of the printmaker. This is what you pay them for.

Step 1: Planning the Print

You still need to plan your print, and this is best done in consultation with the printmaker. Dimensions and prices will come into play to determine the perfect size, medium, inks, and method to be used. "Size is a primary consideration," says Pixel Place's Chris Wade.

"To keep the cost per print to a minimum, an artist needs to understand that they are paying by the sheet or roll width. Prints should be sized to minimize the waste."

This planning is the preliminary step where all the issues between artist and printmaker should be laid out on the table and thoroughly discussed. If you develop a bad feeling about this particular printmaker, now is the best time to pull out, not later.

Step 2: Digitizing the Image

Each printmaker will have his or her own way of turning the original artwork into a digital file. Some prefer a traditional photograph taken on medium- or large-format transparency film and then scanned. Others will direct-scan the original artwork with a digital scan back or other high-resolution scanning method (see Figure 10.5). If the piece is small enough, it could even be put on a drum (if it's flexible) or flatbed scanner. The final result is a high-resolution digital file that has faithfully captured all the details and colors of the original work of art.

Figure 10.5 The ZBE Satellite digital scanning system at Harvest Productions. Note artwork on riser under camera.

Courtesy of Harvest Productions Ltd. www.harvestpro.com

Step 3: Image Editing and Color Correcting

Color corrections and other image editing are done on computer workstations by the printmaker's staff. Out-of-gamut colors are adjusted in comparison to the original material provided, whether that's the artwork itself or a photograph of it. The main point of this step is to match the original, and any deviations from this goal should be approved only by the artist.

"Your print provider should be operating a full color-managed system," advises Pixel Place's Chris Wade. "Ask first and verify that they are not simply guessing at color management."

Step 4: Proofing

How proofing is handled can vary widely among printmakers, but the purpose is to show you one or more proof prints so that you can see with your own eyes how the final prints will look. (The number of proofs will be determined by the policy of the printmaker and what level of service you've purchased.) The best scenario is for you to view the proof in a professional viewing booth at the printmaker's facility. This way, the people working on the print can be brought out to discuss any alterations or "moves" with the image.

When does the reproduction proof match the original? "When the artist says: 'That's it—print it!'" explains Chris Wade. "Ultimately for us, it's all about understanding the client's expectations. We have some who want 'as close as possible' and others who see the print-making process as an extension of their artistic process. The latter group usually wants us to make the prints bolder and brighter than the originals, or they have some other concept in mind for the prints. Others forgo proofing with us entirely because they know our standards and accept them. The amount of time we spend in preparing an initial proof is relative to our clients' needs, budgets, and expectations."

Proofing can be the most time-delaying part of the process when working with outside print providers. Typical turnaround time is one week between proofs, and there can be more than one round of proofs, depending on any problems encountered. Note that preliminary proofs are typically returned and remain the property of the printmaker.

The final, approved proof is called the BAT or *bon à tirer*, ("good to pull or print" in French). The artist signs this print and returns it to the printmaker. It's then used as the guide to which all subsequent prints are matched.

Step 5: Printing

The final print or prints are then output. The advantage of digital printing is that prints can be made one at a time, and it's normal to print in small groups, depending on the discount the printmaker offers for quantity. Jim Davis does not recommend printing more than 10 prints at once. "Unless the artist is well-known, it will take them some time to sell those 10 prints," he advises. "Financially, it's not good business to carry unsold inventory."

Step 6: Finishing and Curating

Curating is what happens to a print after it's output. This is the step where each print is inspected for quality (and fixed or rejected if any major imperfections are found), cleaned, finished with any protective coatings, mounted, and framed, as needed. All trimming or special edge tearing or deckling is also done at this point. When the printmaker uses a chop (an embossed, identifying printer's mark), it is applied in one of the lower corners. If the prints are to be hand-embellished, that is also done at this stage.

John Hughs trims inkjet prints at
Adamson Editions in Washington, D.C.

Courtesy of David Adamson
www.adamsoneditions.com

Step 7: Shipping and Storing

The job is not complete until the prints arrive at their destination, safe and sound. Unless an artist can physically go to the printmaker's place of business for a pick-up, most prints are rolled and shipped in tubes, although they can be shipped flat, too. A good printmaker will use only the strongest tubes with plenty of slip-sheeting and end-stuffing to protect each print. There's nothing worse than to have otherwise-perfect prints ruined in shipping. It's happened to me, and that's why I always insist on the use of overnight air shipping. It's worth the extra expense.

If files or prints are to be stored or "archived" at the printmaker's shop instead of being returned to the imagemaker, make sure you understand the storage policies and costs involved.

Working with Non-Inkjet Providers

Many of the larger print providers now combine both inkjet and non-inkjet output at one facility to cover an evolving market for digital imaging and printing. Companies like Calypso Imaging (Santa Clara, California), Digital Pond (San Francisco), Duggal Visual

Solutions (New York City), and Photo Craft Laboratories (Boulder, Colorado) have one or more LightJets, Lambdas, Frontiers, wide-format inkjets, laser printers, or whatever digital devices they need to satisfy their customers' imaging needs.

Digital Photo Print

One important non-inkjet technology that photographers are especially fond of (although non-photographic digital artists can use them as well) is digital photo print (described in Chapter 2). This print process requires outside service providers since the cost of the equipment is too high for self-ownership. Photo labs, service bureaus, imaging centers, online vendors, and even retailers like drugstores and large discount chains are where you'll find this type of print service. Imagemakers typically submit final, RGB, digital files on CD/DVD or online. Scans from reflective art, slides, or negatives are usually also available.

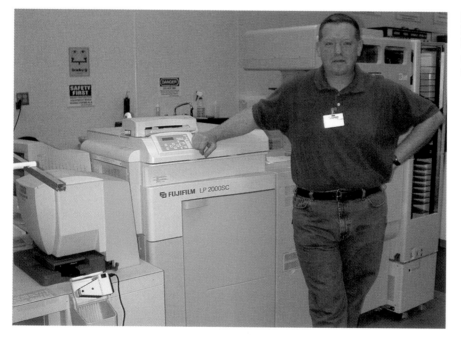

Kevin Scanlon managed the Costco Frontier lab in Cranberry Township, Pennsylvania (outside of Pittsburgh).

Courtesy of Larry Berman
www.LarryBerman.com

Wide-format LightJet, Lambda, or Chromira prints are output to regular photographic paper (only), and print prices can range from $20 to $500 depending on the final size. As with some inkjet printmakers, digital photo print providers like Calypso Imaging will allow 4-up ganging of multiple images on one sheet at no extra cost.

New Jersey photographer Paul Eric Johnson loves his LightJet prints on Fuji Crystal Archive paper for their "sense of a pureness" in his photography. He scans his transparencies at NancyScans in New York, does the image-editing on his computer, and then ships his images on CD all the way to Calypso Imaging in California for output. (Calypso has set up an FTP account for Johnson so he can upload his images to them.) Calypso also produces inkjet reproduction prints on Epson inkjet printers.

Johnson explains that "while the printer is remote, the relationship hasn't been. With good technical support, I've been able to keep close to the action. There's a consistency and an understanding of just how important the work is to the art photographer. The printing itself is one thing I don't have to worry about." Calypso also offers exhibition framing, "so prints now can be shipped direct. However, when signed prints are required, they must still go back and forth."

Paul Eric Johnson's Pearly Everlasting (named for the white flower) is output on a LightJet printer, which he prefers for its chromagenic depth, especially in the dark shadow areas.

© 2000-2004 Paul Eric Johnson
www.paulericjohnson.com

Digital photo process is a subset of digital photo print that applies to smaller-format sizes and involves the use of digital minilabs that employ the Fuji Frontier, Noritsu QSS, Agfa D-Lab, or similar devices. There tends to be less customer interaction with these smaller formats since volume and lower prices are more important. But you can still make your voice heard, and the better providers will listen. Photo Craft Laboratories' Ron Brown explains that, even though they use the Frontier as their main consumer device for smaller prints, they look at and customize every job that comes in the door. "The Frontier has an Auto mode, and a high-school student running one at the corner drugstore may be more prone to use it. But, with our qualified technicians, everything is custom."

Profiles for Digital Photo Print: Printer profiles (see Chapter 4) can be just as important for digital photo printing as they are for inkjet. Unfortunately, your success in finding service-provided profiles from digital photo print shops will be hit or miss, and even an understanding of what profiles can do is scattered. My local pro photo lab, for example, doesn't provide them for either its LightJet 5000 or its Fuji Frontier. Larger providers like Calypso Imaging and Photo Craft, however, provide their clients with calibrated workflows, and they make it very easy to download profiles from their web pages.

There are several ways to deal with any non-profiled lab devices. One workaround is to do what's called *reverse proofing*. Send the lab a small target-test file to print. If you like what you get back, either adjust your monitor settings or your image file *to the print*. Yes, this is a backwards way to do color management, but it can work if you are pleased with the test prints, and the lab stays consistent.

Kiosks to the Rescue

If you're desperate to have a while-you-wait print made, you can always run over to your nearest drugstore, consumer electronic store, Kinko's, or discount retailer to use a self-service *photo kiosk*. These kiosks are all the rage (in the U.S.) and are made by manufacturers such as Kodak (Picture Maker), Fuji (Aladdin), Sony (PictureStation), and Olympus (TruePrint). They offer a touch screen interface for basic image editing including cropping, red-eye removal, brightness adjustment, etc. The Olympus TruePrint kiosks come in two models with dye-sublimation printers that sit behind the counter and that can output 4 × 6 or 8 × 10 prints.

Kiosks accept CompactFlash, SmartMedia, and PCMCIA memory cards and Photo CDs, and some have optional scanners for inputting hard copy. Some now include interfaces for printing from camera cell phones. The Kodak Picture Maker Film Processing Station even lets you quickly develop and print pictures from 35mm, without ever having to "turn in" your film to a lab. (See Figure 10.7.)

You're not going to get a lot of expert advice or hand-holding in this situation, but for a $2.99 print at your local Sam's Club in three minutes, what do you expect?

Figure 10.7 The Kodak Picture Maker Film Processing Station is the first self-service, film-processing kiosk for consumers. It functions as a low-cost, self-contained minilab when connected to a retailer's Kodak Picture Maker G3 kiosk, allowing users to print both film images and digital images themselves.

Courtesy of Eastman Kodak Company

You can also custom profile your lab. Take, or e-mail, one of the RGB profiling target files that comes with your profiling software to the lab and have them make a normal print *with no color management* (this is the key point). Specify the size print that you need, or you may get a target print too small to work with. Back at your workstation, use your scanner- or spectro-based profiling package to build a custom printer profile for that lab printer. Convert to this ICC profile (in Photoshop: Image > Mode > Convert to Profile) and instruct the lab not to make any automated corrections, but to print the file just as it is. It may take a couple of trial runs and some back-and-forth communication, but the lab should eventually understand what you're trying to accomplish.

Another way of working with digital lab printers is now available through Oregon photographer Ethan Hansen of Dry Creek Photo. Hansen has created an online database (www.drycreekphoto.com) of ICC printer profiles for *local* Fuji Frontier, Noritsu, Agfa

D-Lab, LightJet, Lambda, and Chromira lab printers worldwide. In the U.S., this includes many Wal-Mart, Costco, and Ritz Camera locations. If your local minilab provider is listed, you simply download the profile (it's free) and install it on your computer to do your image-editing.

Hansen used to offer a service where if your local operator was not on the list and you wanted to profile them, you could download Dry Creek's profile target, print it at the minilab, and mail the print back to Dry Creek who created a profile at no charge and added it to their database. That service is no longer offered (although those profiles are still available), and Dry Creek is now only accepting targets submitted by the labs themselves to create what it calls "enhanced accuracy profiles." Dry Creek also provides custom printer profiles for individual photographers.

Keep in mind that the accuracy of these profiles is dependent upon how up-to-date they are since lab conditions can change. As Hansen explains, "Some of these labs update their profiles on a regular schedule. If the lab shares this information with us, we give an 'expiration date' for the profiles. Check back around that date for updated profiles. The date information appears in Photoshop or other ICC-compliant applications using profiles."

Online Printing Services

One example of the inroads that the Internet has made into our lives is the business of online processing and printing. While this is mostly applicable to photographers, it doesn't have to be, especially now that the larger print service providers have every type of digital output device including wide-format inkjets.

More and more, the trend is for imagemakers to work with this type of provider electronically or online. What this usually means is that image files, typically TIFFs or JPEGs, along with order forms are either sent via e-mail or uploaded to company websites for image-processing and printing. Some companies also offer a related service for photographers who can send in film for processing and scanning (or hard-copy artwork). The scans are then uploaded to their secure websites where the photographer-artist can download them, image-edit as needed, and either send them back for printing or print them on their own desktop printers.

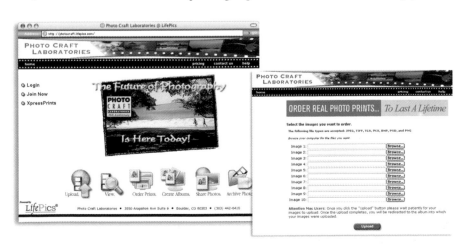

Photo Craft Laboratories' online imaging, archiving, and printing services are accessible through its website.

Courtesy of Photo Craft Laboratories, Inc. www.pcraft.com

Some image-editing software programs such as Adobe Photoshop Elements even have plug-ins to simplify the image-uploading process.

One result of all this online activity is that the physical locations of both the providers and the customers is becoming irrelevant. Where before labs were receiving and sending shipments by walk-in or air courier, they now receive uploaded files to their website and only need to return the finished prints the traditional way.

Image Sharing and Printing

If there's one thing that makes print-service providers nervous—besides the tidal wave of people doing their own printing—it's photo or image sharing. This is the process of uploading images to one of the free hosting services so they can be stored, organized, viewed, and shared. You can assign a password to your "albums," and only those you give the password to can see your images. This has become a popular way to avoid the time and trouble of e-mailing pictures and images to family, friends, and other contacts.

But, that's not all. Since most people still like to have a real print in their hands, companies like Shutterfly, Kodak's Ofoto, EZ Prints, and dotPhoto not only offer image sharing but also print ordering. Once you've added images to your personal album, you can "enhance" them (crop, rotate, add borders and effects), instruct the service which image to print and in what size, and the prints arrive a few days later. Shutterfly even has online resolution guidelines to tell you if your images are too low-res to print well on their Fuji Frontier printers (see Figure 10.8).

For Pros Only

One popular development for professional photographers is the online image viewing, ordering, and printing solution. For example, Fujifilm's StudioMaster PRO is an image presentation and ordering software package that lets professional photographers build a customer order that goes directly to a Fuji Pictrography or Frontier-equipped lab. The software is provided by the lab (sometimes for a fee), and it allows for color-managed, onscreen image-editing, slide shows, and albums.

Figure 10.8 Shutterfly's initial print-ordering screen (top) and the actual prints after they arrived in the author's mailbox.

Courtesy of Shutterfly
www.shutterfly.com

Pictage offers a similar service for wedding photographers. The workflow steps are: (1) digitization of film or uploading digital files, (2) online editing and proofing, (3) ordering and fulfillment. As soon as the event is released, an automatic e-mail is generated providing instructions and access to the event at Pictage.com, where attendees can instantly view and purchase the images. Pictage not only processes the credit card transaction but then produces the finished prints (digital photo print) before shipping them directly to the customer.

Shutterfly has its own version of this type of service with its Shutterfly Pro Galleries. They can handle everything from ordering, payment, printing, and shipping.

Gary Goldberg, Toronto professional photographer featured in Chapter 1 who shoots weddings, portraits, and events in addition to creating his fine-art work, uses the services of California-based DigiLabs (see Figure 10.9). "I control the e-commerce website galleries using DigiLabs' software," Goldberg explains. "I can integrate a PayPal shopping cart into the site, and instead of having another company do the order fulfillment, the order comes to me from PayPal, and I send it to my local digital lab (Pikto), which uses the Agfa D-Lab system for final prints up to 12×18 inches. Anything bigger than that I do myself on my Epson 7600. I then send the final prints to my client."

Goldberg also orders double-sided "proof magazines" from DigiLabs that are printed with HP Indigo printers.

Figure 10.9 DigiLabs software allows Goldberg to upload customized e-commerce web galleries with his personal look and feel; DigiLabs is invisible to his customers.

Courtesy of Gary Goldberg Photography
www.garygoldbergphoto.com

Whether you make your own prints or have a print service do it for you, you'll eventually want to push the limits of digital printing. Read on to find out how.

11

Special Printing Techniques

While the majority of people are content—and adequately challenged—to output a normal digital print, there are others who want to step outside the box, to go beyond the basics, and to stretch their abilities. Here are some ideas for doing just that.

RIPs and Special Printing Software

While virtually all digital printers come ready to print with the required software, there are options that can take you to a different level of printing.

RIPs

Some people swear by RIPs (Raster Image Processor), some swear at them, and the rest just don't understand what all the ruckus is about.

Very basically, a RIP is a group of software tools that allow you to have more control over your printer. In the past, RIPs were primarily associated with CMYK inkjet proofing and printing for commercial graphics. However, RIP makers have wised up to the booming interest by photographer-artists in high-quality digital output (primarily inkjet), and there are now many more RIP options aimed at this growing market. (For monochrome choices, see "The Secret World of Digital Black and White" below.)

All printer drivers (also known as "raster drivers"), in fact, act as RIPs, converting a file ("ripping") for printing. Ripping includes telling the printhead where and how to place the dots and remapping the RGB colors to CMYK or whichever subtractive colors are used. RIPs, however, go a few steps further, becoming, in essence, the brain of a digital printer, taking over that role from the normal printer driver. Here are just a few advantages of RIPs.

- *Screening:* Each RIP has its own way to create an image's screening pattern (there are hundreds of screening patterns registered with the U.S. Patent Office). These screening or dithering formulas replace those of the normal printer driver's, and most RIPs offer a selection from which to choose.

- *Color Management:* One area where a RIP can be a definite advantage is with color management. Instead of relying on a standard inkjet printer's hidden or "black box" conversions going from RGB to CMYK, a good CMYK RIP will give you much more control and power over the output process. As one RIP-maker said it, "This is very different from 'pretty picture' color management where you only need a couple of good ICC profiles to produce predictable, pleasing results." Most RIPs can work seamlessly with standard ICC profiles. Linearization (a calibration step done before profiling to assure consistent print behavior) is frequently an added feature of RIPs.

- *Ink Control:* With most inkjet printers, the main control you have over such things as ink-limiting is with the crude Media Type or paper stock selection (some of the newer printers also have a Color Density or Ink Density slider to help accomplish this). You have only a few choices, and they affect all ink colors across the board. However, with a full-featured RIP, you can specify ink percentages for each ink channel supported by the printer. With this kind of precision, you can avoid oversaturating paper stocks with inks and optimizing ink laydown. This also includes ink mixing, which defines the points at which, for example, the light magenta and light cyan inks come into the image.

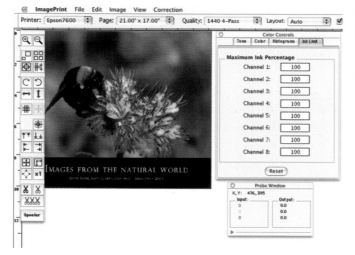

ColorByte's ImagePrint RIP helps photographer David Saffir control his ink densities per channel for his Epson 7600 printer.

Courtesy of David Saffir
www.davidsaffir.com

- *Press Proofing:* If you're doing proofing to emulate another type of printer (an offset press, for example), RIPs usually provide the best way to do this.

- *PostScript:* Many RIPs are PostScript enabled (see "What About PostScript" box).

- *Enlarging:* RIPs use their own proprietary software algorithms to scale up or interpolate a file's data, and some claim their methods are superior to other methods. In addition, some RIPs allow you to make prints larger than you can with standard printer drivers. (See "Printing Big!" for more.)

- *Grayscale:* Some specialized RIPs give you a lot of control in making very neutral grayscale or black-and-white prints. See "The Secret World of Digital Black and White" later in this chapter for more about this.

- *Production Tools:* There are many production aids RIPs provide that most normal printer drivers do not. These include such things as *nesting* (arranging multiple images to reduce paper waste), *tiling* (breaking apart very large images into smaller pieces), rotating, cropping, adding trim marks, queuing/spooling, and more. You will have to decide how important these features are to your digital workflow since some of these production-oriented tools are wasted on individuals doing single prints.

Are there *disadvantages* to RIPs? Of course, and the primary one is cost. RIPs are priced by the size, type, and number of printers supported, and you can figure on spending several hundred to a few thousand dollars on one. RIPs are also complicated to learn, may require training, and require a longer, more complex process to set up for a new paper, ink, or printer than a standard driver. You will have to decide if the added benefits and features of a RIP are worth the price.

Finding a RIP

Most wide-format inkjet printers either come with RIPs as options, or you can purchase a third-party RIP separately. For desktop inkjet, only Epson and HP currently make optional software RIPs for certain models (Epson 4000 and HP Designjet 130, for example), but again, you can find third-party solutions for this category (RIP makers will tell you which printers are supported, and many desktop versions have a scaled-down feature list to lower the price). Epson claims that more than 50 third-party RIPs are compatible with their various printers.

RIPs come in different types ranging from software-only to integrated stand-alone devices. Providers of popular third-party software RIPS include: American Imaging Corp. (Evolution), ColorByte (ImagePrint), ColorBurst Systems (ColorBurst), ErgoSoft (StudioPrint), Onyx (PosterShop), PosterJet, and Wasatch (SoftRIP).

Another option is to use a dedicated PostScript printer model such as the HP Designjet 5500ps or the Roland Hi-Fi JET Pro, each of which has its own PostScript RIP built right into the device. Many laser printers also come in PostScript versions. See the "What About PostScript?" box next for more about PostScript.

RIPs and PostScript

Do all RIPs work with PostScript? No. But to take advantage of what PostScript offers (such as the ability to render PostScript files cleanly), many outside RIPs you might consider will undoubtedly be PostScript RIPs or, like ImagePrint or StudioPrint, come in PostScript and non-PostScript versions.

What about PostScript?

Adobe PostScript refers to both a page-description language and a processor that "interprets" PostScript data. PostScript files describe and locate all bitmapped images, vector art, and type on a rectangular page by X and Y coordinates. You can create PostScript files by saving files created in drawing and page-layout programs through a PostScript engine in your imaging application, or as a stand-alone application.

Do you need to be worried about PostScript? If you're creating professional graphics, color separations, or contract proofs destined for the commercial pre-press or printing industry, then yes, you'll need to involve PostScript somewhere in your workflow. However, if you are printing normal bitmapped files to your own non-PostScript printer (which is what most desktop inkjet printers are), you won't need it.

If you're dealing with PostScript files or files that have EPS graphics included, then you may need to have either a PostScript printer or add a PostScript interpreter to the computer or the printer. Or, use what I like to call the "PDF PostScript RIParound" trick. PDF ("Portable Document Format") is a file format that is built on PostScript language. By taking your digital file and going through Adobe Acrobat and its Distiller program, you can convert the file into a PDF that will render all EPS elements cleanly (see Figure 11.1).

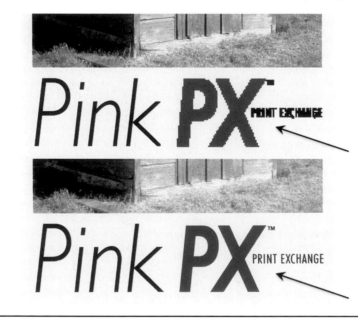

Figure 11.11 Top: bitmapped image with type and EPS logo printed from QuarkXPress to a non-PostScript inkjet printer. Note jagged logo (arrow). Bottom: same image except printed from a PDF version of the same file. Note how logo cleans up.

Do You Need a RIP?

As with PostScript, it all depends. For normal desktop printing of bitmapped images, a RIP is not required. But, if you want access to advanced color management with individual ink limits and channel controls, if your files are very large or complex, if you need to print to unusual output sizes, if you have PostScript elements in your file, or if your printing crosses over into the commercial pre-press world at all, then you will want a RIP. In general, the larger the printer, the more specialized the printing needs, and the more likely a RIP will be appropriate.

Special Color Printing Software

There is another option that falls somewhere between the default printer drivers and RIPs, and that is specialized color printing software. (For more about printing software for producing black-and-white prints, see "The Secret World of Digital Black and White.") Following are a few examples:

Qimage

Qimage (from Digital Domain) is a popular viewing and printing software package. Sold direct and only for Windows 95/98/NT/2000/ME/XP operating systems, Linux systems running Wine, and Macs running Virtual PC, it's reasonably priced at $45 (from www.ddisoftware.com/qimage), and it has avid supporters. "Qimage is just the greatest printing software," says artist Linda Jacobs. "I could probably trade Photoshop for some other image editing program, but I'd never be without Qimage."

Qimage calls itself a "printing application" for improving print quality using internal print-optimization algorithms. It functions as a combination RIP and an image-editor, and where it really shines is with "auto-sizing" or interpolation in order to make large prints. (See more about this feature in "Printing Big!")

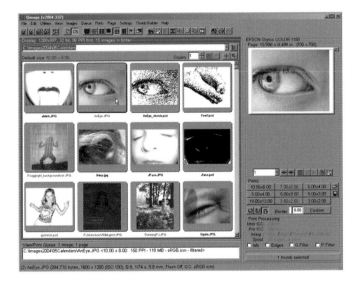

Artist Linda Jacobs prints custom, holiday wall calendars using Qimage and an Epson 1160 inkjet printer. "I have a low-end digital camera that I use for close-ups," she says. "Without Qimage I could never get by with such low resolution."

Courtesy of Linda Jacobs

ILFORD GALERIE Professional Printer Drivers

ILFORD was planning (at this writing) to launch GALERIE Professional Printer Drivers in North America in the fall of 2004. These drivers are designed for GALERIE paper customers looking for a simple and automatic way to achieve better color control and consistency without having to use ICC profiles. After these printer drivers are installed on your computer (PC or Mac), you select the one for your printer and the GALERIE media type when you're ready to print, and the driver takes over the printing control to produce optimized color for that combination. The drivers will be available for a limited number of Canon, HP, and Epson inkjet printers; however, ILFORD promises continuous updating for more printers. For those who prefer to use ICC profiles, ILFORD offers more than 120 profiles for free download from www.ilford.com.

Gimp-Print

Gimp-Print started off back in 1999 as a plug-in for The Gimp, the open-source image-editing program mentioned in Chapter 3. This explains the name, but Gimp-Print has now evolved into an independent printing package; installing The Gimp is not required.

Continuously upgraded by a group of like-minded volunteers and software tinkerers, Gimp-Print is a package of high-quality printer drivers for Linux, BSD, Solaris, IRIX, and other UNIX-like operating systems (and now Mac OS X, which ships with Gimp-Print). "Our goal is to produce the highest possible output quality from all supported printers," says the Gimp-Print team. "To that end, we have done extensive work on screening algorithms, color generation, and printer feature utilization. We are continuing our work in all of these areas to produce ever-higher-quality results, particularly on the ubiquitous, inexpensive inkjet printers that are nonetheless capable of nearly photographic output quality. Additionally, Gimp-Print provides excellent drivers for many printers that are otherwise unsupported on Mac OS X."

Gimp-Print printer drivers can be used with all common UNIX print spooling systems, by means of either CUPS (Common UNIX Printing System) or Ghostscript (an open-source PostScript interpreter). Gimp-Print is supplied in source-code form under the GPL (GNU General Public License).

The Gimp-Print website (www.gimp-print.sourceforge.net) has a long list of the printers (500+) that are supported with separate drivers, and they can be especially useful with old printers that technology (and driver support) have passed by. As UK photographer Keith Cooper puts it, "I use Gimp-Print for handling several old or PC-only printers that sit on my network. It's nice not to have to consign printers to the scrap heap just because the manufacturers have moved on."

Keith Cooper uses Gimp-Print to keep older printers running. Here, he's working with Gimp-Print 5.0 (beta2) for Mac OS X 10.3.5 to print to an Epson Stylus Color 3000.

Courtesy of Keith Cooper
www.northlight-images.co.uk

Printing Big!

With super-sized prints all the rage in the fine-art world, especially photography, there are many ways to break out of the confines of a small page. For wide-format digital photo printing, each brand has its own maximum size. The Océ LightJet 430 can output a single image up to 50.5×120.5 inches, and the newer 500XL model can do 76×120.5 inches; the Durst Lambda 130 can make one seamless print the entire length of a paper roll, or 164 feet.

With inkjets, and this applies especially to imagemakers printing digital panoramas on roll paper or long cut sheets, the maximum printable area is dependent on three factors: the printer driver, the operating system, and the software application.

Driver/OS Limits: The printer driver and the operating system both interact to form the printer's *maximum custom page size* (this does not include margin area, which could make the maximum image size slightly smaller). For example, with the Epson Stylus Photo 2200, the maximum page length (Epson calls it the "maximum printable area") using the normal driver is 44 inches (129 inches with Windows 2000, Me, or XP). Using the CUPS Gimp-Print drivers as described earlier, the maximum is 1,200 inches! However, that's only in theory, because you may also run into the limits of the application you're using (see "Application Software Limits").

One way to exceed driver/OS limits is by using a PostScript RIP or application-direct export module. Once you've handed off the file to the RIP or export module, it takes over by rendering the page to a potentially wider range of maximum sizes, primarily through the action of *tiling*. Tiling means breaking up the image into smaller panels that overlap seamlessly, if desired.

An HP Designjet 5500ps (PostScript model) can print an image with a maximum length of 200 inches. Take that same printer and replace the on-board driver with something like the PosterJet RIP, and the maximum size increases to 50 meters!

Application Software Limits: If you're using the *standard* printer driver, you may reach the limits of the software application before you reach the driver's maximum printable area. (This doesn't apply to RIPs, which trump the application software limits.) Photoshop, for example, used to have a limit of 30,000 pixels in any one dimension. Because of the way Epson drivers interface with Photoshop, the maximum page length for an Epson 2200 (to continue with the earlier example) was 41.67 inches, which was determined by taking the 30,000 pixel limit and dividing that by Epson's desktop "input resolution" of 720 ppi. Now that Photoshop CS has increased its maximum to 300,000 pixels, the theoretical length limit of that Epson 2200 is 417 inches. However, that's still just theory since you may run into the driver limit before you reached that length.

One way around these application limits is either to use a PostScript RIP or to save the file to a page-layout or drawing program that does not have the pixel limit (but which may lead to other problems with color management; you just can't have it all sometimes!). QuarkXPress 4.x only goes up to a maximum page size of 48 inches. Illustrator 8.x/9.x goes up to 227 inches, and CorelDRAW 8.x/9.x can hit a whopping 1,800 inches. You are, however, still restricted by the printer's maximum custom page size—unless you do what I call *application tiling*.

This single image was output 50 feet long in one piece from an HP Designjet 5500 printer using the German-made PosterJet RIP. PosterJet has the ability to print a single image up to 50 meters in length!

Application Tiling: If you're not using a RIP, you can use application tiling to exceed the print device's maximum page-length limit and print in banner mode up to the application's maximum. This neat trick divides the image into smaller pieces that, when laid end-to-end, form one long image without breaks. Both Corel Draw 8.x/9.x and Adobe Illustrator 8.x/9.x allow you to do this. Figure 11.2 shows how Adobe Illustrator 8.01 would be set up to print a tall banner that's 44 inches wide and 227 inches tall on an Epson 10000 under an older OS.

A PostScript RIP, however, gives you even better control over tiling and may eliminate the need to use a page-layout or drawing program in the first place (unless you're creating your image that way).

Another way that application tiling can be done is by breaking up the image into individual tiles that are printed separately and physically reassembled by either butting or slightly overlapping the edges with tape or adhesive. The downside to this type of image tiling is that there will be visible seams.

This is how ceramic tile murals are done, and another good use of this technique is for making full-size mockups. This is also how intentional "collage art" images and super-large images like billboards that are meant to be viewed at a distance are created.

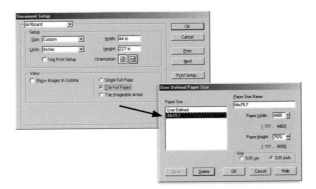

Figure 11.2 At left is the Adobe Illustrator 8.01 Document Setup screen with Tile Full Pages checked in the View section. The right screen shows the custom page size (75.7 inches), created by dividing the banner size (227 inches) by 3 to yield 75.7, which is under the printer's maximum.

Courtesy of Epson America, Inc.

Panoramas

Keeping in mind all the restrictions that limit the size of large prints, some of the most dramatic examples of digital printing are panoramas. There are many ways to accomplish this, usually either by manually blending digitally captured or scanned images (see Figure 11.3) or by using an automatic "stitcher" software program. Photoshop Elements and Photoshop CS both have a Photomerge function, and there are also many third-party software programs that seamlessly combine many separate images into one. Some of the variables that must be understood and conquered include: distortion, image equalization, rotation and horizon line-up, and many other factors. However, there is nothing like a long, seamless, horizontal (or vertical) panorama to show off the advantages of digital printing!

Figure 11.4 Photographer Ralph Cooksey-Talbott creates panoramic prints by manually combining a number of Nikon D-100 frames. Counter-clockwise from top: the final 120-MB *Dry Creek Hills image composed of six separate frames,* a 72-inch version of the print coming out of an Epson 9600 printer, mounting the print with a back brace, and the finished print on the wall of the photographer's studio.

Courtesy of Cooksey-Talbott Gallery/www.cookseytalbottgallery.com

Cheating Pixels

When you're stuck with a given resolution of an image, but you want to blow it up and print it big, Photoshop's Bicubic Resampling function does a fair job—up to a point. It creates interpolated pixels in an attempt to trick your eyes into seeing more detail than is actually there. However, the image soon begins to break down as you increase the enlargement. There are several software products that try to improve on the basic Photoshop interpolation method; each has its own group of believers. Here are three:

FM Stair Interpolation: Photographer Fred Miranda used to offer a Photoshop *action* (automated series of commands) that broke Photoshop's Bicubic interpolation method into small steps, which is why it was called *Stair Interpolation* or *SI*. At this writing, Miranda had replaced all the older versions with *Stair Interpolation Pro*, a Photoshop plug-in (supporting 16-bit in CS) for PC and Mac that has options to interpolate images based on either paper size, pixel dimension, printer resolution, or scale. SI Pro is available via download (www.fredmiranda.com) for a nominal fee and works with all digital image files.

(Photographer Glenn Mitchell offers a free version of his *TLR ImageResizer* for Photoshop as an action set for enlarging in small increments. Downloadable from www.thelightsright.com)

Genuine Fractals: LizardTech's Genuine Fractals (GF) is a Photoshop plug-in that enlarges images using proprietary fractal technology. You first encode the image in GF's .STN format and save it with a choice of Lossless compression (2:1 savings) or Visually Lossless (5:1 savings). You then enlarge it: 150 percent, 250 percent, or more. The PrintPro version supports all Photoshop color modes including RGB, CMYK, and CIE-Lab, and it encodes and renders 8- and 16-bit images. How well GF works depends on the to-from file size and the type and quality of the image involved. For Windows and Mac.

Qimage: Qimage, the stand-alone image-editing and printing software, has nine different interpolation algorithms (including Lanczos, Vector, and Pyramid) to "res up" images. Many users feel that Qimage's interpolation methods are better than those used in most image editors for making large prints from small files.

Qimage developer Mike Chaney explains the differences among the main interpolation functions. "Most interpolation methods including Bicubic and Lanczos use a 'windowed' function to look at pixels in a square window, say 7×7 pixels. The interpolated pixel's value is computed using mathematical functions that apply a weight to each of the pixels in the window. The function itself is what determines how much weight each pixel contributes to the final interpolated (target) pixel, and therefore what the final image will look like. *Bicubic* usually produces smoother results, but less sharp, while the *Lanczos* function produces sharper results because it uses the mathematical sin function, which has a natural tendency to sharpen edges due to its repetitive or 'cycling' nature. *Vector* is a different kind of function that looks at geometric shapes produced by pixels and interpolates by looking at the target pixel's position inside a plane formed by several adjacent pixels in the source/original image. *Pyramid* is a complex extension of the vector algorithm. It basically refines the vector approach by considering many more complex shapes when creating the planes and doing the geometric placement of pixels.

"It's important to note that all interpolation methods have their pros and cons. Some are better for some types of images while others excel with different ones; for example, images with a lot of diagonal lines versus fine mesh patterns like screen doors versus 'random' details like sand on a beach. There is only so much that can be predicted through interpolation, and interpolation definitely has its limits, with each algorithm offering a different bias on the tradeoffs. When going beyond about 4x enlargements (which is a hefty stretch), you can smooth out the jaggies, but you'll never get even close to the amount of detail that you would have had if you were able to capture or create at that 4x size without interpolating!" (See Figure 11.4 to see how these main interpolation methods stack up in one sample image.)

Figure 11.4 Comparing interpolation methods: A–original with $1/4$x downsample (inset) used as input to the other 400-percent upsamples), B–pixel resize (simple 400-percent zoom), C–Photoshop Bicubic Smoother, D–Lanczos, E–Vector, F–Pyramid.

Courtesy of Mike Chaney, author of Qimage www.ddisoftware.com/qimage

The Secret World of Digital Black and White

There is an entire subculture of photographers doing super high-quality digital black-and-white imaging and printing. Following are some key techniques (mostly inkjet) from this hidden world.

What Are You Afraid Of?

Quality, permanence, and unfamiliarity are probably the three biggest fears or concerns—real or imagined—preventing imagemakers from heading down the digital black-and-white path.

Looking at quality first, Florida pro photographer and master printer Steven Katzman describes his own recent conversion experience: "After spending 30 years in the darkroom," he explains, "I was reluctant to try something new. Early on, I had seen some digital black-and-white prints, but was not impressed. Then, I attended a scanner seminar and brought along one of my black-and-white negatives with a selenium-toned darkroom print. They scanned in and inkjet-printed the image for me on the spot, and I realized in that moment that the digital age had caught up with traditional black-and-white printing. The comparison of the digital print with my silver print that had taken hours to pull can only be described as profound, the quality was that good."

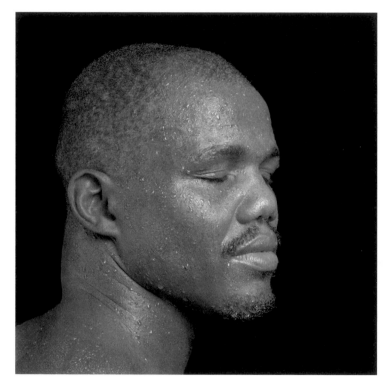

Steven Katzman turned heads at a trade show in New York City when he exhibited his large-format digital black-and-white prints including Young Joe Louis (shown), which is in the Eastman Kodak corporate collection. "People said that they had never seen digital prints with such a neutral color and smooth transition of tonal values," says Katzman, who uses the ImagePrint RIP from ColorByte with Epson wide-format printers.

Courtesy of Steven Katzman Photography www.stevenkatzmanphotography.com.

Regarding permanence or longevity, photographer and digital black-and-white printing expert Paul Roark admits that "until recently, digital black-and-white prints have not been as durable as silver prints," and fiber-based silver or platinum prints are the standard for longevity against which all else is compared. "Unfortunately," he continues, "the older black-and-white inksets were not as good as originally represented because they contained dyes and were not pure pigments, and as such, some people saw their allegedly 'archival' materials turn brown or fade."

However, things are definitely improving. "My tests indicate that the best modern, carbon-based monochrome inksets (MIS UltraTone, Cone PiezoTone) do not warm up like the old inks and are extremely stable; more stable in fact than color pigments," says Roark. "So, in my view, digital black-and-white printing has come of age."

And finally, "familiarity with darkroom ways and unfamiliarity with the computer tools necessary for a digital workflow is another fear," says fine art photographer and consultant Robert Morrison. A different set of skills is definitely required, and this creates resistance to change.

Getting Results with Digital Black and White

Acknowledging that this book can only be a snapshot in time as technology evolves, here are some equipment, supplies, and workflow choices to get you on the road to great digital black and white.

Image Capture

While you could certainly use a high-end digital camera or scanning back, many digital black-and-white pros shoot film and then scan it.

"Start with a well-cared-for black-and-white negative that is carefully scanned," says Los Angeles photographer and printmaker Antonis Ricos, who, with fine-art photographer Martin Wesley, runs one of the most important e-mail discussion lists for digital black-and-white pros (http://groups.yahoo.com/group/DigitalBlackandWhiteThePrint). "For large prints and 8 × 10 negs, drum scanner technology may still have significant advantages over a CCD, depending on the neg and the size of the final print. Scanning at resolutions beyond what the best CCDs offer and doing so with a single, focused point of light extracts more accurate information from certain originals like large format or high-contrast negs. Drum scanning is also able to keep any film (especially 35mm) flatter and therefore sharper than other scanners. However, for formats up to 4 × 5, you can get very decent results with the Imacon scanners, especially the latest models that offer autofocus and a cooled CCD."

Converting Color and Printing Monochrome

If you're starting from a color capture or scan, there are numerous ways of converting color images to monochrome for digital black-and-white printing, and Adobe Photoshop is the preferred software to do it. (There are some excellent Photoshop plug-ins for even more sophisticated conversions of color to black-and-white, too.) "Photoshop is the industry standard for image editing and with good reason," says black-and-white, fine-art photographer Amadou Diallo. Rarely a week goes by that I don't stop and say 'Wow' at the level of precision and control it affords. Because of its widespread use, Photoshop also provides a common language among imagers. I can talk about shadow values, gamma densities, and ink percentages with another photographer, and we're actually talking about the same numbers."

RGB > Grayscale

It's easy to convert a color image to a monochromatic grayscale in Photoshop (Image > Mode > Grayscale), but how you print this neutral image makes all the difference.

Print Grayscale with Black Ink Only: Most inkjet printer drivers give you a choice of "color" or "black" ink when printing (see Figure 11.5). Selecting the black-ink-only option might seem like a good way to print a monochrome image, but there are drawbacks. With the exception of newer printers using the smallest dot sizes, the prints sometimes lack detail and may have a course dot pattern since you're only working with one ink. Yet, some think black-ink-only prints on certain printers and on certain papers are beautiful. A lot depends on the image characteristics. Test it for yourself.

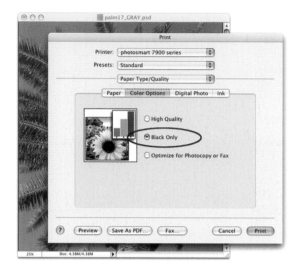

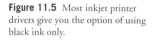

Figure 11.5 Most inkjet printer drivers give you the option of using black ink only.

One advantage with black-ink-only printing is that the prints are going to be fairly neutral, with only the color of the paper and the inherent tone of the black ink (usually warm, or possibly changing to warm) being the variables. And, any concerns about metamerism with pigment inks are reduced since that problem with shifting neutral tones is caused primarily by the colored inks, not black.

Print Grayscale with Color Inks: If you print a grayscale image selecting the color-inks option in the normal printer driver, you can usually see the difference in quality (see Figure 11.6). The image is smoother and fuller due to the added ink colors. (Even though the image is in Grayscale mode, most printers still recruit the color inks.) The major drawback to this method is that you will invariably get an overall color cast (the color will vary depending on the paper and the inks), and the ways to fix that problem are limited. In Grayscale mode, color-based adjustment layers in Photoshop are unavailable, and so are the Color Control sliders in the printer driver settings. A solution is to convert the image to a duotone or back to RGB (see below). Using specialized drivers or software is another solution; see that section later in this chapter.

RGB > Grayscale > Duotone

You can change the color balance of a grayscale image by converting it to Duotone mode in Photoshop (Image > Mode > Duotone) and selecting any custom color to go along with the base black (see Figure 11.7). If you then print the image with "color inks" selected, all the ink colors are used as above. The same lack of color image-editing adjustments exist, but now you have access to the color slider adjustments in the printer driver for tweaking the overall color balance.

Using the same technique, a Photoshop Tritone or Quadtone adds even more color options to the mix.

Figure 11.6 The coarseness of a grayscale image printed with a single black ink only (top) can be pronounced compared to the same image printed with color inks (bottom), depending on the type of printer.

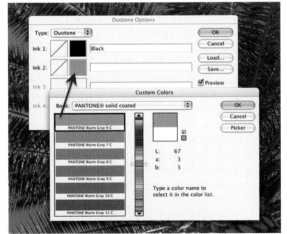

Figure 11.7 Switching from RGB to Duotone mode in Photoshop opens up interesting color possibilities for grayscale images.

RGB > Grayscale > RGB

This is similar to the first method, but by converting the image back into RGB mode, you have access to all the other colors to increase the tonal range. The result is much more color flexibility. If you don't like the overall color balance, it's easy to make it be either more or less neutral. For a sepia effect, for example, add a Color Balance adjustment layer and move the sliders to something like -15 Magenta and -15 Yellow (see Figure 11.8). The same effect can be achieved by using the color control sliders in the advanced section on most inkjet printers. This is similar to darkroom photographers selecting warm or cool papers or toning chemicals to shift the overall colors of a black-and-white print. (You can also use canned printer presets like "sepia," but these have limited use since you typically have no ability to adjust the settings.)

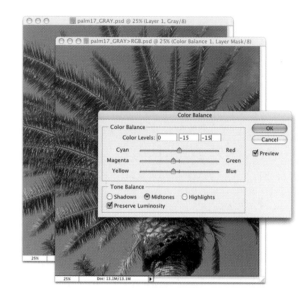

Figure 11.8 Converting a grayscale image to RGB allows for a full range of color adjustments such as this sepia effect with the Color Balance tool.

You could also create a modified printer profile that automatically makes the same color shift for all your prints.

RGB > Desaturate

A simple way to remove color from an image is by desaturating it. Photoshop has a good tool for this: Hue/Saturation. Here's how it works with a slight twist:

Add a Hue/Saturation adjustment layer (Layer > New Adjustment Layer > Hue/Saturation) to the image. (I always use adjustment layers instead of making the adjustment directly to the image.) In the dialogue box, and with the Edit pull-down menu in the default "Master" position, move the Saturation slider to the left and watch the effect. A maximum saturation level of -100 is basically a grayscale image with no color. For an interesting multi-toned option, you can change the saturation of the individual Edit channels instead of the Master (see Figure 11.9). Alternatively, you can shift the colors by adding a separate Color Balance adjustment layer and playing with the sliders.

One drawback to this desaturation method is that you lose the distinction between some colors. To fix this, try the Channel Mixer technique next.

RGB > Channel Mixer

This is a good way to change the relationship of or to emphasize certain colors in monochrome. To do it, make a Channel Mixer adjustment layer, and in the dialogue box, check "Monochrome." The image instantly changes (if Preview is checked), and now the fun

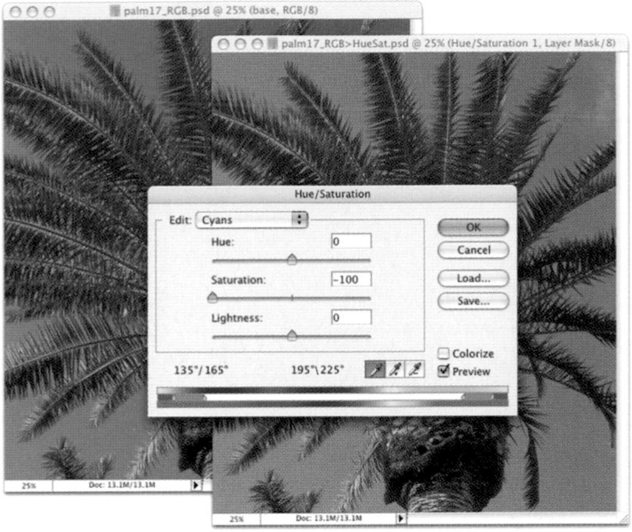

Figure 11.9 Desaturating the individual Edit channels of an RGB image creates an interesting multi-toned effect.

can start. Use the Source Channels sliders to adjust the individual Red, Green, and Blue channels while watching the image change. Make sure that the three Channels add up to 100% if you want to hold the overall lightness-to-darkness range of the image.

For my palm tree, I wanted a dark, brooding sky. To accomplish that, I adjusted my Red, Green, and Blue Source Channels in the Channel Mixer to be +55, +55, -10 (see Figure 11.10).

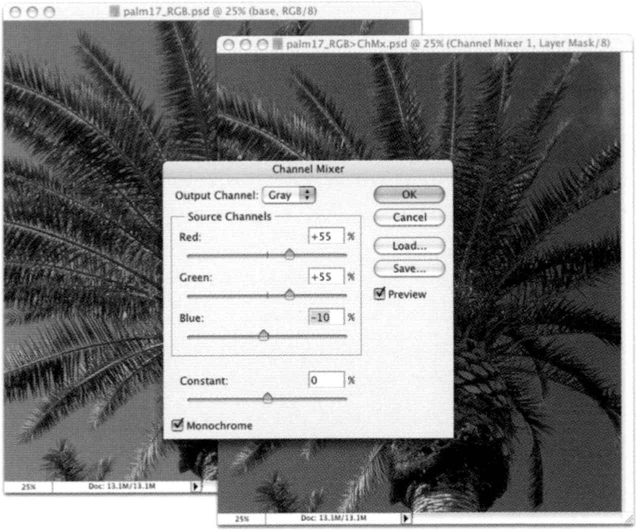

Figure 11.10 Photoshop's Channel Mixer with the Monochrome option checked helps change the relationship of the color values.

RGB > Hue/Sat > LAB

(This is adapted from R9 Corporation's BWBatch program.)

With a flattened, color image open, create a new Hue/Saturation Adjustment Layer with the following settings: Hue—-180, Saturation—-100, Lightness—+100, and Mode–Saturation. Then convert to LAB mode (Image > Mode > Lab Color), selecting the flatten option, if needed. Next, open the Channels menu and get rid of the a and b color channels by simply trashing them. You'll be prompted to flatten the image, which leaves only the Lightness—now called *Alpha 1*—channel that contains all the light-to-dark information (see Figure 11.11). Convert to Grayscale and print.

Figure 11.11 Using Hue/Saturation and then LAB mode is another monochrome conversion technique.

Using Specialized Monochrome Inksets

An improvement in the digital printing of black-and-white images is the development of third-party, multi-toned, monochromatic inks that replace the color inks in inkjet printers. This is also called "quadtone" or "hextone" printing; the printer thinks it's printing in color, but the inks that come out are all shades of black or differing densities of gray. Popular inksets include: Lysonic Quad Black and Small Gamut (Lyson), PiezoTone (Inkjet Mall), Preservation Monochrome (Lumijet), the Quadtone B&W and UltraTone families that include both Monotone and Variable Tone inksets (MIS), and Septone (Sundance).

"Depending on a photographer's needs," says digital expert C. David Tobie, "a quad-tone/hextone gray ink system, or a tinted version of one, may be an excellent choice, although unless it is purchased at a significantly increased price as a proprietary matched system, it will require special knowledge and a fair amount of work to get ideal results. A small-gamut color ink system that uses CMYK-tinted gray inks requires a far less specialized process and offers a broader range of user-determined tint choices (warm, cool, sepia, platinum/paladium, etc.)."

Warm Neutral   Cool Neutral   Selenium Tone   Carbon Sepia

Inkjet Mall's monochrome PiezoTone inks are 100 percent pigmented and come in different Hue Sets.

Courtesy of Jon Cone.
www.inkjetmall.com

One thing that some monochrome printmakers who use these special inks often do is dedicate a separate printer for the job. That way, they don't have to continually switch back and forth between color and monochrome inks, which is a lot of trouble and wastes ink. The older Epson 1160 and also the 3000, both four-color printers, are popular choices, although just about any inkjet printer will do, taking the restrictions of chipped-ink cartridges into account. If you have a thermal inkjet printer with replaceable heads, you could have one set for color and another for monochrome. Bulk ink systems are also popular add-ons for more efficient ink use.

Dedicating a separate printer to black-and-white makes sense for desktop inkjets, but doing so with wide-format becomes very costly.

The popularity of monochrome inks has not gone unnoticed by the OEM printer manufacturers. Epson introduced its seven-color, pigment inkjet printers (2200, 7600, 9600) in the spring of 2002. With these printers, you now have the option of using an additional low-density black ink (only in color mode), which helps improve both metamerism and the monochrome image quality. (HP offers a similar solution with printers such as the Photosmart 7960, which includes three blacks.)

Even with these printer improvements, many experienced black-and-white pros, however, opt for all black-and-white, third-party systems. "For the best image quality, you need to use a dedicated black-and-white inkset," states Paul Roark. "As much as you try, the color insets always end up with color cross-overs and tints. Even if they look great at first, printer instability and differential fading cause the problems to surface with time. Color insets also suffer from metamerism (shifting colors under different types of lights). With a neutral black and white, the eye is extremely sensitive to slight color shifts. No color inkset has been able to solve this problem, whereas it is not a significant issue with the black-and-white pigment insets. Most of us who print with black-and-white 'quad' insets tried color first and just gave up on that approach."

Using Specialized Drivers and Software

Some of the highest-quality black-and-white digital prints being made today are the result of specialized printer drivers or RIPs. Popular examples include: ImagePrint (ColorByte), InkJet Control/OpenPrintmaker (BowHaus), PixelPixasso (R9), QuadToneRIP (Roy Harrington), and StudioPrint (ErgoSoft).

Brooklyn, New York, fine-art photographer Amadou Diallo uses ErgoSoft's StudioPrint RIP to produce his digital black-and-white prints on an Epson Stylus Pro 9000 using PiezoTone inks. Sunflower is shown. "With StudioPrint," says Diallo, "quadtone printmakers now have unprecedented control over their printer's behavior combined with the production gains offered by professional layout features. The output is among some of the finest printing I've ever done, darkroom or digital."

© 2001 Amadou Diallo
www.diallophotography.com

Using Specialized Printers

Non-inkjet printers have their own quirks when it comes to monochrome printing. "With LightJets, Lambdas, Frontiers, and other similar digital imaging devices," explains C. David Tobie, "the trick for black and white is to get a really accurate color profile for the device made and edit that profile yourself, if necessary, to nail the black-and-white or near black-and-white tones you want. And then apply that profile to your images before sending them out for printing on the machine you have built the profile for."

Inkjet is not the only way to print digital black-and-white, but for many, it's currently the method of choice. While there are no (at this writing) true, all black-and-white OEM inkjet printers, Epson raised some eyebrows with the introduction of its UltraChrome inkjet printer line a couple of years ago. As already mentioned, the Epson Stylus Photo 2200 and Stylus Pro 7600/9600 were groundbreaking by including the first use of seven ink colors (in separate tanks) with two different blacks—one full-strength, one diluted.

HP then raised the bar even further when it introduced several color/black-and-white Photosmart photo printers, led by the 7960. This is a desktop inkjet printer with eight ink colors including a separate cartridge (HP 59 Gray Photo) that includes three different black densities, which are only available when printing in grayscale mode (see Figure 11.12). This printer is capable of producing excellent black-and-white prints right out of the box; the primary drawback (besides the high cost of the prints) is the limited output size (U.S. Letter/Legal).

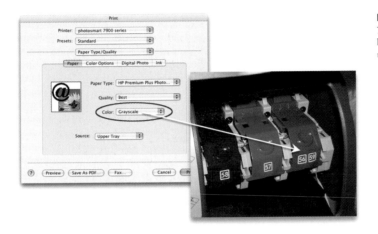

Figure 11.12 The HP Photosmart 7960 Photo Printer has a special 3-black cartridge (#59) that kicks in when the printer outputs in Grayscale mode.

Integrated Monochromatic Systems

Digital printmakers are used to piecing together black-and-white solutions from different sources, but there is a trend toward integrated inkjet systems all under one roof. One example is Jon Cone's PiezographyBW ICC system that combines monochromatic inks (PiezoTones) and Piezography ICC profiles on CD-ROM. (Cone also provides a personalized profiling system through his iQuads program.) In fact, the PiezographyBW ICC entry (also including Piezography Museum Bright White paper) won the 2004 DIMA Printer Shoot-Out award in the black-and-white category. It's currently for select Epson and soon Canon printers from Inkjet Mall.

Lyson's Daylight Darkroom digital black-and-white printing system, newly announced at the time of this writing consists of: (1) Quad Black inks in carts or in bulk feed, (2) printer driver software licensed from BowHaus, (3) Lyson Darkroom range of inkjet media, (4) a set of cleaning cartridges for removal of the standard color inks from the printer, and (5) optional Lyson PrintGuard protection spray. The initial list of supported printers includes Epson 2200, 7600, and 9600, with plans to expand to the Epson 4000 and newer Canons.

Another system is the combination of Sundance Septone inks and R9 PixelPixasso RIP software. It provides wide variation in tonal representation using simple software adjustments. Adjustment of the degree of "warmth" and "coolness" over three density channels is available within the ICQ settings of PixelPixasso." The PixelPixasso RIP, which supports the Epson 2200 and Epson 7600/9600 as Septone printers is Windows-only. PixelPixasso also supports these printers as ICC CMYK printers and as "pure" 7-channel printers (you can send them 7-channel RAW files). A Septone Photoshop export plug-in is available for both Windows and Macintosh. Available from BWGuys.

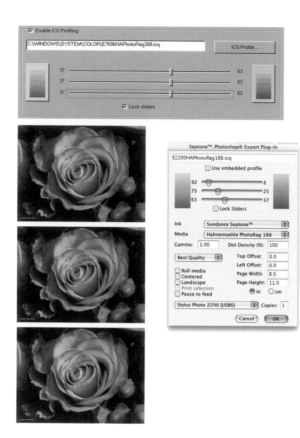

The R9/Sundance black-and-white system includes: (top) the PixelPixasso RIP for Windows with adjustments for selecting warm to cool results; (left) roses show variations of Warm, Mixed Warm, and Cool from top to bottom; (right) the Septone Photoshop plug-in for Mac OS X (the Mac Classic and Win versions have the same functionality but conform to the standards of their respective OS's.).

Courtesy of R9 Corporation. Rose photo © 2001 Ken Niles.

Beyond the Digital Print

Cards, books, portfolios, emulsion transfers, lenticular prints, and other alternative processes—these are just a few of the ways imagemakers are experimenting with the definitions of digital printing.

Cards, Books, and Portfolios

Printing on paper can also take other forms besides single digital prints. Here are some examples to give you a feel for the diversity of paper-print options.

Cards

Greeting, gift, note, and promotional cards are easy to make by self-printers using inkjet or laser printers. There are two basic card-making methods: (1) make a small print and adhere it to the outside panel of a single or a folded card, or (2) print directly onto single or foldable card blanks. (You can also print on a larger sheet and simply fold it down to size by hand.)

Photographer and print-service provider James Respess sends "adhered-print" cards to his clients and contacts. "It just makes sense to please clients," explains Respess. "I always send notes to folks who purchase my art as thank-yous and to keep them informed about my shows. This is also great for cultivating collectors."

Digital artist Teri Brudnak uses the same idea except she hand-folds heavy 7 × 10-inch fine-art paper and then adheres her inkjet print to the outside page. (See Figure 11.13 for examples from both Respess and Brudnak.)

Figure 11.13 Left: A commercial, folded, blank note card with a small canvas inkjet print (*Embrace Me*) attached by James Respess; right: a hand-folded card with a Teri Brudnak *Red Orchids* print attached. Both fit into standard note card envelopes.

For the second "print-directly-on" category, there are many good sources for these cards. ArtZ has three lines of inkjet-printable cards, and in mid-2004, it teamed up with Moab Paper in creating the CardMaker line of fine-art inkjet cards. These are made from 100 percent cotton Entrada Fine Art paper and are printable on both sides (interior and exterior). Cards come in three sizes, and accompanying envelopes are made of pH-neutral and chlorine-free translucent vellum. Downloadable templates and printing profiles are also available.

Other good sources for pre-cut, pre-scored (for easy folding), printable cards include Crane (they have also have a panoramic card), Strathmore, Red River, Photographer's Edge, Digital Art Supplies, Inkjet Goodies, and InkjetArt. Most of these cards come with envelopes.

A final option is to use an outside print service to make cards for you. This is an attractive alternative when high quantities and economics dictate. Printmaker Jan Steinman of Bytesmiths offers color laser cards as a cheaper alternative to inkjet. Andy Wollman of Century Editions prints note cards on 100 percent cotton-rag stock with a natural deckle edge on digital offset presses (see Figure 11.14). He'll do as few as 35 cards in an order with online ordering, and he has cards available in several sizes.

What if you want to sell your cards and need commercial clear envelopes or gift-card boxes for marketing? Clearbags.com has both.

Figure 11.14 Century Editions, a giclée reproduction atelier in Scottsdale, Arizona, prints four-color-process note cards on digital presses with a minimum quantity of 35.

Courtesy of Andy Wollmann
www.centuryeditions.com

Custom Books and Portfolios

Making your own custom books of original digital prints for portfolios, limited editions, bios, family histories—or even as part of an art concept as artist Ed Ruscha did starting in the 1960s—is a great idea.

Books about or by artists are common, but producing books has traditionally been a complicated and expensive proposition best left to publishers and beyond the reach of most photographer-artists. While the print-on-demand technologies now found at any Kinko's and print shops have changed that scenario somewhat, high-quality color bookmaking has remained an elusive goal for most. Until now. It is possible for just about anyone to make custom books of their digital prints with inkjet or other technologies we've been discussing. Here's how:

Fold-a-Book: The simplest way to make a book from your own prints is to fold a single sheet of paper in half. Each sheet now becomes four book pages. (Each side of the paper is one page.) Stack all the folded sheets on top of each other, add a cover sheet, staple, sew, or otherwise hook all the pages together, and presto—you have a book (see Figure 11.15). The trick in doing all this is planning the pages. For that, make a simple mockup using office paper. Just fold pages and start writing or sketching what goes on each page.

To produce this kind of book, you'll need to be able to print on both sides of the page, which, naturally, requires double-sided or dual-coated paper. Be sure to let the ink dry completely between printings.

Bound Books: The trickiest part of bookmaking is the binding step. How are you going to collect and connect all the separate pages into a book that doesn't fall apart the moment you pick it up? The old way was to take your loose pages to an instant print shop or copy center. Staples, Office Depot, or Kinko's all offer the inexpensive and standard office binding methods such as comb, coil, post, Velo, tape, or other types that are typically used by

Figure 11.15 A simple fold-a-book, stapled at the spine.

businesses and students for reports. Commercial book binderies (find them in your local Yellow Pages under "bookbinding") and printers will be able to offer more robust bindery options including sewn, saddle-stitched, or case or perfect binding.

A contemporary option is to print and bind the book pages yourself. There are now several book-binding systems targeted to digital imagemakers who want to make their own hard-bound coffee-table books. ArtZ's BookMaker produces leather-covered digital books with two-sided pages that photographer-artists can print and assemble themselves. The paper is Moab's Entrada Fine Art with acid-free translucent fly sheets to protect the first and last pages (or all pages). There are two sizes: 7×7 and 10×10, and the books can hold 10–20 pages.

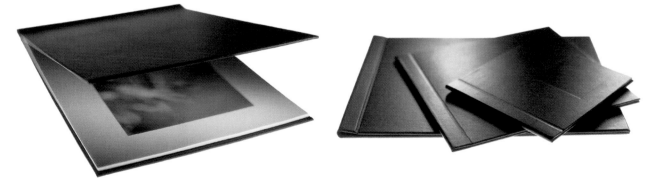

ArtZ's BookMaker system lets digital imagemakers print and bind their own hardbound coffee-table books.

Courtesy of ArtZ/www.artzproducts.com

Bind-It Photo Corp. has a compact tabletop system for binding self-printed, hardbound books. After the images are output onto ready-to-bind, pre-hinged Stone Edition art papers, the pages are placed into the binding unit, which uses an acid-free thermal adhesive in the spine of the cover.

Some imagemakers enjoy binding their own books by hand. I've seen everything from rawhide cords, to steel nuts and bolts, to surgical tubing used. Sometimes, a special binding method can add a lot to the overall impact of a custom book.

Book Services: As with cards, some digital printmakers also offer to make custom artist books. For example, Lynn Lown of New Media Arts in Santa Fe, New Mexico, creates hand-bound inkjet-printed books complete with cloth covers and slip cases (see image).

New Media Arts produces beautiful inkjet-printed books as special projects.

Courtesy of New Media Arts
www.nmarts.com

More commercial and online suppliers of digital books printed mostly by digital offset technology include MyPublisher.com, Snapfish.com, and Apple's iPhoto software and service, which produces (via Indigo printing) linen-covered books in North America and Europe.

A few more comments about custom books:

- Because the pages of books are closed—and therefore dark—most of the time, image stability in terms of lightfastness is less important. However, dark-fading stability as well as ink smearing and rub-off still need to be taken into account.

- Consider making a book of prints and calling that book a limited edition or portfolio. Boxed portfolio sets are nothing new in the world of photography and fine-art, but what is new is the idea of making an actual book of original prints. These prints, then, are not reproductions; they are the originals, no different than if you had made the prints individually, which, in fact, you have done. The difference is that they are now bound together in some meaningful and practical way. Add a bio, artist's statement, and anything else you like, and you now have a portable, permanent art show.

- The most difficult thing about creating books is not their production but their marketing, particularly if you're trying to make it into a commercial venture. Distribution, sales, promotion, and all the rest of the book-marketing process is an ambitious undertaking, and I wish anyone attempting it the best of luck. However, if you're only interested in producing a few books for a close circle of friends, family, clients, colleagues, and buyers, then you are alive at the right time in human history.

Presentation Portfolios: In addition to the limited-edition portfolio mentioned above, more utilitarian portfolios are used by photographers and other artists to showcase their work to prospective clients, gallerists, and other art marketers. Boxes with loose prints, albums with removable pages, and even bound books can be used as presentation portfolios.

Commercial photographers know that if they send out 10 portfolios, they'll be lucky to receive three back. For this reason, and also because portfolio contents are always being updated, image fading is not an important issue, and therefore many choose to print on inkjet printers with dye-based inks in order to take advantage of the increased color gamuts that certain dye-ink-and-paper combinations offer. Canon desktops and the Epson Stylus Photo 1280 have been favorites with portfolio printers for years, although any of the Epson UltraChrome printers can also be used. The HP Designjet 130 printer is also popular with photographers, especially since it can produce prints that are indistinguishable from true photographic lab prints. Photography icon Joel Meyerowitz now prints his commercial portfolios using the HP printers. This was a big step for him, but the reaction of his commercial agent was instant. "They thought they were real photos printed at a lab," Meyerowitz says. "They couldn't believe that I was getting this kind of quality from inkjet."

Photographer, editor, and consultant Andrew Darlow, who teaches workshops on digital printing privately and in conjunction with schools and organizations, gives us a final thought about portfolios: "In the past, imagemakers almost always depended on others to produce their portfolio prints. With the advent of affordable photo-quality inkjet and other printing technologies, photographers and other artists are now producing their own prints, with the flexibility to choose a wide range of papers and binding options. Whether prints are produced and assembled loose in boxes or flat portfolios, placed behind plastic pages, or put in library-style leather-bound books, the creative possibilities are endless."

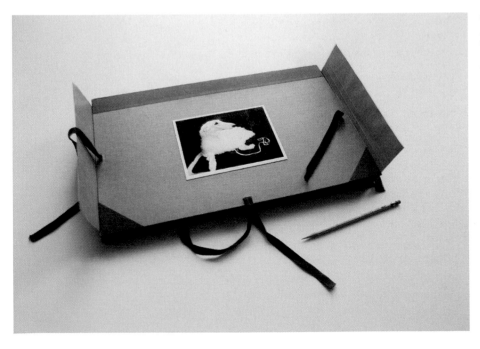

One of Andrew Darlow's favorite portfolios. "I really like to use this type of tie portfolio with flaps, which has been popular for many decades," he says. "The brand is Xonex, from Cleveland, Ohio, and by attaching a print to the cover, I am able to guide the viewer to the content inside and how the portfolio should be opened. The colors and fabric styles are very attractive, and it was inexpensive (under $20). Lineco and other companies offer similar portfolios. I recommend coating the cover print with Liquitex Acrylic Gloss Varnish (item #5016), which results in a beautiful protected image with a semi-gloss finish." (This photo was taken before coating.)

Portfolio photo and image on portfolio
© Andrew Darlow

Digital Mixed Media

For some, a digital print that comes out of a printer is not the end point of a process but only the beginning. Three pioneering artists who have been pushing the digital edge the longest and the farthest were founding members of Unique Editions, which ultimately became known as the Digital Atelier: Dorothy Simpson Krause, Bonny Lhotka, and Karin Schminke (see Figure 11.16). In keeping with their tagline, "a printmaking studio for the 21st Century," even the organization of the group is modern: Each member lives in a different part of the U.S. (Boston, Denver, and Seattle, respectively), and they come together in person only for educational forums, workshops, seminars, and artists-in-residence classes. Their work is in more than 200 corporate and museum collections including the permanent collection of the Smithsonian American Art Museum.

Krause, Lhotka, and Schminke are well-known for combining traditional and digital printmaking to produce their own original digital prints. Although they each use the computer as a tool, their work and media choices are as varied as their backgrounds. It includes one-of-a-kind paintings, collages, image transfers, monotypes, and prints on all kinds of surfaces as diverse as plywood, silk, rusty metal, and handmade substrates.

Figure 11.16 Digital Atelier, from left: Dorothy Simpson Krause, Bonny Lhotka, and Karin Schminke.

"When people see our work, they don't think digital," Schminke says.

Using a digital print as a base or ground, they usually end up with something totally unique. Digigraphs, digital collages, and digital mixed media are some of the terms they've used over the years.

The wide range of their work includes these processes:

- Creating customized surfaces (see "inkAID Precoats").
- Underprinting digital images as a base for and overprinting images onto other media.
- Wet, dry emulsion, and gelatin transfers (see "Clear Emulsion Transfers").
- Layering prints with collage and paint.
- Printing on fabric (see "Fabric Printing").
- Exploring three-dimensional art including lenticular technology (see "Lenticular Prints").

As three of the primary investigators and pioneers of digital mixed-media printmaking, they finally published their own book about it—*Digital Art Studio: Techniques for Combining Inkjet Printing with Traditional Art Materials* (Watson-Guptill, 2004). Rather than cover territory that they have done so well in their book with illustrated steps and a broad range of techniques, I will only hit a couple of the highlights of this fascinating subcategory of digital printing.

inkAID Precoats

Digital Atelier have been "application development specialists" for the inkAID line of *precoats* that give artists using inkjet printers a wider range of substrate options. inkAID can be applied by brush, roller, or spray to a wide range of materials including papers of all kinds, aluminum, acrylic sheets, wood, and more.

In addition to precoating custom materials, inkAID allows adding an inkjet printed image to the composition when working with paintings, collages, or other mixed media. The coatings are compatible with dye and pigment inks.

Bonny Lhotka says, "inkAID fills in the missing link that artists have needed to create multilayered mixed-media art."

inkAID is available in liter and gallon containers from the Ontario Specialty Coating company.

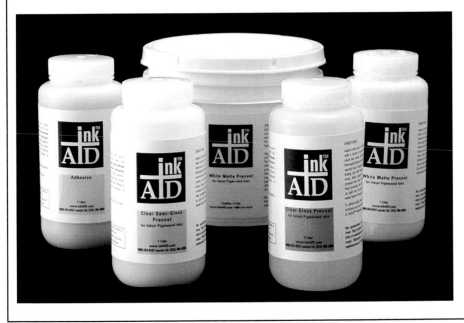

inkAID precoats can be used on almost anything that can be fed into an inkjet printer.

Courtesy of Ontario Specialty Coating www.inkaid.com

Clear Emulsion Transfers

To give a feel for the varied approaches that the Digital Atelier artists take in exploring these hybrid methods, here is one step-by-step workflow from Dot Krause for creating a clear emulsion that will accept ink and then be adhered to another surface.

(All images and following text © 2001-2004 Dorothy Simpson Krause)

Happy Home, final inkAID "decal" transfer with encaustic, 48 × 48 inches.

Happy Home was composed from two scans: a collage using a package of "Happy Home" needles and an icon, *The Twelve Feasts of the Church*, from The Art Complex Museum, Duxbury, MA.

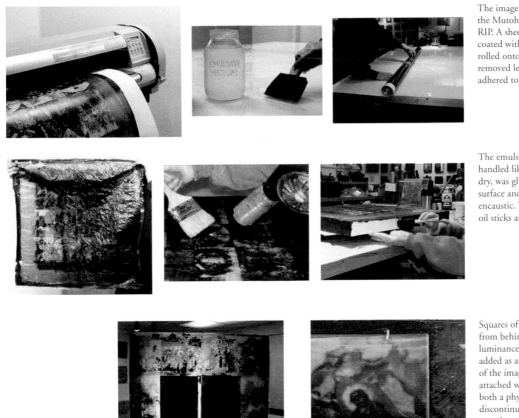

The image was printed onto film using the Mutoh Falcon printer and Wasatch RIP. A sheet of polypropylene was coated with inkAID and the print rolled onto it face down. The film was removed leaving the transferred image adhered to the inkAID emulsion.

The emulsion layer, which can be handled like a large decal when it is dry, was glued to the hardened fresco surface and burnished down with encaustic. Touch-ups were made with oil sticks and paint.

Squares of metallic papers were added from behind to give additional luminance (left). A lenticular print was added as a separate layer to the center of the image. The lenticular overlay, attached with brass brackets, creates both a physical and metaphorical discontinuity between the sacred and mundane.

Lenticular Prints

A lenticular image allows the viewer to see a series of "frames" (usually 2 to 24) sequentially. By carefully crafting these frames, the artist can create animation, depth, and/or morphing of images. To create lenticular images, the source images are developed in image-editing software like Adobe Photoshop. A series of variations on the image are saved as separate files. Each of these variations becomes a frame in the finished lenticular print.

(All images and following text © 2002-2004 Karin Schminke)

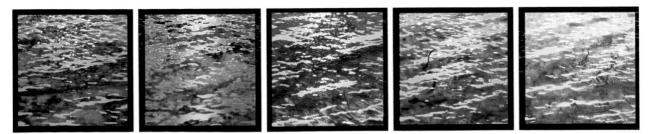

Sound Waves #1–5. Five 36 × 36-inch panels.

The hypnotizing movement of light on water was the inspiration for this installation in the library of a new college campus located just outside Seattle (see Figure 11.17). The five 36-inch square panels utilize lenticular technology to capture movement, transformation, and depth.

Schminke began *Sound Waves* by photographing light playing on waves at various locations around Puget Sound. She created layers of water shapes based upon these photo studies (see Figure 11.18). Linear seaweed forms photographed on a beach at low tide were integrated into each panel to create a minimal focal point and help

Figure 11.17 Permanent installation by Karin Schminke at the University of Washington, Bothel/Cascadia Community College Campus.

define the illusion of deep space. Hand-drawn light reflections were added in such a way that the viewer would see them for only a moment as they passed by the installation, thus mimicking the fugitive nature of light dancing on water.

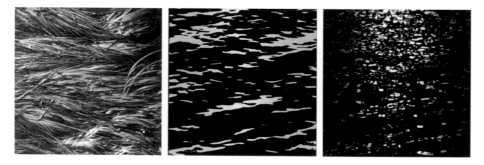

Figure 11.18 Three sample source images and layers used in creating *Sound Waves #5.*

Next, a series of frames (like frames of an animation) were created from the layers. The frames were interlaced into a single image using Flip! software and printed on an Epson Stylus Pro 9500 large-format printer (see Figure 11.19).

MicroLens Technology, Inc. donated a portion of the lens as well as the lamination of the print to the lens. As viewers pass by the finished art, each of the 24 frames is viewed in quick succession, creating an illusion of depth and movement.

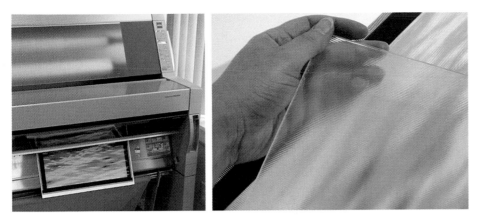

Figure 11.19 Epson 9500 printing the image (left) and the special lenticular lens.

Other Alternative Processes

This is only a quick overview of a few contemporary hybrids where digital printing is playing a strong role.

Dye Sublimation Transfers

The transfer dye-sub process involves printing an image onto a medium and then transferring that under heat and pressure to the final surface. Dye sub is a substitute for silk screening, which usually requires higher quantities, and while there are plenty of businesses that provide this service, I'll focus on doing it myself.

The simplest way to produce dye-sub transfers is to buy special transfer paper and print on it with an inkjet printer using dye-based inks. Then, all you need is a hot iron to transfer the image. Epson even sells packages of Iron-On Transfer Paper in 8.5 x 11" sizes for image-transferring to T-shirts, canvas tote bags, placemats, and other craft and decorative fabric accessories.

For a more professional approach to self-printing dye-sub transfers, consider something like the Sawgrass Systems' Sublijet (for inkjet printers) or SubliMAX (for laser printers) process. For inkjet, patented heat-sensitive sublimation inks are printed on any coated inkjet paper. The inks come in carts for select Epson desktop printers and carts and bulk bottles for wide-formats including Epson, Roland, Mimaki, Encad, and Mutoh. The printed image can then be transferred to a variety of surfaces including wood, synthetic fabric, glass, plastic, ceramics, and metal.

Tropical Graphics and TSS-Sublimation are two other companies that provide dye-sub systems for inkjet printing. They sell their own sublimation inks plus special software and printer drivers for various desktop and wide-format printers.

A ceramic tile mural created by sublimation transfer using Tropical Graphics' Mural 7 imaging software.

Courtesy of Tropical Graphics

Fabric Printing

Inkjet printers can be used to print on fabric with either textile dyes or pigmented inks. The former are specialty inks (acid or reactive dyes), and they can be made washable with post processes such as steaming. Pigmented inks on fabric are stiffer and not really washable. Precoated inkjet textiles are available from a number of sources including DigiFab and Jacquard. Futures Wales Ltd. is another source, and they claim that their Futures Fabrics can be printed with ordinary dye and pigment inkjet inks with good durability.

Two examples of inkjet printed fabrics by Bonny Lhotka. Left: bag printed with pigment inks on cotton; right: dress and jacket made with acid dyes on crepe de chine.

Courtesy of Bonny Lhotka
www.Lhotka.com

Printing on Metal, Wood Veneers, and More

You can print directly onto thin substrates that can fit through your printer if you coat the material first. Bonny Lhotka has printed on thin metals and even tiles by using an inkAID precoat. This is where printers with wide media clearances are a requirement. Lhotka and the rest of the Digital Atelier team have used inkjet printers such as the Encad 880, and they are currently experimenting with other "flatbed printers" that can print on exceptionally thick media.

Dennis Brooker of Imaging Alternatives has created an inkjet-printable, real wood veneer. Called SMartGRAIN, it can be used with normal inkjet printers and requires no special inks (see Figure 11.20). In addition to reproducing exotic wood grain patterns, regular images can also be printed. Applications include: furniture, cabinets, clocks, marquetry, flooring, wall paneling, signs, displays, and more. You are only limited by the size of the printer.

Figure 11.20 *SMartGRAIN is an inkjet-printable real wood veneer.*

Courtesy of Dennis Brooker
www.imagingalternatives.com

A related application is with the use of decal paper transfers provided by UK company Lazertran Inkjet. They have one version of a water-slide decal that must be used with color laser printers. They also offer another version of the decal paper that is only for ink printers, including inkjets. These decals can then be transferred to ceramics, wood, paper, cork, plaster, glass, metal, stone... you name it.

Digital Negatives for Photography

There is a mini-renaissance of antique printing methods going on in the photographic world. Cyanotypes, kallitypes, gum bichromates, bromoils, and platinum and palladium prints are popular examples. While many of these traditional photo techniques can now be emulated or recreated digitally with image-editing software like Photoshop, purists stick to the old-fashioned methods, which many times require contact printing with full-size negatives. The modern-day twist on all this is that many of these photographer-artists are now turning to digital printing to make the digital negatives.

Fine-art photographer Dan Burkholder pioneered the use of digital negatives in 1992, and he helped popularize the process with the release of his groundbreaking book *Making Digital Negatives for Contact Printing* in 1995, now in its second edition. Burkholder, who states that "over a decade has passed since I made my last traditionally enlarged negative via wet processing," also maintains an active website (www.danburkholder.com) with updates to his custom Photoshop Curves that are crucial to the process.

There are two basic ways to print full-size digital negatives: sending a file to an imagesetter or digital photo print device, and printing on an inkjet.

For the highest quality—for example, in printing to silver gelatin black-and-white paper—you can't beat a service bureau imagesetter, especially one running at 3600 dpi or even 4800 dpi resolution. Grayscale images are used to create either a *diffusion dither bitmap* in Photoshop or a traditional but high LPI output to a full-size film negative that is then contact-printed to the final paper. Finding a service bureau that understands this process is not easy, and the negatives are not inexpensive to produce, especially at large sizes, but the quality is excellent and the result can rival the best optically made prints.

For the inkjet version, here are two basic methods: (1) For silver-gelatin printmakers, images are converted to grayscale, adjusted with Curves, inverted to negative (in Photoshop: Image > Adjust > Invert), and printed on Epson's Glossy Film or Pictorico Hi-Gloss White Film with all four or six printer colors; or (2) for an alternative process where white films would block the UV light, images are adjusted with Curves, inverted, and then *colorized* using 0/55/55/0 CMYK values to produce an orange negative (Burkholder calls them "orange, spectral-density negatives") that holds back some of the UV light used in platinum/palladium, cyanotype, etc. photo printing. This orange mask effect is needed for the heavier ink loads of printers like the Epson 1280 when printing on Pictorico OHP film, although Burkholder admits that the Epson 2200 "is making terrific negs for both silver and platinum prints with no colorization of the neg needed."

Burkholder has a supplement to his book (*Inkjet Negative Companion*) that describes a semi-automatic way to do the required steps in making digital negatives.

While the quality of a typical inkjet negative is not as good as one made with an image-setter (some users report a certain graininess with inkjet negatives), this method is very adequate for alternative-process printing. Burkholder also suggests improving the tonal range by making two negatives that are pin-registered when exposing the final prints—one negative just for shadow detail and one for the highlights.

Dan Burkholder's method for creating colorized digital negatives includes using the correct orange Foreground color in Photoshop, then filling the image with it in Color mode. You end up with what Burkholder calls an "orange, spectral-density negative" (right).

You have now reached the end of this book's regular chapters. But, we're not done yet. Turn the page so you can explore the resources in the Appendix.

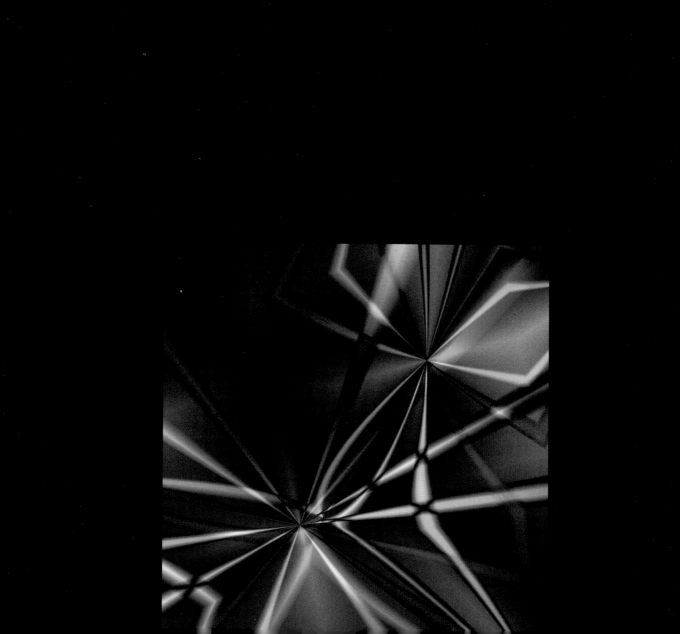

Appendix

Gallery Showcase

There is no printed Gallery Showcase in this edition. Instead, the Gallery is going multi-media! Gallery pages featuring the best examples and the variety of digital imaging and printing being produced with the latest technology and techniques are found on the author's DP&I website: www.dpandi.com. (In case you're wondering, DP&I stands for Digital Imaging and Printing, and this site is an internationally recognized resource for photographers, digital/traditional artists, and printmakers.)

These showcased examples, along with the descriptions of how they were created, are divided into four main categories or types: photography, digital art, digital mixed media, and giclées (reproductions from other media). As mentioned in Chapter 1, digital categories and classifications are a risky undertaking since they are constantly changing and inherently blurry around the edges. This, plus the ability to keep things fresh and up-to-date, is one of the reasons for putting the Gallery online.

Log on and enjoy the show!

© 2003-2004 Harald Johnson

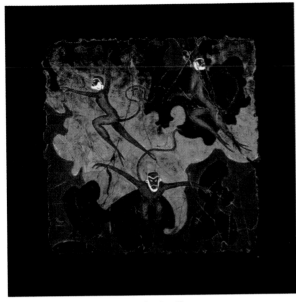

Courtesy of Bogdanoff Gallery/www.bogdanoff.com

Courtesy of Ileana Frómeta Grillo/www.ileanaspage.com

Courtesy of Dorothy Simpson Krause/www.dotkrause.co

Resources

Consider this book the base camp for your digital explorations. If you want to go further afield in search of more in-depth information, additional resources are located on the DP&I website (under "Resources") where they are continually updated. Resource categories include: photographers-artists; print-service providers; vendors of equipment, supplies, software, and related services; researchers and consultants; online discussion groups; festivals and contests; online galleries and showcases; digital-friendly organizations; workshops, classes, and schools; tradeshows and conventions; and publications and other reading sources.

James Mollison's exhibition at the 2004 Arles Rencontres Photo Festival. Photo by Harald Johnson.

Glossary

Courtesy of Dorothy Simpson Krause/www.dotkrause.com

A glossary can be a useful tool for readers puzzled about strange words like *metamerism*. A glossary of important terms for the high-quality digital output field is included on the DP&I website (www.dpandi.com). This lexicon has been prepared with the assistance of the Digital Art Practices and Terminology Task Force (DAPTTF), whose goal is to help counter the general misunderstanding about the terminology and production practices of the digital art industry and to develop a terms-of-reference document that will provide a common ground of accurate communication.

Index

*if you
were here*

Also by Alafair Burke

Long Gone

THE ELLIE HATCHER SERIES

Dead Connection
Angel's Tip
212
Never Tell

THE SAMANTHA KINCAID SERIES

Judgment Calls
Missing Justice
Close Case

A NOVEL OF SUSPENSE

if you were here

ALAFAIR BURKE

HARPER

www.harpercollins.com

HarperCollins books may be purchased for educational, business, or sales promotional use. For information, please e-mail the Special Markets Department at SPsales@harpercollins.com.

FIRST EDITION

Designed by Yvonne Chan

Library of Congress Cataloging-in-Publication Data has been applied for.

ISBN: 978-0-06-220835-4 (Hardcover)
ISBN: 978-0-06-227236-2 (Signed Edition)

13 14 15 16 17   OV/RRD   10 9 8 7 6 5 4 3 2 1

In Memory of Judge Betty Binns Fletcher

if you
were here

PART 1

PART I

All around me are familiar faces.

—Tears for Fears

CHAPTER ONE

Nicky Cervantes smiled to himself as two Wall Street boys pressed past him, one reporting excitedly to the other that Apple stock was up six percent with the release of the company's new iPhone. He could tell from their tone that the good news for the market meant a hefty check for the duo.

Nicky was smiling because one might say he was sort of invested in the market himself these days. And those boys in suits and ties might be whistling over a six percent bump, but Nicky's own pay-back on the brand had nearly tripled in recent days. When demand for the latest gadget was this red-hot, no one seemed to care where the hardware came from. No additional work for Nicky, either. If anything, he felt a little less guilty about it. Anyone dumb enough to buy jack the day it came out deserved to lose it, was how he figured.

In truth, he never had felt much guilt over it. The first time, he expected to feel real bad, like maybe the lady would start crying or there would be pictures on there of her baby that she'd never get back. But when he finally worked up the courage to do it—to just grab that shit out of her hand while she was preparing some text message to send aboveground—the girl didn't seem to care. He still remembered her reaction. One hand protecting the thousand-dollar bag, the other covering the cleavage peering from the deep V in her wrap dress. In her eyes, he was dirt, and the phone was a small price to pay to protect the things that *really* mattered.

He knew he wasn't dirt. But he also knew he wasn't VIP, like those Wall Street dudes. Not yet, anyway.

He was just a kid whose mom needed the six hundred dollars a month he'd been able to kick in to the household since he'd been working at Mr. Robinson's paint store on Flatbush the past year. And he was the star pitcher for the Medgar Evers High School baseball team with a .6 ERA, an 88 MPH fastball, a .450 batting average, and a sweeping curve and change-up that consistently racked up strikes. With numbers like that, the nine bucks an hour he was getting from Mr. Robinson had to go once the coach told him he was spread too thin. If all went according to plan, Nicky might even be drafted right out of high school. He could donate a thousand phones to charity out of his first paycheck to make up for what he was doing now.

Nicky was already fifty reach-and-grabs in, but he was still careful, compared to some of the dudes he'd met who also sold hardware. Tonight he was waiting on the N/R ramp at Times Square, six-thirty P.M. Packed trains. High ratio of Manhattanites to outerborough types. Low odds of resistance.

It really was like taking candy from a baby. But the candy was a five-hundred-dollar phone, and the baby was some hot chick whose sugar daddy would buy her a new one. The standard play was to linger on the platform, like he was waiting to get on the train. Look for someone—inattentive, weak, female—standing near the door, fiddling with a gadget.

Reach. Grab. Run. By the time the girl realized her phone was gone, Nicky was halfway up the stairs. Easy.

He heard the rattle of the approaching train. Watched the lights heading his way. Joined the other cattle gathering close at the edge of the platform in eager anticipation of scoring a New York commuter's lottery ticket—an empty seat.

Six trains had come and gone without a baby and her candy.

This time, as the train lurched to a halt, Nicky saw what he'd been looking for through the glass of the car doors. Eyes down, phone out.

Reddish blond hair pulled into a ponytail at the nape of her neck. Long-sleeved white sweater, backpack straps looped over both shoulders. Despite the train's lurch, she typed with two hands, stabilizing herself against the bounce with her core strength.

Maybe that should have been a sign.

He stepped one foot into the car, grabbed the phone, and pivoted a one-eighty, like he had fifty times before. He pushed through the clump of angry riders who had followed him into the car and now stood before him, all hoping to secure a few square feet on the crowded train before the doors closed.

Had he known what would happen next, maybe he would have run faster for the staircase.

It wasn't until he hit the top of the landing that he realized he had a problem. Somehow he heard it. Not the sound of the shoes but the sound of surprised bystanders reacting.

Hey!

What the . . .

You lost your shoe, lady!

Oh my God, David. We have to leave the city.

Nicky sneaked a glance behind him to see the woman kicking off her remaining ballet flat as she took two steps at a time in pursuit. She had looked sort of average middle-aged through the subway doors, but now she had a crazy look of determination on her face. In her eyes. In the energy of her forearms as they whipped back and forth at her sides.

At the top of the stairs, he spun left and then right, up the ramp toward the electronics store positioned between the N/R tracks and the 1/2. Why were some trains labeled with letters and others with numbers? Strange how random thoughts popped into his head when he was stressed.

He could hear the thump of an old Run-DMC song that his father listened to when he was still around. Nicky was in luck. The break dancers always attracted a dense semicircle of onlookers.

He leaped over a stroller on the near side of the audience, evoking an "oooooh" from viewers who thought his vault across the make-shift stage was part of the act. Picked up the pace once again, gaze fixed on the stairs that would take him to the 1/2 platform.

He heard more shouts behind him. The crowd hadn't stopped her. A kid cried as he fell to the ground.

Girl wasn't messing around.

He sprinted down the stairs, hoping to hear the familiar clack of an incoming train. No luck.

He thought about abandoning the phone, but the platform was too packed. The phone would fall to the ground, unnoticed by her, scooped up by someone whose good luck today rivaled his bad.

He decided to use the crowd to his advantage. He analyzed the platform that awaited him like an obstacle course, plotting out three or four weaves to maneuver his way to the next exit.

He risked another look behind. The woman had gained on him. She was just as fast, maybe faster. And she was smaller, more nimble. She was finding a more direct path than he'd navigated.

Up ahead, he spotted a busker warbling some "Kumbaya" song behind a cardboard sign he couldn't read from his vantage point. The music was shit, but something about the message must have been magic, because a mass of people huddled around the open guitar case.

They were spread out across the platform. No gaps that he could see.

She was still gaining on him.

He heard the distant clack of a train. Saw lights coming on the left. A local train north.

One pivot around the crowd and he'd be fine. He'd keep running until the train stopped. Hop on board at the last second. Wave goodbye to all this once the doors closed behind him.

Almost over.

He dodged to the left, turning sideways to scoot around a pillar.

He saw a lady's long black hair swing like a shampoo ad. He heard himself say "sorry" on impulse as he felt the heavy thud against his right hip. As he fell backward, he saw the object that had bumped him—the brunette's hot-pink duffel bag—followed by the message on the busker's cardboard sign (THE PREZ AIN'T THE ONLY ONE WHO NEEDS CHANGE), followed by a sea of shocked faces as his body hit the tracks.

It was funny what he thought of in the few seconds that passed as he lay there. His right arm. Would his right arm be okay? As the sound of the train grew louder, he wondered whether his mother would find out why he'd been in the Times Square transit station after school instead of behind a cash register at Mr. Robinson's paint store.

Reflexes kicked in. More than reflex: a deep desire to live. Without any conscious thought, he pressed himself flat between the tracks. More screaming.

He closed his eyes, hoping he wouldn't feel the impact.

And then he felt something he hadn't expected: his body being lifted from the ground. He opened his eyes but saw only white. Was this heaven?

The plane of white moved, making way for the scene of the subway platform again. People staring. Screaming. Asking if he was okay.

He looked toward the blurred, fading plane of white. It was her sweater, topped by the strawberry-blond ponytail, still tightly in place. The forearms were pumping again as she took the stairs two at a time, no pause in sight.

She held her recovered iPhone in her hand.

And Nicky?

Nicky was going to live.

CHAPTER TWO

Sitting in a borrowed Chevy Malibu outside Medgar Evers High School, McKenna Jordan thought that kids sure had changed in twenty years. Twenty-five, actually, she realized, since she was their age. How was that possible?

The last bell had sounded only three minutes earlier, and the street in front of the block-long brick building was filled with boys in low-slung pants and ball caps and girls in baby tees and skinny jeans. Some lit cigarettes before hitting the bottom step of the school entrance. Public displays of affection ran rampant—full-on make-out sessions, complete with roaming hands. Even with her car windows up, McKenna had overheard just about every obscenity with which she was familiar, plus a couple of new ones. (At least when one girl called another a "dick trap," McKenna assumed that wasn't a good thing.)

It wasn't as if McKenna and her friends had been angels: smoking, drinking, cussing, even a few teen pregnancies at the school, as she recalled. But at 3:03 P.M.? Right outside the school building? In open view of parents, teachers, and administrators? No way. They'd been too afraid of the consequences.

Maybe the kids hadn't changed after all. Maybe it was the adults who were different.

She checked her phone again for messages. Nothing. McKenna hated waiting for the cooperation of fickle sources. She owed the magazine an article for the next edition. One possibility involved the kid she was here to see at the high school. The other was about Judge Frederick Knight, a notoriously offensive judge who should have been thrown from the bench years before. Both stories needed significant work before she could go to print—work that required information from people whose conduct she couldn't control. That saying about letting go of the things you couldn't control? Not McKenna's motto.

She jerked at the sound of knuckles rapping against the glass of the passenger-side window. She clicked the doors unlocked, and Dana Frazier hopped into the seat next to her. The dark colorful ink that spiraled up her left arm was in stark contrast to the rest of her appearance. Standing barely five feet tall with a blond pixie haircut, Dana was one of those people who looked like she might fit in your pocket. She was so compact that her tiny torso was dwarfed by the enormous Canon hanging from her neck.

McKenna reached out and flicked the camera strap. "You had a two-thousand-dollar camera bouncing around you on the F train? Haven't you heard? Apparently people actually *steal* things on the New York City subway."

Dana flexed her tattooed arm. "I've got mad self-defense skills."

McKenna handed her the car keys. "You mind waiting here after the pictures? I want to talk to the kid alone before we go."

"No problem."

When McKenna had called Dana to ask if she could snap some photos down in Fort Greene, the photographer had said she was taking shots of the Occupy Wall Street protestors, hanging out in the Financial District months after the national attention had passed. McKenna had offered a ride in one of the magazine's fleet cars, but Dana declined, most likely because she had been somewhere else entirely, probably working on the avant-garde photographs she took on the side.

Good for Dana, McKenna thought.

"Speaking of theft," Dana said, holding up the iPad that Mc-Kenna had left on the car dash. "I'm putting this under the seat. These ruffians will grab anything that's not bolted down."

The high school didn't have its own baseball field. McKenna and Dana found the team practicing on a square of concrete that served the triple function of baseball diamond, basketball court, and playground to the neighboring grade school.

A well-built man with a shaved head and a golf shirt stretched tight around his biceps watched his suited-up team jog laps around the bases. Once the two women hit his periphery, he rotated toward them, hands never leaving his hips.

McKenna handled the introductions. "Hi there. I'm McKenna Jordan, a writer for *NYC* magazine. This is Dana Frazier. We were hoping to get a word with one of your players, Nicky Cervantes."

The coach sighed. "Been doing everything I can to make that boy famous for his right arm. Now he's the klutz who tripped onto the subway tracks and had to be saved by a *woman*."

McKenna threw Dana a warning glance. They were here to make friends, not change gender attitudes.

"Mind if we pull him away for a few minutes?" McKenna asked. "We'll be quick. Who knows, maybe all the attention will help him in the draft come June."

The coach bothered to look at McKenna instead of his team. He smiled beneath the bill of his blue Mets cap. "You know anything about Major League Baseball?"

"Not a damn thing. I texted my husband from the car to make sure I had the right lingo. Oh, and I know Jeter's the one who looks like a Cabbage Patch doll."

That earned her another smile.

"Cervantes!" the coach yelled, holding up a hand. "Five minutes, okay, ladies? Don't want his arm getting cold."

Nicky didn't seem surprised that a reporter and a photographer wanted his attention. "Already had three newspapers come by my mom's place last night. A magazine now?"

The night before last, a story started making the rounds on the Internet about a teenager saved from a subway splat by a woman's brave heroics. By yesterday morning, a more detailed version documenting the teen's promising baseball career and the mysteriousness of the unidentified woman had hit the front page of every local paper.

The upcoming edition of *NYC* magazine wouldn't be printed for two more days. McKenna needed to find a long-form angle on the fleeting tale du jour. So far journalists had described Nicky as an honor student and star athlete who'd lost his footing on the platform. McKenna already knew from talking to Nicky's mother that the honor-student label was pure spin. The only academic recognition Nicky had ever received was a certificate of perfect attendance the fall semester of his sophomore year. And when McKenna tried to interview Nicky's boss, a storeowner named Arthur Robinson, she learned that Nicky—unbeknownst to his mother—had quit the job three months ago.

There was another angle to the story. McKenna just had to find it.

She watched as a beaming Nicky struck a series of poses for Dana's camera. Hands on hips. Looking earnestly at the sky. Mimicking a windup.

She didn't really need the pictures, but the modeling session had him in the groove, feeling important. She gave a nod to Dana, who took her cue and headed back to the car, supposedly to grab another lens. Once they were alone, McKenna asked Nicky how he'd slipped.

"What do you mean? I just fell."

"But how? Was the platform slick? Did you have a seizure or something?"

The kid shrugged. "Not sure. Just went down."

"I've seen the MTA's incident report. Bystanders said you were running frantically down the platform right before you fell. One said it was almost as if the woman was chasing you."

If the subway Superwoman actually knew Nicky Cervantes, the story would take on new complexity. Why were they running? Had they been fighting? Why did she leave? And why wouldn't Nicky admit he knew her?

"Whatchu trying to do here, lady?"

What *was* she trying to do? She knew this was the kind of story everyone would forget in a month, like most of the garbage she wrote. She'd like to say she was fostering civic involvement through journalism, but she was simply doing her job: blurring the lines between news, voyeurism, and entertainment. The most entertaining stories needed a protagonist. So far the media coverage of the "1 train tragedy averted" had focused on the good fortune of Nicky Cervantes. McKenna wanted to know about the woman who'd saved him only to sprint away.

The MTA's security cameras had failed to capture any footage of the incident, but McKenna had the advantage of time. Her best lead was a comment posted online by someone claiming that his girlfriend had video of Nicky's fall on her cell phone. McKenna had sent an e-mail to the commenter, hinting at the possibility of payment for the clip; she was still waiting for a response. In the meantime, her firsthand contact with Nicky was leading her to believe that her instincts were on track.

"I know you give your mom money, Nicky, even though you have no obvious source of income." McKenna also knew that, despite New York City's record-low crime rates, robberies on the subway system were on the rise. The story of a mysterious Superwoman saving a promising young teen was media gold. But the story of a female crime victim who simultaneously pursued—and saved—her robber? Pure platinum.

Nicky finally spoke. "You know what? Forget about the pictures, okay? I just want to live my life."

"And I'm trying to find the woman who made it possible for you to do so, Nicky."

"More power to you, then. If you find her, tell her I said thanks. And tell her I've changed. Don't forget, okay?"

"Why'd you need to change, Nicky? Was there a reason the two of you were running through the station?"

He gave his right shoulder a quick massage. "Gotta get back to it now." He returned to practice without another glance in her direction.

CHAPTER THREE

McKenna checked her cell as she walked to the car. No calls but two new e-mail messages, both from the same unfamiliar address, both with the same subject line: Big Pig. She skimmed them quickly.

One of her contacts at the courthouse had come through. Big Pig was one of many nicknames Judge Frederick Knight had earned among the local bar, this one referring to both his massive girth and his blatant sexism. The messages were forwards of e-mails Judge Knight had sent from his judicial address. They must have come from someone with access to the network. If they were authentic, they were tangible proof to confirm rumors that had been whispered for years. She would have enough material to expose Judge Frederick Knight as the lazy SOB he was.

When she took the driver's seat, she could feel Dana staring at her. "What?"

Dana continued to look at her expectantly.

"I've worked with you for two years, Dana. If I've got something funky on my nose, you're supposed to tell me." She rubbed her face with her index finger.

"You're snot-free. I'm just wondering if you want to talk about anything."

"Such as?"

"The article?"

"We work for a magazine, Dana. There are a lot of articles out there."

"Your article. *The* article."

"No. I most definitely do *not* want to talk about the article. No one should talk about the article. I'm starting to think I made a huge mistake writing the stupid thing."

"Tammy told me you got a call from a literary agent. And from HarperCollins." Tammy the editorial assistant always knew something about everything. Those calls had been to McKenna's direct line.

"Stop listening to Tammy. She's a noodnik."

"Can a woman be a noodnik?" Dana asked.

McKenna had no clue. She grew up in Seattle. Went to college and law school in the Bay Area. A dozen years since her move to New York, her Yiddish still couldn't be trusted. "Whatever. Tammy's not exactly an accurate narrator."

"Well, the narrator says you have a book proposal that goes to auction next week. The magazine piece was to start the buzz rolling."

As usual, Tammy knew just enough to get the story wrong. The publishing house had asked about a proposal, and the agent had talked about the possibility of an auction, but a proposal going to auction next week? Not even close. Not to mention, the agent had made it clear that the book would need to be more than an extended version of the magazine article. It would have to be personal. "Intimate." "Maybe even in the first person." "Like a novel but true." "You were barely thirty years old—dating and drinking at night, facing down cops and DAs by day. *That's* the book!" The dreaded "memoir" word had been raised.

At first, when McKenna thought she'd be reporting real news, she saw journalism as an extension of her original work as a prosecutor. Attorneys and reporters both investigated facts and wove them into a compelling—and often spun—story. Ten years ago, when McKenna was an assistant district attorney, she made the mistake of becoming a character in one of those stories she was supposed to narrate. Two weeks ago, she had repeated that mistake as a journalist by writing a ten-page feature article about the same case. But a *memoir*? What was that saying about the definition of insanity: making the same decisions over and over, yet expecting a different result?

McKenna's phone rang from her jacket pocket. She didn't recognize the number on the screen but answered anyway, eager for the distraction from Dana's interrogation.

The voice on the other end of the line sounded like a young woman. She said her name was Mallory. She talked the way all young women seemed to these days, slowing the pace of her speech and dipping her voice low into a "fry" at the end of her sentences.

"Hiiii. My boyfriend said to call. I was on the subway the other day when that lady pulled that kid off the traaaacks."

"Has anyone else contacted you about it?" It seemed like every witness expected to be paid for an interview or at least to get on television.

"No. After you e-mailed my boyfriend because of that comment you saw online, I told him to delete it. It happened so fast, the video doesn't even really show anything."

"Well, I'd love to see it." McKenna tried not to let her tone reveal her excitement. It was a stupid story, but at least it was a story. First Judge Knight's e-mails, now a video of the subway incident that had the entire city talking. She might have enough material to meet her next *two* deadlines.

"Yeah, okay."

"Can you e-mail it to me?" McKenna rattled off her address, but next to her in the passenger seat, Dana was shaking her head.

"Our e-mail system's for shit," she said. "Won't accept a big video file. Have her send it to my Skybox."

The details that came tumbling from Dana's mouth were Greek to McKenna. Her attempts to repeat them to young Mallory were reminiscent of the slumber-party game Operator, where words lost all meaning when passed down a line of communicators. Frustrated, Dana finally extended a hand for the phone so she could speak to Mallory directly. Whatever had seemed so complicated to Mc-Kenna was cake to the two of them; Dana soon returned the phone with a satisfied smile.

"Thanks for that, Mallory. Do you mind if I ask, have you shown this to anyone else? Put it on YouTube or Facebook or anything?" Nowadays, anyone with a phone was an amateur reporter. The video wouldn't be of any value to McKenna once it hit a public website.

"That's so last year. Social networking is social *not*-working. I'm more into, like, privacy, so just leave my name out of it, okay? It was cool and everything, but I can't believe people are making such a big deal out it. I mean, you're a reporter. Last time I checked, our country was still at war, you know?"

It wasn't the first time McKenna had wondered about the merits of her career choices.

Once McKenna was off the phone, Dana retrieved the iPad she had stored beneath the seat for safekeeping. "Don't want to forget this when you return the car," she said. "You got 3G on this thing? I can hook you up on my Skybox action."

McKenna nodded for Dana to work her magic, marveling at the woman's ability to use the virtual keyboard for real typing. "I told Mallory to send the video to my public directory," Dana explained. McKenna caught a quick peek at two heavily pierced twins holding fire hoses. She really didn't understand Dana's artistic impulses. "And I'm hitting bookmark so you can find it online without having to download to your device."

Within seconds, Dana had tilted the screen toward her so they could watch together. The video was typical cell-phone footage: shaky, staccato, grainy. A close-up of someone's back. The cement platform. McKenna turned up the volume. Voices, mostly inaudible. Screams. Someone yelling, "Oh my God!" Someone else yelling something about the train.

By the time Mallory had managed to point the lens toward the tracks below her, a woman in a white sweater, backpack secured tightly on her shoulders, was lifting a stunned Nicky Cervantes to his feet. As she grabbed him around the waist and hefted him halfway up the height of the platform, Nicky's body blocked the camera's view of the woman's face. A man in a denim jacket took Nicky by the wrists and rolled him onto the concrete.

The cell phone jerked toward the woman just as she finished hoisting herself onto the platform unassisted. She turned and sprinted barefoot toward the stairs, ponytail bouncing at the nape of her neck, just above her backpack. The footage returned quickly to Nicky before going black.

Dana let out a whistle. "That chick's kickass. Nicky probably weighs one-seventy. Did you see how she dead-lifted him?"

McKenna wasn't interested in the woman's strength. She rewound the video and tried to stop on the brief glimpse of the woman's face before she turned to run away. After three attempts, McKenna managed to hit pause at just the right moment.

She couldn't believe what she was seeing.

She hit replay and watched the entire clip again.

"So much for identifying Superwoman," Dana said. The image was grainy at best. "Don't worry. You'll find another way to hook in the masses. You always do."

But Dana had misinterpreted McKenna's expression. She wasn't disappointed. She was in shock.

She never thought she would see that face again. Susan Hauptmann had disappeared without a trace ten years ago.

CHAPTER
FOUR

McKenna automatically clicked to her computer's screen saver when she felt Bob Vance walk into her office, looming over her.

Her editor laughed. "If you're going to keep doing that, could you get some pictures of something that's *not* food?" Her current wallpaper was a photograph of a fried-egg pizza. "When are you going to realize that one of the advantages of being a journalist is that you can look at whatever the hell you want and call it research. If you believe Walt, he's been working on a big exposé of the porn industry for the past seven years."

Stanford undergrad. Boalt Law School. A federal judicial clerkship. Four years at the district attorney's office. It had been a decade since she'd left those uptight surroundings, but old habits died hard. McKenna was a natural rule follower. Even as a child, she would lecture her parents for parking in loading zones.

Today, though, she had a reason to hide the screen from her supervisor. She had spent the last hour searching for current information about Susan Hauptmann. There was nothing. In a sadly familiar pattern, Susan's disappearance had consumed the media for a few weeks, with coverage steadily waning in the ensuing months. Now a search for her name pulled up only isolated comments from bloggers and true-crime addicts asking, "Whatever happened to that girl?"

"I hear there's talk of a book," he said.

She rotated in her chair to face him. "You were the one who suggested the article, Bob, and you know how I felt. I don't think I'm up to writing an entire book about it, so don't make me do it."

"I'm not your daddy, Jordan. I can't *make* you do anything, especially when it's not for the magazine. I'm just saying that if the rumors are true—if there's that kind of interest from publishers—something like that happens once in a journalistic career, and only if you're lucky. And this is real news, not the kind of stuff we usually get to do around here."

When McKenna had left the district attorney's office nearly ten years ago, she had vowed not to do any further damage to the people and institutions she had harmed. But somehow, the career moves she'd made in the aftermath had managed to alienate her even more from a job that once was the core of her identity.

It was Bob Vance who had given her a start at a new one. After McKenna had published one not so successful legal thriller and a few pieces on spec about city crime issues, he'd brought her on as a full-time writer. She had fantasized about specializing in local crime and courts, but had come to accept that it would be hard to provide legitimate coverage of the criminal justice system when almost every cop in the city hated her. Instead, she was a features reporter. Given the increasingly silly tone of the barely afloat magazine, she felt more like a paparazzo.

The saving grace was that Vance was a real journalist at heart. The recent article had been his suggestion: a retrospective of the case that had ended her career at the DA's office—a police officer's shooting of a nineteen-year-old named Marcus Jones.

"It's a bad idea," she'd told Vance when he'd proposed it. "Honestly, no one will be interested in Marcus Jones all these years later."

"Ten years. It's an anniversary, so there *will* be interest. People like anniversaries. They distract themselves with the controversies of old rather than fight the battles of today. In my humble and not so ignorant opinion, I think that if anyone's going to tap in to whatever you might have to say, it should be you. You can control the story."

"I tried to control the story ten years ago, and look where it got me." It wasn't only McKenna's prosecutorial career that had taken a hit. It was her general credibility. After her first big feature for the magazine, online commentators gleefully celebrated the irony that a woman who'd made false claims at the DA's office was supposed to be a journalist. The criticism had been so intense that she'd stopped reading the comments before she broke down at her desk.

Although McKenna had written the ten-year anniversary article reluctantly, Vance's instincts had been right. There had been interest, so much that McKenna was getting calls from agents and publishing houses about possible book deals.

"Look," Vance said now, slapping a hand against the desk for emphasis, "all I'm saying is that if I were you, I'd jump at the chance. As your boss? I guess I'm here to tell you that anything you write for the magazine belongs to the magazine. A book's got to be on your own time. You know what I'm saying?"

He didn't wink, and he didn't nod, but he may as well have. Writing for a magazine wasn't a nine-to-five gig, so they both knew that her time was fungible. Just like Dana—working on her artistic photography when she was supposedly photographing Zuccotti Park—McKenna could easily sneak in a few pages of a book during her daytime hours.

"Got the message, boss."

"So you going for the book?" When she didn't respond, Vance held up both palms. "Fine, I tried. I still need four thousand words from you by end of day tomorrow. You working on this subway mystery gal or what?"

Was it work, or was it personal curiosity? Was she seeing things in that grainy cell-phone video? She wasn't ready to talk about it yet.

"I was hoping to find a different angle on the story, but there may not be much more to it."

"I thought you told me someone might have a video."

"It didn't pan out."

"Did you get the video or not?"

Sometimes McKenna wondered whether Bob Vance should have been a lawyer instead of a magazine editor. "The girl sent it, but it was just a bunch of shaking and bumping around."

"Better than nothing. Let's pop it on the website and see where it goes."

"I promised the girl I wouldn't post it," she said, stretching the truth. "Trust me, it's so useless that people would scream at us for wasting their time." At a time when print media was still trying to find its way in an online world, the specter of anonymous Internet vitriol was enough to make Vance back down.

Her first big feature as a journalist had happened because Bob Vance had taken a chance on her. He'd given her a paycheck and a new start. Now she was looking the man straight in the eye and lying to him: "The subway story's not going anywhere."

Alone again in her office, she pulled up the video on her screen and hit replay to view it from the beginning. She hit pause at just the right moment to freeze on Susan's face. Maybe Susan's face.

One thing she hadn't lied about to Vance: the quality was crap.

But there was something about the face that was so distinctive. Susan was one of those naturally beautiful women with clear skin, wide bow-shaped lips, and a knowing smile. Her bright green almond-shaped eyes always glinted with the humor of a silent joke. Her appearance gave off alertness and intelligence. Somehow, despite the video's poor quality, McKenna could make out all of this. Above her left eye, right by her hairline, wasn't that the same small scar?

Or maybe she wasn't seeing anything. Maybe she was projecting the resemblance. Had all this talk about the ten-year anniversary of the Marcus Jones shooting pulled her memory back to the time when she left the DA's office? Was that why she was thinking about Susan? Missing her. Wondering about her. Seeing her ghost in grainy images.

She let the video play and watched the ghost turn from the camera and sprint up the stairs. Even the sprint was familiar. While many women ran with arms swinging side to side as if rocking a baby, the ghost pumped her arms like an Olympian, fingers outstretched like knife blades. How many times had Susan lost McKenna with those effortless dashes? She would wait patiently outside the subway entrance until McKenna emerged from the darkness, slightly out of breath.

McKenna paused it again. There was something in the woman's right hand. Something black and rectangular.

She hit rewind and watched from the beginning. There. Pause. It was right after the woman had hoisted her weight from the tracks to the platform. Both palms were braced past the platform's edge. She swung one leg up to the side. As she pressed herself to standing, she reached her right hand along the cement. Grabbed something.

McKenna had her suspicions that Nicky Cervantes was not the honor-student athlete the morning papers had made him out to be. Now she thought she might know why this woman had been chasing him.

She dialed Nicky's home number. When he answered, she said, "Nicky, it's McKenna Jordan. I talked to you today during baseball practice."

"From the magazine. The lady with all the questions."

"I need to know something very important. And I promise not to tell anyone."

"There's nothing else to tell. I fell."

"Just listen, okay? I need the *real* truth, Nicky. And I won't print it."

"Right. 'Cause reporters are all about keeping things on the down-low."

"I'm also a member of the New York bar." She wasn't. Not anymore. "That means I'm licensed as a lawyer. I will get disbarred if I repeat anything you say to me."

"Will you give me legal advice for free?"

Sure, why not? "I need to know the truth. You took that woman's cell phone, didn't you?"

"Why you asking me that?"

"I need to know." She realized she sounded desperate. She tried to calm herself, but she knew her instincts were right. That rectangle in the woman's hand. The city's familiar warnings to commuters not to use their handheld electronics on the train. "You took her phone, didn't you? And she was chasing you to get it back."

She knew from his pause that he was about to come clean. "Yeah," he finally said, his voice quiet. "And then when I was down there, thinking about that train, she jumped in like Jackie Chan. Threw my ass to safety."

Fast. And strong. Like Susan.

"Now what?" he asked. "What's your advice?"

"Keep it to yourself, Nicky. Don't tell a soul. And don't *ever* do something so stupid again. Snatching a phone from a distracted commuter might seem minor to you, but the state of New York views it as robbery in the third degree. It can land you seven years. Bye-bye baseball, hello prison yard."

"I'm done with all that. Told Coach I need to go back to the paint store. He says we'll work something out on practice. Like I said today, I changed. Laying there next to the rats, the sound of that train—I changed."

Though McKenna had heard so many defendants say the same two words at countless sentencing hearings, she actually believed Nicky. She gave him her number in case he ever needed a favor, then she wished him luck with the season.

She watched the video one more time. There was no way to be certain, but the woman in the video looked more like Susan with every viewing. If Susan were alive, where had she been all this time? Why did she leave? Why didn't she tell anyone? And why was she back now?

McKenna thought about the wealth of information stored on her own phone. Text messages. To-do lists. Voice mails. Call logs. Notes to self. E-mails. Whoever Superwoman was, she had gone to tremendous lengths to get that little black rectangle back.

CHAPTER FIVE

An hour later, McKenna gave up her surfing efforts, no closer to learning anything about Susan's disappearance than when she'd started.

McKenna used to think about Susan constantly; then, with time, for only a fleeting moment per day. Like she'd pass the bar where Susan had been asked to leave after breaking multiple strings of Mardi Gras beads on the impromptu dance floor she had created. Or McKenna would see a trailer for a new comedy aimed at teenage boys and think, Susan will see that with me. Or her phone would ring a little too late for any polite caller, and she'd expect to hear Susan's voice on the other end of the line. In retrospect, McKenna struggled to pinpoint the last time her mind had really focused on a memory of her friend.

If forced to guess, she would have to say it was five years earlier—on a Sunday morning, two days after McKenna and Patrick's wedding. She remembered because she hadn't meant to think about Susan that day. She hadn't meant to cry. Even five years ago, the tears had been less for the loss of her friend than for her guilt at having moved on without her.

The morning hadn't started on a heavy note. She and Patrick were next to each other on the sofa, opening the wedding gifts their friends had given them, despite pleas to the contrary. She could still picture Patrick blushing as he pulled a hot-pink rabbit-shaped vibrator from its beautiful wrapping.

"All righty, then. This one's clearly for the wife," Patrick announced, wiggling the rubber device in McKenna's direction.

Husband. Wife. After five years of playing other roles in each other's lives, boasting that marriage was only a piece of paper, McKenna and Patrick had pulled the trigger. As a lawyer, she should have realized earlier that papers mattered. Papers created rights and responsibilities. Papers defined families.

Today, she couldn't imagine a world in which she wasn't married to Patrick Jordan, but that morning she and Patrick were just beginning to enjoy their new spousal titles. She'd shaken her head and pursed her lips like a stubborn child refusing a floret of broccoli. "But I would never stray from my husband," she'd said in a Scarlett O'Hara voice. "Not even with a battery-operated bunny."

The pink toy was from Emily and Glenn. McKenna could barely imagine reserved, preppy Emily perusing the aisles of a tawdry adults-only shop.

McKenna and Patrick hadn't wanted a wedding. Just a couple of rings, a few nice words, and a great party. No walking down the aisle. No puffy dresses. No white tulle vomit. And no gifts.

As a pile of wrapped packages accumulated in the corner of their private dining room at Buddakan, they'd realized that their friends hadn't complied with the request. "What part of 'no gifts' do our friends not understand?" Patrick whispered. "There better not be a toaster oven in there. Where in the world would we put a toaster oven?"

As it turned out, their friends may not have obeyed the stern no-gifts admonition, but they'd known better than to clutter the overstuffed apartment with nonsense like crystal vases and bread makers. Instead, they had conspired to find the tackiest gag gifts imaginable.

The rabbit wasn't the only X-rated toy. There were the his-and-her G-strings. The bubblegum-flavored massage oil. The "just married" condoms. Especially creative: the pasta shaped like boy parts.

That Sunday morning, their two-day anniversary, Patrick and McKenna were showing their gratitude in a similar spirit, giddily opening the presents while sipping champagne and taking turns writing ironic thank-you notes. *Dearest Emily and Glenn,* McKenna had written. *Thank you so very much for the delightful personal massager. Its rabbit-like shape is at once both whimsical and bold. We would be remiss, however, if we did not ask: where is our fucking tea set? Lovingly, McKenna and Patrick.*

McKenna had saved a special present to give to Patrick last. She reached over the edge of the sofa and lifted a shoebox-sized gift from the floor. "The final one."

"Feels pretty hefty," he said. "If it's another one of those"—he gestured toward the personal massager—"you're going to be walking funny for a week."

"This one is for the husband from the wife."

He tore away the elegant white-and-silver wrapping paper, opened the box, and removed a tight mass of bubble wrap. Beneath the transparent layers, the shape of a glass beer mug was visible.

"Is this like when Homer Simpson gave Marge a bowling ball for her birthday?"

McKenna was the beer drinker in their household. Patrick was strictly a Scotch and wine man.

He placed the beer stein on the coffee table. Pint-size. Thick handle. A shield insignia on the side, embossed with Westvleteren, the manufacturer of a Belgian Trappist beer.

"So what gives?"

For the first time, McKenna told Patrick about the night she and Susan wound up with that mug. And then she felt guilty for not thinking more often about Susan over the years. And then she cried. And then she apologized for ruining the last day of their wedding weekend with silly drama. Then she blamed it on too much champagne.

That was five years ago. How could she have gone five years without thinking about Susan?

Susan and that stupid mug. The night McKenna met Patrick. The year Susan left. The year her job fell apart. The stories all belonged together.

She heard once that a novel was really a collection of fifty to seventy scenes that could be woven together at the author's will. The agent wanted McKenna's book about the Marcus Jones case to read like a novel.

She opened a file on her computer and typed: "Chapter One."

CHAPTER SIX

*I*t was a Thursday, right around the time when single, childless city dwellers had labeled Thursday "the new Friday," meaning it was the night to go out, get drunk, and forget that one more day of work—albeit a casual-dress one—still awaited us.

It wasn't just any Thursday but a first Thursday of the month, meaning it was the night of a Susan Hauptmann happy hour.

I arrived late, even relative to the obscene hours we all kept back then. I had been burning the midnight oil that entire week. I told my colleagues I was taking the extra step of preparing written motions for all my upcoming trials. Their deadpan looks were the silent equivalent of "Whatever, nerd." But I'd been in the district attorney's office for four years and was still trying drug cases. I had vowed that this would be the year when I got some attention.

By the time I made it to Telephone Bar, it was well past ten o'clock. The party was in full swing, meaning fifty or so friends and at least three times as many drinks consumed.

Susan raised her arms in the air and reached across two guys from the usual crew for a long-distance hug. "McKenna! You made it!"

Vocal exclamation points were a sure sign that Susan was getting her drink on. The girl worked her ass off at one of the biggest consulting firms in the world. She deserved to cut loose every once in a while. Back then, we all did.

"Pretty good turnout," I yelled over the thumping soundtrack. That was the year when you couldn't help but Get the Party Started with Pink everywhere you went.

Susan was beaming, which made her even more gorgeous than usual. She was always so proud when the happy hours went well, as if they somehow validated all the steps she'd taken in life to lead to all those friendships. Now some people were leaving the city. Others were getting married and having children. They couldn't stay in their twenties forever. That night, though, everyone seemed to be there, just like the old days.

"McKenna, this is my friend Mark Hunter." He was one of the two guys I recognized next to us. "McKenna was my roommate the first year I came to the city. She went to Stanford for undergrad and law school at Berkeley. Mark just left a dot-com, but his MBA's from Stanford. You guys could have bumped into each other at a Stanford-Cal game."

And then off she went to introduce some other solo attendee to another friend. That was Susan's thing. She collected friends. Back before random strangers "friended" each other online after a chance meeting, Susan was that person who found something interesting about every person she met, then pulled out her cell phone with an easygoing "Give me your digits. I'm getting some friends together in a few weeks. You should join us."

Unlike most of the people who do those things, Susan would actually cultivate the friendship. As a result, her happy hours brought together an eclectic crowd that mirrored the divergent pieces of Susan's impressive life: military friends, business school friends, gym friends, "just started talking at the bookstore one day" friends, childhood friends from all over the country, thanks to her army-brat youth. Her capacity for socializing had earned her the nickname Julie the Cruise Director, at least among those friends who remembered The Love Boat.

Unfortunately, Susan didn't always recognize that she was singular in her ability to connect to people. To her, my non-overlapping undergraduate years at Stanford should have been common ground to bond with Mark the former dot-commer. Instead, the two of us stumbled awkwardly through a series of false conversational starts before Mark pretended to recognize a friend farther down the bar. I let him off the hook before he felt pressure to pay for the Westvleteren Trappist I had just ordered.

As I took the glass from the (of course) scantily clad bartender, a small wave of foam made its way over the rim onto my hand. I was licking away the spilled beer—and not a sexy, titillating, "I'm coming for you next" lick but a spazzy kid with jam on her hands kind of lick—when a girl yelling "Woooo" bumped into me. A second, larger wave of beer foam cascaded onto the man next to me.

"Sorry. Oh my God, I'm so sorry." I patted at his sweater futilely. Again, not a sexy, titillating, "I'm taking my time" pat, but a clumsy, ham-handed, "this might really hurt" pat.

"Ah, beer and boiled wool. That'll smell great in the morning." Another person might have made the comment sound prissy or even cruel. Thanks to the friendly smile that accompanied the words, I found them comforting. It also helped that my beer-soaked victim was six feet three with wavy dark hair and hazel eyes. After getting a better look at him, I registered how firm his stomach had felt beneath that wool sweater.

"Seriously, I'm really sorry."

"It's not a problem," he said, accepting a bar towel from the bartender, who apparently noticed the needs of this kind of man without request. He wiped the beer off my hands and shirtsleeves, ignoring the drops of ale on his own clothing. It sounds corny, but there was something familiar about the feel of his skin against mine. "You're here with Susan, right?"

"Um, yeah. I guess you are, too?"

"Patrick Jordan." He offered a firm handshake. "Susan's pointed you out a couple times at these things, but we've never managed to meet."

"Oh sure, you're Patrick from West Point."

That's right. Susan's wildly diverse and impressive background included college at the United States Military Academy at West Point. According to her, the predominantly male student body might not have treated her as well if it hadn't been for a popular trio of supportive cadets led by Patrick Jordan.

"And you're—"

"McKenna Wright. Susan and I lived together for a while a couple of years ago."

"Wait. Are you the one who calls her Bruno?"

Yep, that was moi. "The first time we met, she said her name—'Nice to meet you, I'm Susan Hauptmann,' like any normal person. And then I go and blurt out 'Bruno!' It was the first thing I thought of."

"Of course, because doesn't everyone know the name of the kidnapper of the Lindbergh baby off the top of their heads? Basic knowledge, really."

He raised a finger toward the bartender and I soon had another West-vleteren Trappist in my hand. The truth was that I usually dreaded Susan's parties. I'm neither a mixer nor a mingler, so a night of serialized chitchat, yelled between casual acquaintances, was my version of being poked in the eye with a needle for three hours.

But that night involved no further mixing or mingling. I barely noticed as the crowd thinned and familiar faces paused for a quick shoulder grab or a "Sorry we didn't get to talk more." Before I knew it, the bartender was announcing last call.

Patrick and I paused our conversation only when Susan showed up and squeezed between us, throwing an arm around each of our shoulders. "Yo, I've been sippin' on gin and juice."

Yes, the song was already old by then. It didn't matter to Susan. It was newer than her other hip-hop standby—"Rapper's Delight" by the Sugarhill Gang, the long version if she was wasted on mojitos. She gave Patrick a peck on the cheek. "That's your prize for keeping this one here so late. She's not usually a closing-time lady. Let me get you guys another round."

The bartender shook her head and made a cutoff motion. Susan made an exaggerated sad face. "Party pooper."

Patrick patted his hands against his pant legs. "Well, I guess that's a sign that we're out of here. Any interest in sharing a cab?"

The words were spoken to both Susan and me, but his gaze was directed at me.

Susan made a loud buzzing sound. "Not tonight, Patrick. She's heading downtown. And not in the dirty way, like you're thinking," she said with a devilish tone and an accusatory index finger. "You can get to the Upper East Side on your own."

"All right, then. Very nice to meet you, McKenna." We ended like we began, with a handshake, but this time I didn't want to let go.

Susan hugged me as we left the bar. "Aw, you look like a puppy who got left at the shelter. Don't worry, girl. I just did you a favor."

"How's that?"

"You don't get out enough. You don't know the rules."

"What rule was I about to break?"

"You put out on the first date, and a guy never respects you. And don't you go looking at me with all that virgin-y indignation. If you'd left with him, you totally would have dropped those drawers. Knowing what a dry spell you've been in, they're probably granny panties, aren't they?"

All I could do was laugh.

"Ah, see? I did you a favor. Don't worry. He knows how to find me, and I know how to find you. He'll call."

As crass as Susan could be, she always managed to do it in a silly way that was never threatening or offensive. When we were roommates, I had hoped that her brand of infectious directness might rub off on me, but no such luck. She told me once that her sense of humor had gotten her through army culture. Susan was by no means the first female West Point cadet, but even now women made up only a tenth of the class, and cadets still referred to military-issued comforters as their "green girls."

As one of the most attractive women on the West Point campus, Susan could have had her choice of boyfriends. But she was the daughter of a general. All eyes were on her. She had to choose her company carefully. For the most part, she stuck with the "Dykes in Spikes," as the female athletes were called, but got along with the men by joking around like a kid sister.

I thought Susan had fallen asleep in the cab, her head resting on my shoulder, but then she reached into her briefcase and handed me something wrapped in a white cloth napkin. She pulled out a Westvleteren beer stein.

"You stole a glass? That's a Class A misdemeanor, I'll have you know."

"Then you're about to commit receipt of stolen property." Her speech was slurred. "Because I saw how you were with Patrick. And I saw him with you. And neither of you is ever like that with anyone. Someday you're going to marry that man, and you're going to want a souvenir from this fateful night."

Five years later, on my two-day anniversary, I gave that glass to my husband as a wedding gift.

I saved that beer stein for five years, through three moves, two changes in profession, and countless on-and-offs with Patrick. I saved it because I wanted more than anything for Susan to be right.

When the cab stopped that night outside my apartment on Mott, Susan tucked the beer stein into my bag as I kissed the top of her head. "Drink some water when you get home. I love you, Bruno."

I made sure the cabdriver knew Susan's address, and I covered the fare plus a generous tip before hopping out.

I was too distracted to take seriously Susan's prediction about Patrick and me. At the time, my entire focus was on making this the year when I finally got the attention I deserved at work.

Both Susan and I turned out to be right.

McKenna stopped typing and read the last sentence again. *Both Susan and I turned out to be right.* Neither McKenna nor Susan had been prescient enough to realize that 2003 would also be the year when Susan would disappear without a trace.

Now McKenna wondered if Susan was finally back, resurfacing to pull Nicky Cervantes from the tracks of a 1 train.

CHAPTER
SEVEN

McKenna was sitting on a stool at the kitchen island, hunched over her laptop, when she heard keys in the front door. Patrick maneuvered his bicycle into the apartment, careful not to let the tires bump the walls, a practice that had taken months of training after the building had sacrificed the bike storage room for an expansion of the laundry room.

"Hey, you're home!" Patrick said, surprised at the sight of her there.

Theirs was one of a growing number of households in which the female half tended to work later than the male half. Patrick was almost always home in time for the six P.M. episode of *SportsCenter*. He was not only fine with a routine, he liked it. If every single day could be the same for the rest of his life, Patrick would be happy as could be.

But today she was the one who had wrapped up work early, wanting to be alone with that video from the subway platform.

For as long as she had known him, Patrick had insisted on riding his bicycle to work. Another part of the routine. The very idea of riding a bike in Manhattan—the fumes; the horn blasts; the texting, Bluetoothing drivers—scared the bejesus out of McKenna. But Patrick insisted he was safe. Helmet. Side-view mirrors. And though his office closet at the Metropolitan Museum of Art was stocked with conservative suits, for the commute, he donned the look of a badass bike messenger, complete with fake tattoo sleeves on his arms. According to him, drivers were less likely to mess with a cyclist who looked like he might slit a throat over a near miss.

As Patrick carried the bicycle to the far corner of their open loft, he paused behind her for a quick kiss on the cheek. "You started cocktail hour without me?"

She let out a distracted "Huh?," then realized he was referring to the beer stein resting beside her computer on the granite counter-top. "No, it's empty. I was just looking at it."

The mug had felt like such a special possession when she'd given it to Patrick, but five years later, McKenna had located it at the back of a kitchen cabinet, blocked by a panoply of coffee mugs and the cheap glasses that emerged only when they had more guests than good stemware. The beer stein deserved better placement, but a lot had changed since they got married.

"Why would you—" His bike propped safely against a wall of bookshelves, Patrick turned his full attention to her. "Oh, it's *the* mug. That was sweet." He wrapped his arms around her waist and gave her a kiss on the neck, letting his breath graze her ear.

She spun around on the stool to face him. "Actually, I was think-ing about this mug because I was thinking about Susan."

His expression went blank. Apparently McKenna wasn't the only one who hadn't thought about Susan in a long time.

"*Susan.* Susan Hauptmann. She's the one who stole it from Tele-phone Bar that night."

"Oh my God, that's right. I always thought of it as the mug *you* stole." He took a seat on the sectional sofa, extending his legs in front of him. "Why were you thinking about Susan?"

She carried her open laptop to the couch, scooting next to him. The video was cued up. "You know that story about the woman who pulled the high school kid off the subway tracks?"

"I believe you tried to bet me twenty dollars yesterday morning that the kid wasn't really an honor student. I didn't take the bet. Plus, we're married, so it doesn't matter. Besides, twenty dollars in this city would barely fill that beer mug."

"Well, a girl on the platform managed to get it on videotape." She hit play.

Patrick chuckled as the scene played out on the screen, a subtle twitch in his face each time the cell phone jerked in a new direction. "You can't use this, McKenna. Did you try the MTA? They have cameras in the stations."

She held up a finger to cut him off. Listening to the now-familiar audio, she prepared to hit pause. The high-pitched scream. The "Oh my God." The something-something "train!" A thump as another passenger bumped into the amateur cinematographer. The "Don't go down there." "Grab him." "Get his wrists." "I've got him, I've got him." "Is he conscious?"

And . . . pause.

"Look. Do you see it?"

"I can see why everyone's calling her Superwoman. Takes a lot of strength to lift a person like that. Hard to tell, but the kid didn't appear to be helping any. Probably suffering from shock."

"Look at the woman, Patrick. Look at her face."

He leaned closer to the screen and shook his head. "I know the MTA's video coverage is spotty, but really, did you at least check? Maybe you'll get lucky."

"Yes, I checked. Just look at her face, okay?"

He raised his brows at her snappish tone. At least he hadn't called her shrieky, as he was prone to do when her tone became too strident for his tastes. "I'm not sure what I'm supposed to be seeing here, McKenna, and I'm obviously frustrating you. Just tell me. You said something about Susan." He looked at the image on the laptop screen again. "Oh, McKenna, no. There's no way."

"The face. The face is the same."

"You can't even *see* her face."

"The shape, like a heart. The lips. And the arch in her brow. Plus, look." She pointed to a spot just beneath the woman's hairline.

"You can see that scar, from when she fell running across campus—during the Maharathon or whatever."

"The Mahanathon," he said, correcting her. The cadets called the sprint from the West Point gym to Mahan Hall the Mahanathon. Despite Susan's usual speed and dexterity, she had managed to trip on a curb and wipe out face-first. "You can't tell that's a scar. It could be a loose hair or a splotch or something. This woman could be anyone. Seriously, the MTA must have better footage."

"They don't, okay? The guy said an entire hotspot or something crashed. This is all I've got, but look at it. You said yourself the woman would have to be incredibly strong to lift a kid like that. Fast, too, to be chasing a high school athlete. You should see her haul ass up the subway steps. Susan is strong and fast. The only female cadet in your class to get that prize—"

"The Commandant Prize. Because Susan *was* fast. She *was* strong." He placed a hand on her knee and gave it a squeeze. "And she's been gone for a really, really long time."

"People aren't just gone. They never found a body. I don't even think she's been declared dead legally."

He pulled his hand away and shook his head. "You're contradicting everything you've ever said since Susan disappeared. 'She'd never just leave.' That's what we *all* said. It's what we *all* told the police. That somebody must have done something terrible to her. Now you're saying she's alive and well and living in New York after all these years?"

"I didn't say she was *well*. Maybe, I don't know, you hear these stories about people with head injuries who don't even know who they are. They eventually start life all over again."

"McKenna, amnesia? Come on." He walked to the refrigerator and grabbed a bottle of water. When he returned to the sofa, he didn't sit quite as close to her.

"She's just *missing*, which means she's somewhere. She could be back in New York. You can't ignore the fact that the woman in that video looks exactly like Susan."

"We haven't seen her in ten years, McKenna. And that picture—

it's like a blur. You went through all of this before, all those years ago. You cried every day for a month. You stopped eating. You were walking around Hell's Kitchen at all hours of the night, trying to find her."

She remembered those nights. She had wanted so desperately for Patrick to comfort her. He was the only person McKenna knew who was also close to Susan—they never would have met if not for Susan. They had taken very different paths to New York City. Patrick had attended West Point and served in the army before going to work at the museum; McKenna had gone to school on the West Coast and was working downtown as a prosecutor. They had tried the game of tracing six degrees of separation between them, but the one and only direct route was Susan Hauptmann.

So if anyone could help her through the grief of Susan's disappearance, she had assumed, it would be Patrick. And McKenna knew that Patrick felt a sense of loyalty to Susan.

She had heard both versions of the story about the beginning of their friendship. According to Susan, she had pulled the old West Point trick of stuffing her bed, tucking laundry beneath her blanket for bed check so she could celebrate her twenty-first birthday in Chelsea. Nights in the city with the friends she'd made outside the army were an escape for her. They helped remind her that she had a life beyond the one she'd chosen in order to please her father. She used those nights to doll herself up and blow off a little steam, to nurse a side of her personality she could never show the other cadets. That night, she wasn't the only cadet who'd left the grounds. When Patrick Jordan walked into the same city bar at one in the morning, she was sure her reputation was done.

In Patrick's version, the only reason he ever walked into a club like the Limelight was because he had a two-day leave from campus for a cousin's wedding, and the bride and groom decided to go bar hopping after the rehearsal dinner. His ears were beginning to adjust to the thumping music when two of the bridesmaids began gossiping about the girl "slutting it up" on the dance floor with two different men. When he looked at the woman grinding against her dance partners, something about her seemed familiar. He recognized Susan just as she made eye contact with him.

He was aware of the whispers about her on campus—the General's Daughter, they called her, or sometimes Hot Lips Hauptmann—but he knew that cadets routinely exaggerated their sexual accomplishments where the female cadets were concerned. Now it appeared that in Susan's case, the whispers might be kinder than the real thing. And as the son of a mere colonel—though a full one, a "bird"—he could only imagine the panic going on behind his classmate's mascara-laden eyes.

The two versions of the story converged from there: Patrick turned around, left the club, and never said a word to anyone on campus about the encounter. Not even Susan. Back at West Point, popular, trusted Patrick found subtle ways to bring outsider Susan—female, attractive, last name Hauptmann—into the fold. Susan knew she had a real friend.

So when Susan disappeared, McKenna knew Patrick cared. They had been friends long before McKenna was in the picture. But he had been almost angry about it. Not angry at Susan or even about her disappearance. Angry at McKenna. At her reaction. At the crying and the sobbing and the picking at food and the inability to sleep. At what he saw as overly dramatic displays of emotion. At her expectation that it was up to him to make her feel better.

"What you're doing right now isn't about Susan," he said to her at last. "I'm worried about her, too. So is her father. So is everyone who knows her. But you're making this about you. Things suck for you at work, and you're using this as an outlet."

That statement—and the hour-long yelling match that followed—marked the first of many offs in their relationship. Ten years later, he was clearly worried that she would unravel once again.

"I'm not doing any of that now. I just— You know, even if the woman on the subway wasn't Susan, it doesn't matter. She's been gone all this time, and I haven't even *thought* of her in years. I want to know what happened to her. She deserves for someone to still be looking."

He started to push back but thought better of it. "So what should we do about it?"

We. Patrick was like that. He could play devil's advocate. He could try to convince her to pursue another path. And then just like that, he could climb aboard and support the mission. That was probably how he'd been able to make it through the army. It was why he was still at the Met—his first civilian job out of the military—after all these years. What were *we* going to do about it. She didn't give him enough credit for that loyalty.

"Her dad started getting sick years ago, and he was the one putting pressure on the police. For all I know, no one's been looking for her. Maybe her loser sister knows something. What was her name again?"

"Gretchen."

"Right. Maybe you can contact the army crowd. See if they know anything?"

"I think I would have heard—"

The expression on her face stopped him. "I'll call around."

"I'll start with the basics. Public records. Credit reports. We can play it by ear."

Playing it by ear sounded so simple. No promises. No rules. Just following intuitions on a lark. As though, if the melody didn't work, you could simply walk away from the piano. But searching for answers wasn't like fiddling with notes on a keyboard. Once you started asking questions, it could be impossible to stop, even when you knew you should.

CHAPTER EIGHT

The man behind the reception desk at the Four Seasons was oily. Not literally. He wasn't shiny or glistening or greasy. But the way he peered out and up beneath thick black eyelashes, not even bothering to lift his chin despite speaking to a man six inches taller than he; the way he smiled without parting his lips; the way his clenched jaw failed to hide the grinding of teeth behind the forced smile—all of it reeked of unctuousness.

"No reservation, sir?"

"I'm afraid not. Thought I'd be back on the train to New Canaan tonight—deal sealed—but I guess the lawyers had other plans. Guess that's what happens when you let these firms bill you by the hour. How can you tell when an attorney's lying? His lips are moving." He dropped an American Express card on the counter. The name read Michael Carter. That would be his name for the foreseeable future. Until he needed to be someone else. "I'll take whatever room you have available. Beggars can't be choosers, right?"

There was that sealed-lip smile again, as if the request didn't bother him a bit. The clench in the jaw told a different story while he tap-tap-tapped away at his merry keyboard.

"Our standard rooms are all sold out tonight, sir. We do have a city-view executive suite. This would be your rate, exclusive of taxes, of course."

The clerk pushed a piece of paper discreetly across the counter: $995 per night. Exclusive of taxes. Of course.

Carter nodded his approval and watched the black card swish through the reader. Beneath the name Michael Carter was the name of a company: Acumen Inc. The company was real, incorporated as a shell, permitting him to funnel untraceable money through a series of offshore accounts. Panama was popular these days.

"How many keys, sir?"

"Just the one, please." One was the right answer for a business-man unexpectedly stuck in the city for an evening. It struck Carter that two was probably the more typical request, given the liaisons he'd observed so many times in high-end hotel lounges. But a re-quest for two keys by a solo traveler was interesting. It provoked curiosity. Carter made a very nice living—with unplanned and unexplained expenses part of the package—by being completely, entirely, and utterly uninteresting and unprovocative.

He returned the clerk's smile while accepting the room key. Throughout the entire transaction, Carter remained angled away from the security camera that hung on the wall behind and to the right of reception. Now he pivoted to his left, depriving the lens of any look at his face.

Not that it mattered. Just habit.

His fib to the reception clerk hadn't been too far from the truth. He was, in a sense, a businessman with an unexpectedly long detour in New York City.

Compared to the work that had gotten him here, Carter's current position was practically a desk job. His job was to watch. To moni-tor. To stand to the side and make sure there were no problems. He thought of himself as an auditor hired by people who didn't want the audits discovered.

He had mastered the language used to describe his line of work. People paid him a lot of money as a *precaution*. For *peace of mind*. For *comfort*. They paid Carter to watch for *red flags*. *Alarms*. People used these terms to describe what they believed to be a feeling of gut instinct. Carter knew there was no such thing. Facts raised flags. Events sounded alarms. Carter knew how to articulate the subtle culmination of facts and events that caused lesser people to experience an inexplicable "feeling."

Usually he could tell when a target was going to be a problem. Living a life filled with secrets required highly choreographed management of both time and physical location. It meant sneaking away for a supposed bathroom break but placing a brief phone call from the men's room. It meant telling your coworkers you had a headache and needed to turn in early, then driving to a rest stop thirty miles out of town for a clandestine handoff of a package.

He had no problems locating the subject of the audit, thanks to the GPS tracker that she didn't know she was carrying. Carter had been hired because the GPS tracker had traced the woman to other parts of the New York metropolitan area. Carter's boss wanted a better idea of what those side trips entailed.

The first two days had been like punching a clock. No gut feelings. More important, no facts to raise red flags or alarms. Just a lot of time out in Suffolk County, where she was supposed to be.

On the third day of observation, she hopped on an Amtrak to Penn Station. He followed. She didn't seem to notice.

But he noticed her. He noticed that she was using a second phone. Not the one with the GPS tracker in it. A different one.

She'd been typing away on it when that boy had grabbed it from her hands. And then she was gone, barely making it past the subway doors before they slammed shut, sealing him inside that crowded tube. Unknowing. Without eyes or ears. Utterly useless for a moment.

He had hopped off at the next stop, Herald Square, then headed north to Times Square. Clipping through the station, he could overhear the leftover rumblings of commotion. *Did you hear? Some guy fell on the tracks! Someone saved him.* It hadn't taken him long to find the two EMTs at the foot of the platform stairs, one flashing a penlight in the kid's stunned eyes.

The kid was fine. The woman he had robbed was gone.

Carter called his boss from aboveground.

Yesterday morning the papers had called the woman the 1-train heroine—an unidentified mystery woman. She had Carter to thank for her continued anonymity. It had taken some persuasion, backed by cash, for Carter to render the MTA's security footage unavailable. What seemed like a lot of dough to an MTA technician was chump change to the kind of people who hired Carter.

He knew what the mystery woman called herself. And where she was supposed to be. He did not know why she had come to New York City or why she had been so desperate to recover her second telephone. But he had a very strong, and very bad, feeling.

And if Carter had learned anything in his forty-two years, it was never to accept the unknown.

CHAPTER NINE

McKenna went to the office early to sneak in some work on her book proposal. As much as she had been telling Dana and Bob Vance and the agent and the editor that she was on the fence, she was beginning to think of it as *her book*.

Vance's advice the previous day had gotten to her. This could be a once-in-a-lifetime opportunity, a chance to make something of her time at the DA's office. A chance to write something other than marshmallowy fluffs of city gossip. She had to admit, she'd felt good writing those few pages the previous day, even though she had no idea what role they'd play in the end product. Her plan was to jot down a few more sample scenes here and there. Just enough to figure out whether she wanted to go all in.

She had written a book before. She was a published novelist, after all. But that was different. She'd started writing her novel after she was forced to leave the district attorney's office. She had taken two years off to write it, and she hadn't even begun to try selling it until it was completely finished.

According to the agent, the nonfiction book that she couldn't bring herself to call a memoir could be sold off of a proposal. It should have a "jazzy"—she hated that word—overview, a table of contents, and a summary of each chapter.

She had no idea how to outline the events that had led to the end of her legal career. So far, she had been working on the overview, but instead of jazz, it was turning into cacophony.

*I*t was the gun. Not the gun itself—not at first—but Tasha Jones's insistence that her son, Marcus, didn't carry one. She never vouched for Marcus's character. Neither did I, not once. The case was never a matter of character. Marcus Jones was only nineteen years old, but he had eleven juvie interactions with law enforcement and was out on bail pending felony theft charges when a bullet from Officer Scott Macklin's gun killed him.

"My boy stole," Tasha told me when she cornered me on the courtroom staircase. "Always did and always would. The schools said his IQ was only seventy-eight, but he knew robbery was harder time than theft, and armed robbery, more trouble still. He didn't have no gun. He didn't have no gun, because he never wanted to be in a position to be pointing one, let alone at the po-lice. He went to the docks that night to meet his girlfriend. What he need a gun for?"

Police never found any evidence of a girl. They did, however, find eighty bucks in Marcus's front pocket, despite the fact that the kid had no lawful means of income. I truly believed I would find evidence connecting Marcus to that gun.

I never thought of myself as the most talented trial attorney in the office. It always seemed to be the lawyers from the local schools who were labeled real naturals or geniuses in the courtroom. But I was a hard worker. I was thorough.

And so I traced the gun, hoping (and expecting) to prove Marcus's mother wrong. Hoping (and expecting) to strengthen Macklin's claim of self-defense. Hoping (and expecting) to make the grand jury's job that much easier.

But the gun had another story to tell.

*T*his wasn't working. McKenna was supposed to write about the case from her own perspective. Her excitement as a relatively junior lawyer to be working on her first homicide—and an officer-involved shooting, at that. Her loyalty to the officer involved: Scott Macklin. The stress of being in the middle of a news story that had taken on unmistakable racial tones. The gradual onset of doubts about his side of the story. Her decision to come forward.

And her utter shock when that decision nearly tore the city apart.

How could she do that in a synopsis? She could never pull it off.

She closed the file. The truth was, she couldn't look back on that time in her life without thinking about Susan. And any thought of Susan pulled her back to the infuriating video. She opened the video again and hit play.

Bob Vance gave a cursory tap on her office door before entering. "Four thousand words. You promised yesterday. Whatcha got for me?"

"I'm going with Judge Knight."

"He's the fatty, right?"

"More important, he's lazy, offensive, and—according to the smoking-gun evidence I now have—disdainful of the public he's supposed to serve."

She handed him printouts of the two e-mails she had received the previous day. "Frederick Knight has been on the bench for five years. From the beginning, there were questions about his intellectual heft—no pun intended. Last week, I got an anonymous call from a woman claiming to have been a juror in one of his recent cases. She said he was rolling his eyes and cutting off witnesses. He'd go off-record, but she heard him tell a domestic-violence victim that she was *too attractive* to get beaten. And he spent most of the trial fiddling with his phone and laptop. I've heard these kinds of things about him before, so I decided to put out some feelers at the courthouse to see if anyone might come forward."

"And?"

"Those appeared in my in-box yesterday."

The messages were short but damning. One, sent by Knight three days earlier: "Can't stand these people. Dirtbags hurting dirtbags. Lock them all in a cage together and give them bats and chain saws. The world would be better off." And the other, sent just yesterday morning: "Going out on a ledge here because I feel like I'm on a ledge. You guys have space for special counsel? I go on civil rotation in two weeks and can throw your firm some bones until the transition's official. I'm serious: I can't take this anymore."

"Can this be four thousand words?" Vance asked.

"No question. Knight came to the bench after practicing only two years as a law firm associate and then serving for nine years as the judicial clerk to Chief Judge Alan Silver. Clerks are supposed to be clerks, but it's become common practice for judges to grease the wheels for lower-level judicial appointments as a reward for their most loyal clerks. Knight was on the criminal court for two years and then got bumped up to felonies. I can have a section about other clerks who found their way to the bench with questionable credentials. I've got a pattern of Knight always siding with the state against criminal defendants, sexist comments—even on the record—and resisting the appointment of defense counsel to the indigent. These e-mail messages would be the nail in the coffin."

Though the smoking-gun e-mails would be the bait to sell magazines, the story was substantive. It was the kind of thing she'd hoped to do full-time when she'd accepted the job.

"They're legit?"

"That's what I wanted to talk to you about. I knew it would be hard getting anyone to go on record about a sitting judge, so I reached out to a network of potential sources and promised anonymity. Unfortunately, instead of trusting me to protect their identity, someone opened a free e-mail account and sent these to me. They deleted the address information of the recipients, so I can't look there for confirmation."

"Stands to reason that whoever sent you these was probably the original recipient, right?"

"It could be one of his clerks or his secretary. Or, because he was stupid enough to use his public e-mail account, a public employee with auditing abilities could have lawfully obtained access. Or someone could have hacked in."

"I get the point. You're making me nervous."

"I'm trying to nail it down. I confirmed through the court system's directory that the e-mail address listed on the two messages is in fact Judge Knight's. I did some digging, and three days ago, when the 'dirtbags hurting dirtbags' comment was sent, Knight was hearing a bench trial of a shooting arising from a drug deal gone bad. I got the attorneys on both sides to confirm that Knight pressured the prosecutor to come up with a plea because it was a—quote—'who cares' case. I also confirmed that Knight is indeed scheduled to start hearing civil cases in two weeks, where he'd be in a position to help big-firm lawyers."

Vance smiled. "Jeez, Jordan. It's like you're a real journalist or something. The messages are self-authenticating when you put them in that context."

"That's what I was thinking. I figured I had enough to call Knight. All he gave me was a 'No comment.' "

"All right, then. Let's run with it."

She was relieved when Vance left without further mention of the subway video.

CHAPTER TEN

When McKenna was in the zone, she could write almost as quickly as she could talk. Two hours after getting the go-ahead from Vance, she had transformed the notes she'd been keeping on Judge Knight into a full-length article. Although block quotes from the e-mail messages in 28-size font would be the red meat to pull in readers ravenous for easily digestible scandal, she had used Knight as a case study to delve into the cronyism that perverted the court system and a culture in which lawyers were too afraid of retaliation to blow the whistle on bad judges.

She hit the submit key on the article. The modern publishing process moved so rapidly that the article would be online by afternoon.

She turned her attention back to the video. She had seen it so many times, she knew where to stop for any single moment that interested her, but she was still at a loss as to how to confirm that the woman was Susan Hauptmann.

Her eyes were beginning to cross from squinting at the screen, as if that could make the images any clearer. This time, when she hit pause, it wasn't to study the mysterious woman's blurry face. Mc-Kenna was focused on the very end of the video, pausing as Nicky's rescuer sprinted up the stairs.

There was something attached to the woman's backpack. A button. Round. About four inches wide. Some design on it, maybe a few letters at the bottom.

She pulled out her cell and sent a text message to Dana.

Before I give up on that video from yesterday: Looks like there's a button pinned to Superwoman's backpack. Can you try to get a better look?

The phone pinged a few short seconds later.

You know it ain't like TV, right?

McKenna smiled. Recently, she and Patrick had tried to watch a series about a hotshot security team at a Las Vegas casino. Only half an episode in, Patrick had flipped the channel when the security team, suspicious of a drop-dead-gorgeous woman at the nickel slot machines, enlarged the house camera's glimpse of the woman's unzipped purse to zoom in on a perfectly legible handwritten note inside—all in about five seconds.

With Patrick incapable of tolerating shows about security, the military, or law enforcement, and McKenna refusing to watch anything about lawyers, they were on an eternal search for television shows they could enjoy together. Most recently, they had tried watching a show about zombies, but Patrick kept interrupting with surefire plans for battle. Note to self, McKenna thought, scythes are apparently the key to surviving a zombie apocalypse.

She sent a return text to Dana:

Got it. I'll take whatever you can give me.

When McKenna didn't receive an immediate response, she used the wait time to cull through her in-box, under constant attack by an ongoing assault of unwanted messages. Vance had just fired off a reminder about the importance of filing deadlines. Human

Resources was admonishing the staff once again not to abandon food in the refrigerators. Then there were all the irrelevant mass mailings she received by virtue of being listed as a retired member of the New York State Bar: the American Bar Association's report on electronic discovery, a continuing legal education session on accounting for lawyers, a last-chance offer for a personalized plaque to commemorate her fifteenth year as a lawyer—now, how in the world was *that* possible? Delete, delete, delete.

She'd paused to check out a book recommendation e-mailed to her from a friend when a new message arrived from Dana.

> This is what I have for now. Try running it through Google Images. And don't say you don't know how. I showed you myself. I'll work on your girl's face tonight—an image of it, not a makeover. You know what I mean.

Dana had warned McKenna not to expect a miracle, but the snapshot attached to the e-mail wasn't too shabby. McKenna's guess had been correct. Pinned to Superwoman's backpack was a round button, the background plain white, the abstract design a blue circle with a series of lines inside it. Two lines formed a cross in the middle of the circle, dividing the circle into four quadrants. Three of the four quadrants contained curved lines, creating the impression of half circles.

The image on the button meant nothing to her. That was where Dana's suggestion of Google Images came in.

McKenna pulled up Google Images on her computer. Inside the bar where she was used to typing search terms was an image of a small camera. She clicked on it and was prompted with "Search by Image," followed by "Upload an Image." Dana had walked her through these steps last month when McKenna was trying to locate the driver of a delivery truck outside the townhouse of an actress constantly rumored to be planning another march down the aisle. By searching for the logo printed on the side of the truck, they managed to find the name and phone number of a bakery in Brooklyn.

Turned out the driver was delivering tasting samples for a wedding cake. It wasn't the kind of scoop McKenna was proud of, but the magazine tripled its newsstand sales that week.

She uploaded the digital image that Dana had extracted from the video and watched Google work its magic. She immediately got a perfect hit: PEOPLE PROTECTING THE PLANET. The picture on the backpack button was Planet Earth behind crosshairs. The three semicircles had transformed the straight lines of the crosshairs into three P's—an acronym for the organization.

She ran a separate search for information about the group. According to a sympathetic website, PPP carried out "direct actions to defend the planet by liberating animals, disrupting the activities of polluters, and depriving predatory corporate entities of their ill-gotten gains." Another website called the organization "eco-saboteurs." Another claimed the group was on the government's ecoterrorist watch list.

Whether People Protecting the Planet were saviors or a domestic threat, they didn't sound like Susan's crowd. She was from a military family and had gone to West Point. Even after leaving the army for business school, she'd kept a toe in the water through the reserves. She was deployed for nearly a year in Afghanistan through the Civil Affairs Brigade, completing her service as an economic development officer, helping the Afghanis stabilize their banking system.

After all those years in uniform, Susan had enjoyed her freedom from a dress code. She was more of an Armani-suit-and-Prada-handbag woman than a button-adorned-backpack type.

The observation sent McKenna's mind back to one of her last memories of Susan, teetering on sky-high Jimmy Choos. A few years earlier, the heels would have set her back close to a month's take-home pay. Even on a consulting firm salary, they were a splurge, but Susan was so proud, strutting around the store while other women marveled at her ability to maintain balance. "I'm taking these bad boys home. And for the right bad boy," she added with an out-thrust hip, "I'll wear them with nothing but a thong."

The other customers hooted their support. Susan had that way about her.

Those shoes—along with the rest of her belongings—were found in her apartment after her disappearance. It made no more sense today than it had all those years ago.

McKenna dialed a number she had looked up an hour earlier but hadn't had the guts to call.

"Scanlin."

Even ten years ago, McKenna had figured the guy to be close to his twenty-two years of service. Some cops couldn't leave the job.

"Detective Scanlin, this is McKenna Jor—McKenna *Wright*. Please don't hang up. It's important."

"As I recall, everything you believe to be true is always so . . . darn . . . *important*."

"I'm calling about Susan Hauptmann. Can you meet me in person?"

CHAPTER ELEVEN

McKenna scoped out the landscape at Collect Pond Park. The good news was that the city was experiencing a warm, bright, beautiful October day. The bad news was that the unseasonably pleasant temperatures had brought out the masses. The place was hopping.

She opted for a bench holding one other person. His one person managed to occupy more than half the bench, but there was enough room for her to sit, and he was far too preoccupied by his newspaper to give her a second glance.

Scanlin was the one who'd chosen the park for the meet, placing her smack-dab in the middle of a strip of action below Canal Street that was the heart of the Manhattan criminal court system. This territory used to feel like her heartland, too, pumping blood through her system. How many times had she carried a yogurt down to this park, or a bit farther south to Foley Square, just to breathe some fresh air and enjoy a brief respite from the courthouse's fluorescent lighting?

She used to know all the hot-dog vendors—not by name but by face, cataloged mentally by the characteristics that really mattered. Good mustard. Softest pretzels. The guy who stocked Tab.

She knew which homeless people were regulars on the civil commitment and misdemeanor dockets, and which were harmless enough to become part of the daily banter. Back then Reggie was one of her favorites. "Whatchu gonna use to eat that salad with, my dear?" "I'm going to use this here fork, Reggie." "Well, go on, then. Fork yourself!" Reggie would laugh and laugh and laugh, even though he used the same line four times a day, every single day.

She looked around, wondering what had become of the man. She didn't see him. She didn't recognize anyone.

She felt like an outsider. She *was* an outsider.

When she'd caught Scanlin on the phone, he was just leaving the squad room to give testimony in a motion to suppress. "If it's so important," he'd said, "why don't you meet me downtown?"

He initially suggested meeting in the courtroom where he'd be testifying. But while she used to be able to whisk past security, asking the guards about last night's Giants game, giving a self-satisfied wave to the defense attorneys waiting to enter, McKenna now had to line up with the rest of the citizens to be cleared for entry. Wasn't there a more convenient place to meet? she had asked Scanlin. She'd been hoping for a coffee shop near the precinct, but he had insisted on a location by the courthouse, finally selecting the park. "You said it was important. I'm just trying to make sure you see me as soon as I'm done testifying."

She knew he took a certain pleasure in beckoning her to hostile territory that once was her home.

She wouldn't have recognized him if he hadn't looked directly at her from the courthouse steps and made a beeline to her park bench. "You need to be here, guy?" Scanlin asked. From behind his open newspaper, McKenna's neighbor on the bench threw her an annoyed look. She shrugged, but one glance over the paper at Scanlin sent the man shuffling in search of a new spot to crash.

"Well, how about you? You look pretty much the same. Not too many people can say that after a decade. You should be proud of yourself, ADA Wright."

McKenna didn't know what to say. Scanlin had to know she

wasn't proud. She wasn't an ADA anymore. She wasn't even a Wright anymore. When she and Patrick married, she picked up on his preference that she change her name. In his world, that was what wives did. In her world, the whole thing seemed ridiculous, but she made the change anyway. Maybe her name wasn't the only thing she was trying to change at the time. Her writing name would be McKenna Jordan. Not McKenna Wright, the disgraced prosecutor.

She couldn't return Scanlin's compliment. She'd met him in person only twice, right after Susan disappeared—once when she'd shown up unannounced at Susan's apartment, insisting on speaking to the detective in charge; and a week later, when she appeared un-announced at the precinct, accusing him of avoiding her phone calls based on what she'd considered a conflict of interest.

The man she remembered had been close to fifty years old, with a well-groomed mustache that matched his dark hair. She remem-bered that he wore cuff links and a subtle cologne that smelled a little like pine. He was the kind of man who made the effort.

Now he took up nearly as much room on the park bench as its previous resident. No mustache, just the graying stubble of a skipped day or two from shaving. No cologne or cuff links. His tie was loose, and the wool of his navy sport coat was beginning to shine from too many cleanings. No, she couldn't say that he looked pretty much the same.

"Thanks for meeting me, Detective."

"What detective doesn't want a face-to-face with a member of the illustrious media?"

She could tell from his smile that he was enjoying his barbs. "I'm not here as a writer. Or as a former prosecutor, for that matter. Is Susan Hauptmann's case still open?"

"It was never cleared, so it was never closed. Last time I checked, not closed means open."

"But is anyone working it? Is anyone looking for her?"

"Not my case anymore. I'm in homicide at the Twelfth now."

"You never considered the case a homicide even when she was in your jurisdiction."

"I know *you* did. You made that clear the day you came storming to my lieutenant accusing me of stonewalling you."

"I'm not trying to relive the past, Detective. I'm asking you why you were so sure that Susan up and left when everyone who knew her said otherwise."

"We never found evidence of foul play. I guess you didn't need much in the way of evidence to go around making claims."

McKenna ignored the superfluous dig and tried to focus on Susan. She could feel the stirrings of all those old frustrations. "To the people who knew Susan best, her sudden disappearance was the strongest possible evidence. She would never put her friends and family through that kind of uncertainty."

McKenna remembered the few basic facts she'd been able to glean from Susan's father and her own queries: Susan's gym card had been scanned at Equinox on the Saturday morning after Thanksgiving. One of the trainers remembered waving hello as she cranked away on the treadmill, seemingly lost in the beat of the music pumping into her headphones. She had RSVP'd to a friend's Sunday card game as a maybe, so no one gave her absence any thought. It wasn't until Monday night that a coworker dropped by Susan's apartment building, assuming she must be incredibly sick to miss work and not call in. At the end of Tuesday, the building superintendent unlocked the apartment door at the request of Susan's father. The police took two hours to show up, and only after ADA McKenna Wright made a phone call.

Though there was no point in rehashing all of the details with Scanlin, McKenna highlighted the key points. "She left her purse, her passport, her wallet."

"You don't have to remind me, Ms. Wright. I know that you, of all people, don't hold the police in the highest regard—"

"That's not fair—"

He waved a hand, not to concede the point so much as to signal his unwillingness to debate it. "I remember my cases. I can tell you the life stories of missing people—men *and* women—that I still wake up wondering about. And I can tell you that I believe I failed by moving on without them, without answers for their families. But I never felt like that with your friend. You know why? Because you and I view the same facts in a different way. Every single thing was in its place at her apartment. You see that simple fact the way you see it. But I've been a cop for over thirty years, and I know that a woman who goes somewhere takes her pocketbook with her. She takes her wallet. Hell, she at least takes her damn *keys*. And there was no sign of disruption to the apartment, even though, by every account, Susan Hauptmann was an athlete. A trained soldier. A fighter."

McKenna thought about the woman in the white sweater, pulling Nicky Cervantes from the tracks and sprinting up the subway staircase. Fast. And strong. A fighter. She knew where Scanlin's reasoning was headed.

"No blood. No knocked-over furniture. Not even a pillow out of place. No sign of a struggle means that no one harmed a fighter like Susan Hauptmann in that apartment. We've got no evidence of harm *inside* the apartment. We've got no evidence that she was surprised on some normal kind of outing *away* from the apartment."

"People don't just evaporate."

"That's where you're wrong. Not physically, not like abracadabra. But that's exactly what they do. Or at least *want* to do. Evaporate. Susan Hauptmann left behind her passport, her wallet, her pocketbook, her keys. She left behind her life. She . . . *left*. You didn't want to believe that."

"I didn't *want* to believe it because I couldn't believe it. I *knew* her."

Scanlin said nothing, but his gaze, though focused across the street at the courthouse, grew sharper. For a moment, behind the razor stubble, sloppy tie, and extra layers of fat, McKenna recognized the intensity she'd sensed in him so many years ago.

"Why are we talking about this now?" he asked.

"Because I think you were right. I think Susan's still alive. I saw her."

"I'm glad to know it. It's too bad her father didn't live to hear the news." Susan and her father always had a difficult relationship, but he was the one who pushed the investigation and worked the media, even though he had just been diagnosed with cancer. McKenna had seen his obituary in *The New York Times* two months ago.

"Aren't you even curious about what I just said?" she asked.

"I don't need to be. I know if you ran into her at the movies and caught up like old pals, you wouldn't be here talking to me. Why don't you go ahead and get to your point. What do you want from me, Ms. Wright?"

She opened her iPad and pulled up the link for the public drive of Dana's Skybox to play the video clip. She hoped that Scanlin had studied enough pictures of Susan back then to recognize her now.

The connection was timing out. Maybe Dana had changed the settings. Or maybe the iPad wasn't getting a good enough data connection to access the Internet. Or, more likely, McKenna the Luddite had managed to do something wrong.

"I'm sorry. I have a video here. I want to show it to you."

"Just tell me what I need to know, all right?"

She started to speak but realized how ridiculous it sounded. He needed to see the actual image.

"I'm so sorry. I'll go back to my computer." The only still photograph Dana had e-mailed her was of the button on the woman's backpack; Dana hadn't yet created a still version of Susan's face. Maybe once she did, she could enhance it for better clarity. "If I e-mail it to you, will you please just look at it?"

His gaze moved to the distance again before speaking. "Yeah, sure. Send whatever you want."

He handed her a business card, and she automatically responded with one of her own. "Thank you, Detective. Really. I know what you must think of me, but I always cared about Susan, and I need to know what happened to her."

He fingered the edges of her card. "I noticed the name change when you started at the magazine."

She held up her left hand, ring forward. "Five years now. To Patrick Jordan. You might remember him from the investigation. He was another one of Susan's friends."

"Seems like you've got a good thing going for yourself now. The writing thing. A husband. I would've thought, of all people—after everything that happened—you would've learned that some things are better left alone."

Scanlin pushed himself off the bench as he stood. She watched him walk to his fleet car, parked just outside the courthouse.

Scanlin resented her. He still had the same conflict of interest she'd raised with his lieutenant ten years earlier. He looked at her and saw his friend Scott Macklin on the front page of a newspaper, beneath the headline Cop Hero or Murderer?

But Scanlin was on the job, he remembered Susan, and McKenna had gotten somewhere with him: he'd look at the video. That was all that mattered. It was a start.

She was about to walk to the subway when she looked again at the courthouse. There was another conversation she needed to have in person.

CHAPTER TWELVE

Assistant District Attorney Will Getty rose from his desk to greet her with a warm hug. "McKenna Wright." Everyone from the DA's office—at least the people willing to acknowledge her existence—called her by her maiden name. "Speak of the devil."

She returned the hug and took a seat. This was the same chair she sat in a little over ten years ago, when Getty called her into his office to offer a chance to work with him on an officer-involved shooting. A cop named Scott Macklin had shot a thug named Marcus Jones at the West Harlem Piers.

"Was someone speaking of me?" she asked.

"The chattering classes are very excited. Rumor is you've been asking for dirt on Judge Knight. You can't possibly expect me to help you with that hot potato."

His conspiratorial smile brought out lines that hadn't been there when she'd first met him, but he was still handsome—more handsome than he ever wanted to let on. Neat haircut, but not too fashionable. Respectable suit, but not showy, and probably a size bigger than the salesperson recommended. Will Getty was the kind of trial lawyer who knew that jurors were distrustful of men who were too good-looking.

"I am here about a hot potato—just not that one."

"I saw the article. I was wondering if I might hear from you."

McKenna had thought about calling him before the Marcus Jones article went to print. But he was her superior ten years ago. She was a journalist now and didn't need his permission to publish a story.

And yet.

"I don't know if you noticed, but your name wasn't in the article."

"You don't need to explain anything, Wright. And not that my opinion means squat, but I happen to think that you handled it very professionally."

Her article had focused on the protests following Marcus Jones's death and the eventual exoneration of Officer Macklin. She had disclosed the fact that she—the author of the piece—was the junior prosecutor who had raised doubts about Macklin's self-defense claim. There had been no reason to bring Getty's name into the piece.

She knew Getty well enough to get straight to the point. "I've been asked to write a book. Not write but propose. Who knows what will happen—"

"A book about the Marcus Jones case?"

"Not about the case itself but my place in it. It would be a more personal account than the article. A thirty-year-old woman who, for a couple of months, was in the middle of—I think at one point we agreed to call it a shitstorm?"

The problem boiled down to the gun. Scott Macklin claimed Marcus Jones pulled one, and the gun was found resting in Jones's limp right hand. Jones's mother insisted her son did not own a gun and accused Macklin of planting it. The pistol was a Glock compact with a filed-down serial number. McKenna had recently read an article about the ability of crime laboratories to restore obliterated serial numbers. Eager to prove herself, she'd filed a request with the local field office of the ATF, which was able to determine the last four digits. A search of the ATF's database scored a match, meaning that the gun was used in a previous crime.

McKenna remembered the adrenaline rush that had come with the news. She wanted Marcus's mother to be wrong and Scott Macklin to be right. A boy was dead, killed by a good cop. Mc-

Kenna wanted proof that Marcus was the bad guy. She wanted proof that he had left Macklin with no choice. The gun in Marcus's hand had been used in a previous crime. Marcus, at only nineteen, was a longtime criminal. She knew she'd find the connection.

But the connection between the Glock and that night at the West Harlem Piers wasn't the one she'd expected to find. The serial number of the handgun was in the ATF's database because the gun had been seized by the NYPD in 1992 after it was found in a garbage can. It was slated for destruction in accordance with the NYPD's weapons disposal policy. As part of a public relations campaign called Safe Streets, the police department would make a show of feeding that gun—and hundreds of other seized weapons—to a smelter, subjecting them to three-thousand-degree temperatures until liquefied. But the gun never made it to the smelter. It wound up next to Marcus Jones's body eleven years later.

Eleven years before his death, Marcus Jones was only eight years old. There was no reason to believe that he could have come into possession of the gun back then, and certainly no explanation for how the gun could have made its way to him from an NYPD property room.

But eleven years earlier, Scott Macklin was already a police officer, two years into his service. More notably, he was one of the young, enthusiastic, telegenic officers who had served as the face for Safe Streets. A *New York Post* article about the program showed Macklin delivering a truck full of guns to the smelter. *Officer Scott Macklin said that more than four hundred guns would be destroyed. "Any day we can take guns that might be used in crimes or accidental shootings and turn them into manhole covers and chain-link fences is a good day for the citizens of New York City."*

All these years later, she remembered the sick feeling in her stomach when she'd learned that Marcus's gun—Marcus's *supposed* gun—had a direct connection to Scott Macklin.

Macklin was third-generation NYPD. His grandfather and father and uncles would have told him about the days when every cop carried a "drop gun," an unregistered weapon to toss at the side of a suspect to justify a shooting, if needed. Macklin was a newer breed of police, but tradition in blue families could be deep, as if passed by blood. It would have been easy to slip a gun from the Safe Streets pile.

She'd taken the evidence to the prosecutor in charge, Will Getty. He was one of the most respected lawyers in the office. He had become something of a friend after accompanying her to one of Susan's happy hours. She trusted him.

But as she explained to him all the work she had done—the serial-number recovery, the ATF database search, the old newspaper article connecting Macklin to Safe Streets—she realized how ridiculously eager she sounded. After all, she was a mere drug prosecutor, and her special assignment of second-chairing this investigation was a glorified term for carrying Getty's bags. She had been hoping to be rewarded for taking the initiative, but instead, she'd made herself look like a total freak by pursuing a side investigation into a politically and racially sensitive case without any input from the lawyer in charge.

She could remember what he said to her. "We don't want to do anything rash. But good work, Wright. You've got a good eye for detail."

He told her he would recess the grand jury for a couple of days while he looked into it.

Days went by. Then a week. When she asked him for an update, he explained that things took time and that he was working on it.

And then she'd heard nothing. Hearing nothing wasn't McKenna's forte. With each passing day, she became more convinced that Getty was finding a way to steer the grand jury in Macklin's favor without her.

At the end of the second week, she met with Bob Vance at a dive bar in the East Village and told him everything she knew. The papers depicted her as a whistle-blower. She declined offers to appear on cable news and at protest rallies, but the people who accepted those invitations made a point of crediting her for revealing the "truth" about Marcus Jones's shooting.

And then Will Getty figured out how that gun really had gone from Safe Streets storage to the right hand of Marcus Jones's dead body, and McKenna wasn't so beloved anymore.

Ironically (or maybe predictably), Will had always been supportive of her. He was the one who told everyone who would listen that she'd been trying at every moment to do the right thing. Even as it was becoming clear that McKenna had to leave the DA's office, he had gone so far as to write an essay for the *New York Law Journal*, arguing that she epitomized the ideal version of a prosecutor who was doing justice. He called her at home and conceded that if he'd communicated with her better after she'd gone to him with the Safe Streets connection, he could have prevented the "tragic misunderstanding."

"Have you ever stopped to think," he asked her now, "that in a weird way, that case helped you find your true calling. You were a good lawyer, Wright, but do you know how many lawyers would kill to write? I don't care how much trash the people around this place were talking. They were all reading your novel, they were all loving it, and they all would have given their left nut to be in your shoes."

Her first career move after leaving the DA's office was almost accidental. After two months of wallowing on her sofa, she had started tinkering with a short story on her computer. As the story slowly blossomed into a book, she lived off her modest savings, supplementing with credit card debt as necessary.

The book was her escape from the real world—pure, unabashed, relentless fiction. When *Unreasonable Doubt* came out, her former coworkers nevertheless chose to see the book as an attempt to cash in on her platform as a scorned ADA.

As it turned out, there was no real profit involved. Despite every lawyer's fantasy of writing a novel and retiring, she'd earned barely enough on the advance to pay off the debt she'd racked up while writing. But she had written a novel. It had gotten good reviews.

She felt better about herself. She let herself be happy for a while, which seemed to stabilize what had been an erratic relationship with Patrick.

Then she took another two years to write a second book, and by then the publishing industry had changed. Stores were closing. Sales were down. Apparently the legal thriller was dead. That book was sitting on her hard drive, unpublished.

By then she was a thirty-five-year-old lawyer with a five-year gap in her résumé; well educated but with only one real interest: in crime.

No prosecutor's office would have her. Even defense firms didn't want her because they believed prosecutors would blacklist her on plea bargains.

She'd written a novel (two, if an unsold book counted), so she knew she could write. And she knew how to tell a story. She wrote a few pieces on spec, and then Bob Vance gave her a chance at a full-time job. That was career change number two. She despised the fluff pieces that dominated her work, but at least she had a paycheck until she figured something else out.

Back in Getty's office after all these years, she felt herself gripping the worn upholstery of the chair arms, knowing she was doing the right thing but wanting to get it over with. Getty was a good lawyer. She could see him processing the information. Considering his words carefully.

"Do you want to do it? The Marcus Jones book?"

"I think so. If I can find a way to do it that is respectful of the people who deserve respect." She patted his desk.

"What you're saying is that the article didn't mention my name, but a book would."

"I wanted you to hear it from me first. And I promise to treat you fairly."

"Okay, then. Can't ask more than that, can I?"

The hug he gave her when she left wasn't quite as warm as the one she'd received when she arrived.

CHAPTER THIRTEEN

Two hours later, Joe Scanlin was back at the Twelfth Precinct. The estranged wife of a suspect in yet another drug-related killing had agreed to come in for questioning.

He knew the history. Six 911 calls made from their shared address just in the last four years. Three arrests of the husband for domestic violence. One time she went to the hospital with a broken jaw. No charges ever filed.

She moved out two months earlier when Child Protective Services threatened to take her kids if they continued to witness the violence against her.

But "separated" and "separate" weren't synonymous.

"Kenny don't sell," the woman insisted. "He don't even use. No way he'd have something to do with *that*. His no-good friends always dragging him down. That's all that is. They the ones did this. Don't you listen to their noise."

Scanlin walked out of the interrogation room while she was talking. He didn't need to hear the rest. Been there too many times. She wasn't under arrest, but he knew she'd stay there in the box until he told her she was allowed to leave. No one ever tried to leave, certainly not a woman who'd gotten used to being beat on.

Back at his desk, Scanlin found himself fiddling with McKenna Wright's—Jordan's—business card. Since she'd called that morning, he had felt off his game. Like he was walking and listening and talking through a filter, smothered by a layer of dust. He was trying to pinpoint the reason why. The moment she'd said her name, he had been pulled into this cloud.

Even as he was insisting that she meet him downtown—at the courthouse, near the courthouse, anywhere that would remind her of her former existence—he had known he was being transparently vengeful. But there were legitimate reasons to remind that woman of the past. She was a vulture. A user. A one-lady wrecking ball. Like so many lawyers before her, she had tried to build a career on the backs of decent men. Everyone knew that most prosecutors worked the job as a stepping-stone to the bench or elected office, and the fastest shortcut was across the back of a dirty cop. If you had to make up corruption where none existed, so be it.

Even with the disappearance of her friend, she never seemed as interested in the truth as she was in telling Scanlin how he should do his job. For a moment down there at the park, he had let his guard down. He'd felt the hardness that he'd readied in the courthouse elevator begin to soften at the sight of her business card. Changed job. Changed name. She was a woman who cared about her friend after all these years.

Now he found himself wondering whether her phone call had anything to do with Susan Hauptmann. All those years ago, she was so convinced that something horrible had happened to her friend. Now she pulled a one-eighty: not only had Scanlin been right back then; now she had a firsthand eyewitnessing of the long-missing woman. No details, mind you. Just the promise of a video he was never shown.

He wouldn't put it past her to dangle the promise of photographic evidence as a carrot. She could pretend to be tracking down Hauptmann as a pretext to talk him up. That was how users like her worked. They saw people as chips that could be cashed in for a favor.

Scanlin knew that Susan Hauptmann was out there somewhere,

hopefully living a happier life. Regardless, Scanlin could die satisfied if he never heard her name or McKenna Jordan's again.

Scanlin had been all too aware of his age the moment McKenna Jordan recognized him across the park. He saw himself through the younger woman's eyes. It wasn't just that years had passed since she'd last seen him. He had changed.

There was a time when Scanlin worked the job a hundred percent, knowing that at the end of the day, Melissa would be waiting—makeup on, hair curled, dinner either on the stove or ordered from one of their favorite Italian places on Arthur Avenue. They weren't rich, but they managed to make their life glamorous. His life was different now, and those differences had manifested themselves in his appearance.

He'd seen the Jordan woman's big article, of course. The story meant nothing to the new cops, but the guys who'd been around for a while paid attention. Scanlin had read it online for free, refusing to shell out six bucks at the newsstand.

He was too smart not to wonder whether her phone call had something to do with her newfound interest in rehashing the past. For all she knew, Scanlin could get her access to the man he suspected she was truly interested in—the man whose career she'd ruined, the man she could use to help sell more magazines.

Scott Macklin was an old friend in both senses of the word. Over a decade had passed since Mac decided to cut off ties with his NYPD buddies. He was an aged friend because—well, because they both went and got old.

Scanlin checked his e-mail. No video from McKenna Jordan. Not even an e-mail. Maybe she had imagined seeing her friend and come to her senses. More likely, the woman was working an angle. The less he thought about her and the trouble she brought down on those around her, the better.

CHAPTER FOURTEEN

McKenna never voiced the opinion aloud, but she believed that she excelled at everything she did. Even thinking it, she realized how narcissistic it sounded. She didn't mean it in a boastful or arrogant way.

To say that she was good at everything she did wasn't to say that she was good at *everything*. The assertion said very little about her natural talents but spoke volumes about something she wasn't good at—taking risks. McKenna excelled at everything she did because she'd spent her life avoiding the things she could not do.

She remembered returning her flute to that tiny old music store in Seattle. Her parents had bought the instrument used, on an installment plan. They were only on the fourth payment by the time it was clear McKenna was no longer interested, deciding that she had a better chance of mastering the violin. The sympathetic owner agreed to rent the family a violin. Then a viola. Then a saxophone and a trumpet. McKenna wound up in debate club instead.

She was no more tenacious as a grown-up. One of her female law professors led a series of golf lessons for the Woman's Law Association, plugging the sport as a way for women to spar with the boys in law practice. For three weeks, McKenna watched as, one by one, her peers got the hang of the swing plane, the cocked wrists, the release of the club, the follow-through. When it was McKenna's turn, the ball would roll forward a pathetic ten feet, as if felled by her wood-chopping swing. No more golf for her.

Her predilection for favoring skills based solely on mastery had almost led her into a math major. She couldn't imagine a life crunching numbers, but they came easily to her, so she'd stuck by them. Lucky for her, she had also been a good writer, a good arguer, and a pretty decent speaker. Even luckier, she happened to live in a world where good writers, arguers, and speakers could usually find a place for themselves.

As a result, even while her career had taken turn upon unpredictable turn, McKenna had always believed that everything would turn out okay because she had been good at enough things to patch together a facade of effortless talent. She was still waiting for that faith to prove well placed.

It seemed these days that her natural talents for breaking down facts and weaving them into a story collided increasingly with her fundamental inability to understand computers. To break down facts, one first needed to gather them. And where gathering facts used to involve questioning witnesses, subpoenaing documents (as a lawyer), or talking her way into file cabinets that were meant to be off limits (as a reporter), now it seemed like every time she needed a piece of information, technology got in her way. McKenna was barely forty years old, but with a librarian mother and an English-teacher father, she was one of those rare young people who was more comfortable with microfiche and dusty notebooks than WAV files and thumb drives.

Today it was this stupid Skybox program, or website, or app— *whatever*—that was making her crazy. She had watched the subway video from the link Dana had given her at least a hundred times, but now all she was getting was an error message informing her that the link was invalid.

She had seen Scanlin's skeptical look when she promised to send him the video. Now hours were ticking by, and she had bupkes.

So much for her credibility—not that she had any with the man.

She had rubbed Scanlin the wrong way from the minute she badged her way into Susan's apartment, insisting that the police brief her on the status of the investigation. It had been a rookie move, but she'd bought in to the idea that her position as an assistant district attorney for New York County entitled her to a certain amount of respect as a law enforcement officer. She hadn't been around long enough to realize that the general maxim didn't hold true with the other half of the equation—cops.

To make matters worse, Scanlin had spent four years in a precinct with Scott Macklin. It hadn't taken Scanlin long to make the connection between the nosy ADA pushing her way into his investigation and the bitch who was accusing his old friend of lying about an officer-involved shooting. She remembered the way Scanlin had raised the issue. She had called him the day after storming into Susan's apartment. The point of the call was to apologize for her heavy-handed approach, but she never got the words out. Instead, she got an earful from Scanlin about the honor, integrity, and courageousness of Scott Macklin, followed by a warning that she was "nobody" as far as Susan's case was concerned, followed by a prediction that karma would catch up with her, followed by a *click*.

She remembered her response to the click in her ear. She had run to the ladies' room down the hall at the DA's office and held her hair back while she vomited. Susan was missing. McKenna had publicly accused a police officer of homicide and perjury. And now the Marcus Jones mess was keeping her from helping Susan.

She had wanted to call Scanlin back. She wanted to explain to him how hard it was to come forward with her suspicions about that shooting. She wanted him to know that she liked Scott Macklin. He'd been a regular in her office at the drug unit. He had shown her the pictures of his new wife, Josefina, and her eight-year-old son, Thomas. He had talked to her like a friend.

So, yeah, she wanted Scanlin to know that she didn't need a lecture about honor and courageousness and karma. All she wanted was to do the right thing, but locked in that bathroom stall, sobbing into a ball of toilet paper, she had known that the Scott Macklins and the Joe Scanlins of the world would forever see her as a back-stabbing, ladder-climbing careerist.

Now Scanlin would think she was yanking his chain once again with the promise of a video that McKenna could no longer find. Another fucking error message on the computer.

McKenna had called Dana twice, and both times got voice mail. She normally approved of Dana's ability to disappear from the reservation with no accountability, but now she was beginning to understand Bob Vance's frustration with her freelancing ways. It was four o'clock. Where was Dana?

She hit redial on her cell. This time she recognized Dana's ring tone—a snippet of the Blondie song "Call Me"—chirping from the pool of desks beyond her office.

"Dana?" she yelled, hitting refresh on her keyboard in a futile attempt to pull up the link. "Is Dana back?"

She was answered with the blurt of a "fuck"—Dana's voice—followed by an explanation from Pete the junior assistant: "You might want to lay low. She's having, like, a meltdown or something."

McKenna found Dana bent over the computer in her cubicle. "I can't *believe* this. It's gone. Every freakin' thing is gone."

"Your Skybox? That's what I've been calling about. I can't pull up that subway video."

"Screw the video. My photographs. My entire backup account. The entire thing is wiped out."

"It's not just the link?"

Dana looked at McKenna as if she were a child asking why dogs couldn't talk. There was no need to provide a response. Instead, she continued ranting to herself. "I'm going to have to call them. You know there won't be a live person. Fuuuuck!"

McKenna could tell it wasn't a good time to press the subject of the video. She turned to Pete. "Do you know anything about this stuff? Why would her account be down?"

"It's not down," he whispered. "It's deleted. It's like someone logged in as her and erased the entire thing. That was her *backup*. She's totally screwed."

CHAPTER FIFTEEN

Carter was situated comfortably in the second-to-last row of the PATH train, by all appearances deeply interested in the *Wall Street Journal*'s analysis of the latest tech-industry initial public offering. There had been a time when Carter followed the markets, squirreling away his few extra dollars in an IRA, hoping that sensible choices would create slow, steady gains that would lead to a comfortable retirement long down the road. That was when he bought in to the idea that if you were a good person and tried hard enough and kept your head down, everything would work out in the end. That was back when he believed in institutions and loyalty and hierarchies. That was back when he believed in . . . anything.

Carter was a different person now. Now he was the kind of person who stayed liquid.

He knew that most of what was covered in this newspaper was irrelevant to the way the world actually worked, but the paper served its current purpose of helping him blend into a sea of commuters departing Penn Station.

The woman's *People* magazine served a similar purpose. It was four o'clock, and commuter traffic was already getting heavy. She could be calling it an early day after a long presentation at her job in marketing. Or heading back after those part-time classes she was taking to get that advanced degree she was always talking about. Or going home to her kids from her monthly mommy day in the city for a facial and a haircut. She looked like any other woman. You'd never know that three days earlier, she had chased a kid onto the tracks of the subway only to rescue him seconds later.

Carter had to hand it to the woman. She was good. The casual observer would think she was genuinely engrossed by the latest celebrity baby bump or ongoing love triangle involving a teen mom. But he could see her eyes sweeping the car, monitoring the platform at each stop. So far, she hadn't noticed him. She was good; he was just better.

What was she looking for?

He almost missed it. The man stepped into the train right before its departure. He sat in the seat behind hers, so they faced opposite directions. He sported earbuds blasting metal that was loud enough for other passengers to hear from a comfortable distance away. He even threw in an occasional mock air drum. He didn't seem like Miss *People* Magazine's type.

But then Carter saw the woman's left hand move ever so quickly to her side, just as his right hand swished down from the drum solo playing in his head. He had given something to her, as if they were two grade-school children passing notes. Very skillful grade-school children.

When the heavy-metal guy stepped from the train at Thirteenth Street, Carter stepped off, too. When he walked up Sixth Avenue, Carter followed. The earbuds stayed in. The metal kept playing.

Carter pulled his cell phone from the breast pocket of his cashmere sport coat. Pretended to send a text but zoomed in and took a quick snapshot once the man's head was turned to the side.

Carter watched the man enter a residential building. He noted the address. He watched through the glass as the man stopped to retrieve his mail from the wall of boxes.

Other people would have called it a gut feeling, but Carter knew it was all about facts. He did not like the facts he was gathering.

He waited for the man to leave the lobby and then entered. He approached the doorman with a friendly smile. "Hi, there. I'm looking for a rental. Wondering if this is a rental building or only ownership?"

"Ownership. It's a co-op."

"Ah, okay. Thanks." He turned to look at the building's mailboxes. Four rows over, three boxes down. That was the one the man had opened. Apartment 602.

It was time to call the client.

He knew by now that the preferred reporting style was to use as few words as possible. Train. Man. Address. "I have his picture."

"Send it. You know the number."

That cell phone number—untraceable—was pretty much the only thing Carter knew about his client. "Sure thing."

He texted the man's photograph.

Two minutes later, Carter's phone rang. The client used the same crisp style—no extraneous words. A minute after, Carter hung up, knowing that his mission had just changed. So much for the easy life.

CHAPTER
SIXTEEN

It was four o'clock, and Scanlin still had that funny feeling in his head. He had to admit that his annoyance with McKenna Jordan was just part of the reason. Her reappearance had not only reawakened his antagonism toward her and his memories of Scott Macklin; it had also triggered a look back at his life.

When he caught the Hauptmann disappearance, he was no longer that hundred-percent detective at the top of his game. Oh, he looked the part. He was physically fit, with the clothes and the watch and the swagger. But on the inside, he realized now, the change had started, because Melissa's changes had started.

At first her problems were hardly noticeable—little verbal tics. In their circle of fast-talking New York friends, Melissa had been the most manic chatterer of all, but he started noticing occasional uncharacteristic pauses. Proper nouns that once were as familiar as her own name were replaced with descriptions like "that restaurant you like with the squid-ink risotto" or "your partner from back when you worked in the Bronx."

Initially Melissa attributed her "offness" to sleep deprivation. Or sometimes to one too many glasses of Chianti. They used to joke, after all, that a bad hangover temporarily suppressed twenty points worth of IQ.

The doctors would tell him later that it wouldn't have mattered if he'd gotten her to experts earlier, but sometimes he wondered whether they said that in a failed attempt to make him feel better.

The pauses in her speech got longer. Her extensive descriptions to compensate for the loss of proper nouns became more vague: "That place—the one where you—have food." A restaurant? "Yes, the one with the—small white food, but dark." Squid-ink risotto? "Right! That's the one." By then she would have forgotten why she was trying to remember the restaurant at all. Was she remembering their second date there? Craving a dish they served? Interested in the dress shop next door? Whatever it was, the moment was gone.

And before he knew it, so was Melissa. The fast-talking friends were polite at first, pretending not to notice that she could no longer follow the conversation. And then pretending not to mind. And then pretending to support his efforts to maintain some semblance of normalcy in their marriage. But his patience for Melissa had outlasted theirs with him, so then they were gone, too.

He could look back and see it all so clearly. A beginning, a middle, and an end to the arc in their lives together. Ten years ago, when Susan Hauptmann disappeared, he had no idea what would happen later and how it would affect him—was already affecting him.

As he recalled it, Susan disappeared just after Thanksgiving. Scanlin got Melissa's initial diagnosis on October 24. Every week she had appointments with specialists. The doctors were constantly changing her medications, trying to wean her from the antidepressant/antipsychotic cocktail they put her on before realizing that frontal-lobe changes were to blame.

And Jenna. Oh God. Jenna. Scanlin loved Melissa more than he could ever love another woman, but no one loves a woman the way a child loves a mother. Maybe in some families, one parent's illness brings the healthy parent closer to the children. That wasn't how it worked for the Scanlins.

Scanlin remembered the initial interview of Susan Hauptmann's sister. What was her name? Gertrude? Gwendolyn? Guinevere? G-something, if he had to guess. See? He couldn't remember. At the top of his game, he could remember the name of a victim's sister. Somewhere right between her last high and the next one, the sister had been a font of information, motivated by concern for her sister but probably also the hope of getting on the good side of a police officer.

As she'd droned on and on about the pressures their father had placed upon Susan—no sons, only one "good girl" to count on—Scanlin had felt himself coming to conclusions. If Scanlin's own daughter, Jenna, could push him away, why wouldn't a woman like Susan, with an SOB father like that, make a clean break of it and start over again?

And then he was getting pushed in a different direction by the likes of some cop-hating prosecutor. Not to mention constant phone calls from the pushy father who had pushed his daughter to the brink and was now pushing him.

All that pushing at a time when Scanlin was in no mood to be pushed.

The truth was that, back then, the only way he found the time to deal with Melissa, her doctors, and his pissed-off daughter was by phoning it in on the job. Susan's father obviously had enough money and connections to pull out all the stops for reward offers and private detectives, so what more could Scanlin do? Writing off Susan Hauptmann as a grown-up runaway made his life easier.

Now his mind was in a fog because seeing McKenna Jordan was forcing him to ask whether he'd rushed to judgment. He could think of only one way to be sure he could stand by the choices he'd made so long ago. He made a call to the Records Department. "It's Joe Scanlin, Homicide, Twelfth Precinct. I need an old case. The name on it is Susan Carol Hauptmann."

He'd take a quick look. Just for peace of mind. Just to be sure he hadn't missed anything.

CHAPTER SEVENTEEN

Dana was still freaking out in the pool reporter room. At one point, she began to screech like a stepped-on cat until Bob Vance stuck his head out of his office and threatened to remove her vocal cords with a letter opener if she didn't shut up.

Her meltdown had sent McKenna into a panic, futilely opening windows on her own computer, hoping that the video had cached itself somewhere in the computer's memory. As if McKenna even knew what "cached" meant.

That video was the only proof—if she could even use that word—that Susan was alive. Even after seeing the video, Patrick had been dubious. Now she had nothing.

She was starting to wonder if she truly remembered what Susan looked like. She had pictures, of course, but pictures were never the same as the real thing. They were a more perfect version—images that were saved for a reason. Photographs were never enough to catch the facial expressions, subtle reactions, and other idiosyncrasies that defined a person's appearance.

McKenna had first met Susan through an e-mail forward. Susan had found a two-bedroom in Hell's Kitchen but needed a roommate to split the rent. Her e-mail blast about the rental landed in the in-box of an ADA who knew that McKenna's tenancy on the sofa of a college friend was wearing thin.

When McKenna went to see the apartment, she couldn't believe her luck. The condo was clean and bright with floor-to-ceiling closet storage and a tiny slice of a Hudson River view. And her new roommate was smart, nice, and hilarious. What could be better?

But just as cameras failed to capture a person's real appearance, first impressions usually didn't reflect real character. Over the next twelve months, McKenna's opinion of Susan evolved. At first she was drawn to Susan's boldness. She was beautiful and magnetic and always spoke her mind. When the man who lived upstairs listened to a Dave Matthews CD on repeat one too many times, Susan managed to sneak into his apartment and swipe the offending disc. She wasn't just funny; she was a good person. Not in a flashy show-off way; she was someone who constantly thought of others. Reaching down to help a fellow subway rider carry a stroller up the stairs. Bringing a flashlight to the widow on the third floor during a power outage. Carrying an extra umbrella on a rainy day in case a coworker forgot one. Answering the door for unannounced visits from her screwed-up sister, despite the hour. She had a big heart and a big sense of humor. It wouldn't be an overstatement to say that McKenna idolized her.

Then one night McKenna found Susan—always so busy, always buzzing with energy—sitting alone on the kitchen floor, a bottle of wine in one hand, the cordless phone in another. Her father had called. There had been a fight. He was the one person who could shut Susan down with nothing but a stern glance. This time he'd gone much, much further. Joining her on the cold tile, McKenna knew she was seeing a side of Susan rarely shown to anyone.

Which side of Susan was McKenna remembering? Did she really remember her, or only snippets of time, artificially frozen in the recesses of her brain?

If she couldn't trust her memories of Susan, how could she possibly begin to recognize the ghost on the 1-train platform, whom she'd seen only in grainy, shaky footage? She had to find that video.

She called Patrick to see if he knew anything about Skybox storage. No answer on his cell, and his secretary said he'd left work early. Just her luck to need him the one day he skipped out before five.

She heard Vance yell another warning at Dana, this time to shut up before he choked her with her own tattoos. With Dana momentarily silenced, McKenna realized that, unlike her photographer colleague, she had a backup plan. She flipped through her phone, found the incoming call from the previous day, and redialed the number. "Is this Mallory? It's McKenna Jordan from *NYC* magazine. You were nice enough to send me a video clip yesterday."

"Sure. I remember."

"I hate to bother you, but we're having some computer glitches on my end. Is there any way I can get it from you again?"

"Same thing with the Skybox account?"

Apparently everyone understood cyber storage except McKenna. "No, that's where the glitch happened. I know it's an imposition, but can I meet you somewhere in person? I'll upload it to my laptop directly, just to make sure I don't mess something up."

There was a pause before Mallory responded in her low drawl. "I guess that would be okay. I'm at work. There's a Starbucks at Forty-fifth and Sixth Avenue. Call me when you're there, and I'll come down."

"I'll be there right away."

McKenna was pulling her jacket on when her cell phone rattled against the desk. This time she recognized Mallory's number.

"I'm just heading out, Mallory. See you in a bit."

"Don't bother."

"What do you mean?" McKenna heard her own voice jump an octave and hoped Bob wouldn't appear, letter opener in hand.

"The girl in the next cubicle overheard the call and wanted all the details. I went to show her the video, but it's gone."

"What do you mean, it's gone?"

"I don't know. It's just not there anymore."

"Is your phone working?"

"I called you, didn't I?"

McKenna could tell that her persistence was irritating the girl, but she didn't understand how Mallory could erase the video and not know about it. "I'm sorry, but I really, really need it. Is it possible you overlooked it?"

"No. I'm positive. I only took one picture since then, and it's gone, too."

"Did you erase them?"

"Not intentionally. I think some dipwad I lent my phone to must've deleted them."

"What dipwad?"

"My friend Jen and I were in line at Margon. Line's always halfway down the block at lunch. Some dude said he needed to call his wife and left the office without his phone. Maybe he accidentally erased it or something."

McKenna was certain that nothing involving this video file was accidental. "What did he look like?"

Another long pause. "I have *no* idea."

"Anything at all that you remember would help, Mallory. Anything."

"Jen was telling me about her douchebag boyfriend, who tried to justify cheating because she gained seven pounds when she quit smoking. I wasn't paying attention. Honestly? I couldn't pick the guy out of a lineup if my life depended on it."

Whoever "borrowed" that phone probably planned that, waiting until Mallory was completely distracted.

"Wait a second. Is this really such a hot story?" Mallory asked. "Is this like some rival reporter stealing the video so you can't have it? That totally blows for you."

McKenna thanked Mallory for the sympathy, figuring there was no harm in leaving the girl under a mistaken impression. Mallory had already served her purpose to whoever had erased the video from her phone. There was no need for her to know the bigger picture.

Not that McKenna had any idea what the bigger picture was. As she hung up, she realized she was in way over her head. Someone had wiped out Dana's media storage account. Someone had tracked down Mallory's phone. Someone definitely did not want that video to be seen. She found herself wondering whether the malfunction in the MTA cameras might be related, before she realized how insane that idea was.

She rushed to her desk and e-mailed a file on her computer to her three different e-mail accounts, saved it to a thumb drive, and then hit the print key. She watched the photograph churn from the printer.

A picture of a button pinned to a backpack. The logo for a group called People Protecting the Planet. This was her only image of the woman on the subway. It was all she had left.

PART II

Girls, you've got to know when it's time to turn the page.

—Tori Amos, "Northern Lad"

CHAPTER
EIGHTEEN

When Scanlin took the Hauptmann file home, he wasn't entirely sure he would even open it. As he drove to Yonkers, the box from the Records Department filling his passenger seat, he scolded himself for letting McKenna Jordan into his head. Thanks to budget cuts, he had enough work to fill his hours. He didn't need the added burden of dusty files detailing a perfectly capable adult's voluntary disappearance.

I'm a good cop. He had repeated that phrase mentally like a mantra, all the way up the West Side Highway onto the Henry Hudson Bridge. I went through hell back then, but *I was a good cop.* I've always been a good cop. Even then.

Now that good cop's dining room table was covered in paper. The DD5s documenting each witness interview. The crime lab reports. Inventories of items seized during searches of Susan's apartment and office. The file from the investigation had been organized by type of document. Scanlin had rearranged the documents in strict chronological order, refreshing his memory of the case from beginning to end.

When he'd told the former prosecutor—emphasis on "former"—that he remembered the case well, he'd believed his own words. But he'd learned through years on the job that memory was a fragile thing, more like a crime scene that had to be protected and preserved from alteration than a fixed, permanent object that was impermeable over time. Usually the evolution of an eyewitness's memory helped the prosecution. He'd seen it so many times. The witness, reluctant and uncertain as she perused the six-pack of suspect photographs. A tentative finger moving toward a candidate, the witness searching for some kind of affirmation from police that she had the right guy. "I think he's the one."

"Good job" was Scanlin's standard response. A small reward, but he could see immediate effects in the relieved witness: a nod, a small, satisfied smile. By the time the prosecutor asked the witness how sure she was of the identification, she would be "extremely confident." And when she pointed that accusatory finger at the defendant—in person, at trial—it was as if the suspect's face were emblazoned on her visual cortex. "I'm absolutely certain."

Say something enough and it not only sounds true, it becomes memory.

Everything he had said to McKenna Jordan about the disappearance of Susan Hauptmann had come from memory. It all sounded true. It all *was* true. And he had been able to recall those facts effortlessly—to pull them from memory—because he had repeated them so many times to General Hauptmann in those first years after Susan disappeared.

Susan Hauptmann was last seen on a Saturday, following her usual routine of a long workout, even on Thanksgiving weekend. No one had any inkling of a problem until she failed to report to work the following Monday morning. When Scanlin was called to her Hell's Kitchen walk-up on Tuesday night, he found the one-bedroom apartment in what her friends described as its usually tidy condition. Neighbors reported no known visitors, noises, or other noteworthy observations. It was as if, as her friend McKenna said so sarcastically, Susan simply evaporated.

But in less obvious ways, Susan had left behind evidence that pointed Scanlin to his eventual conclusion that she had disappeared of her own volition. Her consulting firm's managing partner reported that the firm recently notified Susan that she was underperforming, not living up to potential, and unlikely to be a serious candidate for partnership. After her "noble" service in the Middle East, she had failed, in her boss's estimation, to transition from her military background into the culture of a private firm, where billable hours were more important than efficiency, and the most successful associates understood they could forge their own version of a chain of command.

At the same time, according to Susan's sister, their father was pushing her back into that familiar culture. "The General," as the girls had learned to address their two-star father, had been temporarily appeased by Susan's following his footsteps to West Point, but he had never accepted her decision to go to business school. He'd hoped that her stint in Afghanistan would persuade her that life was better spent in service to her country than as yet another corporate lackey. His words, recited by Gretchen, were right on Scanlin's dining room table, staring at him from her DD5: "Our father would always say, 'The only thing lawyers and consultants have ever created is more work for lawyers and consultants.'"

After a full career in the military, George Hauptmann was launching his own firm to do contract work for the government. One of Susan's friends from West Point had already signed on, and the General was pushing Susan to make the move or, at the very least, go back on active duty. Scanlin had his fair share of problems with Jenna, but he could not imagine wanting to send his daughter to war—especially the two wars that were raging when Susan Hauptmann disappeared.

She had a million friends, but none of them close. She dated, but no boyfriends. Two careers, but no successes. She was a woman who had nowhere to belong. How many times had Scanlin restated these facts, cementing them into his memory with each new recitation? No sign of a struggle. No sign of foul play. A woman in a time of "emotional and professional crisis"—those were the euphemistic words Scanlin had used gently with the father when what he'd really wanted to say was "You drove your daughters away, the ways fathers can. Now one's a junkie, and one has run away from you."

All those facts were true. But memory was malleable. It was selective. Some facts hardened, and others fell away. As he relived the course of the investigation from beginning to end, he found his present self arguing with his former self. How did she leave New York? There were no plane tickets, bus fares, or car rentals on her credit cards. No large cash withdrawals. She'd left behind her driver's license, passport, and every other possession. When did she leave? Perhaps most important, if she really did leave of her own accord, why had she never resurfaced? Runaways, whatever their age, eventually returned, but even after the death of her father, Susan remained missing.

MISSING.

That was the header on the flyers plastered on telephone poles and parking meters across Manhattan as November turned into December. Basic data: thirty-two years old, white female, five feet seven, 140 pounds. In the photograph, shoulder-length blond waves encircled her wide face, marked by a broad smile and gleaming green eyes. She was beautiful. And she was a missing young white woman with an impressive background and influential father. The case had gotten attention.

He remembered all the wack-job calls to the tip line: spottings at bodegas, bookstores, Knicks games. None of them panned out. Well-intentioned but mistaken tipsters believed she was a current coworker, classmate, fellow yoga aficionado. As he leafed through the old notes, he saw that one guy (anonymous) had claimed to have had sex (anonymously) with the missing woman six months earlier in a restaurant bathroom. No information about her current whereabouts.

The tip—viewed in the context of a fresh look at the entire file—reminded Scanlin of another piece of paper he had just seen. He pulled the DD5 of one of Susan's colleagues, Jared Klein. Like most everyone else who knew her, he was utterly perplexed by her disappearance. Scanlin remembered prompting Klein, as he always did, to think of anything—*anything at all*—that might have been unusual. Klein had shaken his head, but Scanlin could tell he was holding back.

"Now's not the time for secrets," Scanlin had warned.

"It's not a secret. It's just— You know, maybe I misunderstood."

"Misunderstood what?"

"Last year, we were working late, as usual. We had a couple glasses of wine at dinner. Everyone else left, and it was just the two of us. She leaned in and—I don't know, it was like she was going to kiss me or something. I stopped it. Last thing I needed was a sexual harassment suit or worse. I expected her to brush it off like a stupid late-night moment, but she got—well, I guess I'd say aggressive. Like, who was I to reject *her*? The next morning she seemed totally normal, and I've always thought maybe it was me who had cloudy judgment that night. But now I'm wondering if maybe I saw a hidden side of her. Jeez, I feel bad saying this about her now."

It had seemed like a stretch at the time. And the anonymous tip about the anonymous sex had seemed like nonsense. The neighbors' observations about all of the people—mostly men—coming and going from her apartment had seemed totally consistent with the depiction of a woman who socialized regularly and operated in male-dominated work settings. The half-empty box of condoms in the nightstand had seemed like a standard precaution for a heterosexual adult woman.

But all of it together? Maybe there had been a side to Susan Hauptmann that her friends and family didn't know.

His thoughts were interrupted by a knock on the door.

CHAPTER NINETEEN

McKenna looked at her watch. Five-ten P.M. Patrick would be leaving work soon. She sent him a text.

> Guess who pulled a pop-in on the Upper East Side? Meet me in the modern wing.

He responded immediately.

> You're here?

> Yes. Modern. Electric chair.

> Bike gear or no?

He was asking whether he should change into his usual commuter wardrobe, or if they would be going somewhere that required proper attire.

> Cleaned-up version requested, por favor.

The Metropolitan Museum of Art was almost a quarter mile long and occupied over two million square feet. When McKenna first moved to New York, she would roam the hallways, thinking about Claudia Kincaid, the runaway preteen heroine of one of her favorite childhood tales, *From the Mixed-Up Files of Mrs. Basil E. Frankweiler.* She would imagine what it would be like to live in the depths of this huge museum, as Claudia had with her little brother, scrounging coins from the fountain and sleeping on the historic beds.

Now McKenna was one of those locals who hopped into the museum a few times a year to see a special exhibit or favorite sections—or, in her case, favorite section, the modern wing. On this particular day, she was taking in one particular piece—Andy Warhol's silkscreen of an empty electric chair. A friend had published an entire essay dedicated to this little silkscreen's implications about humanity's fascination with death.

Of course, her visit had nothing to do with art. She was here for Patrick.

When Patrick first told her he worked at the museum, she was so jealous. She also came to realize how much his continued employment revealed about his values. About a quarter of West Point graduates opted for lifelong military careers; those who didn't had their choice of lucrative professions. Corporate headhunters jumped at the chance to land the kind of leadership skills found in junior military officers. Private security firms paid top dollar for ex-military types willing to provide protection work in dangerous locations. One of Patrick's army friends insisted he was a makeup importer and exporter, but when McKenna asked about the merits of mineral foundation, he looked at her as if she'd asked about soaking her hair in gasoline. When she pointed out his lack of cosmetic expertise to Patrick, he gave her a list of friends who probably shouldn't be questioned too closely about their work. CIA, perhaps. Maybe sensitive cultural liaison work for the State Department? she wondered. Hopefully not hired mercenaries, but she kept her distance just in case.

Patrick, on the other hand, had gone directly from the military to security management for the museum. She'd heard him justify the choice to his wealthier, faster-living friends more often than he would have liked. He felt good working for a nonprofit. He enjoyed the diverse cast of characters who filled the building. He was surrounded every day by some of the most impressive art on the planet. But what had struck McKenna the most about Patrick's employment when they first met was its stability. He wasn't one of those people always trying to climb to the next step, who saw the present as a bridge to the future. He wasn't like her.

On the other hand, she hadn't realized that ten years would go by without even one change.

"We do have other collections in this museum, you know." Patrick took a seat next to her on the bench across from the Warhol.

She rested her head against his shoulder. "Good day?"

"Fine. We had a close call this afternoon with a girl who fell into a Matisse, but luckily there was no damage."

Thanks to films like *The Thomas Crown Affair*, the average person believed that museum security was all about high-speed, high-tech heist prevention. Little did they know that the most significant losses came from damage, not theft. The water delivery guy rolls a flat of Poland Spring bottles into a Renoir. A fresco is hung on too small a hook. A Rodin sculpture's pedestal simply gives out one day. And every year, a big chunk of damage was inflicted by girls who drank too much, ate too little, and insisted on tackling the city in five-inch heels. One little topple and suddenly Philippe Bertrand's sculpture of Lucretia is missing a foot.

"How about you? I've overheard a few people in the museum talking about your Big Pig article."

McKenna had filed her article about Judge Knight with the title "Should This Man Be Calling Balls and Strikes?" It was a reference to the confirmation testimony of the current chief justice of the United States Supreme Court, who had stated that a good judge was like a neutral umpire. To jazz it up, *NYC* magazine had gone with a close-up photograph of Knight's bloated face, the words BIG PIG stamped across him like a USDA beef rating.

The response to the story had been swift. A spokesperson for the chief judge had promised a thorough investigation. Reacting to speculation about his resignation, Judge Knight had issued a statement attacking the tabloid culture of the media and promising full vindication.

But McKenna wasn't here to talk about Frederick Knight. "You too tired for a little outing?" she asked.

"No, I'm good. What were you thinking? Dinner? A celebration?"

While Patrick's moods were ever constant, hers were frustratingly tied to external achievements. In light of the Knight article, he assumed she'd want to spike the football.

"Dinner does not count as an *outing*. Dinner is just . . . dinner. This is an actual *outing*." It dawned on her that she'd never asked him why he had left work early the previous day. "Speaking of which, what was your outing yesterday?"

"What do you mean?"

"I tried calling when Dana's Skybox imploded, and your office said you left early. It was right after four."

He gave her an exasperated look and shook his head. "Incredible. I leave my desk to walk the floor, and they tell people I'm gone. One of our trustees nearly stroked out when he thought I stood him up." He got up from the bench and held out his hand. "Now, what is this about an outing?"

"You're not going to like it, so I'm officially cashing in a chip." She had no idea whether chips were currency in their household, or how she might have earned one, but it seemed like the right way to ask for a favor. "It's about Bruno."

"Uh-huh."

Not mad. Not annoyed. Just processing the bad news.

"I can't let it go, Patrick."

"Yeah, I've been getting that impression."

"I keep seeing her face. Not that I can actually look at it anymore. You have to admit, it's pretty bizarre that the original and the copy of the subway video both got wiped out yesterday."

"Well, if I have to admit it, then . . ."

She smiled. That piece of banter was a staple in their repertoire. "I'm serious about cashing in a chip, Patrick."

"And I was serious when I told you I'll do what I can. I already sent out an e-mail to the West Point crowd. No one's heard anything. I got the impression they were kind of freaked out that I was even asking. It probably seemed a little out of the blue."

"I got an address for Gretchen." Susan's sister was two years older than Susan. A quick search had turned up a marriage license and an address. "She's living out on Long Island. Nassau County," she added quickly, distinguishing it from more distant parts of the island. "Barely past Queens. It's only an hour by train."

"Gretchen's a junkie, McKenna. We go to her, and there's no telling what she'll try to drag us into."

"I know. She's also Susan's only living family member."

She knew he didn't want to go. She also knew he wasn't going to fight about it. Fifteen minutes later, they had purchased their Long Island Rail Road tickets and were ready to roll.

When the cabdriver completed the short ride from the Roslyn train stop to the address she'd given him, McKenna checked the house number against the slip of paper in her hand. "You're sure this is it?" she asked.

"I guess that would depend, miss, on your definition of the word '*it.*' If what you mean is whether this house is the place you want it to be, I guess that's for you to know and you to find out." He was obviously amused by the choice of words. "But if what you're asking me is whether this house is the property located at the street address that you provided upon entry into my cab, why, then, I can say definitely that yes, this is *it.* Now, are you going to pay the fare or keep asking me silly questions?"

Patrick answered before McKenna readied her verbal retort. "We're going to need you to wait," he said.

"As long as the meter's running."

"What an ass," McKenna said as they stepped out of the cab.

"Suck it down, M, or we'll end up stranded here. Can't exactly hail a taxi on Long Island."

He was not happy to be here.

They took in the house where Susan's sister supposedly lived. Two-story brick Tudor. Manicured lawn. Volvo sedan in the drive-way. Unless Gretchen was stealing this family's mail to fund her drug habit, McKenna couldn't imagine the connection.

Patrick gave the heavy brass knocker on the walnut door three sturdy raps. They heard a child's voice inside. "Mom. Moo-oooom. The dooo-oooor."

"Did that video game somehow bust your feet, Porter? See who it is. And if it's those Bible thumpers again, tell them even Jesus had his limits."

"Mo-om. It's not funny to make jokes about Jesus."

The boy who answered the door was about nine years old, give or take. He seemed frightened by the sight of a man on his porch but then softened when he saw McKenna. She spoke up first.

"Hi, there. No Bibles here, we promise. We're looking for a woman who used to be a friend of ours. Gretchen Hauptmann?"

"My mom's name is Gretchen. And her dad's name was George Hauptmann. But now her name is Henesy, just like mine."

McKenna had been so thrown off by the suburban perfection that she'd forgotten that the state's record of Gretchen's marriage to a man named Paul Henesy had been the item that led her to this address in the first place.

"Porter, who is it?" Gretchen was folding a towel when she ar-rived at the bottom of the stairs. Most people looked like a worse version of themselves after ten years. Not Gretchen. Gretchen looked the way she should have looked but couldn't a decade ear-lier. Her long dark hair was tied into a loose bun at the nape of her neck. She was dressed comfortably in a pair of blue jeans and a long purple T-shirt, but she still had the trim, athletic body she'd had in common with her sister, even as she tried to destroy it with drugs.

Patrick was the one to say it first. "You look good, Gretchen."

Her nod was barely perceptible. "I've got a phone number. E-mail. Hell, even a Facebook page."

"It's about Susan," McKenna said.

She stepped aside to invite them in.

CHAPTER TWENTY

Gretchen led McKenna and Patrick into a brightly lit living room but did not take a seat or invite her guests to do so. "The house is a mess right now. If I had known you were coming—"

McKenna had to search for any signs of imperfection. A few toys littered the floor. The throw pillows were scrunched into the corners of the sofa. Pizza crumbs were scattered across the glass coffee tabletop. An open box next to the corner bookshelf was half packed with CDs.

What was more apparent was the care that had been put into the room. The vase on that same bookshelf was color-coordinated with the unfluffed pillows. Silk rug. Leather chairs. Nice place.

"I can tell you want to ask," Gretchen said, "so I'll give you the short version. I'm clean. Have been for some time now—eleven years this December. I met Porter's father—my husband, Paul—in a program. He was more a recreational coke guy, not the garbage can I was."

McKenna ran the math in her head, wondering about the age of Gretchen's son, the timing of the pregnancy, whether it had been the thing that finally kept her clean.

"I was sorry to hear about your father's passing," Patrick said.

"Thanks, but we weren't exactly in touch anymore. Not like you two, I guess. Even after all these years?"

"Married," McKenna said, holding up her ring. "Five years already."

"Susan always said the two of you were meant to be." Did McKenna imagine the sarcasm?

"I've been thinking about Susan a lot lately," McKenna said. "I want to finally find out what happened to her, Gretchen. You see all these cases solved decades later. New DNA evidence. New witnesses. I want to look."

"You're not exactly the FBI."

"No, but I still have some contacts. And I learned a lot about investigations at the DA's office and as a reporter. Patrick will help."

"Will Scooby and Shaggy be there, too? Maybe get yourself a little Mystery Bus?"

Nope. Sarcasm was not imagined.

"McKenna's not asking for much," Patrick said. He was using what she referred to as his military voice. The one he used with the uniformed guards at work. The one he occasionally invoked at home if frustrated with her. Now he was using it to defend her. It was a voice that quietly projected command in the culture that he and Gretchen knew. McKenna understood that world better now than most nonmilitary people, but she would never be an insider.

McKenna tilted her head, trying her best to appear sympathetic. "I figured you'd be the one the police would have called with any new information."

"Well, I haven't heard squat. Not that I'm confident the police would even tell me."

"You're her closest relative."

"You know what I was like back then. Not to mention whatever my father probably told them, which would've been even worse."

Susan had filled McKenna in on the Hauptmann family dynamics that night on the kitchen floor, one hand still gripping the phone after the call from her father. The General used to joke openly that he'd wanted to name the girls George and Mercedes. George for

Gretchen, because he'd wanted a namesake son over a daughter; and Mercedes for Susan, because he'd wanted a new car over a second girl.

Their mother, Carol, had done her best to protect them from his poison, at least in the beginning. Susan had early memories of dark looks across the table, followed by screaming matches behind her parents' closed bedroom door. But the General wasn't a man who could be reasoned with. He listened to complaints, in the sense that he could repeat them back—word for word, usually to mock the sentiment—but he lacked the empathy to truly understand another person's perspective.

One summer Susan had taken to calling him General YB and refused to explain the significance. Her sister knew that YB stood for "Yes, but." Each of the girls at various times in their lives had steeled themselves to have a true conversation with the General. They would strategize their talking points, searching for the softest possible expression of the deepest emotions. No matter how well— and how tactfully—they articulated a perspective, being careful to say nothing that might make the General feel judged, their father would always respond with a quick "Yes, but—."

Susan had all her reasons for wanting to go to a private liberal arts college. "Yes, but nothing prepares you for leadership like a military education." Her sophomore year in high school, she wanted to spend a semester as an exchange student in Denmark. "Yes, but it's the pinnacle of privileged indulgence. You should be at home, working."

The way Susan told the family history, for her first twelve or so years, Susan and Gretchen had been bonded by their shared experiences in the Hauptmann household. But when Gretchen hit high school, that bond began to tear. It started with the death of their mother. For whatever reason, the girls developed different ways of responding to their father's solo parenting.

Susan was the more rebellious one, at least initially. She was a good student but had no interest in history, world events, American exceptionalism, or any of the things that engrossed her father. She broke curfew to hang out with her friends and spent the rest of her time looking at fashion magazines and watching reruns of 1970s sit-coms.

Gretchen, on the other hand, tried to please their father. She was one of the few girls in their high school's JROTC, the junior version of the Reserve Officers' Training Corps. She was at the top of her class, both academically and athletically. She took her father up on every opportunity to know his work and his colleagues, practically deposing them about the details of military life and the doors it could open for a promising young person. She was gunning for a spot at West Point, not that anyone doubted she would get it. She was the heir apparent.

"It used to drive me crazy," Susan had confessed the night McKenna found her in tears in their apartment. "The way Gretchen kissed up to him. When Mom died, it was supposed to be the two of us against the General. He'd have to learn how to take care of us. But then she took his side. It was like she abandoned me. And he didn't have to try anymore with me because he had *her*."

Then the high school principal found a plastic bag of pot in the heir apparent's locker. The General had been so convinced of his daughter's innocence that he insisted on a fingerprint test of the bag. The lab found not only Gretchen's prints but also cocaine residue. The drug test that the General forced on his daughter revealed not only pot and cocaine but also speed and LSD.

A year later, the ex-boyfriend who tipped off the principal mysteriously had all of his college applications withdrawn and twelve thousand dollars of credit card debt racked up in his name.

Revenge was probably sweet, but it hadn't saved Gretchen from her first trip to rehab, nor had it made that trip her last.

"I used to give Gretchen so much shit for trying to suck up to him," Susan had told McKenna that same night. "But look what it did to her. It broke her. And the minute she was out of the picture and he set his sights on making me the golden child, what did I do?"

Off to West Point she went.

Though McKenna had gathered that life with General Haupt-mann wasn't easy, Susan always seemed to bring an annoyed but ultimately optimistic eye to the relationship with her father, choos-ing to believe that the tough, gruff, antiquated geezer had a softness that only his daughters knew. Gretchen fostered no such fantasies.

"Did Susan tell you about my arrest?"

McKenna could tell from Patrick's blank expression that he hadn't known, either.

"Oh yeah. Got caught in Alphabet City with enough crack that they accused me of intent to distribute. I used my one phone call to ask Dad to bail me out. You know what he said? 'I accepted a long time ago that you would wind up in jail or dead. It's time for you to go your own way, Gretchen.' And then he just hung up, leaving me there to get strip-searched, not to mention ogled and pawed by the guards and one of my new roommates. I remember every word of that call, because it's the last time we spoke. But you know what? It's true what they say—you've got to hit rock bottom. I was looking at ten years in prison, but I got lucky. The case kept getting pushed over for trial, and in the meantime, I cleaned up—started working a program. Finally swung a plea deal for rehab and probation at the state level. Two months before Susan—before she was gone. Guess she didn't want you guys knowing about her jailhouse sister. Those cops who investigated her disappearance sure knew. I'd been clean nearly a year by then, but they never treated me as anything but a junkie. I guess that's what I was."

The next half hour felt more like a therapy session than an unex-pected drop-in from two old acquaintances as Gretchen devolved into a monologue about the dysfunction in the Hauptmann family. How her father could be kind to everyone except the wife and children he saw as nothing but an extension of himself. How his love—if you could call it that—had always been conditional. How the estrangement from him had finally been her key to getting clean.

"Susan did everything she could to become the child he'd always wanted. It was never enough. He at least talked to her—unlike *moi*, the bad-seed daughter. But she could never really please him. No one could."

"I'm glad you've found a better life for yourself," McKenna said. She gave Patrick an apologetic look. Coming here had been a mistake. Hearing the details of a broken relationship between a dead man and his daughters was the kind of psychological drama Patrick hated. Searching for a way to end the conversation, McKenna pulled a folded sheet of paper from her purse. "Do you recognize this? It's a logo for a group called People Protecting the Planet."

Gretchen shook her head. "Susan wasn't much of an environmentalist. Why?"

"I'm not sure. Just something I'm working on."

In her periphery, McKenna noticed Gretchen's son craning his neck around the corner of the hallway, eavesdropping. He tucked his head back like a surprised turtle, then poked it out again. "Mommy, is Daddy coming to see us tonight, or is he staying at his new house?"

"We'll talk about that later, Porter." Gretchen offered an embarrassed smile. "Paul and I are going through some changes right now. I'm afraid I need to ask you to go. The truth is that I know nothing more about what happened to my sister today than I did ten years ago."

She led the way to the front door, but only Patrick stepped outside.

"Sorry," McKenna said, "but just one more thing. What happened to Susan's stuff?" She immediately recognized the irony of saying "sorry, but" to a woman who had been raised by General YB.

"What stuff?" Gretchen asked.

"Your dad waited six months, I think, and then packed her apartment up."

"I don't know. Ask Marla, his nurse. She took care of him at the end. She also got a huge inheritance, unlike, oh, his daughter. Like I said, the old man could be kind to people who weren't related to him. If anyone would know, it would be her."

"You were really that estranged?" McKenna asked.

"Jesus, did you not listen to anything I just said?"

McKenna asked for Marla's full name and number. Gretchen didn't hide her frustration but excused herself to the kitchen and returned with a document whose pages she was flipping through. "I was served a copy of the will as a courtesy. Nice, huh? Here you go." McKenna jotted down the information—Marla Tompkins, a Manhattan phone number—and thanked Gretchen once again.

Patrick was waiting for McKenna on the porch. As she joined him, she promised Gretchen she'd call if she learned anything more about Susan's disappearance.

"Don't," Gretchen blurted. "I mean, I wish you wouldn't. I wish you wouldn't call, but mostly I wish you wouldn't do any of this. Just let it be."

"Don't you want to know what happened to your sister?"

"You don't get to say that to me, McKenna. Who are you? You were roommates for, what, a *year* before you decided that even the good Hauptmann girl was a little too wild for your taste. You thought you were some hotshot DA when Susan disappeared, and where did that get any of us? You don't think I know what happened to you at work? You think you can solve this like some cold case on television and try to get your career back? And, Patrick, don't even get me started on you. I'm her only family now. I'm the one who gets to say that it's okay to move on. And I've moved on."

Patrick was the one to speak up first. "We didn't handle this well, Gretchen. Try to enjoy the rest of your night."

McKenna could tell he was speaking to her just as much as to Gretchen. She couldn't let it lie, though. "Back then you told the police she wanted to get away from your father. To start another life. I think you were telling yourself that because you wanted to believe she was okay. If she is, don't you want to know that? Don't you want her to see how well you're doing and to meet her nephew?"

"See, you just don't get it, do you, McKenna? If you really knew my sister, you'd realize that if she were alive—if she were here— she'd know exactly where I was and how I was doing. She would know about her nephew. Hell, she'd probably have Porter's schedule down to the minute. She'd know that you were here right now. And yet I haven't heard one thing from her in ten years. Either she's dead, or she's got a damn good reason to keep her distance. Do you seriously think that, after all these years, you can take care of something that Susan Hauptmann couldn't? Please. Don't."

As they walked toward the cab, they heard the bolt lock behind the closed door.

CHAPTER TWENTY-ONE

Scanlin should have anticipated the knock, but it annoyed him all the same. "Come in," he called out, trying to hide the frustration in his voice.

Jenna had lived in this house for twenty years. When Melissa was home, their daughter had walked in and out as if it were still her home, too. Now she insisted on knocking, no matter how many times he told her not to.

"Sorry I'm late, but we better get moving." She looked at her watch. "They won't let us in after eight."

The nursing center had told them four months ago that it "would be for the best" if Scanlin timed his visits to see Melissa with their daughter. He had read somewhere that architects considered triangles the strongest base of support: something about symmetry aiding in the distribution of weight. He saw that in his own family. His visits to Melissa depended on all three points of their family triangle. Melissa no longer remembered him as her husband. But she remembered Jenna and understood in their daughter's presence that Scanlin was Jenna's friend. Without Jenna, he was a stranger to Melissa. And without Melissa, Jenna wanted nothing to do with him.

He realized that the scenario was a triangle only from his perspective. From theirs, did he matter at all?

"Dad, are you coming?" While he was pulling on his jacket, she had stepped into the dining room. "Big surprise. Work. Well, at least the table's being used for something. God knows you never had dinner at it."

She laughed, but he knew that the joke was based in the ugly truth. He had been a shitty father. He'd been always working or trying to live the hotshot life he enjoyed more in his imagination than in reality. Nice suits. Cologne. Beautiful wife. Dinners at favorite restaurants, talking up the waiters who'd worked there since he first trotted in with Melissa on his arm.

He hadn't left any time for Jenna. He'd seen the parenting duties as Melissa's domain, something to be done while he was at work.

Now his daughter's comment made him self-conscious about the files sprawled across the table. He did a quick tidying of the documents, putting the coworker's DD5 on top as a reminder. He was a good cop. He'd always been a good cop. Even then.

But he hadn't pulled at every thread. Given where he was in his own life ten years ago, he had seen Susan Hauptmann primarily as her father's daughter. One daughter was a drug addict, and the other daughter was a runaway. But she was an adult woman with no boyfriends and yet an open box of condoms in her nightstand. Maybe Jared Klein—the co-worker who'd said Susan had put the moves on him—really had seen another side of her. Maybe that was the side that had put her in danger. Maybe Scanlin had missed it.

He had been so convinced that Susan left town to get a fresh start away from her father. Even if he'd been right, what if it had been Jenna? What if Jenna—instead of pretending he did not exist when she first learned of her mother's diagnosis—had walked away in disgust, leaving without a trace? He would want someone to find out what happened to her.

Susan Hauptmann's parents were both gone. Her sister was a screwup. If someone were going to search for the girl, it would have to be Scanlin.

CHAPTER TWENTY-TWO

Marla Tompkins had a broad caramel-colored face. Deep lines were beginning to set in, but the retired nurse's most noticeable features were the dark freckles across her nose and the warm smile that greeted McKenna at the front door.

When McKenna had called the woman from the train back into the city and asked to meet with her, she had jotted down the address without realizing it should have been familiar.

She noticed the wedding ring on the woman's finger. "Thanks for seeing me, Mrs. Tompkins. I came here once with General Hauptmann's daughter Susan. I was very sorry to hear about his passing."

Susan's father had lived in the family's home near West Point, but kept a one-bedroom Upper East Side pied-à-terre in the city.

"Your friend's father was a very generous man. He knew things weren't easy for me after Harold—my husband—passed away. He always told me I had nothing to worry about, but it never dawned on me he would leave me an apartment of my own. Well, it's not mine yet. But it's going to be, and the executor of the estate saw no point in evicting me in the meantime."

"I'm wondering where I can find any of Susan's belongings that General Hauptmann may have had. Susan's older sister, Gretchen, suggested that you might know."

"By the time I started to care for the general, he had already packed up most of his things, preparing for the end. That's the way he was. Very unsentimental about death. Stoic. He kept the basic necessities—a television, pots and pans and dishes. A couple of pictures of his wife on the nightstand. His personal belongings were already in storage."

"And after his death?"

McKenna remembered Susan's breakdown over the news that her father had cancer. They had spent nearly four hours downing every variety of vodka on ice at Pravda. McKenna could tell that Susan was unwavering in her commitment to get obliterated, but she had no idea why until Susan held up yet another shot glass: *To the General. He's human after all.*

McKenna had tried consoling Susan with the usual clichés about advancements in medical care, but she soon realized that Susan was crying more from anger than fear or sadness. She was angry because her father had managed to use his cancer as one more way to pressure her to join his firm. News of his illness would kill the effort before it was off the ground. The firm had secured respectable work for a new player, but it would never land the more lucrative government contracts without assurances that the man himself—or his daughter—would be around for the long haul.

And she was angry because she cared. Despite it all, she cared about her father and did not want him to die.

Mrs. Tompkins offered McKenna a seat in a leather recliner. "I was very surprised when he left it all to me. Not the entire estate, of course. He had his charities and whatnot. But I'll get this apartment and a bit of cash to help cover the maintenance."

"What about the things he put in storage? Are they available? I'd be happy to go through it to see if anything of Susan's—"

"I don't know precisely, but Adam would. Adam Bayne. Do you know him?"

"Of course." Adam was one of Susan and Patrick's classmates from West Point; he had been the closest thing Susan found to a boyfriend among the army crowd. Despite attempts to make their relationship work over the long haul, the two were strictly platonic by the time McKenna came on the scene. Susan used to joke that her relationship with Adam had been doomed the minute her father decided to call Adam "son." "If he's the General's son, that makes him my brother. Which means no more playing with his pickle." That was Susan.

Adam had stayed friends with Susan but had found a true mentor in her father. Unlike Susan, he had signed on to work at his firm. Adam may have been the one to extinguish any chance that she might join him there when he told her about pulling "tub monkey" duty in Afghanistan—peering out with an M-60 from behind hill-billy armor, playing rear guard for a private convoy in the exposed bed of a pickup. Susan had heard too many stories about the dete-riorating picture on the ground. She had no interest in heading back to the Middle East, even to help her father.

Now McKenna was wondering whether George Hauptmann's special relationship with Susan's ex-boyfriend had been one more step in the man's search for a legacy—from Gretchen to Susan to Adam.

"Adam's the executor. He was so close to the general; plus, they worked together and such. He took responsibility for going through the storage unit. I believe he kept a few mementos and some rec-ords from their business but got rid of most of it. He could tell you more."

McKenna thanked Mrs. Tompkins for her time and said she'd follow up with Adam Bayne. The woman stopped her before she left the apartment. "You saw Gretchen? How was she?"

"Very well," McKenna said. "Healthy. Happy. She has a beautiful son." She saw no reason to mention that Gretchen's husband was in the process of moving out.

"She visited him. Just once, shortly before he died. He was in terrible pain by then, but he was so happy to see her. I gave her his diary. He wasn't writing in it anymore, and it seemed like she should have it. I was hoping she'd come back. That maybe they'd made peace. But she never returned. Not even an appearance at the funeral." Mrs. Tompkins shook her head. What a shame.

It was just like Gretchen to not want anyone to know that she had found a single moment of softness for her dying father. Despite the estrangement, at least she had made one exception to say goodbye.

No one ever had that chance with Susan.

CHAPTER TWENTY-THREE

Carter watched the house from the curb in his rented Chevy Malibu. He had watched the house before. He knew the woman shared it with three other people—two female, one male. He knew that one of the women was currently at work as a desk clerk at the local U-Haul branch. He had seen a second woman leave fifteen minutes earlier on her miniscooter. That left two at most inside—the woman and the man who had recruited her. Or at least, according to Carter's client, the man had been led to believe he was recruiting her.

Because Carter had done independent research, he also knew about the house. He knew from property records that it was a three-bedroom, two-bathroom split-level ranch built in 1954. It belonged to the grandmother of Hanna Middleton, the girl on the scooter. Hanna had spent a year at the University of Oregon but now lived in this house in Brentwood with three of her friends. The grandmother had gone into a nursing home last July, perfect timing for Hanna to drop out of college and pursue other passions on Long Island.

Because Carter had already been inside, he knew the place was just how the grandmother must have left it, except for the attic's acquisition of agricultural fertilizer, diesel fuel, and a mess of chemicals that shouldn't be under one roof together.

He got lucky. The last remaining occupants of the house—the woman and the man—walked out the front door, got into an early-model Honda minivan, and drove away.

When he'd seen the woman yesterday on the PATH train, she'd been on alert. She had pretended to read her gossip magazine, but he was certain she knew precisely the number of people on that train with her, where they were sitting, and what they were wearing. Today she walked straight from the house to the car, her eyes only on her companion. Yesterday she hadn't wanted to be seen with the heavy-metal guy on the train. Today she was on home turf. She wasn't worried.

Once the minivan turned the corner, he moved quickly. He walked to the front door, duffel bag in his right hand. The bottom lock slipped easily with a pick. It was probably the same one Grandma had, back when no one bothered. Though the top lock was a more sophisticated bolt, they'd left without securing it. Easier entry for him, but their carelessness could be a sign that they'd be returning soon.

Thanks to their own handiwork, rigging the place for explosion was relatively simple. They'd lacked a couple of key ingredients, but he had what he needed in the duffel. The technical name for the fuse was an anti-handling device, but it was essentially a booby trap.

He took one last look at his masterpiece as he started down the attic steps. He knew he was crossing a line. He was no longer a mere observer. He was using tactics learned in another world.

They had crossed a line, too. He'd seen the evidence with his own eyes. If they didn't go into the attic—if they didn't handle the anti-handling device—they'd have nothing to worry about. And if they did? That was their decision, not his.

CHAPTER TWENTY-FOUR

Patrick was waiting for her with two seats at the bar at Union Square Cafe. Their favorite bartender asked if she wanted the usual. She gave him an enthusiastic yes. A minute later, Bombay Sapphire with a twist appeared in front of her.

While McKenna had been visiting General Hauptmann's nurse, Patrick had gone back to the apartment to change out of his suit into his usual weeknight fare of button-down shirt and blue jeans. She noticed he was already eating a salad.

"Sorry, I was starving. Your errand go okay?"

She updated him on her visit to Marla Tompkins. "I feel like I missed something. Like there was a question I should have thought to ask but didn't. I guess all I can hope for is that Susan's father held on to some of her things and that Adam might have them. Would you mind calling him in the morning to check?"

"No problem. Is that it?" he asked. "You seem upset."

"Sorry. It's just that you know you've had a bad day when Gretchen Hauptmann, of all people, looks at you like *you're* the selfish one."

"She didn't say you were selfish."

McKenna hadn't wanted to talk about their visit to Gretchen's house while they were in the cramped quarters of the train. She had hoped that the view of Nassau County whizzing past them to the steady rhythm of the car against the rails would calm her. Instead, the hour-long trip had given her time to fume over every aspect of the conversation.

"She accused me of looking for Susan to advance my own career. She can try to convince herself she's moved on and has her whole Volvo-driving-mommy life now, but I remember what she was like. She'd call Susan at all hours of the day and night, and Susan would never know what she was going to get when she picked up: Gretchen bitching about their father, Gretchen strung out and barely able to talk, Gretchen so manic that Susan could set the phone down to go to the bathroom and her sister wouldn't even notice. And now *she's* judging *me*?"

McKenna initially had felt bad for not telling Gretchen what she'd seen on the subway video. But her instincts had been right: Gretchen wouldn't have believed it. What she hadn't expected was Gretchen to make her doubt her own loyalty to Susan. The accusations weren't entirely misplaced. The truth was, McKenna and Susan had been roommates for only a year, and McKenna had been the one to initiate the split. She had told Susan that it was because she was about to turn thirty and thought she should live by herself for the first time in her life. But the reason McKenna had splurged on her own place was to avoid admitting to Susan that she just couldn't live with her anymore. She was too frenetic. Constantly buzzing around. Always planning the next outing. Staying out until three in the morning or not coming home at all. She couldn't sit and watch television or read a book. She couldn't be alone. She couldn't just . . . be.

"Fine, she came off a little self-righteous, but is it really a surprise that she doesn't want to dig all this up again?" Patrick asked.

"A *little* self-righteous? And what was that comment about you?" Patrick said nothing, but McKenna could remember the acidic tone of Gretchen's voice. " 'Don't even get me started on you'? What was she talking about?"

"Who knows, and who cares? Gretchen's the kind of person who isn't happy unless everyone is as miserable as she is. I could tell the first time I met her. On campus visits, families would bring care packages and games and stuff, and Gretchen would just sit there and run Susan down in front of her classmates. She's a button pusher. She may be clean, but she's probably still totally fucked up. Maybe that's why her husband's bailing on her."

Such a cutting comment was out of character. Patrick was annoyed about the wild goose chase.

They were cut off by their bartender friend asking if they were ready to order. McKenna didn't need to look at the menu. Patrick might be starving, but she was too stressed out to eat. A half serving of pasta would be more than enough for her tonight.

Unfortunately, her dinner order said more than she'd meant to reveal. "You need to eat," Patrick warned. "And don't even try to convince me you ate lunch, because I know you never do when you're obsessing."

"I'm not obsessing."

"Um, hello? Train ride? Long Island? A sudden drop-in on Susan's sister? And then Susan's father's *nurse*? How far are you going to take this, McKenna?"

"It's only been two days," she said.

"Three. Three days when you've done nothing but read old newspaper articles about Susan and look at pictures of her from a decade ago. You don't think I noticed that you got up in the middle of the night to pull out yearbooks from my storage trunks? You haven't slept, and you're not eating, but you seem to have no problem drinking."

She didn't like the sound of the pissy sigh that escaped her throat, but she also didn't enjoy getting lectured.

Patrick placed a hand gently on her knee. "The woman on the subway was fast, and she was strong, and with your mind on the past lately because of the Marcus Jones anniversary, it's not surprising that you thought about Susan. She was a big part of your life when you were at the DA's office. But I saw the video, McKenna. And I knew Susan a lot longer than you did. It wasn't her."

"What about Dana suddenly losing all her files?"

"Computers crash all the time."

"The same day the girl who took the video had her phone tampered with?"

"She *thinks* it was tampered with. How many times have you accidentally deleted something from your phone? And you said yourself the girl sounded like a ditz. Try and take a break from this, okay? Eat a little. Get some sleep. Stop tearing the closets apart in the middle of the night." She returned his smile. "Things will look different in a couple of days."

Everything Patrick said made sense. As she watched him finish his salad, she made a point of nibbling some bread, just to prove she could.

P atrick was already removing his coat in the elevator.

"A strip tease? All for me?" She feigned a seductive tone.

"Nothing sexy about it. I'm exhausted. And I need to drop a—"

She held up her palm. "No. Don't even say it." She was well aware of his many sayings for what it was he needed to do in the privacy of their home, and she didn't try to hide her disgust. When they first got together, she was mortified by Patrick's comfort with physiological realities. Peeing with the bathroom door open. Smelling his underarms on a hot day. Farting, no question. When she found him fanning what he called his "undercarriage" in front of her air-conditioning unit after a bicycle ride, she finally had to say something. "How in the world do you expect someone to put up with this? Where's the romance? The mystery? You mean to tell me you'd still find me attractive if you walked in here to find me doing something like that?"

"I don't believe in being anything but myself. Besides, I like the idea of walking in to find you doing all sorts of things you never planned on anyone seeing." It was a good line, and it had worked. For a while. For a few years, she had found his frankness charming. Now she was rolling her eyes.

As previously announced, Patrick was tired. He crashed as soon as they hit the bed. But she was high from running around all night. She was also more than a little buzzed from her martini and the bottomless glass of wine that had accompanied her pasta.

Patrick reached for her as she slipped out of bed. "Don't. You promised."

She hadn't promised, but it wasn't Susan's case that she wanted to work on. Her book proposal wasn't getting anywhere. Maybe if she made some progress on it, her thinking would be clearer. She didn't bother turning on the living room lights as she flipped open her laptop. She worked best this way. She'd written at least half of her novel while drunk between bouts of crying on the sofa, just her and the dim illumination of her computer screen.

She reread what she had written the previous day. *It was the gun.*

No shit, it was the gun. She had been so damn proud of her investigative skills for tracing that stupid gun. The serial number. The hit in the ATF database. Hell, even when she realized the eleven-year-old connection between Scott Macklin and the gun, she hated the implications but felt certain she had uncovered a truth that would have remained buried without her industriousness.

Only problem was, she was wrong. How in the world had she been wrong?

Her fingers flew above the keyboard as she recalled the story of that damn gun.

*T*he *serial number was a match. The Glock next to Marcus Jones's body had been seized by the NYPD eleven years earlier and scheduled for destruction as part of the city's Safe Streets program. Only four of the NYPD's 34,800 police officers had been assigned to that year's gun destruction project. And one of them was Scott Macklin.*

Coincidence? Impossible.

I brought the information to my supervisor, Will Getty. We had to take the evidence to the grand jury. It was a no-brainer.

But the funny thing about odds is that even if it's one in a million, there is a distinctive one, apart from the 999,999 others. There's always an ex-

ception. Some poor schmuck golfer gets struck by lightning in his backswing. A lucky waitress actually wins the Powerball. And eleven years after Scott Macklin worked the Safe Streets gun destruction program, he looked down the barrel of one of those guns that was supposed to have been liquefied.

For Macklin, the odds of being one of the cops who had unmonitored access to the guns scheduled for destruction in 1992 weren't one in a million. They were four in 34,800. Macklin was one of the four. That left three others.

I never stopped to think about the other three. Will Getty did.

One of the other cops on gun-smelting duty in 1992 was Don Whitman. By the time Macklin shot Marcus Jones, Whitman was already serving six to eight for selling tips, favors, and other forms of support to the Crips in their effort to dominate the Latin Kings in a deadly turf war during the late 1990s.

A cop on a gang payroll had been given access to truckloads of weapons slated for destruction. That at least one went missing no longer seemed shocking. It was inevitable. From a dirty cop to the Crips to the streets to Jones's hands over a decade later.

When Will Getty finally found James Low—the kid in the neighborhood who admitted selling the gun to Marcus—the truth became clear: I had accused a cop of murder and sent the city into race-based tensions and protests, all over a coincidence.

McKenna always wondered what would have happened if she'd stopped to think about the other three cops who'd had access to that gun. She could have been the one to prove that Marcus Jones had carried that Glock to the docks that night. She could have cleared Macklin of any suspicion in front of the grand jury, instead of running to a reporter with specious claims.

Those two weeks—after she'd gone to Getty and before she'd gone to Bob Vance—had been wasted. Instead of checking out the other Safe Streets officers, or at least pushing Getty to update her, she had treated his silence as conspiratorial. She had assumed that he was burying the evidence.

By then McKenna had known Patrick for three months. She con-

sidered asking his advice before going to the press, but he had worries of his own. It had been six months since a banner on the deck
of an aircraft carrier declared mission accomplished, but Saddam
Hussein hadn't been captured, and a suicide bomber had attacked
the UN headquarters in Iraq. There were rumors that the army—
struggling to fight two wars in the Middle East—was pulling retired officers back into active duty. McKenna's problems had seemed
minor in comparison.

She pulled her thoughts back to the book proposal. She knew the
facts cold. She suspected that she always would. But this book was
supposed to be more than facts. It was supposed to be the human
story behind the events. She needed to focus on the *people*.

While writing her novel, she'd thought of the characters as living,
breathing, sentient beings and had let them drive the narrative. If
she were going to write a book about the Marcus Jones shooting and
its aftermath, she would be a character, though not the only one.
Perhaps not even the main character.

She needed to write about Marcus, initially labeled a thug based
on his criminal history but who had been known in his neighborhood as Patches—the sweet but strange boy whose face was spotted
from a skin condition called vitiligo. She needed to write about
Marcus's mother, who once chased members of the 137th Street
Crew down Madison with a broom when she found out they were
pressuring thirteen-year-old Marcus to join their gang. McKenna
needed to write about Will Getty, of whom she'd assumed the worst
but who was simply being cautious with the investigation of a politically sensitive case.

And she needed to write about the man she had accused of perjury and murder. She pictured Scott Macklin's face and began to
type.

CHAPTER TWENTY-FIVE

I *never wanted to be the prosecutor who brought down a cop. If anything,*
I needed Scott Macklin to be vindicated. I became a prosecutor because I be-
lieved in a firm line between right and wrong. I wanted to help crime victims.
I wanted to punish bad people who did bad things. But a prosecutor is only
a lawyer. Though I had the legal knowledge and training to help the truth
navigate its way through the justice system, every single one of my cases relied
on police officers to educate me about the truth. They were the ones who
questioned witnesses, interrogated suspects, and gathered physical evidence. If
I couldn't trust them, my job meant nothing.

And this wasn't just any cop. It was Scott Macklin. He was a member
of the Drug Enforcement Task Force of the Narcotics Division when I
was trying drug cases. That meant I saw him more than other cops. He'd
been in the grand jury room with me at least thirty times, testified in five
of my trials, and come to my office for search warrants and legal advice
dozens of times. And it wasn't only about the work with him. He perused
the frames on my office walls—the college and law school degrees, the cer-
tificate commemorating my time as a clerk for a federal judge, the absence
of any personal photographs. One day he asked if I was married, quickly
apologizing if he was being inappropriate. I assured him it was fine, but
no, I wasn't married. He told me that love had changed his life. It became
a running joke. Whenever he was at the courthouse, he'd pass my office

door: *"You're. Still. Here. You need to leave this office if you're going to find love."*

He talked to anyone who would listen, including me, about his gorgeous wife, Josefina, and his new stepson, Thomas. Then one day he came to my office to tell me he was moving out of Narco into a new federal-state team formed through Homeland Security. He might not be around the drug unit so much.

I made some lame joke about him movin' on up to a badass Homeland Security gig with the feds. Then he abruptly changed the topic. He asked me, "speaking of the federal government," if I had learned anything about immigration law during my judicial clerkship. When I said that I hadn't but had taken a course in law school, he closed my office door and told me that he was worried about some "complications" with Josefina's legal status inside the country. Complications. *I remember that word in particular because his voice broke when he said it. Her young son was at risk of being deported. He looked away from me, trying to regain his composure, but his emotions failed him. He shook his head in frustration and wiped away the tears starting to pool in the corners of his eyes. I offered him a Kleenex from my purse. I also wrote down the name and number of an immigration lawyer I knew from school.*

Neither of us ever spoke of that day again, not even after I accused him of lying about Marcus Jones.

He trusted me. He talked to me like a friend, and he trusted me. I needed to believe cops, but I really needed *to believe this one.*

Dammit. Now she was the one wiping away a tear. That moment in her office had gotten to her. Her memory of the details was fuzzy at best—something about Josefina entering the United States lawfully but her son being brought into the country later—but she remembered Macklin breaking down. He didn't want to lose the family he'd only recently found. He didn't want Josefina to get in trouble. He made too much money to qualify for free legal aid and not enough to retain a private lawyer.

She'd never seen a man cry, let alone a man like Macklin. He was at least fifteen years older than she was. Six-one, probably 220, he had a square head and thick hands like two baseball gloves. She had wondered whether he might resent her later for witnessing him in that state. She felt like she had emasculated him in some way. That night after work, she had talked to Susan about it, thinking that she must have seen men in vulnerable moments during her time in the army.

Susan had told her that men moved past their emotions. Though McKenna was sitting in the bar that night, reliving and question- ing every second of that brief office interaction, Macklin was a man, and men, Susan explained, didn't pore over every millisecond of every human encounter. Just then McKenna's cell phone had rung—an incoming call from a lawyer she had just started seeing. When she rejected the call, Susan reiterated her point: "See now? If the tables were turned, and you had been the one calling him, you'd spend the rest of the night wondering why he didn't pick up, what he was doing, and what you'd done wrong. A man won't do that, not even a wussy man like Nature Boy. Nature Boy will just hang up and assume you'll call him back later. We could stand to learn a few things from men."

Nature Boy. Susan never seemed to approve of any of McKenna's potential suitors—except Patrick, of course. She called poor Jason Eberly "Nature Boy" because he was a lawyer for an environmental nonprofit. A noble choice by any measure, but the nickname did manage to sum up Jason's penchant for reminding everyone that he was more benevolent than they. He'd openly note that it was only through a loan forgiveness program that he was able to work for a nonprofit. When private lawyer friends would complain about an unreasonable client or nightmare partner, he'd say things like "That's why I'm glad I work for a cause." McKenna had nothing against his chosen cause, but Susan was right: Jason reeked of do- gooder-ness.

Jason. Benevolent, noble, earth-loving Nature Boy. If he was still working for environmental causes, he might know something about the organization whose button had been on the subway woman's backpack.

She opened Google and searched for Jason Eberly. Up popped a slew of information about an up-and-coming teen singer. Who knew? She tried again, searching for "Jason Eberly attorney." She found a hit at the website for the law firm of Walker Richardson & Jones. It was one of the ten largest firms in the country.

She clicked on the link. Gone were goatee and shaggy hair. From the looks of his closely shorn head, he'd lost most of his hair entirely. According to the bio, he was a new partner at the firm and had counseled clients on hundreds of transactions and litigation matters across all industries, nationally and globally, including chemical refining, oil and gas, mining, heavy manufacturing, and toxic torts. So much for saving the planet.

She jumped at the feeling of a hand on her shoulder.

"Patrick. Sorry, you scared me. Did I wake you?"

"My alarm went off. You've been up all night?"

She hadn't noticed the sunlight beginning to make its way into the living room. "I was writing."

"Looks to me like you're surfing the Internet. Who's Jason Eberly?"

"A lawyer I used to—"

"Oh, wait. That's the guy you were dating when we first met, right?"

She knew how it looked. How many stories had she heard about extramarital affairs that began with an innocent "I wonder whatever happened to so-and-so" Google search? First comes Facebook, then comes Betrayal.

But her husband's expression wasn't jealous. He looked tired. And worried. And at least a little angry. He was looking at her and remembering all those nights when she drank too much, ate too little, and couldn't sleep. She didn't want him to think she was going back into the dark place that had kept them apart for so long.

"I really was working on the proposal. Then I realized I need to produce something for the magazine. I thought I could do a story about these people who are trying to reduce their carbon footprints to zero. One guy even stopped using toilet paper for a year. I thought Jason might know something about the movement. Turns out he's gone to the dark side." She rotated the laptop in his direction, making clear she had nothing to hide.

He took a quick look at the lawyer's head shot. "Guess I don't have anything to worry about there."

"Never," she said, arching her neck back and giving him a soft peck on his navel.

"Cold face," he said, giving her hair a quick stroke. "I need to get to the museum a little early today. The queen of Jordan is supposed to be in. Can you grab a little more sleep before work?"

She nodded. She was tired, and the reception desk at Walker Richardson & Jones wouldn't pick up until nine.

"You'll remember to call Adam Bayne today?" she asked. "See if he still has Susan's father's stuff?"

"I really wish you'd rethink this. Last night it was Gretchen on Long Island, then the old man's nurse. Look at you. You're already exhausted. Just give it a rest, okay?"

"I just want to see if Adam has any of her things. If there's nothing there, I'll let it lie." At least for a while, she told herself.

He assured her he would make the call, but she could tell he wasn't happy about it. She climbed back into bed, working her way into the warmth Patrick had left under the blankets.

When Patrick kissed her on the cheek before he left, his lips felt soft and he smelled like toothpaste. She kept her eyes closed, pretending to have found sleep.

CHAPTER TWENTY-SIX

The slam of Scanlin's coffee mug against his desk was harder and louder than he'd intended. One desk over, Ricky Munson—always trying to earn a reputation as the squad's funny boy—couldn't resist a comment. "Whoa, whoa, whoa. Stop the clock. Haven't you heard that it's 'be kind to dishes' day?"

There was a reason Munson hadn't yet achieved squad-comedian status.

Scanlin had slammed the mug for a reason, and the reason was that people were stupid. They were stupid, and they were assholes. Sometimes they were both. He'd just gotten off the phone with some finance guy whose in-home chef was found dead in the family townhouse the previous day. Odds of homicide were low, but thanks to an ambiguous bump on the woman's head, Scanlin had to wait for official word from the medical examiner before releasing the crime scene.

It had been under twenty-four hours since the woman's body had been wheeled away—a woman who'd cooked for this d-bag's family for sixteen years. And the man wasn't even in the city. He was calling from East Hampton, natch.

Didn't matter. He insisted on a guarantee that his caterers would have access to the kitchen the following weekend. The best part was when he tried to defend himself against Scanlin's suggestion that his priorities might be a bit *off*. "I'll have you know we treated Rosalyn as family, Detective. She even stayed overnight in the pool house when she cooked for us in the summer."

When Scanlin slammed the cup on his desk, maybe he was picturing the guy's skull.

Now he welcomed the distraction of the delivery he had just received from the Records Department. He had reached out to Jared Klein, Susan's former coworker who had mentioned her late-night attempt to turn work into pleasure. Klein remembered little about the night beyond what he'd said during the original investigation, but after some pressure, he repeated his suspicion that he had seen an entirely different side to Susan's personality. "She was always such a—" He stopped himself from using the word he was undoubtedly thinking. "She was, you know, hard. Tough. Obviously came from a man's world. She was fun, always trying to fit in, not like a feminazi or anything. But not a *seductress*. More like a raunchy kid sister. That night? God. I admit I still think about it sometimes."

Maybe Klein realized it was more than a tad creepy to be fantasizing about a missing woman, because that was all he had to say about Susan.

The documents on Scanlin's desk were copies of any and all reported incidents within a block of Susan's building in the three weeks preceding her disappearance. It was the kind of step he should have taken at the time, but he couldn't swear that he had. Neighborhood canvass, yes. A search for incidents involving her or her apartment, yes. But a three-week record search? Maybe not. Neighbors occasionally saw male guests coming and going at Susan's apartment. Maybe one of them had gotten a parking ticket or had witnessed a neighborhood altercation.

As Scanlin flipped through the pages, he realized why he may have skipped the step ten years earlier. In densely packed Manhattan, a whole lot of podunk idiocy went down in a three-week period. A shoving match at Taco Bell when two customers simultaneously reached for the same root beer spigot. A couple of graffiti cleanups, courtesy of AmeriCorps, because the complainants had uttered the magic phrase "gang symbols." One week must have seen particularly good weather because reports of ranting homeless people skyrocketed. A whole slew of noise complaints but remarkably few parking infractions. Were meter maids slacking, or had people figured out that even sky-high garage rates were better than the city's $265 parking tickets?

Scanlin flipped back to two noise complaints that had originated from Susan's apartment building. They were both called in by the same tenant—Vera Hadley, apartment 402. Same floor as Susan, who was in 406. The first complaint was about a loud stereo from the apartment downstairs at 10:40 P.M. Twenty minutes later, Hadley called back to say that the music had stopped, "no thanks to you people." The second complaint came in two days before Susan was last seen at the gym. According to Hadley, a man and a woman were screaming inside apartment 404. For reasons that weren't clear, the call was logged in as possible DV—domestic violence— triggering a response from patrol officers. When police arrived, the hallway was quiet, no one answered the door at 404, and Hadley had no further information to offer. Call closed.

Scanlin shifted his attention to a separate pile of documents: summaries from the neighborhood canvass conducted after Susan was reported missing. No response at 404 over the course of four different days, at four different times. The tenant on the lease was a man named Paul Roca. According to the mailman, Roca had left "last week," and his mail was being held for a month.

If the blockhead patrol officer talking to the mailman had thought to ask whether Roca had left before or after the next-door neighbor had disappeared, he hadn't thought to make a note of it. A stupid mistake. And yet Scanlin had let it slide.

He did a quick search for Paul Roca. Still at the same address. Arrested six years earlier for hitting a girlfriend. The charges had been dismissed without prosecution but were enough to pique Scanlin's curiosity.

Mr. Roca was worth a visit.

CHAPTER TWENTY-SEVEN

McKenna's love life had never been noteworthy until she met Patrick. Two college boyfriends. A shack-up for the last two years of law school, more to save rent than as an audition for marriage. She was starting to get into a relationship with Jason Eberly, aka Nature Boy, when Patrick came around and ruined her for anyone else. Until she met him, breaking up meant exactly that. No polite holiday cards. No phone number stored in the cell. No staying friends. She and Patrick kept going back to each other until they finally got it right.

When she called Jason that morning, it was the first time she had spoken to him in over a decade. She used her maiden name, and even then, there was an awkward silence on the other end of the line. Too composed to ask, "Who?," Jason obviously needed a moment to place the name. There was another long pause when she asked to see him. "McKenna, I'm, um—I'm very flattered, but I'm married. Two kids. I don't know how my wife would feel about—"

She resisted the urge to blurt out, "In your dreams!" She was the one who'd broken it off. "Oh, I should have explained. It's about a group called People for the Preservation of the Planet—for a story I'm working on. I work at *New York City* magazine now."

"Given that you called me at the firm, you probably know I'm not at the epicenter of the conservation movement anymore. I sold out to the man."

"Really, I just want to pick your brain. Fifteen minutes. You can bill me if you want."

From the looks of his office, she was thankful he hadn't taken up her offer of payment. His sleek glass desk was the size of a queen bed. Floor-to-ceiling windows offered an unobscured view of Central Park. He greeted her with a quick hug, more a pat on the back than an embrace. "You look great, McKenna. Getting out of the hellhole that is legal practice must be the secret to the fountain of youth."

"The law thing seems to have suited you well." She was telling the truth. Where he'd been a bit shy and goofy-looking as a younger man, he now appeared confident and comfortable in his own skin.

"You're interested in the P3s?"

"Is that what they call themselves?" she asked.

"Guess it's supposed to sound more hard-core, reminiscent of a gang name like the 18th Streeters. They're an offshoot of the Environmental Liberation Front, or ELF. Even ELF is considered an eco-terrorism group, but the rumor is that P3 was formed by a couple of guys who found ELF's practices a bit too . . . tame."

She couldn't imagine how Susan could be connected to such a group. "How big are they?"

"I don't know a lot about them," he said. "The groups I associated with stayed away from ELF. And we were just beginning to hear whispers about a more radical offshoot. These days, the only time I give groups like that any thought is if they're causing problems for my clients."

"What kind of problems?"

"Protesting a nuclear power plant, trespassing to collect water samples they hope will validate some conspiracy theory about toxins. But some of these groups go off the deep end. Bomb threats. Chaining themselves to trees scheduled for a chainsaw. Burning down new construction. Breaking animals out of research laboratories."

"Are they national or located in a certain region?"

"Like I said, I'm no expert. Are you focusing specifically on the P3s, or is your article about ecoterrorism in general?"

She tucked her hair behind her ears—an action that Susan once called her "tell" when trying to teach her poker. "Ecoterrorism in general, but I've found that focusing on one example, then placing it in a broader context, can be really effective."

"Ah, right, like your article on Judge Knight. Excellent job, by the way. Well, if the People for the Preservation of the Planet are going to be your next Big Pig, I think I've got the right contact for you. I had to hammer out a document subpoena with an FBI agent last year when one of our cosmetic clients was targeted by activists for testing mascara on rabbits."

McKenna knew that her face revealed her disgust.

"Never gave any thought to where your makeup comes from, huh? Anyway, the agent knew this ecoterrorism stuff backward and forward. I could give her a call and grease the wheels. Maybe you can get a sit-down."

He dialed a number and put his phone on speaker. Four rings. "You've reached Special Agent Jamie Mercado."

At the beep, he picked up the handset. "This is Jason Eberly. We worked on the . . ." He said the first half of the name of a well-known cosmetic company, then smiled at McKenna. "That matter involving the rabbit research last year. I have a friend here—McKenna Jordan with *New York City* magazine. She's been research-ing a group called People for the Preservation of the Planet. She was hoping to get some background information, and I thought of you." He left his number and asked for a return call.

McKenna was thanking him for his time when his phone rang. "Well, that was quick," he said, looking at the caller identification screen. "This is Jason. Thanks for calling me back so quickly, Agent Mercado. I've got McKenna right here. I'm going to put you on speaker, if that's okay."

"Ms. Jordan, this is Jamie Mercado with the FBI. I'm going to need you to come into the field office to see me. We're at 26 Federal Plaza. You can check in on the twenty-third floor."

McKenna could tell by the tone of the agent's voice that she was not offering a friendly sit-down for assistance with an article.

"I appreciate the offer, Agent Mercado, but would tomorrow work for an appointment? I want to make sure I'm thoroughly prepared so I can make the best use of your time."

"Am I correct that you have been investigating the People for the Preservation of the Planet? Known as the P3s?"

"I wouldn't call it investigating. I've been researching an article."

"And how exactly did you end up focusing on that group?"

"I don't know what you mean."

"I can play back Jason's message if necessary. He said you were interested specifically in the P3s."

"Is there something wrong, Agent?"

"Like I said, Ms. Jordan, I'm going to need you to meet me at the field office. And just to be clear, I can get a grand jury subpoena if one is required. There is no privilege that protects journalists from testifying."

McKenna couldn't imagine what this FBI agent thought she could possibly offer. It looked like she would find out soon enough. "I'll be there in fifteen minutes."

CHAPTER
TWENTY-EIGHT

As Scanlin approached apartment 404, he heard the repetitive thump-thump-thump of generic dance music. He rapped the base of his fist against the front door to the beat, then heard the volume drop. A voice behind the door yelled, "Wrong apartment, man."

"Police. Just a couple quick questions, Mr. Roca."

Roca was tying his black silk robe when he opened the door. Scanlin was overpowered by the oaky smell of cologne.

"Sorry," Roca offered as he turned to primp his hair in a full-length mirror just inside the entrance. "Running late for a date. The smell fades fast. I swear."

Roca didn't seem interested, but Scanlin flashed his badge out of habit. A quick look around the studio apartment revealed more tasteful choices than Scanlin would have expected, given the first impression. Natural wood floors. White walls. Neutral furniture. What Melissa would have called "pops" of color from matching pillows and accessories. Had to be either a girlfriend's or a decorator's touch.

"You sure you're at the right place?" Roca asked. "Can't think of anything police would need here."

"It's an old case. Taking a new look. You remember Susan Hauptmann?"

Roca shook his head immediately, then paused as the name sank in. "Oh yeah. That's the girl from next door. What happened with that?"

Scanlin shrugged. "That's why I'm here. We never talked to you back then."

Roca laughed nervously. "You're kidding me, right? That was, like, eight years ago."

"Ten."

"Talk about taking your time." Roca walked to a double-wide closet and began flipping through a row of neatly hung dress shirts. "What do you need to know?"

"Did you know her?"

"No. I mean, by sight, yeah. Exchanged pleasantries in the hallway, that kind of thing. But I didn't even know her name until after everyone was looking for her."

"You were out of town when that happened."

Roca squinted, searching his memory. "That's right. Got sent to L.A. on a client project for over a month. When I got back, the posters were still up. That kind of thing."

"Susan was a pretty girl," Scanlin said. "*Really* pretty. Liked to date, from what I heard."

"Yeah, I'd see her come and go with guys. Girls, too. You know. Social, like that."

"How about you? She never came or went with you?"

"This has to be a joke. Seriously, is someone punking me?"

Scanlin took out his badge again so Roca could get a better look. "No joke. Just crossing all the T's. Making sure we didn't miss anything. Turns out one of your neighbors heard you arguing in here with a woman two nights before Susan disappeared. Sounded to her like domestic violence. Lo and behold, after Susan disappears, you up and leave for a month. Then there's that pesky arrest you had for assaulting a woman a few years ago."

"That girl was crazy. She found lipstick on some cigarette butts in my garbage and started trashing the place. I was trying to calm her down, and she called 911 on me. You can't think—"

"I'm just trying to make sure the lady you were fighting with two nights before your neighbor disappeared wasn't Susan Hauptmann. So why don't you give me a name, and I'll be on my way."

"It was ten years ago. I have no fucking clue."

"So *think*, Roca. And I'll make it easy for you. It was November twenty-seventh, on Thanksgiving."

"Dammit. Fine, okay. Um, wait. I was gone by then. Figured I was starting the L.A. gig December first, I might as well make it down to Santa Fe to see my folks for Turkey Day. I left the day before. Hold up. Who called the police about this supposed argument at my place?"

Scanlin didn't respond.

"Was it that crazy bird in 402? Had to be. Now she's nearly deaf, but yeah, she was still calling the cops constantly back then. She was always getting the apartments mixed up. Apparently directional hearing wasn't a real strength."

Scanlin gave closer thought to the layout of the small complex. Four apartments on one floor. Five floors total. Two voices fighting inside an apartment. The echo of the stairway running floor to ceiling through the center of the building like a fire pole. Thanking the man for his time, Scanlin left Roca to his primping and crossed the hallway to apartment 402.

Her neighbor had been right: Vera Hadley was nearly deaf. She was also a hoarder. What probably began as small stacks of magazines, newspapers, collectibles, videotapes, out-of-season clothing— just waiting for the right moment to be sorted through—had grown into layers of padding throughout the apartment. From what Scanlin could see, the poor woman had enough free space to navigate from the entrance, to one empty spot on her sofa, to the kitchen, and—God willing—to a bathroom.

They'd been making progress since Scanlin had given up any semblance of speaking in a normal voice and begun screaming into her hearing aid. Yes, she remembered Susan Hauptmann from down the hall (followed by a saddened *tsk* and a shake of the head). Yes, she remembered frequently calling the police over the years. Yes, she supposed it was possible that if an argument had erupted in that "nice woman's" apartment, she might have attributed it to the "carouser" across the hall.

When he gave her the date of the noise complaint and asked what she recalled about the incident, he expected either a blank stare or a long recitation of every dispute she'd ever overheard. What he did not expect was the woman to stand up from her cubbyhole on the couch and say, "Let me get my notes."

CHAPTER TWENTY-NINE

Too familiar. Recast." McKenna remembered her editor's comment, red-penciled in the margin of the manuscript for *Unreasonable Doubt*. The note was in response to McKenna's depiction of an FBI agent who appeared at the local police precinct to exercise federal jurisdiction over the investigation.

But McKenna had met a few FBI agents in her time at the district attorney's office, usually when the feds were cherry-picking her best drug cases, and they'd all been straitlaced, clean-cut, and rigid. They had deep voices, didn't laugh, and favored midpriced suits from places like JoS. A. Bank. Just because it was a stereotype didn't mean it wasn't true.

But Jamie Mercado didn't fit the mold. She was petite, with long, dark, wavy hair and a full face of makeup, complete with cherry-red lipstick. Like agents McKenna had worked with in the past, she wanted answers, but instead of resorting to legalese and bureaucratic officiousness, Mercado leaned across the table toward McKenna, raising her voice in obvious anger. These were moves McKenna associated more with the NYPD than the FBI, and she had experienced them only from the other side of one-way glass.

"For a full-time reporter with a reputable magazine, you don't seem to know much about a topic you're supposedly investigating.

Not the name of a single person associated with the group. No information about the organizational structure or geographic focus. Not the details of even *one* of their suspected anti-industry missions."

"I told you," McKenna said, "I just started looking into it."

She knew that any false statement to a federal agent—even outside a courtroom, whether she was under oath or not—was a felony. She was not required to offer information, and she could refuse to answer, but she had to ensure that every utterance from her mouth was true—at least technically.

"Yes, you've said that so many times, you're beginning to sound like a windup doll. So, fine. I went to college. I remember what it's like to write a paper. You think you have an idea, so you dig around a bit to see if you're interested, if there's enough material to merit a deeper search."

McKenna nodded in agreement. No falsity there.

The college Mercado was referring to would have been the University of Idaho. In a quick briefing from Jason Eberly, McKenna had learned that Mercado was a good and thorough agent who treated her hunt for ecoterrorists as a personal calling. With the resources of a large law firm and their corporate clients behind him, Jason had done some digging into Mercado's background to get a better sense of the woman who had been his bunny-blinding client's best ally against the protestors. After two years of full-time college, she took another four to graduate because she had to help raise her younger sister. Her father, a logger, went on disability after his chain saw hit a railroad spike that activists embedded in the trunk of a western red cedar in the Nez Perce National Forest.

"But from what I remember," Mercado continued, "you still have to get the idea from *somewhere*. A newspaper article. A comment made by a friend. A report on the radio. How did you come to hear about the P3s? They're one of the lesser known militant environmental activist groups."

"I don't always remember where ideas come from." Technically true.

"When you say you've just begun your research, what do you mean? What precisely have you done?"

McKenna could refuse to answer, but there was no privilege to avoid testifying if Mercado got a grand jury subpoena. And this was her opportunity to learn more about the P3s and why an FBI agent was so determined to talk about them.

"I'd be more comfortable sharing my work product if I knew you had a real need for it, Agent. My understanding is that the FBI is prohibited from engaging in general information gathering about political groups."

McKenna's lawyering skills weren't entirely rusty. The statement was perfect. An offer to cooperate. The reference to work product, suggesting she had something of value to offer. The not so veiled threat to expose the FBI's activities if they ran afoul of federal restrictions against domestic spying.

"You can rest assured that we don't gather intelligence against American citizens based on their exercise of First Amendment rights. Maybe if we did, I wouldn't need to question a private reporter for essential background information after a bomb comes close to wiping out an entire residential block."

McKenna felt the air leave her throat. She couldn't breathe. A *bomb*? When her mouth finally opened, she felt herself wanting to tell Mercado everything. The subway video. The P3 button on the backpack. McKenna's suspicion that the woman carrying the backpack was Susan Hauptmann. What had Susan gotten herself into? What had *she* gotten herself into?

Then she remembered all those interrogations she had watched from behind the one-way glass. Just as McKenna had chosen her words to convince Mercado to reveal her motivations, a good agent might say anything to test McKenna's resolve. How many times had she seen detectives lie to get a confession?

"What bomb?" she asked.

"An explosion in Brentwood—out near Islip—last night. We've managed to keep it quiet so far. The Long Island papers are calling it a suspected gas leak." Mercado pulled a photograph from a file folder and slid it across the table toward McKenna. The second level of the house was gone, replaced by shards of wood and drywall.

"The next-door neighbor's air-conditioning unit blew out of its casing. The expert tells me anyone within six feet of the epicenter would've evaporated into a 'pretty pink mist.' Those were his exact words—the kind of juicy tidbit you'd like for an article. It'll be a while before we can identify them or know the number of bodies."

McKenna had no way of verifying Mercado's story. Was the agent holding up her half of an information-exchange bargain, or laying on the details to give a lie more credibility?

"What about the neighbors?"

"Got lucky. We found some other bombing materials at the site, but those didn't ignite. Looks like the bad guys were building something and set it off accidentally. One of the surviving residents is a dumb little thing—barely drinking age, searching for an identity. Maybe thirty years ago she would've ended up with the Krishnas. Now she's a so-called 'environmental activist.' She shacked up with a group of older P3s. Denying any knowledge of the bombing materials, but . . ." She trailed off, as if everyone knew that denials were predictable, false, and temporary. "They had enough fertilizer to take out an entire warehouse when mixed with the right ingredients. We don't know the intended target, the date of the planned attack, or who else might be out there to complete the job. So I'm thinking that for a reporter who wants to do the right thing—a former prosecutor, to boot—that might be a good enough reason to answer a few questions."

McKenna slid her iPad from her bag. "You remember last weekend a woman pulled a teenager from the subway tracks at Times Square?"

Mercado nodded.

"A girl on the platform tried to get a cell video of it. The video's been deleted, but I managed to get this still shot of the woman's backpack."

"That's the P3 insignia," Mercado said.

"I didn't know that at first, but yes. I read a few articles online about the group and then went to Jason this morning to see if he could point me in the right direction."

"So you were just looking for the subway woman?" Mercado was clearly disappointed that McKenna didn't have a more ambitious research project in the works.

"That's all. I went to the kid who got rescued. I tried the MTA's security cameras. This was just one piece of a wild goose chase. If it makes you feel any better, I won't be writing about the bombing. Unless something goes down in the city, our magazine treats it like it didn't happen." McKenna didn't know the area well, but Brentwood was out in Suffolk County, forty-plus miles from Manhattan.

"And you still don't know who the woman with the backpack is?"

"No." The denial was legally permissible, since McKenna didn't *know* anything, but after the word came out, she wondered if she had done the right thing.

She could tell that Mercado believed her now. "When you were looking for your mystery girl, did any of these names come up?" The agent pushed another sheet of paper across the table.

McKenna didn't recognize any of the four names—three female, one male. "Who are they?"

Mercado heard the question but didn't answer.

"I told you, Agent, this isn't on my magazine's map. To be honest, most of what we print these days is what we call 'lifestyle.' What you'd probably call gossip. You won't see a story from me on the bombing."

"Doesn't mean I need to share my sandbox, though, does it? You mind showing yourself out?"

McKenna could tell there was no point in arguing. She wished the agent the best of luck with the investigation and made her way back to the reception area.

She knew from her time as a prosecutor that the federal building was closely monitored. Her descent in the elevator, her march through the lobby, her traipse to the next block would all be on screens for Mercado and her pals to view, if they were interested.

So McKenna gave them no reason to be interested. She did her best to appear calm. Indifferent, even. But mentally, she was repeating the four names Mercado had asked her about, over and over again, committing them to memory.

CHAPTER THIRTY

McKenna ducked into a deli two blocks from the Federal Building and quickly jotted down the names from Mercado's piece of paper. She had just finished scribbling when her cell phone rang. She recognized her editor's number.

"Hey, Bob. I'm just on my way in. I should be there in fifteen—"

"Where are you now?"

"Not far. Downtown. I'll be right—"

"Don't come in."

"You've got something for me?"

"No, I mean, we've got something of a shit sandwich here." He sounded strange. Panicked. Vance didn't panic. "Look, I can only say so much."

"Why, Bob? Are the aliens listening?"

"This isn't funny, McKenna." Usually Bob Vance could find anything funny, and he wasn't the one who'd spent the morning being grilled by an FBI agent. "I can't say much because the magazine's counsel doesn't want me to."

"Counsel like an attorney?"

"Attorneys. Multiple. There are—some issues."

"Issues?"

"Jesus, please stop repeating everything I say. These obviously aren't my usual word choices, all right? Our lawyers got an affidavit this morning from the state court's tech people. They inspected the primary e-mail database for the judicial system, and those Big Pig— The e-mails we ran in your piece about Judge Knight didn't come from his account."

"I don't understand. I thought he was a no-comment."

"Well, after he gave you a no-comment, he called a lawyer who was able to do what we couldn't. The judiciary keeps complete records of all e-mails sent through its systems. They checked the dates and times when Knight supposedly sent those messages, and there was nothing. And they did a text search for the content of the messages. Nothing."

"But why would someone—"

"It gets worse, McKenna."

"I published forged documents. I have New York State's court system saying I got a story wrong. I'm not sure how it can be worse, Bob."

"Knight's attorney used the affidavit from the court system to go to the free e-mail service that was used to forward you the supposed messages. They have IP addresses. That kind of junk."

"Okay. And?"

"Jesus, McKenna. If there's something you need to say, tell me now. I can still fight for you. If I'm in front of it, I can control the damage. I mean, did I push you too hard? Were you spread thin with the pressure to write a book?"

"Bob, I swear to God, I don't know what you're talking about."

"I can't believe I'm saying this. The IP address. The 3G connection or whatever used to access the anonymous e-mail account that sent you those messages about Knight? Your so-called anonymous source e-mailed you from your own iPad, McKenna."

"No. There's no way that's right. I'll take a lie detector right now, Bob. Tell them."

"It's ironclad. Your IP address. Your iPad."

"I'll find some tech geek to fix this. There's no way—"

"It's not going to be that simple. I was on the phone, weighing the options with counsel. I thought I could hold them at bay, but there's some serious shit going down here. I've got an FBI agent searching your office right now, McKenna. They're saying that opening an account like that to forge e-mails could amount to a felony—"

"Wait, Bob. Who's saying that? Is it an Agent Mercado? Female? Dark hair?" Mercado would have to be Wonder Woman to have gotten to the magazine with a warrant already. She must have applied for it the second she got the call from Jason Eberly.

"No, the agent's a man, and he's not saying a word. It's the lawyers who are calling the shots."

"Listen to me, Bob. The FBI thing has nothing to do with Knight. It's a story I was working on about environmental terrorism. There was a bombing or something late last night." As she tried to tell him about her call to an old friend who was an environmental lawyer, and the road to her interrogation with Mercado, she realized how crazy it all sounded. So much for Mercado pretending to believe McKenna when she said she didn't have any information.

"There's nothing I can do, McKenna. The lawyers are going into bunker mode in case Knight sues. They were saying it was worse than Jayson Blair and Stephen Glass." Given the kind of fluff work the magazine had steered her toward, she never would have expected to be compared to two of journalism's most infamous liars.

"So what are you saying?"

"You're terminated immediately until further notification. Your entry card into the offices has been deactivated. Your press credentials are revoked. Your log-in to our databases will no longer work."

"Bob, my work. My e-mails. All of my data—"

"I'm sorry, McKenna."

She could tell that he was, in fact, sorry, but it was the kind of regret that came from trusting a person only to be disappointed. Bob Vance didn't believe her.

CHAPTER THIRTY-ONE

Everyone was a liar.

Carter had no shortage of examples. The Bible-belting, Jesus-loving politicians who got caught with hookers and rent-a-boys. The fat housewives who swore they kept a reasonable diet and a regular exercise regimen but breezed through the McDonald's drive-through three times a week when no one was looking. The spoiled trust-fund kids who held themselves out as writers and artists and "entrepreneurs."

Most people didn't really mean to lie. But the story they told themselves and the world was a better version of the truth. It was as if they implicitly measured themselves against a bell curve of human behavior created in their own minds. By imagining others as worse, everyone could say they were above average.

As a result, Carter knew that what people believed to be true about themselves was rarely the absolute truth. It was the relative truth. Carter's own identity—these days, at least—was very much about the tricks he had learned in the positions to which he'd been trusted. Tricks like explosives.

Carter thought of himself as one of the best in his line of business. He certainly knew more than the average bear. He was smart. He was ambitious. He was willing to sell his skills to the highest bidder.

The actual skills? His talent was understanding people. Including the people who had started hiring him once he realized there was money to be made on the skills he had acquired. But when it came to his knowledge of explosives, he may have exaggerated. Sure, he knew more than the average person, but the average person could barely light a match. And he hadn't set up explosives since 2007.

He had moved to the Marriott after one night at the Four Seasons. The Marriott sucked, but it could be counted on to forget its guests. Given the change in mission, he needed to be forgettable.

Now he was sitting at the built-in desk in the corner of his room, with those stupid outlets at the base of the lamp that never worked. He was checking the tracker on his laptop again, hoping to get an update on the woman's location. Nothing.

He checked the news reports again, too. The explosion had definitely taken place. Two women were in custody. No reports about the other two occupants, in particular the one he was interested in.

He shouldn't have driven away. He should have waited nearby. Watched the explosion. Made sure no one walked out alive.

But any decent emergency response to a bombing would have been quick and overwhelming. And if he'd gotten stopped? Toast.

The time estimates varied by news report. Ten-thirty P.M.? Ten-forty? Eleven?

He hadn't made the explosion big enough. He'd wanted to make sure the investigators found evidence that the people who lived there had been stockpiling bomb materials—that they were the ones who had done this.

She must have seen the detonator. She could have leaped from a window at the last minute and escaped the blast.

All he knew for sure was that her phone somehow made it out of that house. The woman—Carter didn't know her real name, so he just called her "the woman"—didn't know it, but his client had installed a GPS tracker in her phone.

Carter knew he had a problem when the woman's phone moved from the house, down the block, to the left, and then to the right. It was a route toward the Long Island Expressway, 1.6 miles. It took about ten minutes. She was probably running. Fast. And then she stopped. And then she turned off the phone. Twenty-two seconds later, she realized that killing the power wasn't good enough.

The tracker went dead. Maybe she threw the phone under the tire of an eighteen-wheeler. Or pulled out the SIM card and lit it on fire. Whatever, the tracker was now dead.

The woman wasn't. She was alive. And she knew she was being hunted.

This had gone very, very wrong.

Carter set aside any inch of doubt he had allowed to creep in and replaced it with the confidence that had come with fifteen years of work, training, and specialization. There was a reason he had his job.

Because he was an expert, he knew that the tracker in the woman's phone had been put there by his client, which meant his client would be monitoring it, which meant his client would know what Carter knew.

He called the special number.

"We have a problem," he said. "She's alive."

PART III

You stepped out of a stranger.

—Kate Bush

CHAPTER THIRTY-TWO

Though she'd admit it only to her closest friends, McKenna had a Google Alert. A million years ago, when "Google" still sounded like a masturbation euphemism, McKenna was publishing a debut novel. In awe of the fact that newspapers, magazines, and trade reviews would weigh in on the value of her wee little book, she had set up the ongoing search service. Every time her name appeared on the Interwebs, she got an alert.

Today the Google Alert was going wild. If only her novel had brought so much buzz. Since *New York City* magazine had posted its retraction of the Knight story, her name had gone viral. Print media. TV. Blogs. Twitter. It was a weird feeling to be sitting at her familiar spot on the living room sofa, knowing at only the most abstract level that her name was rapidly becoming a part of the zeitgeist outside the bubble of her home. The first telephone call was from the literary agent who had been so damn hot to see a book proposal about the Marcus Jones shooting. *Needless to say, the timing's probably not great right now. If anything changes, I'll be sure to give you a call. But until then— Well, I wish you all the best.*

No bueno.

She finally closed her e-mail to avoid the incoming Alerts. She was interested in an entirely different news story. Word of the explosion in Brentwood had gotten out, as Agent Mercado had predicted. Although details were fuzzy, multiple media outlets were reporting that the FBI had two people in custody on suspicion for possession of weapons of mass destruction.

When her cell phone rang, she was tempted to ignore it but checked the screen to see if she recognized the caller. Patrick. She had tried to sound cool when she left a message earlier, but he had probably heard about her firing.

"Hey," she said.

"So it's true?" They'd been together long enough that apparently "hey" could say everything.

"How much have you heard?" she asked.

"Someone burned you on the Knight e-mails, and the magazine's throwing you under the bus."

"That's— Well, no. It's worse. It started when I went to see Jason Eberly this morning—"

"Your secret boyfriend?"

He was trying to cheer her up, but he had no idea how much her world had changed today. That was her fault. She hadn't even been honest with him about her reason for contacting Jason. "He called an FBI agent for background information about that environmental group." She didn't bother to say "the group I thought Susan might be part of." She knew his thoughts on the issue. "The next thing I know, the agent was hauling me in for questioning because they're a bunch of ecoterrorists. There was an explosion at a house where they were storing bomb materials. Then the FBI showed up at my office with a search warrant, right when Knight was bringing down the hammer on those e-mails. Plus, the magazine is saying there's evidence that I was the one who fabricated the e-mails. Bob actually asked me if I was under too much pressure. They think I'm going crazy."

"I'm coming home."

"Are you sure?"

"Of course. I'll be right there. I know it's bad, McKenna, but everything's going to be okay. I promise. We're going to be fine."

Those words brought more comfort than McKenna ever could have predicted. She found herself watching the clock on her computer, counting down the minutes she had to sit here alone. She needed someone with her right now. Not any someone—Patrick.

She finally forced herself to pull her attention back to the real world. *The New York Times* seemed to have the most detailed coverage about last night's explosion. McKenna recognized the names of the two women in custody—Carolyn Maroney and Andrea Sanderson—from the list that Agent Mercado had shown her.

That left only two more names, one male and one female. She typed the man's name, Greg Larson, into Google, but the search brought up too many results to be helpful. She narrowed it down to "Greg Larson and People for the Preservation of the Planet." She found a few hits quoting Larson at various environmental protests. According to several reports, he was the de facto leader, even though the group eschewed any hierarchical structure.

The remaining female name on Mercado's list of names, Pamela Morris, also proved too common to be of use. Even when McKenna coupled it with the environmental movement, she found nothing.

She called a homicide detective she knew at the Thirteenth Precinct. Female. Youngish. Most important, Detective Forbus owed her a favor for running a story three months ago about a gang killing that no one cared about until it consumed four full pages of a widely circulated magazine.

Forbus picked up on the second ring. "Forbus."

Though McKenna started in with introductions, but Forbus remembered from the earlier case. "Tough break about the magazine," Forbus offered. "If it helps any, everything you said about Knight is a hundred percent accurate. If he didn't write those e-mails, I guarantee you he thought every last word."

"Put it this way," McKenna said. "If you framed a guilty man, would his guilt really matter?"

"Nope, but like I said: *if* it helps."

"What would help is a search. Greg Larson. Forty-six years old.

Has at least one arrest, for criminal trespass at Oregon Health and Science University in Portland in 2007."

"Yep, got him. And that's one of many. All misdemeanors—petty stuff. Trespassing. Vandalism. Public disorder. Disobeying the order of a police officer. Oregon. California. Arizona. Montana. Illinois. D.C. D.C. D.C. D.C. Texas. D.C. Busy guy."

If Larson was running the movement and had been willing to face arrest so many times for his beliefs, he was unlikely to divulge any information. McKenna had to hope that the last person on Mercado's list might know something—and had lived. "One more name?" she asked. "Pamela Morris."

"And?"

"That's all I've got."

"Date of birth? State? Something?"

"Nothing." She thought about the age ranges of the other residents in the house. The youngest was Carolyn Maroney, twenty-two. Greg Larson was the oldest. "Between twenty and fifty," she offered. "And probably in New York, at least until recently."

"Very helpful," Forbus deadpanned. McKenna waited as she heard fingertips against a keyboard. "Yeah, what I thought. I've got fourteen driver's licenses in New York alone. And just to be clear, this counts as a favor—an actual call-it-even favor, whether it helps you out or not."

"Fine. Um, narrow it down to criminal histories."

More typing. "Yeah, okay. Down to one, but it's way back. Pamela Morris. Thirty-nine years old. Two prostitution pops in the late nineties. Nothing since. Maybe got out of the life. Happens sometimes, even outside of Hollywood fairy tales."

"Can you run her with the date of birth in the general databases? See what you find?"

"Look at you, little Miss Jessica Fletcher." More typing. "Yep, I got her. Huh."

Huh? *Huh* was usually bad.

"'Huh'?"

"Well, it could be anything. But your girl's very low-radar. No driver's licenses. No car registrations. No NCIC hits." Meaning no involvement with law enforcement. "Very minimal. Like, off the grid."

"Does she have contacts in the area?" Pamela Morris might be able to confirm that Susan Hauptmann was the woman from the subway platform.

"All right. Let me see." More typing. "I've got a mom here. Arresting officer called her after one of the two prostitution busts. Loretta Morris." She rattled off an address in Jersey City. More typing. "From what I can tell, the mom's still at the same address. That's all I've got, Jordan."

"What about a booking photo on the prostitution pop?"

"*Pop.* Listen to you with the cop talk." More typing. "Looks like she was cited and released on her first arrest, but yeah, she got booked on the second *pop.* I'll shoot it over to you. E-mail okay?"

"I'll take it." McKenna started to recite her work address out of habit, then caught herself and provided her Gmail account instead.

"I'll make a note of it. And best of luck. Because if you ask me? Whoever Pamela Morris is, she doesn't want to be found."

CHAPTER THIRTY-THREE

Scanlin wasn't usually the type to cheer on members of the judiciary. Judges sat behind their benches, literally elevated above the courtroom and clothed in antiquated garb to remind the world of their superiority. Yet they knew nothing about the real world affected by their rulings. (Even the word played into the myth of judicial superiority, as if they actually "ruled" over others.) How many times had Scanlin seen routine consent searches bounced, all because some lefty judge who had never been north of Eighty-sixth Street believed that no one who was carrying would be stupid enough to let a cop check his pockets? Judges were glorified lawyers who didn't know the unwritten rules of the streets. Even the judges who tended to rule for the state—judges like Frederick Knight—did it more for political popularity or disdain of criminal defendants than respect for police work.

But what was that saying about the enemy of my enemy being a friend? The maxim must hold water because, on this particular day, Scanlin found himself hoping that Frederick Knight was out there somewhere, treating his gluttonous self to all the fried eggs and bacon in lower Manhattan.

Just that morning, *New York City* magazine had issued a retraction of a hatchet job they'd run against Knight the previous day.

The language on the website was formal but apologetic, explaining that the contemptuous e-mails supposedly authored by Knight were apparently fabricated; offering sincere regrets about the story; and promising a thorough investigation and complete transparency as additional information was gathered. Scanlin's favorite line was the final one: New York City *magazine has terminated its relationship with the author of the article, McKenna Jordan.*

In the cutthroat world of New York City media, the circling sharks smelled fresh, oozing blood. Several other media outlets— the *Daily News, New York* magazine, Gawker, Mediabistro—were comparing the emerging story to other journalistic scandals, but it was the *New York Post* that went furthest, not only digging in a knife but giving the blade a vengeful twist.

Although NYC magazine promises its readers a thorough investigation into the events that led to the fabricated article, critics will argue that the scandal should be anything but a surprise. The reporter in question, McKenna Jordan, née Wright, made headlines a decade ago as an assistant district attorney. Wright was the junior prosecutor who went to the press with evidence that she claimed would prove that a twelve-year police veteran's shooting of nineteen-year-old felon Marcus Jones was not justified. Her allegation poured fuel on a fire simmering between civil rights activists and supporters of the NYPD. She resigned from the district attorney's office when an investigation revealed further evidence to back the officer's self-defense claim. She subsequently published a novel that was a thinly veiled depiction of her former life as a prosecutor. And the reporter who ran with her claims all those years ago? His name was Bob Vance. That's right: the same Bob Vance who now sits as editor in chief at New York City magazine.

Scanlin wondered if the demise of McKenna Wright Jordan would provide any kind of karmic justice to his old friend Scott Macklin.

Scanlin couldn't remember the last time he'd seen Macklin. It must have been about six years ago, after Mac heard that Melissa finally had to go to the home. He stopped by with a casserole from his own wife. Scanlin didn't mention that he already had a freezer full of Pyrex dishes. Apparently Scanlin was going to be treated as the neighborhood widower, even though Melissa was very much alive—at least to him back then.

Even six years ago, Mac's decline was obvious. It had been fast. If anything, age had taken hold of him even faster than it had Scanlin. Before, when Mac announced that he was marrying Josefina, he was like Benjamin Button, aging backward, whistling like a giddy newlywed. He insisted that life with Josefina's young son, whom he treated as his own, only made him feel younger. The guys who sported bags under their eyes from trying to keep up with their own growing broods begged to differ, but no one begrudged Mac his happiness. How could you carry one ill thought about a man who'd do anything in the world for his family and the fellow officers he treated as such?

But then Marcus Jones pulled a gun, and Mac became the white cop who killed a black teenager. Throw in the reckless, grandstanding antics of McKenna Wright, and Mac's miraculous reverse aging reversed itself again and then some. By the time Mac came to see Scanlin with the casserole, he just seemed old and sad.

Now Scanlin opened the second drawer on his desk and pulled out a Rolodex that had been made obsolete by electronic databases. Miscellaneous business cards were stuffed randomly among the yellowing notes. He skipped to the tab marked M and flipped through the entries. MAC. It was the only name the man needed.

Josefina picked up the phone. She sounded distracted but happy. Harried but not annoyed, like maybe she was balancing the phone between her cheek and shoulder while unloading a bag of groceries. He wished Melissa were still around to answer their phone that way a busy woman does. Before the diagnosis, Melissa had gotten crabby, snapping at the mildest irritation. He chose to think it was the dementia setting in and not the changes between them, but there was no real way to know.

Mac wasn't home. His wife asked if she could take a message.

"I was hoping to talk to him. To, I don't know . . . catch up."

"He's helping Tommy move a mini-fridge into his dorm room. He should be back in an hour or so."

"That little rug rat's off to college already?"

"Freshman at Hofstra. He wants to be called Thomas now, but I can't help it. Mama's always going to call him Tommy."

"I'll give Mac a call later, then. I don't know if this is a touchy subject, but it's about that prosecutor who tried to jam Scott up back when—you know, when he was still on the job."

Her end of the line went silent. He pictured her freeze, momentarily distracted from the groceries. Her voice was lower when she spoke. "I don't know who you're talking about. Scott— You know how a man is. He shielded us from the details. We don't like talking about that."

Scanlin regretted mentioning it. He should have ended with the polite chitchat and a routine message. "Sure, I totally understand. Trust me, this is a good thing. Karma's biting the ass of someone who deserves it big-time." He felt uncomfortable about using profanity with her. "I'll let you get back to what you were doing. I'll give Mac a call later."

He hit the print key on the *New York Post*'s delicious massacre of the reporter and former prosecutor in question. He'd bring it to Mac in person. It was even better than a casserole.

CHAPTER
THIRTY-FOUR

Maybe if Patrick had come home at that moment—right when McKenna ended the call with Detective Forbus—everything would have been different. But that wasn't what happened. She was left there in the apartment, alone with her thoughts.

And when McKenna was alone with nothing but time and energy, she had to stay busy. She stayed busy by opening the box that had arrived via messenger, courtesy of Adam Bayne, while she was talking to Agent Mercado that morning. According to what Adam had told Patrick, George Hauptmann had one box in storage marked SUSAN. Adam could never bring himself to dispose of it.

The box was small. If Susan's father were alive, McKenna could ask him why he had chosen to keep these six cubic feet of his daughter's belongings. Photographs, school merit certificates, the West Point degree—those items made sense. But as McKenna unpacked the box, she also found a commemorative plate from the Mount Vernon estate, a wine opener from Napa Valley, and a pink plastic Slinky. Were these items from special moments they had shared together? Or had the best intentions to preserve treasured memories collided with the last-minute realities of packing up an apartment?

McKenna set aside the bulkier items and made a stack of photographs—some framed, some bound in albums, many thrown haphazardly into the box. Flipping through the completed pile provided an escape, a reprieve from reality, while she waited. Waited for what, she didn't know. For Patrick to come home and make her feel better? For someone to realize that the Knight e-mails were legit? For the mysterious subway woman to emerge, bearing only a superficial resemblance to Susan Hauptmann? For the FBI somehow to *un*search her office? There wasn't always an end point to waiting.

She almost missed the picture. So many of them were of people she'd never seen. Or they were old, old, old pictures of the Hauptmanns—George, Carol, Gretchen, and Susan, looking like any other 1970s family in polyester shirts and flared pants. But McKenna paid slightly more attention to the pictures from the college years. West Point. Those beautiful, rolling hills next to the Hudson. The tanned, hard-bodied, buzz-cut men in tank tops and shorts, arms around shoulders, wrestling, tackling each other to the ground. How many times had she teased Patrick that the U.S. Military Academy was the gayest place on earth?

Of course, the entire campus wasn't all young men. Some of the cadets were tanned, hard-bodied young women. Women like Susan, far outnumbered by her male colleagues.

It shouldn't have bothered her. The photograph was taken twenty years ago. But the look on Patrick's face. The smile. The twinkle in the eyes. The joy. She loved seeing that look, which she had always thought was reserved exclusively for her.

The way his hands rested so comfortably on Susan's stomach as he hugged her from behind. Susan's lips on his neck. McKenna's mind filled with other images of the two of them together. Laughing. Kissing. Removing clothes. Her own intimate memories of her husband, but with Susan.

Those weren't the only thoughts pulling at her. From the minute she had shown him the video of the woman on the subway, Patrick had been steering her away from looking into Susan's death. He had insisted that the woman didn't look like Susan, even though the resemblance was so clear.

She felt her fingers shake as she scrolled through her contacts list, searching for Adam Bayne's phone number.

He sounded cheerful when he answered. "McKenna, I'm so glad you called. I wanted to make sure that you got the box we sent over. I'm not sure what you were looking for, but that's all the General kept from Susan's things."

"Yes, it's here. Thanks for sending it."

"Look, McKenna. I—I heard about your situation with the magazine." She wondered whether there was anyone in America who hadn't. "Our firm has investigators, computer experts, that kind of thing. Let me know if we can do anything to help."

From what McKenna gathered, it was no surprise that Susan's father had invited Adam to work for him. Adam had been a West Point "Star Man," a cadet entitled to wear a small star on his uniform collar, signaling his place in the top five percent of his class. Other cadets called them "star geeks" on the assumption that all they did was study, but Adam's skills went beyond book smarts. He was fearless and decisive, traits that would later serve him well in the Special Forces.

General Hauptmann's contracting firm had never lived up to the man's goals, but Adam had managed to land on his feet. After winding down the General's active work in the Middle East, Adam returned to New York to launch his own private security firm. Adam's clients tended to be sports teams, celebrities, and other "high-value" clientele.

"Thanks, Adam. I appreciate it. I actually have a question for you. And I feel kind of weird asking it, but were Susan and Patrick ever . . . together? I found a picture of them—"

"I thought you were trying to write about what happened to Susan. I'm not sure how old flirtations could have anything to do with that."

"So they were a couple?" McKenna tried to block out the mental images.

"If you can even call it that. I guess I assumed you knew. I mean, *I* certainly knew."

"No, I didn't. I thought she was with you in college."

"She was. Mostly. But we were on and off. We were young. You know how it is. Didn't you and Patrick go through the same thing? Sometimes being together isn't as clean as we'd like to think. Things worked out for you guys. Not that it's my place to give advice—we don't know each other well, and God knows it took me long enough to settle down—but it's never helpful to start thinking about your spouse's exes. Isn't that the whole point of being married? You're there for each other from that point on, and the past doesn't matter."

"I was with Patrick for *five years* before we got married. Were they together even after he met me?" She thought about the weeks that would go by when they were taking a break. How stupid she felt sitting at home, wondering whether he would call. Wondering whether she should call. Where had Susan been all of those nights? She remembered Gretchen's comment to Patrick at her house: *Don't even get me started on you.*

Adam sighed loudly. "Look, McKenna. You know how Susan was. I loved her, but she had problems, and needing the attention of men was one of them. It was a big part of the reason it didn't work out for us. She couldn't be with one guy, so yeah, sometimes she was with Patrick. She was with a lot of guys we knew. But it was never serious. It was just— Well, you know."

"If the sex didn't matter, how come neither of them ever told me?"

"I should've gone through that stupid box myself before sending it over. No offense, McKenna, but if you ask me, you've got bigger things to be thinking about right now. Again, let me know if we can do anything to help. You take care, okay?"

CHAPTER THIRTY-FIVE

McKenna had heard the sympathy in Adam's voice before he'd hung up. She could imagine him thinking, Poor thing. Poor, pathetic thing.

She was pathetic, sitting here alone on the living room floor, frantically sorting through old photographs, wondering how long Patrick's relationship with Susan had lasted. How happy they had been together. What trips they may have taken.

She looked at the clock. She had time for a quick walk before Patrick got home. She needed to clear her head before she saw him.

She headed up toward Madison Square Park. This stretch of Broadway, between Fourteenth and Twenty-third, once was so congested that you literally had to press yourself sideways against adjacent buildings to pass another person on the sidewalk. A few years ago, the city had closed most of the street to car traffic, forming a pedestrian walkway complete with tables and umbrellas for shade. It was all part of the ongoing campaign to make the city more *livable*.

Her mother always said to her, "I love visiting you, but how long are you going to continue *living* there? The crowds and the honking. All that noise. It's so *stressful*." But Manhattan's packed sidewalks had always been a kind of comfort to McKenna. Losing herself in a crowd allowed her thoughts to roam free. Some of her best ideas—whether for a closing argument, her novel, or story concepts—came when she meandered anonymously among the thousands of other tiny specks of humanity occupying this little island.

She still felt shamed by Adam's admonishment. He was right, of course. Everyone had a past. She certainly hadn't been a virgin when she met Patrick. When they started dating, she began the whole "what's your history" conversation. When she asked about his last girlfriend (first name Ally, last name unknown), he described her as "a big-boned girl. Not in a strong way, either. Soft. Smushy, if you will. With red frizzy hair. Lots of brown freckles. Moles, too. Big ones, on her nose and chin. Not the brightest bulb. And a voice like a horse. A real doll."

Point made. There was nothing to be gained by hearing details about former lovers. No one else mattered once they met each other.

At the time, it had seemed like such a sweet and simple solution to avoiding petty jealousies. Now McKenna wondered if, at some level, he had been avoiding the truth about his past (present?) with Susan. But why did any of it matter? Like Adam said, she had bigger problems to deal with.

Yet there was a reason the picture of Patrick and Susan had shaken her. If he and Susan had been that close, they could still be in contact. He may have known this entire time that Susan was out there. He could be making sure that McKenna didn't search for Susan—or publish the subway video.

He had seen her log in to Dana's Skybox account, which meant he could have signed in to wipe it out. Once she thought of that possibility, she realized he also had access to her iPad, which meant he could have been the one to send the forged e-mails about Judge Knight. Without the video, no one would believe she'd seen a woman who'd been missing for ten years, and the Knight e-mails had put the nail in her credibility's coffin.

Okay, she was seriously losing it. If she said any of that out loud, the listener really would call the nice men with the butterfly nets and a white van.

She was at the park now. She smiled as she looked at the long, winding Shake Shack line, extending from the hamburger stand, across the south side of the park, and turning north toward the dog run. If Patrick were here, he'd have something funny to say about New Yorkers being like cattle, standing in lines only because they existed. Two summers ago, he had nearly thrown a woman out of the five-hour line for the Alexander McQueen exhibit when, two hours in, she said, "Wait. You mean it's dresses?"

She gave herself a mental pep talk before heading home. She liked to say she'd been with Patrick for ten years, but becoming a couple was never as clean as you liked to remember. They were different people ten years ago. Neither was ready to do the work that came with a real relationship. They took breaks. A lot of them. She spent nights with other men. He was with other women, and Susan might have been one of them. It didn't matter.

But that picture had taught McKenna one thing: she didn't know Susan very well. They were friends. They drank together. Giggled. Partied. Commiserated over their jobs. She'd known Susan had no problem with one-night stands or "no commitment" hookups, but Susan had always given McKenna the impression that her relationship with Adam was stable and monogamous before they broke it off. Similarly, McKenna had known about Gretchen's drug problem, but Susan never told her about Gretchen's arrest, even though McKenna was a prosecutor when it happened. What other information had Susan been keeping to herself?

Then it dawned on McKenna that she might not be in this mess if she hadn't been playing so close to the vest herself. She should have posted the subway video to the Internet immediately, asking people to identify the mystery woman. She should have told Scanlin, Vance, and Gretchen about the sighting. Even that morning, she should have told Mercado about the link between Susan and the P3s.

Instead, she had held back. And where had all the secrecy gotten her?

It was time to try a different route.

She pulled out her iPad and opened her Twitter app. She typed as quickly as she could before she lost the nerve:

Contact me w/ ANY info about disappearance of Susan Hauptmann ('03). There's a connection b/w past & present. Help me find it.

She ended with an embedded link to her e-mail address. Thanks to her active efforts, nearly ten thousand people followed her personal Twitter account. Still, the odds of one of them knowing anything helpful about Susan were minuscule. She needed an even bigger audience. Then she realized she probably had one.

She switched accounts and logged in to the official *New York City* magazine feed. She watched as the little thinking wheel at the top of her iPad turned, a sign that it was processing the request.

She was in. They hadn't thought to change the password.

NYCM changed its locks but not Twitter password. Please RT any & all of my messages before they delete & change PW. —McKenna Jordan (fired)

She included a link to her e-mail account, hit send, and began typing a second message.

NYCM not telling full story. Help me do it. Contact me w/ ANY info about disappearance of Susan Hauptmann ('03). RT b4 they delete! McK J

In the abbreviated world of Twitter, with its 140-character limitation, she had asked her fellow Twitter users to "retweet," or repeat her message to their own followers, before the magazine could delete it. She wished she could be a fly on the wall when Bob Vance gave the magazine's lawyers the news.

She made her way back down Broadway, feeling confident that she had her head on straight. She didn't know why someone had gone to such lengths to erase the subway video. She didn't know how the video was connected to this morning's explosion on Long Island. And she was still unemployed and disgraced, thanks to someone's efforts to make sure she looked like a total loon.

But at least she was doing something about it. She wouldn't stop until she answered every last question. And Patrick would help her.

She was about to slip her key in the front door when she heard Patrick's voice inside. He'd beat her home.

Maybe the internal pep talk to quell the paranoid voices hadn't worked after all, because she didn't insert the key. She paused. She paused to eavesdrop on her own husband in their own home.

"I don't know where she is," Patrick was saying inside the apartment. "I told her I was coming home."

Silence.

"I'm about to call her. I just walked in. She's not here. Her purse is gone."

Silence.

"I *know* it could be nothing. But she's got a bunch of your old stuff scattered all over our living room floor. Is there something in here that could be an issue?"

Silence.

"Fine. I'll let you know when I find her. But don't worry. I have it under control. Problem solved. Just take care of yourself."

Silence. Silence. Silence.

CHAPTER THIRTY-SIX

McKenna was frozen in the hallway, the apartment key hovering one inch from the lock.

She had to get out of here. She took the stairs one floor down, to be sure Patrick wouldn't hear the elevator ding on their floor, and then she headed straight to the Union Square subway station to lose herself in the nearest crowd available.

I have it under control. Problem solved.

There was only one person who could have been on the other end of that phone call. Those paranoid voices were making more sense.

I have it under control.

She made her way into a pack of subway commuters standing just inside the turnstiles to watch a guy playing an electric violin on the makeshift staging area at the southwest corner of the station. McKenna had seen the performer before. He favored recognizable rock anthems, punctuating the high notes with eccentric moves like side squats and karate kicks. She knew he'd draw a large enough crowd to keep her concealed. She also knew she could get a phone signal this close to the station entrance.

She checked Twitter. Her blasts were working. The magazine had deleted her posts from its official feed, but there had to be nearly a hundred retweets already. Those people's friends would continue the pattern, and then theirs, and so on. She also had eight hundred new followers to her personal account. If the trend continued, she'd have a healthy platform to communicate directly to the public as more information came in.

She checked her e-mail next, in case any tips had come in. There was a message from Detective Forbus. The attachment was a booking photo for Pamela Morris from a prostitution arrest in 1998. Morris would have been twenty-four at the time but looked at least thirty. Three inches of roots revealed her to be a natural brunette, but the rest of her hair was bleached and processed to the texture of straw. Her face was simultaneously drawn and sagging. Although she'd clearly tried to put on a tough face for the camera, black smears around her red eyes revealed that she'd been crying. It looked like she was recovering from a fat lip.

That was fifteen years ago. No arrests since, but that morning an FBI agent had mentioned her name in the context of a weapons explosion at the suspected site of domestic terrorists. McKenna reminded herself that she had no way of knowing whether this Pamela Morris was the same Pamela Morris.

This particular Pamela Morris had been—in Forbus's words—keeping a low profile. Plus, Mercado had said that the college student who owned the house had been shacking up with a group of "older" P3s, and this Pamela Morris was closer to Greg Larson's age than to a college student's.

McKenna's cell phone rang. It was the home number. She almost answered it. Maybe Patrick would have an explanation.

But she knew what she'd heard. And now she was hearing those voices in her head again. The picture of him with Susan. All his attempts to talk her out of looking into her disappearance. The afternoon when he left work early but denied it later. The worst-case scenarios.

She waited for the voice-mail alert to flash on her phone and then checked the message. "Hey, babe. I got home as fast as I could, but now you're not here. Let me know where you are, okay? We'll figure this out. Try not to worry."

How could his voice sound so different than it had a few minutes earlier? When she'd heard him inside their apartment, his voice had been crisp. Stern. The way people sounded when they were alarmed or angry or frantic but struggling to maintain control. His military voice.

And now? When he called her? *Hey, babe.* Like, Hey, let's go grab some enchiladas and margaritas and make everything better. Even the tone of his voice was a lie.

She thought about calling Adam Bayne. He did private security. He had offered to help.

But he already thought she was nuts for asking about Patrick's past with Susan. If she started talking about erased Skybox accounts and forged e-mails from her iPad, he'd think she was certifiable. And he'd known Patrick a hell of a lot longer than he'd known her.

She was on her own.

CHAPTER THIRTY-SEVEN

The address McKenna had gotten from Detective Forbus for Pamela Morris's mother turned out to be a brick duplex south of downtown Jersey City. Two symmetrical halves. Fifty-fifty odds.

The east side of the porch was adorned with an array of well-maintained potted plants. A plaster frog sat next to a teak rocking chair. The welcome mat read, HI. I'M MAT. The west side of the porch was . . . a porch.

McKenna was looking for the mother of a middle-aged former prostitute. She played the odds and rang the west bell.

The woman who came to the door fit the role. Probably only in her mid-sixties, but hard years. She wore sweatpants and a New York Jets T-shirt and smelled like an ashtray. Despite the age difference, she bore a strong resemblance to Pamela Morris's booking photograph. Pale eyes and thick eyelids. Wide bridge of the nose.

The look she gave McKenna made her feel like she was supposed to give the woman something.

"I'm looking for Loretta Morris," McKenna said.

"You can stop looking, because I'm right here."

"My name is McKenna Jordan. I'm trying to find an old friend of mine, and I think she might be connected to your daughter, Pamela. I'm afraid it's a bit of a long story, ma'am."

"I've got nothing if not time, and you look harmless enough." She stepped aside to usher McKenna in.

The house was dated and cluttered but otherwise well maintained. Linoleum entranceway. Fake brick fireplace. Brown carpet in the living room. Probably typical of the homes built in the neighborhood in the 1970s.

Loretta let out a small groan as she lowered herself to the sofa. McKenna took a seat next to her. "Is there any way I can get in touch with your daughter? That might be the easiest way to find my friend."

"Is your friend in Pamela's church?"

McKenna couldn't imagine trying to explain: *Well, you see, I think I saw my long-lost friend, but the only lead I have is a button for a batshit-crazy environmental group that blew up its own house this morning. And someone named Pamela Morris—who may or may not be the same Pamela Morris as your daughter—had something to do with that bombing. But now the house is blown to bits, and the people inside—including maybe your daughter and maybe my friend—are now pink vapor.*

Instead, she lied. "My friend is missing, and I'm trying to find her. She told me she was doing some kind of work with a woman named Pamela Morris. It might not be your daughter, but I figured if I find every Pamela Morris in the area, I'll eventually find the one who knew my friend."

"Sounds sensible enough, but my Pamela's not in the area."

"Is that right?" Her one lead was fizzling out.

"She travels. Found herself a nice man some years ago. He's a preacher. They're sort of like missionaries, I guess—going around the country, converting people or whatever. I was never much for religion, but I guess it works for them."

If Pamela were tied up with the head of the P3s, she could have sugarcoated it for her mother. In the fictional version of Pamela's life, the lead organizer for an ecoterrorist group became a preacher. Attacks on research laboratories and oil refineries became missionary work. Protests became proselytizing. "Do you know where she is now? It would be helpful to contact her."

"No. We don't check in day-to-day. She mostly sends me Christmas cards. Mother's Day. Just to let me know she's doing all right."

"Maybe I can give her a call?"

Loretta shook her head, as if realizing that a mother should have her daughter's telephone number. "I've never been much for the phone." She waved a hand for emphasis.

"I see. The Pamela Morris I'm looking for had a couple of police interactions back in the nineties. For—" She struggled for a euphemism. "For being a lady of the evening." She cringed at the sound of it.

Loretta's gaze moved to the fake brick fireplace. "That was a long time ago. Pamela's doing better now. Turned her entire life around. This area was a bad influence on her. When she left, everything changed. Has a man. Has her church. No more police. No more— lady of the evening." She returned her gaze to McKenna with a twinkle. She'd known it was a corny phrase.

"So, I'm sorry . . . when did you last see her?"

"It's been a while."

The woman did not want a stranger to know she never saw her daughter and didn't have her phone number. "I'm so sorry to press, ma'am, but my friend is missing. It's important."

"I haven't seen her in person since—I guess it would be fall of 2003. Doesn't seem that long ago, really."

"That's—um, that's quite a long time not to see your daughter."

Loretta's breezy tone became stern, and her face darkened. "Maybe in some families. Not this one. Pam started running away when she was fourteen years old. Dropped out her senior year. Moved out right after. Seemed the only time I ever saw her was when she needed money. Or bail the one time. I guess I suspected the kind of life she was living, but at least when she got arrested, she came clean with me. I let her move back in while she tried to get her act together—went to counseling for girls trying to get out of that . . . lifestyle. It would last a few weeks at a time, then she'd be gone again and we'd start the cycle all over."

"That must have been hard for a mother to see." McKenna didn't know what else to say.

"You have no idea. I just kept thinking every time the phone rang, it would be the police telling me my baby girl was dead. At one point I let her stay with me even when she was in the life. It was a terrible compromise to make, but at least I knew every night that she was alive and in one piece. And because she didn't need as much money, she promised me she'd only see her regulars, not the kind of guys who would beat her up. She told me a couple of the guys were married with sick wives and told themselves that being with her wasn't the same as cheating, since it wasn't emotional. One guy was a funny-looking dude—and a little slow—but she said he'd bring her flowers and love notes and stuff. One guy paid her just to talk to him and watch movies. That kind of thing."

"How did you go from that . . . arrangement to her leaving?"

"She was getting a little too comfortable telling me about the work. I lost it one night and told her it was still— Well, that's not what I said. I told her *she* was still a whore. It would've been better for me to just slap her across the face. She walked out, and that was the end of the—arrangement, as you called it. Frankly, the cards she sends a couple of times a year, that's about as much as I heard from her when she was living two miles away."

"Did you ever hear her mention a woman named Susan Haupt-mann?" McKenna pulled up a picture of Susan on her iPad, the same one that her father had used for the reward posters.

Loretta shook her head. "Nope. Pam never had many female friends. Or male ones, for that matter—at least I wouldn't call them friends."

"How about the People for the Preservation of the Planet?"

Loretta chuckled, then covered her mouth. "Sorry, but that's quite a tongue twister, isn't it? Nope, never heard of that one, either."

"Would you say Pamela was an environmentalist? Or passionate about animal rights?"

"She had a hamster in the fourth grade and traded it to the boy next door for a Popsicle. You sure you've got the right Pamela Morris? You might want to try the other ones."

But McKenna left Jersey City with a feeling in her gut that she had the right Pamela Morris. Happy talk in holiday cards might keep a mother at bay, but the fact remained that Loretta hadn't seen her daughter since 2003, the same year McKenna last saw Susan Hauptmann. Something had happened. Something to explain both of them leaving. Something to explain their shared connection to the P3s. Something that had changed life for both of them forever.

CHAPTER THIRTY-EIGHT

Carter lit yet another match. Dammit. That was the problem with these enormous hotels. The windows didn't open. Too many concerns about liability.

No open windows meant no fresh air. Which meant that Carter's room at the Marriott smelled like vomit.

Three times on his knees in front of the toilet bowl. The last time had been dry heaves, but still.

He had even given himself the talk, the one from two years ago, when he'd made the decision to go private. He saw what was happening. Other people were doing the same work for ten times the money and without all the bullshit.

Since then, the line had gotten blurred. What had been a government job became private. Some of the things he couldn't do then he was allowed to do now, but other things he was authorized to do then were now off the table. The geography changed, but the skills were the same. Usually the same cast of characters, too. Different theaters but somehow still all connected. Working for the same people. Playing the same angles.

The explosion out in Brentwood was a perfect example. He'd killed people before. In Kandahar, he'd started thinking of it like a video game. They had all signed on to the game. Some people won, and some people . . . didn't.

But in Brentwood, he'd screwed up. The woman who was part of the game had won. She'd made it out of the house before the explosion, run 1.6 miles in ten minutes, and now she was in the wind.

In response, the client had tweaked the mission once again. The client had new, undisclosed information. There was a third party in the picture. He was a threat, too.

This time, Carter's usual pep talk wasn't doing the trick. This latest mission wasn't the war zone come home. It wasn't a situation where everyone had signed on to play the game.

He wasn't sure why he had puked. Was it the realization of what he'd already done? The pressure of what was expected of him next? The fact that, as hard as he had tried to become the man who'd accomplished what he had in the past two years, he'd been given an assignment that he couldn't bring himself to execute? If this job crossed the line, where was the line? And how many times had he already blazed right over it?

He had lived the last two years in a lie. Lying to the clients. Lying to himself. He wasn't the man who'd earned all that money. He wasn't the hired gun who could carry out this next job. He wasn't . . . Carter. And he had no idea what he was supposed to do next.

He walked out of the hotel without checking out. He went to a cash machine and withdrew the maximum amount of four hundred dollars. He had a foreign bank account under an untraceable name that he could get to later. He had saved about four hundred grand so far. It wouldn't last a lifetime, but it was enough. Enough for him to walk away.

In about ten minutes, the client would figure out that a man who was supposed to be dead was still alive.

He passed a thrift store and remembered a book he'd read about an ex-military drifter who traveled the world with nothing but a toothbrush. Five minutes later, he paid twenty-eight bucks for a pair of used Levi's, a white canvas work shirt, and a pair of Timberland boots. He stuffed his own clothing in a trash can on Forty-fourth. He'd learned that GPS devices could be planted anywhere. He wasn't taking any chances.

A bus was heading his way on Seventh Avenue. The advertisement plastered across the side promised a new beginning through weight loss.

He threw his phone under the front tire as it passed. Heard the crunch. Looked down over the curb to make sure it was in pieces.

A kid stepped out of Chipotle shoving a football-sized burrito in his face. "Dude." He spoke through a full mouth. "Your gear is toast. Bummer."

As Carter passed a pay phone, he thought about calling in an anonymous tip about his client and the man Carter had been instructed to kill. But they wouldn't believe him. And they'd trace the call. Police response in midtown could be fast.

It was time for him to walk away. Carter was free.

CHAPTER THIRTY-NINE

By the time McKenna got back to the city, it was after nine o'clock. She felt like she'd been awake for four days straight. Had it really been only that morning that Agent Mercado had summoned her to the Federal Building?

Patrick had called her eleven times and had left three additional messages.

Hey, it's me again. Where are you? Call me at home, okay?

McKenna. You're starting to worry me. You had a shitty day. I know. I want to help. Call me, okay?

All right, I'm trying not to lose it here. But you call me at work telling me you were questioned by an FBI agent about some ecoterrorism group and had your office searched. Someone's setting you up at work. And now you're gone? For hours? Maybe you're working on something. I don't know. Just call me. Even a text. Something. I'm still home. Okay. Bye.

She would have to face him eventually. She stepped outside to make the call. There was no answer at the apartment. When she tried his cell, she heard a ring, followed by a long tone, a ring, followed by a long tone. He was on the phone.

If he were home and on his cell, he would have picked up the apartment phone when it rang. At this time of night, he would know it was McKenna. He'd want to know where she was.

Which meant he wasn't home. Maybe he was looking for her? But that wouldn't make any sense. If he were so worried, wouldn't he be glued to the apartment, waiting for the phone to ring? But he wasn't, which meant that he was doing something besides waiting for her. He was doing something that he'd lie to her about later.

He was probably talking to Susan again. She tried to tell herself there must be an explanation. Maybe Susan had a good reason for leaving, and he was doing the right thing by helping her now. The fact that Susan had jumped in front of an oncoming train to save Nicky Cervantes suggested that she was the same kind person at heart. Her instinct to rescue others was ingrained.

But to leave like that? To let missing posters go up all over the city? To watch as her friends and family mourned her? To keep that a secret for ten years?

McKenna could still hear the coldness in Patrick's voice. *I have it under control. Problem solved.* And then to call her moments later with *Hey, babe.*

Maybe he and Susan were spies. Maybe Patrick was a national hero. Maybe he had a secret storage unit filled floor to ceiling with war medals for saving the country from alien invasion time and again. But to bifurcate his life that way? To know her for ten years—marriage for five—showing one face to her and one to Susan and whomever the hell else who knew whatever secrets they were carrying?

It didn't matter why he had lied to her. She was afraid of him. She was afraid of her own husband.

She was so tired. She couldn't think straight anymore. She needed to sleep. Where the *hell* was she going to sleep?

She was checking out last-minute hotel offers online when she realized she wasn't sure how she would pay for it. All of their credit cards were in both of their names. Patrick would be monitoring her charges.

She had friends, but they were all "couple friends" at this point, which meant making up a story to explain her need for a crash pad, then having to explain why she'd lied once Patrick started calling around for her.

Fuck!

She scrolled through the contacts on her phone. Who the hell could she call? And then she knew.

Dana picked up on the second ring. "Holy hell, woman. All hail the renegade! Who knew you could go all gangsta?"

"I know," McKenna said. "It's absolutely insane."

"That stunt you pulled with the magazine's Twitter feed? Freakin' brilliant!"

McKenna hadn't checked the Twitter progress since she'd left for Jersey City. "Are people retweeting?"

"Oh my God. You've *totally* gone viral. Huff Post even put it on the front page of the Media section. Please tell me you've got your whole revenge plan up and ready to roll. Is it going to be like that TV show where the crazy bitch goes after a different enemy every week? You bringing a fire to their house or what?"

McKenna had always suspected that Dana's passion had nothing to do with the magazine, but she never would have guessed that the usually unanimated hipster would be so enthusiastic about a workplace scandal.

"No fires. But I do have a huge favor to ask."

"Hit it."

"Can I crash at your place? I know it's a lot to ask, but Patrick's out of town, and a reporter just showed up at my apartment wanting to talk about the Knight e-mails. I just need a break, and seeing as how I don't exactly have a salary anymore, a hotel would—"

"Just stop, okay? Of course it's fine. Not exactly the Taj Mahal, but I got a sweet daybed from CB2 that should suit you fine. When are you coming?"

"Soon. If that's okay."

"No problem. And I've got a surprise when you get here."

"Okay. Um, where am I going?" She'd never even been to the woman's home and was inviting herself over for a slumber party.

"Oh, duh." Dana gave her an address in Brooklyn. "Call me when you're out front."

CHAPTER FORTY

Dana's address turned out to be for a three-story townhouse in Prospect Heights. McKenna called upstairs from the street, and Dana soon appeared at an open window on the top floor. "Catch!"

McKenna dodged to the left before the key chain hit her in the kneecaps. Upstairs, Dana was cracking up. "You can't catch for shit! Third floor. Hopefully you can walk better than you field."

At the apartment door, Dana said, "Come on in. I'll give you the tour. This is— Well, this is pretty much it." She had already opened the daybed and made it up, leaving barely enough room to walk between the open bed and the small TV stand in front of it. Beneath the window was a large desk with two laptops, a giant printer, and stacks of prints. To the side was a narrow galley kitchen.

"Oh, no. Am I taking your only bed?"

"In your dreams, McKenna. Your suppressed lesbian dreams. Nope, over here." Past the desk, she opened two sliding doors that McKenna had assumed belonged to a closet. Inside was enough space for a full-size bed and a dresser. Compact but efficient, the way a starter New York City apartment should be.

"Thanks again for letting me crash. I promise it'll just be for the night."

Dana handed her a full glass of wine from the kitchen counter. "Figured you could use this after the day you've had."

McKenna was happy to accept the offer. Dana clinked her own glass against McKenna's. "To unemployment."

The wine was awful, but McKenna said, "Mmm, nice." She hadn't known what good wine tasted like when she was twenty-five years old, either. "Word to the wise, though. Don't joke about unemployment, especially in this economy. Take it from me."

"Not just you. Me, too. I quit today."

"What?"

"Solidarity, sister." Dana held up her fist in a power salute. "Fuck the man. The way they threw you out with no notice?"

"Oh, no, no, no, no. *Please* tell me you're joking."

"No way. I'm out of there."

"You can't. Call Vance tomorrow morning and tell him you were mad and made a mistake. He'll take you back. He's a good guy."

"Yeah, right. He was really good when he was shoving a knife in your back."

"Do *not* do this for me." Dana was just a dumb kid with a degree from the New School in some kind of art thing that McKenna had never heard of. A heavily tattooed photographer wouldn't exactly be a hot ticket on the job market, and—based on her digs—she didn't seem to have a trust fund lying around. "I'll be fine. I can always go back to practice. Last time I checked, people still needed lawyers to get them out of jail and whatnot."

"I didn't do it for you. I mean, yeah, today seemed like the day to pull the trigger. But I hate it there. I only do it for the paycheck, and it's not even a good paycheck. I just want to take my weird pictures and make cool stuff that oddball people like me will want to hang on their walls."

"Yeah, but you were doing that stuff on the magazine's clock, anyway."

"Caught me. Really, though, it's fine. My friend's dad owns this huge photography studio—one of the big factories that does a ton of weddings and bar mitzvahs. He said he'll let me do assistant stuff to help pay the bills. It's better dough than the magazine, so I was already thinking about doing it. But telling Vance it was because of the way they were treating you made it seem a lot more rock-star."

McKenna could see the appeal. "All right, then. Solidarity, sister." She drank more of the wine, suppressing a wince at the paint-thinner flavor.

Dana took a seat on the unfolded bed. "Sorry, only place to sit without going in the bedroom, but, don't worry, I don't like you that much." McKenna laughed and joined her. "Now, please, please, please tell me what's going on. I know there's *no. way.* you doctored up those e-mails about Judge Knight. At first I was thinking it could have been Knight himself who set you up. Like, he heard you were running a story exposing all his courthouse crassness to the world, so he decided to discredit the messenger."

"It's a little more complicated than that." Based on Dana's comments, McKenna assumed that Vance hadn't told the magazine staff that the bogus tip had supposedly originated from McKenna's own iPad.

"Well, that's what I figured once you hijacked the magazine's Twitter feed. I hadn't heard of that Susan Hauptmann before, but I was reading up today. Sounds like it's an old cold case." Thanks to the proliferation of television procedurals, everyone with a cable box knew law enforcement lingo. "What the hell does the Knight story have to do with her?"

"I don't know. I'm still figuring it out."

Dana reached for a laptop on the floor and opened it. "You've certainly gotten people's attention. Take a look." She had opened four different windows on her Internet browser. Huffington Post. The Daily Beast. Gawker. Gothamist. It was a story ready-made for the rapid-fire, speculation-heavy world of media driven by social networking. McKenna's sudden firing from a traditional media outlet. The high-profile backstory. Her turn to Twitter to communicate with a curious public. The dangling of a "cold case" and the promise of more information to come.

The story was so weird that commenters were beginning to speculate that the entire thing was a high-concept media hoax to build buzz for *New York City* magazine.

If only that were true.

When their wineglasses were empty, Dana offered her a refill. McKenna declined. "I'm sorry. I'm just really, really tired."

"Sure, of course. I'm going to hit the hay, too. I'll see you in the morning."

Once she was alone in the living room, McKenna checked her e-mail account. She had more than a hundred new messages, almost all of them along the lines of: *Brilliant PR move. Can't wait to see what you're up to. You've got a reader for life. Who needs old-school publishing anyway?* Three media requests. A disturbing number of comments about the hotness of her publicly available head shots and the things she might have time to do with strangers now that she was unemployed.

Sometimes the Internet sucked.

She picked up her cell phone and thought again about calling Patrick, wondering what she could say. More important, she wondered what *he* could say. She wasn't ready to face the truth yet. That he had been lying to her from the minute they'd met. That he'd known more about Susan's disappearance than he'd ever let on. That he had done something terrible that they could never undo.

As long as she could tell herself that she was still looking into things, she could try to believe that everything might be okay.

She typed a new text message:

Sorry, I left the apartment because reporters were showing up trying to get a statement.

Dana had bought the story without a hitch. Hopefully Patrick would, too. Just for the night.

Felt overwhelmed and got a little hammered with a friend and fell asleep.

A friend? Nope, that wasn't going to fly. She went back and erased.

> Got a little hammered with the magazine crowd, trying to make me feel better. Fell asleep on the couch.

Whose couch? It was the kind of detail that got skipped over in the shorthand of texting, especially if she were drunk.

> Really sorry. Don't want to wake you and am too drunk to be walking around anyway. Going to crash here, but I'll see you after work tomorrow. I'm fine. You were right. Everything's going to be okay.

She turned off her phone before it could ring again.

CHAPTER FORTY-ONE

She felt the cold steel bars in her palms. She heard the clink of manacles clamping around a prisoner next door. In the distance, jail keys rattled. Then a loud beeping sound filled the block. Inmates began to yell and bang objects against bars. Something was happening. But she wasn't a prisoner. She was a guard. She opened the cell door and saw Patrick.

McKenna opened her eyes, the sound from her dream filling her head. The source of the steady staccato beeping turned out to be a work truck backing up outside Dana's building. She hadn't realized she had fallen asleep, and now it was morning already.

Dana's sliding bedroom doors were closed. McKenna stepped quietly to the bathroom, pulling the door closed gently. Her face was puffy, her eyes were red, and her mouth felt like it was coated with flour. She found Dana's toothpaste in the medicine cabinet and scrubbed her teeth with her finger.

At Dana's desk, she scribbled a quick note. *Eternal thanks for the crash pad. I'm ready to face the world again. Owe you big-time! —McK*

Dana had come through in a pinch, but her eagerness for every last detail had been a little overwhelming. McKenna didn't want to start the day with a new round of questions. She folded the sheets neatly in a corner and let herself out.

The sign outside a coffee shop on Atlantic Avenue touted free Wi-Fi. She ordered a large coffee and a breakfast sandwich. She was finally hungry. That had to be a good sign.

It was eight-forty-five. Unless Patrick were skipping work, he'd be on his bicycle. She took a chance and called his cell phone. No answer. "Hey, it's me," she said at the tone. "Sorry again about last night. They say drinking can't solve your problems, but turns out that four ginger martinis can dull the pain. A sure sign of alcoholism, huh? Anyway, I crashed at Dana's and am ready to face the world again. I'm going to see what I can find out about Judge Knight's supporters at the courthouse. My best guess is that he got wind of the questions I was asking and forged the e-mails himself in an attempt to make the entire story seem false." No mention of Susan. She was just an unemployed reporter trying to clear her name. "Hope work goes okay. Sorry I'm a lush, but I'll see you at home tonight."

That gave her about nine hours to clear or confirm her worst suspicions.

She started by calling Mallory. "It's McKenna Jordan again. We talked about that video you had of the subway rescue?"

"Yeah, sure. I just saw something on Gawker about you." The girl's flat affect made it impossible to know whether she saw McKenna's newfound fame as a good thing or utter mortification.

"I'm sorry to keep bothering you, but do you have some time this morning for a quick meeting?"

"A meeting? I sit in a cubicle all day and proofread copy for fashion auctions on the Internet. I don't exactly have a secretary keeping a calendar for me."

"I meant a few minutes to talk in person. I want to show you a picture to see if you recognize it."

"Can't you just e-mail it to me?"

McKenna wanted to make sure the girl took a close look. This was important. "It'll only be a few minutes. I'll come to you. You said something about a Starbucks near your office?"

"Yeah, I guess. Forty-fifth Street and Sixth Avenue. Call me when you're close, and I'll meet you."

McKenna hung up and made another call. She got lucky. Nicky Cervantes was at home. He remembered her. "What time do you need to be at school?" she asked.

"I don't. Teacher prep day. Got practice at one, though."

"Any chance you can meet me near Times Square? I'll make it worth your time. Twenty bucks?"

She could tell he was thinking about negotiating.

"Yeah. A'ight. Subway, too?"

"The Starbucks at Forty-fifth Street and Sixth Avenue. No problem."

Those pictures don't look right," Nicky said. "They look old or something. Like her hair and clothes and stuff."

To McKenna, ten years ago didn't seem that long ago. Sure, pictures from the 1980s? Peg-leg harem pants, Madonna bangles, and Cyndi Lauper hairdos were instant date-setters. But 2003? McKenna was certain she was wearing some of the same clothes. To a teenager like Nicky, 2003 probably looked as retro as Woodstock would have seemed to McKenna at his age.

"She'd be ten years older now," she said, pointing again at the photograph of Susan. Ten years to a teenager? Unimaginable. "She'd be my age. Could this be the woman from the subway station?"

"I don't know. She was— Damn, she was chasing me most of the time."

"You must have looked at her in the beginning, scoped her out for at least a second."

"Let me see again. Yeah, okay. I got it. Her hair's not as blond now, maybe there's more red in it or something. But the face? It could definitely be her."

"Does that mean it *could* be her, or it's *definitely* her?"

He looked at her like the question made his head hurt. "What do you *mean* what do I mean? I guess I'm saying that lady in your pictures looks a lot more like the lady on the subway than you do, or my mother, or that lady over there, or that lady, or that one. So, yeah, it could *definitely* be her."

She'd take what she could get. At least he hadn't ruled out the possibility. He grabbed the twenty-five dollars like it was the easiest money he'd ever made, even though McKenna knew it wasn't.

She called Mallory and said that she was waiting at the coffee shop. A few minutes later, a woman in her mid-twenties walked in, scanning the place with uncertainty.

"Are you Mallory?" McKenna never would have expected from the girl's voice that she'd be so attractive. She had clear alabaster skin, strawberry-blond hair, and big pool-blue eyes.

"Yeah. I didn't realize until I opened the door that I had no idea who I was looking for." Mallory took a seat at the bistro table across from McKenna. "I made the mistake of telling my friend you called again. She wants me to ask whether your whole Twitter campaign is a PR thing for the magazine. She's got some idea about doing the same kind of thing for her boyfriend's band. Like anyone would care if there was a feud between members of some band no one's ever heard of."

"It's no stunt," McKenna said. "Someone gave me a bogus tip for a story and tried to make it look like I made the whole thing up. It's complicated, but I'm starting to wonder whether the same people wanted to make sure I didn't get a lead on the subway video you shot."

"Whoa. That's intense." The woman had a way with understatement.

McKenna pulled up the photograph of Susan that she'd showed Nicky Cervantes. "It's over ten years old, so you've got to do some mental age progression. But is this the woman from the subway station?"

"Oh my gosh. I think that's her. I really think that's her."

McKenna noticed then that Mallory's coloring was close to Susan's. It made sense that she might be better able to discern among similar-looking women than Nicky. They all looked the same when "they" didn't resemble "you."

Nicky and Mallory had both seen the subway woman in person, and neither of them had ruled out a match. They were validating what McKenna had believed all along.

The real reason she'd wanted to see Mallory in person was for another photograph entirely. McKenna scrolled through her photographs until she found one of Patrick alone.

"You said you loaned your phone to a guy in the lunch line the day the subway video got erased. Could this be the man?"

Mallory took a quick look, much shorter than her inspection of Susan's picture. "Nope. Not him."

"You're sure? You told me before that you couldn't pick him out of a lineup."

"Exactly. Which is how I know this isn't the guy. This guy's pretty hot. I'd remember him. And my friend Jen? She would have found a way to give him her number. Trust me."

McKenna had never been so relieved to get a negative response. Whoever had borrowed Mallory's phone must have been the person who deleted the subway video. It stood to reason that the same person had wiped out Dana's Skybox account and fabricated the Knight e-mails sent to McKenna. Patrick had physical access to McKenna's iPad, but a decent enough computer expert could have pulled it all off virtually.

She needed to find the man who'd gotten into Mallory's phone. "You said the man borrowed the phone while you were in line somewhere? That was on Wednesday, right? Do you happen to remember the time?"

"Margon. Some of the city's best Cuban food, tucked away in that wasteland of Times Square. The lines are massive, but it's cheap. We were at the start of lunch break. It must have been between one and one-fifteen."

The man might have wiped out the video that McKenna was most interested in, but there were other cameras in the city. McKenna was going to start using that to her advantage. She was turning the tables.

CHAPTER
FORTY-TWO

Some people would have been puzzled by Mallory's description of Times Square as a wasteland, but those people would be exposing themselves as non–New Yorkers. To non–New Yorkers—people who called the city the "Big Apple," who thought of it as stressful, a place to visit but not live, people like McKenna's mother—Times Square *was* New York City. But to people who lived here, Times Square was the place that gave their hometown a bad rap. It was like Disney World or Costco or the DMV—places you probably went but only under protest, for a very specific purpose.

A few times a year, like every good New Yorker, McKenna ventured into this combat zone for an especially lauded performance or to meet an out-of-town friend at some ghastly hotel bar. Today she had a very different reason.

It was only eleven-thirty, and a line had already formed outside Margon. As McKenna bypassed the line to the entrance, responses ranged from the passive-aggressive ("I didn't think they took reservations") to the aggressive-aggressive ("You're not that special, lady! Back of the line!").

McKenna had assumed from the restaurant's demand that it was the latest celebrity-soaked Manhattan hot spot. When she reached the front, she realized it was barely a restaurant at all. The long, narrow space was occupied primarily by a food counter with cafeteria-style service, complete with a sign reading LINE START HERE. The early birds had grabbed the few tables available for dining.

The cashier seemed as in charge as anyone. It took a few tries before he understood McKenna's request. When he finally did comprehend the question, he laughed quietly and shook his head. "No. No cameras." He gestured around like, *Look at this place.*

When McKenna walked out empty-handed, some of the line occupants gained newfound faith in karmic justice. "Yep, back of the line!"

She followed the line, scoping out businesses whose security cameras might have captured the interaction between Mallory and the man who'd borrowed her phone. Nail salon. Indian restaurant. Tattoo parlor. Three strikes.

Her next try was a parking garage. It was well past the length of the current line, but Mallory had been here during rush hour. It was worth a shot.

The entrance to the underground garage was a steep, narrow ramp. A row of cars was backed up, waiting to be worked into the Tetris-like clump of vehicles squeezed into the cramped garage. She found herself cringing in anticipation of a crunch as the parking attendant lurched a Porsche Carrera from the line. With authority. Nothing but net. It would have taken her fifteen minutes of wiggling to free that car from its knot.

She waited patiently while he retrieved cars for four customers standing nearby with claim tickets. People who needed favors couldn't be pushy. When she got his attention, he was more than happy to chat. He probably didn't get many opportunities to socialize in his profession.

"Yeah, we got cameras. A bunch of them. Two years ago, some madman pulled a woman from the street and raped her right there on the ramp. My guy was down here the whole time, but he was washing cars and listening to the radio. Didn't hear a thing. Me? If I'd heard something like that? Guy wouldn't have gotten out of here alive. Now we got a bell that rings whenever anyone sets one foot inside the ramp—you walked down here, right? Yep. I heard the bell. Knew someone was coming but didn't see a car. Works good. Plus we got cameras. A big system. Catches everything."

"What about outside the ramp? On the sidewalk?"

"Yeah, sure. I mean, not like all of midtown or whatever. But yeah, sidewalk on both sides of the garage."

"Do you have tape?"

"For fourteen days, then it cycles. Not sure I'm supposed to be showing it to anyone. No one's ever asked."

She'd heard the anger in his voice when he spoke about the madman who attacked the woman two years before. "I'm on something of an amateur sleuth venture. My little sister was waiting in line for Margon—"

"Oh, man, those rice and beans . . ."

"Well, some guy borrowed her phone, saying it was an emergency. And when she got it back, he had put these crude pictures of himself on it."

"Now, see? What the hell is wrong with people? Who does something like that?"

"That's what I'm trying to find out. The police say they can't do anything about it, since the pictures he left—they're not exactly of his face, you know? But maybe your cameras caught it on film."

"Say nothing more. I got you. We're gonna catch this fucker."

The number of drivers waiting to drop off keys continued to grow as the attendant scanned through digital video files in the back office. "Just a second, guys. I've got a big emergency here. I'll be right out. Promise!" He had queued up the feed from the camera on the west side of the garage from Wednesday, starting at one, the beginning of Mallory's lunch hour. They could see people waiting in line on the sidewalk. He played it at high speed.

"There!" McKenna saw Mallory deep in conversation with her friend. "That's my sister," she said. "Slow it down." They watched at regular speed as a man in the line said something to them. Mallory barely looked at the man before handing him her phone.

"Oh yeah." The parking attendant was now her full partner in the investigation. "There's the sicko. Yep, he's doing something. Not taking pictures but fiddling with the controls. Probably had the pictures all ready at some website to download on the phone or something."

In the video, the man handed the phone back to Mallory and stepped out of the line. "Stop!" McKenna said.

"We got him," her partner announced, pausing the screen.

McKenna had no idea who the man was.

CHAPTER FORTY-THREE

Before Scanlin even opened the glass front door, the two women at the reception desk of Comfort Park exchanged a glance. In that shared look, he overheard their entire unspoken conversation.

Here he comes again.

We keep telling him—

But he doesn't listen.

It was true. They had kept telling him. They told him Melissa didn't remember him. They told him she really was happy here; he didn't need to worry. They told him it was best to come with Jenna.

Easier said than done. Despite all of Jenna's resentment of her father for putting his work before family, she—in her words—wasn't "a morning person." It was all she "could do" to get up in time to make it to her job as a corporate accountant. Her visits to Melissa were strictly in the early evening.

Scanlin, on the other hand, was a cop with comp time that he had to use or lose. He was also the one who'd taken care of Melissa, even after everyone said she needed to move into a "facility." No one had believed him, but there were minutes back when she was home—sometimes over an hour—when she was almost normal, and it was always in the morning. She'd wake up before him and find him sleeping in Jenna's room and ask whether he wanted pancakes. Didn't she have to remember him to know that pancakes were his favorite?

"Good morning," he said. "I'm here to see Melissa Scanlin."

Comfort Park. He hated the name. It sounded like a combination of "comfort station" and "trailer park." He hated the place itself when Melissa moved in. The exaggerated attempts to make it look cheerful—flowered upholstery, flowered curtains, plastic floral centerpieces in the dining area. The dated furniture. The weird smell.

He eventually realized that his discomfort with the place was all about him, not Melissa. He wanted Melissa to be the kind of woman who would hate living here. But she wasn't. She was a woman who acted like a child due to her dementia. And much like a child, she didn't care about design or upholstery or even the people around her. She liked arts and crafts sessions, music days, and the fact that the ladies at Comfort Park constantly brought in a rotating collection of hats for her to wear.

"Of course, Detective Scanlin. I believe she's in the group room right now."

The group room was a bright, open room filled with nonmatching chairs, small tables, and activity pods for drawing, puzzling, clay molding, and reading. The woman led the way to his wife, who was sitting by herself in front of a TV tray, playing solitaire. It wasn't actually solitaire, but for some reason, the practice of placing piles of cards in seven columns and then turning over the remainder of the cards, three at once into the waste, remained a familiar pattern.

"As we talked about, Detective," the woman whispered as they approached.

"I know. Just keep her company. No reminders. No prodding."

"Exactly," she said, like he was a student who had recited the alphabet correctly for the first time.

"Not to worry. I'll act like a complete stranger."

He couldn't help himself. He recognized that the people who worked here—most of them, at least—truly cared about the patients. But at the end of the day, their jobs would be easier if the husbands and the parents and the siblings would just go away. Then they could run Comfort Park like a day-care center with giant toddlers and would not have to be reminded that the people in this room used to be adults. A woman like Melissa used to be a mother, a wife, and a kickass cook. Until she agreed to marry a cop, she liked to sneak a toke of doob. And though no one but Scanlin would ever know it, she was sexier than any porn star in the bedroom.

"Hi, there," he said. "Good game?"

"Oh, yeah. I like this a lot. I always win, too."

She *never* won, not even when she knew how to play.

"You know how to—you know." She gestured to the cards.

"I used to play. I could never win, though. Too hard."

"Doesn't seem so hard to me."

"You must be very good at it. My name's Joe. I was born in Pittsburgh. I'm a police officer, and I have a daughter named Jenna."

He'd learned that he could recite basic biographical facts without triggering a series of events ending with a staff member asking him to "come back later" with Jenna. As long as he acted like a talkative stranger, Melissa was calm, even mildly entertained. But any statements like "I'm your husband" or "We lived together for twenty-three years" or "How can you not remember?" were quickly followed by stressful pacing around the room, tears, or—the worst—accusations that he was trying to "steal" her.

"When Jenna was little," he continued, "her appendix almost burst, and we almost didn't know. Other kids yell and scream the second they get a tummyache, but all Jenna said was that she must have eaten too much pizza. She kept saying it for over an entire day"—twenty-four hours wouldn't mean anything to Melissa—"and even when the pain got really bad, she didn't scream or even moan. She said, 'Daddy, the pizza moved to the right side of my body. I think that means I need to go to the hospital.' "

There was a certain irony to the Comfort Park staff's cordial relationship with Jenna. By the time he decided to place Melissa in a home full-time, everyone they knew could barely contain their relief. *Better for both your sakes. Long time coming. Had to be done.*

Everyone but Jenna. If he could undergo a lobotomy to forget all of the hateful words that had spewed from his own daughter that night, he'd happily make the first cut.

"Does Jenna have a mommy?" Melissa asked.

He knew it. Mornings were always better for Melissa. He believed it was because the sleep refreshed her. If it were true that most people used only ten percent of brain capacity, maybe Melissa was able to use more when she was rested.

"Yes, she does. In fact, her name is Melissa. Isn't that your name?"

Melissa's brow furrowed, and he wondered whether she was about to have an episode. "That's nice that you have a—" She waved her hand in the air, the way she did when she couldn't conjure an appropriate word. "I used to have one. But he's gone now."

Melissa could not remember him, but she did seem to remember that she'd had a boyfriend at Comfort Park until he had passed away four months earlier. For her sake, he hoped she would forget. And that she'd forget the ones who were likely to come after. Melissa had long outlived the average life expectancy of patients with her diagnosis.

"It was nice talking to you, Melissa. Have a good time finishing your game."

"I always win."

He thanked the women on his way out, who gave him the sympathetic but impatient look they seemed to reserve for him.

He had an entire afternoon in front of him. He wasn't good at taking a day off. No job. No family. No hobbies.

For a while, he'd thought the Hauptmann case might become his hobby, but he'd hit a wall with Vera Hadley's notes. So maybe the nosy neighbor had heard Susan argue with a boyfriend. He still didn't know who the guy was. And he didn't know whether Susan was dead or alive.

The final straw had been the stunt McKenna Jordan pulled. Most people caught red-handed printing libelous information about a judge would lie low and take their lumps. But hauling out the name of her missing friend on Twitter to try to save herself? The woman would do anything for attention.

The thought of McKenna Jordan reminded him that he wanted to check in with his old friend Scott Macklin to make sure he had heard the news that she had imploded once again.

Mac's house was pretty much as Scanlin remembered it. He was never one to swear by his memory, but it was possible they had added the dormer windows to the second floor. Maybe the cedar fence around the side yard was new, too.

The door of the single-car attached garage was closed. The driveway was empty.

He rang the doorbell, expecting Josefina to greet him with that cheerful but busy voice. No answer. Another ding-dong. More silence.

The twenty-five-minute drive had seemed like nothing when he left Comfort Park. But twenty-five minutes times two was close to an hour. An hour of time wasted in the car.

He walked to the side of the house and peered into a window. If the television was on, he'd at least know they were on their way home. He could grab some McDonald's and come right back.

He tried the phone number and heard it ringing inside. No answer.

He went to his car and found an old oil-change receipt in the glove box and a pen in the console. *Hey, Scott. A voice from your past. Called yesterday. Popped in today. By next week, you'll need a stalking order. Give me a ring when you have a chance to catch up.* He scrawled his name and cell number and made his way to the porch to drop off the note.

There was no logical place to put it. No screen door to hold it in place. The bottom of the door was weather-sealed, so there was no slipping the note beneath. The mailbox had a lock on it, thanks to identity thieves.

He tried the door. If it were unlocked, he'd leave the note in the front hallway and get on his way.

It opened.

The house smelled like crispy bacon. Scanlin couldn't think of a better smell.

He bent down to place the note on the hardwood floor in the foyer. That was when he saw the bare feet protruding from the living room doorway.

CHAPTER FORTY-FOUR

McKenna knew her suspicions were right the second the transit agent saw her. He recognized her. And her return trip to the video monitoring center for the subway system had him very nervous.

"Hi, Frank. Remember me? I was here last weekend looking for camera footage of that kid who fell on the tracks at Times Square."

"Yeah, sure. Sorry about the glitch. People want low taxes. Want to keep the fares down. When crap starts breaking, they act like they're all surprised."

"Back up and running again?"

"Last I heard. All set to go."

"Good. So if someone gives me a bribe on the platform down there today, you'll catch the whole thing on film?"

"Umm . . . yeah, sure, I guess. Something I can help you with?"

"I mention the possibility of a bribe being caught on film, Frank, because that's basically what happened to you."

"I think you better leave, lady. I've got work to do, and you're obviously under a mistaken—"

"Don't. Just don't, okay, Frank? That man who paid you to wipe out the footage from that day? He was an undercover reporter."

"I don't know what you're talking about—"

"He's a bit of a lowlife but fancies himself an investigative journalist. An amateur Geraldo Rivera type. He doesn't actually have the *ethics* of a legitimate reporter. See, most reporters—if they're going to do a story about corruption among low-level city employees, people like you—they actually need to *know* about the corruption first. Not Hank the Tank." No clue where the nickname came from, but she was rolling with it. "That's what he calls himself. Because he's sort of a tool. Anyway, Frank, reporters like me are pretty sick of tools like Hank running around making up stories. Not to mention that this time around, he fucked me by wiping out the subway footage I needed for my Superwoman article."

"What kind of story is he making up?"

"Well, he didn't really make it up, did he? But he did entrap you. You were just sitting here minding your own business until he came around making an offer no reasonable person could refuse. Like you said, people want low taxes. They want cheap fares. That leaves hardworking guys like you holding the bag, working more hours for less pay. He played you, Frank. He took advantage of you, paid you off, and now he's going to use you as the centerpiece of a story—like *you're* the big problem in this city."

"But that's— He can't. I'll get fired."

"And that's why I'm here, Frank. I've always suspected this hack of pulling the strings on his stories. This time I figured it out. He's already bragging that he got a city worker—on tape!—to wipe out security footage from one of the biggest terrorist targets in the world. Well, I put two and two together, and I want to reverse the sting on him. I'll show that he set you up. That he overcame your resistance by upping his price over and over until you relented. That's what happened, right?"

"*If* it happened, then yeah. But, um, does my name have to be used?"

"Nope, not at all, Frank. If everything goes to plan, my story—no names—will be the end of Hank, and that will kill his story about you."

"Okay, let's do that, then. He entrapped me. Just like you said. He came in saying that he was married to the lady in the tape. That all she was trying to do was help a person, but after the fact, she realized reporters would make a big deal out of it and everything, and she just wasn't interested. I told him there was nothing I could do, but like you said, he kept pestering me. I figured she was a hero and all. What was the harm in protecting her privacy?"

"Okay, and to be clear, Frank, this is the guy we're talking about, right?"

She showed him a still photograph from the parking garage's security camera. In her head, she had started thinking of the man as the Cleaner.

"Yeah, that's the guy, all right. Can't believe he played me like that."

"And he gave you"—she took a guess—"five thousand dollars?"

"No. It was only a grand. He's telling people *five*?"

Frank was cheaper than she would have expected. Someone needed to explain to him the value of a union job these days.

She was no closer to identifying the Cleaner, but she was now sure of two things: he was thorough, and he did not want anyone to know Susan Hauptmann was alive.

CHAPTER FORTY-FIVE

Twenty-two minutes.

Scanlin knew, because after calling 911, he waited by himself on Scott Macklin's porch for what seemed like an eternity before checking his phone log to see how long it had been since he'd made the call. Then he heard the sirens. Then he saw the ambulance turn the corner.

Twenty-two minutes for someone to show up to the scene of a dead cop.

Scanlin had seen a point-blank head shot before. He wished he hadn't, but he had. He'd even seen a self-inflicted one—another cop, in fact. That image might have been what saved him when things got really bad with Melissa. He couldn't stand the thought of someone finding him like that.

But that was how he'd found Scott Macklin. His friend had been sitting in the recliner. The bloodstains on the chair and the wall behind it made that much clear. His arms had probably fallen to his lap. The gun was in his right hand. The movement of his head backward had pulled the weight of his body forward in the chair. He eventually slid onto the floor, where Scanlin discovered him.

By the time Josefina pulled up in front of the house, the ambulance had been joined by a fire engine and two marked police cars.

She recognized Scanlin standing at the curb and greeted him with a smile. She was wearing what looked like a yoga outfit. "Oh my goodness. You weren't kidding when you said you wanted to see Scott. What's all the commotion?"

"It's Scott. I'm so sorry, Josefina."

She dropped to her knees when he told her.

Scanlin stayed with her through the entire process. The moving of the body. The questions from responding officers and detectives. The call to Tommy who now wanted to be called Thomas. The clearing of the house for entry, even as Josefina realized there was no way she was going to spend the night there.

They wound up at a Denny's, where they waited for a church friend whom she was going to stay with.

"I don't know why he'd do this." She used her fork to push the scrambled eggs of her Grand Slam to the edges of the plate. "I didn't even know he still had a gun. He seemed so happy about Tommy going to college. Maybe it was because he was out of the house? Maybe the idea of just the two of us—"

"Aw, don't start talking like that. Mac was crazy about you." Scanlin had no way of knowing whether that was still true. Hadn't the most bitter, unhappy couples been wild about each other at some point? But he couldn't imagine Mac falling out of love with the woman who had brought him to life back then. Scanlin could think of only one reason Macklin would have been so desperate, and he wasn't sure how to broach the subject with Josefina.

"I know Scott tried to protect you from the details, but I assume you know something about the shooting he was involved in before he took early retirement."

"I was a new immigrant, Joe, but I wasn't illiterate. Of course I knew the basic facts. That boy reached for a gun, and Scott had to shoot back. But the boy was black, and Scott was a white cop, and so—That's how this country still sees things. Maybe it will always be that way."

"The DA's office took it to a grand jury. The lead prosecutor was all set to steer the grand jury to uphold the shooting as justified, but then a younger prosecutor claimed that Scott had used a drop gun. That's what it's called when a police officer takes an extra gun and plants it—"

"Yes, I knew all of this. It's ancient history. They cleared Scott, but all that digging around in his past exposed other problems. People he arrested from years ago came out of the woodwork. He eventually cut a deal to leave the department and keep his retirement."

He was tainted goods by then.

"You're right," Scanlin said, "it is ancient history. Or at least it was. I called you yesterday because that same prosecutor—the one who started the whole scandal—was reviving the story for the ten-year anniversary. She's a reporter now. She wrote a big article in a magazine, trying to get attention."

"Ay, ay, ay. The reporter lady. She was out here yesterday. I come home from getting the oil changed, and there she is in my living room." Josefina was speaking more quickly now, her Mexican accent more noticeable. "I told Scott, 'What are you doing talking to some reporter?' He thinks he can be nice and charming and show her how we live a normal life, how he raised a good boy, maybe she'll leave him alone. Oh my God, do you think that's why he was so upset? Is the *reporter* the reason he would do this?"

He hadn't answered the question when he saw Josefina's attention shift to the sound of bells ringing at the Denny's entrance. A plump middle-aged woman walked in and spotted Josefina immediately. He saw tears begin to form in both women's eyes.

"That's my friend. She'll drive me to her place. I need to lie down for a while."

"Of course." He walked Josefina to her friend and waited while the two exchanged a hug. "Call me if there's anything I can do to help. Anything at all."

She nodded, but he could tell she would be more comfortable relying on people who had been a part of their lives more recently.

As the friend backed her MINI out of its parking space, he watched Josefina place her face in her hands and begin to sob.

He dropped a twenty on the table and headed to his own car. He was surprised at how hard he slammed the car door. How tight his grip was on the steering wheel. How he could almost hear the blood pounding through his veins.

A good man was dead. This wasn't right.

He found her business card crumpled in his jacket pocket. McKenna Jordan. Cell number scribbled on the back. As he listened to the rings—one, two, three—a lump formed behind his Adam's apple. He tried to swallow but felt a gasp escape from his throat. Dammit. He was not going to cry. He would *not* allow this woman to hear him cry.

CHAPTER FORTY-SIX

It was amazing how much a hot shower had done to calm Mc-Kenna down. Being here, in her own apartment, surrounded by the little reminders of her everyday life—her life with Patrick—was helping, too. Patrick was gone, presumably off to work, which meant her phone calls had reassured him that everything was okay.

The contents of the box that Adam Bayne had sent over seemed to be just as she'd left them. Granted, she hadn't memorized the exact placement of every item, and she had taken the picture of Patrick and Susan that had gotten her so worked up. But if Patrick had really been as anxious as she thought he'd sounded the previous night—*Is there something in here that could be an issue?*—surely he would have torn through the belongings, searching for whatever it was he thought could be so damning.

In retrospect, it was the phone call that had set her imagination running wild. What had she really heard? She mentally replayed his side of the conversation. *She's got a bunch of your old stuff scattered all over our living room floor.*

He had said *your stuff*. She had assumed the "you" was Susan, but maybe he'd called Adam when he saw the messenger labels on the box. *Is there something in here that could be an issue?* Okay, so he didn't want her to know that he'd had a fling or whatever with

Susan. McKenna was mad—pissed—that he hadn't told her, but she could see how it would happen. They met. They liked each other. It wasn't like "Hey, I used to sleep with your friend" was a great pickup line. A lie about a past lover was nothing compared to the scenarios she'd been playing in her head.

And then there was the last part of the call: *I have it under control. Problem solved. Just take care of yourself.*

He could've meant "Fine, if she found out about me and Susan, we'll work through it." And *Just take care of yourself* could have been a jibe, as if to say "Take care of your own house and mind your own business."

Her thoughts were interrupted by the trill of her cell phone.

She didn't recognize the number. She hesitated. Every moment of the last two days had brought nothing but more horrible news. She didn't think she could take any more. She was also screening incoming tips about Susan. Maybe someone had gotten her number from the magazine.

Three rings. She had to decide. "Hello?"

"You've got blood on your hands, Jordan."

There was something familiar about the voice, but she couldn't place it. "Excuse me?"

"You're like a one-woman wrecking ball. You should come with a warning label: human destruction will follow. Do you even *stop* to think about the way your choices affect other people? Killing his job wasn't enough, was it? It's all just publicity to you, but you cost a good man his life. His *life.*"

She should have known that a public call for information about a decade-old death would bring out the nut jobs. "Who is this?"

"It's Joe Scanlin. That stunt you pulled going to Macklin's house? I hope it helped you with whatever story you're trying to publish, because you pushed him over the edge. I just found him. He ate his gun."

She felt a lurch in her stomach at the imagery. "Oh my God. Scott Macklin?"

"He's dead. You pushed him over the edge. Are you happy?"

"Of course I'm not happy. He was—I *knew* him, whatever you might think of me. And I don't know what you mean by any stunt. I didn't go to his house. I haven't seen him since I left the district attorney's office." She pictured Macklin, beaming as he described the strategy he used to teach his stepson the perfect spiral football pass. That sweet man killed himself?

"His wife told me everything. She saw you there yesterday in the living room. He just wanted to be left alone. Why'd you have to—"

"She said *I* was there? I wasn't. I swear to God, Scanlin."

"I don't believe you."

"Yeah, well, I'm getting used to that these days. Did she say me specifically? Maybe it was another reporter. It's the ten-year anniversary, after all."

"She said she came home and saw a woman in the living room, and that it was a female reporter. Of course it was you. What other female reporters are going to bother a cop who left the job a decade ago?"

A woman. An unidentified woman asking questions about something that happened ten years ago. It didn't make any sense, but she could think of only one person it could have been.

"Are you there? Fucking bitch hung up—"

"No, I'm here," she said. "And it wasn't me at Scott Macklin's house yesterday. But if Scott Macklin is dead, I'm not sure it was suicide. I need you to meet me. Right now. I promise I'll tell you everything."

CHAPTER FORTY-SEVEN

It's said there are certain moments in history that everyone remembers. The moon landing. The day Kennedy was shot. The night the United States elected its first African-American president. The day the towers came down.

The first reports came in right around nine A.M. on September 11. McKenna was on her way to the morning plea docket. Heading from her office to the elevator, she passed a lounge area for civilian witnesses—the most luxurious area on the floor, complete with a television set—and saw early reports of an airplane colliding with the World Trade Center. The anchors were trying to calm the worldwide audience: "The most likely scenario is that this is a private commuter plane that left its intended route. City officials are encouraging everyone to remain calm."

From there, McKenna went to the courtroom of Judge John DeWitt Gregory to accept routine guilty pleas from routine defendants on routine charges. Forty-five minutes passed without interruption. It was a different world then. It was a world without an omnipresent information stream playing constantly in the background via phones and other devices. It was also a world where the date she wrote on each of those plea agreements, September 11,

2001, was just a date. By the time she was done taking that morning's pleas, the world and America's place in it had changed.

She sensed something was wrong the minute she hit the hallway.
Usually lawyers piled up outside the sluggish elevators, no matter
how long the wait, because people, let's face it, are lazy. That morning, people were sprinting up and down stairs. She remembered
the panic on the face of a former coworker turned defense attorney
who passed her in the hallway: "We've got to get out of here. Leave
downtown. Leave the city. This is really, really bad. They're saying
there are eight other planes unaccounted for."

It wasn't until McKenna got to her office that she connected the
frenzy in the courthouse to the television report. Her mother had
left a panicked voice mail. "Kenny, we just heard the news. Aren't
you right down there by the towers? I think you are, but your daddy
says you're a ways away. Let us know you're safe, okay?"

By then, McKenna couldn't get a dial tone. She did manage to
find a cabdriver filling up on the Lower East Side. "Stupid day to let
the tank go low," he was muttering. He didn't want to take a passenger, but she begged, then offered to pay for the entire tank plus
fare to go anywhere outside of Manhattan. She and the cabdriver
actually argued about which route to take. Some attributes of city
life were truly ingrained.

And now here she was again. It wasn't 9/11, not by a long shot,
but she did feel like her life had changed forever. She'd lost her job.
Susan was back, possibly tied up in a Long Island bombing. The
FBI had searched McKenna's office, when she still had one. And
once again, she was bickering with a freakin' cabdriver who could
not accept that the best way to Forest Hills was the LIE and not the
Fifty-ninth Street Bridge.

It had taken her enough work just to get Scanlin to agree to meet.
Even after he relented, their conversation had turned to a geographic
bartering of the metropolitan region. Surely it was easier for Scanlin
in his own car to meet her in Manhattan than for her to leave the
island. But he was in Forest Hills, having spent the day consoling

Scott Macklin's widow. Yep, that was the moral high ground. Scanlin got to name the spot. She was schlepping to Queens.

In retrospect, she was grateful he had a head start. By the time she met him at the Irish pub he had chosen, he was at least two Scotches in and no longer sounded like he wanted to pound her skull against concrete. She took the seat across from him in the booth. She didn't bother with introductions or even words of solace about the death of Scott Macklin.

She started with the absurd chase to determine the identity of the subway Superwoman and summarized every last detail until he called her with the news of Mac's death. The face that looked like Susan's. The missing video. The button that linked the woman to the People for the Preservation of the Planet. The bombing in Brentwood. The extremely coincidental timing of the fake tip about Frederick Knight. Even her stupid suspicions about Patrick. Everything.

"What does any of this have to do with Mac?" Scanlin asked.

"I have no idea."

"Nice."

"Hear me out. If I'm right, if Susan is alive, it means that for ten years, she was perfectly happy doing whatever it is she's been doing. But now, after a decade, she's back in New York. And look at all of the things that have happened since then." She ticked off the points on her fingers. One. "The man I call the Cleaner did not want her to be seen." Two. "Deleting the video of her is one thing, but someone also set me up with those forged e-mails from Judge Knight." Three. "Which means I no longer have a book deal about the Marcus Jones shooting, and everything I say from now on will be considered false." Four. "Now Scott Macklin is dead, and someone claiming to be a female reporter was at his house yesterday."

There was only one conclusion. "Susan being back has something to do with the fact that it's been ten years since the Jones shooting. Maybe my article triggered something."

She could tell from his expression that Scanlin didn't want to buy it.

"The timing works," she argued. "Susan disappeared not long after the Jones shooting. Look, I'm the last person who thought I'd say this. I was sure someone killed her. We all said she'd never just walk away—"

"Not *everyone*."

"Not you, of course."

"Not her sister," Scanlin said. "And not your husband."

"Patrick never thought Susan would leave. He still insists that she must be dead."

"I know you think I'm incompetent—"

"I never said you were incompetent."

"Close enough. But I'm quite sure Patrick was the one who told me that Susan had major issues with her family, hated her job, hated the pressure to work with her dad. He told me that in his gut, he thought she just started over again."

She had set aside her doubts about Patrick, and now they were back.

What had he said to her the other day? *She'd never just leave. That's what we all said. That's what we all told the police.* Yet another lie she'd caught him in.

When she looked at Scanlin, he was taking her picture with his cell phone.

"What the—"

His phone was against his ear now. "You have a picture of Susan Hauptmann on that gadget of yours?" he asked, gesturing to the iPad sticking out of her purse.

"Yes, but—"

He held up a finger to cut her off. "Josefina, this is Joe Scanlin. I'm so sorry to bother you, but it's really important. That reporter at your house yesterday? You remember what she looked like? Okay, I need you to look at a couple of pictures for me. I wouldn't ask if I didn't think it was urgent. Do you have an e-mail address?"

They sat in silence after the pictures had been sent. There was nothing more to say until they had their answer.

He picked up his phone the second it chimed. "You got the pictures? You're sure? Okay, let me see what else I can find out. Try to get some sleep." He set his phone down on the table. "Tell me everything again. From the beginning."

"What did she say?"

"That she was a hundred percent certain the woman she saw with Scott yesterday was Susan Hauptmann."

CHAPTER FORTY-EIGHT

Carter should have left town. He should have gone to his safe-deposit box, pulled out his passport, and taken the first flight from JFK to Switzerland.

But some part of him—the part that had puked his guts out at the Marriott, the part that had started to reach for the pay phone yesterday, before it was too late—had kept him in New York. And the same part of him brought him to the Apple store in SoHo to search the latest local news updates.

"Good afternoon, sir." The kid who greeted him wore a black T-shirt and a giant ID badge around his neck. He looked entirely too helpful. "What can I help you find today?"

"To be honest? I'm not buying. My phone's almost dead, and I'm hoping to check some game scores."

"No problem. I hear ya. All our demos are hooked up to the Web, so have a go wherever you'd like. No pressure."

Carter picked a laptop at the far corner of the display table. Scott Macklin. Enter.

It had already happened. The suicide of a retired cop wouldn't necessarily be newsworthy, but reports had identified him as the police officer whose controversial shooting of Marcus Jones incited city-wide protests, widespread racial tensions, and his early retirement. Macklin's former partner was quoted as suspecting a connection between the suicide and the ten-year anniversary of the shooting.

Carter knew better. He knew because he was the one who was supposed to have killed Scott Macklin.

The story was accompanied by two pictures of Macklin with his family—one at his wedding, and one at the son's high school graduation last May. In both, the boy looked at his father like a hero.

Was it too late for Carter to be a better man?

When Carter started thinking about going private, all the work was international. That was fine. After three deployments, Carter was used to it. He would do the same job in the same hellhole and earn a hell of a lot more dough.

Then more and more people took gigs working the homeland. Now they didn't even call it the homeland. It was just home.

Police were estimating that Officer Macklin had taken his life at about nine o'clock this morning. Carter had killed his cell phone at eight o'clock the night before. Even if the client had figured out immediately that Carter was off the rails, that left about thirteen hours to line up another doer. No way.

That confirmed what Carter had suspected the minute the client had changed the mission the first time. What had been a surveillance job had become an order to blow up a house in the suburbs. He was willing to do it. The woman was fair game. The rest of them were domestic terrorists, as far as he was concerned.

But the order didn't sit right with him. Carter worked best when the people giving the orders were as calm and rational and dispassionate as he was. The house explosion was about emotion. So was the order to kill Scott Macklin.

For Macklin to have died this morning without Carter pulling the trigger meant that the client had done it personally. And the client would know that Carter knew.

Carter had seen firsthand what the client's strategy was for people who knew too much. The woman. The retired cop. It was time to clean house.

It was unavoidable: Carter would be next. And he had no interest in spending the rest of his life in hiding.

Carter was a firm believer that any mission required complete knowledge of all available facts. Usually his mission was narrow—watch someone, break through a security alarm, find out a true identity. Here, it had escalated from following the woman, to planting the bomb, then taking out Scott Macklin. It was not his job to know the larger "why" behind these assignments.

Now that he was on his own, the "why" was precisely what he needed. But the two people who could have helped him were gone.

He should have called Macklin yesterday, before it was too late. He could have warned the man. Maybe it wouldn't have saved him, but it would have given him a chance to protect himself. And Carter could have asked Macklin why someone wanted him dead.

The woman might know, but Carter had no idea how to find her.

Without the woman, and without Macklin, Carter lacked the information he needed to get himself off whatever hit list the three of them shared.

He could think of only one other person who might be able to help: the man he'd seen meeting the woman on the train. Carter remembered his address.

He searched for the apartment's sales history online. Bingo. Purchased five years ago by Patrick Jordan and McKenna Wright.

He did a Google search of both names. Ah, a very nice wedding announcement in the Sunday Styles section of *The New York Times*. He was West Point, army, museum security. She was Stanford, Boalt Hall, prosecutor, writer.

Prosecutor. Carter clicked back to one of the stories he had read about Scott Macklin's suicide. *Last week* New York City *magazine published a ten-page article about the Marcus Jones shooting. The article was authored by McKenna Jordan (née Wright), the former prosecutor who initially raised doubts about Mr. Macklin's claim of self-defense.*

Interesting.

Was it too late for Carter to be a better man? He was about to start finding out.

Their phone number was listed under P. Jordan, same address.

"Hello?"

Carter was calling from a pay phone. Even if Patrick Jordan had caller ID, the number would mean nothing to him.

"You're going to be very interested in what I have to say."

"If that's a sales pitch, you need to work on it."

"Your girl is in danger," Carter said. He wanted to get this guy's attention. Patrick Jordan had to believe he needed Carter's help.

"Who is this? Do you have her?"

Huh. Carter had been hoping Patrick could lead him to the woman. Was Patrick looking for her, too?

"I'm not interested in hurting anyone. But you and I need to talk."

"We're talking now."

"In person," Carter said. He didn't know how Patrick might fit in to the picture. He didn't know where his loyalties were. He needed to meet him—alone. To read his body language. See his expressions. Figure out if they could trust each other.

"Leave McKenna out of this. She doesn't know anything."

Carter heard the break in Patrick Jordan's voice. He wasn't worried about the woman. For some reason, he was worried about his wife.

"If you care about her, you'll come," Carter said. "Trust me."

"Those two sentences don't belong together, guy."

Carter could see Forty-second Street and Lexington from the pay phone. Occupy Wall Street protestors were beginning to stream out of the 6 train exit. Others were pouring into Grand Central up Park Avenue. He'd selected the train station for the meeting because there was an unauthorized OWS flash mob scheduled to start in an hour. Big crowds. Big police presence. Big chaos. If he needed to get lost in the mob to get rid of Patrick, the protestors would provide cover.

"Grand Central Station. The north side, by the MetLife escalators. I'll come to you. One hour." He hung up, hoping that would do the trick.

He should have realized that he wasn't the only person who might be interested in the whereabouts of Patrick Jordan. Or that his attempt to get the man's attention would be so successful that Jordan would be too worried about his wife to notice he was being followed.

CHAPTER FORTY-NINE

Three more drinks in, McKenna and Scanlin were hammering out wild scenarios that could connect Susan's disappearance with her reappearance and, most challenging of all, Scott Macklin's shooting of Marcus Jones.

Her phone buzzed on the table. It was Patrick. She let it go to voice mail.

"The timing between the Jones shooting and Susan's disappearance was close," she pointed out.

"I remember," he said. "That's part of the reason I hated you."

"I'd like to think I'd do things differently now."

He surprised her. "Me, too."

She was allowing herself to think aloud for the first time in two days. "The big debate was whether she left voluntarily or something bad happened to her. But if she's still alive? And if she has some kind of tie to Scott Macklin? You were the lead investigator. What do you think?"

He shook his head.

She was looking down at her gin, feeling the fatigue of the last two days. There was nothing she wasn't willing to say right now. "Look, we only got this far because I was willing to tell you that I basically saw a ghost. You have no idea how good it felt to talk about all of the insanity that has poured down in the last two days. And I'm not talking about therapy or purging or anything like that." She leaned forward intently and realized what a clichéd, intoxicated gesture it was. "But you and I are the only ones who know anything about this. You know about Susan. And Scott. We have to tell each other everything. Because you know things that I don't know. And I know things that you don't know." She was aware of the couple next to them, eavesdropping. She recognized that shared look—yep, she was wasted.

Scanlin was in the same zone. He needed to talk. To unleash. He was spinning the edge of his empty Scotch glass against the table. "After you called me last week, I asked for the cold-case files on the Hauptmann case."

She put down her gin and switched to water. "You did?"

"To tell you the truth, I wasn't my best back then. Family stuff." He waved a hand as if she'd know what he meant. "In retrospect, there were things I missed."

"See? This is what I meant. We need to work together."

"I didn't get anywhere."

"What is it they say about opting for the simplest explanation for multiple problems? Pretty much since I left the DA's office, I've lived in a world where every single day ends the same way it began. My world just happens to be falling apart at the same time Susan Hauptmann is running around on the New York City subway system wearing propaganda from a group involved in bomb-making, and when Scott Macklin just happens to decide to kill himself. There has to be a connection."

Her thoughts moved back to her husband. Patrick knew she'd been considering writing a book about the Macklin shooting. Patrick had been closer to Susan than she had ever allowed herself to recognize. But why would Susan care about the Macklin shooting? Her head was cloudy. Too much speculation. Too much gin.

Scanlin turned his glass upside down and slapped it on the table. "I got bupkes."

Her cell phone rang. It was Patrick again. She turned it off. She was on her way home. She was finally ready to talk things out in person.

"*And* I'm going home," Scanlin added. "Let me kick it around in my head some more. I'll check in with you tomorrow if you want."

"I'd like that, Detective. Thanks. And I'm really sorry to hear about Mac."

He started to throw cash on the table, but she insisted on paying.

She should have answered the phone when Patrick called. Or maybe it would have been enough had she checked her messages once she was alone in the bar. If she had, she would have called him back. He would have known she was okay—that she was on her way home, ready to talk to him. Ready to tell him that he needed to trust her with the truth. Ready to hear his side of the story and find a way to understand whatever role he had played in a ten-year lie.

But she didn't answer.

So he left a message, left their apartment, and walked into the night to meet a stranger.

It wasn't until she got back to their empty apartment that she checked her voice mail.

"Call me as soon as you can, if you can—if you're okay. Dammit." His voice cracked. "I got your message earlier and thought you were fine. But—I should have known. I should have told you. I should have—I'm so sorry. Fuck. I'm—Fuck!"

She listened to it again, and it made no more sense the second time.

She played a second message, assuming it would be from Patrick. It was Bob Vance. "McKenna, hi, it's Bob Vance. Um, I know things aren't good right now, but I thought you should know—Patrick just called me. I guess he'd been trying to get ahold of Dana with no luck, but he wanted to know whether you were out with the magazine crowd again like you were last night. I told him I didn't know what he was talking about. Dana quit, and—Sorry, the magazine's lawyers are requiring every employee to notify them about all contact with you. Anyway, I don't know what you told him about where you've been the last couple days, but I thought I should let you know he called me. I hope things work out for you. Sorry, I'm rambling. And now I guess I'll have to tell our lawyers about this stupid message. Bye."

Patrick had caught her in a lie, too. What was happening to them?

She tried his cell. Straight to voice mail. Either he had turned it off or was somewhere without reception.

She finished a quick walk through the apartment. The Susan box still open in the living room. The blankets pulled hastily over the bed, the way Patrick did it on weekdays. Not exactly hospital corners. Not exactly unmade.

Then she saw the note on the kitchen counter. *Phone call from unidentified man claiming to have my wife. Meeting him at Grand Central.* Patrick's signature, followed by today's date and the time, half an hour ago.

He had left the note behind in case he never came home.

She called Scanlin. She'd never heard her own voice sound like that before. Loud. Shrieking. Hysterical. "It's Patrick. He left. Someone said they'd kidnapped me. He's gone—a meeting at Grand Central Station. We have to find him."

"All right, just calm down. I'll call it in. They'll have someone there to look for him."

She was already out the door.

CHAPTER FIFTY

McKenna let out a groan in the backseat of the cab as the light at Thirty-fourth and Park turned red once more. She could have subwayed it faster than this. "Can we go around or something?"

"Your noises don't make the cars move any faster," the driver said.

"You don't understand. It's an emergency."

"Everyone believes everything is an emergency these days. Turn on the TV if you'd like. Some people find it makes the time pass more quickly. Or take deep breaths and count. That's what I do."

Great. She had the only yoga-practicing cabbie in New York City.

"Please. Go in the right lane. It's faster. And if you take the next turn, we can go over to Third. I'll pay you double the fare."

"You have to let me do my job. I hear it on the radio. Big protest at Grand Central. It's a traffic jam all the way around."

"Fine. I'll go on foot." She tossed him a twenty through the window of the plastic partition.

"Wait. You can't get out here. I need to pull to the curb."

She stepped out into the middle of the street, weaving her way to the sidewalk through the gridlocked, horn-blasting cars. She could jog to Grand Central in five minutes.

She noticed the first protestors on Thirty-sixth Street. She could tell from their signs. One said: HONK IF YOU'RE IN DEBT. The other was: SAY NO TO TRADE DEALS, YES TO U.S. JOBS.

By the time she hit Forty-first, protestors outnumbered regular commuters, many dressed to make their point. Union workers had come in factory and trade uniforms. Others wore red, white, and blue to emphasize patriotism. McKenna spotted one couple dressed in full business attire but with makeup to create white faces, black undereye circles, and bloody mouths. Handmade signs around their necks identified them as Corporate Zombies.

By far the most common accessories were masks. Halloween masks with dollars taped over the mouth holes. Black bags over heads to simulate images from Abu Ghraib. And the most popular staple of the Occupy crowd: the pale-faced, rosy-cheeked, soul-patched masks of Guy Fawkes from *V for Vendetta*. In typical New York City fashion, an entrepreneurial street vendor was selling the masks on the corner. Apparently the irony of purchasing a mask licensed by a multinational media conglomerate to participate in a 99-percenter protest was lost on some people.

As McKenna tried pushing her way north through the crowd, she realized that just as many protestors were trying to leave Grand Central as were heading there. As she got closer to Forty-second Street, the individual comments became more specific.

Forget it, too crowded.

They've got it blockaded. That's bogus. They can't keep us from gathering in a public place.

This is getting crazy.

It's got to be the cops, man. They're probably beating on people again.

Holy shit. People are, like, running *out of there.*

I just heard there were gunshots. We've got to get out of here.

Oh my God, people got shot.

They're saying he was in a Vendetta *mask. You know they'll try to pin this on us.*

As the words rippled through the crowd—gunfire, gunshots—a consensus built to move south. She pushed against it, turning sideways as necessary to press between protestors. She could see Forty-second Street now. She was almost there.

A wall of police officers behind barricades greeted her at the corner.

"I've got to get in there," she said to the nearest one.

"Not gonna happen."

"My husband's in there—"

"Well, he won't be for long. We're evacuating the station. You need to leave, ma'am."

"There was a shooting?" She said it like a question, then realized there was only one way she was going to get past this barrier. "I got a call that there was a shooting. It's my husband, Patrick Jordan. My husband's involved. I need to get in there. *Now!*"

The officer disconnected two of the barriers, allowing her to pass. An older officer, also in uniform, wasn't happy about the development. "Mario, what are you doing?"

"This lady says her husband's one of the guys got shot."

More than one person shot. More than one male.

The two officers led her through the press of people being cleared from the train station. She found herself praying. Please don't let it be Patrick. I'll do anything. Please not him.

The older officer seemed to be the one who knew where they should go once they were inside Grand Central, heading directly to the stream of yellow crime tape that formed a large right triangle from the west balcony staircase to the circular information booth and over to the escalators. She spotted a huddle of three people in the center of the marked-off scene. One was crouched on the ground.

She cried out when she saw the puddle of blood behind them.

The huddlers turned toward her.

"I thought we were clearing this place out." The man wore plain-clothes. Badge on belt. Shoulder holster. He had to be a detective.

"This lady says she got a call. Said her husband was one of the shooting victims."

The detective walked toward her and stopped at the crime tape.

"What's your angle, lady? You with the protestors or something? Because we haven't called anyone."

"It's my husband. He got a phone call telling him to come here." She handed him the note Patrick had left in their apartment. "I think he's in danger."

The officer who originally let her through the barricades sighed. "Dammit. I'm sorry, Detectives. She told me *she* got a call. I swear to God. I should have confirmed it with you before bringing her back."

"Get her out of here," the detective said.

"My husband's name is Patrick Jordan." McKenna fumbled for her phone and showed him the screen saver—it was a picture of them together at the High Line. She was kissing his cheek. There was a rainbow over the Hudson River.

"Hold on just a second," the detective said. He walked toward the balcony staircase. She watched as he made a call. She couldn't hear the conversation, but she could imagine the words. Because she knew. She already knew. The way he looked at that picture. The way he stopped the officer from walking her out of the station. He must have recognized Patrick.

When he turned back toward her, something in his face had changed. Serious. No longer annoyed at her presence. Even sympathetic.

Oh my God. Not Patrick. Please, God, no.

PART IV

So much past inside my present.

—Feist

CHAPTER FIFTY-ONE

McKenna's shoulders began to shake as the detective delivered the news. "Two men were rushed to the hospital with gunshot wounds. One was dead on arrival."

She felt one of the uniformed police officer's hands grab her under the arm as her knees gave out beneath her.

"Because they were rushed by ambulance," the detective continued, "we didn't have identification on either man. But I just phoned the hospital. One of the men had a wallet in his back pocket. According to his driver's license, his name is Patrick Jordan."

"No. Oh God, no."

"He's in critical condition. They're operating on him now, but he's alive. Your husband's alive."

The prayers started all over again. Prayers that surgery could save him. Prayers that she would see him again. Prayers that they would have a chance to fix whatever they'd gotten themselves into.

"We'll get you to the hospital right away."

"Thank you."

"Of course, it would help if you could answer some questions we have. You said he got a phone call instructing him to come here? Was he part of the protest?"

"Please, Detective, I need to get to the hospital. I need to be with my husband."

"Mrs. Jordan. While I sympathize with your situation, another man is dead. And we're looking at some very strange facts. The deceased victim had a gun in his waistband. We have witnesses who saw him reaching for it. And here's the thing—the reason your husband's alive and the other man is dead? Your husband came here with four thick law books strapped around his torso with duct tape, like a makeshift bulletproof vest."

She would have laughed at the ridiculousness of the image if this weren't really happening. In the ongoing negotiations that determined their household TV-watching schedule, he'd tolerated her passion for a show about a burned spy. In one episode, the main character wrapped himself in books from the law library to protect himself from a knife. Patrick had known what she was going to ask before she'd even opened her mouth. *Yes, that would work.* She couldn't imagine how desperate Patrick must have been to try something so haphazard.

"This doesn't appear to have been a random incident. We need information."

She knew now that Patrick had been lying to her. He'd known that Susan was still alive, and he'd known for perhaps the last ten years. She also knew from his note that Patrick had come here expecting to face danger. And he had come in a rush. No time to go to the museum for the gun he stored in a locker there. No time for real body armor, just stupid books. And he had done it not for Susan but for her.

Ten years. If Patrick had lied to her, to the police, to Susan's father for ten years? He must have had his reasons.

"What did you say your name was, Detective?"

"My apologies, ma'am. I'm Tim Compton."

"I hope you won't take offense at this, Detective Compton, but there's only one police officer I'm willing to talk to right now. His name's Joe Scanlin. I can give you his number if you need it. Now, are you going to help me get to the hospital, or do I have to get there myself?"

She woke up on a chair in the corner of the waiting room outside the Intensive Care Unit at Lenox Hill Hospital. Someone had placed a man's sports coat over her body. She recognized it as the jacket Joe Scanlin had been wearing earlier that night.

Or was it last night? Was it morning now?

The clock above the double doors into the ICU said 6:20. Light seeped through the waiting room blinds. It was morning.

She was at the nurses' station trying to get someone's attention when Scanlin walked in with two Styrofoam cups of coffee. He handed her one. "Hope black is all right."

She nodded her appreciation and took a quick sip. "Where's Patrick? Any news?" She remembered being awake in the same waiting room chair at one-thirty in the morning, when the doctor emerged from the double doors. Patrick had two gunshot wounds. One in the torso, one in the neck. The damage was severe, but the surgery had gone well.

"What does that mean?" she'd asked. "He'll make it? When can I see him?"

Everything the surgeon had said was straight out of the bedside-manner handbook. Have to wait and see. Up to his body to determine how he responds. Not yet conscious. She wanted to punch him in the throat when he used the phrase "cautiously optimistic."

Scanlin shook his head. "Nothing new. Sorry."

"When did you get here?"

"Just a couple of hours ago. I'd passed out at home by the time Compton started calling. He said you wouldn't talk to him without me? Not a way to make friends with the police investigating your husband's case."

"Compton told me that Patrick had taped some of my law books to his body like a makeshift protective vest. He has a gun, but it stays in a locker at work. Obviously he expected danger but didn't have enough notice to get to the museum. And he didn't call the police. Patrick is the bravest person I've ever known." The kind of person you'd want in charge of the planet if it ever got invaded by

aliens. *That* kind of brave. "He had to have his reasons for not calling the police." She suspected the reasons were related to Susan's
decision to fake her own death.

Scanlin cut her off. "All right, I get it. But Compton wants some
answers. And maybe you and I have reached some kind of truce, but
I'm still a cop. I've got to tell him what I know."

She nodded.

"By the way," he said, "those law books you mentioned? Compton says they saved your husband's life. The torso shot would have
been fatal, but it was barely a puncture wound by the time it passed
through all those pages. If it hadn't been for the neck shot, he would
have walked away from the entire thing with nothing more than a
bandage."

She remembered the surgeon telling her the same thing. How
many times had Patrick asked her to throw out her old casebooks?
Every time she'd moved, he'd said it was like lugging around six
boxes of bricks.

The books may have protected his body, but they hadn't covered
his neck. A gunshot in the neck. They were talking about it like it
was something he could live through, but she could tell they were
hiding the truth. Was there any part of the body that was more vulnerable than the neck?

"Did you get any information from Compton?" she asked.

"He showed me a photo of the man who was DOA. Not just a
bystander. He's the same guy who wiped out your video of Susan
on the subway platform."

The Cleaner. "So who was he?"

He shook his head. "No cell phone on the body. No ID. So far
his prints have come up *nada* in the databases."

"Is he the one who shot Patrick?"

"No. Based on what Compton knows for now, Patrick and the
mystery man were standing in the same vicinity, which was packed
with Occupy protestors. Gunshots rang out. The shooter was in the
crowd wearing a Guy Fawkes mask and cape. He got lost in the en-

suing chaos. I saw some video footage. Trying to track the guy on the tape was like keeping your eye on one bee in a hive."

Her husband's shooting was on tape. At some point, she would see a man in a mask walk up to her husband and put a bullet in his neck.

"I know you need to brief Compton," she said. "But he won't be any closer than we are to understanding what's happening. There has to be some connection between Susan's disappearance and Scott Macklin. There's no way around it. You worked Susan's case ten years ago. And I was the one who basically ended Macklin's career. You knew him, and I knew her. If anyone's going to figure out the connection, it's us. You said last night you had the case file on Susan's disappearance. Where is it?"

CHAPTER FIFTY-TWO

If anyone had told McKenna a week ago that she'd be standing in Joe Scanlin's living room, she would have checked his pupils.

The house was clean but dated. An entire wall was nearly covered with framed photographs. A young Scanlin in uniform, probably right out of the academy. Scanlin in a tuxedo next to his gorgeous bride on the church steps. The young couple with their little girl in front of a muted blue background, probably at a JCPenney picture studio. She noticed that the wall-size scrapbook seemed to end abruptly. In the most recent photographs, Scanlin looked the way she remembered him from when Susan disappeared. It was as if life in this house were frozen still.

He caught her checking her cell phone again for missed calls. "I can take you back to Lenox Hill," he offered.

"No. I'm fine. They said they'd call if they had any news." Scanlin had the files from Susan's disappearance at his house. By coming here with him, she'd given them an hour's head start.

He spread the files across the table and gave her an overview. Most of it was information she'd been able to glean at the time: No blood, semen, or other physical evidence at Susan's apartment. No financial problems. No enemies. No obvious motive for anyone to want to hurt Susan Hauptmann.

Tell me again about the men," she said.

He shrugged. "Well, from what I can tell, she may have been . . . a little open with her sexuality."

McKenna looked away. It was no easier for her than for Scanlin to have this discussion. That side of Susan had always been there, but McKenna had never wanted to process the reality.

"It's like a dark side," she said. Since Susan's disappearance, Mc-Kenna had been carrying around all the best memories of her friend. Her unparalleled generosity. Her courage. Her disarming humor.

Now she was recalling another side. "She seemed like a strong, independent, self-respecting woman, but at a certain time of day, all she really wanted was the attention of a man. She hid it from me, but there were signs. I just didn't want to see them."

How many times had an exhausted McKenna left a bar alone at two in the morning, a pit in her stomach because Susan insisted on staying behind for "one last drink," almost always with some guy she'd just met. And what about all those late-night phone calls? The ones Susan would answer out of earshot, only to announce within the next few minutes that she needed to meet an old friend who was having a rough time.

Susan may have tried to hide her promiscuity from her girl-friends, but McKenna had suspected. Men, after all, weren't so discreet. She'd heard the talk at happy hours. McKenna knew that Susan had hooked up with at least a couple of prosecutors she had met through McKenna, including Will Getty.

"You know, it's funny," Scanlin said. "Usually when we talk about a dark side, we're talking about a man who turns all that anger and destruction against other people—his wife, his children, a stranger out of nowhere. But I used to see it back when I was in vice. These women with dark sides, they rarely turned against other people. They took it out on themselves."

Scanlin pulled out another manila folder, this one less yellowed. "A neighbor in Susan's building called in a noise report two days before she disappeared, but got the wrong apartment number. I talked to the neighbor, and it's likely that what she overheard was a fight between Susan and a man. Take a look at some of the words she wrote down." He pointed to the word "smack." "Maybe one of Susan's boyfriends had started getting physical with her, and they were arguing about it after the fact." He pointed to another word. "Important." "Maybe something like 'It's really important that you never smack me again.'"

"I think it's safe to say that Hollywood won't be calling you to write dialogue, Scanlin. Besides, if any guy raised a hand to Susan Hauptmann, he'd need a new set of teeth by the time she was done with him. But you mentioned working vice and how the prostitutes had a dark side." She realized that in giving him her rundown, she'd left out Agent Mercado asking about Pamela Morris and Greg Larson. She told him about going out to Jersey City to talk to Pamela's mother. "Susan was always trying to help lost souls. Maybe she crossed paths with Pamela. They both disappeared at the same time. Pamela Morris's mother hasn't seen her since the fall of 2003."

"Then how does she know her daughter's alive?"

"She gets letters a couple times a year. Pamela says she's married to a preacher and travels around the country. I thought maybe that was her way of describing life with the P3s."

"What does Pamela Morris look like?"

McKenna shrugged. "I've got one booking photo from 1998, and she's got on a pound of makeup and sporting a fat lip. Brown hair, dyed blond at the time. Kind of regular."

"Age? Height? Weight?"

She searched her memory for the details and saw where Scanlin was going. "Oh my God."

"A couple cards a year to Mom are a small price to pay for a stolen identity."

She remembered the fat lip lingering in Pamela's booking photo. It wasn't her first bust. She was deep into the life. And then she turned over a new leaf? That happened only in Hollywood. In real life, women who took the road chosen by Pamela Morris did not get happy endings. "You're saying that the Pamela Morris who was living with the P3s out in Brentwood was actually Susan."

"Hate to say it, but prostitutes die all the time," Scanlin said. "A lot of them are never identified. Taking a dead person's identity is one of the easiest ways in the world to get a fresh start."

Susan had been at Scott Macklin's house the day before he died. If Susan was the woman who had been living with the P3s as Pamela Morris, she must have survived the explosion on Long Island.

"But to take over Pamela's identity, Susan would have to know that she was dead."

She was looking at the papers spread across the dining room table, hoping an answer would come to her.

Then she saw it. "The neighbor. Susan's neighbor who called about the noise from the argument. You said she reported the wrong apartment. Is it possible she made other mistakes? About what she actually heard?"

"Sure. She's practically deaf now."

"Look, Scanlin. Right here." She jabbed her index finger against the page on the table. "Smack. But not *smack*. Mac! We know Susan went to Mac's house the day before he died. But if she was arguing with him—or *about* him—two days before she suddenly disappeared? There's a connection between Susan's disappearance and whatever happened on that dock between Macklin and Marcus Jones."

"And you're trying to say that the connection—whatever it may be—would somehow explain why Susan is now using Pamela Morris's name?"

He meant the statement sarcastically, but hearing him say the words out loud made all the difference. Scott Macklin. Pamela Morris. Together. Connected.

P amela's mother told me that toward the end, before she rode off into the sunset with her knight on a white horse, she was only seeing her regulars. Harmless, lonely married guys. That kind of thing. She specifically said that one of the guys was strange-looking and slow but nice to Pamela."

Scanlin's face didn't register the point.

"Marcus Jones," she said. "The pigmentation of his face was blotchy because of a skin condition called vitiligo. And his IQ was around seventy-five, placing him at what's considered the border-line. His mother always maintained that he'd gone down to the docks to meet his girlfriend. We never found the girl, but he did have eighty dollars in his pocket."

"And the docks are a frequent cruising spot for working girls," Scanlin added.

"If Susan took over Pamela's identity, she'd have to know that Pamela wouldn't need it anymore. Maybe Marcus Jones wasn't the only person who died at the pier that night. What if Mac's shooting of Marcus Jones was bad, and Pamela Morris saw it?"

"You're saying Mac intentionally killed her to cover it up? You've *got* to be kidding me. You know, this was a bad idea. I should have known—"

"Hey, we're just talking things out, Scanlin. There are other ex-planations. Maybe Marcus was involved in something going down on the docks—selling stolen merchandise or something. Pamela Morris is there to meet him but sees something she's not supposed to see. Marcus, or maybe someone else, hurts her. And then Mac comes along, and Marcus pulls the gun on him."

"Mac never said anything about Marcus being with a girl, let alone someone killing her."

"You see my point, don't you? If something happened that night on the docks that we don't know about—whatever *it* might be—that would explain the timing of Pamela going off the grid. And Susan's disappearance, if she found out about it. And the fact that someone doesn't want me rehashing that night."

Scanlin was out of his chair, pacing. "Except—one—you don't even know what the 'something' that happened might be. Two—

you have no reason to think that Susan Hauptmann was connected to it. Look, no offense, but I think we've done all we can here. Compton's a good cop. He's going to look for whoever hurt your husband, and once he has some answers, maybe that will shed some light on Susan and everything else." He took a look at his watch. "I've got a shift. I'll drop you back in the city. You'll feel better once you get an update about Patrick."

The car ride was silent but for the adult contemporary radio station that Scanlin turned on to fill the void. When she thanked him as she got out at Lenox Hill, he simply nodded an acknowledgment.

The ICU was busier than when they'd left. The halls were filled with nurses and interns in scrubs. People stepped aside to make room for patients being moved on gurneys. McKenna got the attention of a nurse. There was no new information, but they had moved Patrick into a patient room, where she could sit with him if she'd like.

As long as she had known Patrick, he'd been healthy. He was just one of those people. He could pig out for four straight days over Thanksgiving and not gain a single ounce. He could stay up until two and wake at seven, looking refreshed, his eyes circle-free. If he got a cold, it came and went with a few sneezes, a couple of coughs, and a handful of over-the-counter meds. And though he had aged in their time together—the lines around his mouth, the gray hair at his temples—it wasn't in a way that made him appear weak or frail; it made him look like a man who spent time outdoors.

So when she saw him in the hospital bed, she wanted to find the nurse and explain that she'd been sent to the wrong room. The man attached to all those tubes and hoses couldn't be her husband. Just above the edge of his baby-blue polka-dotted gown was a wad of gauze taped around his neck. She knew that the gown and the gauze covered the gun wounds and surgery scars. If he managed to pull through this, those marks would be there forever, constant reminders of the events that had put him in this bed.

She looked at his pale, stubbled face beneath the oxygen mask. How could he have lost so much weight in one day? Was that possible? She wanted to see his eyes open. To watch him smile when he recognized her. To see *him*. To see him and know that they were going to be okay. That whatever secrets he may have been keeping were for all the best reasons. He would wake up and tell her everything, and then they could somehow make this right.

But he didn't open his eyes.

She felt herself starting to shut down from the inside like a child's toy whose battery had died. They'd find her body, slumped and nonresponsive, in this orange vinyl visitor's chair.

She reached out and placed her hand on Patrick's bicep, the only part of his body exposed between the blankets and the cotton gown. She tried to remember what it felt like to place her head on that exact spot as he slept, their bodies pressed together like spoons.

She never should have gone to Dana's. She should have gone home and confronted him. Torn off the bandages and learned the truth, however ugly. She hadn't, and now he was here, and she might never know why.

She leaned down and kissed his forehead. No response, not like a fairy tale, where the prince awakes. Not even a fleeting moment of comfort in which she magically knew that everything would be okay. It was just her dry lips against his warm skin.

She was not going to stay here and collapse out of helplessness. Only two weeks earlier, she had published a six-page article to commemorate the tenth anniversary of the death of Marcus Jones. Now Scott Macklin was dead. So was the man who had wiped out the videos of Susan on the subway platform. Patrick was in critical condition. And it all had something to do with the night Marcus Jones died.

She had missed something. Ten years ago, her suspicions about the gun next to Marcus Jones's body had briefly shone a light on the events that had transpired on the docks the night of October 16. But then she was disproved and the lights went dark. A decade later, with the publication of a six-page article, she had managed to lose her job, her reputation, and most important, her husband's safety. Someone wanted the lights to remain off. She was going to turn them on again.

CHAPTER FIFTY-THREE

As McKenna stepped off the elevator on the basement level of the courthouse, she heard two women whisper as they passed: "That's the magazine reporter who teed off on Knight." She couldn't make out the second woman's complete response, but she did hear "he had it coming" and "basically true."

That was the way the truth worked sometimes. An eyewitness might make a mistake about the color of the gunman's shirt but still pick the right man. Maybe McKenna had been wrong ten years ago when she claimed that Macklin had planted a drop gun on Marcus's body, but maybe the core of the allegation had been on the mark.

The woman at the front desk of the Supreme Court record room was reading a novel called *Criminal*.

"How about that," McKenna said. "A real, live hardcover book with pages and everything. Nice to know I'm not the only person around who likes my reading old-school."

Instead of leaving the book open with a broken spine, the woman carefully placed a Post-it note to mark her spot. "My son bought me one of those e-readers for Christmas. It was good for my summer cruise. On that tiny little machine, I took a book for every day of the trip. But there's something about turning the pages of a hefty book."

McKenna had learned the fine art of talking up administrative staff during her judicial clerkship. She could call for district court records and have pages faxed within the hour. Her coclerk, Richard, who made it clear in every call that he was a very, very impressive young lawyer working for a very, very influential appellate court judge, never understood why his requests took a week to answer. It wasn't about power or authority or official obligations. It was basic human nature: people wanted to help the nice guys and shaft the douches.

"I'm hoping you can help me out with something. I need the court file for *People* v. *Scott Macklin*. It's an old one, I'm afraid." McKenna gave the month and year for the original opening of the file.

"Oh, sure. I remember this one." The woman must have been too engrossed in her novel to have read the news about Macklin's death. "You think that's old, I had a girl in here this morning asking for a forty-year-old landlord-tenant dispute. Her building is claiming that her grandmother was evicted from a rent-controlled apartment back in the seventies, which would mean she had no right to live there now. Poor thing couldn't stop crying. I found the file, though. Turns out the eviction was never finalized. It's nice when you actually get a happy ending."

"Well, if you could find that, my file should be a cinch."

"Is there a specific document you're looking for, or do you want the whole thing? Keep in mind that photocopies are a quarter a page. And no, in case you're wondering, the money does not go to the nice lady who runs the copies."

"Wouldn't that be nice. I want the whole file, but trust me, it's a thin one."

"My favorite kind," the woman said with a smile.

Twenty minutes later, McKenna had what she needed. A twenty-minute wait at the courthouse was the equivalent of the speed of light in the rest of the world.

McKenna found a bench at the far end of the basement hallway and settled in to review the file.

The stack of pages was, as expected, thin. The file was thin because there had been no charges at all. Typically there would be no documentation other than a single slip of paper with a checkmark from the grand jury, indicating that it had not true-billed the case—a fancy way of saying flushed. But the Marcus Jones shooting wasn't typical, especially after a young but respected ADA stuck her neck out and claimed that the grand jury hadn't heard all the relevant evidence.

Because of the intense public scrutiny, the district attorney had taken the extra step of filing a memorandum declining to pursue the case further, complete with a detailed justification. It was signed by the lead prosecutor who had presented the case to the grand jury, Will Getty.

She skimmed the introduction. Scott Macklin. Thirteen years with NYPD. At the seaport that night for a routine assignment pursuant to a federal-state cargo inspection program.

The report moved on to Macklin's version of the night's events. He noticed Marcus near the inland edge of the dock. Marcus appeared to be monitoring the movement of computer parts into a shipping container. Because the docks still saw the occasional snatch-and-grab, Macklin approached the teenager as a precaution. When Marcus saw Macklin heading his way, he turned and ran. Macklin pursued him, turned a corner around a shipping container, and saw Marcus reach for a weapon. He had no choice but to shoot.

The next section of the report summarized Marcus Jones's background, his mother's insistence that he did not own a gun, and McKenna's tracing of the gun back to Safe Streets, the police-sponsored gun destruction program. Only four NYPD officers had been scheduled to transport the Safe Streets guns from a locked property room to the smelter. Scott Macklin was one of them.

The report did everything it could to make McKenna's inference appear reasonable, which it would have been if not for Don Whitman. As the report went on to explain, Whitman was one of the other three Safe Streets cops. More significantly, he was convicted a few years later for being on the Crips' payroll.

When Getty realized that Whitman could have walked off with a Safe Streets gun just as easily as Macklin, he sent investigators back into Marcus's neighborhood, searching for someone who could tie Marcus to a gun slipped eight years earlier to the Crips.

The witness was James Low. The twenty-two-year-old lived in the same housing project as Marcus Jones. He testified to the grand jury that he'd sold the gun to Jones for two hundred bucks after finding it in his father's dresser following his father's death. Before his uneventful death from acute myocardial infarction, James Low, Sr., was considered a "five-star universal elite" in the New York City Crips hierarchy.

When McKenna had heard the news, only one word captured her surprise: "Un-fucking-believable."

The grand jury testimony of James Low, Jr., completed the chain from property room, to junk pile, to Officer Don Whitman, to James Low, Sr., to Jr., to Marcus Jones. In comparison, Macklin's connection to the gun was a fluke.

Or was it? McKenna had been so mortified by her rush to judgment that she had never stopped to question the alternative. She had simply assumed that Low was telling the truth.

She made her way back to the file room. The nice reading lady was back into her novel. "That was quick," she said.

"I've got another request, if you don't mind. Can you tell me whether you have any cases involving a James Low?"

The woman typed a few commands into a computer on the front desk. "I've got a few, all criminal. Starts back in 1972, looks like the most recent is 2004."

"There was a Senior and a Junior. I'm interested in the kid."

"Got it. Yes, the younger was charged as Junior. I got three cases, all resulting in convictions—theft in 1999, assault-three in 2001, and an assault-three in 2004."

McKenna already knew from the Marcus Jones case that by the time Low testified before the grand jury, he had two misdemeanor convictions—a shoplifting incident in 1999, and a misdemeanor assault in 2001 for punching a guy who spent too much time checking out Low's girlfriend at a bowling alley. McKenna asked the nice reading lady for a copy of the 2004 file.

This time McKenna didn't bother to resume her spot on the hallway bench. She skimmed the file at the counter. The nice lady, returning to her novel, didn't seem to mind.

According to the probable-cause affidavit filed the night of Low's arrest, Low had been one of several men in the VIP lounge of a hip-hop club in Chelsea. An argument broke out between two groups of customers. The genesis of the dispute was stupid, as usual—something about a member of the other group insulting the ex-girlfriend of Low's cousin's friend's brother—but it culminated in Low's side attacking the rivals with liquor bottles.

The arresting officer booked Low for felony assault. A bottle was a weapon. Multiple perpetrators made the assault a gang attack.

McKenna knew the district attorney's filing policies. This was definitely a felony. Low's misdemeanor assault only three years earlier would have made him an unsympathetic candidate for plea bargaining and sentencing.

And yet.

Low pleaded to a misdemeanor. Seven days in jail, which in reality meant a night or two before early release. Instead of doing real time in state prison, he chilled out in local for a few hours and walked away without a felony conviction. In highbrow legal terms, it was a sweetheart deal, and it came only a little over a year after Low's grand jury testimony had saved New York's law enforcement community from a scandal whose toxicity would have lingered for a generation.

Even before she turned to the last page of the file, where the attorneys of record were listed on the final page of the conviction order, she knew what name she would find there. For the people of New York County: Assistant District Attorney Will Getty.

CHAPTER FIFTY-FOUR

Susan had her fair share of dalliances, and Will Getty was on the list.

Neither of them flaunted that fact, but McKenna wasn't blind. She had been the one to introduce them. She remembered the night.

McKenna didn't know Getty well yet. It was about four months before the Marcus Jones shooting. He was one of the lifers, already handling major crimes. She was only four years in, handling drug cases but beginning to eye more serious assignments.

She had worked late, as usual. When she left, Getty was also heading out. It began with chitchat in the elevator.

"Not that I'm monitoring you or anything, but I'm pretty sure this is the first time I've seen you leave the office. I was starting to think you lived here."

"That's a hologram to fool people into thinking I'm actually working."

"I'll deny it if you ever tell anyone I said this, but take it easy. You don't want to burn out before you get to the fun stuff."

"Duly noted."

They stepped out on the ground floor.

"You heading to happy hour?" he asked.

"I am heading to *a* happy hour but not the *office* happy hour."

"Another piece of unsolicited advice: spend less time at your desk and more time drinking with your coworkers. Friendships matter."

"Trust me. If you knew how much I drank my first two years in this office, you'd sign me up for the liver transplant waiting list."

"Ah, but that's when you were just a baby ADA, playing with the other kids. We career guys know how it works. Most of the newbies are here for a couple years of trial experience, then jump ship to make some dough. We don't bother getting to know people until they've been around a while. Now you need to jump in with the older generation. Graduate to the lifer crowd."

"Can you seriously tell me that hanging with the lifer crowd is any different than the usual scene in this office?"

"Did you really just use the word 'scene' to describe the DA's office?"

"You know what I mean. The war stories. Who crushed which defense attorney at trial. Who hauled out the most badass line during plea negotiations. Everyone's always trying to out-macho each other."

Wincing, he started to offer a retort but stopped himself. "Yeah, that does sound familiar, doesn't it?"

"At least when I play, I do it with people who don't talk shop all night."

He looked at his watch. "They're probably all gone by now. Damn, I could use a drink. I had a cooperating codefendant retract his confession on me today. Total nightmare."

"Well, my happy hour's just getting started. You should come."

"Nah, I'd be crashing."

"No such thing." She explained the concept of Susan's monthly the-more-the-merrier gatherings. "Seriously, you should come. It's my chance to convince you that I do have a life outside this office."

She could tell he was on the fence. She pressed him. "I wouldn't ask if I didn't think you'd have fun. And you did say you needed a drink."

"Sold."

Susan had been delighted to see McKenna arrive with a guest in tow—a decent-looking male guest, to boot. Despite McKenna's assurances to Getty, she had not enjoyed much of a life beyond work recently. After a long dry spell, she had met Jason Eberly (aka Nature Boy) two weeks earlier at a city bar event, but it was nothing serious. And it never would be, because McKenna would meet Patrick at the next Bruno happy hour.

In typical Susan fashion, she wasted no time jumping into the gutter once Getty broke away to the men's room. "I knew you wanted a faster track to trying homicides, but sleeping with your boss? A bit unseemly for you, dear."

"Not funny, Bruno. That's how rumors get started."

"He's single, right?"

"To my knowledge."

"And he's not technically your boss."

"No, but he could be down the road."

Though the conversation could have ended there, Susan went on. "You're absolutely certain you're not interested? Hundred percent?"

"A hundred and ten percent. Nothing good comes from interoffice romance."

When Getty returned to the table, Susan moved her chair a hair closer to his and laughed at his jokes with a little more enthusiasm. McKenna had seen the transition before. And she could tell Getty liked it.

Four months later, Scott Macklin would shoot Marcus Jones, and Getty would select McKenna to assist with the grand jury investigation. She would wonder at the time whether she got the assignment because of her hard work or because she'd inadvertently gotten him laid.

She wouldn't really care. She had a homicide—the sexiest kind, an officer-involved shooting. Her career was finally starting. And then it ended. And Susan was gone. And now McKenna was wondering if it was all because she had bumped into Will Getty on that elevator.

Thanks anyway," McKenna said to the nice reading lady. "Thanks for everything."

The woman hadn't found any record of a conviction for the final name McKenna had asked about. There was only one person who could provide the information she needed.

McKenna couldn't get cell reception in the file room, so she took the elevator up to the ground floor of the courthouse. Gretchen answered on the third ring. "I told you I don't want to be involved."

Stupid caller ID. Given how their last encounter ended, it was a wonder that Susan's sister had picked up at all.

"It's one question, Gretchen. I promise. You said you almost got prosecuted federally when you were arrested, but you worked out a plea deal for a state conviction with rehab and probation."

"It's all ancient history, McKenna."

"You said the case was pending for a while, but you got the deal just a couple of months before Susan disappeared?" There was no record of Gretchen's conviction in New York County, which meant she had gotten her record expunged—a lenient outcome considering the severity of the initial allegations.

"Glad you were listening."

Damn, she was a bitch. "Do you know if a local prosecutor was involved?"

"Sure. My attorney did a full-court press. Finally found a guy willing to make a call to the feds—someone Susan knew. I was surprised she didn't go to you. She must not have wanted you to know."

McKenna didn't have the kind of network that a more experienced prosecutor would have. Like Getty had said, sometimes the job was about the friendships you'd made. The question was how close a friend he'd been with Susan before she disappeared.

"Was the prosecutor a guy called Will Getty?"

"My record's supposed to be clear. How did you know?"

The night Susan and Getty met couldn't have been a one-night stand if Susan had reached out to Getty for a favor four months down the road. Maybe they'd had something resembling a relationship. If Getty was involved in covering up the Marcus Jones shooting, Susan could have found out about it.

A beep-beep from her phone notified McKenna that another call was coming in. She assured Gretchen that there was no record of her drug case and ended the call.

"This is McKenna Jordan," she said.

"Ms. Jordan. My name is Mae Mauri. I'm a physician at New York Family Medical."

"Is this about Patrick?" She started rushing toward the courthouse exit, hoping he was conscious. Hoping she could finally talk to him.

"No, I'm—" She sounded confused by the question. "I hope you'll forgive the intrusion. I contacted your former employer for your number."

"I'm sorry, Doctor. I'm waiting for some very important news about the health of a family member."

"Of course. But I believe you're looking for Susan Hauptmann. I may have information you'll be interested in."

CHAPTER FIFTY-FIVE

The receptionist at the front desk of the New York Family Medical practice greeted McKenna with a warm smile and a soft, soothing voice. "Good morning. You're here for a wellness visit?"

McKenna felt like she was checking in for a spa appointment. "I'm here to see Dr. Mauri. She's expecting me."

"Of course. Are you a new patient? I usually recognize everyone. I'll just need your insurance information."

"No, I'm not a patient. It's a different kind of appointment. Please, if you could just tell Dr. Mauri I'm here. McKenna Jordan."

"No worries. I'll let the doctor know."

No worries. When did that ridiculous sentence become an acceptable thing to say to another person? As far as McKenna could tell, the phrase was used most frequently when there was, in fact, a reason to worry, and almost always by the very person who was the source of the current worry. This annoying woman had no idea what worries McKenna was harboring.

The woman returned. "The doctor's ready for you," the worry-free, calming voice instructed. She led the way to the doctor's office.

Dr. Mauri rose from behind her desk to shake hands. "I'm sorry that I wasn't able to tell you more over the phone, Ms. Jordan."

"I'm sorry I was so insistent. Someone close to me is in the hospi-tal right now. I'm— Well, let's just say I'm juggling a lot."

"I gather. At least, based on the little I know. I met my niece last night after the theater. She's an intern at *Cosmo*. She was telling me how difficult it is to make a career in print media, and as an example, she told me about your recent departure and the ensuing controversy on—is it called Twitter?"

McKenna nodded. Apparently the receptionist's insistence on a calm demeanor came from the top. The way Dr. Mauri had worded it, McKenna's professional implosion sounded like any regular day.

"In any event," the doctor continued, "my niece became quite enraptured with your story and its apparent connection to a missing woman. Then she asked me whether I remembered anything about the disappearance of Susan Hauptmann. She's nineteen years old, so for her, ten years ago is like the Ice Age. She caught me off guard with the question. I had no idea that the missing woman she kept talking about all night was Susan."

McKenna had been hoping to get more information out of the doctor in person, but so far the woman still hadn't confirmed the basics of what McKenna suspected. She tried another tack. "I was Susan's roommate and one of her closest friends. I already know she was your patient."

Dr. Mauri looked relieved. "If only all of my patients gave so much care to their own health. Annual physicals, no smoking, reg-ular exercise. Most people insist that they eat healthy and work out, but I can tell—well, my point is: Susan was a real delight. Very gregarious, with that salty sense of humor; our conversations often went beyond the narrow confines of doctor-patient treatment. I think it's fair to say I knew her."

"You said you might know something relevant to her disappear-ance?"

"Given my situation, I was hoping that perhaps you had seen the police file and could confirm that anything I might know was al-ready considered a part of the investigation."

McKenna had not seen the doctor's name in Scanlin's file, or anything related to Susan's physical health. She took a guess. "She had an appointment with you, not long before she disappeared."

The doctor smiled politely.

"Look, I know you're restricted by privacy laws, and I respect that. How about this? I'm not asking about any individual patient. I'm interested, hypothetically, in what may have happened *if* you had a patient disappear."

"Without using names, let me say that *if* I ever had a patient go missing, it was twelve weeks after she was scheduled for an office visit. I assumed when I saw her name on my calendar that she was coming in for her annual physical because she was about due for one. But my assistant alerted me that the appointment was actually forty-nine weeks after her last annual, meaning it was too early for her insurance company to cover it. They're sticklers about that. I called the patient to suggest rescheduling, but she told me it was important. I thought, well, even my healthiest patient has finally gotten sick. But when she came in, she wasn't *sick*."

But she'd been *something*. "She'd been assaulted? Victimized somehow?"

No response.

"She was pregnant?"

Dr. Mauri smiled again. "Let me just say that by the time most unmarried women come to me for a pregnancy test, they have already taken multiple home versions and are looking for a different result."

"This particular patient wouldn't have been happy about the news."

"I'm always careful not to say anything loaded when I deliver the results, because many women have no idea how they're going to feel about an unplanned pregnancy until they've had a chance to digest the reality of the situation. So I simply tell them that the test is positive and ask whether they have questions. That's usually my first indication of what direction the woman is leaning."

"And did this hypothetical patient have questions?"

Dr. Mauri pressed her lips together. McKenna had crossed whatever line the doctor had drawn for navigating this conversation.

"What types of questions do you think a single, pregnant woman might have?"

As much as she was beginning to doubt how well she'd known Susan, Susan had always made her views on the most obvious subject very clear. Susan would not terminate a pregnancy.

"Paternity," McKenna said. "She wanted to know whether you could determine paternity."

Dr. Mauri gave a small nod.

McKenna did the math in her head. She had introduced Susan to Will Getty four months before the Marcus Jones shooting, which was six weeks before Susan disappeared. Getty could have been the father.

"She would have been close to four months pregnant when she disappeared." It was only as she said the words that McKenna remembered Susan drinking club soba at a happy hour. *My thirties are gaining on me. Got to take off some L.B.s before I turn into a Fatty McFat.*

If Susan knew that Getty was involved in a cover-up, and she was pregnant with his child, that might explain why she would leave New York. Whether she liked it or not, Getty would have parental rights. She'd spend her entire life permanently connected to him.

"Did the patient happen to say anything about who she thought the father might be?"

"I've already stretched quite a bit on what I should probably say, Ms. Jordan. But when a patient asks about a paternity test—"

"It means she had multiple sexual partners. I need to know who they were."

"I don't know," the doctor said sadly.

"When Susan first went missing, you never thought to tell anyone about Susan's pregnancy?"

"Of course I did," she said. "I must have called the police three different times. But no one ever called me back. I eventually gave up, assuming that they must have already heard the news from someone else. When my niece told me you were looking for Susan, I needed to make sure it hadn't slipped through the cracks."

Scanlin had said that the police tip line had been overwhelmed with harebrained, bogus, and wackadoo calls. He'd also pretty much admitted that he had done a crappy job on the case. Dr. Mauri was making that clear.

As McKenna walked through the doctor's calming lobby back to the real world of honking cars and bus fumes, she tried to black out the images that had been flashing in her visual cortex for the last two days. Susan catching Patrick's eye with that sexy sideways smile—her go-to man-eater move. Patrick responding. Susan whispering in his ear, *McKenna doesn't feel like this, does she?*

Stop it! She replaced the imaginary images with a real one: Patrick in a hospital bed.

Just because Susan was unsure about the father of her unborn child didn't mean that Patrick was one of the contenders. It was as Dr. Mauri had quietly confirmed: Susan got around.

Sometimes beliefs came not from facts or proof but from faith. McKenna had always had faith in Patrick. She would choose to have faith in him now. He was going to survive. He was going to wake up, he was going to be okay, and he was going to have an explanation for everything.

In the meantime, she needed to make another trip to the courthouse.

CHAPTER FIFTY-SIX

McKenna sat on a bench at the far end of the fourth floor. She was out of the flow of traffic but had a clear view of the entrance to Judge John DeWitt Gregory's courtroom, where Will Getty was arguing against a defendant's motion to vacate a jury's guilty verdict.

McKenna had gotten lucky when she arrived to find Berta Ramos outside for one of her hourly smoke breaks. Ten years later, the woman still hadn't kicked the habit.

"Ay, Mamí," she had called out when McKenna waved at her from the sidewalk. Though their kinship had started with an un- likely shared love of *Buffy the Vampire Slayer*, Berta had become one of McKenna's better allies among the DA support staff. She barely had an accent but liked to pepper her conversation with Spanish slang. "Your ears must be burning. Lots of talk about you around here this week."

"I can only imagine."

"Don't you worry. Berta knows you wouldn't make up a story. Besides, all these people"—she used her manicured blood-red fin- gernail to draw a circle in the air—"they know that Judge Knight is just how you say he is. *Cerdo sucio.*"

"I need to talk to Will Getty, but I'd rather not plant myself in the DA waiting room like a goat at the petting zoo."

"Don't you even worry about it. Give me your number and I'll report from inside."

Now Getty walked out of the courtroom, carrying only a single file folder. His back was straight, shoulders squared, steps even and proud. Defeating the motion clearly was a cakewalk.

McKenna pretended to be composing a text and then faked a double take in his direction. She smiled, gave a wave as an after-thought, and caught up with him.

"Bold move, being here," he said. "The courthouse staff is se-cretly cheering you on, but Knight's still got friends."

"I know. I thought if I came and talked to my sources, I'd figure out who burned me." *Was it you?* She searched his eyes for some sign of nervousness. "No luck yet."

"I have no doubt you'll get to the bottom of it."

"Hey, it dawned on me when I saw you that you'd be a good person to bounce some ideas off of. You have a second?"

He looked at his watch. "Sure. Gregory calendared an hour for a motion that took ten minutes."

"Coffee? My treat."

Getty opted for a Chinese bakery on Canal. Once they were set-tled in with a tray of roasted pork buns, Diet Cokes, and egg tarts, she continued the I'm-just-bouncing-some-ideas-off-you talk.

"Sorry if I sound a little scattered, but my thoughts are all over the place. Did you hear about Scott Macklin?"

"Fucking awful."

"I know. The first thing I thought was, Oh my God, what if this is because I was digging up the whole Marcus Jones issue again. I mean—"

Getty was shaking his head already. "You can't try to figure out why someone does that. Otherwise, everyone who ever met the guy could say, What if I had done something different? I'm sorry.

I liked Macklin, rest his soul. But what he did is on him and him alone."

"I hear you, and I appreciate that. But like I said, my mind went there. And maybe it's because I didn't want the weight to be on me, but I started thinking, No, someone doesn't shoot himself because of a magazine article or even a book. I mean, he didn't do it back when protestors were waving pictures of his face behind bars and the city was close to rioting. So, I hate to admit it, I started wondering—you know—what if it was because he thought if I looked again, I'd find something new. Something I missed. Like maybe the hammer was finally going to come down."

Getty washed down some pork bun with a big gulp of Diet Coke. "That's a lot of wondering, Wright."

"Here's the thing. I went back and took another close look at the case. It's a long story, but it turns out that a prostitute who used to meet tricks down at the piers went missing the night Mac shot Marcus Jones." McKenna glossed over the uncertainties in that part of her theory. "According to her mother, the prostitute was meeting a regular that night—someone slow and strange-looking. I think she was meeting Marcus Jones."

"Possible, I guess. Makes sense that the kid would tell his mom he was meeting a girl, not a working girl. Plus, he had cash in his pocket." Getty's lightning-quick reasoning had always been amazing. "What about it?"

"The girl never came back. I'm thinking, What if she saw something that night?"

"The shooting?"

"Or maybe she saw something *before* the shooting. And so did Marcus Jones. And they both wound up dead. You can get rid of the hooker without raising too many questions, then drop a gun next to the body of the kid with a criminal record."

Getty balled up his napkin and tossed it on the plastic tray. "I'd keep this to yourself. This on top of the Knight article? Jesus, we went through this ten years ago. You made a mistake. I thought you'd moved on."

"I know, I know. Hear me out. It was that kid James Low who saved Macklin's ass. Low's testimony put the gun right in Marcus Jones's hands. Mac's access to the gun through Safe Streets was just a coincidence."

"And yet?"

"If it weren't for the kid's testimony, it would be one major hell of a coincidence. What I want to know is, how did Low come to you? Did someone bring him in? Did he call out of the blue?"

Getty blinked; she could see him searching his memory for the details. "When you came to me about the gun coming from Safe Streets, I told you I'd look into it. And I did. I looked up the other cops in the program. Saw that one of them was on the Crips' payroll. What was his name?"

"Don Whitman."

"Right, Don Whitman. I figured a guy who took money from bangers wasn't above slipping a few guns. So I sent three DA investigators to talk to the usual suspects in East Harlem. Try to find someone from the neighborhood who knew anything about Jones and a gun. I was giving it a few days to sink in. But then you went public."

She resisted the urge to remind him that he'd locked her out of the case for two weeks before she took the evidence to Bob Vance. That was an argument they'd had ten years earlier. Getty's regret about his lack of communication was supposedly the reason he'd always defended her.

He continued, "It was a few days after the story exploded when Low showed up at the courthouse, asking who was in charge of the case. Once he got to my office, he told me he didn't want to say anything bad about Marcus, that he"—Getty let out a laugh, remembering the moment—"he *certainly* didn't want to help the cracker cop who killed him, but he didn't want to see Harlem burn." The remainder of his recitation came in clipped, just-the-facts fashion. "He asked whether I was going to arrest him if he confessed to a gun charge. I made a quick decision to give him a pass if it meant I'd get the truth. He said the gun had been his dad's, but he'd sold it to Marcus a month before the shooting. I ran his dad. Big-time Crip, which connected the gun back to Safe Streets through Don Whitman."

"Did you ever think it was weird that a hard case like Low would walk into the courthouse out of the goodness of his heart?"

"I've been doing this job a long time, Wright. Those kids don't give a shit about themselves, but they care about their neighborhoods and their mothers and their friends. Things were getting bad. You don't think I know how the NYPD was cracking down in the face of those kinds of protests? Yeah, I believed Low when he said he wanted it all to stop."

"Fair enough. But here's a thought experiment, nothing more. What if he played you? What if someone realized that Don Whitman's bust provided an alternative explanation for the gun making it out of Safe Streets? It wouldn't be hard to find a kid who knew Marcus Jones and had some connection to the Crips."

"And that someone would be Scott Macklin?"

McKenna shrugged. Other people might berate her for raising such thoughts about a man who had recently died, but she knew that after nearly a quarter of a century at the DA's office, Getty didn't dwell on death like normal people did.

Getty said, "You know, when you first came to me, you said you thought Mac panicked when he saw Jones reach into his pocket, so Mac dropped a gun to cover up his mistake. Your little thought experiment sounds a lot worse. Plus, this stuff about the prostitute. Why would Macklin kill her?"

"Maybe the prostitute and Jones saw something they weren't supposed to see."

"It wasn't mistaken self-defense but cold-blooded murder?"

She shrugged again. "Still could have been a panic thing. Trying to keep them from getting away. I know it's crazy. But you know the facts of that case better than anyone. I'm just asking you to think it through with me—as a friend, not a source. I'm not going to quote you. But as a huge what-if, what could Jones and the girl have seen that would make Mac panic that way?"

So far the words had come out exactly as she'd planned them. The right delivery. The right tone. Just a friend thinking out loud. If Getty blew her off because he was too busy, she wouldn't know what to think. If he became defensive or angry, she'd assume he was hiding something.

Instead of offering either of the anticipated responses, Getty surprised her. He played out the thought experiment. And damn, he was smart.

"Let me start by saying that if you *ever* try to make it sound like I *believe* any of this shit, I will drop-kick your ass back before the day I met you. But if we're really playing what-if, I'd say it was all about the pier."

"Because Mac thought Marcus was planning a grab?"

"No, because piers are where we import and export. I don't know all the details, but Macklin was on the docks that night for some kind of inspection program. If he was on the take, Marcus Jones and the hooker could have seen illegal cargo coming in. Drugs. Maybe people."

The theory was coming together even as she articulated it. "Mac heads over to make sure they're not a problem, but they're not having it. He panics, pulls his weapon . . ."

"Total fiction, if you ask me," Getty said. "But yeah, it's possible."

Depending on the role Macklin played in the cargo inspection, he could have been the one person standing in the way between seized cargo and a free pass. She remembered Macklin asking her about immigration law. The situation was complicated, he had said. She searched her memory for the specifics. Josefina had entered the country lawfully but failed to return to Mexico when her visa expired. Even worse, she had her sister bring Thomas into the country illegally when he was five years old. Macklin was pretty sure that the marriage resolved any of Josefina's immigration problems, but he was worried about Thomas getting deported. He'd said he needed money for an immigration lawyer.

Thomas, now starting college at Hofstra, obviously remained in the country. Maybe Mac had found a way to fight for his stepson.

"But once James Low stepped forward, we stopped considering the possibilities," she said. "Do you know what ever happened to him?"

"Been a long time."

McKenna knew. She'd done the research. Killed in a gang shooting two years earlier in Atlanta. "He got picked up in a bar brawl a year after he testified before the Marcus Jones grand jury."

"Sure, I know about that. I handled it, in fact. But since then? No clue."

So much for catching Getty in a lie. "I looked at the police report," she said. "It was an easy felony. Plus, he had priors. Why'd you plead it to a misdemeanor?"

"Because I have a bias against cases that are cluster fucks. There were thugs on both sides. Complete pandemonium. All the witnesses were drunk, and none of them wanted to testify. The so-called victim had a record six feet long, including multiple assaults. His lawyer—Bernadette Connor, you know her?"

McKenna nodded. Telegenic and straight-talking, Connor was her law firm's go-to person for high-profile criminal trials. Nine years ago, she was a midlevel associate at the firm but already had a reputation as a hard charger in the courtroom.

"Bernadette came to me early and made it clear the case wasn't winnable. I'd dealt with him on the Marcus Jones thing. He had a clean sheet during the year in between, and I thought he might not be a lost cause. We pleaded him out to the misdemeanor and moved on."

Getty's explanation was plausible, but it was raising questions she hadn't considered. "Did you ever wonder how a kid like James Low had enough money to hire a private lawyer? Or to get VIP bottle service in a club?"

"Not really. Club night could have been a hookup by a doorman, for all I know. And a firm like Bernadette's does a ton of pro bono."

Or James Low had been paid off to say he gave the gun to Marcus Jones.

"Speaking of pleas," McKenna said, "I saw Gretchen Hauptmann this week."

His face was blank before the name registered. "Sure, Susan's sister. How's she doing?"

"She said you helped her out of a federal drug indictment. I didn't realize you knew her."

"I didn't. I knew her sister. You're the one who introduced us, remember?"

"Sure, that one night. I didn't know you stayed in touch."

For the first time since they'd sat down, he looked offended. "Where's this coming from?"

"I just found out that Susan was pregnant when she disappeared. And I assumed from your helping Gretchen that you and Susan must have . . . connected after I introduced you. In light of the timing, I thought it was kind of weird that you never said anything to the police when she went missing."

"Look, not that I owe you an explanation, but I saw her a few times after we met at the bar. It obviously wasn't going anywhere— she had a lot going on in her life. She was looking at another deployment. By the time she disappeared, we weren't together that way. I helped her sister because she asked me to review the case and it seemed like the right thing to do."

Susan had never mentioned anything about deployment to McKenna. And she'd just seen Susan's file. Scanlin had checked with the military: Susan's service was done; she was free and clear. Was Getty lying? Or had Susan made up the deployment to break things off with him? Or had Scanlin made yet another mistake?

"Did Susan tell you she was pregnant?" she asked.

"No. Obviously not. I would have told the police."

If Getty knew more than he was letting on, she hadn't caught him. "So, you need to get back to the courthouse?"

"After the big interrogation, that's all you have to say?"

"I figured you were busy, that's all. I really appreciate the time, Will."

She could tell he wanted to say something, but he pushed the tray in her direction, shook his head, and left without a word. He let the bakery door slam behind him. So much for her last remaining ADA friend.

The meeting hadn't been a complete bust. She had been thinking so much about the gun next to Marcus Jones's body that she'd completely glossed over the reason Scott Macklin had been at the pier in the first place. She remembered the bits and pieces of the argument that Susan's neighbor had overheard. "Smack" and "important." Smack was Mac. Important? Could have been "import." If Macklin had been involved in a smuggling operation at the piers, that would explain how Marcus Jones and Pamela Morris had become a threat.

McKenna found the business card she was looking for in her purse.

"Agent Mercado, this is McKenna Jordan. I want to propose a deal."

CHAPTER FIFTY-SEVEN

I want to propose a deal. McKenna thought the line was pretty good bait. The promise of a swap. A quid pro quo. She thought it would draw the FBI agent in.

Once again, Mercado wasn't like other FBI agents. She hung up.

At least she picked up the phone on the second try. McKenna forewent the cool pitch, trying an earnest approach. She actually said, "Cross my heart, you'll want to hear this." Combined with the desperate tone, it probably amounted to groveling. But it worked. She was back at the Federal Building and had Mercado's attention.

"I have information for you."

"Good. Let's hear it."

"Because I'm a lawyer," McKenna said, "I know I'm not obligated to turn over information out of the goodness of my heart."

"I can subpoena you to testify in front of the grand jury."

"You can. But then I'll move to quash that subpoena, and you won't be able to tell a judge what you even want to ask me. Even if you do haul me before the grand jury, once again, you don't know what to ask me."

"So, just like some scumbag codefendant invoking the Fifth Amendment, you want a deal."

"Call me what you want, Mercado, but I've seen the look of an investigator who's hot on the trail, with every piece falling into place, and it's only a matter of time before the entire thing comes together. I've also seen the opposite, where every road is a dead end, every promising tip a brick wall. You look like you've been hitting dead ends and brick walls."

Mercado held her gaze for a few seconds, then gave her a grudging smile. "What do you want? "

"The morning after the bombing in Brentwood, you asked me about four names. I know that two of them are already in custody. I assume the other two were cohorts?"

"Again, not sure why I'd tell you anything. I've heard about your brand of journalism. Not real interested."

"Fine. Just listen. I know that Greg Larson is the de facto leader of the P3s. That leaves one other name on your list—Pamela Morris. It sounded like you didn't know where Larson and Morris were or whether they died in the bombing. I have information about Pamela Morris. And I mean rock-solid information."

"Is she with Larson?"

Mercado's question meant she had not yet received confirmation that Larson or Morris had died in the explosion.

"I don't know, but—" McKenna stopped when Mercado got up to leave the conference room. "Hold on, hear me out. I know *who* she is, and her real name's not Pamela Morris. And because I know who she is, I know a context to her work with the P3s that, frankly, you're clueless about."

Finally, McKenna had gotten her interest. Jamie Mercado was not used to being called clueless.

"What do you need from me?"

"I need your word that you'll do me a favor."

Another smile, this one condescending. "You've got to understand something. *My* word? In *my* world? It actually means something. I can't give you my word when you ask for something that amorphous."

"Fine. You want specifics? Part one—I show you a photograph

of the woman you've been looking for, the woman you know as Pamela Morris. You take that to the two P3s you have in custody. They'll confirm it's her. That should earn me enough goodwill for part two: you promise to answer two questions for me—one having to do with a cargo inspection ten years ago, and one about a search of my office this week. Since I trust that you're a person of her word, once you promise me that, I'll fill in the connections. Is that specific enough for you?"

"Jesus, Jordan, you're a piece of work. Just give me the picture already."

McKenna handed her a photograph of Susan. "See if they recognize her. But tell them the picture's ten years old."

Mercado took a quick glance and dropped the print on the table. "What are you trying to pull? This is that missing woman you've been Tweeting about—Susan Hopman or whatever."

"Hauptmann. We had a deal, Agent Mercado. Show the two prisoners the picture. You'll get a match. And then I'll explain. I promise. My word means something, too."

"One of them lawyered up, but I still have the younger one hanging on by a thread. We're about to go in for another round with her, in fact."

"It'll be worth your time. I promise."

Ten minutes later, Mercado confirmed it: the woman who'd been living as Pamela Morris was Susan Hauptmann.

"Enough with all the game playing," Mercado said. "What's your angle?"

McKenna told Mercado everything with the linear precision of a lawyer's narrative. Susan's disappearance. The pregnancy. The elderly neighbor hearing an argument with repeated mentions of "smack" (Mac) and "important" (import). Susan's reappearance on the subway platform, wearing a backpack tying her to the P3s, and everything that had happened since: McKenna losing her job; Scott Macklin's supposed suicide a day after Susan visited his house; the

Cleaner who wiped out the subway footage of Susan; the shooting at Grand Central Station; her suspicions about Will Getty.

"Look," Mercado said, "I'm sorry about your husband, but you've mistaken me for someone who cares about your friend's disappearance or whatever the fuck happened ten years ago between a dead kid and a former—and now dead—cop."

"Very sensitive, Agent."

"It's not my job to be sensitive. You came here with a promise of information. Tell me how this jumble of data helps me get to the bottom of a nationwide ecoterrorism organization."

"Weren't you listening?"

"Yes, and patiently, I might add."

McKenna resisted the temptation to use a condescending tone herself. "I didn't see it at first, either. But there's only one explanation for Susan Hauptmann living in that house in Brentwood. She was strictly law-and-order. A hard-core, chain-of-command, work-within-the-system type. The complete antithesis of a group like the P3s."

"So why was she there?"

"Because for ten years, she has somehow managed to support herself. I know Susan. She's industrious. She could take her military experience and talk her way into a decade of work with private security firms without revealing her true identity—the kind of firm that might not ask too many questions if an operative proved she was talented enough. The kind of outfit that might engage in the domestic surveillance you're not allowed to conduct as an agent of the government."

She saw a flicker of recognition in Mercado's face, part excitement, part frustration that she hadn't seen it earlier.

"She was hired to be there," Mercado said.

"I'd bet everything on it. No one's more motivated to bring down a gang of activists than the corporations left paying the bills from their handiwork. And those corporations can afford to hire the best. Once you know who her clients were, you can subpoena them for information. It would be illegal surveillance if it originated with the FBI, but if a private party gathered it—"

Mercado finished the thought. "It's fair game. We're regulated, but they're not. They can pose as sympathizers. Snoop in e-mails. Bug phones."

"They'll have names, locations, dates, target information. The starting point is finding Susan Hauptmann, which is where my questions come in. On October 16, 2003, NYPD Officer Scott Macklin was working on some kind of container inspection at the West Harlem piers. I'm trying to figure out the specifics. If we can tie Will Getty to it, we might have enough evidence for a wiretap. Catch his connection to Susan."

Without a word, Mercado left the conference room. She returned twenty minutes later. "Remember how, after 9/11, we figured out that however high we ramped up security at airports, we still had these gaping holes in our border because of cargo inspection? The newly formed Homeland Security Department cranked up the search requirements but didn't have the systems to keep pace. Containers were getting so backed up at the Port Authority that they literally ran out of storage space. Fancy imported food was going bad. Just a big backlog."

"The NYPD was filling in?"

"To streamline cargo inspection, a federal-state cooperative Homeland Security task force created a preapproval process for shippers and receivers." When Mercado described the program, McKenna felt a tug at the threads of her long-term memory. "Frequent importers and exporters could get prescreened to receive cargo with less rigorous inspection. Shipments could skip the usual receiving ports for spot-checking at local piers, and then the approved receivers would conduct a full search on their own and certify that they didn't receive any unauthorized items. Participants were high-volume, high-credibility entities."

Mercado was blabbing along, living up to her end of the bargain, when McKenna realized that Patrick once told her that the museum was authorized to participate in the preapproved cargo program. She remembered him working nights, inspecting art shipments.

She tried to retain control over her own thoughts. She tried to stop the images of Patrick with Susan. Without McKenna. Talking about McKenna. Enjoying the thrill of getting away with it.

She needed to focus. "Is there any way to find out which preapproved shippers were receiving cargo that night? Maybe we can find a connection to Susan."

"I'll have to reach out to Homeland Security, but I wouldn't bet on it."

"One more thing, Agent. I don't want to push my luck, but why'd you bother searching my office? What did you think you were going to find there?"

Mercado looked amused. "I only *wish* I had the time to care so much about you, Jordan. If someone searched your office, it sure as hell wasn't the Bureau."

McKenna found Bob Vance on his way to Vic's Bagels. Her former editor was Rain Man–like in his consistency. Vic's was known for its multitudinous toppings. Signature menu items included the Tokyo Tel Aviv Express with wasabi and edamame, or the Vermonter with bacon, maple syrup, and cinnamon. You could make your own spread, with mix-ins as diverse as pesto, corn, or potato chips.

Bob Vance? Plain bagel, butter, lox, and tomatoes, untoasted, every day around two-thirty.

On instinct, he smiled when he spotted McKenna, but then he shook his head as reality set in. "Too soon, my dear. Get a lawyer to talk to the magazine's lawyers. Maybe they'll work something out."

"I'm not here to beg for my job, Bob. The FBI agent who searched my office. Was he this man?" She showed him a photograph of the Cleaner. His picture had not yet been released to the press after the shooting.

"Yeah, that's the one. You're not stalking an FBI agent, are you? I wouldn't mess around with that."

Yesterday she would have savored telling him he'd been duped. That his magazine's lawyers were idiots who didn't know enough about criminal law to check out their copy of the warrant, if they'd even been served with one. She would have used the infiltration as proof that someone was trying to discredit her, and she would have insisted on getting her job back.

Now she didn't really care about any of it.

"So who's the guy in the picture?" he asked.

"You'll find out soon enough."

"You should reach out to Dana. She quit in a huff about the magazine letting you go, but I saw her talking to that agent outside the building."

CHAPTER
FIFTY-EIGHT

In a strange way, McKenna had always been intimidated by Dana, who was younger, shorter, and less educated, but bold enough to pierce her tongue and stomp through a newsroom in a tank top with her bra straps showing. She dropped the F-bomb without mercy. And she didn't seem to care that she usually smelled like garlic.

McKenna realized now that all of the brashness was a veil. Dana pretended to place art above real-world concerns like employment, rent, and a retirement account, but she was a phony. She was for sale, no less than the corporate drones she liked to mock.

She wasn't even worth a subway ride to Brooklyn. McKenna could deal with her in a phone call.

"Hey there, M."

One night on the girl's daybed, and Dana was using a nickname that only Patrick called her.

"Do you realize that what you did amounts to wire fraud under the federal criminal code?"

"What are you talking about?"

McKenna gave her a brief tutorial in the law. As an employee, Dana owed the magazine her duty of honest services. By taking a bribe and then using the Internet to delete the magazine's intellectual property (the video of Susan) and to fabricate a false story about

Judge Knight's supposed e-mails, she had committed wire fraud. The maximum sentence was twenty years.

Dana continued to deny it.

"I'm not playing with you, Dana. You are in so far over your five-foot-tall head that you can't begin to understand the rain of hell I will bring down on you. The man who hired you? Bob Vance saw you together. He's dead now. Maybe you woke up long enough today to hear about the shooting at Grand Central? He was killed, and my husband nearly was, too."

Dana was making "oh my God" noises on the other end of the line.

"Shut up, Dana. And grow up. I am giving you one chance to do what I'm telling you. After that, I go to the U.S. attorney's office, and you take your chances with a grand jury."

"I'll do anything, McKenna. I didn't know—I thought it was just one story. Then you got fired. And oh my God, that guy's *dead*? And Patrick—"

"What did that man want from you?"

"At first I didn't know. He offered me two hundred bucks to tell him what you were working on. I told him about the Knight story—your search for a smoking gun. He paid me five grand to make it look like you manufactured your own evidence."

"I got *fired* for that, Dana." Worse. Because of Dana, McKenna had suspected her own husband of being behind the setup.

"I didn't think it would be that bad. It was a *lot* of money. That's like almost three months' pay. I was supposed to keep him updated. When you got the video of the subway lady, he gave me another grand to delete it."

"So the temper tantrum you threw about your backup being deleted was bogus."

"I didn't know you'd get fired. When I quit, it was my way of trying to make it up to you."

"Your being out of a job does absolutely nothing to help me, Dana. Nothing about your life is at all relevant to mine."

"You don't have to be such a bitch—"

"I'm pretty sure that's *exactly* what I need to be right now. Because here's what you're going to do. You're going to go to Bob Vance—in person, at *NYC* magazine—and you're going to tell him what you did. You can make whatever lame excuse you want: alcoholism, bipolar disorder, I'd probably go with a practical joke that got out of hand. You already quit, so I doubt they'll do anything more to punish you. But you *will* make it clear that you were the one who set me up on the Knight article.

"Alternatively, I will make sure the U.S. attorney's office knows that you accepted a bribe and forged e-mails under the name of a sitting New York County supreme court judge. Do I need to ask you more than once?"

McKenna's pulse was just returning to normal when her cell phone rang. She recognized the general number for the district attorney's Office.

"This is McKenna."

Getty didn't bother introducing himself. "You know, Wright, I was the one person in the office who defended you when the Macklin case imploded. I felt responsible for your going public. But you know what? You proved today that my initial instincts were right. Every bad word anyone has ever said about you is right. You've got no judgment."

What comes around goes around. She had just gone off on Dana, and now Will Getty was venting at her.

"Will, you have no idea what I'm dealing with right now. I just had a few questions—"

"That's bullshit, and you know it. You were basically accusing me of knowing something about Susan's disappearance and taking perjured testimony from James Low to cover up for a bad cop. It's ridiculous. But if you want to start throwing accusations at every man who fell into Susan's bed, there's another name you should know about."

Don't say it, Will. Please don't say it.

"I told you before that things didn't work out with Susan and me. I said it was because of the deployment, because I was trying to protect your feelings. But there was something else. She told me she was in love with one of her best friends and wanted to make something work with him."

No, don't say it. Don't say it. No, no, no.

"Guess what, Wright? The friend was none other than your husband, Patrick Jordan. Maybe you better find out what he knows before you weave together your master conspiracy theory."

The line fell silent. She tasted bile in the back of her throat.

Her phone chirped again in her hand. If Getty was calling to apologize, it was too late. Some things could not be taken back.

The call was from a different number.

"This is McKenna."

"I'm calling for Dr. Gifford at Lenox Hill Hospital. We thought you'd like to know that your husband is awake. He's awake, and he's talking. He made it."

CHAPTER FIFTY-NINE

The ICU was marked by the same chaos McKenna had left behind that morning. Same overcrowded hallways. Same loud, scratchy pages over the intercom system. Same weird antiseptic odor.

Patrick, though, had moved. The bed he'd occupied was now home to a twentysomething woman surrounded by balloon bouquets and teddy bears. The smocked staff had changed, too. McKenna didn't recognize any of the nurses she'd ingratiated herself with the previous night. She zeroed in on the sole woman at the nursing station who seemed to be standing in one spot for consecutive seconds.

"I'm looking for my husband, Patrick Jordan. He was in room 610, but he must have been transferred."

The woman gave her a confused look. "Mr. Jordan was moved to a room in our recovery wing. Do you mind if I check your identification?"

McKenna placed her driver's license on the counter.

"Room 640. Just through these double doors, take the first right turn, and then it's the third room on your left. And sorry about the ID check. I could've sworn another woman was just here saying she was the patient's wife, but I must have misheard her. We're a bit swamped today. Probably another member of your family."

Probably not.

For all Susan's talk about how Patrick and McKenna were soul mates, meant to be, it was obviously Susan and Patrick who shared the deep connection. Susan had probably been sneaking around with him the whole time McKenna had been falling in love. Whatever they had for each other could have been going on the entire time Susan was supposedly missing, and she had dragged him into something that had gotten him shot.

And now she had been here. With him. At his bedside, instead of her.

McKenna hated both of them.

How could Patrick ever fix this?

A pair of open eyes and a chapped-lip smile turned out to be a remarkable beginning. All of the horrible mental images she'd been carrying around disappeared. She didn't have any answers, but suddenly, it wasn't about his phone call or leaving work early one day or discouraging her from looking for Susan. Somehow she knew at a basic, cellular level that Patrick would have an explanation.

"You're here," he said. His voice was low and hoarse.

She placed a hand over her mouth and fought back tears. She rushed to him, leaning in to hug him tight, and then froze at the sight of the hoses and tubes. She settled for a palm against his temple and a kiss on his cheek. "You scared me."

"You scared me, too. I guess we're even."

When she'd decided to go to Dana's that night, it never dawned on her that he'd be worried about her safety. The fact that she'd trusted Dana over her own husband made her feel sick. Seeing him now, she knew she never should have doubted him.

"You may need to buy me some new casebooks for Christmas."

His laugh quickly turned into a cough. "Shh," she whispered. "Take it easy. I promise never to be funny ever again."

"The surgeon told me how smart I was. I had to confess I saw it on one of your TV shows. Remember?"

She nodded and wiped a tear from her cheek. "I almost lost you."

So much had changed since they'd gotten married. They had taken the plunge after a year of uninterrupted bliss had convinced them they had finally worked out all the kinks. He'd thought she was over the pain of what had happened at the DA's office. That now that she was happy in her new life as a writer, she could be happy with him. But then her second book got rejected, and she had turned into the same moody, self-centered person she'd been before. When she was unhappy, it affected the way she treated Patrick. His potty humor, once endearing, was immature. His penchant for constancy, so reliable and admirable when they met, was boring.

It was as though she'd gotten married believing he'd change, and he'd married her on the assumption that she'd always be the same. If it hadn't been for the marriage license and the apartment they'd bought together, they might have gone right back to their previous cyclical ways: on, then off, then on. She wouldn't let that happen again. Her professional life was in tatters, but all she cared about right now was Patrick.

He looked away from her. "I'm so sorry, McKenna. I—I don't know how I let this happen. There's so much I need to tell you."

"She was here, wasn't she? Susan. She was here with you."

He started to cry. In all the years she had known him, she had never seen him cry. "How did you know—"

"I know a lot, Patrick. And now I need you to tell me the rest."

She e-mailed me at work last Monday. From an anonymous account." It had been two days after Susan rescued Nicky Cervantes from the subway tracks—the same day McKenna had shown Patrick the video of Susan. The same day he'd pretended the woman looked nothing like Susan. The same day he'd sat next to her on the sofa and lied to her face.

"Just out of the blue? After ten years?"

"She told me that she couldn't explain everything, but I had to trust her: I had to make sure you didn't write anything else about the Marcus Jones shooting. And she said I couldn't tell anyone she was alive. That she was in danger, and you might be, too, if I didn't keep you out of it."

"That's it?"

"Yes. I thought it was someone's sick idea of a joke, so I said I was going to call the police and tell them about her e-mail unless she agreed to see me in person. I was shocked when she sent me instructions about which train to board, which car, which seat to take. She was obviously worried about being watched."

"So you met her?"

"I'm not sure you can call it that. I handed her a flash drive with a letter on it, trying to convince her to come back. To take her life back. I didn't hear from her again until she called me two days later, wanting to know why you were posting calls for information about her on Twitter. I tried telling her that I'd done everything I could—"

"I overheard that call," McKenna confessed. "I found a picture of you together in the box Adam sent over. And then I heard you talking to her. I thought—I thought you'd been in touch with her all this time, and I left. If I had only—"

"Stop it, McKenna. If it's anyone's fault—"

"You know what? Let's not do that right now. Let's not apologize to each other or place blame or any of that. She called you, and then what?"

"I figured she had something to do with those e-mails that got you fired. She swore up and down that she didn't know anything about it, but I didn't know what to believe. All I knew was that you were supposed to be home, and you weren't, and you'd obviously been going through that box. I figured you saw something that upset you. I should have realized she'd have pictures. Jesus, I should have told you at the very beginning, when we met. Because I didn't, it always seemed too late to do it. And then the more time went by—"

"It's not important, Patrick. Not right now, at least."

She could tell he was forcing himself to move along with the facts.

"You finally called me, saying you'd gone out with the work crowd and were crashing at Dana's. I wanted to believe everything was okay, but you didn't come home the next night, either. And then I got that phone call. A guy saying he had you and to meet him at Grand Central. Susan had said that you could be in danger, so I—"

"You taped yourself up in my law books." She took his hand and kissed the inside of his wrist.

"It wasn't the guy I was meeting who shot me. It was a guy who came out of the crowd of protestors. In a mask and a cape. He shot us both."

She told him about the Cleaner. She also told him that he hadn't been as lucky as Patrick.

"Who is he?"

"They don't know yet," she said. "Part of me wondered whether he was someone you and Susan knew."

"No. I mean, when I showed up at Grand Central, I thought he might have been watching me the one time I met Susan on the PATH train. I'd never seen him before that."

"And that's it?" she asked. "You really don't know anything else?"

He shook his head, and that was all it took. She knew Patrick. She believed him.

"I saw her cold-case file," she said. "I know you told the police back then that you thought she'd left on her own. Why didn't you ever mention that to me?"

"I only suspected. I knew she had reupped her obligation to the army in 2001, right before 9/11. She'd already been deployed once, and there would obviously be more where that came from. Remember how worried you were that I'd get called up, and I wasn't even active reserves anymore."

She remembered. As she recalled it, she wasn't the only one who'd been worried. She could still picture Patrick's expression the day he'd opened a letter from the army declaring in official terms that he was "hereby recommissioned" as a captain in the army and ordering him to accept the commission by signing the enclosed documents. It was only on more careful inspection that she had seen the small type at the bottom of the form: if he failed to accept the commission by the stated date, the offer would expire and there would be no guarantee that he could rejoin at his former rank.

By the time Patrick received the letter, the news was reporting stories of the army pulling in forty-year-old officers who had been out of the military for a decade, under a program called the Inactive Ready Reserve. The military's position was that any officer who retained a single benefit of military service—including a military identification card—could be activated at will, whether duped into signing a recommission letter or not.

"A lot of people were looking for ways to get out. We had a classmate who hired a lawyer to make sure he had severed all possible connections to the army. Even that was enough for the crew to write him off, like some draft dodger running to Canada. But Susan? Given who her father was? If she didn't want to go back? Part of me could imagine her just starting over."

According to Will Getty, Susan had been pulled back into active duty. "Did she say anything about getting ready for another deployment?" McKenna asked.

"No. We talked about the possibility. She was headstrong about not going back if that happened."

"If she had been activated, would pregnancy be a basis for getting out?"

"No. Women can defer depending on the due date and the timing, but it's just a deferral. But Susan wasn't—"

He could see from her face that Susan, in fact, had been pregnant. Was McKenna only imagining it, or was he mentally running the math, counting the weeks? They were still together, even then. When, Patrick, when? Was it the entire time? But they weren't going to talk about that. Not now. Not yet.

"She still would have owed the army her time," he said.

"Giving up her identity seems like a drastic way to get out of service."

Then McKenna realized that she'd been looking at everything wrong. She'd been trying to work out how Susan might have stumbled upon whatever happened at the docks that night. She had never seen that Susan could have been the one to make it all happen.

"Do you remember that cargo import program you told me about?" she asked. "Where the museum's shipments got spot-checked, and you were certified to do the complete inspection on your own? Did you ever mention that program to Susan?"

"Yeah, I guess I did. Some night when I had to bail on one of her parties because I was working late."

McKenna remembered the night she'd told Susan about Macklin breaking down in her office. He'd just been moved into the state-federal team working with Homeland Security.

Between the two of them, McKenna and Patrick had told Susan everything she needed to exploit a potential hole in the country's cargo inspection. By turning Macklin, she could have sneaked anything into the country.

"Is it possible Susan was involved in some kind of smuggling operation? Maybe with Gretchen's dealers?"

Patrick looked at her as if she had proposed a move to the ocean to live with the mermaids. "First of all, I think Gretchen's dealers were more corner hustlers than Pablo Escobars. Besides, Susan had her problems, but something like that? No way. She was more her dad's daughter than she wanted to admit."

He was starting to speak more slowly. She could tell he was getting tired. "I hate to ask you this," she said, brushing his hair with her fingers, "but the police want to talk to you about the shooting. Are you sure there's nothing else to tell? Because now's the time to say so. We'll hire a lawyer."

He gave her a tired smile. "I swear. There's nothing else. I'll talk to the police."

"What about today? Susan was here at the hospital?"

"I thought I dreamed that. When I first woke up, it was— God, McKenna, I thought I was dead. It was like I could see things, but then I'd fall back asleep. And I couldn't talk. I thought I saw you, too, and we were in Cinque Terre, popping open that bottle of prosecco and letting the cork fly below us to the Riviera."

She remembered the exact spot and wished they were there again. "You thought you saw Susan?"

"At one point, she was in that chair when my eyes opened. She looked relieved, and I was sure we were both dead, like she was welcoming me. But then she started crying uncontrollably and saying she was going to end this. No matter what. I thought maybe she was going to hurt herself, but I couldn't move. The next time I woke up, she was gone."

He was fading back into sleep even as he finished the sentence.

CHAPTER
SIXTY

McKenna tracked down a nurse in the hallway. "He's groggy again. Does the doctor need to check on him?"

"No, that's natural. He's on a morphine drip. Your husband's very stoic, not a complainer, but he's in a lot of pain. It's better for him to rest."

Stoic. Marla Tompkins had used the same word to describe General Hauptmann's acceptance of impending death.

McKenna told the nurse she'd be in the lobby if Patrick became alert again. When she got there, she found Joe Scanlin waiting. He greeted her with a "hey," and she took the seat next to him.

"You okay?" she asked. "I should have backed off this morning. Macklin was your friend. And I didn't say enough about how sorry I am about his death. Or that you were the one to find him."

He held up a hand. "Your husband was in critical condition, and you wanted to know why. I was an ass. And I put my blinders on about Mac. I promised to see this through, and I dropped the ball."

She nodded. "You can tell Compton he can question Patrick as soon as his doctors think he's up for it."

"Compton won't need to talk to your husband."

"He needs to know about the phone call Patrick got. The Cleaner said I was in danger—"

"First of all, you don't need to call him the Cleaner anymore," Scanlin said. "We've got a name. I figured if he was connected to Susan, I'd check military fingerprints. Prints taken for military personnel before 2000 aren't in AFIS. But with the military, I got a hit. Our guy's name is Carl Buckner. Direct into army in 1995 after ROTC at Texas A&M. He put in sixteen years—military intelligence—and then quit. Honorable discharge."

She knew from Patrick's friends that twenty years of service meant retirement pay for life. "Did any of his service overlap with Susan's?"

He shook his head. "No, but I talked to his most recent supervising officer. Apparently Buckner was brilliant. And a true believer. A lot of guys entered the army in the late nineties thinking they'd never see real danger. A little UN peacekeeping here and there, with all the benefits of service. Not Buckner. When other soldiers started silently cheering on the 'bring home the troops' crowd, Buckner wanted to stay in the Middle East and finish what we started."

"And what exactly was that?"

"More than six thousand service members lost their lives for freedom, Jordan. For men like Buckner, that means something. When we decided to pull out with the job unfinished, he quit. Told his friends he'd spent sixteen years watching government contractors get rich without the sacrifices made by true soldiers. They got the impression he was moving on to the private sector, but we can't find any evidence that Buckner used his social security number to earn a single dime, or rent a house, or buy a plane ticket since the day he came home from Afghanistan."

For anyone who'd earned a reputation for brilliance among military intelligence, living off the grid for a couple of years must have been like tying shoes.

"I talked to Patrick." She gave Scanlin an abbreviated version of her husband's interactions with Susan. "He thinks he saw the Cleaner—Buckner—on the train but doesn't know anything else about him."

"I'll get the full story from him," Scanlin said. He saw the confusion register on her face. "I got the department to reassign the case to me. I told them it was connected to Susan Hauptmann's disappearance. Do I have his lawyer's permission to see him now?"

She placed a hand on his shoulder. She thought it was the most affection Scanlin could handle.

While Scanlin went in search of Patrick's doctor, McKenna placed a call to Marla Tompkins, the nurse who had taken care of George Hauptmann during his illness. Something had been bothering her about their earlier conversation, though she hadn't put her finger on it until now.

"Mrs. Tompkins, it's McKenna Jordan. I came to your apartment earlier this week."

"Of course. I remember."

"You mentioned that General Hauptmann's daughter Gretchen visited him shortly before he passed away and that you gave her his diary as a memento."

"Yes, that's correct. He was so very happy to see her. I don't think I'd ever seen him filled with that kind of joy."

"Had you met Gretchen before?"

"No, it was the first time. She was very emotional also. It was— Well, General Hauptmann came to depend upon me, and he treated me so very, very well. But his daughter—she was family. I was surprised they remained estranged after she visited. I hoped at the time that I was witnessing a thawing of the ice."

"Had you seen pictures of the Hauptmann daughters before?"

"No, ma'am. As I mentioned, he had already packed away most of his belongings, and I was told when I showed up for the home care that he found photographs of his family upsetting. Though he did have a wedding portrait of his wife right next to him on the nightstand. I saw him looking at it often."

McKenna had seen that photograph before, on Susan's bookshelf. She'd commented once on how much Susan looked like her mother.

"When Gretchen came to see her father, did you happen to notice if she looked like the late Mrs. Hauptmann?"

"Oh my goodness, yes. Isn't she just the spitting image of her mother? I couldn't stop commenting on it, but then I realized she seemed a bit uncomfortable with my remarks. My, yes, that's the woman's daughter, no question."

It was one of Mrs. Hauptmann's daughters, all right, but it hadn't been Gretchen. Just like Gretchen had said, she had left the cord to her father severed, even as he'd been dying. Susan had been the one to see her father one last time, to let him know she was alive. Susan, the same woman who told Scott Macklin's wife that she was a reporter and the Lenox Hill ICU that she was Mrs. Patrick Jordan, had told her father's nurse she was her older sister, Gretchen.

"Mrs. Tompkins, I hope you won't take my question the wrong way, but it's important that I ask. I can tell that you were a complete professional in your care of General Hauptmann, but I imagine that when you gave his daughter that diary, you had your reasons."

"I thought she would want it. That's all."

This proud woman did not want to admit there was more to the story. McKenna pressed again. "Wouldn't it be part of his treatment for you to have a sense of his mental state as he was reaching the end? Or maybe you had seen him write something about his daughters, and you wanted Gretchen to know."

"I don't snoop, if that's what you're saying."

"Of course not." What sane person sharing a house with a lonely, decaying old man—a man who'd lived a life filled with power, politics, and international travel—wouldn't sneak a peek at his journals? "But this is important, Mrs. Tompkins. Was there anything in the general's journal about his other daughter, Susan, and the end of her military service?"

"Not really. No."

"Not really" did not mean the same thing as "no." "Did Susan ask him for help getting out of active duty?"

The silence confirmed it. It was only because McKenna knew the truth that the nurse was considering putting aside her loyalty to her former patient and friend. "I cared very much for General Hauptmann, and he was a brave and good man, but I never understood the hardness he showed toward his girls. You see, that's why I read his journals. To see if there was something I could use to bring Gretchen back into his life—something he had written that he could not say to her directly. But all he wrote about was their shortcomings and his disappointment in them."

"Like Susan leaving the military?"

"Yes. According to his journal, Susan came to him and begged for help. He pulled strings for her that regular people do not have access to. He said it reminded him of the senators' sons and corporate nephews who got deferments in Vietnam. He said he had no regrets cutting off Gretchen, and now it was time to do the same with Susan. They never spoke again. He was so ashamed for helping her that he didn't tell her himself. He said that he could find no way to deliver the news without sounding like he approved of her decision. He had his business partner tell her instead. She disappeared three months later."

"Business partner? Do you mean Adam Bayne?"

"Yes, that's right. I guess that was a long time ago, but Adam was like a son to General Hauptmann. Mrs. Jordan, if you talk to Gretchen, please tell her how sorry I am for giving her that journal. I wasn't thinking about her feelings. I was thinking about the general."

McKenna's mind was racing. She didn't understand the nurse's last comment. "How were you helping General Hauptmann?"

"He was an important man, the kind of man people write about when they die. I didn't want anyone to see what a terrible father he was."

McKenna mumbled something to the nurse about being a good person and disconnected the call. Before she knew it, she was pulling up Adam Bayne on her phone and hitting dial.

"McKenna. I saw the news. They said Patrick was in critical condition. I didn't know if it was okay to call. Any updates?"

Die. Die, die, die. You shot my husband, you evil motherfucker.

"He's going to make it." The catch in her voice wasn't feigned. "He's out of the woods."

"Oh, thank God. If there's anything at all I can do—"

You can go to hell, right after you die.

"Right now it's only immediate family, but visiting hours start at six." That gave her two hours. "Patrick's asking for visitors. I think he'd really like you to come."

"Oh. Well, absolutely, then."

He was good, but she could hear the skepticism in his voice. At one point, Patrick and Adam had been close, but these days they were barely beyond holiday-cards friendship.

"In fact," she added, "you're the only person he asked me specifically to call. Maybe after that kind of danger, he just wants an old military friend to talk to."

"Of course. Anything he needs. I'll see him right at six."

Scanlin was just finishing up with Patrick when she entered the hospital room. "How soon can we get a wire set up in here?"

CHAPTER
SIXTY-ONE

McKenna held Patrick's hand tightly in hers. "Are you sure you're willing to do this?"

He flashed her a look that revealed the ridiculousness of her question. Her plan for Patrick to coax Adam into incriminating himself was the equivalent of a luxury cruise compared to what Patrick really wanted to do to his former college buddy.

"You can't show that anger," she warned. "He'll know." She hadn't prepped a witness to wear a wire in ten years, but she remembered the basic talking points from her prosecutor days. Get the subject to talk on his own rather than merely acquiescing to your suggestions. Don't be too eager to lead. Be passive. You're the one who's scared. You're the one who's vulnerable. You're the loose cannon. Once the target feels the need to take control, he'll start talking.

She did one more test of their phones to ensure that the connection would work. Two hours' notice hadn't been enough to get NYPD approval for a recording device. McKenna had taken the situation into her own hands.

It was 5:53 P.M. She hit the call button on Patrick's phone, dialing herself, and then answered the call, activating the record function she'd installed for source interviews. "Detective Scanlin," she said, "my husband is clearly fatigued."

Patrick voiced weak protests that he was fine.

"In light of the fact that you haven't yet identified the gunman who nearly killed my husband, I assume you'll be here to frisk anyone who attempts to visit him in the hospital."

"Of course, Mrs. Jordan." Scanlin rolled his eyes, but he sounded perfectly obsequious. "I plan to stay during visitors' hours. Given the gunman's attempt to conceal his identity at Grand Central, I'd be surprised if he showed up here, but I've got two officers standing by just in case."

The real reason for the officers' presence was to back up Scanlin in the event that Adam Bayne was arrested. If Adam tried to argue later that the NYPD had orchestrated the recorded conversation with Patrick, this prologue would prove that she and Patrick had acted independent of the police.

Once she and Patrick were alone, she held his hand again and whispered in his ear. "Be careful, babe. Nothing you get Adam to say is worth the risk."

"He already shot me, M, and I'm still good. He won't be armed. I'll be fine. Now get out of here."

She paused at the door, knowing they had so much more to say to each other. But every word was being recorded, and Adam would be here any second. Patrick could see all of it on her face. *I know,* he mouthed.

Later. They would work through it later. All of the pain—Macklin's death, Patrick's shooting, even Susan's so-called disappearance—could have been avoided if people didn't always put off the problems that needed to be worked through right away.

Now it was 6:02 P.M. Adam was coming. It was time for her to go.

She played her assigned role when Adam appeared, gargantuan iris in tow. "Thank you for coming. You're such a good friend." She felt like the widow at a funeral.

Detective Scanlin played his part, too. "Sorry, sir. Routine for crime victims. Just a quick weapons check."

She stared at Scanlin as he stepped away from Adam empty-handed. As a detective, the man had missed a lot at one point in his career. But he had made a promise to her, and she'd made a decision to trust him. She had to believe he was capable of finding a weapon in a frisk. If he put Patrick in danger, she'd never forgive either one of them.

She listened to her cell phone four chairs away from Scanlin in the ICU waiting room. If Scanlin were ever asked, he could testify under oath—with no chance of contradictory evidence—that he had no idea she was eavesdropping on her husband's conversation with his friend. If something went wrong on the other end of the line, all she had to do was give Scanlin the signal, and he'd intervene.

She had one final idea. She pulled up her Twitter account on her iPad and posted a message:

> Susan, you promised P you would end this. Time is NOW. We know about AB; he's here. Come to hospital. P needs you NOW.

According to Will Getty, at one point Susan had been in love with Patrick. As careful as she'd been about hiding, Susan had come to the hospital today to check on him. She had told him she was going to end this, no matter what.

McKenna had to hope that Susan was still the same person, hardwired to do the right thing.

There was nothing more to do but wait.

CHAPTER SIXTY-TWO

Buddy. You look fucked up." McKenna nodded to Scanlin; she could hear Adam's voice clearly. The record function was working. "Not to rush anything, but if you die, is McKenna fair game?"

They called it the sickness, and supposedly Patrick's circle of army friends had it to a person. For someone with the sickness, nothing was off limits—profanity, incest jokes, even necrophilia jabs. It was all comedic fodder.

"You know nothing about true love," Patrick said. "It's in our vows. Promise to love, honor, obey, through sickness and health, richer or poor, and to do me, alive or in rigor mortis. Once the hard, high one wears off, that's another matter."

"What the hell happened?" Adam said. "They're saying it was some mind blow at an Occupy flash mob." The local news had made it sound like a random shooting during the Occupy protest. If McKenna's suspicions were right, Adam knew otherwise.

"Don't bother with the act, Adam. Susan told me everything. I just wanted to see you before it all went down. To try to understand how you could do this to me."

"I know we joke, but that shit's not funny, bro."

"I have a bullet hole in my neck, *bro*. You think I'm playing? It's just you and me here. For now, at least. Didn't you recognize the cop who searched you for weapons? Same guy who handled Susan's missing persons case. But Susan's back. And she knows you set her up. She's going to the feds."

"Set her up for what? Seriously, man, they may need to cut you back on the morphine—"

Scanlin looked at McKenna for an update. She shook her head. Nothing yet.

"It took ten years, Adam, but you can't keep a secret forever. Susan knows that her dad's the one who got her out of the military. Free and clear. No active duty; she could walk away."

For the first time, Adam didn't have a quippy response. That was good.

"The general couldn't bring himself to tell her. You were supposed to be the one. You didn't exactly convey the message."

She and Patrick had pieced together the theory after McKenna had spoken to General Hauptmann's nurse. If Susan had been under the mistaken impression that she was being called into active duty, it was because Adam hadn't told her that her father's intervention was successful. McKenna had been searching for a reason why Susan would have gotten involved in a smuggling operation at the piers; now they believed they'd found one.

Patrick continued to push Adam for a response. "What did you do, tell her she could satisfy her deployment by doing something closer to home? Just a few little shipments at the port? She always was a good implementer. And why shouldn't Susan have to sacrifice? She was the one who refused to save her dad's firm—the firm you'd been working your ass off in Afghanistan for. Just when you were about to cash in, the old man went and got cancer. All Susan had to do was lend her name to the enterprise—a name you'd never have, no matter how hard you tried—and she couldn't even do that."

"I don't know why you're doing this, Patrick, but I'm calling bullshit. Susan's dead. Or in the wind. Never coming back."

"You don't believe me?" Patrick asked. "Go check hospital security. She came when McKenna was out. Hospital security will have a tape of her coming in."

That was a mistake. If Adam took Patrick up on the suggestion, he'd go straight from the security office to the hospital exit, and they'd lose their shot at tripping him up. McKenna let herself breathe when she heard Adam respond. "Anyone who would disappear herself for ten years has obviously lost it. If she's making claims about me, she's got her own agenda."

Scanlin was looking at her more urgently. She shook her head again.

"Look, of all people, I get it," Patrick said. "Other guys post-9/11 were going back in, active duty, getting recommissioned—defend the homeland, get the bad guys. You know what I did? I quit the reserves. That's right. Because I knew we needed to invade someone, no matter what. And once you invade in that part of the world? You were the one who saw it firsthand. The bad guys weren't always bad. The good guys could be the most evil form of life on the planet. With the moral compass upside down, there were plenty of ways to rake in the money. And when the general got diagnosed with the big C, you realized your payday wasn't going to come, and you devised another way. But duping Susan into helping you? Setting off a house bomb to kill her? Shooting a *cop*? Coming after *me*? Taking out the guy you hired to do your dirty work?"

Despite his injuries, despite the painkillers, Patrick was yelling. In his anger, he was saying too much. They had speculated that Carl Buckner worked for Adam and then got scared off, but he also could be connected to Susan. They had wondered whether the Brentwood explosion was Adam's attempt to kill Susan, but it could have been an accidental explosion by the environmental activists Susan had infiltrated.

McKenna was sure Scanlin could see the worry on her face. Should she give the warning sign? Even without a weapon, there were ways Adam could hurt Patrick. The drip. The morphine drip. They should have asked the nurse whether it was tamper-proof.

Patrick must have realized that if he got too loud, the hospital staff would intervene. His voice was quieter, almost pleading. "I mean, Adam, who *are* you?"

"Pat, man, you've got to believe me. Yeah, okay, I got pretty screwed in the head in Afghanistan. And I got greedy. And I made— God, I made some horrible mistakes. But a house bomb? Shooting you? I have no fucking clue what you're talking about. And if Susan's telling you or the feds or anyone those kinds of things, she's lying. Believe what you want, but I'm going to go."

McKenna was shaking her head again at Scanlin. He could listen for himself once the call was over, but she knew they didn't have enough for probable cause. "I really am glad you're okay, Patrick. I mean it, and I hope one day you'll come to believe it."

They were screwed. She would have to play nicey-nice again while the man who shot her husband was allowed to walk away.

But before she saw Adam turn the corner toward the hallway from Patrick's room, she saw another familiar face. Susan's.

For days, McKenna had been convinced that Susan was alive, but she never really expected to see her again. And now here she was, twenty feet away, looking just as she had in the subway video.

Susan obviously recognized Scanlin, because she started to duck back into the elevator. McKenna ran toward her. "No, please!" The elevator doors began to close and then reopened. Susan stood at the threshold. At least she was willing to hear McKenna out.

"Adam Bayne is here but is about to leave," McKenna explained. "I can stall him. Scanlin knows everything, Susan. Just tell him so we'll have enough to arrest Adam right now."

Susan said nothing.

"You've got to do this, Susan. Or Adam gets away with everything. He'll keep coming after you for the rest of your life. And now that Patrick and I know, we're in danger, too."

McKenna could see Susan weighing the options, and for a second, it was like they were roommates again, her friend's face full of concentration as she balanced on a dining room chair to change the bulb in McKenna's closet. She had come here, hadn't she? She still cared. She was still protecting them.

"Okay, stall him," Susan said at last. "Do *not* let him leave. I have enough evidence to bury us both."

CHAPTER SIXTY-THREE

McKenna caught Adam just before he hit the double doors from the patient recovery rooms.

She put on her best tired smile. The loving wife who had spent the night next to her husband's recovery bed. The oblivious wife who didn't know yet that the hunt she'd begun for her missing friend was at an end. "Oh, no. You're done with your visit already? He seemed like he was really looking forward to seeing you."

"It was good to see him, but he's been through a lot. I don't want to push him too hard. I'll come back another time." Adam was walking away; McKenna reached gently for his forearm.

"You know, I wanted to say something. You were right—when I called you, I mean. About that old picture of Patrick and Susan. That was so many years ago, and it was stupid for me to call you that way. Something like this"—she gestured at Patrick's room—"puts things into perspective."

"That's good. I'm so happy he pulled through. I'd expect nothing less from a bruiser like your husband."

She let him hug her. The son of a bitch was actually *hugging* her. She didn't know how much more she could take.

She saw Scanlin entering the double doorways, a uniformed officer at his side. He gave her a nod. Whatever Susan had told him, he had enough.

Confusion, followed by panic, registered on Adam's face as law enforcement surrounded him. She'd never been so relieved to hear the reading of Miranda rights.

As the uniformed officer walked Adam to the lobby in handcuffs, she spotted Susan sitting in the waiting room next to the other officer awaiting Scanlin's orders. Susan's hands were in her lap, covered by a jacket.

She was in cuffs, too.

"What did you think was going to happen?" Scanlin said. "She gave it up, though. You were right. She was pregnant and had been called up to active duty again, this time for Iraq, and the army wouldn't let her out. She could defer, but she'd still be a single mother leaving behind a newborn."

McKenna knew how jaded Susan had been after her first deployment to Afghanistan. By the time she was called back in, people had figured out that the mission wasn't accomplished in Iraq. McKenna wondered if Susan had used the pregnancy as the excuse she'd never had to walk away from a life she'd taken on only for her father.

"Adam told her things had gotten even worse in Afghanistan. The military was cutting deals with opium farmers just to keep the peace. Now the farmers were crossing the line into exporting directly into the United States. He told her it was a way she could get herself out of active duty for good."

"I can't imagine she'd think that was okay."

"We didn't have time to cover all the details. She knew about the cargo inspection program from Patrick. She knew from you that Mac was assigned to the program and had an immigration problem. She put two and two together. Adam told her he got a promise that Mac's kid would be okay if he helped. It wasn't until she got her father's diary that she realized Adam had lied about the entire thing."

"It doesn't make sense," she said. "The military could fly cargo in on its own, no questions asked. And how could Adam get INS cooperation if he was acting as a free agent?"

"Again, details. We've got paper-thin probable cause based on her statements about the smuggling; plus, she says she's got recordings of both Bayne and Macklin before he died. I'm going to bring in Agent Mercado to trace the money. My guess is she'll find unexplained cash flowing to Bayne while he was in Afghanistan, not long after Susan's father found out he had cancer. From there, we'll get a search warrant for Bayne's home and office. Hopefully we'll find something tying him to Carl Buckner. Or proving that he was our shooter at Grand Central. Like I said, it's really thin."

"I know. But as long as you hold on to him, we don't have to worry about him coming after Patrick again. That's enough for now."

This was the bargain they'd struck once she had summoned Adam to the hospital. They were rushing. They had no real evidence to tie Adam to Patrick's shooting. They had to hope the police would find the gun in a search, or a drop of blood from Patrick or Carl Buckner. It was a risk she and Patrick had decided to take. If McKenna was right, Adam was so unhinged that his own Cleaner had defected, trying to turn to Patrick for help. More evidence might never come, but at least they were safe.

Scanlin started to follow the uniforms to the elevator, and then he turned around. "You're the one who made this happen. You want to come down to the precinct? Hear what your friend's been up to for the past ten years? She gave herself up to nail Adam Bayne to the wall. She could probably use the support."

McKenna had been racing from place to place, from lead to lead, for a solid week. And now Susan was alive. After all these years, and all those nightmares, she was alive, and she was in custody. There hadn't been time for a reunion, not even a handshake.

McKenna nearly followed Scanlin on autopilot. Then another instinct kicked in. "No," she said. Scanlin stopped walking, and she put a hand on his forearm. "I'm not sure I care anymore. And I mean this when I say it: I trust you to see it through. All I want is to stay here with Patrick."

The embrace Scanlin gave her was one of those big, strong hugs that certain kinds of men gave only to certain kinds of women. It was absolutely pure.

"Oh, and one more thing, Jordan. Not that it matters, but Susan says she lost the baby a month after she left New York. I got the impression that you might want to know."

Words were spilling from her mouth when she walked into Patrick's hospital room. "Scanlin got him. But Susan had to give herself up. But I can't figure out—"

"Shh," he said. "Just come here."

She kept talking. "Adam told Susan they needed a domestic contact person for drug imports. Couldn't they just fly everything in themselves through the military? And then Mac got a promise about his stepson. I don't know how Adam could possibly deliver."

Patrick was smiling. He was exhausted, and nauseated from painkillers, but he was smiling. He held up his cell phone.

She realized hers was in her pocket and that she'd never disconnected their call.

"A little muffled," he said, "but I got the gist. You did it, M. You did what I couldn't do, and the NYPD couldn't do, and the FBI couldn't do. You did it all."

He patted the edge of the bed, and she managed to lie on her side next to him.

"We're going to be okay," he whispered. He kissed the top of her head and squeezed her arm. "Thank you."

We're going to be okay. She'd been trying to tell herself that for days, but for the first time, she actually believed it.

PART V

SUSAN

CHAPTER SIXTY-FOUR

McKenna never would have thought that the best rest she'd had in a week would be on a narrow sliver of a hospital bed, listening to her husband talk between bouts of morphine-induced sleep.

His reminiscing about Susan was hard to take at first. Through the entire course of Patrick and McKenna's relationship, they had pretended—falsely, of course—that their romantic existences had begun and ended with each other. But once she got past the shock of imagining Patrick with another woman, his drug-addled memories of nights, weekends, sometimes even weeks—but never months—with Susan began to feel like period pieces. Vignettes from another time, featuring two familiar characters, but wholly unrelated to her own reality.

It had started the beginning of their third year at West Point.

Though McKenna had imagined the most passionate hypotheticals between her husband and Susan, she wanted to believe that any physical connection had been fleeting. Awkward. Meaningless.

The first time had been two days after Patrick learned his father died from an aneurysm. The commandant had him pulled from noon formation, shook his hand, and gave him the news. He also gave him the choice of taking the day off or returning to lunch. Patrick was Patrick, so he opted for the latter, then didn't say a word to anyone about the death of his father until two days later, when Susan cornered him after dinner and said she could tell he was feeling blue.

Those were Patrick's words. *She could tell I was feeling blue.* McKenna knew the Susan of ten years ago, who was only eight years older than the Susan who had been there to comfort Patrick when his father died. She had a preferred method for escaping the pains of the world, and that night she'd shared it with Patrick.

At least from his perspective, it had never been a relationship. He was twenty years old, and by that time, Susan had convinced herself that wanting sex like a man—often and without strings— was a form of female empowerment. They were never what others perceived as an official couple.

A year after graduation, Susan had taken a weekend leave from Fort Sill to find him at Fort Bragg, supposedly to escape the Oklahoma heat, though he suspected she was there for more. He told her then that he loved her as a friend, but—And she had cut him off. *As if! Dude, that's like incest.* Except maybe not, since she still wanted to sleep with him. Only for the sex. Because other guys sucked.

"We all chose to believe that was how she wanted it," he said. "We were a bunch of macho kids who thought we could have a friend who was just like us, except she was a woman who would . . . be with us." He brushed McKenna's hair back from her face. She had always known that he'd adopted the move because she'd made it clear that she liked it. "I was such an idiot then."

She'd heard enough for now. "I thought the only woman you knew before me was Ally, the big-boned girl. Frizzy red hair. Freckles and moles. Dumb as a rock."

"A real doll," he said, repeating the joke he'd made so many times when she was still trying to find out about his old girlfriends. "McKenna, I want you to know, however much—"

She shook her head. "It was a long time ago. We started over so many times, even after she was gone. And then we finally got it right." Maybe someday McKenna would press for details about the timing of the end to his hookups with Susan and the beginning of his relationship with her. Right now she didn't want them.

He saw her looking at the digital bedside clock. Susan was giving a complete videotaped debriefing this afternoon. Mercado and Scanlin had said they wanted McKenna there in case she could fill in any blanks. She suspected that Mercado was afraid she'd go public with the story if she weren't kept in the loop.

"I should go. I need to stop by the apartment first. I've been wearing the same clothes for two days straight."

"You're gross." He kissed the top of her head. "You sure you want to do this? You said they'd be fine without you."

"They would. But we're never going to understand what Susan did if we don't hear it straight from her. I'll be back as soon as it's over."

CHAPTER SIXTY-FIVE

McKenna was alone in their apartment, her first time home since she'd learned that Patrick had been shot. Susan's belongings were still scattered across the living room floor. McKenna packed them back in the box that Adam had sent over and pushed it all in a corner behind Patrick's bicycle. She didn't want to see it.

She stripped off her clothing, climbed into the hot shower, and turned her face up into the water stream. She felt the past week flow off of her. As the shampoo suds swirled into the drain beneath her, she imagined their problems carried away through the plumbing.

Adam Bayne was in custody. McKenna didn't have all the details, but Scanlin had told her this morning that he was confident they had enough to hold him for a long time. Carl Buckner—whether he'd been trying in the end to help them or hurt them—was dead. The police department was labeling Macklin's death a murder, so his family at least would be able to collect his life insurance and pension.

Tomorrow McKenna would go to see Bob Vance. By now, the editor knew that Dana had been the one who set her up. McKenna would sit down with the magazine's lawyers to make sure the retraction was sufficient to clear her name. And she would make sure they knew how much she could embarrass them with the fact that they'd allowed someone to search a journalist's office without veri-fying his credentials or the legitimacy of his supposed warrant. She would call the shots.

Did she even want that job?

As she turned off the shower, she let herself entertain the possibil-ity that the district attorney's office might invite her back. Maybe she didn't want that job, either. Maybe it was time for her to write a book. Not on an agent's terms, or an acquiring editor's, but because she really had something to say.

For now, she deserved to sit on her ass for a couple of weeks. Right after she made one last visit to the Federal Building.

Tom the mailman gave her a wolf whistle when she stepped from the apartment elevator. "Take a look at the big shot. You clean up pretty good."

Her usual attire was business casual at best, but she'd hauled out her nice Hugo Boss dress, the one she'd bought when her dog-walker article had earned her a five-minute interview on CNN. (Ever stop to wonder how you know your dog got walked? That's right. You don't.)

"Thank you, Tom. I've got to look like a grown-up today."

"You've got a couple days' mail backed up here. Want me to leave it with the doorman?"

"No, I'll take it." She folded the stack in half and tucked it into her briefcase.

"I mean it, McKenna. Don't let that tough husband know I said it, but you look fantastic."

She left feeling happy about the compliment. And then she real-ized how pathetic she was for caring about her appearance today. She cared because she wanted to look better than Susan.

Mercado met McKenna in the reception area and led the way to her office, where Scanlin was waiting. "Susan spent last night at MDC," Mercado explained. "We transported her this morning to continue the debriefing we began last night."

After four sleepless years at West Point and another five in the army, Susan had always insisted on perfect sleeping conditions: room-darkening curtains, Egyptian-cotton sheets, and absolute silence. McKenna could not imagine her at the Metropolitan Detention Center.

It didn't take long for Mercado to bring McKenna up to speed. "Based on what we got from Susan, we searched Bayne's home and office. Unfortunately, as we feared, the guy is careful. No evidence yet tying him to Carl Buckner or to either Macklin's death or the Grand Central shooting. The better news is that we've got a forensic accountant examining his financial records. He's just getting started on what's going to be a long process, but he tells me he's found discrepancies already. Namely, a fifty-thousand-dollar withdrawal one day before James Low, Jr., showed up at the DA's office claiming to have sold a gun to Marcus Jones. Plus, way more deposits than reported income, and right before Susan disappeared. He used a lot of it to set up his company in New York after he left the Hauptmann firm."

The money would corroborate Susan's claim about the drug importing. The unreported income alone could send him away for a decade. It had worked on Al Capone.

"What exactly did Susan tell you?" McKenna asked.

"You're about to hear for yourself," Scanlin said.

Mercado explained the process. Susan had already been talking for hours. Now they would get a straight, clean narrative on videotape.

McKenna remembered defense attorneys' complaints about videotaped confessions. The cops never recorded the stuff that happened earlier.

"Obviously the tape will be admissible against her," Mercado said. "We'll also give it to Bayne's lawyers to put the pressure on. If he knows for sure that she's flipped and is a compelling witness, he might do the same. My guess is he has names of other private contractors who were involved on the Afghanistan side of the operation."

"How does this work? I'll watch through a one-way glass?"

Mercado nodded, but gave Scanlin a look.

"There's one catch," Scanlin said. McKenna knew they had a reason for asking her here. "Susan's the one who wanted you to come. She wants you to hear her statement—kind of like an explanation, I guess. But she wants a few minutes alone with you before she'll go on tape."

CHAPTER SIXTY-SIX

Susan's orange jail scrubs were at least a size too big. They made her look like a young, waiflike girl. So did her posture—slumped in the chair, hands in her lap. Just a week ago, this same woman had outrun a high school athlete and dead-lifted his full weight.

"They told me you wanted to see me," McKenna said. It was the first time they'd been in the same room since their few minutes at the hospital prior to Susan's arrest.

Susan looked up and smiled sadly. "Of course I wanted to see you. But not to try and tell you what happened. They don't want you knowing anything other than what we're about to put on video. Undermines the evidentiary value or something."

"So why, Susan? Why am I here?" McKenna didn't try to hide the anger in her voice. She had spent the last day wondering whether she would have preferred that Susan had been murdered, as she'd always suspected. Ultimately she couldn't feel that way about anyone, but Susan had gotten people killed. And now she had to drag McKenna into the carnage of her own personal hurricane one last time.

"Because I want to tell you how sorry I am. Not just for—I mean, my God, for everything, but *personally*. I'm sorry for the harm I caused to you personally, McKenna. You'll hear soon enough why

I did what Adam wanted, and why I ran away instead of owning up to it. You can decide for yourself how you feel about that. But I am sorry. I hope someday you'll forgive me."

McKenna stared at Susan in silence. She thought about walking out but took a seat across from her at the table. "Your coming to the hospital yesterday was the beginning," she finally said. It was hard not to feel sorry for Susan. She was looking at serious prison time, and all because she'd chosen to turn herself in. "There was no other way to make sure Adam wouldn't come after Patrick again."

Susan nodded. "Don't thank me. It's only because I reached out to Patrick that he was in danger. I had to stop it."

"Patrick remembers seeing you in his hospital room. Sobbing. You still love him, don't you?"

Susan looked away.

"I know about you two. And I know you told Getty you were still in love with Patrick and wanted to be with him. Why didn't you ever tell me?"

"I almost did. That night we left Telephone Bar together, after the two of you met? I nearly told you. But I knew you'd never go out with him if I did. You'd been alone for a while, and he and I were never right together. I stole that mug for myself at first—like a memento of the night I really lost him. I gave it to you instead."

McKenna shook her head. "You didn't tell me because it would have been selfish." Typical Susan. She could have guaranteed with one sentence that she'd never have to watch the man she loved fall in love with her best friend. She could have sabotaged McKenna's relationship with Patrick before it started. But she wasn't selfish. She never was.

"My intentions weren't always pure," Susan said. "After I told Will I still had feelings for Patrick, I really was going to give it one more shot. I had this whole scene planned where I would pour my heart out, and he'd realize that he felt the same way, and maybe you'd even understand. But when I went to his apartment, all he could talk about was you. You guys had rented a paddleboat in Central Park or something. So *not* Patrick. So *completely* the kind of thing he'd usually mock. But because it was with you—anyway, I knew we were never going to happen."

"Were you pregnant then?"

She nodded.

"They told me you lost the baby. I'm sorry, Susan."

She shrugged.

"Was it Patrick's?" She regretted asking as soon as the words came out of her mouth. She'd been so careful not to press Patrick for the details. The idea of them being together after she and Patrick met had been enough to send McKenna out of their apartment after she'd found a college photograph. But now? She honestly didn't care.

Or perhaps she cared a little, because she felt relieved when Susan shook her head. "Of course not. We stopped crossing that line way before he met you. Or at least *he* stopped crossing that line. Let's just say there would have been a long list of paternity candidates."

McKenna had been idealizing her friendship with Susan, the way people do with friends who die. Now that Susan was back, McKenna realized that the personality differences she'd sensed a year into rooming together were a chasm.

McKenna placed her hands, palms up, on the table. Susan accepted the invitation. The two of them sat there, fingers entwined, in silence. It was the reunion they didn't have time for at the hospital. It wasn't much, but it was all McKenna could give. She wanted to be with her husband.

"Thank you for the apology," McKenna said, releasing Susan's hands. "And for your help exposing Adam. I imagine they'll want to start the taping soon."

"There's something else." Susan's voice dropped slightly. "So far I've been acting without a lawyer because, as you know, the best shot I have at leniency is to give complete cooperation. And I need people to understand how truly sorry I am. I didn't know— Well, again, they don't want me getting into that with you. Just the tape. I'm basically at their mercy."

"Turning yourself in and helping the government is a good start."

"I'm scared, McKenna. I don't want to spend the rest of my life behind bars. I thought about just killing myself, but then Adam would get away with what he did. I know I have no right to ask anything of you, but will you please consider writing my side of the story?"

"I don't know, Susan. I don't even have a job at this point. And Patrick nearly—"

"I know, I get it. But I'm doing everything I can to make sure Adam never gets out. That's why I'm here, probably for good. Just—just stay and listen to what I have to say. You can decide then whether you want to help me. Just listen and think about it." Susan took the lack of opposition as acquiescence. She clasped her palms together in gratitude. "Thank you, McKenna. Really."

"Whatever does happen, you eventually need a lawyer," McKenna said. "I'm sure you'll have people lined up to represent you for free, just for the publicity."

"Actually, I'm planning to hire Hester Crimstein."

The name required no further explanation. If what Susan needed was a trial by public opinion, the larger-than-life Hester was the right woman for the job. Susan's private work during her period of hiding must have been very lucrative.

"You'll be in good hands," McKenna said. "I'm going to let them know we're done here."

"Again, I'm so sorry, McKenna. For everything."

Though Susan had supposedly brought her here to apologize, she had also asked for help. McKenna felt her emotions competing again. Anger at Susan for all the harm she'd caused. The lies. The destruction. Gratitude that she'd come forward to tell the truth. Sympathy.

She would stay long enough to hear what Susan had to say for herself.

CHAPTER SIXTY-SEVEN

It had been a long time since McKenna had watched a confession through one-way glass. She'd never thought that the person on the other side would be someone she once considered to be a close friend.

Susan looked less real than she had fifteen minutes earlier, when they'd been seated across a table from each other. She would seem less human still once she was reduced to a two-dimensional image on a screen with a digital counter ticking off time beneath her chin.

"I was pregnant. I planned to have the baby. Even though I would be doing it on my own, I was required to serve. Obviously they wouldn't force me to deliver the child during active duty, but all I could do was postpone the inevitable. I knew from a classmate that the army had activated his wife even though they had two children under the age of three, and he'd even offered to go in her place. I was desperate."

McKenna knew how this worked. The jurors who would eventually watch this tape would see an uninterrupted narrative, as if Susan were speaking spontaneously to a faceless, nameless, genderless, identity-less biographer on the other side of the camera. It was the talk-to-the-camera format everyone had grown used to in the age of reality TV.

But this monologue—seemingly without a script, without notes—was the fruit of hours of preparation.

"I called my father." Susan provided what appeared to be an impromptu aside about her father's prominence in the military. "Three days later, his business partner—and my former West Point classmate—Adam Bayne called to tell me that I could satisfy my active-duty obligation to the army in an alternative way."

Susan took her time explaining the context surrounding the deal Adam had conveyed. By then, reports were coming out that the U.S. had lost control of both wars. Former Taliban soldiers had infiltrated the new regime in Afghanistan and were attacking from within. Women and children were being used as shields. Troops handing out water and rice had been killed by land mines. The president had declared Iraq the new central front in the war on terror, as anti-American chants and calls for resistance of the "occupation" broke out at the burial of Saddam Hussein's sons. By the time Susan disappeared, Baghdad's Green Zone would have experienced the first of many attacks when twenty-eight rockets struck the Al-Rashid Hotel.

Those were the kind of surroundings that forced governments to weigh ideology against reality. Since Adam's arrest, McKenna had done some research about that reality. After invading Afghanistan, the military largely opted to look the other way when it came to the country's thriving opium business. Opium farmers weren't friends, but they weren't enemies. They tempered local fears. They negotiated settlements. They garnered cooperation.

But they were demanding more than a blind eye, at least according to Adam. With the war impairing the usual means of export, they wanted the military to provide cover for shipments directly into the United States.

"I didn't understand," Susan explained. "I didn't want to believe that anyone in the military would strike that kind of deal, but Adam told me that soldiers' lives were at stake in the arena. It was only supposed to be a couple of shipments. They were buying a huge asset in the field, and in exchange, the influx of heroin into the United

States would tick up by one undetectable notch. It came down to a cold, hard cost-benefit calculation."

McKenna could tell that Susan was forcing herself to slow down. She could almost hear Mercado's coaching during the warm-up session. *You're talking to someone who doesn't know the background. Explain every last detail.*

"I asked him why the military, of all organizations, couldn't bring the shipment into the country on its own terms, with no inspection whatsoever. But this was quasi–off the books. Authorized and yet not. They trusted my father, and therefore they trusted me. They were funneling the job through my father's firm in order to disclaim responsibility if something went wrong. Because I was his daughter, and because I had networks in the city, they thought I was the perfect contact person within the border. This was a concrete way to save the lives of American soldiers. I know it sounds impossible now, but this was 2003—support the troops, us against them, remember the towers. I'll admit it, I didn't want to go to Iraq. This was my out. And I found a way to justify it—I felt for the soldiers who were over there, especially the ones in Afghanistan who had been left while we pursued a different agenda in another country. This was a way to increase their safety."

Adam had played her.

Susan set out the contours of the plan. The truncated cargo inspection program. A cop who needed immigration help for his new family.

"That was the hardest part to justify to myself—involving Officer Macklin. But I really did believe we were saving American lives. And just like I was getting something personally from the deal— freedom to walk away from the army—I believed, because Adam told me, that Macklin was securing citizenship for his wife and son. I realize in hindsight that Adam had no way to help Macklin. He was simply playing the odds that immigration would never come after the wife of a cop or a boy who was brought to the United States at five years old."

Susan's gaze appeared to shift in the direction of the one-way glass. "Ultimately, though, Macklin was my best asset for accomplishing the mission."

She was looking at the glass because she knew McKenna would get the message. Macklin had been the "best" asset but not the only one. Patrick, after all, was the one to mention cargo inspection to Susan. If the appeal to save soldiers' lives in exchange for a shipment or two of heroin had worked with Susan, it might have worked with Patrick, too. Yet Susan had left him out of it. Or at least she had until last week.

"Then the night of the container inspection," Susan continued, "something happened. I was at the end of the docks, watching through binoculars. There was a container filled with heroin. Some men—I don't know who they were—were unloading it into a truck. Officer Macklin spotted two individuals nearby and approached: Marcus Jones and Pamela Morris. He told me later he thought Jones was reaching for a gun, but he was probably reaching for ID, and Macklin was nervous. Jumpy. It was my fault, because I was the one who pulled him into something that had nothing to do with him. He panicked and shot them both. I rushed to the scene, but it was too late. They were both dead."

She exhaled loudly and took two slow breaths. "I'm the one who devised the plan from there. It was clear from Pamela Morris's attire that she was a prostitute. The men who took the cargo—they also took her body. I don't know where. I told Officer Macklin that he could claim mistaken self-defense: it was dark, he thought he saw a weapon. That was when Officer Macklin told me that he had an untraceable weapon, what cops call a drop gun. We placed it in Marcus Jones's hand."

She walked through the ensuing controversy over the shooting. The initial quiet murmurs in the African-American community. The church-led vigil at the piers. And then a young ADA who traced the drop gun back to Safe Streets.

"I was sure that once people began looking at the shooting, someone would start asking questions about the cargo coming in that night. Adam flew back to New York from Afghanistan and met me at my apartment. I tape-recorded that conversation and have given a copy of the recording to the FBI."

The recording was the evidence she'd said would sink both of them. The argument in her apartment. *Mac. Import.*

"Adam assured me that his contact people in the military were coming up with a plan, but I know how the world works. The whole reason the military would use private contractors, off the books, for this quasi-authorized operation was to have deniability. We were on our own. So I left everything I had and walked away. At some level, I was afraid for my life, and for my baby's, because of the secret I carried. I also saw it as an obligation to my country never to get caught."

She'd spent the last decade working private jobs, mostly overseas. She was an especially good catch for the protection market. The assumption was that a woman couldn't pull off the difficult work, let alone one attractive enough to pass for a valued asset's girlfriend or personal assistant. She never had a problem locating people who were willing to use her skills and not ask too many questions about her past.

"Three months ago, I learned it was all a lie." Her tone of voice changed. A flicker of anger registered in her eyes. "There was no *quasi* authorization. And there was no military *team*."

She described the visit to see her dying father and the relevant passages in his diary. "I was free to walk away from the army, and I never knew it. Instead, I walked away from the only life I'd ever known."

She took a job following environmental activists to the New York suburbs. They were buying small quantities of bomb-making ingredients, to locate suppliers in the event of an eventual plan to use them. She was nervous but did not believe the operation had reached a level where criminal investigators could intervene.

One day she came home and saw a fuse, something she was sure that none of the people living in that house knew how to build. She tried to grab Greg Larson, but he resisted, and there was no time. She escaped out the back window on the second floor, convinced that Adam was trying to kill everyone who might be able to expose him.

Her plan was to persuade Scott Macklin to join her in coming forward with the story. Adam would pay for what he did, and they could be free of the secrets they'd carried for a decade. Her incentive was to return to her old life. But Macklin was perfectly happy with the life he was living. He said he needed to think about it. A day later, he was dead.

"Even if it had been my own country asking this of me, it would have been wrong. We are a nation of laws. There are no exceptions. But I allowed myself to believe that we knew right from wrong in a way the general population would never understand. I bought in to the idea that there was a higher law above civil law. If I could do anything to take it back, I would. I'll pay whatever price I need to, if only for the hope that Adam Bayne is punished to the fullest extent possible."

It felt like a natural ending point, even though the moment was entirely manufactured.

Scanlin and Mercado walked out of the room together. "She did a good job," Mercado announced. "I don't know about you guys, but I'm actually rooting for a good deal from the federal prosecutor."

Scanlin patted McKenna on the back. "Your girl did good."

"She's not exactly my girl anymore, but she did. And so did you with the prep."

Despite her words, McKenna still knew Susan Hauptmann. She was the woman who'd pulled Nicky Cervantes from the train tracks when she could have simply grabbed the phone that would have led back to her assumed identity. She was the woman who'd come to the hospital when Patrick was hurt, and had returned again when it was time for her to confront Adam Bayne. McKenna even understood why Susan had never told her about the relationship with Patrick.

It had been ten years, but McKenna knew Susan at her core.

And because she knew her at her core, McKenna understood that—despite the prep, despite the video—Susan was holding back. She knew more than she was saying.

CHAPTER SIXTY-EIGHT

The way her husband was shoveling ketchup-topped tuna fish straight from the can to his mouth, McKenna would have thought he was feasting on the signature dish at a five-star restaurant.

"You must be the only patient who has ever rejected hospital food in favor of something even worse than hospital food."

When they met, Patrick was still in the habit of opening a can of tuna and a deli packet of ketchup and calling it a meal. In the intervening years, most of his other disgusting culinary habits—instant iced tea, three-dollar wine, and Velveeta sandwiches—had fallen by the wayside, but he still loved tuna and ketchup.

"I wish you could go home tonight," she said. "I'd make you a proper meal."

"You mean you'd walk to Union Square Cafe and ask them to pack us up a proper meal."

Patrick's surgeon had been close to releasing him tonight, but they were still monitoring him for the risk of internal bleeding. Tomorrow, they said. No promises, but they'd reevaluate tomorrow.

"I'm getting used to it here," he said. "Adjustable bed. Free sponge baths. All the antiseptic cleanser you could possibly desire. You should go home and get some proper sleep, though. You've been through the wringer this week."

"Which of us has a frickin' bullet hole in his neck?"

"I'm going to be fine. But Susan manipulating you that way? Trying to guilt trip you into helping her? I would have expected better. She's obviously not the person she used to be."

"You weren't there, Patrick. She thought she was doing the right thing. Not just for herself. For everyone. It was almost—messianic." McKenna had conflicting emotions about Susan, but she believed Adam had been able to deceive her only by abusing her patriotism.

Patrick wasn't having it. Internal checks. Chain of command. There was no excuse for going outside the system. In her own thoughts, McKenna heard the counterargument.

The nurse who came to check on Patrick's respiratory strength made a not so subtle suggestion that he could use a night of uninterrupted sleep. Without a visitor.

McKenna kissed him on the lips. She could tell from the way he returned the kiss that he was ready to come home.

In her dream, McKenna was back at the DA's office. She had gone to Will Getty with the link between Safe Streets and the gun next to Marcus Jones. She was back to her drug cases, arriving to work each day, waiting for some word from Getty.

She walked into Getty's office. Susan was leaning over the desk, her back arched, mouth open. Adam Bayne was behind her, grabbing her hair in his fists.

McKenna's eyes opened. The room was dark.

She reached for her cell phone and checked the time.

4:14 A.M.

She wasn't used to sleeping in their bed alone. Outside of an occasional security conference, Patrick was always home at night.

She tried to fall back asleep but kept hearing Susan's voice. *I was having a baby . . . I was desperate . . . a concrete way to save the lives of American soldiers . . . support the troops, us against them, remember the towers . . . I saw it as an obligation to my country never to get caught . . . I walked away from the only life I'd ever known.*

McKenna had left the Federal Building believing that Susan was holding something back. Wasn't that natural, given the unnatural confines of the statement? In custody, on videotape, after hours of coaching? When they'd been alone, without Scanlin or Mercado or the camera, it had been like being with the old Susan. She fucked up, and now she was trying to make it right.

McKenna pulled her laptop into the bed and started to type: *My name is Susan Hauptmann, and on November 29, 2003, I walked away from my own identity.*

By the time she closed her computer, light was peering through the crack in the curtains. She had the first six thousand words of Susan Hauptmann's life as a fugitive, and they were good words. They were the kind of words that would put Susan on the *Today* show, not as a drug dealer but as a woman whose loyalty to her country had been manipulated by Adam Bayne.

What had felt like the middle of the night was now well into the morning. McKenna walked to the kitchen, hoping that caffeine would rouse her from the fog.

Her briefcase, thrown on the kitchen island, was still stuffed with the two-day overflow of mail that Tom the mailman had handed her the previous day. Con Ed bill. Bank statement. Eight furniture catalogs that Tom had been unable to squeeze into their mailbox.

Something for Patrick. Handwritten, no return address. A New York City postmark.

Seven minutes later, she placed the letter in a Ziploc freezer bag and made a phone call to Marla Tompkins.

General Hauptmann's former nurse finally answered after six rings. She sounded tired.

"Miss Tompkins, it's McKenna Jordan. I hate to bother you again, but you mentioned that General Hauptmann was very generous to you by recognizing you in his will."

"That's correct. I didn't feel right about accepting it at first, but I prayed on it. He was a strong-willed man, and it was what he wanted."

"What about the rest of the will? How did he deal with his missing daughter, Susan?"

"I remember very well, because the estate lawyer explained it to me. It was complicated because he never was willing to accept that she was gone. He could have had her declared dead after she was gone for three years, but he never, ever did it."

"Susan was still in the will?"

"Well, yes. In a way. If she was no longer alive, her part would pass to his other descendants, but then he expressly disinherited Gretchen, so it would go to his various charities. Wounded Warriors. Special Olympics. American Cancer—"

"And what if Susan lived?" McKenna felt rude cutting the woman off, but it was the will's other contingency plan that interested her.

"That was simple: if she outlived him, she got her inheritance."

"How much was that?"

"Well, he left a quarter to me, which was just over nine hundred thousand dollars. That's mostly the value of the apartment, but I still can't believe it. Another quarter will go to the charities. The remaining half was set aside for Susan. And there was a deadline where if they didn't find out what happened to her within . . . I believe it was seven years of his death, the money would be divided among his charities."

The General had written off (and out) Gretchen, but he'd never been able to give up on Susan.

McKenna called Joe Scanlin, but got his voice-mail. She typed a text message instead:

Don't make any deals with Susan.

Susan had spent ten years on the run. Her father's death had given her more than 1.8 million reasons to come home.

CHAPTER SIXTY-NINE

Scanlin placed two sunny-side eggs carefully on the plate-size pancakes. Those were the eyes. Strawberry nose. Bacon smile.

"Maple syrup on the side," he announced, positioning the plate and a small pitcher of warmed syrup in front of Jenna at the dining room table.

"You know I avoid carbs, Dad." Jenna picked at the pancake with her fork the way a crime lab analyst would handle a blood-soaked mattress.

"It's almond meal instead of flour," he explained. "Got the recipe off the Internet. Tastes like a hubcap if you ask me, but I know you're always good for eggs and bacon if all else fails."

"You got a carb-free recipe off the Internet?" she asked. "Who kidnapped my father?"

"I know you're not ten years old anymore, and this is my way of thanking you for getting up early to come here before work. It's the last time I'm going to ask you to change your schedule for me."

She gave him a confused look as she scooped up half of a runny egg.

"Your mother doesn't remember me," Scanlin said. "She recognizes me sometimes, but only when I'm with you. You have your own life and need to see her on your own schedule. So that's going to be my schedule, too."

She swallowed her food, taking in his words. "Okay."

"I've been hanging on to the past, Jenna. And simultaneously not taking responsibility for it. I've been blaming you and resenting you for giving me a hard time, without ever admitting that you've got good reason to. And without telling you how much I regret that."

"Dad, I haven't always been fair—"

He raised his hand to stop her. "Whether you have or not, that's not the point. I'm your father. And I owed you more. I owed your mother more. I even owed myself more, but mostly I owed you two. I realized that years ago, when your mother first got sick. But then somehow it became a battle between the two of us, and I was too stubborn to do what I should have done as your father—which was to put you first."

He couldn't remember the last time she'd looked at him that way. No resentment. No fatigue. Just trust. For a second, she looked like her mother.

"This pancake *totally* tastes like a hubcap." But she kept chewing.

His cell phone interrupted the moment. Jenna smiled sadly. "Go ahead, Dad."

"No, I'm not answering it."

"It's probably work."

"Absolutely not." He walked to the freezer and tossed the phone inside. "See? I can't even hear it now."

She laughed the way she usually laughed only with other people. "How am I going to feel if that's a super-secret, super-smart witness who wants to help you catch bad guys. Justice is at stake, Dad."

That was what he had always told her when he was leaving for work, despite her pleas that Daddy stay home. *Justice is at stake.*

The muffled ringing sound stopped. "Too bad," he announced. "I missed it. Justice will have to wait."

"At least take it out of the freezer." She opened the door and grabbed the phone from the top of the ice tray. "You should probably see this."

He stole a glance. One missed call, followed by a text from McKenna Jordan.

Don't make any deals with Susan. Carl Buckner sent us a letter
before he died. It changes everything.

CHAPTER SEVENTY

McKenna met Scanlin at his detective squad. She read the letter over his shoulder, even though she'd already memorized every word.

> *To Whom It May Concern:*
>
> *My name is Carl David Buckner. Two days ago, I rigged a bomb to ignite in Brentwood, Long Island.*
>
> *The target was a woman living there under an alias as Pamela Morris. I do not know her true identity, but I was hired to kill her.*
>
> *Not at first. Initially, the job was to follow her and to discredit a reporter named McKenna Jordan. I paid a coworker of Jordan's to help with the latter. I then learned from Jordan's coworker that Jordan had video footage of Morris. The person who hired me asked me not only to wipe out the video but also to wipe out Morris.*
>
> *When the woman escaped the Brentwood bombing, I was then ordered to kill Scott Macklin, a former NYPD officer. I did not comply with the order, but I also did nothing to save him.*
>
> *It has become clear that the person who hired me is a sociopath willing to kill anyone. I am trying to stop that.*
>
> *If this letter gets mailed (FBI, NYPD, FOX News), it's because I did not make it back to a Mail Boxes Etc. by noon the day after I wrote this, which means I am probably dead.*

*I don't know whether this will be one of those stories on the front
page for a week, or maybe no one will care (except maybe my brother). If anyone does care, I was a good person once and am trying to be
one now.*

*I know about soldiers who have come home and killed their wives
or themselves or a roomful of strangers in a mass shooting. I'm not
going to try to make excuses for myself. I crossed a line when I set that
bomb. And then I didn't do enough to make up for it.*

*I'm trying now. Is it possible to be a good person, then a bad per-
son, and then a good person again?*

*I have close to $400,000 set aside. I want ¾ to go to the family of
Scott Macklin. If possible, I want ¼ to cover college for my nephew,
Carl David Buckner III.*

*As for the person who hired me: I was contacted entirely by un-
traceable phone and e-mail. All I know is that the voice on the phone
was female.*

Signed,

Carl Buckner

*P.S. I sent a copy of this letter to a man named Patrick Jordan
because I saw him with the woman I know as Pamela Morris. He
is married to McKenna Jordan, and I believe he was trying to help
Pamela Morris. Hopefully I will see him in person before I die. I am
going to meet him now at Grand Central Station.*

Scanlin dropped the letter on his desk.

"Female," McKenna said, placing an index finger on the most
important word on the page. "The person who hired him was a
woman."

"It doesn't mean anything," he insisted. "Adam could have used
a middleman—or -woman—to hire Buckner. Or a voice distorter.
I've seen ones from spy shops for a hundred bucks that sound like
the real thing."

"You can't just ignore this," McKenna said. "Whoever shot Patrick and Buckner was wearing a mask and a cape. It could have
been Susan. She could have orchestrated the entire thing. At the

very least, the letter is exculpatory evidence as far as Adam Bayne is concerned. You'll have to turn it over to his defense attorney, who will argue that Susan was behind this from the very beginning."

"Only because you told me about it. You sure you don't want to put it in the recycle bin?" Scanlin was rereading the letter, trying to find some way to prevent it from ruining the tidy package of evidence they had put together against Adam.

"He mailed it to the NYPD, FBI, and FOX News. I just got to the mail a little faster. You said Susan had a recording of the argument she and Adam had before she ran away. Is it enough to sink Adam?"

"Yeah. It's a whole conversation about growers in Afghanistan wanting to cut out their middlemen and import directly into the United States. They talked about Macklin panicking and starting to shoot. Susan felt bad for dragging Mac into it, and Adam tried to calm her down, saying that in the end Mac was an undisciplined cop with a drop gun."

"Does the recording make clear that Adam was the one in charge? That Susan thought she was acting on behalf of the military?"

"No. If he wanted to, he could say they were in it as equal partners. No deception involved."

"If Adam can say that, maybe it's actually true. Under the terms of her father's will, Susan gets half his estate now that it's clear she's alive. You've got to ask her about this. If she's the one who hired Carl Buckner—"

"I know, Jordan. You don't have to spell it out for me. Bayne might be a smuggler, but all the blood from the last week would be on her." He took a deep breath. "Better get it over with. I'll call Mercado."

"I think I have something that might help." She handed him a document from her briefcase.

McKenna was watching Susan through the one-way glass again. Mercado was seated next to McKenna, having decided to take advantage of Susan's daddy issues by letting Scanlin work solo.

Scanlin started by handing Susan a document. It was the thirty-page manuscript McKenna had hammered out on her laptop the night before. The words had flown from her as if from a wellspring. She'd always felt that the best writing required empathy. Those pages were her most empathetic attempt to tell Susan's story.

"Story" being the key word.

Susan was flipping through the pages. "I don't know what to say. Please tell McKenna how grateful I am—"

Scanlin pulled the document from her hands and began ripping the pages in half.

"What are you—"

"No one's ever going to see this. Carl Buckner left behind some evidence of his own. We've been blaming Adam for the Brentwood bombing, for Macklin's murder, for the Grand Central shooting, all because we thought he was the one who hired Buckner. It wasn't Adam who hired Buckner. It was a woman."

"But—"

"McKenna told us you were trying to go the reformed-and-repentant-female-fugitive route on us. Pretty smart, using sexism to your advantage. It's always so easy to believe that a woman is the passive underling. But it's clear that you were the one who hired Buckner, in which case I'd say this week went pretty damn well for you."

Susan miraculously escaped the bombing in Long Island, which set the stage for her to claim someone was trying to kill her. Scott Macklin died one day after she visited his house, perhaps because he refused to go along with her plan to blame the entire operation on Adam Bayne. And with the Grand Central shooting, she silenced Buckner and nearly took out the man who broke her heart.

"Here's the thing, Susan. I don't think you planned for it to go this way. Why'd you hire Buckner? For protection? To watch over you as you reemerged in New York? Make sure Adam didn't come after you? Then Nicky Cervantes stole your phone—a phone that contained incriminating calls and e-mails. You wanted that phone back, and then you did something truly selfless. You saved the kid from the tracks. Buckner managed to wipe out the video footage he knew about, but how could you be sure those were the only copies? So you had to change plans."

Her plan was to play the victim, which would allow her to claim the inheritance and hire the best criminal defense lawyer in the city to get her a deal.

Scanlin dropped a copy of George Hauptmann's will on the table. "McKenna told us you have plans to hire Hester Crimstein. I guess you're planning to pay her with your inheritance. If you'd stayed dead, you couldn't collect. But now you've got half of your dad's life savings. Pretty good time to come out of hiding."

Susan was reading the will with much greater attention than she'd given McKenna's draft article. Her lips parted. McKenna and Mercado exchanged a glance, preparing for the next wave of lies.

Instead, she pressed her lips together and flipped through the pages of the will once again. Then she started to cry. She put her head on the table, hiding her face with her arms, and sobbed.

"It's not too late to cooperate, Susan."

She managed to utter a single sentence. "I want to go back to my cell."

Susan was done telling stories. She was about to start the beginning of the next phase of her life. One that might last forever.

The hospital released Patrick that afternoon. To prepare, McKenna had propped four pillows on his side of the bed and loaded up her laptop with episodes of *Arrested Development* and *The Wire*. "I tried to roll the TV into the bedroom, but the cable cord wasn't long enough."

"It's okay. I've watched enough TV in the last two days to dull my brain for a month."

Once he was comfortable in the bed, she told him about the letter from Carl Buckner and the terms of George Hauptmann's will.

They might never prove that Susan was the masked assailant who shot Buckner and Patrick at Grand Central, but as promised, the tape of her and Adam arguing in the aftermath of the Marcus Jones shooting had been enough to sink them both.

"Do you have any questions for Scanlin or Mercado?" McKenna asked. "They were going to brief you at the hospital, but I told them you were coming home. They said to call if you—"

"You know what, M? I think we're both sick and tired of thinking about Susan Hauptmann. What do you have to say about that?"

"I say you're pretty smart for a guy with a hole in his neck."

CHAPTER SEVENTY-ONE

For five days, they didn't talk about her, and life got back to normal.

Normal except that neither of them was working. McKenna had an offer to go back to the magazine—higher pay, more freedom, a fancy title as a "feature columnist." She told Vance she wanted two weeks to think about it and a paycheck at the new rate while she pondered.

Patrick was using some of the eight million sick days he had accumulated after fourteen years at the museum without a single illness.

She could get used to this lifestyle.

Patrick was eyeing the cardboard box she had placed next to the front door. Susan's things. The box had been sitting in the corner next to Patrick's bicycle for nearly a week, the last visible reminder of the danger Susan had brought into their lives.

"Last chance," he said. "I'm thinking a Dumpster seems like a good idea right now."

Scanlin and Mercado had already inspected the box's contents and determined there was nothing relevant to the investigation.

"I know. But Gretchen might want this stuff someday."

"She was pretty pissed the last time we went out there."

"Maybe she's changed her mind now that she knows her sister is alive."

"Call her and find out. Oh, except then she'll tell you she doesn't want this crap, either. And you'll be stuck with it."

She smiled. He knew her too well. "Yep, it's like a hot potato. I don't care what she says. We're dumping this stuff at her house and then getting out of Dodge. No more Hauptmann sisters in our lives. I can go by myself, though. My dumb idea, my errand." She had a Zipcar waiting downstairs at the curb.

Patrick said, "I haven't been outside in a week. The car ride will be good."

She knew he wasn't going for the fresh air. Gretchen's words had been harsh. He didn't want her facing that bitterness alone. He reached down for the box and jerked back upright. It was too soon.

As hard as McKenna was working to cleanse their lives of every mark Susan had left, some of them would linger forever.

Gretchen's Volvo sedan was in the driveway. "Looks like she's home," McKenna said.

"You could just drop the box on the front porch and run away."

"Yes, that would be a very mature way of dealing with a woman whose sister is probably going to prison for the rest of her life."

McKenna noticed as they walked to the front door that the lawn looked like it hadn't been mowed in two weeks. She balanced the box against the porch rail while Patrick gave the brass knocker a few taps.

They saw Gretchen peer out from the living room blinds. During the delay that followed, McKenna wondered whether Gretchen was simply going to ignore them.

As soon as Gretchen opened the door, McKenna stepped inside.

"Gee, McKenna, come on in."

"Sorry," she said, dropping the box to the floor. "But that's heavy. It's some of Susan's things that your father held on to. I thought you might want to have it. There are some old pictures of your mother. That kind of stuff."

Once her hands were free, McKenna noticed that the living room had changed since their last visit. The black leather recliner in the corner was gone, indentations in the carpet marking the spot where it had been. The wide-screen television above the fireplace was also missing, replaced by a smaller version on a cart against the wall. Gretchen's husband had finished moving out.

McKenna was expecting Gretchen to bawl her out for showing up at the house again without notice, but her face softened. "That was nice of you. Thanks."

They were on their way out when Gretchen stopped them. "The police were here. I know what happened. I'm glad you're okay, Patrick."

Patrick nodded.

McKenna didn't feel right, leaving without saying more. Gretchen lost her father long before his death. Her husband had left her. Now she'd rediscovered her sister only to lose her to a prison cell.

"This has to be hard on you," McKenna said. "There are support groups—for families of prisoners—if you want me to give you some names."

Gretchen's son came running through the living room, banging on the newly delivered cardboard box with a plastic sword. "I thought we were all done with the moving, Mommy."

"We are, Porter. Just give us a second, okay?"

He dropped his sword and started pushing the box down the hallway, making engine noises as he went. "I'm going to put this where Daddy's office used to be. That's where all the boxes go, right?"

Gretchen offered McKenna and Patrick an awkward smile. "We're going through some other changes around here. Figured while my husband's packing up, I might as well do some purging. You wouldn't believe how much stuff a nine-year-old kid accumulates in a lifetime." There was a crash in the next room, and she rolled her eyes. "Porter, stay out of that stuff. I told you, those old toys are going to Goodwill."

"You'll be fine." McKenna realized how hollow the words sounded.

"Mommy," Porter called out from the back room. "There're pictures of your friend in this box."

"Okay, Porter, leave it alone. I'll come see later." Gretchen moved toward the front door. "Really, thank you so much for coming."

McKenna had sorted through the entire box. The only pictures were of Susan's family and her friends from the army. There were no pictures of anyone Porter would recognize as one of his mother's friends.

McKenna remembered what Gretchen had said the last time they were here. *If you really knew my sister, you'd know that if she were alive—if she were here—she'd know exactly where I was and how I was doing. She would know about her nephew. Hell, she'd probably have Porter's schedule down to the minute.*

Gretchen knew. The whole time, Gretchen knew that Susan was alive.

"Your son knows your sister," McKenna said. "Susan stayed in touch with you. That's why you didn't want me looking for her. You knew she was alive. You knew she had her own plan for coming back to New York."

"*Moooooom.* Look what else I found."

"Porter!" Gretchen was screaming now. "Get out of there, I mean it!" Her voice returned to normal. "I obviously have my hands full here. Thank you very much for bringing her things."

They were almost to the front door. McKenna saw no point in pressing the issue. Whether Gretchen knew, whether she didn't. Whether Susan visited her nephew, whether she didn't. None of it really mattered.

They almost walked out.

And then it happened so fast that McKenna would have a hard time later describing the sequence of events.

Gretchen was shepherding them toward the front door. Porter's little feet came storming down the hallway toward them. They all turned to face the sound of his happy, bellowing voice.

"I'm a ghost," he yelled. "I'm a ghost." He ran in a circle through the living room and back down the hall, making "boo" sounds along the way.

He was wearing a black cape and a Guy Fawkes mask.

Gretchen lunged for the console table next to the front door. Patrick saw the movement and charged toward her, but he was too late. She had a gun, and now he was inches from her.

Only one thing mattered to McKenna in that moment: the gun right next to Patrick's stomach, still bandaged from the smaller of his two wounds. There were no books there to protect him this time.

McKenna jumped on Gretchen with all her weight. The three of them fell to the floor in a tangle. The gun. She heard it thud against the hardwood floor.

Six hands groping for the weapon. McKenna was so close. She felt the steel against her middle finger, but then the gun slid from her reach. She saw someone else's fingers wrapped around the grip. She felt her body tuck instinctively into a ball, trying to protect itself from the oncoming shot.

And then Patrick was on his feet. He had the gun.

Gretchen was scrambling toward him, but he took one step backward and pointed the gun directly at her head. "I'll do it, Gretchen. I swear to God, I will do it."

More footsteps toward them. "I'm a ghost, I'm a ghost."

Porter stopped dead in his tracks. He looked at them in terror.

Gretchen put on a fake smile. "Don't be scared, Porter."

He ran back down the hall.

"I'll go," McKenna said. "I'll tell him everything's okay."

She found him curled up on the floor, still in the cape, his mother's mask resting on the top of his head. The room was vacant but for a few boxes and stuffed Hefty bags. McKenna recognized the nearest box as the one she had delivered. It was open, and various pictures of Susan were scattered next to it.

McKenna knelt on the Berber carpet beside him. "Sorry we scared you. You were having so much fun playing ghost that we decided to do a make-believe game of our own. What do you think about that? Now I'm going to pretend to call the police to report the bad man in your living room." She dialed 911 on her cell and made big comic eyes at Porter while she gave the dispatcher Gretchen's address.

He looked at her and laughed. He had big dimples and a heart-shaped face. Almond-shaped eyes. She hadn't noticed it before, but he looked much more like Susan than Gretchen. More like a young, boyish version of the girls' mother than General Hauptmann. The age was right, too—a little over nine years old.

Unlike Gretchen, Susan had not been disinherited. Because she had survived her father, she was poised to come into half of his estate. McKenna had assumed that Susan had come back from exile to cash in on that provision of the will.

But that wasn't the entirety of George Hauptmann's will. As Marla Tompkins had laid it out, because the general did not know whether Susan was dead or alive, he had included an alternative. In the event she was dead by the time the estate was dispersed, her portion of the estate would go to any remaining descendants other than Gretchen.

As she looked at Porter, McKenna realized that she was looking at the person who would have inherited $1.8 million once Gretchen did what her father had never been able to do: declare Susan dead.

McKenna held her cell phone in the crook of her neck, trying to keep a calm voice while she urged the dispatcher to send a car as quickly as possible. Gretchen was crying in the living room. "It's not fair. After all this time, she was coming back and taking every-thing."

McKenna reached for the little boy beside her, wrapped him in her arms, and began removing his newfound cape.

The crime lab would need it for testing.

CHAPTER SEVENTY-TWO

McKenna had not been inside an attorney conference room at the Metropolitan Detention Center since her days in the drug unit.

She jerked at the sound of the door's harsh, continuous buzz as the guard led Susan in.

Susan did not look happy to see her. "I knew something was wrong when I didn't hear someone bark at the guard the instant the door opened. You are definitely *not* my defense lawyer."

McKenna smiled. "I'm not even a member of the bar anymore. Stopped paying my dues two years ago. It's time to start telling the truth, Susan."

It had been Scanlin's idea to let McKenna have the first go at Susan.

"I read what you wrote," Susan said. "That *was* the truth. My mistake was believing Adam. I had no idea how much destruction we were unleashing. When Scanlin showed me those pages, I thought you believed me."

"I do believe you. At least I believe you're telling the truth about Adam and what happened on the docks ten years ago. But I saw how you responded when Scanlin told you that it was a woman who hired Carl Buckner. I saw your expression when he showed you a copy of your father's will. You hadn't seen it, had you? Gretchen received a copy but never told you."

"This is all about my reaction to Scanlin? How would *you* respond if the police accused you of murdering two men?"

"Almost three," McKenna said. "She shot Patrick, too. You went to Scott Macklin—you wanted him to come forward—because you believed that he was fundamentally a good man who would choose to do the right thing. How can you protect the person who killed him and tried to kill Patrick?"

Susan opened her mouth, but no words came out.

"I know what you were about to say," McKenna said. "Because she's your sister. She's blood. For you, that's always come first. You spent your whole life trying to believe that your father loved you, that some part of him was proud of you, even if he couldn't say it. You risked everything to come back to New York City and see him one last time before he died. Because Gretchen's your sister, you kept a connection to her, too. She was the one person who knew you were alive."

Though Susan was shaking her head, McKenna knew her suspicions were right.

"When you saw your father and learned that Adam had lied to you about the military's involvement in the drug running, you decided you were going to get your old life back. You had a plan to have Macklin back you up. The country's immigration policies had changed. His stepson was no longer at risk of being deported. Mac could finally tell the truth without worrying about his family being sent to Mexico. And then you made the mistake of telling Gretchen. She hired Buckner to follow you. When she found out you were going through with it—contacting Mac, contacting Patrick—she tried to kill you. When that failed, she went after everyone else who knew you were alive. You figured it out when Scanlin showed you the will and told you that Buckner was working for a woman."

Susan was working her jaw as if chewing an imaginary piece of gum.

"She pulled a gun on us yesterday," McKenna said. Susan stopped chewing. "The police say it's the same weapon used to shoot Buckner and Patrick. They also found a cape and mask matching those worn by the shooter."

"So why do you need me?"

"Because she can still say you did it. She can say it's your mask, your cape, your gun. You dumped it all at her place with no explanation. She'll claim that when she heard about the shooting, she realized it was you but was too confused to know what to do. Then when we came to her house and saw the costume, she panicked and pulled your gun. She'd probably get attempted assault at best."

In McKenna's short prosecutorial career, how many jailhouse deals had she cut in these attorney conference rooms? In theory, she was rewarding those who were least responsible and most contrite in exchange for their cooperation against the most culpable offenders. Most days, it was a question of which bad guy talked first.

"Susan, you mentioned the destruction you and Adam unleashed. Look at what Gretchen did in the last week. Mistaken or not, you did it because you thought there was a higher good. You thought you were saving lives halfway across the world. And here you are, ready to pay the price for what you did, even though you already paid dearly. You lost your life for ten years. And you lost your child."

Susan looked away. "It didn't mean anything. It was just a clump of cells."

"No, it wasn't. *He* wasn't. You didn't lose your baby. Porter is your son. You couldn't be the person—the *people*—you've had to be for the past decade and also raise a child. But Gretchen could. She was clean. She got married. You're not doing this to protect Gretchen, are you? You're trying to protect Porter. How can it be good for him to be raised by a murderer? By a woman who tried to kill you so she could be the one who inherited your dad's money instead of you? Think about it, Susan: how did she hire a guy like Carl Buckner in the first place? She only knew about that kind of private work because you've been doing it for ten years. Let me guess: she probably hit you up for a lot of extra cash in the last few months. You thought you were helping her through the divorce, but you were paying your own hit man."

Susan was clenching her fists so tightly that her knuckles were white.

"Even if you try to take the fall, the police won't buy it. Gretchen will get indicted. She will go to trial. And Porter will have to testify that he found Mommy's neato mask and cape right before she pulled a gun on that nice couple who came to visit. He'll testify about mommy's friend who always brought him toys and called herself Carol—your middle name, your mother's name. He'll be cross-examined by Gretchen's lawyer. Oh, and don't forget the DNA evidence. Scanlin will get a search warrant authorizing the state to draw Porter's blood. He won't understand why a man in a white coat is poking him in the arm with a needle, but his very biology—the fact that he's your *son*, Susan, not your nephew—is proof of Gretchen's motive. She wanted the money, but she also wanted him. Some lawyer will have to explain to him that his mother is his aunt. That the father who just left his mother isn't really his father. In fact, no one knows who his father is."

Susan jolted upright. "*Stop!* Just stop, okay?" The room was silent except for the sound of her heavy breaths. "Who will take care of Porter?"

Though McKenna had been prepared to use Porter as a chip in this negotiation, she had never stopped to think about what would happen to the boy while Gretchen was serving life in prison and Susan served whatever time she got for her part in Adam's drug scheme. "Does Gretchen's husband know Porter isn't his?" she asked. "He obviously thinks of him as his son—"

"Paul?" Susan shook her head. "Gretchen met him at an N.A. meeting when she was supposedly six months pregnant, thanks to a rubber maternity bump. When she told me she'd met a guy, I wanted to shake her senseless. Faking the pregnancy got a little trickier. Fabricated doctors' appointments. Sham sonogram images. I coached her through all of it. She just had to keep him from seeing her naked for a few months. From what I understand, it's not all that hard once your gut's the size of a beach ball and the only moans you're making are from morning sickness." The momentary smile

brought back memories of a younger Susan. "As far as Paul is concerned, Porter was born three weeks premature, at home in their
bathtub, assisted by the doula I bribed while he was away on business. He's a decent guy—good enough to fall in love with a woman
who was already knocked up. But when they got engaged, I panicked. I figured he'd want to adopt Porter, and then what would we
do? In over nine years, he's never raised the subject. Being called
Daddy is one thing, but being legally obligated? I need to know
Porter will be taken care of. And that he might have some connection with me when I get out."

"I'll make sure of it." McKenna was hearing her own words
before she'd thought them through. But they felt right. At one point
in their lives, Susan had been Patrick's closest friend. Susan had been
the person to introduce them. Susan had cared about them both
enough to sit back and watch as they fell in love.

And now that same friend was trying to take care of a nine-year-
old boy who had no one else to care for him.

McKenna saw the uncertainty in Susan's face. "I promise you that
I'll work with Paul. Any man who married a woman he believed
was pregnant and then spent nine years raising the boy as his own
has to be a decent guy. He'll want to be part of Porter's life. And
Patrick and I will help out so he won't be overwhelmed. Porter
will be taken care of. And loved. When you get out—and you *will*,
Susan—you'll get your life back. You'll get your son. All of this will
be over."

In the silence, Susan imagined Scanlin listening to the trans-
mission of the conversation. With nothing but audio, he would
think they'd lost her, that Susan was shutting down. He could not
see what was happening in the silence: Susan grasping McKenna's
hands across the table. Something had changed. Porter was the key.

"It's my fault," Susan said. "I'm the one who set this in motion.
Gretchen had finally gotten her life together, and I dragged her
into my mess. She raised my son as her own. And when I decided
I wanted to come back, I never stopped to think how much that
must have terrified her. Or how much she resented me. I was the

one who let my father believe I was dead, and yet he continued to hold out hope for me. He searched for me. In his mind, I became the good daughter again, even as he continued to shun the only daughter he had left. In all those years, he could never bring himself to call Gretchen and take back the horrible things he said to her when she got arrested."

"She could have picked up the phone, too."

"But she didn't. Because she never felt like she was loved. And I was just as guilty as our father. When I persuaded Getty to give her a plea bargain, I felt like she owed me, so she was the one who would keep my secret and not tell anyone I had left. When months went by and I still had no way of coming home, she was the one who would raise the baby until I figured something out. I never thought it would be ten years. Even after she got married, I still treated her like a babysitter, a placeholder. Time was frozen for me. I was in limbo. But she became Porter's mother. She *loves* him, McKenna. And she's good with him. She needs him. And now I was coming back, and I never took the time to make her feel loved enough to know that she wouldn't be left alone—no Paul, no Porter, no me. I know you think this was only about the money, but it wasn't. I did this. If I could serve her sentence for her, I would."

"You can't. You know the letter that Carl Buckner mailed before he was killed? He said he was trying to do the right thing even though he was late. He actually wrote, *Is it possible to be a good person, then a bad person, and then a good person again?* It's not too late to start making the right choices. Someone has to be there for the child you and Gretchen both love. Under the circumstances, however we got here, that has to be you, Susan. It's time to start taking care of yourself so you can take care of him."

"Give me five minutes. Then send Scanlin in."

Scanlin was waiting in the adjacent room. He was packing up the audio equipment that had monitored her conversation with Susan. "Good job."

She nodded. Susan's testimony would help seal the case against Gretchen, but McKenna didn't feel like celebrating.

"Please tell me you were shining her on about helping out with her kid."

"Nope. Dead serious."

She allowed him a few sentences to lecture her about the seriousness of child care. The responsibility. The sacrifice. The way children can break your heart. She cut him off. "You don't know everything here."

McKenna imagined a different reality, one in which Susan was never reactivated by the military. One in which she didn't need to call her father for special treatment, and Adam Bayne never ensnared her into his scheme to squeeze every last bit of cash out of Afghanistan while he could. Susan still would have been pregnant and single, but she would have stayed in New York City, parenting a son alone. She would have had help from Uncle Patrick and Aunt McKenna.

If Susan had been here, this boy would have been part of their lives already. It wasn't too late to catch up.

MARCH

At the beginning of this trial, you made an oath to the judge in this case—an oath that you would listen to the evidence and follow the law. And once you were sworn in as jurors, I made a vow to you, as a lawyer for the People of New York, that the evidence in this case would support every representation that I made to you in the People's opening statement."

As McKenna spoke, she made a point to look directly at each juror individually. To a person, they returned her gaze. No nervous glances at their laps. No fidgeting in their chairs.

She had this.

"You have now heard the evidence. And I know you will follow the law. I am confident that you will find I have kept my promise as well. We have played our role in the system, and now it is time for the defendant to learn that this system works. That truth prevails. And the truth is that the defendant is guilty of assault in the first degree. I am confident that your verdict will reflect that truth."

She walked solemnly to the prosecution's counsel table and took her seat. There was a time when she had tried an entire case with nothing except a Post-it note. But this was her first jury trial in ten and a half years. She had memorized that closing argument word for word.

For all she knew, those jurors would look her in the eye, lock themselves away in their little room, and then decide that Martians, not the defendant, had beaten her victim—a homeless twenty-seven-year-old whose only offense was falling asleep on the subway.

But she believed in juries. She always had.

Will Getty was waiting for her, coat draped over his arm, when she emerged from the courtroom. "I stuck my head in. Good closing. Sorry it's not the kind of case you were probably looking forward to handling."

When the district attorney himself called last month to offer her a position, he had explained that her assignment in the office would reflect her prior experience but also the fact that she had been out of practice for so long. She could tell by the cautiousness of his words that he expected her to be insulted. A year ago, maybe she would have been. Now? The events of last fall had taught her that happiness wasn't about titles or acclaim or recognition.

She had spent all those years feeling like a victim, punished for the simple act of pursuing justice. Even though her suspicions about the Marcus Jones shooting proved to be correct, her motivations weren't entirely pure. She could have pressed Getty back then to tell her more, but she used his silence as a justification to play whistle-blower. After so much grunt work, it was her chance to shine. And when her novel came out, she may have told herself that she was trying to start over, but she made a point to take her author photo on the courthouse steps. Her publicity materials talked up her prosecutorial experience, describing her as more experienced than she ever was. She had earned her former colleagues' skepticism.

Now she was just happy to be back in the only job she'd ever wanted.

"Want to walk over to the courthouse together?" She meant the federal courthouse, where Susan was scheduled to be sentenced today.

She noticed then that Will was holding not only his coat but hers as well. "I took the liberty. We need to hurry if we're going to get there on time."

Patrick was already in the courtroom when they arrived. McKenna took a seat next to him. Will Getty chose a spot behind them, next to Gretchen's ex-husband, Paul Henesy. So far, Susan's predictions about Paul had proved an underestimation of his resolve to remain a father to the boy he had always treated as his son. He had moved back into the family's home and was serving as Porter's primary guardian. Porter's biological father, Will Getty, was slowly easing into the boy's life. As of three weeks ago, Porter had taken to calling him Daddy Will.

Susan was wearing the borrowed suit that McKenna had given to Susan's defense lawyer, Hester Crimstein, the previous day. It was a little baggy but better than the jail's coveralls.

Crimstein set forth the conditions of the plea agreement. McKenna already knew the terms. In the five months Susan had been in custody, her attorney had managed to work out a joint deal with federal and state prosecutors. Adam and Gretchen were looking at homicide charges: Adam for setting in motion the events that led to the deaths of Pamela Morris and Marcus Jones; and Gretchen for shooting Scott Macklin and Carl Buckner. Susan would testify against them both. In exchange, she would receive immunity from the state government, serve a year in federal prison, and complete five years of closely monitored probation.

It was a good deal—so good that Susan's lawyer was worried the judge might not accept it. Every observer in the courtroom was willing to speak in support of the sentence if necessary.

The courtroom door opened, and Joe Scanlin entered with Josefina Macklin and a teenage boy McKenna recognized as her son, Tommy. To McKenna's amazement, they had come to terms with Mac's wrongdoing. Now they wanted justice—for him and for them. Learning how to forgive Susan was part of that process.

"Does the defendant have any remarks?"

Susan rose to speak. As she laid out all of the mistakes she had made, and all of the opportunities she had missed to mitigate the harm, McKenna thought about her own regrets. She had spent ten years waiting for her life to change. Waiting for something big to happen, as if she were owed something better. Waiting to be happy—someday, when things were different, when the pieces fell into place.

Susan had described her time away as limbo. McKenna had created her own limbo.

The judge announced that she was accepting the plea agreement and then banged the gavel, bringing a quick end to the proceedings. Susan threw her head back and let out a soft sigh. She was going to jail, but she was finally free.

So was McKenna. She reached next to her and took Patrick's hand in hers. Her wait for the future that would change everything was over. She had been there all along.

ACKNOWLEDGMENTS

Ten years ago, I published my first novel with the enthusiastic support of a smart and perceptive editor named Jennifer Barth. Hitching my wagon to hers was the best non-marital decision I have ever made. She makes every book better. Thanks to her, I now also have the tremendous support of an extremely talented crew at Harper-Collins: Amy Baker, Erica Barmash, Jonathan Burnham, Heather Drucker, Mark Ferguson, Michael Morrison, Katie O'Callaghan, Kathy Schneider, Leah Wasielewski, David Watson, and Lydia Weaver.

I always struggle for words to thank my tireless agent, Philip Spitzer. He is the most loyal champion a writer could ask for. His colleagues Lukas Ortiz and Lucas Hunt round out the team. And, together with his wife, Mary, he has made his agency feel like our second home.

We also had a temporary third home this year, thanks to a storm called Sandy. Thank you, Linda and Mike, for taking us in.

Thanks as well to retired NYPD Sergeant Edward Devlin, NYPD Sergeant Lucas Miller, UC Davis law professor Rose Cuison-Villazor, and Gary Moore for answering questions along the way. Thank you to Anne-Lise Spitzer, Richard Rhorer, and Ruth Liebmann for being good friends who know a ton about publishing. And thank you to my author-friends whose work not only inspires me but sometimes makes cameo appearances in mine, like Easter eggs, to be found by the careful reader. (For this novel, those eggs come courtesy of H.C., L.C., and K.S. Did you spot them all?)

You may recognize some familiar real-life names in this novel, too. One of my beloved former students donated generously to Hofstra Law School's Public Justice Foundation to have a character named for her mother, Mae Mauri. McKenna Jordan, owner of Houston's wonderful Murder by the Book, agreed to let me use her name, because not any name would do for this particular protagonist, a fictionalized me married to my fictionalized husband.

(If reading the story behind the story is too much like knowing how sausage is made, skip the next three paragraphs.) My husband and I met despite completely non-overlapping paths to New York City. I attended a tiny hippie college in the Pacific Northwest before working as a prosecutor and then turning to teaching and writing. My husband went to West Point and served in the army before taking up security management at the Metropolitan Museum of Art. Had we not met online, we might never have met at all. No shared job. No shared friends. No shared past.

In real life, that lack of common history made it fun to get to know each other from true scratch. But as a writer, I have always wanted to find a way to mine the potential for secrecy in a relationship where either party could be lying about the past. How much do we each really know about the lives the other led before we built one together? What events and people have we chosen to filter from the present?

I also felt ready to write about the post–West Point and private security cultures that I've been privileged to learn about second-hand during my marriage. The end product is fiction, which means you won't find details on Google about most of the specific programs mentioned in the novel. However, I hope I've done justice to the cultures, institutions, and time periods depicted.

Given the backstory, I've never been so nervous to have my husband read a manuscript. In some ways, this is probably the most personal book I've written. It also, even more than the others, belongs to Sean. Thanks, mister.

A NOTE TO READERS

I get sad every time I hear a person say, "I don't read." It's like saying "I don't learn," or "I don't laugh," or "I don't live."

I am lucky to have found readers who prove that books make you smarter, funnier, and livelier than the other bears. Writing is solitary work, but I am not a solitary creature. Getting to know readers has been an unexpected perk of publishing. Although I've met some of you personally at libraries and bookstores, I'm thankful that the Internet has made it possible for us to meet on my website, Facebook, and Twitter. I am truly thankful for the ongoing support, and always enjoy hearing from you.

Some of you have gone the extra mile and serve as an online "kitchen cabinet," weighing in on choices like character names, titles, and the funny noises kids make when they think no one is listening. You've driven long distances to serve as unofficial photographers and friendly questioners at author events. Your word of mouth support is better than any publicity machine.

Though I'm sure I'll have some omissions, I can at least try to thank you by name: Adele Sylvester, Alan Williams, Alana Kinney Amaro, Alice Wright, Allen Young, Allison Freige, Allison Russell Smith, Amanda Richards, Amber Alling, Amber Scott Guerrero, Amy Fleer, Amy Hammer, Amy Nagdeman, Amy Turner DeSelle, Amy Williams, Amy Wolf, Andrea Napier, Andrea Stacy Kirk, Andrea Wichterich, Andrew Kleeger, Andrew Morrison, Andrew

T. Kuligowski, Andy Gilham, Andy P Barker, Angie Burton, Angie Thomas-Davis, Ann Abel, Ann Flynt, Ann Hyman, Ann Rousseau Weiss, Ann Smith, Ann Springer Shaffer, Ann Tully, Ann Zerega, Anna Tauzin, Anne Allen, Anne Madison, Anne Mowat, Anne Ward, Annie Goodson Frye, Annie Noll McAvoy, Anya Rhamnusia Gullino, April Smith, Archie Hoffpauir, Arllys Brooks, Art Battiste, Audrey Pink, Barb Bradley Juarez, Barb Finnigan, Barb Kearns, Barb Lancaster, Barb Mullen Gasparac, Barbara Bogue, Barbara Detwiler, Barbara Dux Mullally, Barbara Franklin, Barbara Jarvie Castiglia, Barbara McPherson, Barbara O'Neal, Barbara Rosenbloom Howell, Barbedet Philippe, Barry Allen, Barry Bruss, Barry Knight, Barry Nisman, Basil Tydings, Baxter Legere, Bea Wiggin, Becky Decker, Becky Prater Sullivan, Becky Rathke, Ben Small, Bernard Payn, Bert Walker, Beth Rudetsky, Bethany L.B., Betsy Steele Gray, Bettie Kieffer, Betty Vaughan, Beverly Bryan, Bill Amador, Bill Botzong, Bill Cheney, Bill Hopkins, Bill Horn, Bill Lee, Bill Reiser, Bill Strider, Bill Taylor, Bill Tipping, Billy Paul Craig, B.J. Van Nix, Bob Blackley, Bob Briggs, Bob Dunbar, Bob Fontneau, Bob Horton, Bob Marquez, Bob Rudolph, Bonnie K. Winn, Bonnie Spears, Bonny Carey Sadler, Brantley Watkins, Brenda Curin, Brenda German, Brenda K. Gunter, Brenda LeSage, Brian Corbishley, Brian Fingerson, Brian Highley, Brian Rosenwald, Brian Shrader, Bridget Munger, Bruce DeSilva, Bruce Southworth, Bud Palmer, Bunkie Burke Rivkin, C. Michael Bailey, Cal Thompson, Carl Christensen, Carl Fenstermacher, Carla Coffman, Carmen E. Padilla, Carol Bennett Mason, Carol Clark, Carol Johnsen, Carol M. Boyer, Carol Mcdonnell, Carol O'Gorman, Carole Farrar, Carole M. Sauer, Carole Schultz, Carolgene Bishop Cottle, Caroline Garrett, Carolyn G. Manuel, Carolyn Richmond Parker, Carolyn Schriber, Caron Legowicz Kott, Carrie Brady Lint, Carrie Dunham-LaGree, Cassie Ane, Catherine McDonald Patterson, Cathy Peck, Cele Deemer, Celeste Libert Mooney, Chantelle Aimée Osman, Charlene Wigington Hulker, Charlie Armstrong, Charlie Burton, Charlotte Creeley, Charlotte Marchand, Charnell Inglis Sommers, Cheri Gould, Cheri Hamlett, Cheri Land, Cheryl Boyd,

Cheryl Thompson, Cheryle Meyer Stadler, Chris Austin, Chris Cooper Cahall, Chris Costelloe, Chris Denicola, Chris Hamilton, Chris Holcombe, Chris Knake, Chris La Porte, Chris Martone, Chris Morrison Dougherty, Chris Schuller, Christa D. Paulsen, Christine Jewitt, Christine McCann, Christine Sublett, Christopher Kingsley, Christopher Zell, Christy Schroeder, Chuck Bracken, Chuck Palmer, Chuck Provonchee, Chuck Stone, Cindy Current Griffin, Cindy Spring, Cindy Wexler, Cindy Whitson, Clair Leadbeater, Claire Marie Gudaitis, Clare Kelly, Clarence Davis, Claudia Meadows, Clinton Reed, Connie Camerlynck, Connie Havard Ryland, Connie Meyer, Connie Ross Ciampanelli, Connie Williams Claus, Courtney Clark, Craig Todd, Crystal Haynes Zeman, Crystal Smith Hunter, Cyndie Lamb, Cynthia Diane Gardner Marsh, Cynthia Dieterich Mooney, Cynthia Poley Parran, Dale Glenn, Damon Reynolds, Dana Lynne Johnson, Danielle Emrich, Danielle Holley-Walker, Dannii Abram, Danny Nichols, Danny Prichard, Daphne Anne Humphrey, Darren Eskind, Darryl Johnson, Daryl McGrath, Daryl Perch, Dave Bowen, Dave Densmore, Dave Hall, Dave Kinnamon, David Barnes, David Bates, David Bell, David Bolander, David Cloud, David Dobson, David Greensmith, David Hale Smith, David McMahan, David Michael Lallatin, David Miller, David P. Watson, David Stine, Dawn M. Barclay, Dawn Miller, Dean James, Deana Fruth, Deb Gravette Threadgill, Deb Sturgess, Debbie Clark Trolsen, Debbie Hartley Holladay, Debbie Hoaglin, Debbie Prude, Debbie Rati, Debbie Stier, Debi Durst, Debi Kershaw, Debi Landry, Debi Murray, Debi Sussman, Deborah Sampson, Debra Eisert, Debra Manzella, Deda Notions, Dede McManus, Dee Hamilton-Worsham, Denise Berger, Denise Sargent, Denise Shoup Andersen, Dennis Kerr, Dennis Mullally, Dennis Raders, Desney King, Diana Bosley, Diana Hurwitz, Diana Keenan, Diana Rossbach, Diane Brown, Diane DeArmond, Diane Donceel McDonald, Diane Griffiths, Diane Hilton, Diane Howell-Arp, Diane Lowery Polk, Diane Muscoreil, Diane Sholar, Diane Warrener, Dick Droese, Doc Nyto, Dolores Melton, Don Boynton, Don Lee, Don Nations, Donna Cox Trattar, Donna

McNeal Sannicandro, Donna Reed Enders, Doug Kueffler, Dru Ann L. Love, Dudley Forster, Durella Jones, Dustin Epps, Ed Caldwell, Ed Lopez, Edgar Poe, Edward Foster, Eileen Brennan Locher, El Jackson, Elaine Meehan, Elbre E. Hickerson, Elda Zenn, Elena Shapiro Wayne, Elizabeth Julia, Elizabeth Larson, Elizabeth Salisbury Anderson, Elizabeth Sheppard Cross, Elizabeth Womack, Ellen Blasi, Ellen Montroy Doe, Ellen Sattler Harpin, Ellen Wills Bailey, Ellis Vidler, Elyse Dinh, Emin Guseynov, Emmy Lunatic, Eric Dobson, Erin Alford, Erin Mitchell, Erin Sweet-Al Mehairi, Etienne Vincent, Evelyn Lavelle, Faye DeBlanc, Forrest Croce, Fran Burget, Francena Parthemore, Frank Guillouard, Fred Emerson, Fred Feaster, Fred Hobba Middle, Fred Littell, Fred Pat Heacock, Fred Vinson, Freida D Jensen, Gail Patrie, Garnett Wallace, Garry Puffer, Gary Moore, Gary Morton, Gaye Matravers, Gayle Carline, Gayle Perren Haider, Gene Ruppe, Genevieve Skorst, Geoff Moffatt, George Bennett, George Cunningham, George Reid, Georgia Whitney, Georgie Goetz, Geraldine L. Allen, Gerry Binga, Gilbert King, Glen Manry, Glenda Voelmeck, Glenn Eisenstein, Gloria Haynes, Gloria Ketcher, Gregory S. Hammer, Greta Roussos Cosby, Gretchen Gfeller, Guy Tucker, Hailey Ellen Fish, Hap Louisell, Hayden Wakeling, Heather Bowden, Heather Giles Linhart, Heather Owens Watson, Heidi Moawad, Helen Carlsson, Helen Cox, Helen Perkins, Hilary Garrett, Howard Mills, Hsin Pai, Ike Reeder, Ilene Ratcheson Ciccone, Ilene Renee Bieleski, Inga Lucans, Irene Biggins, Irwin Shaab, Jackie D'Inzillo, Jackie Denney, Jackie Schmidt Welcel, Jackiesue Roycroft Denney, Jacqo Le Bourhis, Jacqueline L. Larson, Jacqueline May, Jame A. Riley, James Amerson, James Brown, James E. Barkley, James Merideth, James R. Bradbrook, Jamie Knight, Jan Wilberg, Jana Johnson, Jane Baker Fryburg, Jane Wise Shear, Janet Brockel, Janet Lindh, Janet McClure Hammond, Janice Gable Bashman, Janie McCue Lynch, Janine Grondin Brennan, Jann Sherman-Lassman, Jay Drescher, Jean Bleyle, Jean Mirabile, Jean Spurvey, Jean-Marc Le Faou, Jeana Burke, Jeane Anderson, Jeanine Elizalde, Jeanne Adcox Lockett, Jeanne King Hendrickson, Jeanne Lese, Jeb McIntyre, Jeff Bettis,

Jeff Nowland, Jen Forbus (yep, that detective is you!), Jen Hansen, Jen Mullins Keane, Jenet Lynn Dechary, Jennifer Abelson Whitney, Jennifer B. Jacobs, Jennifer Barney, Jennifer Ellis Lindel, Jennifer Hudson, Jennifer Irvin, Jennifer Kyles, Jennifer L. Irvin, Jennifer Ledbetter, Jennifer Little Beck, Jennifer Mueller, Jennifer Murtha Kountz, Jerrica Furlong, Jerry Hooten, Jerry McCoy, Jill D'Alessio, Jill Fletcher, Jill Porter Connell, Jim Boylan, Jim Cox, Jim Lewis, Jim Mccarthy, Jim Snell, Jimbob Niven, Jimmie Montoya-Treadway, Jo Ann Nicholas, Jo Boxall, Jo Scott-Petty, Jo Trotter, Joan Hersch Schwartz, Joan Long, Joan Lumb, Joan Moore Raffety, Joan Nichols Green, JoAnn Shapiro, Joanne Benzenhafer, Joanne Comper, Joanne Kaplan, Joanne Rembac Warren, JoAnne Rosenfeld, Joe Carter, Joe Shine, JoeAnn Bruzzo, Joey Mestrow, John and Sheryl Wetmore, John Bednarz, John Buckner, John Chester, John Decker, John Elder, John F. Armstrong, John Hanley, John Jones, John K. Peterson, John Karwacki, John Ketch, John Lindermuth, John Mcdaid, John Moore, John P. Eperjesi, John Paul Farris, John Schinelli, John Thomas Bychowski, Johnny Johnson, Jolene Schlichter, Jon Schuller, Jordan Foster, Jordana Leigh, Josh Lamborn, Josh Tennille Gimm, Joyce Joyner, Joyce Marie Martinko, Joyce Wickham, Juaan Prescott Gibbs, Jude Simms, Judi Burke, Judie Warner Morton, Judith McCarrick, Judith Taylor, Judith Williams, Judy Aschenbrand, Judy Bailey, Judy Easley, Judy Gehrig, Judy Glies, Judy Jongsma Bobalik, Judy Lambert Watson, Judy Pike Smith, Judy Waren Bryan, Jules Davies-Conjoice, Jules White, Julie Bower, Julie Ebinger Hilton, Julie Fragale McGonegle, Julie Gerber, Julie Kosmata Elliott, Julie Ryan, Karen Beaulier, Karen Burke Tietz, Karen Hosman, Karen K. Stone, Karen Lavely, Karen M. Crump, Karen McNeel Meharg, Karen Mitchell Klein, Karen Montgomery, Karen Nason Abdulfattah, Karen Richardson, Karen Ross, Karen Wills Johnson, Karin Carlson, Karin Durette, Karina Cascante Zumbado, Karl Binga, Karla Davis Glessner, Kasandra Maidmentt, Kate Wood, Katherine Wheeldon, Kathi Burke, Kathleen Andrews, Kathleen Geiger, Kathleen O'Brien Blair, Kathryn Witwer, Kathy Collings, Kathy Gabrosek Walters,

Kathy Goodridge Poulin, Kathy Kiley, Kathy Pagel Carle, Kathy Sammons, Kathy Schmidt, Kathy Tidd, Kathy Vraniak Aldridge, Katie Blackmon, Kaye Wilkinson Barley, Kayla Painter, Kelly A. Gunter, Kelly Ballenger, Ken Koziol, Kenneth Johnson, Kercelia Fletcher, Kerry Souza, Kerstin Marshall, Kestrel Carroll, Kim Baines, Kim Bonnesen, Kim Hector-White, Kim Mehr, Kim Rafelson, Kim Roberts, Kimberley Stephenson, Kimberly Hatfield Deighton, Kristen Howe, Kristi Belcamino, Kristy Knox Taylor, Kylo Switzerland Keen, Lance D. Carlton, Lance McKnight, LaRaine Coy Petersen, Larry Prater, Laura Aranda, Laura Bostick, Laura Piros McCarver, Laura Pop, Laurel Haropulos Bailey, Lauren Nassimi Yaghoubi, Laurence Bolzer, Laurie Stone, Leah Cummins Guinn, Leann Collins, Lee Walton, Leigh Sanders Neely, Len Hill, Lenice Wolowiec Valsecchi, Lenny Ferguson, Les Branson, Letty Cortelyou, Liam Moloney, Lincoln Crisler, Linda Careaga, Linda Connell, Linda Ellis, Linda Flannery, Linda Gilmer, Linda Goetz Greenham, Linda Hammitt-Salmi, Linda Hanno, Linda J. Myatt, Linda Jaros, Linda L. R. Roberts, Linda Maxine Williams, Linda McIntosh, Linda Moore, Linda Napikoski, Linda Quinn, Linda Robertson Feaselman, Lisa Bergagna, Lisa Burke, Lisa Ellis Schugardt, Lisa Fowler, Lisa Keller, Lisa Mason, Lisa Minneci, Lisa Sizemore Poss, Lisa van IJzendoorn, Lisa Wilcox, Liz Patruś, Liza Kosiadou, Lloyd Woods, Lois Alter Mark, Lois Roberson, Lois Rosenstein Reibach, Lola Troy Fiur, Lori Homayon-jones, Lori Hutcheson Kwapil, Louis Brunet, Louis Dienes, Louise Maughan James, Lovada Marks Williams, Lucy Limb Edmonston, Lyle Aul, Lynda Davis, Lynda Pendley Bennett, Lynelle Russell, Lynn Ashworth Peters, Lynn Christiansen, Lynn Comeau, Lynn Hirshman, Lynn Murray, Lynne Dalton, Lynne M. Lamb, Lynne Victorine, Marc Davey, Margaret Bailey, Margaret Barnum, Margaret Franson Pruter, Margaret Louise Clarke, Margaret Overstreet, Margie Watts Iverson, Margo Underwood, Maria Aurora Riojas Jackson, Maria Lima, Marianne Wysocki, Maricarmen Romero-Vazmina, Marie Horne Jackson, Marilyn Hambrecht, Marilyn Tipton Keyes, Marion Coro, Marion Montgomery, Marion Shaw, Marjie Satten, Marjorie

Tucker, Mark Go, Mark Gould, Mark O. Hammontree, Mark Smidt, Marlyn Beebe, Martha Lyons, Martha McConnell Greer, Martha Paley Francescato, Martha Stephenson La Marche, Martin Cook, Martin Treanor, Marty White, Martyn James Lewis, Mary A. King, Mary Asbury, Mary Geary, Mary Hohulin, Mary Jo Peterson Rodriguez, Mary Moylan, Mary Parsons, Mary Phillips, Mary Steck, Mary Stenvall, Mary Thompson Bullock, Maryann Mercer, Marylou Hess, MarySue Carl, Matt Foley, Matthew Jeanmard, Matthew Wallace, Maura O'Dea Stevenson, Maureen Fink, Maureen Howard, Maureen Lennon Kastner, Maureen Liske Stavrou, Maureen O'Connor, Maureen Rice, Maureen Wiley Apfl, Mauricia Sledd Smith, Melanie Sumihiro, Melinda Martin McClung, Melissa Costa, Melissa Mitchell Tate, Melissa Simpson-Keith, Melissa Sutton Gaines, Melissa Twingstrom Tomas, Meredith Blevins, Michael Bok, Michael Charles Woodham, Michael Gallant, Michael Haskins, Michael Honeybear Cotton, Michael Ma, Michael Ridout, Michael Rigby, Michael Sladek, Michael W. Sherer, Michele Corbett, Michele Hendricks, Michele Tollie, Michelle Goad, Michelle Martin, Michelle Pabon Pharr, Michelle Phillips, Michelle Waits, Mick Drwal, Micki Fortenberry Dumke, Mike Burzan, Mike Forehand, Mike Harris, Mike Holbrook, Mike Houston, Mike Neustrom, Mike Newman, Miles Powell, Millie Ann Lowry Buck, Missie Silva, Mitch Smith, Mitt Winstead, Molly Cramer Anderson, Monica Niemi, Mysti Berry, Nancy A. Nash Coleman, Nancy Cullen, Nancy Ethier Carrod, Nancy Gillis Cawley, Nancy M. Hood, Nancy McCready, Nancy Rimel, Nancy Ryberg Key, Nancy W. Cook, Naomi Golden, Naomi Waynee, Natalie Chernow, Nathan Danger Conner, Nelda Elder, Nevin Sanli, Nic Wolff, Nils Kristian Hagen Jr, Nisha Sharma, Oliver Shirran, Otis Wayne Hale, Owen Weston, Pam Bieschke-Sebrell, Pam Hughes, Pamela Cardone, Pamela Dawn Williams Montgomery, Pamela Jarvis, Pamela Kelly, Pamela Melville, Pamela Pescosolido, Pamela Picard, Pat Mays, Pat Neveux, Pat Toups, Pat Winfield, Patricia Blackwell-Cox, Patricia Burns Porter, Patricia Eck, Patricia Hawkins, Patricia Medley, Patrick Kendrick, Patrick Riley, Patsy

Green, Patti James Anderlohr, Patti MacDonnell, Patti Neal Blackwood, Patti O'Brien, Patty Hudson, Patty McGuire Moran Kilkenny, Paul Deyo, Paul Hansper-Cowgill, Paul Miro, Paul Renn, Paul Roath, Paul W Stackpole Jr, Paula Daniel Steinbacher, Paula Friedman, Paula Rossetti, Peggy Kincaid, Penny Sansbury, Pepper Goforth, Perry Dugger, Perry Lassiter, Pete Sandberg, Peter Baish, Peter L. Pettinato, Peter Robertson, Peter Spowart, Phil Messina, Philip McClung, Phillis Spike Carbone, Phyllis Browne, R. Bruce Osmanson, Rand Hill, Rebecca Jones Woodbury, Rebecca Roush Aikman, Rebecca S. Autrey, Rebecca Turman, Rebecca Woodbury, Regina McCartt, Reina Schwartz, Renee Collar Sias, Rex Bovee, Rhonda Tate McNamer, Rhonda Thompson, Rich Maxson, Richard Fox, Richard Hurt, Richard Johnson, Richard Sandefur, Rick Miller, Rick Reed, Robert Carotenuto, Robert Carraher, Robert F. Klees, Robert Hartman, Robert J. Scheeler, Robert Ray, Roberta Boe, Robin Hill Sparacio, Robyn Alexander, Robyn Gee, Rodney E. Dodson, Roger Q. Fenn, Roger Vaden, Ron Gilmette, Ron J. Turk, Ron Kaznowski, Ron Kramer, Ron LaBarre, Ronald Clingenpeel, Ronda Smittle Aaron, Rose Quaranta, Rosemary Lindsey, Rosie Richardson, Ruby Martin, Rue Vandenbroucke, Runner Rusty Bostic, Russell Hyland, Russell Meadows, Ruth Mariampolski, Ruth Miller Blackford, Ryan Dorn, Sabine Pilhofer, Sal Towse, Sally Channing, Sally Dorfler, Sam Sattler, Sammi-Rexanne Huskisson-Bonneau, Samuel Perry, Sandra Jean Krna, Sandra Sarr, Sandra Speller, Sandy Cann, Sandy Featherstone Mosley, Sandy Holcombe Olson, Sandy Maines, Sandy Meyer, Sandy Plummer, Sandy Schwinning Hill, Sara Baldwin, Sara Glass Phair, Sara Gremlin, Sara Weiss, Sarah Beckett, Sarah LaPorte Scott, Sarah Pearcy, Sarah R.H., Sarah Tobergta, Sarah Van Zandt, Scott Bristow, Scott Irwin, Sean Neid, Sean Sharpton, Shanna White, Shannon Kenglish, Sharon Brown, Sharon Faith Graves, Sharon Lema Allsworth, Sharon Stewart Walden, Sharon Woods Hopkins, Sheila Arlene Dempsey, Sheila Dawson, Sheila M. Ross, Sheila Sanders Parker, Sheri Carlisle Horton, Sherri Caudill Lewis, Sherri Merkousko, Sherri Young Coats, Sherrie Saint, Sherrie Simmons, Sherrie Whaley Frontz, Sherry Lee, Sheryl Cooper, Sheryl Ditty Hauch, Sheryl J. Dugo, Shirley Anderson Whitely, Shirley Grosor, Shirley Smith Cox Patterson, Simon Cable, Simon Lloyd, Sita Laura, Skip Booth, Skip Crawford, Skye Weber Middle, Sonnie Rix Sullivan, Soules Wanderer, Stacey Oldenburg Robb, Stacy Allen, Stan Finger, Stella Mullis, Stephanie Angulo, Stephanie Doherty Rouleau, Stephanie M. Gleave, Stephanie Smith, Stephanie Stafford Roush, Stephen Burke, Steve Downs, Steve LaVergne, Steve Shreve, Steven Parker, Stuart Spates, Sue Christensen, Sue Cipriani, Sue Hancock, Sue Hollis, Sue McLauchlan Faulkner, Sue Smith Stewart, Sue Stanisich, Susan Collins, Susan Connolly, Susan Cox, Susan Dineen Kritikos, Susan Feibush Braun, Susan Ferris, Susan Hansen Bubb, Susan Jarrett Carey, Susan MacDonnell, Susan Martinez, Susan Pritchett Thomas, Susie Cowan Hudson, Suzanne Abbott, Suzanne Chiles, Suzanne L. Miles, Suzanne M. Watson, Suzanne Perzy, Svend R. Nielsen, Tami Kidd Masincupp, Tammy Dewhirst, Tammy Helms Meyers, Tanya Currin Faucette, Ted Myers, Teri Bass McElhenie, Teri James, Terri Clawson Swift, Terry Butz, Terry Hill, Terry Molinari, Terry Parrish, Tetsu Ishikawa, Therman Jones, Thomas C. McCoy Jr, Tica Gibson, Timothy Daniels, Tina Lee, Tina Marie, Tirzah Goodwin, T.J. Carrell, Tom Measday, Tommye Baxter Cashin, Tonett Mattucci Wojtasik, Toni Kelich, Tony Engle, Tony Sannicandro, Tori Bullock, Tracee Forster, Tracey Edges, Tracey Paveling, Traci Boeh Wickett, Tracy Campbell, Tracy Davison, Tracy Nicol, Trena Klohe, Trish Waldbillig, Veronica Piastuch, Vick Mickunas, Vicki O'Bryant Marston, Vicki Parsons, Vicki Ray Blitenthal, Vickie M. Neyra, Vickie Parshall, Vicky Hatchel, Victoria Waller Ranallo, Viola Burg, Vivian Valtri Burgess, Wade Weeks, Wallace Clark, Wanda Brown York, Wanda Watkins, Wayne Cunnington, Wayne Curry, Wayne Ledbetter, Wendy Brown, Wendy Burd-Kinsey, Wendy Weidman, Wes Comer, Will Boyce, Will Swarts, William Bruner, William Penrose, Win Blevins, Yash Bombay, Yevon Duke, and Zita Fogarty.

Thanks for reading.

ABOUT THE AUTHOR

Alafair Burke is the best-selling author of eight previous novels, including the stand-alone *Long Gone* and the Ellie Hatcher series: *Never Tell, 212, Angel's Tip,* and *Dead Connection.* A former prosecutor, she now teaches criminal law and lives in Manhattan.